WHATLINGTON
SEDLESCOMB
Whatlington
Sedlescombe
Sedlescombe Street
Scrays
Maddomswood
Dorrells
Hoath Cottages
Meth. Ch
Royal Oak Inn
Reservoir
Dukeshall Shaw
Maddoms Wood
Hancox
Herbert Wood
Riccards Lane
Oast Meadow
Mill Cottage
Riccards Farm
Home Place
Cottage Wood
Leeford Lodge
Alder Shaw
Church Room
Rectory
Corn Mill
St. Mary Magdalen's Church
Leeford Farm
Eastlands Farm
Carcombe Wood
Ringlett's Farm
SOUTHERN RAILWAY
Viaduct
Greenbank
New Road Cottages
Riccards Wood
U.D.By.
ROMANO-BRITISH IRON-WORKINGS (Remains of)
Long Wood
Beech Wood
Oasthouse Shaw
Beech Farm
Great Sanders
Combe Wood
Alder Shaw
Spring
Bartlet's Wood
Killingan Wood
Churchland Wood
Hurst Wood
Austford Wood
Hurst House
Mabb's Farm
Sandrocks
Stream Lane
Glebe Cottage
Durhamford
Spilsted
St. John's Church
Castlemans
Pump House
Windpump
Highfield
Waterfall
Long Shaw
Allotment Gardens
Club
Hall
Saxon Coins found A.D. 1876.
Brickwall House
Sch.
Tank
F.P.
F.B.


GW01336680

# TWENTY CENTURIES IN SEDLESCOMBE

*To all dwellers in Sedlescombe past, present and future, and especially to Rory and Jamie who grew up there.*


*My thanks go particularly to Norah and Paul Salkeld for their help and interest; to Pamela, John and Gerald Corbett for their enthusiastic criticism and encouragement; and above all, to my husband, Charles, for his continually supporting role.*

# TWENTY CENTURIES IN SEDLESCOMBE

(*An East Sussex Parish*)

by

BERYL LUCEY

ASSELTON HOUSE
SEDLESCOMBE

© Copyright BERYL LUCEY, 1978

This book is copyrighted under the Berne Convention. No portion may be reproduced by any process without the copyright holder's written permission except for the purposes of reviewing or criticism, as permitted under the Copyright Act of 1956.

First published 1978
Reprinted 1998

The author would like to thank the following for permission to quote from: —

George P. Elphick, *Sussex Bells and Belfries* (Phillimore, 1970).

G. M. Trevelyan's *Social History of England* (Longman).

Published by
ASSELTON HOUSE
Sedlescombe TN33 0QA

Printed by
ST EDMUNDSBURY PRESS LTD
Bury St Edmunds, Suffolk

## CONTENTS

| Chapter | | Page |
|---|---|---|
| 1 | The River | 9 |
| 2 | The Road | 20 |
| 3 | The Village receives a Name | 35 |
| 4 | The Hundred | 40 |
| 5 | The Battle | 46 |
| 6 | The Hidden Treasure | 56 |
| 7 | The Vow Kept | 60 |
| 8 | The Rape | 72 |
| 9 | Sedlescombe in Domesday | 79 |
| 10 | Robertsbridge Abbey | 83 |
| 11 | Who Was Robert Basok, Knight? | 91 |
| 12 | The Bridge and the Mill at Iltonsbath | 93 |
| 13 | The Church | 97 |
| 14 | Four of the Oldest Houses in the Street | 114 |
| 15 | Rebellion | 133 |
| 16 | Back to Iron: Prosperity for Sedlescombe | 137 |
| 17 | Three Families and their Homes | 144 |
| 18 | The Poor | 169 |
| 19 | The Churchwardens | 183 |
| 20 | Parish Records | 187 |
| 21 | The Rectors | 190 |
| 22 | The Year 1632 | 202 |
| 23 | The Houses and People on the 1632 Plan | 213 |
| 24 | The Civil War | 255 |
| 25 | Smuggling: A Sussex Industry | 261 |
| 26 | The Mercers of Sedlescombe | 267 |

| Chapter | | Page |
|---|---|---|
| 27 | The Great Hurricane | 274 |
| 28 | The School | 281 |
| 29 | The Powdermills | 300 |
| 30 | Beauport Park | 307 |
| 31 | The Last Labourers' Revolt | 317 |
| 32 | Oaklands and the Combes | 323 |
| 33 | The New Road | 337 |
| 34 | The Houses of the Street and the Green | 344 |
| 35 | Other Houses in Sedlescombe | 391 |
| 36 | Charcoal-burning in Petley Woods | 413 |
| 37 | Farms and Farmhouses | 418 |
| 38 | Hops | 433 |
| 39 | The Two Inns | 439 |
| 40 | The Chapels | 443 |
| 41 | The Well on the Village Green | 447 |
| 42 | Sports and Festivals | 451 |
| 43 | The First World War | 460 |
| 44 | Beating the Bounds for the last time | 464 |
| 45 | The Village grows | 468 |
| 46 | The Powdermill Reservoir | 471 |
| 47 | The Second World War | 474 |
| 48 | The Village grows again | 480 |
| 49 | The International Children's Village | 482 |
| 50 | The Last of Old-time Labourers: "Bangy" Smith | 485 |
| 51 | The Churchyard | 485 |

*Bibliography*

*Index*

## MAPS AND DRAWINGS

Endpapers. Map A—Part of Map of Sussex by Richard Budgeon, 1724. (Reproduced from E.S.R.O.)

Endpapers. Map B—Part of Map of Sussex.

Map 1—Sketch Map showing Mediaeval and Modern Coastline and Roman Road. (Page 13.)

2—Sketch Map showing Footlands and Detail of Roman Road. (Page 23.)

3—Sketch Map of The Street. 16th and 17th centuries. (Page 237.)

4—Map of Hurricane, 1729, by Richard Budgeon. (Reproduced from S.A.C. Vol. 36.) (Page 275.)

5—Sketch Map of The Street. 19th century. (Page 345.)

Drawing of Coins Discovered 1875. (Reproduced from S.A.C., Vol. 33.) (Page 58.)

Plan of a Hall-House. (By kind permission of David Martin, R.O.H.A.S.) (Page 115.)

Signatures (Reproduced by kind permission of E.S.R.O.) (Page 154.)

The 1632 Church Plan. (Page 217.)

Drawing of "Baby Mary". (Page 400.)

Drawings of Hop Tokens and Hop Tally. (Pages 434-435.)

LIST OF PLATES

(between pages 264 and 265)

The Village from Chapel Hill
Sedlescombe Church in 1738
The Lennard Fireback
The Old Thatch
"Seddlescombe Place", 1738
Spilsteds
Linenfold Panelling
Durhamford
Hercules Brabazon Brabazon
Gregory's Bakery
The Interior of Gregory's Bakery
The Village Green
The Charcoal Burner
Charcoal Burning: The Pet
The Oast-house at Luff's Farm
The Oast-house at Brook Lodge
Hop-picking at Luff's Farm
Bark Flaying for the Tannery
"The Queen's Head"
"Carters": Manor Cottages
A detailed view of the front of Manor Cottages
Brickwall before the fire
"The Coach and Horses" after the fire

*Chapter One*

## THE RIVER

Six miles from the sea and rather more from the eastern boundary of Sussex the green village of Sedlescombe, abounding with antiquities, climbs the two hills (the Church crowning one, the Chapel the other) on either side of the valley. Here are ancient houses of picturesque beauty, a Roman road, traces of Roman-British ironworkings, the site of a treasure-trove and who knows what else besides; but older still and oldest of all is the River, flowing eastwards to the sea beneath the bridge at the foot of the Street.

Inconsiderable and unimpressive, it runs narrowly today, more a brook than a river, thickly whitened with the cups of water crowfoot, along a wide and peaceful valley, some fifteen miles from source to sea, its quiet surface undisturbed from year to year except by the cast of a fisherman or, more rarely, by the wash of an exploring canoe adventuring to Rye between its herbaged banks. It belongs wholly to the brown-eyed creatures housed in its clay sides, the sedge warblers and reed buntings that nest in its rushes and the herons and swallows that sip its water, the loach, eels and trout its most intimate inhabitants and the sheep and cattle whose thirst it quenches.

But in the wild centuries of pre-history this now insignificant stream was a tidal arm of the sea, reaching widely up through the great forest as far as Sedlescombe, filling completely the valley between the villages of Brede, Westfield and Guestling which have grown up through the years. Down from the surrounding hills of the Wealden Forest, thickly set with the ancestral trunks of ash, oak and hornbeam trees and yew, thorn and birch, it and its tributaries ran to flow through the saltings and flats to the sea.

Up its broad waters paddled, in their tree-trunk canoes, the first men to arrive in this parish and, eventually, the first who settled here beside it. (A Celtic boat discovered at Amberley and now in the British Museum is made of the hollow trunk of a single oak tree 34½ ft. long.) Flint tools were made by people living on its banks hereabouts at least four thousand years ago, in 2000 B.C. Who knows how many thousand years before that had people made their homes here? This history, however, is going to start no further back than the year A.D. 1, for we know something about the two groups that lived here beside the river at that date; the river that was their only highway and means of contact with each other, the river that runs red with iron, their reason for choosing to live beside it.

Over a quarter of a mile wide and filling the whole of the valley between the two hills, it was difficult to cross because it was bordered by marshes. On these marshes the first settlers built their huts of woven boughs cemented with mud and clay. With their iron tools they cut down the nearest trees and stockaded their settlement with stout wooden fences as added protection from the dangers of forest and river. From the river alone could come the possibility of attack from other human beings but wild and dangerous beasts, both real and legendary, filled the fearful depths of the forest that both protected and threatened them. The nearest trees became individual and accustomed as any other neighbours, their idiosyncracies of shape or colour familiar; the further ones, strangers, dimly seen, were foreign and sinister.

Clear traces of the main industry, the mining and working of iron, remained for hundreds of years in two places within the parish boundaries; in the Mine-pit field near the drive which now leads up to the Pestalozzi Children's Village and, a mile north, beside one of the tributaries which feed the river; a place to become known as Footlands. Close by is a wood still called Combe Wood, so it is possible that this was the original combe which gave its name to the settlement. Several dozen flints, described by Dr. Curwen as of mesolithic type, including four microliths, were picked up here in 1951; and two years later a hollow-based arrowhead of mottled grey, translucent flint unpatinated; and a broken Neolithic or Early Bronze Age stone axe-head.[1] The two communities were in close contact by river, and later by road too.

[1] Museum of B.H.S.

The mining and working of the iron were simple processes and slow. First the miners had to dig the ore from out of the ground. It must then be heated to make it workable. As the burning of wood could not produce a sufficient intensity of heat, charcoal had to be made. Leaning along the river banks were plenty of alder trees to hand for this, as there still are today, with their round ribbed leaves and tiny berry-sized cones. Dogwood was also greatly used. Charcoal-burning in Petley Woods today is done in exactly the same way, though the containers, now made of metal, are permanent. (Chapter 36.)

The apparatus for producing the wrought-iron was a small hearth or furnace built in the woods close by. Cone-shaped, it consisted of alternate layers of charcoal and iron-ore covered with clay. Some form of bellows made of skins was operated by two men from opposite sides alternately and worked for several days at a time, before the molten iron would collect at the bottom. When it had cooled into malleable lumps these were hammered into bars or "blooms", which gave the name "bloomeries" to the furnaces. This method of iron-smelting remained unchanged for well over a thousand years.

In the early pre-Roman days numerous bloomeries were worked all through this part of Sussex and over the border in Kent. A mile or two south, in what we now call Beauport Park and at Chitcombe, on the northern boundary of the parish, were more. These bloomeries were almost invariably in a valley beside a river; in many cases, and this would probably apply to Footlands, in such a deep ghyll that it would be calm even in the wildest weather, for a constant supply of water was necessary for cooling the tools.

The settlements beside the rivers were ceaselessly busy with industrial activity. There were the miners, the kiln operators, the woodcutters, the charcoal burners, the smiths and metal workers, the hunters and fishermen and also the farmers (for they were good agriculturists); and the clearing round the settlements, as the years passed, gradually increased in size and the sky itself became wider and the river lighter as the walls of the forest slowly retreated. Far removed from the days of woad and short tunics of pelts, the women were skilled weavers; they also made clay pots and utensils, some of the remains of which can be seen now in the Museum of the Battle Historical Society and in the Barbican House at Lewes[1].

[1] Museum of S.A.S.

Their contemporaries, as we know, fashioned delicately patterned jewellery and metal-work.

Because they did not write, no records of them remain save their broken pieces of pottery and iron slag. All their doings were told or sung in poetry or song. The language they spoke was, of course, British, the tongue of the Celts, the origin of modern Welsh. Maybe they already spoke of the "cwm" (combe) when talking of their valley.

It is strange to visualise this river as a highway for commerce, but so it was, and for hundreds of years there was a harbour at Sedlescombe where the small ships of those days could moor and turn. The records say that in A.D. 893 King Alfred drove off the Danes from the Rother estuary, into which they had sailed with 250 ships, destroying an English fleet anchored there. In a Chart Roll of the 13th century in the reign of Henry III, the wide tidal estuary of the River Brede is called "the Sea"; Edward I, while staying at Court Lodge, Udimore, is said to have inspected the whole Channel Fleet within one mile eastward of where the small Brede Bridge now spans the narrow river. (Map 1.)

How did this river of such outstanding breadth, named by the Danes "Brede", meaning broad, shrink to its brook-size winding through the wide, dry valley today?

The answer is that human activities over many hundred years— activities that often conflicted against each other—have contributed to this shrinkage, and nature has given a helping hand.

This coast, from the Rother and Brede estuaries eastwards far into Kent, is open to the sea, lacking the defence against its ravage that cliffs afford to other parts of our shores and, very early in our history, human hands began to build defences to protect the land against the great tides and storms of the Channel that beat so wildly upon it. In the year 1251 a Commission was set up to see how Winchelsea could be saved and the marshes of Winchelsea, Rye and others including those of Brede, could be protected against the sea. An old chronicler describes damage done the year before by storm "at Winchelsea, an eastern port; besides salt-sheds and fishermen's hovels, and bridges and mills, more than 300 houses in this neighbourhood together with certain churches were destroyed by the stormy high tide."[1] Two years later, the year after the formation of

---
[1] Mathew Paris.

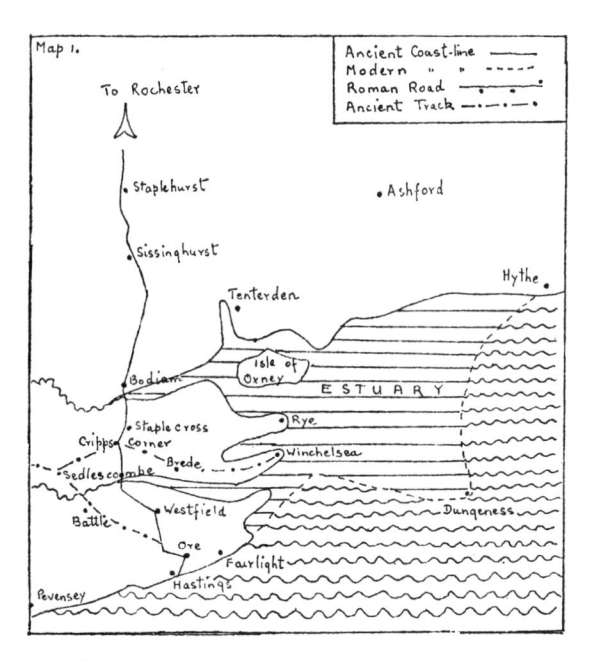

MAP 1. *Sketch Map showing Mediaeval Coastlines and Roman Road.*

the Commission, "at the port of Winchelsea, very necessary to the English and especially to the Londoners, the tide of the sea, as if contemptuous and furious of having been turned back the previous day, by the seizing of the coastal area, flooded mills and houses and swept away and drowned a great number of people". The port of old Winchelsea was set at the wide joint estuary of the Rother and the Brede and the broad channel was known as the Camber, a name usually implying a land-locked harbour.

The town of Winchelsea was not saved. Inundated again and again, it was finally drowned in A.D. 1300. The port was silted up completely about two hundred years later. A sluice had been built across the Brede, where the Ferry Bridge now stands at what is new Winchelsea, the effect of which was to silt up the channel of the river with sand deposits which built up so badly that fifteen years later, according to a Close Roll of 1357, an order was made for the removal of all obstructions, including the sluice, so that "the tide might ebb and flow toward the town of Battle as of old and clean the river and harbour of silt". According to the late Mrs. Brabazon Combe, of Oaklands Park, there was a salt water lake over all the low lying land of Luff's Farm and Lower Marley Farm, which had earlier been this harbour of Battle, called by the Romans "Coldharbour". The late Sir Alan Moore, of Hancox, and others, have thought Battle harbour to have been near Whatlington Church, and Sir Alan had a theory that the ancient yew tree in the churchyard, reputed to be a thousand years old, marked for all comers the fording place.

Two hundred years later complaints were in reverse when Westfield Forge was set up three-quarters of a mile west of Brede Bridge, to work in conjunction with Brede Furnace (where Powdermill Dam now is). The Mayor and Jurats of Rye complained that the diversion of water of the river for this "iron hammer" was "very hurtful to the town". This time nothing was done to make amends and work at the forge continued. It is hard to see how this activity on the river could in any way have hurt the town of Rye, and for several hundred years the forge continued to fill the air with the clang of hammers and the roar of the furnace. Traces of cinder and charcoal can still be found at the site, but there are no remains of the Iron House which was erected at Brede Bridge for storing the cannon and shot, cables, anchors and other manufactures, pending shipment by barges to Rye and thence to the Tower of London or the Continent. (Chapter 16.)

Even as late as the seventeenth century a description of the harbour at Rye states: "There may lie afloat at lowe water 15 or 20 sayle of shippes which draw 12 Or 14 ft. of water, and all without prejudice one to the other. There is a very good conveniency for ships to clean and tallow, careening afloat or groundinge adry which they please."[1] In the early years of the nineteenth century this was put to an end when the Royal Military Canal was constructed as a line of defence and means of military transport along the flat southeast coast, from Folkestone to the cliff-end east of Hastings at Pett Level. The River Brede itself from Rye to Winchelsea was used for this purpose, the true canal branching off from it at the foot of Winchelsea Hill. It was the lock gates of this canal which prevented the water of the Channel at Rye flowing far up the valleys of the Brede and Rother as of old.

[1] S.A.C. 94.

## THE RIVER

During the heyday of smuggling in the eighteenth century much illicit cargo, secreted on board the river barges travelling up the Brede to fetch down the iron guns, helped to stock many a village store-cupboard and cellar, drunk with great pleasure, no doubt because bought cheaply, the Government being cheated out of its duty.

Meanwhile, nature was at work on land and water. Mediaeval maps show a very different coastline in this part of Sussex and Kent from that of today.[1] Because of the whole eastward drift of the Channel, which still continues, the sea receded gradually from the Brede and Rother estuaries and from the marshes, thus slowly, but continuously and fundamentally, altering the beach-line. At the same time continual efforts were made to safeguard the land thus reclaimed. Dykes were built to restrain the sea, and banks to contain the diminished river, for the valley-land was fertile and the increased acreage valuable.

In the village of Sedlescombe itself, the Brede waters had been harnessed for the working of a corn-mill since before the year 1218. (Chapter 12.) Two hundred and fifty years later it was "newly re-built", and for another three hundred years its mill-stones continued to grind all the local corn beside "the bridge at Iltonsbath" till, in 1750, the mill was converted to another use. Europe was at war. For years the River Brede and the people living by it had contributed to the making of instruments of death; guns, cannon and shot. Now the mill at Sedlescombe turned from the peaceful grinding of corn which would feed people to the grinding of saltpetre to make gunpowder which would kill them. Fourteen years later, one day "before breakfast", the early morning quiet of every villager for miles around was shattered terrifyingly by a tremendous explosion, and soon all were mourning the deaths of four men working at the Powdermill, two being James and Thomas, the only sons of the proprietor, James Gilmore. (Chapter 29.)

Two miles away along Powdermill Lane the river was being put to the same use; a powdermill had taken the place of the Furnace and two or three times in the years following the same noise of shattering explosions sent trembling men and women hurrying for news. (Chapter 29.)

[1] Map 1.

During the eighteenth century the Brooks were again drained and reclaimed and the river seems to have been divided into several channels for agricultural purposes, and the valley was given over until recent times to the growing of hops. (Chapters 37, 38.) Far into the nineteenth century coal barges, each with its small dog like a figurehead, were still travelling up and down the river to Sedlescombe's little harbour, now not much more than a landing and turning place, but all the time the tidal flow was growing gradually less. There were fewer days each month when the barges could make the trip, till at last came the day when the bargee for the last time brought his load as far as Sedlescombe; henceforth he would bring it only as far as Brede Bridge. He drank his last pint at the "bottom-house" and people turned home after cheering him away, shaking their heads sadly at a chapter closed, a source of news and gossip and a reason for comfortable loitering at the bridge on regular days of the month gone.

In 1875 John Catt built the new bridge over the narrowed river to replace the old larger wooden one which had to be repaired nearly every spring.

Three-quarters of a mile upstream from Brede Bridge, not far from the old Forge, stands on the riverside a brick building with a 99-ft. high chimney. This is an engine-house and boiler-house built in 1902 by the Waterworks Department of the Hastings Borough Council, together with filters and a 115,000-gallon capacity underground pure-water storage tank. Into this, water was pumped, after treatment, from three wells 270 ft. deep, two on the north and one on the south side of the river. A 500-ton coal store was built, to which the coal was brought by a small steam locomotive and wagons running on 18-inch gauge tramway from a wharf constructed at Brede Bridge. The river was then navigable for two consecutive days each fortnight from Rye to the Bridge, and coal was brought up in 20-ton bargeloads and transferred by a travelling steam crane to the wagons. On arrival at the Pumping Station, each wagon was lifted by a hydraulic hoist to discharge its load through the roof of the coal store. This building was demolished and replaced by an additional engine-house in 1939, the smaller coal for the new chain grate being stored in the open.[1]

[1] Coleman.

## THE RIVER

All the water from Brede Pumping Station was pumped to Hastings, including that routed vîa the Station from the Powdermill Reservoir built in 1929. One of the tributaries of the Brede, with two sources (one flowing from Cripps Corner and one from near Chitcombe), was formed into the catchment area. (Chapter 46.) Sedlescombe continued for another quarter of a century to take its water supply by bucket from the Brede or by bucket from the village well on the Green, or from private wells.

In 1928/29, a borehole had been sunk at the Bowlings, Blackbrooks, from which, too, water was pumped to Brede Pumping Station to supplement supplies for Hastings.

However, in 1954 the Battle Rural District Council purchased the borehole and small pumping station to develop into a large installation to supply an area, including Sedlescombe, with mains water. Buckets and shoulder-yokes then soon faded into folk-lore.

In the autumn of 1951 Brickwall, the old sixteenth-century house at the head of the Green, had burned while firemen from Hastings, Battle, and Broad Oak hurried to unroll their quarter-mile of hose downhill to the river before they could pump water into the destroying flames, which thus had time to rage beyond control.

Still, as of old, several streams bring their waters down into the River from the surrounding woods and hills. The Brede itself rises between Marley Lane and Mount Street in the farm land in Battle owned by the National Trust. Before it has run a mile it is joined by another stream whose source is only about a half-mile distant from the Brede's; also in Battle east of Mount Street. Together their waters skirt Felon Wood in one narrow stream, thickly fringed with purple-catkinned alder trees. Flowing under the New Road, it leaves the woods and as it runs through the water-meadows of the Brooks it receives the waters of three more streams. The biggest of these, the River Line, rises near Mountfield in Limekiln Wood near the Gypsum Mines. Flowing to the Mill at Whatlington, it is joined there by a rivulet having two sources, one in Burnthouse Woods (also close to the Gypsum Mines) and the other half a mile away between Ivyland Farm and Netherfield Place. Together the River Line and its tributary drove the mill-wheel at Whatlington. Flowing on, they watered the hop-gardens that once were part of Riccards Farm, before they joined the Brede just above the Sedlescombe millpool at the Powdermill. There for hundreds of years their power turned another wheel, assisted by the water flowing down from Footlands Farm, where the first settlers worked—the stream that gives its name to Stream Lane.

After flowing under Sedlescombe Bridge the character of the Brede changes. No longer do alders or any other trees shade its banks; from here down to the sea they are open, growing gradually wider apart, and are thickly covered with herbage and wild flowers in great variety, purple, yellow and white. Twisting and winding towards Brede Bridge it receives water, collected in Powdermill Reservoir from streams rising in the woods behind Hurst Lane, at Cripps Corner and near Goatham Green. Out of the reservoir this water flows down southwards, passing by the site of Frymans Farm, blown up by a land-mine in the 1939-45 War, into the Brede, which runs on through the sheep-scattered meadows. In the woods near Chitcombe, rises yet another tributary which meanders down through Steep Hill Wood past Brook Lodge and into the Brede beside the Waterworks building.

From the south one stream only brings its water into the Brede; from its source in Battle Great Wood, not far from Telham Hill, it collects in its course three rivulets running out of Beauport Park. It twists and turns for two and a half miles before it flows under Sprays Bridge (where once it turned another mill-wheel) and thence into the Brede also beside the Water Works.

Between Sedlescombe Bridge and Brede Bridge there used to be two field bridges, built for the convenience of workers on Oaklands and Westfield Place estates. Solid little bridges, these were of brick and turf, demolished in recent years. A path follows the course of the Brede along its south bank for a mile or so, and then leaves it at right-angles to edge a field and join a wide path coming down from Westfield Place. At this point there used to stand the largest wild cherry tree that I have ever seen or hope to see. Every spring our family would walk across the fields to enjoy this loveliest of trees "wearing white for Easter-tide". The girth of its trunk was more reminiscent of an oak than a cherry tree, for two adults, standing one on either side with outstretched arms around its trunk, could barely touch fingertips. Beside it was another but half its size and yet still unusually large for this species. One disappointing year, making our usual expedition we found the cherry tree was gone; only the flat stump, like a large round footstool, remained where it had been sawn to the ground. Its fellow too had disappeared.

# THE RIVER

Lacking now sufficient tidal power to keep its bed scoured, the river is dredged at regular intervals and, for a while after, its banks are high and naked, their clayey sides denuded of their cream and purple covering of meadowsweet, willow herbs and loosestrife and its surface cleared of water crowfoot and forgetmenot. The water population of fish, water voles, otters, and immigrant mink is disturbed, and the larvae of dragonflies and caddis flies and other immature creatures; but, however that may be, the tiny demoiselle dragonflies can still be seen flying over the water or resting on the herbs with vibrating wings of emerald, turquoise or indigo. Occasionally still a kingfisher, brighter even than they, streaks by, but not for a decade now has the nightingale sung beside the mill-pool.

Improved drainage prevents the river, even in the wettest years, from overflowing the road beside the bridge, as it so often did in the not distant past. I well remember in 1945 the Rector, Mr. Noble, helping an old lady, Kate Bryant, to climb down the ladder from a room in the upper storey of Riverbridge Cottages, where she had taken refuge from the downstairs flooding.

But in the fill-dyke month of February, the floods sheeting the Brooks still give some idea today of what the valley looked like in the former days of the river's greatness, when without it the village would never have been.

*Chapter Two*

## THE ROAD

First the River, then the Road. Forcing its way between the massed trunks of forest trees ran the Roman road, the second most ancient thing in the village today and the oldest made by man.

With the coming of the Romans the legendary haze of pre-history gives place to definite events, since we know that they landed unopposed on our southern shores in the year A.D. 43, though they met resistance further inland round the River Medway and also from the famous British Queen Boudicca, nearer London. After several victories and some diplomacy, the British rulers in the South at last made peace and this peace lasted for four hundred years; the Romans, as we know, bringing law and order, unity and the beginnings of Christianity; building towns and roads and developing old and new industries all over the island.

Amongst the old ones that particularly interested them were the numerous iron-workings which the British had established beside many rivers throughout the Forest, which the Romans called Anderida. We cannot know when their first reconnaissance party reached the British settlements beside the River, as yet un-named, and its tributary.

The transport of such heavy material as iron required good roads and, although by this time there was a considerable number of tracks from east to west through the Forest, what was needed were north and south roads from the coast, to bridge the Forest and carry the iron to the growing city of London, which had become the centre of the Roman road system. After, therefore, they had built the military roads to ensure the speedy movement of troops to all parts of the country, they started making the commercial roads, and the Street through the village is part of one of these. Because of its object,

## THE ROAD

the linking of the various iron-workings, it was not so ruler-straight as the military roads which used the shortest route wherever possible, regardless of difficulties. Estuaries then ran far inland and there were harbours at Sedlescombe and Bodiam, the navigable limits of sea-borne traffic on the Brede and the Rother respectively, and with these and the iron-workings here and over the border in Kent the Road made connection.

Both for look-out purposes and for greater ease of road-building and drainage, the Romans built their roads well above the level of the surrounding country (hence the term "highway"), so the roads made through the great Forest of Anderida kept to the ridges and high ground wherever possible.

Mr. Ivan Margary has traced the road's course from Ore, along the present road through Little Hides Wood to where Westfield Church now stands (where a straight length of Roman road from Brede Harbour joined it—the main road of today). Still following the line of the present road, from Westfield it continued past Spray's Bridge along the ridge above the Brede valley through Hart's Green and down the hill to cross the river at Sedlescombe, where the breadth of the valley narrowed to about two hundred yards in width before opening out again to the harbour over the Brooks. The river probably could have been forded here at low tide, but at high tide, when all the level ground would be deep water, there was a ferry, (Map 1.)

Following the present Street, the road climbed the hill (passing probably behind the church of today) as far as Hurst Lane and along what is now the curved drive of Great Sanders (an interesting stretch, because never tarmacked)[1] It crossed the present road at Compasses and took the line of that old road for a few hundred yards, curving back to rejoin the route of the present one, which it took to Cripps Corner, crossing there the old east-west ridgeway track that ran across East Sussex from Rye to Heathfield. It then pursued its course on through Staplecross to the harbour at Bodiam, and over the River Rother into Kent to serve the iron-workings at Sandhurst, Benenden and elsewhere, until at last it joined the London to Dover road, Watling Street, at Rochester. Made of iron waste and iron slag (the refuse from the iron-workings) and wide enough—14 to 16 ft.—to allow two columns of legions to pass

[1] Map 2.

without breaking formation, it was as hard and compact as the hardest modern road. Magnificently constructed, it lasted for centuries in spite of the utmost neglect.

The Roman-British bloomery at Footlands was known to have been flourishing in the first century and there must have been a loop road connecting it with the main road. So in May and June 1951, six members of the Battle Historical Society examined the line of a possible road running from Little Castlemans to the south end of Beech Wood, which was indicated by a stretch of ploughed up cinder, some apparently low aggers in the Alder Shaw and in Beech Wood, and a row of rabbit holes in a slight fold of the Lavix field[1].

Trenches were opened and, in the Aldershaw, under a topsoil of 10 inches of loam, a road surface was exposed of iron cinder 14 ft. 8 in. wide, well cambered and 28 in. thick, resting on a subsoil of clay. The great thickness was to lessen the steepness of the bank down to the stream.

In the Lavix field, a trench 4 ft. wide revealed, at an average depth of 30 in., the road surface, 11 ft. wide; again composed of iron cinder. When cut through it showed a section with little camber, 7 in. thick in the middle, lying on a clay subsoil covered by loam. The ground here had a slope of 1 in 11, and, in order to level the road, exactly one half had been laid on a dug-out foundation and the other half brought up to the same level by extra metalling. (Map 2.)

In the south end of Beech Wood, a flat surface of rammed sandstone 10 ft. wide was found under 14 in. of top soil. There are traces alongside of a small quarry where the sandstone may have been dug. Mr. Ivan Margary took photographs and measurements, and confirmed that the road exposed was indeed a Roman vicinal road to the iron-works.

As this approach road follows the course of a public footpath, it was decided to examine also the one leading from Footlands Wood to the former Compasses Inn near Cripps Corner. An outcrop of cinder was found in the bank of the stream where the footpath crosses it, and from that point, by probing, the line of a road 2 ft. underground and about 20 ft. broad was found to run straight across the field into the corner of Kemps Wood. Running parallel

Trans. B.H.S. 1952.

THE ROAD 23

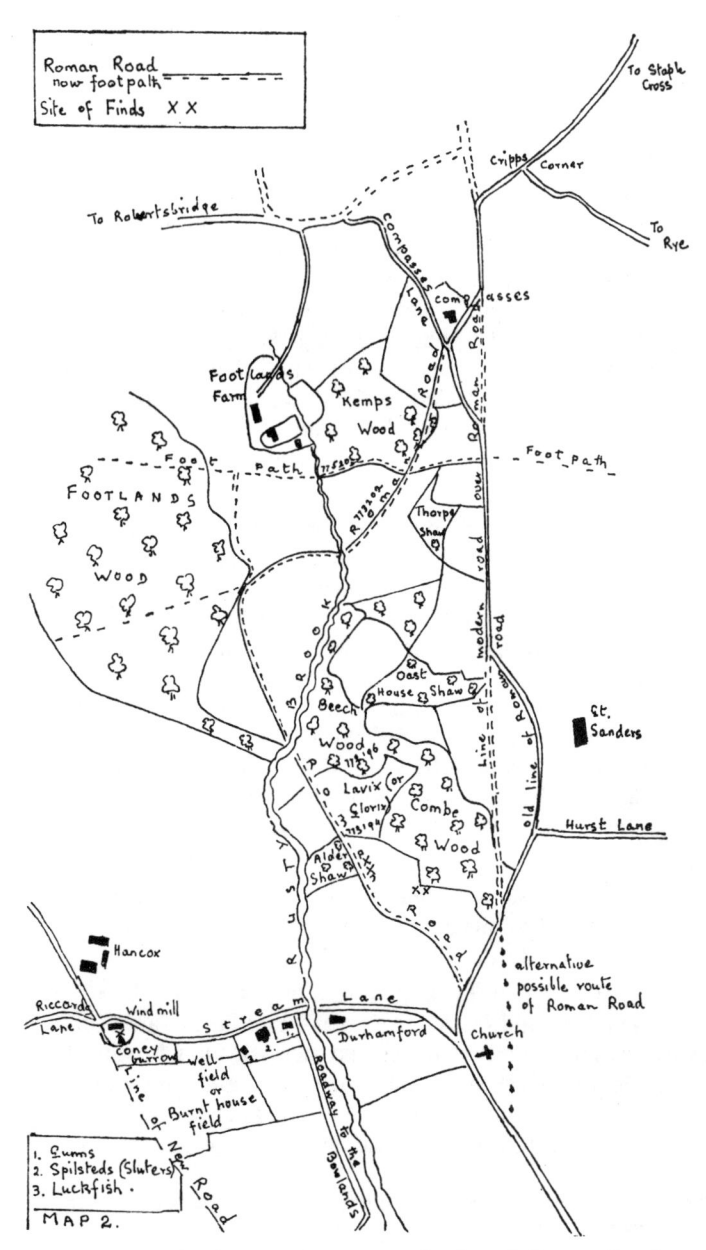

MAP 2.  *Sketch Map showing Footlands and Roman Road.*

to the eastern edge and about 10 yards from it, the road emerged to pursue a straight course to the entrance of Compasses Lane and the main road. At one point in Kemps Wood, the removal of a few inches of topsoil revealed a flat road surface of iron cinder no less than 25 ft. broad.

A field on Footlands Farm, bounded by the western end of this path (where some excavation had been carried out in 1925), showed some rectangular bare patches among the bean crop. On June 11th the footstand of a small Roman Samian dish and several other small fragments of Samian and local British pottery were picked up beside this path. It was in the hope of finding the foundations of a building that two small trenches were dug two months later. The footpath, on probing, was found to lie above an iron cinder road, just as it did on the east side of the stream. The eastward line of this road remains to be found, as inclement weather put an end to further exploration that season.

A year later, Eileen Chown, of Combe Cottage, found, near the spot where the buried road emerges at the east corner of the Alder Shaw, a metal disc, sometimes known as an "Abbey Token". These were used on a "chequer board" to facilitate the reckoning of accounts while Roman numerals were still the only ones used.[1] It bears the inscription "IE IOVGE TOVT POVR VOVS CE DII." (I reckon everything for you today.) She found also at the same place two sherds of late Saxon or early Norman pottery. While removing cinder for road-making, Mr. Wilmshurst, the farmer, found also on top of the metalled surface running through the same wood a piece of a twelfth-century pot.[2]

These objects, separated in time by 300 years, found not far from each other on the same Roman road show the continued use of that road and therefore suggested that Footlands iron bloomery continued to operate during the Middle Ages.

During World War Two, quantities of pottery had been found in the stream bed and banks from near Footlands farm for a mile downstream by Eileen Chown and her friend, Christine Kirk of Beach House. Most of it was early—1st and 2nd century—but some of it was 3rd and 4th. Some was dated before the Roman occupation, proving that the iron had indeed been worked on the site

---

[1] This is said to be the origin of the title The Chancellor of the Exchequer.
[2] Museum of B.H.S.

THE ROAD 25

before the Romans came; there was a lot of red-glazed Samian ware imported from Gaul, some with patterns on. One small cup, nearly complete, had the potter's name Vitalis, stamped on the bottom. There was also a quantity of rough native pottery, mostly grey and brown; and some quite delicate black-glazed pieces, probably Castor ware from near Peterborough. There were necks and handles of vessels and even a colander; and also a tile such as would be used for the roof of a Roman villa. Some of this pottery is in the Museum of the Battle Historical Society; but the bulk was loaned to Dr. Lowther of the Surrey Archaeological Society, who was preparing a paper to be read to the Society of Antiquarians. Christine and Eileen were invited but no more was heard of the invitation or the pottery. The latter at last, in the nineteen-seventies, has turned up at the Barbican Museum at Lewes, *on loan* to the Sussex Archaeological Society by the *Surrey Archaeological Society*.

It is noticeable that a great many footpaths meet at Footlands, near which was found so much of this pottery. The sophisticated Romans with their advanced methods of building and architecture would hardly have been happy living in the cramped mud and wattle huts, however well built, that satisfied the native British. No doubt some of them lived in camps and barracks, but there has long been a tradition of a Roman villa in Sedlescombe. Various sites seem connected with this tradition. Hurst Lane is one and Footlands, where so many ways meet, is another. Such a villa would have probably looked something like an extensive bungalow built with a wooden framework, filled with daub and wattle and roofed with the usual heavy clay Roman roof tiles. The Rusty Brook, flowing close by, was then considerably more of a river and the villa would have been flanked by out-houses, farm buildings, granaries, barns and corn-drying ovens, the normal features of Roman farms. This would have been the first large dwelling-place in the village; close to the iron-workings and the huts of the early British settlement we know to have been built there.

A mile or so to the south in Beauport Park (which was carved out of Bathurst Wood in the late 18th century) beside the bloomeries there, have now been discovered the site of an extensive settlement with Roman baths; much remains still to be found in that area, including possibly a barracks. (Chapter 30.)

So the gift the Romans made to the early inhabitants and to us was the road. To these early predecessors of ours a hard, wide road through the deep forest must have been a gift indeed. Gradually, with the introduction of the heavier Roman plough, the cultivation of the ground increased, so the clearings round the settlements widened and the crops improved. Work must have been plentiful with road-building, farming, iron-working and its attendant industries of charcoal burning and the making of tools and implements from the iron; also the moulding of clay tiles, bricks and pottery utensils. The settlements, though small, seem to have been busy and comparatively prosperous, the Britons gradually absorbing the Roman civilisation during the occupation of three hundred and fifty years (that is, as if from the death of Elizabeth I to the accession of Elizabeth II) and coming to look upon themselves as part of the great Roman Empire in the same way as men of other races have been eager to claim citizenship of the British Empire with the right to a British passport.

Towards the end of the third century, when the Saxons first began to raid these shores, the Romans erected a series of forts along the coast, of which the castle of Anderida (Pevensey) was one, and a Count of the Saxon Shore was appointed to guard them and organise their defence.

At last in the year A.D. 410 tragedy and despair hit the Roman-British population, for the Romans were recalled by their Emperor, Honorius, to defend their native land. Some may have been well-pleased to see their departure and some glad to go, but there must also have been great sorrow, with tremendous separations of families and friends, sometimes of whole communities. As many British looked upon themselves as Romans, so for many Romans Britain must have been the country of their birth.

So the British were left to defend their own shores from the attacks of Saxons and Danes; they had little energy, inclination, knowledge or resources to repair the roads, the existence of which must have been sometimes a positive danger as being a means of rapid approach for raiders pushing in from the coast. The incoming Saxons were a race of seafarers who took naturally to travel by river rather than by road and so gradually the forest closed in again over the road, as the bushes, trees and undergrowth reached towards each other across it, leaving it little penetrated by sunshine. Though never again till the twentieth century had it so smooth a surface, the road was there; muddy, dangerously rutted and founderous though it was, it was used through hundreds of years between then and now by all the inhabitants and most of the animals of the village. Carts and wagons brought goods and commerce along it. Soldiers on horseback and soldiers on foot—possibly Harold's army—used it; travellers to and from London, mostly on horseback, complained of its terrible state and that dangerous robbers and outlaws lurked in the bordering tangle of trees and undergrowth that narrowed it year by year.

Thus it was that in the year 1285 Edward I passed the Statute of Westminster, which ordered that all highways must be widened, and the bushes and trees "where a man may lurk to do hurt" be cut back a bowshot (200 yards) from each side; for England was full of outlaws, offenders against the many harsh feudal laws who, seeking the ample harbourage of the forests, must poach and steal in order to live. Robbers were the greatest danger with which travellers had to contend. This was no new hazard, for King Alfred had passed a law: "If a man from afar, or a stranger, travels through a wood off the highway and neither shouts nor blows a horn, he shall be assumed to be a thief, and as such may be either slain or put to ransom."

Homewards along the road to Sedlescombe one autumn day in 1415 rode Richard Oxenbrigge, booted and spurred, returned from the victorious fighting of Agincourt to a hero's welcome in the village.[1] Back along it too with lightened heart some thirty years later, travelled Richard Beche of Sedlescombe, with many another pardoned rebel from Jack Cade's revolt. (Chapter 15.)

Full of sticky mire, obstacles, ruts and pitfalls round which travellers had trodden out curving tracks, it remained hazardous, particularly for wheeled traffic; the roads of Sussex were so notoriously bad that they passed into a proverb—"as bad as a Sussex road". Sussex women, it was rumoured, grew longer legs than others of their sex, in order to be able to go about in the deep mud that filled their roads.

The Dissolution of the Monasteries was a calamity as far as the roads were concerned, for the Church had interested itself in their upkeep and alms had been collected for road maintenance, dispensations being given to those who contributed either in money or service. Thus legacies were not infrequently made toward their upkeep. In 1528 John Browne, of Sedlescombe, left in his will:

[1] S.A.C. 15. P. 137.

"to the reparation of the King's Highway between Wykham Hille and Sedlescombe Hill 6/8d.". How far would that small sum of money have gone even in those days? At the end of the fifteenth century, London had about 50,000 inhabitants. A hundred years later this number had more than trebled, so there had been naturally a tremendous increase in the volume of traffic on the roads, wheeled vehicles being used more and more. The roads were, like those of today, unfit for them and the damage to them was immense. The Highway Act of 1555 made each parish responsible for its own roads and every inhabitant could be called upon to perform six days personal labour a year. A surveyor was to be appointed by the Magistrates to oversee the work; unpaid, he could be heavily fined if he refused to accept the post, and he could be fined if he neglected the job; if he carried it out he could be very unpopular! So the Act failed and the responsibility passed to the parish officers, the churchwardens and constables who, particularly in this part of the country, must have had a well-nigh impossible task, for every year bad was made worse by the transport along the roads of heavy guns to London from the Wealden furnaces. In a wet year their carriage wheels could be bogged down, immovable for months or even the whole winter, before the road dried out enough for them to be dislodged to continue their journey. So it was that, wherever possible, the rivers were used; the Brede and the Rother transported the guns to Rye from Brede, Chitcombe, Beckley and Robertsbridge Furnaces.

The local landowners at Great Sanders, Hancox, Beech and Castlemans and all the others in Sedlescombe were assessed at so many shillings in the pound on the value of their land, once or twice a year and sometimes, in bad times or for a special purpose, as often as four times.

Among the Parish Records are some of the Accounts of the roads:—

"The Assessment made by Surveyor and Overseer on the Inhabitants of the p'ish of Sedlescombe for and towards . . . the highways at the rate of 12d in the £. The A/C of George Biggs, one of the p'ish surveyors of the highways . . . for the year 1655 made in April 1656:—
*Receipts* 7.14.08.
*Expenses* 7.06.11.

# THE ROAD

June 1. Jo Baker for spreading 25 loads sinders and healing them with gravel. 00.02.01
To P/ish Sedlescombe for a slab to make a footbridge. 01.00
Jo Baker for 2 days ½ in ye way of getting for filling and carrying sinders. 02.10.00
More to him for 3 days and ½ in the way. 4.00
To Mr ffarnden for 3 Courts (carts?) a day for 3 days of sinders 2 days for Court. 18.00
more for . . . work 3 days filling of ye said sinders. 4.6
Jo Grantham for 1 day filling of sinders. 1.6

1656 A/C of Henry Barns of the Surveyor for ye Highways in the p'ish of Sedlescombe. *Recd.* 08.00.10.
*Expenses* 08.13.00.
Pd. to Mr. Bishop for carrying 19 loads of sinders. 01.17.08
Pd. for carrying 80 loads of sinders from R/bridge Furnace. 04.00.08
Carrying of gravell. 00.12.00
Tho. Sorrall for 3 days work. 00.04.00
Nicholas Eardenbus 13½ days. 18.00
ffor one court 3 days to carry gravell. 6.00
Rich. Eatonbury 4 days. 05.04
John Stonham carrying of sinders. 4.00
John Baker 2 days. 2.00
5 days for Henry Barnes. 5.00

1657 A/C of Rich. Bysshop and John Everndon surveyors of the highway of ye p/ish of Sedlescombe.
*Recd.* 8.13.1.
Rec. by Rich. Bysshop 3.6.4. (of Great Sanders)
Rec. by John Everndon 4.10.11 (of Beech House)
*Disbursements by R.B.* 7.17.03.
Pd ye 15 day Nov. for 6 rods of new ditch at 2d foot 2/8
for scouring of 36 rods of ditch 1d ye rod 4/6
paid for 3 (carts?) 2 days ½ at 2/6 ye day 18/9
paid for ½ day and 2 cart 2/6
pd to . . . for carrying sinders 1/6
*Disbursed by John Everndon junior*
To Rich. ffoster and Jo Rolfe 1 days work at 1/4 4/-
To John Rolfe 1 days work 1/4
Mrs. ffarnden for carrying 10 loads sinders 4/

| | |
|---|---:|
| More to her for sinders carried by others | 2/ |
| John Dubbie (Darbie) for carrying sinders 2 days | 8/ |
| John Goding carrying load of sinders | 4/ |
| More to him for 45 loads | 17/6 |
| To J . . . for scouring of ditch | 5/9 |
| More to him for loading of sinders | 2/6 |
| Jo Stonham for cart load of sinders | 1/4 |
| Jo Grantham for making a ditch at 2d. | |
| Jo Baker for digging a way down ye gravell bank | 8d. |
| John Baker for a journey to Battle about ye bridge | 1/. |
| Totall | 3.14.9. |

Signed by Edmund Thorpe, Will Fowle, Wm. Woodhouse J. Everndon. Will Bysshopp."

The first of these signatures is that of the Rector, the second the blacksmith (Chapter 18), the fourth the farmer of Beech (Chapter 23) and the last the ironmaster of Great Sanders (Chapter 17). Very many of the other names too are to be found in the "Sittings Plan" of 1632 (Chapter 23). Those receiving pay for the carrying of cinders, etc., are not poor labourers, they are mostly farmers, tradesmen or landowners, who were performing their statutory duties of personal labour on the parish highroad.

Frequently along this road, in the reigns of the first two Stuarts, rode Sir Thomas Sackville, Knight of the Bath, to London and back from his house, Hancox, on affairs of State and to forgather with his relative, the Earl of Dorset, for entertainment and business, which included the supplying of guns to the Government from his furnace along Brede Lane (Chapter 16) which was under the management of the King's own Gunfounder, John Browne. During the Civil War Parliamentarian troops must have ridden or marched along it, cursing its sucking mud and roughness; and guns and more guns from Brede Furnace, now one of the chief suppliers to the Roundheads, churned up its surface more and more completely with the wheels of their carriages.

Back along it rode the Cavalier officer, Colonel Thomas Sackville (Chapter 17) home from exile, fined and pardoned by Cromwell, to live at Hancox again, his childhood's home.

In due course soldiers off to fight Napoleon were cheered as they marched south to the coast, and signal beacons were again built along its course on high places, such as Beacon Hill at Staplecross, where more than two hundred years earlier they had flashed warning of the Armada's arrival.

The post horn of stage coaches echoed along it. The postilion sounded it loudly as he passed Castleman's Oak, so that it could be heard in the village at the two inns, the "Queen's Head" at the top of the Green and the "King's Head" at the bottom. By the time the coach drew up at either food and drink would be laid and waiting so that no time was lost. At some time in the nineteenth century the name of the lower inn was changed in its honour to the one it bears today the "Coach and Horses" (Chapter 39).

When an Act was passed in May 1836 for making and maintaining a turnpike road from St. Leonards and St. Mary Magdalen to the "Royal Oak" at Whatlington (Chapter 33), it included a branch "through Sedlescombe to Cripps Corner", thus making the old Roman road part of the turnpike system, with a toll-gate at Blackbrooks, at the bottom of Chapel Hill and at Compasses Lane.

A turnpike road was a main road or highway which was maintained by a toll, levied on the cattle and wheeled vehicles which used it. It acquired its name from the pikes which in early days were stuck in the ground to form a barrier till the toll was paid. Up to this date travellers from Sedlescombe to Hastings must either follow still the old Roman road to Ore or, for the more westerly end of Hastings and for the new town of St. Leonards, they could turn off that road at Spray's Bridge, going south to join Moat Lane, and up through Beauport on to the Battle road, where a road went south again from the "Harrow Inn". In order to get from Sedlescombe Bridge to Blackbrooks, from whence went the old road to Battle, it was necessary to go up what is now Chapel Hill and down Crazy Lane.

The plan of "new Line of the Kent Road" shows a piece of new road cutting round Whydown Hill (on the slope of which Luff's Farm now stands) "through lands of Hercules Sharpe, Esq." owner of Oaklands, "to Sedlescombe Bridge", an older one than the present one, which was not built till forty years later. At the same time the road was straightened at Castleman's Oak where, instead of going down the hill towards Stream Lane, round the trees and up again, the road now cut through Glebe land straight across the top, thus creating the Castleman's triangle of today. At the corner of Hurst Lane too it took a straighter course, cutting off the curves of Great Sanders drive and at Compasses.

James Byner, whose family later built Miller's Stores, was Parish Surveyor and thus responsible for the upkeep of the roads and for finding the necessary material, as in earlier days. For the new stretch to be built round Whydown Hill from Blackbrooks, he found to hand close by a plentiful supply of the same material as the Romans had used, in the shape of a 30 ft. pile of iron-slag and waste from the ancient Roman-British iron-workings just inside Oaklands drive (Chapter 1). There he found six coins of Hadrian (A.D. 117-138) and some pottery. Out-of-work soldiers were employed in the building of this road.

The Act ruled that "all his Majesty's Justices of the Peace acting for the County of Sussex be Trustees, together with all owners of the land through which the road passed"; all told they must have numbered, for the two roads, nearly a hundred people. They were directed by the Act to hold the first Meeting "at the Queen's Head Inn, Sedlescombe, or some other convenient place in the neighbourhood on the third Tuesday after the Commencement of this Act . . . between the hours of 10 and 2 of the clock . . ." It looked as if the "Queen's Head" would be unlikely to be able to contain them all. However, at the Annual General Meeting held in March 1837 and in the five years following there was no seating problem; the last of these years showed a bumper crop of nine Trustees present; in all the other years there were either five or seven! Truly times do not change as much as is sometimes thought.

In 1875 John Catt, the Sedlescombe builder (Chapter 34), built the new brick bridge across the river, where the road was flooded nearly every year, and put his name clearly on it, unashamed, and there it stands a hundred years later as good as ever.

An old man vividly remembers the arrival of the coach from Hastings in later years, the coachman and guard wearing grey flat top hats. As the coach passed Oaklands the guard blew with a flourish the coach-horn, which was carried in a long basket. By the time it arrived at the "Queen's Head" a pint of ale and a cigar each was ready for them and tea on the lawn laid out for the passengers.

Over the bridge to Hastings three days a week went the Carrier's van. In the memory still of some today, Nelson Baker and his son would arrive in Sedlescombe from Ewhurst at nine o'clock, with their two fine horses, one a grey and the other a chestnut. At the bottom of Ebden's Hill, so called after Mr. and Mrs. Ebden who had recently built Baldslow Place (now Claremont School), they and any weighty passengers would climb down from the van and walk up the long hill to lighten the load for the horses of which he was so proud. For children in the summer the journey was wholly delightful, made longer by the stops to deliver parcels, to take orders and to pick up passengers; but in the winter, in spite of the warm rugs and thick mufflers wrapping each one, it was so bitter-cold that it was hard for freezing limbs to unstiffen sufficiently to climb down at the journey's end at Hastings Memorial, three-and-a-half hours from the start.

Still the road's rough surface through Sedlescombe was toilsome as ever, white with a smother of dust in dry weather and thickly sticky with mire in wet. "The stretch known as the Pinnock, just north of the school, was in summer inches thick in dust and, having been taught in Sunday school that God made Adam out of dust, I thought that was the place where He came down from Heaven and made him", remembers an elderly villager today. As late as the beginning of the twentieth century the Minutes of the Parish Council show what condition the road was in.

"Ditch very deep and dangerous on the East side of the main road abutting onto the Village Green. Complaints received of great damage to vehicular traffic, which is greatly increasing from Hastings through Sedlescombe. Several accidents to horses and traps getting into ditch recently. Several people during the past winter have fallen into the ditch and hurt themselves considerably. Formerly a similar ditch on the opposite side of the road filled up now, and large drain pipes put in to take surface water from main road. Ask County Council to do this. Agreed. 8th August. 1902."

These ditches were from time immemorial the only drainage system for the old road. Now at last the parish had help from the county in its road care. Among oxen being driven to market within the memory of many still alive, one fell in the ditch at the bottom of Church Hill, possibly from exhaustion, broke its leg and had to be pole-axed on the spot by the village butcher, Mr. Holmes.

Among the steps taken to celebrate the coronation of King George V was the tar-spraying of the Street at a cost of £32, of which the Parish Council paid £9, so at last, for the first time since its hard Roman-laid surface deteriorated a thousand years earlier, it received again a firm surface that was impervious to rain; its swirling white summer dust was laid, its rain-slimy ruts filled and its colour changed from light to dark. It was in honour of this coronation that the seat on Church Hill was first put there, made by Herbert Dengate, whose daughter still lives in Sedlescombe.

In 1911 again there was an accident in the winter because of "the dangerous ditch on the E. side of Church Hill. Suggested drainpipes", tersely reports the Parish Clerk; in 1912 again "a system of drainage is absolutely necessary". Thereafter this was soon laid.

From then on the story is of vehicular traffic, ever-increasing both in volume and in weight, and of gradually decreasing pedestrian use. For more than a thousand years it had been the highway for feet, the feet of the people of the village and the feet of their animals; for their children walking to school, skipping and bowling hoops; for themselves walking to work, walking to visit friends and relations, walking to fairs, to harvest homes and to November bonfires, walking every week to church, once, twice and three times a Sunday. Children living as far away as Staplecross and Swailes Green would walk to church and back along it in the morning, to Sunday School and back along it in the afternoon, and often again to evening service with father and mother.

Every foot of it was known; the trees beside it were friends, the nest-filled hedges continuous discoveries, the cold mist-filled hollows expected; the light of glow-worms regular in their own places and the first primroses and white violets and the earliest wild strawberries in theirs. All were part of daily activity. So too was the excitement of winter, the regular flooding of the road at the foot of the village, tobogganing down the snow-covered Church Hill or, more steeply and shortly down Balcombe Lane to swing out into the road, and in the twentieth century was added the thrill of spinning down the same hills on a bicycle.

Today it is no place for play, being full of danger but, like most of Britain's roads, it is still beautiful and it is still also romantic, as cars stream by with boats on trailers, or with caravans behind, rushing to the adventurous sea and its clean, salty air.

In the evening, with lights shining, they return northwards to air-stale London, and the cats-eyes shine like the forgotten glow-worms in the centre of the black road.

*Chapter Three*

## THE VILLAGE RECEIVES A NAME

With the departure of the Romans in A.D. 450, Britain broke up into several self-governing Roman-British kingdoms, preserving Roman ideas and the Christian religion. Sussex, however, was particularly vulnerable to attack from the Vikings, Danes and Saxons who had been harassing its shores during the latter years of the Roman rule, when a Count of the Saxon Shore had been appointed and the fort of Anderida built, among others, with the express object of guarding the coast from these raiders.

The first two hundred years of this period have no written record. The earliest reference to Saxon settlement in East Sussex is under the date 477 in the Anglo-Saxon Chronicle (compiled and perhaps partly written by Alfred the Great).

"Aella and his three sons, Cymen, Wlencing and Cissa came into Britain with three ships in that place which is called Cymensora and there killed many Britons and drove some into flight into the wood which is called Andredslea." Aella met with much resistance and it was thirteen years before he completed his conquest of the South by finally defeating the British at Andredcaestre (Pevensey Castle), and became King of the South Saxons.

What happened to the iron-working people living and labouring in the forest beside the road and river, described in the last two chapters? We do not know whether they were all killed, put to flight or absorbed into the way of life of the incoming Saxons. Stories of the ruthless massacring of the British, who were very small men, by the huge, fierce, blonde Saxon warriors are now queried. Doubtless those who resisted were killed or put to flight and at least some of those who did not continued to live and to conform, in part, to the changed ways. There were many certainly who did flee and who hid themselves deep in the forest, where as far as the eye could see trees stood behind trees clothing the hollows and the slopes with their thick pelt, and there led secret lives. These little men, surviving perhaps for several centuries in small groups, could have been the origin of the Little People of the fairy tales; Puck, Robin Goodfellow, Brownies and their like; sometimes mischievous, sometimes malevolent and sometimes helpful. The fleeing British took their language and the Christian religion with them into the forests and hills, ever westward. As each piece of country was torn from them, it was formed into a new pagan Saxon kingdom, Essex, Sussex and Wessex, the kingdoms of the East, South and West Saxons, and these wild and warlike men are our own ancestors, who gave us our language, our love of freedom and the basis of many of our methods of governing ourselves.

The Saxons gave us our language; thus it was that the village and river received their names. "Combe", as we know, means "valley"; a steep-sided valley, different from a "dene". "Sedle" comes from their word "Setl", meaning a seat or residence; Sedlescombe "the valley of the residence". Did they find in our valley a building of sufficient importance to dominate and identify the area? Did they find a Roman villa? The name they gave to the valley points fairly strongly to this conclusion and is an important argument in favour of the suggested villa at Footlands, named by them, for the first time, "Foda Lands", later corrupted to Footlands. (Chapter 8 and 23.)

The only other possible reason for such a name as the Valley of the Residence is that they themselves put up a particularly large house in the valley.

The Saxons, who were afraid of ghosts, seldom built, it is said, where others had built before them, but chose a new position, though they might raid and destroy and use material from an old site. They erected log huts of wattle and daub, shaped like ridge tents, the steep thatched roofs sloping right down to the ground; and they built them in a circle for protection, thus enclosing a central space. Did they, avoiding the original settlement beside the south bank of the river (to which the Danes before them had given the name Brede, meaning "Breadth") build it on the north bank beside the road, clearing away the trees as they built? Did they thus, with their enclosed space, lay the origins of our village green? It could well be so.

The important men, the thegns and earls, built themselves great halls which were the centre of Saxon life, where virtually all the business of living took place, including sleeping and feasting. No feast was complete without a minstrel to sing or tell of heroic deeds of themselves or their ancestors. There was little privacy even for an earl or thegn; all living was communal, in a hall. If such a hall were the reason for the name, the Valley of the Residence, it would have to be a particularly large one in order to be an identification, where many other such were built in the country all around.

The Saxons, who colonised this area, seem to have been a tribe whose original leader was called Haesta, said to have given his name to Hastings. The original form of the name was Haestingas, and names ending in "—ingas" (a very old type in Sussex) are, according to the experts, those of groups or tribes. The Haestingas inhabited an area which included both the place now called Battle and the village of Sedlescombe and it is highly probable that at an early date they possessed a dynasty of their own[1]. Sir John Thorne wrote, "I think that I may have tracked down someone (Wattus Rex) who was a ruler of Haestingas in our neighbourhood. In the south-west corner of Northiam parish there is a hill called Watts Hill and beside it a lane called Watts Palace Lane which, going southwards, crosses the Staplecross-Rye road (B2089). It used to continue across what is now the catchment area of the Powdermill Reservoir. Where it comes out now on the public road a little outside the parish, the now abandoned track is still known by local people as Watts Palace Lane. I have long tried, without success, to get a clue to the name. Watts Hill 'is probably to be associated with William Watts who occurs in a document of 1392':[1] but the personal name goes back much further, for the same authority quotes a Charter of the year 1672 in which Wattus Rex attested a grant made by another Saxon king, and a connection between that name and Whatlington is surmised. If this King Wattus was one of the kings ruling the Haestingas people in this neighbourhood, it is conceivable that his home (long ago vanished) was known as Watts Palace—a name which seems otherwise inexplicable."

[1] Pl. N. of S.

There is still a farm and cottages, just outside the parish of Sedlescombe, marked on the six-inch Ordnance Map as Watts Palace Farm and Watts Palace Cottages, in the middle of Watts Palace Lane[1], a very fascinating name into which further research could be made, though a search at the British Museum has so far failed to produce any mention of Wattus Rex.

The Anglo-Saxons, essentially an agricultural people, avoided life in the cities and towns which had been built by the Romans. The first people to recognise the fertility of the river valley, they cut down the close-set trees, slowly pushing back the forest walls to increase the cultivated strips and meadows round the village, tilling the rich soil with their heavy ploughs driven by eight oxen. The edges of the forest gave pasturage for their pigs. The villagers were not allowed to move away to another village without the lord's permission. There was small need for roads, since the village was self-supporting, requiring little from outside but salt, which could be obtained by a short journey down-river to the salt-pans at Rye. The farmers used sledges to carry their crops. Road-making was one of the labours owed by the peasants to their lord but they seem as a race to have had little skill in it.

The village became divided into three areas, the Street (a name that is nearly always an indication of a Roman road) in the south; Hurst, the "wooded spur", in the centre; and the northern part, Fodilant, the "land of Foda", who is thus the first named human being to be immortalised in Sedlescombe, but about whom we know absolutely nothing. The Saxons chose their names to describe the lie of the land or some outstanding characteristic of it. When you give a name to something you immediately give it an identity, so the village is no longer a nameless settlement, it is Sedlescombe—however it be spelt—for evermore, and the river is the River Brede, in the "broad" valley. On the crown of the hill where the three areas met, they built in the course of time, a small wooden church or chapel.

Over the six hundred-odd years that passed between the departure of the Romans and the Norman Conquest, the Saxons fought among themselves for supremacy of the several kingdoms, till at last the country was united under one king. Gradually there developed a strong system of local government, the smallest unit of

---

[1] Map A: marked W.P.L.

## THE VILLAGE RECEIVES A NAME

administration apart from the village itself, being the hundred, which consisted of a small group of villages (Chapter 4). In due course Edward the Confessor became King of England, a man who had spent his boyhood and youth in Normandy and who naturally liked to have Normans about him. In the year 1020 Canute had made a Saxon, called Godwin, Earl of Wessex (which included what we know as Sussex and Kent), where he owned much land. He was succeeded by his son Harold who, among his possessions in Sussex, owned land in Crowhurst, Whatlington, Bodiam, Northiam and Sedlescombe.

So the Saxons left in Sedlescombe perhaps the origin of the Green, the first Christian church, the names of the river, village and places in the village, the Hundred of Staple and, over the whole country, the basis of much of the methods of government in use today, not to speak of their influence on the language. It is said that the men who fought under Harold would have understood many of the terms in use today for the simple but fundamental facts of existence, such as birth, life and death.

*Chapter Four*

## THE HUNDRED[1]

The Hundred, a very old territorial division made up of a small group of villages known in some counties of England by other names such as "watentake" or "ward", is still in existence today. Concerning the origin of the name, the old theory is still considered the best, that it denoted a group of a hundred families and, from this, the area occupied by them. Another view, that it was a term of measurement consisting of a hundred hides of land, is not contradictory; for it is held by many that the area of a hide was the amount of land which would support one family—a family in its widest sense, almost a tribe or clan, which included every relative or dependant. The exact measurement of a hide has been much debated, 120 acres being most generally agreed, so that the area of the Hundred would have been roughly 12 thousand acres.

A Tithing was a yet smaller Saxon grouping, within the Hundred, of ten men and their families, the members of which were bound to stand security for, and pledge themselves for each other's good behaviour.

The Hundred of Staple, stretching from the river at the foot of Sedlescombe Street to the Kent border at Bodiam, was made up originally of two pairs of villages: Ewhurst and Sedlescombe; and Chitcombe and Northiam. Chitcombe, now a tiny hamlet close to Broad Oak, but still in the Hundred of Staple, was from Roman days and for long years afterward an important iron-works above the river Tillingham.

The meetings of this Hundred in Saxon days took place at the crossroads at Staple, a central point in the Hundred, under the chief official, called the Hundredsman or Elderman. Every inhabitant of the villages had to be a member and to attend the Courts, which

[1] Map B.

were held in the open air each year in April and October, with less important meetings sometimes in between. In October, the officials for the year were appointed, the Hundredsman and the two constables. As today, offences against the highway laws took up much of the court's time; these charges being largely of neglect against people responsible for the upkeep of roads and bridges who had allowed them to become 'defective, noisome and noxious', or had neglected to top trees, clear ditches or keep their animals from straying into the neighbouring Hundreds of Godstow (at Brede), Baldslow (at Westfield) and Battle (at Whatlington). Minor justice also was dispensed; all cases of theft were in the first instance taken to it. More serious cases were heard at the Shire Moot.

The names of a great many hundreds are still in use and it is easy to see how the village of Staplecross got its name. The Cross, where the Hundred Court of Staple met, may simply have been the crossroads but some think that in the course of time a wayside cross had been planted there. The meeting-place of the adjoining Hundred of Godstow was at the Hundred House which still stands today at the corner of Hundred House Lane at Brede; though in earliest years it met in the open air.

After the Conquest the Count of Eu, as Lord of the Rape, received liberty and franchise within the Hundreds; he could claim all the waste land and, after Hastings Castle was built, he received guard-rents for it for various lands within the Hundreds including some in the Hundred of Staple.

The Court of the View of the Frank Pledge, a Norman institution, was to a great extent the old Court of the hundred held at the meeting-place at the crossroads at Staple twice yearly at Easter and Michaelmas, and it lasted for about a week. A Court of record, its duty was by inspection to make sure the pledge existed. This was the old Saxon custom taken over by the Normans, whereby all the inhabitants of the Tithing were responsible for any crime committed by any of their number. William the Conqueror ordered that "everyone who wishes to be regarded as free must be in a pledge, and that the pledge must hold him and bring him to justice if he commits any offence". For the purpose of the Court, the Hundreds were divided into groups of, usually four, tithings. The Tithingman was the officer who made the presentments and was responsible for the presence in Court of all offenders. He also collected the fines (known as Justicyeld) and he could be called on in a crisis by the two Constables of the Hundred to assist in the arrest of prisoners in his tithing.

There were constant complaints of the tithingman, that he concealed offenders or, alternatively, made false presentments. Twelve Swornmen confirmed, contradicted or supplemented these presentments, as the case might be, during the hearings. The penalties seem to have been mostly fines.

Bodiam was originally included in the tithing of Ewhurst; for instance, the records say that the total King's tax collected in 1334 from "Iwhurst, Selscombe, Chitcombe and Northihamme" in the Hundred of Staple was £14.17.6 but a hundred years later (probably as a result of the building of the Castle by Sir Edward Dalynrigge in the fourteenth century which had increased the village's importance), it became a separate tithing.

The cases occurring in the rolls of the Court of the Frank Pledge are very varied being concerned with "defaulting suitors, assize of bread and ale, market regulations, overcharging in buying and selling, false weights and measures, setting corrupt victuals, waylaying on the highroad, bawds, eavesdroppers and chatterboxes, upkeep of bridges, roads and rights of way, diverting of highways and watercourses, cutting of trees in the highway" (these now belonged by right to the Lord of the Rape, even though the adjoining lands were not his), "fouling of springs, removal of boundary marks, rape, sorcery, fishing and poaching, keeping of nets, dogs and ferrets, waifs and strays, treasure-trove, and goods of felons".[1]

In view of this very comprehensive list of dealings it is not surprising that the Court sat for a week at least twice a year. Much of the interest which their activities hold for us today is in the names which occur in their lists.

In a Court of the View of the Frank Pledge for Staple Hundred held in 1392, three of the twelve Swornmen were Thomas Beche, John Kirsford (Crisford) and William Frensham, all names to become familiar in later Sedlescombe records. The Tithingman for "Setlyscombe" was William Geffray, who presented among others the following cases:[1]

(1) "the default of Thomas Mot . . . , that William Geffray junior . . . Thomas Beche . . . Thomas Mot . . . and Nicholas Thorpe . . . have brewed and broken assize, therefore they are in mercy . . .

[1] S.R.S. 37.

that there watch is not kept, and therefore the whole tithing is in mercy."

"The phrase 'in mercy' meant that the defendant was guilty and therefore at the mercy of the Court, which in this case included the whole of Sedlescombe, as the pledge had not been kept.

(2) "that as continually, the Abbot of Battle has withdrawn the tenants of Telscombath" (Iltonsbath) and Popynoth (Poppinhole) "as had already been presented and therefore counsel must be taken." (Iltonsbath and Poppinhole were by this time part of the Manor of Battle Abbey and, as the Abbot claimed "liberty from the Hundreds Courts, there was constant friction.") "Counsel was taken."

(3) "Iwherst have brewed and have not sent for the taster and therefore in mercy."

At a Court held at Easter of the year 1400 concerning "Setlyscombe it was presented: (1) that John Randecombe has encroached from the highway over against Wellefeld", a piece of land, measurements given, "which the Hundred is ordered to take back under penalty." Wellfield is still on the Tithe map. At Michaelmas in the same year it was presented that: (1) "Adam Corner was rebellious to the tithingman while doing his office and therefore he remains in mercy."

Michaelmas 1409: (1) that "Margerie Swyst of Ewhurst had made an assault against the peace on Isandra Jarye Hour'" as also had Isabella Freeman and that the said Isandra is a "common chaterbox'.

Michaelmas 1415 "Setlyscombe":

(1) "that Isabella Akedenne" (already in trouble for breaking arrest) "threw mud into the King's high road to the destruction of the aforesaid way and of her neighbours".

(2) "that a sheep value 9d is in the custody of Thomas Bisshop whereof the received is charged".

(3) "That Richard Curteys of Battle . . . entered the liberty of the Lordship" (of the Rape) "and made an assault on Richard Knyght against the peace by night; and with a strong hand, with force and arms, to wit with swords, bows and arrows, they unjustly took him off to Battle within the liberty and town of the Abbot of Battle, against the peace. And be it remembered to enquire of the

lord's tenants concerning the encroachments made by the Abbot of Battle as in Basokysse and Whatlingtonese". (Here is clearly another case of the Abbot interfering with a tenant, and removing him forcibly; and the older infringement is not to be forgotten.)

Three years later, early in the reign of Henry the fifth, on the Tuesday before Palm Sunday:
"for Setlyscombe, that Richard Bartlet of Battle broke the arrest of John a Lyghe and John Bathurst (subcollectors of the Lord King for the township of Setlyscombe) of 20 sheep and 11 beasts arrested and assessed for his goods there." (Bartlot Woods and Bathurst Woods are today local names.)

1447 Easter, a complaint was made that:

(1) "Thomas Bras of Ewhurst has encroached upon the highway between his house and the house of Simon Bisshop over against Mordantes" (the measurements of encroachment are given) "and order is given to amend it under penalty of ½ mark."

(2) and the twelve say that Thomas Bras has stopped up the highway over against Mordons with oak.'

(3) "that the same Thomas . . . keeps a bushel which is not sealed and order is given to amend it." The name Thomas Bras is interesting in view of Brasses Farm in Ewhurst; and that of Simon Bisshop because it is one of the earliest mentions of the family which came to own so much property in that part of Sedlescombe . which adjoins the parish of Ewhurst.

"John Castleman, tithingman of Sedlescombe presents:

(1) the default of John Botehurst and Edward Motey . . . from their view (of the Frank Pledge);

(2) that William . . . and Alexander Bysshop are tanners

(3) that Richard Beche has brewed commonly and he is a baker," (and so has no right to brew for public use).

(4) "John Westbourne has brewed commonly

(5) that the highway between Geffrays and Bisshopes is noxious in default of the whole tithing." Here is an example of the use of personal names for property. The house, Geffrays or Jeffreys—named, it could be presumed, after William Geffray, the aforementioned tithingman who had lived in it some fifty years earlier—today unidentified, figures frequently in early records of the property of the Bishop family. Did John Castleman, also a tithingman, give his name to Little Castlemans and so to Castlemans?

(6) "Richard Beche has a day to amend his ditches on the other side there under penalty of 12d."

(7) "default of the Rector of Sedlescombe' (James Fyndward) "in scouring the ditches against Preshousfeld 12d." (This is the first mention of the Precious field which adjoins the churchyard on the north side.) "The twelve jurors of the said Hundred of Staple say upon oath that all the above presentments are true. Affeerors, 4, one being William Bisshop sworn."

This Court continued through the centuries to sit, but the importance of the hundred gradually declined as the manorial and parochial administration became stronger and the status of Justices of the Peace increased. As a unit of government it existed until late in the 19th century when the Local Government Act of 1894 set up the District Council which is its logical successor. Until the development of the police forces this collective responsibility for apprehending offenders and bringing them to book was a dominant part of English country life. It would be interesting to know at what date the last Hundred Court was held.

So Staplecross must have been for a week, on these twice-yearly occasions, as busy as a market-place, with officials of the Court and others riding up from Bodiam, Sedlescombe, Chitcombe and Northiam. Many a small lad tarried expectantly in the hope of being called to hold a horse. Other travellers arrived in farm-carts or wagons and many on foot. An alehouse and stables would be a necessity so that those attending the Court could put up their horses, eat, quench their thirsts and gossip.

The present "Cross Inn" goes as far back as the fifteenth century replacing no doubt an earlier and more primitive building. Its sign today is a Cross formed from the four sails of a pictured windmill, a representation of the fine octagonal smock-mill which stood for 140 years but a stone's throw away. Built by a millwright, Thomas Martin, in 1815 to replace an earlier mill, it towered over the village in a row of other buildings, a splendid white windmill which was a landmark for miles around as had been its predecessor, marked on a map of 1783. In the late nineteenth century it was worked by Henry Richardson; and during World War II by Messrs. Banister and Co. After the war it ceased working and was finally demolished in 1952 because it was pronounced unsafe for the buildings beside it.

The sign of the inn was in earlier days too, surely, a cross, probably a more simple religious one.

*Chapter Five*

## THE BATTLE

Does an account of the battle, which took place outside the actual boundaries of the parish of Sedlescombe, have a place in a book about that village? Since it undoubtedly had a devastating effect on the people and the lands of the village before, during and after the battle, I think it does. Fuller calls it "the most famous and important battle ever fought in England, and one of the decisive battles of the world". It is also a fascinating story, about which millions of words have been and are still being written. With its fantastic trappings of a "hairy comet" and a "Hoar apple-tree", oaths broken and oaths kept, it is of the stuff of which sagas are made. With the illustrated story (the Bayeux Tapestry), the near contempory account from the Saxon side (in the Anglo-Saxon Chronicle) and the contempory account of it from the Norman side (in the Carmen de Haestingae proelio, or Song of the Battle of Hastings, written before 1070) we have three detailed early descriptions of the battle which agree surprisingly well.

Sedlescombe must have suffered before the battle for, while William remained near the coast for a fortnight hoping to draw Harold to fight him there (since the further he himself went into the interior the more dangerous would be his situation and his communications), he began a systematic destruction of the villages around, pillaging, killing and burning, and the result is noticeable in Domesday Book, where village after village is recorded as devastated or laid waste, including Sedlescombe and Whatlington. This was not just a matter of foraging for a hungry army, taking cattle for food; it was burning of villages and harrying of inhabitants, the victims being Harold's own people, since he was Earl of Wessex and Sussex was part of his inheritance. The Tapestry shows clearly the firing of a house, from

## THE BATTLE

which a Saxon woman and child are being driven. William hoped thus to entice Harold down to the coast to rescue and avenge them, so bringing him to battle there. His strategy was successful.

Harold's army consisted of (a) professional soldiers, (b) select Militia and (c) untrained Militia. The professional soldiers, called House-carls, a highly-trained Royal bodyguard of a few thousand well-equipped men-at-arms, paid in peace time as well as in war, wore a uniform, if it can be so called, of close-fitting leather jerkins to below the knee, on to which were sewn iron rings for better protection. Their head-gear was of steel with nose-pieces. The pointed wooden shields they carried were a yard long and their weapon was a long battle-axe. There were also javelin throwers and swordsmen in support. All are illustrated in the Tapestry, a strip cartoon of the battle.

The Militia was called the Select Fyrd. There has been much debate recently but it seems that every five hides of land in the country had to provide and support one soldier for two months every year. These formed the Select Militia, partly-trained men who could be called on to fight for sixty days at a time and could be called up again and again provided they could be provisioned and paid for by those they represented. There must have been in England at that time many thousand such part-time warriors (perhaps as many as 48,000).[1]

Finally, there were the untrained men, the ordinary Fyrd; villagers aged between 16 and 50, liable to serve as a Home Guard in their own district during the day, without pay. (If they were employed too far from home to return there at nightfall, they were paid.) These

---

[1] Lemmon.

were the ordinary able-bodied villagers with little discipline and no equipment. Their importance was that they could be quickly mobilised to repel coastal or local raids and were very useful, since they knew so well the locality, their own, in which they fought. They would be armed with anything they could lay hands on, clubs, scythes, axes, sharpened sticks, hooks, pitchforks or poles.

And so the able-bodied of Sedlescombe certainly fought in this famous battle. They may have already been driven by the devastation of the village to take their families and belongings for refuge into the surrounding forest.

Harold, hoping to surprise the Norman army, as he had surprised that of Hardrada and Tostig a few weeks earlier, hurried to Sussex with the half of his army most recovered from the recent battle, leaving the rest of it straggling, to join him as it could. They collected with the local Fyrd at the Hoar Apple-tree, well known to Harold and appointed for such a purpose some months before. This apple-tree, clearly a landmark, grew on Caldbec Hill near to where the boundaries of three Hundreds met;[1] always called the "Haar". I think that the Haar Apple-tree has over the years become corrupted to Hoar Apple-tree, aged and lichen-hung. There are many instances of apple-trees having been planted at the Haar as landmarks.

Harold drew up his army about one mile from the forest edge along the ridge of hill that is covered today with the Abbey buildings and the houses of Battle High Street and Mount Street, which was then rough untilled ground, though the eastern and southern slopes were cultivated. This was shortly after sunrise on the morning of Saturday, 14th October.

Meanwhile, in the Norman camp seven miles away, the soldiers had been busy preparing themselves and their horses for battle, and fitting on their helmets. They must have moved from camp before the sun rose at 6.20, marching quickly along the ridge to the hill now known as Black Horse, or Telham Hill, about a mile from Senlac where Harold's army was arrayed.

When the Norman host appeared, advancing over Telham Hill into Harold's view, he seems to have been taken by suprise. He had expected a large army of foot soldiers and archers, but not an immense number of horsemen such as he now saw before him.

[1] Lemmon.

# THE BATTLE

William had achieved the impossible by transporting hundreds of animals over the Channel in flat-bottomed boats. Also, according to the Anglo-Saxon Chronicle, the Normans appeared before Harold's army was set in order.

So Harold called his men to battle, riding among them and giving his final orders, which were that they must keep together at all costs and defend themselves as a body, none to move from his own place, which he must defend to the last. The Saxons did not fight on horseback, preferring to fight on foot. The Norman cavalry, he emphasised, would be at a disadvantage having to charge uphill from low, marshy ground. If the English foot stood firm together the horsemen could not penetrate them.

William had achieved his wish. He had brought Harold to fight him near the coast. Harold had not succeeded in his desire to surprise, but he did have an ideal position for battle, on ground of his own choosing.

So the trumpets sounded and the battle began. The Norman archers advanced to within bow-range, a hundred yards from the Saxon line (the Bayeux Tapestry shows them sticking their large quivers in the ground) and they began to shoot, uphill, as needs must.

"Preparing to meet the enemy", the song of Guy of Amiens relates, "the King (Harold) mounted the hill . . . on the highest point of the summit he planted his banner. . . . All the men dismounted and left their horses in the rear and taking their stand on foot they let the trumpets sound for battle. . . . First the bands of archers (Normans) attacked and from a distance transfixed the

bodies with their shafts and the crossbowmen destroyed the shields as if by a hailstorm, shattered by countless blows. Now the French attacked the left, the Bretons the right; the Duke with the Normans fought in the centre. The English stood firm on their ground in closest order"—as Harold had commanded them. "They met missile with missile, sword-stroke with sword-stroke; bodies could not be laid down, nor dead give place to living soldiers, for each corpse though lifeless stood as if unharmed and held its post; nor would the attackers have been able to penetrate the dense forest of Englishmen had not guile reinforced their strength. The French, versed in stratagems, skilled in warfare, pretended to fly as if defeated." Some authorities say that this was not a stratagem but

## THE BATTLE

a genuine panic; whichever it was, it had the effect of making the English peasantry, not the Select Fyrd or House Carls, "rejoice and believe that they had won; they pursued in the rear with naked swords . . . each wing of the English vied to be first to slaughter the scattered enemy in various ways. But those who feigned flight wheeled on the pursuers and forced them, held in check, to flee from death. A great part fell there . . . (but the part in close order stood fast)" so the trained troops still obeyed Harold's command, standing together behind him "for indeed ten thousand suffered destruction in that place." These were the untrained, the Great Fyrd, the villagers. "But the very powerful force that survived in the battle attacked more furiously and counted their losses nothing. The English people, prevailing by their numbers, repulsed the enemy and by their might compelled him to turn . . . and then the flight which had first been a ruse became enforced by valour. The Normans fled, their shields covered their backs."

William had to move fast to save the day. "When the Duke saw his people vanquished, he rushed to confront the rout. . . . He spoke words of entreaty. 'Where are you flying? . . . It is hard to return home, the sea lies behind you . . . hard and long the voyage; here no way of escape remains for you! You will fight to conquer if you only want to live! . . .' Their faces grew red with shame. They wheeled, they turned to face the enemy. The Duke as leader was the first to strike; after him the rest laid on. With drawn sword he hewed to pieces helms and shields, and even his war-horse slew many. Harold's brother, Gyrth by name, born of a royal line, was undaunted by the face of the lion; poising a javelin, he hurled it from afar with a strong arm. The flying weapon wounded the body of the horse and forced the Duke to fight on foot; but reduced to a foot soldier, he fought yet better, for he rushed upon the young man like a snarling lion. Hewing him limb from limb" he killed Gyrth, "and very many souls he sent to darkness."[1]

The battle lasted for eight hours. Colonel Lemmon says that there must have been long pauses in the conflict, since soldiers cannot fight hand-to-hand for eight hours on end. After the struggle just described both sides must have had to re-form, fill their gaps and recover and redistribute their weapons, not to speak of providing themselves with time to snatch food and drink.

[1] Wace.

Attack after attack took place, but the House Carls with their wall of shields stood firm. "The Norman archers with their bows shot thickly upon the English, but they covered themselves with their shields, so that the arrows could not reach their bodies, nor do any mischief, how true soever was the aim or however well they shot. . . . The battle was up and down, this way and that, and no-one knew who would conquer and win the land. Both sides stood so firm and fought so well that no one could guess which would prevail. They were ever-ready with their steel, these sons of the old Saxon race, the most dauntless of men." So wrote the near contemporary Englishman, Wace, and the Norman, William of Poitiers.

The Normans seem then to have staged another feigned flight. "The Normans saw that the English defended themselves well and were so strong in position that they could do little against them, so they consulted together privily and arranged to draw off, and to pretend to flee till the English should pursue and scatter themselves over the field. . . . And as they said, so they did. The Normans by little and little fled, the English following after them. . . . Thus they were deceived by the pretended flight and great mischief thereby befell them; for if they had not moved from their position it is not likely they would have been conquered at all".

"The Normans, retreating slowly, so as to draw the English further on; as still they flee, the English pursue, they push out their lances and stretch forth their hatchets . . . scattering themselves over the plain. . . . Then the Normans resumed their former position, turning their faces towards the enemy; and the men were to be seen facing round and rushing onwards to a fresh melee, the one party attacking the other . . . one hits, another misses; one flies, another pursues . . . on every hand they fight hard, the blows are heavy and the struggle becomes fierce."[1]

The Normans failed to break through the firm standing Fyrd. All were exhausted. Nearly despairing, William called to his archers for a last effort; they had all to win, nothing to lose. Could they shoot, he asked, over the Saxon shields up into the sky?

"At one hundred yards short of the English line," records Wace, "the archers halted. Crouching beneath their quivers, elevating their bows . . . the arrows swept over the massed line of shields and in their falling they struck the heads and faces of the English and

[1] Wace.

put out the eyes of many. . . . To protect their faces from the falling shower, the Englishmen were forced to raise their shields, exposing their bodies to the thrusts of lances and preventing them from using their axes."

One of the eyes that was pierced was the right eye of King Harold. The Bayeux Tapestry shows him clutching the arrow's shaft, as he falls to the ground at the foot of his standard. The fight went on thickly and fiercely around him, the House Carls defending him as the Normans fought their way to the crown of the ridge, to the ring of House Carls, to the Standard, to the still breathing King. The Tapestry shows the last act, the killing of Harold and finally a knight hacking off his left leg.

It is all over. Harold is dead. The battle that was so nearly won is lost. "Many of the richest and noblest Englishmen fled," says Wace of those that were left.

But even at this final hour the Englishmen that remained, even though in flight, had some fight in them. William of Poitiers writes: "They began to fly as swiftly as they could, some on horseback, some on foot, some along the roads, but mostly over the trackless country. . . . Although ignorant of the country, the Normans eagerly carried on the pursuit. The tapestry shows the English flying, some on the horses of their leaders . . . other Normans strip the dead of their valuable mail shirts."

The Chronicle of Battle Abbey, which was written before 1180, states: "Between the two armies lay a dreadful chasm, of broad extent when seen at close quarters, a wide ravine formed either by a natural cleft in the ground, or perhaps by being hollowed out by storms, yet so overgrown in its vast expanse by bushes and brambles that it was not discernible, so that it destroyed large numbers especially of the pursuing Norman horsemen. For as in their wild unwitting charge they galloped headlong into this place, they perished terribly, dashed to pieces. And so this abyss is to this day called by the name derived from this disaster—Malfosse." In the hour of victory the Normans thus lost more men than they had during the battle.

For years there has been a search for this place, and three of the sites which have been identified with it in the past have one by one been questioned and found wanting. The late Mr. C. T. Chevallier, Clerk of the Battle Rural District Council for many years until 1958, studied all the evidence exhaustively, and in a lecture delivered to the Battle & District Historical Society on February 27th, 1953, spoke thus: "All, or nearly all, the features of the Malfosse, as described by the Chroniclers, such as multiple ditches, a defensible far bank and a causeway crossing the ravine, apply to the Oakhurst Gill, running 1,500 yards north of the Abbey, a sufficient distance for the English 'to suffer countless casualties in their flight' before they got there.[1] Unfortunately, the causeway, if in the situation suggested by the map of 1724, is buried beneath the higher and wider embankment of the Turnpike road to London, constructed in 1836 on the line slightly oblique to that of the track leading to the causeway. Factors of line and visibility connected with the course of the battle suggest that Oakwood Gill was Malfosse. The episode could only have occurred when, to excited victors, it seemed just light enough to make a heavy charge, but when in fact it was just too dark. On that moonless evening corresponding to October 20th (new style) dusk was about 5.35 p.m. Harold fell about 4 p.m., as time was then roughly judged. The intervening period would be fully occupied by the mopping up on the battle ridge, a running fight back to Caldbec Hill and final victory on its summit.

"On several grounds it is likely that the last stand was made there. It was this hill, and not the battle ridge below, that earned the name Mount of Joy, which it still carries. That Edith Swan-Neck was so early available to seek out Harold's body suggests her capture here, at Harold's assembly post. . . . We can infer that William himself reached the summit and saw the fleeing English seeking shelter in Oakwood and its gill. Down the slope he set his mounted knights in motion. Very soon, but when it was quite dark, Eustace of Boulogne hastened back to report the disaster in the valley and to urge that it was death to go on. As he spoke, Eustace was struck down in the dark by an unknown hand. If before the Malfosse charge began William had not taken his stand at a point where he could be found, Eustace would not have known where to find him. As it was, Eustace had only to climb the hill, aided, it may be, by a victory fire on the Mount of Joy, to find the Duke there. It is hard to conceive," concluded Mr. Chevallier, "any satisfactory basis for these occurrences other than that William was on Caldbec Hill and that the Malfosse episode took place at the wood, gill and causeway of Oakwood, down below."

[1] Map A on A2100 between Le Rette Farm and Woodsdale.

"The Duke," wrote Freeman, "allowed the women of the countryside to remove the bodies of their husbands, sons, brothers and fathers for Christian burial in nearby churches." It is not hard to imagine the stunned despair of the remaining inhabitants of that countryside when the autumn morning dawned. The day had been so nearly theirs. The disaster was so complete, so utterly final. The King and all his brothers dead, together with many of the aristocracy. There was no one to gather the remnants and to give a new lead. The English were a conquered race; the foreigners who now ruled were French-speaking, who regarded every native as an inferior. Yet England remained England.

Though no national leader emerged to save the English heritage, the ordinary folk stayed firmly English, never allowing themselves to be made into French peasants, and it was the language of these inarticulate countrymen (though it was much influenced by the Norman-French which was for years the language of the new aristocracy) which eventually triumphed.

*Chapter Six*

THE HIDDEN TREASURE

The village and the fields around Sedlescombe suffered badly after, as before the battle, for it was on the line of retreat. Edith Swan Neck, Harold's handfast, or morganatic wife, is described by Hope Muntz in her book *The Golden Warrior* as having hidden after the battle in a wood near Sedlescombe. Survivors of the ordinary Fyrd, the men from the village who had fought in the battle, must also have hidden in the forest till it was safe to return to what was left of their huts, when the Normans had gone further afield. Some of the women braved the dangers abroad to go and search for the bodies of their missing men on the field of battle. Everywhere was mourning and fear, despair and the shock of defeat, with the death of the King and all his brothers. Many had no homes to return to and no food to eat. Crops and cattle were gone. Saxons of all ranks were fleeing and in hiding. moreover most of Harold's best soldiers, the House Carls, had died with him.

On a summer's day more than eight hundred years later a villager in Sedlescombe made a very strange and surprising discovery. Boyce Harvey Combe of Oaklands described how on "Thursday afternoon of August 24th 1876 a labourer, whilst digging a drain in a grass field,"[1] (No. 458, on the Tithe Map known as Street or Barber's Field, Barber of Homestall being the tenant), "struck his spade against some hard substance; on looking down he saw what he took to be a hop tally. On further search he discovered in a small hole the pieces of a small iron pot, and inside the pot the pieces of a leathern bag with about a pint of coins—the iron is quite oxidised and the bag quite rotten[2] The coins are of three or four different

[1] Map 5.
[2] S.A.S. Museum.

sorts and sizes, but apparently all of Edward the Confessor, (1041-1061). They are of very thin silver in tolerably good preservation but are very common and of no great value . . . The soil is light sand and very dry and the hole in which the coins were found is about 2 ft. from the surface. The field has been in grass for a great many years."[1] The coins, still mistaken for a time for hop tallies, were greedily appropriated by the village children for playthings until their real character was discovered, when they were promply exchanged for current coin. Mr. Raper of Battle found it therefore impossible "to arrive at a reliable estimate of the number of coins composing the hoard, but I surmise", he wrote "that there were probably between two and three thousand.[2] "After considerable labour and delay I have succeeded in tracing a large number of the coins . . . and have catalogued in all 1,836 perfect coins, and have examined the fragments of 50 more, which were too minutely divided to permit of their being catalogued. The oxide was easily removed by hot water, soap and a soft brush, but the operation was delicate and tedious, owing to the extreme brittleness of many of the coins. Many were considerably worn, showing that they had been long in circulation, but many were as fresh, and their impressions as clear and perfect, as on the day they left the minter's hand; these latter were not of any particular mint. All the coin's were found to belong to the reign of Edward the Confessor . . . , minted at no less than 44 cities and towns scattered over the length and breadth of England, from York in the north to Exeter in the south-west and Dover in the south-east; and, considering the comparative slowness of inter-communication in Saxon times, one may fairly conclude that such a varied collection of the same reign could only come together in some great centre such as London, or perhaps . . . a port of communication between this country and the continent; such as Hastings.

"The fact that they all belong to Edward the Confessor's reign points strongly to the conclusion that they must have been concealed either during his reign or very shortly after, while their vicinity to the field of Senlac suggests some connection with that memorable battle . . . It represented so large a sum in those days that one can scarcely suppose it was private property, but that it rather belonged to the Public Exchequer. The fact that three-fifths of the

[1] S.AC. 27.
[2] S.AC. 33.

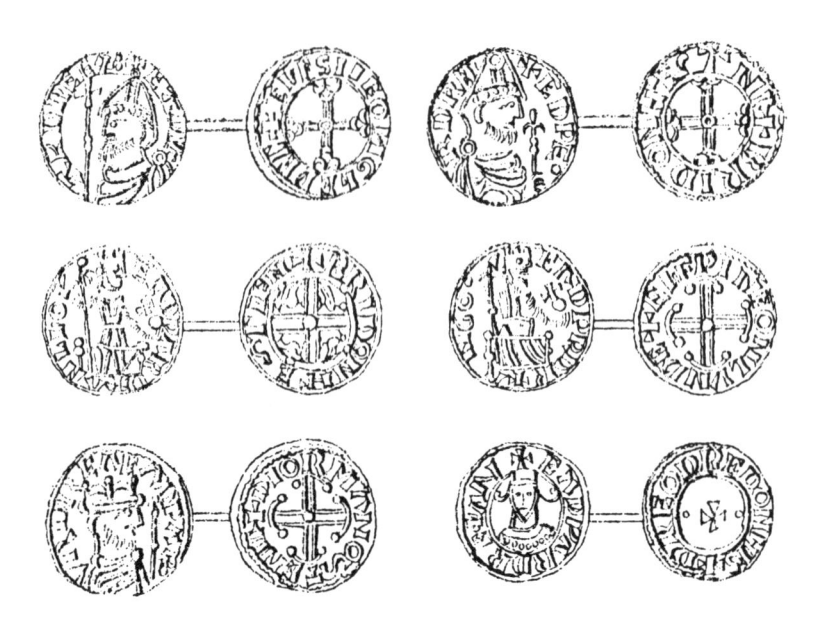

coins were minted at Hastings favours the theory that they came from that port, and may well have been Crown Revenue, despatched inland for safety when Duke William appeared off the coast, or that they may have been sent, later on, to replenish Harold's military chest and, after his defeat and death were carried off by some of his followers to prevent their falling into Norman hands. The spot where they were found lies to the north-east of the battlefield and in the direction in which the greater part of Harold's followers fled after his death, for it is recorded that the fugitives turned on their Norman pursuers and inflicted great slaughter on them in a ravine, which acquired in consequence the name of Malfosse, and this ravine is situated in a direct line between Senlac and the spot where the coins were discovered.[1] Possibly he who buried the chest may have been prevented by death or some other cause from returning to recover it; or, returning, may have failed to recognise the spot where he concealed it."

This location of Malfosse has since been disputed. Ch. 4.

## THE HIDDEN TREASURE

Mr. Ernest Willett, F.S.A., an authority on coins of that date, adds: —"The enormous proportion of coins from Hastings, the comparatively large number from the rare mint of Romney and the representation of all mints in the immediate neighbourhood, together with the absence of all early-struck types, points to the hoard being, as Mr. Raper suggests, hastily collected in an emergency, and there is little doubt but that it was part of the treasure belonging to that ill-starred host which fought so gallantly at Senlac."

What a thrilling find! What a fascinatingly romantic story. The discovery of Harold's pay chest within a mile or two of the most famous battle in English history! All the coin experts flock to the spot; the reporters, the television cameras, the buzz of eager excitement, the fuss, the locals wishful to be in it! Sedlescombe on the map for ever—Sedlescombe in the news and in the national papers —if the discovery had been made 100 years later in 1976!

As it was—the treasure was handed out to school children and would never have been recognised but for the eagle eye of Mr. Raper of Battle. The only national notice of it, even so, seems for some reason to be on the Ordnance Map, where the site and date of the find is marked. In 1947 the British Museum had never heard of it!

Perhaps we can be glad to have been spared all the notoriety and the price that has, in modern days, to be paid for it!

Of the coins, two or three can be seen in the Museum of the Battle Historical Society, two in the Hastings Museum and two in the Barbican Museum at Lewes; and that is the end of the fascinating little contact with a very enthralling chapter of early English history.

*Chapter Seven*

## THE VOW KEPT

"I make a vow that on this place of battle I will found a suitable free monastery for the salvation of you all and especially for those who fall." Thus spoke Duke William on the eve of the battle.

To his credit, in victory King William the Conqueror remembered his vow (partly perhaps with thoughts of his system of defence) and one of his first acts was to found and endow the monastery which was to be "the token and pledge of the royal crown" and, according to the words of its foundation charter, the "one great chantry for the souls' health of those who helped to win by toil and aid the kingdom for him and especially for those who died in the battle."[1] A solemn Mass of Requiem was to be offered up in the Abbey, year in, year out, for all the souls—of English and Norman alike— who had fallen on the field.

The endowment was magnificent and the privileges and immunities unique, generous and very extensive; his gratitude proven. To the monastery he granted and gave the Leuga lying round it (this was all land within a radius of one and a half miles). Within this territory the Abbot of Battle was to be sole sovereign, holding his own Court free of the jurisdiction of Rape and Hundred; the priviledge valued before all others was his exemption from all spiritual jurisdiction. He was as supreme in his monastery as was the Primate of Canterbury in England. Battle has through the ages remained a 'peculiar'. A note in a book, still preserved, dated May 1844, records: "Whereas I am desirous . . . to hold a Confirmation in the Parish Church of Battle, I do hereby declare that I do it not by virtue of any Episcopal Authority which I lay claim or intend to

[1] Ch. B. A.

## THE VOW KEPT

exercise there, but by the consent of Revd. Jno. Littler, A. M. Dean of Battle, to whom that exempt Jurisdiction is granted. A. T. Chichester.' " To this day the Bishop still knocks on the church door for permission to enter before he takes a Confirmation; a tradition greatly cherished by Battle with its long history. At the Silver Jubilee, the Advowson was offered to and very graciously accepted by her Majesty, Queen Elizabeth the Second.

All these privileges made a grand foundation, but the material foundations were slower to achieve. Monks came from France to superintend the building, but the site on which the King had determined—the crown of the hill where the battle had been won, the high altar to be on the exact spot where the English standard had been captured and Harold killed—was exposed and waterless and did not please the monks. They settled for a more sheltered site, protected from the winds and gales, and began to build themselves temporary dwellings and shelters, until the King came to see for himself the progress of the work. His anger was great when he saw that they had changed his site, and he commanded them to build where he had planned, waving away complaints concerning lack of water and lack of stone. "I will so amply provide for this place," he cried, "that wine will be more abundant here than water in any other abbey" and as for stone, he would himself send ships to bring Norman stone from Caen at his own expense. As he said, so he did; but still the building rose too slowly. "A goodly number of men were brought hither out of neighbouring countries and some even from foreign countries." Did any men from the devastated little village of Sedlescombe, after putting their homes to rights, find work for their hands in the erection of this great building?

William never saw its completion. He died where he was born, in Normandy. Had he died in England he might well have been buried in his own abbey, the fulfilment of his vow.

William Rufus, his son, visiting the Abbey in 1090, was impatient and annoyed to find the work of building still progressing far too slowly. Five years later he was waiting at Hastings with 20,000 troops for a fair wind to carry him across the channel to invade Normandy. For six weeks he was forced to wait, and during this time the dedication of the still unfinished Abbey took place in his presence, with the support of Gundred, Bishop of Rochester, among five others, clergy and, no doubt, some of his soldiers, possibly a few proud veterans of that epoch-making battle, now thirty years away.

Beside the Abbey and only because of the Abbey the settlement, which quickly became the town of Battle, grew up to provide goods and services for the Abbey. Here was a great opportunity for the enterprising; for craftsmen and merchants as well as for labourers, and the weekly market established by Henry I throve. The Community was tightly knit with that of the Abbey for the Abbot was lord of both, administering justice in his court, confining miscreants to his own prison, and giving the final punishment on his own gallows; and at the same time presenting a centre of employment and settlement, security and defence. Family relationships between monks and burgesses, too, were often close and town and abbey were interdependent.

The criticism by the first four monks that the earth of the site was dry with no nearby source of water and with only miles of primeval forest surrounding it was true; and, but for William the Conquerer's decision, would not have been a natural choice for either an abbey or a town. Thus, in this difficult country, the early Abbots concentrated on settling and extending the small clearances of land, often just swine pastures, closest to the Abbey; but their eyes turned naturally with desire towards the river pastures with their cattle-grazing potentials which, already partly cleared, lay in the parishes of Sedlescombe and Whatlington and just outside the leuga; and which had the additional advantage of giving access to the river and its means of transport to the coastal ports. An Abbot early purchased 30 acres of low-lying meadow on the North bank of the Rother as far away as Bodiam with the same object, and one of his successors built a wharf there for the loading and unloading of goods to be shipped down the Rother. By 1124 the fourth Abbot, Ralph, a Norman from Caen, had acquired Sedlescombe lands in Wickham which lay alongside the stream from Durhamford to the Bowlings, and also in Iltonsbath, thus enlarging the Leuga lands to the East and gaining those desired water-meadows and river lands. Both Robert Basoc (chapter 11) "Lord of Sedlescombe," and Alicia, Countess of Eu, gave holdings of land at Iltonsbath 100 years later where the Abbey established a corn mill and a tannery. These lands were not, at first, outright gifts, for the same gifts were made more than once, but were grants of the rents only. The Abbey policy in the early thirteenth and fourteenth centuries was to bind these and other holdings to the Abbey by a much firmer tie. John, the Abbot from 1308-1311, was a native of Whatlington, his family being cattle-raisers there, and he bought up for the Abbey the lands of his own family including the grasslands of the Bowlings, the early holdings of the de Beche family, and also some peasant holdings.[1] Abbot Walter de Luci, 1139-1171, one of the ablest of the Abbey's administrators, continued the process, buying the church of Westfield and its wist (about 82 acres)[2] which lay close to the Leuga boundary.

Somehow in the course of the fourteenth century these lands with those of Iltonsbath and Wickham in Sedlescombe were turned into copyholds and the Abbots successfully imposed heriots on lands which had never previously known them. There is no record of how this was achieved but it may well have been the result of the Black Death which, in the two years 1348-1350, reduced the number of monks from 52 to 34. It is likely therefore that the countryside around suffered comparative losses, leaving many holdings of land empty. With no heir, copyhold was easily achieved and the peasants of the Leuga lost their old freedom to buy and sell customary land by charter. The Abbey's policy of bonding the lands firmly to it had succeeded and from henceforth till the twentieth century all the Abbey lands, held for rent or service directly from it, paid heriot or heriot relief.

Those lands eventually included all the houses on the East side of the Green as far as Harriet House; all the Brooks and the Bowlings and nearly all the meadows beside the Stream between them and Spilsteads Farm. In the deeds of the houses on these lands (described in later chapters) it is frequently recorded how when a tenant or owner died the heir, on being admitted as the new occupier, had to pay fine and often heriot or heriot relief. Heriot was "an obligation, derived from Saxon times, on an heir to return to the lord the war apparel of the deceased tenant originally supplied by the lord. This military gear, depending on the status of the tenant, included a horse, harness and weapons. This obligation applied to both freeman and villein. At about the time of the Norman Conquest, the custom was being superseded by a tenant's

---

[1] Searle.
[2] "Wist" may well be the origin of "wysse" and "wish" as a suffix to field and land-names: e.g. "Gorwysse, Basocwysshe" etc.

heir giving his lord the best beast of the dead tenant, and later this became simply a money payment and, in effect, a fee to enter the estate."[1]

The Abbots were now landlords with a rent-roll, within and without the Leuga, of farms and smallholdings as well as of burgesses' houses and shops.

Under the Abbey patronage, Battle became the finest town in Sussex after Chichester and its market drew from long distances both buyers and sellers of high-class goods, as did its twice yearly fairs held in July and September.

The sixteenth century brought its cataclysmic change. By 1538 every abbey in Sussex had been dissolved except those of Battle and Robertsbridge. By the 27th of May the King's officials had received the charter of voluntary dissolution, sealed and signed by the Abbot of Battle, John Hamond, and his eighteen monks. All received pensions save only one monk, a young man not much above twenty-one years of age.

In early August the site, buildings and Leuga, with other Sussex lands of this Abbey, were granted to the King's friend, Sir Anthony Browne, son-in-law of Sir John Gage of Firle; Master of the King's Horse the following year and, in 1540, Knight of the Garter, and later to be Lord Montagu. He preferred his other country house of Cowdray and pulled down the church cloister and chapter house at Battle, selling the material to help to finance his building works at Cowdray and Southwark.

The last of the thirty-two Abbots who had ruled the Abbey for 471 years, John Hamond, lived in Battle until he died one year before his King, in 1546, leaving the last of the Abbey possessions to the parish church.

Lord Montagu's descendants converted the remaining Abbey buildings into a mansion-house where generations of them lived, and the gateway keep was used as a prison right into the nineteenth century. The Lord or his Steward presided, as had the Abbots, at the Manorial Courts held in the Great Hall, taking over the copyhold customs and heriots introduced by them. It is amazing to read in the *Deeds of Spilsteds* (Chapter 23) that as late as December 1835 when the owner, Tilden Smith, died 'there happened to the Lord for Heriots five horses which were seized and compounded

---

[1] L. Hist. Enc.

for £61.6s.8d.' and, in 1857, the Auction Schedule informed all possible buyers that the farm buildings were subject to 'the annual quit rent of 11/8d and to heriot of best beast on death . . . and the remainder of the farm to quit rents of £1.19s.10d. per annum and . . . to six heriots of the best beast at death.' When Hercules Brabazon died in 1906 his heir too paid heriot, on part of his lands, to the Battle Abbey Estate. Heriot was a fair enough demand when the horse had been originally supplied by the lord, but it seems completely unjust when this was not so, and an iniquitous demand from a farmer.

*Marley Farm*[1]

The Manor and farm of Marley was created in the first years of the fourteenth century entirely as a demesne farm to supply meat and food to the Abbey; and it was worked at first by the monks themselves with the assistance of wage labour. There were at the beginning no tenants, for customary work had always been paid with a meal and a few pence per day; and, with the price of food rising, this became less profitable for the Abbey, so wage labour with no meals was a better deal. Therefore, customary labour was little by little commuted to wage labour.

Abbot John de Whatlington systematically acquired for his Abbey, to the loss of the poorer peasants, the lands which followed the course of the tributaries of the Line and the Brede lying between the villages of Sedlescombe and Whatlington. These were the old lands of Robert de Basoc and Olivia de Wickham, where clearing had been easiest and which were rich pasture land, the very best for raising cattle for meat and dairy produce; for horses, ponies and oxen for work on the farm, which could find sheltered winter grazing in the surrounding forest of Petley Woods and Bathurst Great Wood.[2] Felons Wood, divided from Petley Woods by Marley Lane, is in early records "Fellands Wood", a word which denotes land bordering demesne land. Hangman's Croft carved out of it may well be that of the Abbey hangman in days when the Abbot's justice held sway.

In the last quarter of the fourteenth century after the Black Death, holdings in the Marley demesne were taken by tenants and accepted as hereditary copyholds, that is, "held by copy of the Court Roll". One of these tenants was a Hamond.

[1] Marley House. Map A.
[2] Searle.

Tradition has it that Marley farmhouse was built with stone from those parts of the Abbey which were demolished by Sir Anthony Browne in the middle of the sixteenth century.

Marley Farm was added to over the years and included all the lands of the Bowland Brooks and Black Brooks with the farmhouses of Beanford, Battle Barn Farm and Lower Marley. At the beginning of the twentieth century Horsmans, Magazine Farm and the Bowlings were built by the Estate. During the next twenty-five years all were sold and for the first time became entirely independent of Battle Abbey, which had for hundreds of years given employment to farm labourers and many a skilled man from Sedlescombe; hedgers, ditchers, thatchers, carters, horse- and cattle-breeders and blacksmiths. Among these were George Simmons and his son who for two generations did all the smith's work on the farm; and Bert Wilson who was gardener at Marley between the wars, the owners then being the Pears family (of soap fame). Since that day it has had little connection with Sedlescombe.

*The Bowlings and Blackbrooks, or Hamond Land*

In 1367, the Hamond family was the second largest renter of land in the Abbey demesne, and in 1450 John Hamond, jointly with his wife, still held "the tenement, Bowland Brook and Blackbrook, formed by his great grandfather out of Marley demesne." In April of that year,[1] the Tithing headman distrained several of Hamond's cattle for non-payment of his share in the communal tithe; his successor at the Michaelmas Court refused to return them until the debt was paid. In November, Hamond fought back, suing the two Tithingmen for trespass. He admitted that he owed the tithe though he had paid his rent, for he denied that such customs as the tithing-fine were a charge on his land. A jury of twelve burgesses of Battle ordered the return of the beasts to the headman of the Tithing and cleared him of trespass. Ten years later the fines were being paid. This case shows that, though Hamond lost, seignurial rights could be queried in open court in a democratic way without fear.

Robert Hamond married Florence Gunne, heir to her brother's lands which also lay in Wickham. One of their grandsons became the last Abbot of Battle while his brother, Richard, inherited the lands which continued in the family for a long time after the Dissolution and which are frequently referred to in deeds as Hamondland.

---

[1] Searle.

In 1656 Bowland Brook figures as an old parcel of Marley demesne. In Deeds of Spilsteds 1785, Little Bowlands, Bowlands alias Hamonds, and Wickhamsland appear as part of its farm lands. The Battle Abbey Estate Map of 1811 shows Rough Bowlings, a field of 4 closes, and Smooth Bowlings, of 2 closes, totalling 20 acres each. The Tithe Map of 1840 shows how the New Road, the Turnpike from St. Leonards to Whatlington, split these Brook lands in two; those on the East side, Battle Abbey brookland and Riccards farm, and those on the West being of Spilsteads and its neighbouring farm, Beech (temporarily Street Farm). During these years cattle gave place on a large part of these pasture lands to hops. During the present century they have gradually reverted to cattle pasture, which is what the original word "Buland" meant: cattle land.

Mr. Jack Johnson until 1930 farmed 25 acres of the Bowlings, probably the Rough Bowlings of the early records, while the Smooth Bowlings are part of Spilsteads.

The present Bowlings House was built in 1956 replacing a pair of cottages built by the Abbey Estate towards the end of the nineteenth century. These may well have replaced an earlier building, for farm sheds still stand a few yards away, cut off by the "New Road".

The cottages now house employees of the Waterworks Department of the Eastbourne Corporation and the 25 acres of land have been added to Leaford Farm of Whatlington.

*Lower Marley Farm*

This farm was cut off from Marley farm by the Turnpike Road, the New Road. The house, part of which is very old, was sold by the Battle Abbey Estate to the Waterworks Department of the Hastings Corporation in 1926. They sank a borehole on it unsuccessfully and built on to the house, which is now let with 41 acres of surrounding meadow to a local farmer whose father farmed both it and Luff's.

*Little Powdermill Farm*

After the closing down in 1825 of the Powdermill (Chapter 29), always part of the Battle Abbey Estate, the old mill-house became a farm labourer's house with a smallholding attached, once part of Hamonds land. The Dallaways were the last family to live in the old house, and Miss Dallaway, now at Cripps Corner, remembers being woken one midnight by the noise of many feet rushing along the mill lane which passes across the Brooks close by the house. "What's all that running?" cried her mother, and then through the window they saw that westwards the sky was flaming bright where it should have been black. The great barn of Lower Marley farm on the far side of the Brooks was ablaze. The hay was all burnt to ashes but the house was saved.

In 1905, after the Dallaways had moved to Little Castlemans, the old mill-house was pulled down and four years later the present one was built on the same site by the Websters of Battle Abbey, leaving most of the old powdermill buildings, used for years as farmsheds, standing. A family of the name of Parson started a laundry business, with a pony and trap to fetch and deliver the laundered clothes. Gypsies did a good business selling clothes pegs to them. In about 1920, Frank Thomas, the builder, moved in with his family. After World War II, it became for some years tea-rooms, its name changed to The Waterfall, and a popular place it was with expert Yorkshire home-baking. Now once again it is a private house.

One by one the old mill-sheds have, over the years, been pulled down; but there still remain to tell the tale the old powdermill runners or grindstones; and the fall of water which turned the old mill-wheel still splashes down into the mill-pool, where trout lurk.

Up another tributary to the Brede, the Black Brook, lay a small cleared valley cut out of the northern end of Bathurst Great Wood, known often in Battle Abbey records as North Bathurst. Here lie the farms of Beanford, Horsmans, Magazine; and Battle Barn (Chapter 32).

*Beanford (Map A)*
Beanford is by far the oldest of these farmhouses and has been standing for around five hundred years in a fold behind Black Brooks where the old road from Westfield down Crazy Lane to Battle forded the Chanse stream. In a later record it is Beauford, the easy misprint of 'u' for 'n' creating a lovely though erroneous picture of the "beautiful ford". The old crownpost and heavy beams still remain in the house, supporting it; and the roof, once of thatch, spreads itself far down over the walls in the ancient way. It was

always held of Battle Abbey and "Notices under Marlye" for 1530 include "Beneford and the Watermill near Iltonsbath."[1]

In 1700 there were three holdings: one with cottage called Avans, one with house Beanford, and another with cottage called Greens. In 1569 the heirs of Laurence Avann and later of Robert Avann were recorded as holding Blacklands, the heirs of John Boyes held Beneford, and the heirs of Richard Bishop Greens. In 1433 Richard Grene had held 'a messuage and garden' bordered on the north by 'the royal street'—the King's highway— 'from Botehurst to Westfield'[2] the now overgrown lane leading into Crazy Lane at the Blackbrooks Garage. In maps of the late eighteenth century, Beanford farm is marked Evans or Avans and Horsfield in 1824 follows suit. But at a Court Baron of Godfrey Webster held in 1792 there is no mention of Evans by name when "At this Court came John Pollard Crouch of Hastings, a customary tenant of the Manor and surrendered . . . all that . . . cottage and garden lying near Bathurst Wood . . . and also . . . Beanford . . . and also one other customary messuage . . . called Greens . . . to the use and behoof of Jeremiah Skinner . . ." By 1815 all three had become part of Marley Farm, the Home or Demesne farm, and continued so for about a hundred years. Beanford was then sold as an independent farm and has remained so ever since. It is possible that the old cottages of Evans and Greens may have degenerated into farm buildings and cartsheds.

*Magazine Farm*

These farmlands were probably originally divided between Horsmans and Lower Marley whose lands were separated by the New Road after 1830. There seems no record of it as an independent holding, though there were certainly buildings there before the present house was built at the turn of the century for the Battle Abbey Estate. Its name indicates that it was connected in earlier days with the Powdermill in the Brooks below it, for a Magazine is defined as a building or room where the supply of powder is kept. Tradition has always said that this is what it was, following the principle of keeping powdermill buildings well apart. There are stories too of entrances to subterranean hiding-places. Magazine Stream and Magazine Wood are close by.

[1] Thorpe.
[2] S.B.A. 1433.

When the present farmhouse was built, the farm was largely used for cattle-rearing for Marley Farm. Soon after World War I it was sold, and has since continued as an independent cattle farm under successive owners.

*Horsmans*

An entry in the list of rentals in Thorpe's Catalogue records in 1457, "Receipts of rents of lands in Little Uckham, the farm called Cheverles (Chevaliers) . . . meadow near Petlet, lands designated as Sandpettes and Northbotehurst, Pasture called Botehurst, the farm of a garden called Grene's."

It is possible that this Chevalier is the origin of the name Horsmans, since the latter is a literal translation. Botehurst has become Bathurst and Uckham is identifiable with Wickham. However, another possible origin of the farm's name is to be found in a thirteenth-century record that certain lands in North Bathurst were leased to a Henry Horsman among other Sedlescombe men.

In 1569 "the heirs of Richard Bishopp" (who held also Greens and Whitefield) held "other lands herefore called Horsemans by estimation xllj acres", bordered on the south by "a lane leading from Bothurst Wood towards Westfield." (See Beanford.)

In 1700 "a holding without a cottage, called Horsmans" is recorded. Eighty years later, Robert Pollard left in his will to his grandson, John Pollard Crouch, then an infant, "all that copyhold messuage . . . farm buildings and premises situate in Battle in the tenure of Samuel Cook or his assignees". In 1792, J. P. Crouch, come of age, surrendered to the use of Jeremiah Skinner of Crowhurst "two messuages, 1 orchard, 50 acres". The tenants who followed Skinner were in turn 1793 Edward Milward, 1796 John Phillips and 1811 Joseph Tilden.

In 1815 Horsmans with Beanford, always copyhold of Battle Abbey, was merged into the demesne lands and so became part of the home farm, Marley. "All that customary cottage and garden lying near Bathurst woods in Battle and also one other messuage . . . called Greens and also 1 other customary parcel . . . of land called Horsmans and one other parcel . . . containing together 80 acres more or less" still belonged to the Crouch family in 1841; "who paid annually 4/8. Gives a fine 6 Heriot assest 4 pence each" on the death of the owner.

# THE VOW KEPT

In the very first years of this century, the present Horsmans farmhouse was built by the Websters and part of the Marley lands were transferred to it. The Crouches had disappeared and 'Bumper' Sheather, a horse-breeder, was the tenant farmer. Horsmans was used for the sportsmen's mid-day refreshment when the Abbey Shoots took place; the gentry in the dining-room (now the south end of the sitting-room), the gamekeepers in the kitchen (now the office) and the beaters in the scullery (now the kitchen). These shooting parties were jolly occasions for all, food was not stinted, game pies and other delicacies being sent round from the Abbey, and laughter and gaiety rang out.

Encouraged perhaps by this use of his home, Bumper 'spoke forceful' about the disgraceful state of the old farm buildings behind the house and eventually, with the additional use of guile, he got the new buildings he wanted; for he quietly moved his landlord's stakemarks, thus getting bigger sheds than the 'ridiculously small' ones which Webster had intended.

The place was full of animals; horses, goats, cats and dogs. Among the horses was a small brown one called Tommy, who, harnessed to the cart, would take Sheather into Hastings to get the meat for the Sunday joint. Such was the complete stillness round the farm that the sound of Tommy's hooves could often be heard along the New Road before he turned into the long farm road. "Bumper" loved eating and his wife, tiny against his largeness—she weighed only 7 stone—delighted in feeding him, and baked plentiful buns and pies which filled the place with their warm smell.

Ants were specially bred in the West Strip, close against the wood, to feed the pheasant chicks reared for the Shoots, and when the father of the present owners planted orchards some fifty years ago a crowd of ant-hills plagued the Strip.

Fruit the farm has grown ever since, its orchards rising and falling on the undulations of land between Battle Woods and Petley Woods, a foam of blush-white in the spring. After the war, an effort was made to combat the threat of damage by frost by burning cans of diesel oil between the rows of trees. The lively flames from below and the moonlight from above shining on the snowy blossom filled the dark hours with magic, enhanced by the heart-piercing songs of nightingales from the hedges.

In these surroundings the five grandsons of the fruit-farmer, Gay, have been reared. The farmhouse is now owned separately from its surrounding land.

*Chapter Eight*

## THE RAPE

Because Sussex was of first importance to the defence of England, William put each of the six rapes into which the county, uniquely among all the counties of England, was divided (either by him or earlier by the Saxons) into the hands of a well-trusted Norman lord. It is possible that the word Rape is derived from the Saxon one "rap", a measuring rope, or "reaps", a space. Sedlescombe is in the Rape of Hastings, which consisted anciently of $9\frac{1}{2}$ Hundreds, but now of 13; parts of Battle outside the Abbey and its leuga made the $\frac{1}{2}$ Hundred. William gave this Rape to his cousin, Robert, second Count of Eu, who took his title from the little port, still in existence across the Channel opposite Hastings, in the north-east corner of Normandy, where he held extensive lands. It was in the church at Eu that Duke William and his wife Matilda had been married. Robert had helped in the invasion of England by providing sixty ships and also by fighting "gallantly" at Senlac.

The boundaries of each Rape, which ran parallel north and south across Sussex, contained a town of some importance with harbour and market, and a river, near the mouth of which each Lord of the Rape built a castle for its defence; in later years a second castle was built a few miles inland as the next line of defence. Robert of Eu and his successors built and lived in Hastings Castle. (Bodiam Castle, built in 1385 by Sir Edward Dalyngrygge, was later to be the supporting one.) Of all these great forts of Sussex, Arundel is the only one which, in its renovated state, is still inhabited, and furthermore by the descendants of those to whom the Conqueror gave it.

The Lords of the Rapes gave of their lands to 50 or more knights in return for their knights' service—their feu. These in turn let part of them again to sub-tenants also at a feu, part of the service they themselves owed to their lord. Thus did each Lord of the Rape produce the requisite number of knights and men for the defence of the land when called upon by the King to do so. These knights of Hastings Rape had to do regular stints in guarding Hastings Castle.

Count Robert expressed his gratitude for the lands that came to him after the Conquest by founding in his castle on the cliff the Collegiate Church of St. Mary-in-the-Castle in Hastings, and he made provision for the endowment of the secular canons, who lived there in community, out of the tithes and rents from the neighbouring villages. Geoffrey, the Canon, mentioned in Domesday Book as holding 50 or 60 acres in Sedlescombe on which lived two cottagers, was one of these. The College was dissolved early in the sixteenth century at the time of the dissolution of the monasteries by Henry VIII, but there is still a church of the same name built later beneath the cliff.

Hastings Castle is said to have been the scene of the first tournament held in England, at which the Conqueror's daughter, Adela, presided as Queen of the Joust.

After the Conquest, Sedlescombe had an independent status and some importance as one of the two or three places in the Rape of Hastings where the Court Leat met. Separate from other jurisdictions such as Abbots and Bishops it was under the authority of Hastings Castle. Its desolated lands were tilled again and gradually began to recover their value.

Robert of Eu died in 1090, three years after his liege lord, and his son, William, succeeded him. The Conqueror, by bequeathing Normandy to his eldest son, Robert, and England to his younger son, William, at one stroke divided again the loyalty of his Norman barons, who had lands in both countries, which he had been at such pains to build and on which he had so greatly relied. In 1088, Robert of Eu tentatively joined with other lords of the Rapes in Odo's rebellion but deserted it the following year. His son, William, too, six years later, joined a rebellion in favour of Robert of Normandy, was captured and, for punishment, both blinded and castrated. Not long after he died in Hastings Castle. In 1100 there was yet another rebellion for Duke Robert and, not surprisingly, the loyalty of the new young Count of Eu was suspect. Rebellions ceased with Henry I's successful invasion of Normandy in 1106 while his brother, Duke Robert, was away on a crusade.

Henry, 4th Count of Eu, married the widow of his king, Henry I, but, their son Raoul dying as a minor without issue in 1186, Henry's brother, John, succeeded as 5th Count. He had married Alicia d'Albini, a daughter of the Duke of Arundel, who after this her first husband's death, married Alured de St. Martin, Sheriff of the Rape of Hastings and flag-bearer to Richard I. Together they founded Robertsbridge Abbey in 1176, bestowing on the monks some of their lands in Ewhurst and Sedlescombe.

Under King John—Normandy having been reconquered by Philip of France in 1205—there was again a fear of French invasion. Since several lords, including the Lords of the Rape of Pevensey and Hastings, had already been in arms for the French against their king, John summoned a council of Barons, who agreed that an oath to keep the peace and to defend the kingdom should be taken by all over the age of twelve throughout the realm; also that head constables should be appointed for every county, and under them a constable for every Hundred (in addition to the usual constables of the castles) and that lists should be made of armed men under each constable, who was to be empowered to summon such levies when required for defence. In addition to the infantry and irregulars thus provided, it was enacted that every nine knights throughout the country should equip and maintain a tenth, on penalty of losing their feus. The Count of Eu provided 56 knights.

Henry, 6th Count, had no son, his heir being his only daughter, Alicia, named after her grandmother. Alicia became Countess of Eu in her own right and married, probably when she was very young, a man named Ralf of Issoltun or Yssoltun (Chapter 14). They with their son, William of Ysselton, were the last people to live in Hastings Castle. When in 1218 Ralf died, William became 8th Count, his mother being Dowager Countess. They had, of course, still their lands in Normandy only a few miles distant across the Channel and once again, three years later, the family was found to be in league with the French against the English King, Henry III. As a result of this final treachery all their lands and the Lordship of the Rape were forfeited to the Crown (Chapter 13). They retired to their lands of Eu.

The King for a while kept the lordship of the Rape of Hastings in his own hands; his son, Prince Edward, later gave it to the Earl of Brittany. In 1412 it was granted to Sir John Pelham, Constable of Pevensey Castle and Sheriff of the County of Sussex, for himself and his heirs in perpetuity. Notwithstanding, on his death it passed to Sir Thomas Hoo (Seneschal to the Pelham family) by Royal Grant. The Pelhams, not unnaturally, disputed this so that for some years the Rape was in dual ownership until the Pelham family recovered it by purchase in 1591 and have held it ever since, the present Lord of the Rape being John Buxton Pelham, 8th Earl of Chichester.

*The Court Leat or Lathe Court*
This Court is said to be of very great antiquity and, whether or not it was pre-Norman, it was certainly the earliest for jurisdiction within the Rape and independent of later local courts. Justice within it belonged completely to the Lord of the Rape. It was unique in the County of Sussex to two Rapes, those of Hastings and Lewes; though in Kent, where the geographical divisions are themselves called Lathes, these courts are numerous.

The King, however, complicated the jurisdiction of the Count of Eu by planting within his Rape the Liberty of Battle Abbey where the Court of the Abbot was supreme. In view of this the choice of Sedlescombe and Derfold (to be identified with Darvel in Netherfield) as the meeting-places of the Lathe Court was a carefully considered one; they were the villages closest to the Leuga boundary of the Abbey on the east and west respectively. The Count thus endeavoured to ensure that the Leuga remained firmly part of his Rape, for the Kings more than once confirmed and strengthened the Liberty of the Rape.

"Know that I have not conceded to Robert Count of Eu," wrote William I to the Archbishop of Canterbury, the Count of Eu and others, "the hunting rights of the monastery of my monks at Battle. On which account if either he or any of his men start any beast there and which they take there . . . receive his gage and place him under pledges. Do this upon his men unless the Count wishes to vouch for them."[1] The King then adds, "But you, Robert Count of Eu, I pray you as my faithful vassal to make a gift from your forest to my monks for use in my Church at Battle for love of me, and likewise something for their fire. And it is my wish you should look after them in my place." Later Henry II commanded that all land and men of the Abbey be "free of all Shires and Hundreds pleas and plaints, tolls and customs", a situation which caused constant

[1] Searle.

friction between the Abbot and the Courts of the Hundred and the Rape (Chapter 5).

While the Court of the View of the Frank Pledge sat independently for each Hundred in its own meeting-place, at the Court Leat all the Hundreds under the Lordship of the Rape of Hastings met together on every third Monday throughout the year in Sedlescombe and Netherfield alternately and, once yearly, at Hastings Castle. There is a note of a "Lathe Court held at the gate of Hastings Castle"[1], proof that it was held, in early days at least, in the open air. A Seneschal presided, Beadles were the Court Summoners and Aldermen the executive officers.

The 52 Knights and their successors, to whom Robert 2nd Count of Eu had given of his land in return for their knights' service, had to attend the Court Leat, in which were heard all pleas of life and member. They must gather there to report and exchange information on the state of their district, which was not confined to one Hundred only.

So for several hundred years the village green in Sedlescombe was a very noisy and crowded place every six weeks, with the hooves of the horses, which brought the knights and bustling officials, throwing up the mud from the road in wet weather and clouds of dust in dry, and flattening the long rough grass on the green; with bunches of local boys competing to lead off and tether the horses; with creak and squeak of wagons and carts bringing defendants and plaintiffs; and raucous clamour of voices shouting, talking and gossiping; the landlord and his womenfolk at the alehouse hurrying to bring out food and drink for the more important arrivals while poorer folk munched from their wallets and the cottagers hung around their doors eager to gather and pass on any news and to watch and comment on the proceedings. In bad weather, the officers may well have retired into the alehouse, and in later years into the nearby Hall-place, the plaintiffs and defendants being called inside by turn.

The following are a few cases concerning the Hundred of Staple in the fourteenth and fifteenth centuries that are interesting (as were those of the Court of the Frank Pledge) chiefly because of the names of those involved[1]. Most of the pleas were concerned with debt, trespass, covenant, unjust detention and similar matters.

[1] S.R.S. 37.

At Sedlescombe in 1392 "John Jerways complains of Nicholas Bachelor on a plea of trespass that Nicholas and his son led his horses away six separate times out of the pound he had put them in. Nicholas is present and denies."

In 1395 "Richard Bourne complains of John Sandre on a plea of debt."

At Sedlescombe in 1443 when the officials of all nine Hundreds were present—quite a conclave in itself—"John Fynhawe, labourer, had to answer the executors of the will of William Cheyne de Smallhyde on 2 pleas of debt and detaining chattels. Order given to levy upon the goods and chattels of John Crips, to the use of John Drynher, carpenter . . . John Drynher is essoned against John Crips." (Essone meant that the plaintiff or defendant could send someone in his place to excuse him from appearing.) Here is one of the several mentions of Crips as a personal name.

1445. John Broke and John Brayleshaw, constables of the Hundred of Staple have offered themselves against John Jeffray, tithingman, and the whole tithing of Sedlescombe in a plea of debt wherein he complains and says that he owes him 18d scot assessed for 'le standerd' in the aforesaid Hundred in the 23rd year of the present King, which they should have paid before Lent the next following. (He asked for damages 14d.) "The defendant comes and says that he owes nothing and thereupon he has waged his law fourhanded. Defendant won."

Here is Jeffrays the tithingman again, and the first mention of the name Sander, perhaps the origin of Great Sanders (Chapter 17).

John Pralle appears more than once as an attorney at the Court Leat held at Derfold. There is still a house called Pralles in Ewhurst.

When the Court Leat was being held on the green at Sedlescombe in Easter week in the troubled year of 1450, a great commotion occurred as a threatening crowd of hostile men, followers of Jack Cade, who had mingled with other onlookers, suddenly fell upon some of the officers and gentry, striking right and left at them with sticks and staves, successfully and triumphantly breaking up the Court as was their intention. They had no enmity against the villagers, nearly all of whom, whether openly or secretly, sympathised with them; when the vanquished officers had discreetly ridden away there was great celebration, acclamation and applause, and, no doubt, excited talk for many weeks, if not years, after as the anniversary of the sensational occasion recurred.

The Courts Leat of the Rape of Hastings and the Courts of Battle Abbey came to be held for convenience sake on consecutive days and often with the same officials. Eventually the Court Leat lapsed as the judiciary system became centred more on the county, but the Abbey Court lasted into the twentieth century.

*Chapter Nine*

## SEDLESCOMBE IN DOMESDAY

Domesday, eight hundred years old, shows the amazing continuity of the English countryside for almost every obscure hamlet of today is mentioned in it, the owners, tenants and villeins of every parcel of land, together with the ploughs, oxen, horses, pigs, sheep, mills and fishponds—and what it was worth. It was an enquiry, written in a strange sort of Latin, used by the scribes of that day, in a neat and legible hand, into the value and tenure of lands, for the main purpose of assessing taxation by the Crown, especially the Danegeld (a tax originally imposed to raise money to buy off the Danish raiders), which the Conqueror revived. He appointed four Commissioners, persons of the highest standing, who took the sworn evidence of sheriffs, lords of manors, church officials, officials of Hundreds, and also of six villeins in each village. All this was sent to Winchester, where it was put together and copied; and so the final register, Domesday Book, was made.

The lands of Sussex are listed in it under fifteen heads, the names of the fifteen owners. Of these one was the King, two were the original Saxon owners, five were the Norman Lords of the Rapes, and the rest, five Bishops and two Abbots. These latter were the Abbot of the Norman house of Fécamp, to which Brede and its neighbourhood was given, and the Abbot of the new Abbey of St. Martin at Battle, to which William gave all lands within a one-and-ahalf mile radius of the spot where his victory was won. Sedlescombe was thus only just outside the estate.

Out of a total of 386 Lordships in Sussex, as many as 353 appear to have been taken from their Saxon owners and bestowed on the five Lords of the Rapes. At first after the Conquest there had been confiscation only of the lands of Englishmen who had fought against William, but some time during the ensuing twenty years the apparent intention of leaving Englishmen in possession and of ruling through them seems to have been changed because of the numbers of risings against the Normans during these years. William had had to establish a "murder-fine" to protect his followers. By this, if a Norman were found killed and the slayers were not produced, the eventual responsibility of paying the fine of forty marks fell on the inhabitants of the Hundred where the crime occurred.

The Anglo-Saxon Chronicle describes William's survey thus: —

"He sent his men over all England into every shire and had them find out how many hundred hides there were in the shire, or what land and cattle the King himself had in the country, or what dues he ought to have annually from the shire. Also he had a record of how much land his archbishops had, and his bishops and abbots and his earls . . . though I relate it at too great length . . . what or how much everybody had who was occupying land in England, in land and cattle, and how much money it was worth. So very narrowly did he have it investigated that there was no single hide nor yard of land nor indeed (shame it is to relate it, but it seemed no shame to him to do) was one ox or one cow or one pig left out that was not put down in his record. And all these writings were brought to him afterwards."

Not only was the value of lands and possessions at the date of Domesday catalogued, but also the value before and immediately after the Conquest.

The resentment common to all men through the ages when questions have to be answered about their possessions comes vividly through. The enquiry was in fact so unpopular that in some places it led to violence.

Domesday gives us the information that Sedlescombe, in the Rape of Hastings and the Hundred of Staple, belonged to the Countess Goda, the sister of Edward the Confessor, before the Conquest, and that the holder under her was a Saxon called Lefsi, who was dispossessed—or maybe he was dead—by the Count of Eu, who put in his place a Norman called Walter, son of Lambert, who was given property also in other parts of Sussex. It is noticeable that these men who held land from the Lords of the Rapes (no doubt as a reward for loyal and good service) were not given it in one large area each, but in smaller parcels widely separated from each other, possibly to prevent their owners from becoming too powerful. The Count's land in "Selecombe" was assessed at "one hide" (about 120 acres) "and three rods outside the rape, before the Conquest, and now for one hide."

The land is described under three headings, arable, meadow and woodland. The area of arable was estimated by the number of ploughs which would be required to till it. In the land held by Walter, son of Lambert, "there is land for 4 ploughs; in demesne is one; and six villeins with two bordars have 5 ploughs." There were therefore six ploughs altogether in the village, one on the home-farm (the demesne) and five among the eight small tenants who held land from the lord. It is said that the plough of those days was drawn by eight oxen (horses very rarely). Up to the last years of the nineteenth century and later, oxen were still being used for ploughing on the South Downs near Beachy Head, and an ox-plough, though drawn by horses, was still then in use at Norton's Farm (see chapter 37).

Domesday continues: "There are 7 acres of meadow and wood for 6 hogs." This was, as could be expected with the forest all round, a good extent of woodland, not just enough to feed pigs, but an area for which villeins would pay their lord six pigs for the right of feeding their herd of swine in the woods. (Pork was probably the only meat the poorer people would get).

"There is a little church." Of this no trace has ever been found, and it is therefore assumed that it would have been of wood; we take it for granted that it was on the hill site where met the three areas into which Sedlescombe was divided, where the church stands today.

The value of all this had been "in the time of King Edward 60 shillings and afterwards 20 shillings. Now 40 shillings." It had not yet fully recovered from the devastation of the Conquest.

Walter, son of Lambert, held another piece of land in Sedlescombe "one rod. It never paid geld and was always outside the Rape. There is land for one plough. There it is in demesne" (in other words, this was another part of the home-farm), "and 3 acres of meadow and wood for one hog. Then and afterwards 10 shillings. Now 20 shillings.". It was clearly well cultivated and rising in value.

Geoffrey, "the canon", also held land in Sedlescombe, about 60 acres and woodland which had been "laid waste" but was now worth 10 shillings. He was one of the secular canons who lived in community in the Collegiate Church of St. Mary-in-the-Castle in Hastings, founded by Robert, Count of Eu.

The Count of Eu himself "holds on his demesne 1 villein who belonged to Sedlescombe and he holds 1 vergate" (about 30 acres) "outside the Rape". (These references to being "outside the Rape" and yet in Sedlescombe are a mystery.)

"In the same Hundred Wenestan held $\frac{1}{2}$ hide" (about 60 acres) "at Fodilant and could betake himself whither he would. It is possessed for 2 vergates" (60 acres). Fodilant is, of course Footlands, the land around the tributary of the Brede where the Roman-British iron-workings and settlement were. Clearly Wenestan had been a Saxon with an apparently unusual privilege, who had also held Lordstreet nearby, "nor could he go where he pleased" there. He had been displaced by a Norman named Anscitel who had one plough and one villein (no one else beside the Count of Eu had a villein). Anscitel also had woodland for 4 swine.

The Saxon who had held Hurst, Ulwin by name, had also been dispossessed, or perhaps killed fighting for King Harold. Ednod, who now held it, was also a Saxon, one of the very few who held land at the time of Domesday. It was quite a small property, having "on the demesne 1 plough and 1 acre of meadow. It is and was worth 10 shillings." Oddly enough, no woodland went with Hurst or Herste, "the wooded spur".

Though not actually concerned with Sedlescombe, there are two other items of interest to be found in the Domesday entries for the Hundred of Staple. "Earl Harold held Whatlingstone. It was worth 50 shillings and has been waste." There is no mention of a church.

The other item of interest is: "Of the land of this manor Werste (Ewhurst) Oasbern holds 1 hide and 3 rods in Bodeham and it always lay in Werste and there was the hall," and again of Waliland, before the Conquest, "four brothers held this and could go where they pleased. There was only one hall." No hall is mentioned in Sedlescombe. Werste is Ewhurst but Waliland remains unlocated. Though probably not far distant it does not seem to have been within the bounds of Sedlescombe. The question of the whereabouts of the hall has a bearing on the Saxon name of "Sedlescombe" as described in Chapter 3.

Strangely, but with an unmistakable echo of modern times, Domesday Book was never used, never corrected, never brought up to date.

*Chapter Ten*

## ROBERTSBRIDGE ABBEY   (Map A)

It may seem strange that Robertsbridge Abbey should be included in a book on Sedlescombe but, as much of the land in the South of the parish became held of Battle Abbey by gifts of Alicia, Countess of Eu (daughter of the sixth Count), so land in the north of the parish became held of Robertsbridge Abbey through the gifts of her grandmother, Alicia, widow of the fourth Count. She had married as her second husband Alured de St. Martin, flag bearer to Richard I (Chapter 9), and with him founded the Abbey in 1176; it was built close to the site of the "George Inn"; but was later rebuilt beside the Rother at Salehurst, away from the noisy bustle of the little town, where the white monks could have scope in the meadows around for the manual labour and field work, with severe simplicity of life, which their Order demanded. When the King was captured and imprisoned on the Continent, the Abbot was one of those who was sent to search for him, and Alicia's son, Henry, now the seventh Count, provided £60 towards his expenses. The story of how Richard's minstrel, Blondel, discovered his master at last at Oxefer Castle in Austria by singing outside the walls a tune known only to the two of them is famous. Count Henry followed so freely his mother's example in generosity of gifts to the Abbey that, by the advice of the Abbot Denis, the Abbots of Citeaux and Clairvaux conferred upon him and upon his mother's soul the "benefits of the Cistercian Order". His brother John, inheriting, confirmed the gifts.

In 1332 Walter Krips was one of the Abbey monks, a surname which reappears in records over the years. Doubtless one bearer of the name is immortalised in Cripps Corner.

Henry III twice visited the Abbey, the second time just before the Battle of Lewes, when he extorted large sums of money from the monks, in return for which he granted to the town, as was frequently his habit, the privilege of a yearly fair to be held for three days from September 14th. This Holy Cross, or Abbot's Fair, was a privilege well worth having and everyone for miles around benefited from it. It remained a holiday and festival of merrymaking looked forward to with happy anticipation and excitement year after year through the ages.

In 1449, when discontent was rife all over Kent and Sussex (Chapter 15), John Cotying, a yeoman and captain of a band of followers of Jack Cade, led his men with sticks and staves to break up the fair. It is not clear what exactly his object was, for, though the fair was a source of great profit to the Abbot who ruled it absolutely, it must also have brought gain to the stall-keepers, craftsmen, pedlars, players, minstrels and entertainers of all kinds who paid him their dues. It is possible that these had become unduly oppressive and intolerable. While the Abbot of Battle and the Prior of Lewes with all their monks supported the rebellion of Jack Cade in the following year, the Abbot of Robertsbridge did no such thing. Eventually the attackers were driven off, for the Abbot had his own officers and constables to enforce his laws during the festival.

In 1539 the last Abbot, Thomas Taylor, surrendered the Abbey to the King on April 6th. He was granted a pension of £50 a year with smaller allowances of £4-£8 per annum to his eight monks. This might be thought not to be the full complement but the number was the same in another reference to them in 1417. According to Horsfield these were still being paid fourteen years later to the Abbot and four surviving monks.

Henceforth the Holy Cross Fair became just "Robertsbridge Fair" but was still a holiday of fun, and a place for profit-making, to enjoy every year. After the change in the calendar its annual date became September 25th and so it remained until the Fair was killed by World War I. Fair Lane still stands as a memorial to it. In September 1975 for one year it was revived with pageantry and success.

King Henry VIII granted to Sir William Sidney and Agnes, his wife (the parents of the famous Sir Philip), Robertsbridge Abbey with all its lands, which included Footlands and practically all of the land in the north of the parish as far as Hurst Lane. Strangely enough, another Sedlescombe name appears in the charters of the Abbey at that date: "Robertsbridge: late Monastery: Fee Richard Sackville Kn. Steward of all the possessions of the said late monastery."

The manor of Robertsbridge was divided into five boroughs for rental purposes, the borough of Streatfield being composed of parts of Ewhurst, Northiam, Whatlington, Sedlescombe and Brede. The tenants of Streatfield combined with those of the borough of Puryfield (Northiam) to choose at the yearly Court of Robertsbridge "a bedell to collect the monies; he to be taken 2 years from Streatfield and the third from Puryfield,,[1] Streatfield is still to be seen on the Ordnance Map.[2] By the time of Sir Philip's death in 1586 much of his estate in Sedlescombe and Ewhurst, amounting to 300 acres or more, was in the hands of the Bishop family, members of which had lived in Sedlescombe for over a hundred years already (Chapter 17). Streatfield, for instance, had been held leasehold by John Bisshop in 1528 and before that by Thomas Bisshop; passing in 1538 to Laurence and 31 years later to Richard, at which time the copyhold is described as "3 parcels of pasture, Stretfields (late Laurence Bishop) lying in Ewhurst at a place called ye Gallows of Hoorne between ye highway from Cripses to Breadhith."

This landmark, the Gallows of Hoorne, with its sinister implication, is mentioned several times in the Robertsbridge Charters when boundaries were delineated, so that it must have been a very conspicuous and well-known place, as most certainly a gallows would have been. Brede High is about two miles from Cripps Corner on the road to Broad Oak, so the Gallows of Hoorne was somewhere on that road not far from Cripps Corner.

Another document describes the boundaries of the "house and one croft belonging to John Darbie" of Footlands lying between the highway from Staplecross to Sedlescombe West; and the highway leading from Staplecross to the Gallows of Horne and so to Bredehith, Est: and abutteth to the lands of Darby of Footlands ... and contains by measure 1; (51) acres dl (550) xv dayworks". Another boundary description is: "in ye parish of Ewhurst between ye highway from Swale to a place called Gallows of Hoorne."

[1] S.R.S. 47.
[2] Map A.

By 1660 the Gallows of Horne had become Hoorn Oak. From all these boundary descriptions it can be deduced that the Gallows of Horne stood at the crossroads just east of Cattsgreen Farm on the Cripps-Rye road.[1] Horn was in earliest documents spelt Whoorne and meant iron. It is worth noticing that the wood beside Cattsgreen Farm is Ellenwhorne Wood (earlier Horn Wood) abutting Ellenwhorne Farm. Streatfield Wood forms the southern border of the road at this point. (In the nineteenth century the Bishops still owned Catts Green Farm.)

A crossroads was a customary place for a gallows to be erected. It may well be that this gallows was simply an oak tree and, as the summary hanging of felons ceased, the name Gallows in time fell out of use and the landmark was referred to simply as Hoorn Oak and eventually Horn Oak. A natural assumption was at first that Broad Oak, nearby on the same road, had been the "Horn Oak", but the continual mention of Brede High on the east threw this out of court; so also with Horns Cross to the North.

Robertsbridge Abbey Estate was rich in iron and the Furnace and Forge, together with subsidiary ones like Panningbridge, became famous and prosperous. Detailed account books were kept both under the Sidneys and later under the management of John Fuller of Brightling. Some of these can be found in Straker's book *Wealden Iron*.

Two further records from the Robertsbridge charters show something of the similarity of its manorial customs with those of the Battle Abbey Estate. "One croft called Motyes in ye parish of Ewhurst between ye highway leading from Wattlehill" (still marked on the map as a farm) "to Hoorne Oke, West; ye lands of Edward Easton, East and North; and ye feu farmlands of Derby of Footlands, South; and contains 1 acre and payeth by yere vs. vld (5s 6d.) and for heriot, at ye death and change of every tenant, as his best beast." Another small property, "sometime Martyn Brasses lying in ye parish of Ewhurst between the highway leading from Staplecross to Bodiam on West; and lands of William Bishop South, containing by measure 1 acre and xvl (16) days work, and payeth by the year xviid and, for heriot, his best beast." Brasses Farm can be seen standing exactly there today. Finally, one other record of interest from the Robertsbridge Abbey Estate reads thus: "Black-

---

[1] Map A.

brooks in Westfield is divided into five holdings, each ⅛ of a knight's fee, and two are assessed at 3d. each for eelsticks." An eelstick, states a dictionary, was a measure of quantity, one stick containing 25 eels: (could an eel be connected with an ell—25 in.—which gave rise to the saying "give him an inch and he'll take an ell"?) It is strange to find Blackbrooks, mentioned so often as Battle Abbey Estate, now part of Robertsbridge.

In 1726 Sir Thomas Webster, owner of Battle Abbey and its estates, added those of Robertsbridge Abbey to his possessions by buying its lands from Lord de L'Isle and Dudley, descendant of the Sidneys, with its ironworks and timber resources and some 1,000 acres of land in various neighbouring parishes, including Sedlescombe. Twenty years later Sir Thomas's son, Sir Whistler Webster, leased the Robertsbridge furnace to a Staffordshire ironmaster, John Churchill. But fourteen years later it was in the hands again of Sussex ironmasters, William Polhill, David Guy and James Bourne, the latter a Salehurst man. By this time the Sussex iron industry was on the wane and Sir Godfrey Webster, always short of money, sold the Robertsbridge Abbey Estate. Its farmlands in the parish of Sedlescombe became part of the Vinehall Estate under its various owners until that estate in its turn was broken up. The law of copyhold being brought to an end, the farms became freehold and independent of the Abbey, the buildings of which had become a farmhouse and farm buildings.

*Footlands (Maps A and 2)*

Footlands, 60 acres at the time of the Conquest when it was taken from its holder, Wenestan, and given to the Norman, Anchitel, by the Lord of the Rape, increased over the years, extending northwards. On Anchitel's death, it passed to another Norman, Inglegram de Freisenville, and so to his son-in-law and daughter, Rainald de Meiniers and Matilda. Welland, a knight's feu and part of Footlands, was granted to Alured de St. Martin (who founded Robertsbridge Abbey 16 years later) by his father or brother, Geoffrey, in exchange for land he held in Normandy.

After Rainald's death, it appears that his widow, Matilda, sold the lands of the "manor of Footlands", 244 acres, to the Abbey, which was confirmed by Henry Count of Eu in 1195 and again by his brother, John, in 1200. The lands of Footlands now included Badlands and the Morgay Woods over the border in Ewhurst parish. Morgay was written "Morgheve"[1] and derived from the word "morgen-gifu" which means "morning gift", a charming custom by which on the morning after the bridal night a husband sometimes gave his bride a gift of land to be her very own, at a time when all the bride's property became her husband's. It is attractive to ponder that the Morgay Woods, which lie along the east side of the Hawkhurst Road just beyond Cripps Corner, may have been just such a gift long, long years ago.

In 1537, the year before the closing of the Abbey, an Abstract of Letters Patent shows that there was granted "to Laurence Derbye of 10 pieces of arable, 4 woodland, 5 arable, and 2 woodland lying altogether and called 2 Welland Fields". These were tenanted at the Dissolution by Bartholomew Clerk, "the 2 wattell fields, Tanners Croft, Grete Morgays Wood, Lyttell Morgayes Wood, 5 other pieces of arable and 2 of Woodland lying together and called Long Whalehose, Whale Two Jenslynge, Calcotts, Wymblecotts and Cotterells lying in Wherste" (Ewhurst) "and Whatlington". Most of these names are still to be found, with slightly different spelling, on the ordnance map.[2]

"The lands of Darby of Footlands" are mentioned many times in sixteenth-century deeds of the estate of Robertsbridge Abbey; Laurence Darby in 1536 "and before that John Darbie" and twenty-five years later "lands of Derby of Footlands" and "John Darbye holdeth by copie Braylshaws (late Laurence Derby)". In 1566 mention was again made of "Derby of Footlands".[3] In 1607 John Darby of Footlands gave one of the first of the Church bells (Chapter 10). By 1624 the name was William Darby but in 1632 it was once again "John Darbie of ffootelands".

In the marriage registers there are, as might be expected, several Darby weddings recorded. In 1641 Elizabeth Darby married Thomas Newnham and four years later William Derby married Susannah Wood.

In 1666 "ye fee lands of Derby of Footlands" figure in deeds and from 1708 to 1726 another William Derby is in occupation. In 1715 Susannah Darby, daughter of William and Susannah, married John Waghorne. In 1712 and again in 1722 William Darby was Church-

[1] Pl. N. of S. Vol. 2.
[2] 6 in. to 1 mile.
[3] S.R.S. 47.

warden and in 1724 overseer. But prosperity was leaving the family. In 1671 Footlands was mortgaged to Sir John Lades (Chapter 23) (or Leeds) and time was running out. William Darby lived on at Footlands until he died in 1784 but it was being farmed for Leeds by Thomas Kedwell. And that was the end, after 260 years, of the Darbies of Footlands.

*After the Darbies*

For twenty years Thomas Kedwell farmed the land for Mr. Leedes, living in one of the cottages till William Darby died, when he and his family moved into the old farmhouse. In the churchyard beside the path that runs between it and the main road stands a tombstone with the inscription:

>            Elizabeth...............
>            Alexander ............
>            daughter ...............
>             Elizabeth Kedwell
>          died 1744 aged 22 years
>      All ye that see me as I lie
>      Remember this that youth must die.
>      For as you are so once was I
>      As brisk as any lark that flies
>      As you see so must you be
>      Prepare your soul (self?) to follow me.

Samuel Baker followed the Kedwell family, living in Footlands and farming its acres for another twenty years. By the end of the 18th century William Collins had bought it from the Leedes Trustees, "when 609 loads of cinder was taken from Footlands Farm for the making of the Turnpike road at 2d. per load." These were the cinders and slag from the old Roman British bloomery and the turnpike was the one from Cripps Corner to Whatlington.

All through the nineteenth century Footlands was farmed by tenant farmers. Tilden Smith, of Vinehall, bought it from William Collins and it became for the next hundred years part of that estate, inherited by Tilden's son, Richard, and lost by his bankruptcy. While Vinehall was owned by William Rushton Adamson (Chapter 17) in the second half of the century it was renamed, somewhat confusingly, Rushton Park. In the twentieth century under Lord Ashton of Hyde, it reverted to Vinehall again. Thanks to his daughter, the

Hon. Mrs. Whistler of Battle, all the Deeds are deposited at the Record Office at Lewes, and are full of information concerning the farms in the north of the parish.

Between the wars Footlands was farmed by the Dallaways, late of Little Castlemans. In 1949 it was sold to a family called Dickinson. When he died his son ran it as a turkey farm.

At what date the house itself was built is not exactly known for, like all the other old houses in the neighbourhood, it has been added to and altered by succeeding generations of owners and occupiers. A beautifully mellowed rusty colour, it looks as though it were growing in its wide wooded hollow. It was "built round a tree-trunk", Miss Dallaway informed me. "You went up the stairs up the tree to bed. The attic was always apple-scented with the rows of fruit on its floor. There were three front rooms as well as the dairy with benches all round its walls."

Seeing it in its seclusion, settled so firmly, it is easy to imagine a Roman villa spreading there in the ancient days. Much of archaeological interest has been found in its fields and along its streams and more certainly remains to be discovered yet. The fields bordering the stream have the names Cinderbury and the hopgarden which flourished there in the eighteenth and nineteenth centuries was called Cinderbury Hopgarden. Other field names were Stumbletts, Calves field and Pennygrove Wood.

*Chapter Eleven*

## WHO WAS ROBERT BASOK, KNIGHT?

One hundred and twenty-five years after Domesday, the lands of Sedlescombe were still in the hands (under the Lord of the Rape) of the descendant of Walter de Lambert, Peter de Scotney by name, who sublet them to Robert Basok, knight, son of Adam Basok; and the greater part of Sedlescombe was known as the feu of Basok. The Victoria County History states that his name was probably originally Robert de Baroches who held 2 virgates of the Count of Eu by service of supplying 2 brackets and 4 harriers when required.

The whole system of tenancy was complicated, or so it seems to us who look back, by gifts of land being made both by the tenants and sub-tenants to the adjacent Abbeys for 'the health of their souls' or those of their relatives. Robert Basok both leased and sold lands to Battle Abbey. He held and disposed of more than a quarter of a knight's feu and was referred to as lord or "dominus de Sedlescombe". After his death his widow, Milisent, sold to the Abbey her rights in his land for a half-merk and a life corrody.

Among many references to Robert Basok in Thorpe's Catalogue is one dated 1238 which refers to: "a meadow near the church of Sedlescombe and 3 acres of meadow between Sedlescombe and Wickham." (Chapter 7).

Another is to:
"feoffment to John Haremere by his homage of the hundredsland in Sedlescombe called Scottesland with the Brook . . . " and again "feoffment to the monks of Battle Abbey of land called Scottesland and Hundredsland . . . " Land lying along the north of Brede Lane, opposite Blacklands, is known today as Scotch Down.
"feoffment of certain rents arising out of land held by Joscelyn,

sone of Thomas of Haremere; Wecke," (probably the same as Wick or Wickham) "Bruere, Spliceregge and the Blanchelonde of Sedlescombe"; and finally

"feoffment to the Abbey of Battle of all his lands called Scottesland and Hundredsland." All these records are of the thirteenth century but are not precisely dated. Blanchlond, translated 'Whitelands' might well be identified with the lands close by the Brooks on the south, called variously in later records, Whiteacres, White Down or Whydown.

In spite of all his generosity to the Abbey, Robert Basok lost his case when the Prior of the Knights Hospitallers claimed the advowson of Sedlescombe church from him in 1225 (Chapter 13).

A record of the Manor Court of Wode (a borough into which the Manor of Battle Abbey was for a short time divided) states that in 1369 "on the Monday, St. Alphage's Day, Philip Gyfarth did service for land in Sedlescombe at Tyltonsbath etc . . . " So the 'feu of Basok' had passed away from that family. The name Robert Basok however continued long in the district for, over 200 years later in 1595, a marriage licence was granted "by John Prescott vicar of Rie to Robert Basok and Agnes Buckland". A less happy notice of the family name is in the Battle gaol delivery rolls which record the trial of a local man, Walter Wardun, "for having received the two fugitives, John and Laurence Basoc, now hanged."[1]

[1] Searle.

*Chapter Twelve*

## THE BRIDGE AND MILL AT ILTONSBATH

Iltonsbath or Hiltonsbath is one of the oldest names still in use in Sedlescombe. The name, variously spelt in old records as Iltonsbeth, Hiltonsbeth, Heltongsbath, Taltonsbath, Tiltonsbath and Tyltonsbath, is now used only for the cottage next to the disused chapel at the south end of the Street and under the same roof as Barracks Cottage, but once upon a time it was a manor consisting of acres of meadows and woodland edged by the Street and including the bridge, mill and tan-yard. As lately as 1834 a property in the Street is described as "situate in Iltons Bath Sedlescombe".

The earliest reference I have found to it is in the Catalogue of the Rents and Muniments of Battle Abbey in the following entry: — "In 1218 Alice Countess of Eu made deed of confirmation for the health of her soul to the Church and Monks of the Abbey of St. Martin at Battle the following gifts, grants and feoffments: land, the scite of the Mill of Iltunesbath, with land called Scottesland; part of the Meadow of Gorwisse, and Foss, with reflux of water to the Mill pool of Iltunesbathe, lately the Gift of Robert Basoke, free of all services, for the salvation of my soul, and for the souls of my father and mother, and for the soul of my Lord, Ralph de Issolden, of good memory, late Earl of Ou and for the souls of all my antecessors and successors, in free, pure and perpetual alms." (Chapter 9).

The actual deed, with all the others belonging to the Battle Abbey Estate, was sold in 1835 by Sir Godfrey Webster, the spendthrift owner of the Abbey, to Huntingdon University in California, and the Catalogue published by Thorpe's in the year of the sale is all that we have left in this country. It is, however, a mine of information. Another entry 21 years later states, "Robert Basok, Feoffment, for the health of his soul, etc., to the Monks of St. Martin at Battle of a Water Mill near the Bridge of Iltonsbed or Iltonsbath." So by the year 1238 there is both a mill and a bridge at Iltonsbath in Sedlescombe. A later record says: "Robert Basoc, Feoffment to the Church and Monks of St. Martin at Battle, of all his lands lying in the King's Highway of Iltonsbathe"—the King's Highway being, of course, the old Roman road, the Street.

Yet another record says: "Robert Basoc of Sedlescombe, Feoffment to the Church and Monks of St. Martin at Battle, of all his lands close by the Royal Manor of Iltonsbethe . . ." It is interesting and noteworthy that, having been the Manor of Iltonsbath, it has now become the "Royal Manor", which sounds rather important. It was, in fact, the result of treachery. Alice, Countess of Eu, widow of Ralf d'Issoltun, Count of Eu and Lord of the Rape of Hastings, who had made gift of the land of Iltonsbath to the Monks of Battle Abbey for the good of her soul, had with her son, William of Issoltun, the eighth Count of Eu, been in league with the French against the King of England, Henry III. William was deprived of the Lordship of the Rape of Hastings and the family lost all its lands in the Rape, including the manor of Iltonsbath, which reverted to the Crown, So that was how it became for the time being a Royal Manor. Forty years later in 1288 it was gifted by Prince Edward (later Edward I) to the Duke of Brittany, who became also the Lord of the Rape.

By 1242 Robert Basoc had transferred to the Abbey of Battle 106 acres of land, 8 acres of meadow and 8 acres of wood in Sedlescombe.

There are numerous references during the next three hundred years in the Catalogue to Iltonsbath: In 1471 the lease of a Watermill, near Tiltonsbath in Sedlescombe, then newly rebuilt, to Richard Shepherd of Battle is recorded, "dated from the Chapter-House of the Monastery at Battle, April 3", and in 1483 reference is made to "land in Iltonsbath a garden called Collys garden near Iltonsbath brigge." Iltonsbath had become, thanks to Robert Basoc, part of Battle Abbey Estate and remained so until 1924. We can therefore trace in its records from that date the tenant-millers, most of whom lived in Sedlescombe, and a list of them will be found at the end of this chapter.

# THE BRIDGE AND MILL AT ILTONSBATH

For nearly fifty years, from 1707 till 1750, the millers belonged to the Lingham or Langham family and one of them, John Lingham, was prosperous enough to hold a mortgage on Beech House, the property of John Everndon, for £200. He was also churchwarden. In 1745 his widow was still living at the mill, but three years later she had moved to "Abraham Bodle's new house" and John Lingham junior was at the Mill. Abraham Bodle's grave is in the churchyard (Chapter 35).

For five hundred and fifty years there was a watermill at Iltonsbath in Sedlescombe which year after year ground the local corn, and miller succeeded miller; yet today hardly a trace remains but the mill-pool and the groove in the brickwork where the mill-wheel turned. It has been suggested that the Tithe Barn opposite was where all the grain was stored to await grinding, but it is more likely that it was where the skins for the Tannery were stored.

It is interesting that in the last hundred years a bakery was established by the Gregory family close to the bridge at Iltonsbath. It might be thought that there was some relationship between the old corn mill and the new bakery and that this had been a natural development, but there is no connection whatever, for in the year 1750 a tremendous change took place at the watermill at Iltonsbath. Instead of grinding corn it began to be used to grind powder (Chapter 29).

### *Millers of Iltonsbath Corn Mill*

1471   Richard Shepherd of Battle.
1619   John Levett of Sedlescombe, Gent.
1657   Lease for twenty years of the Water Cornmill commonly called Tiltonsbath Mill with Mill-house or Tenement and all lands, etc., belonging to same, in Parishes of Battle and Sedlescombe to
Stephen Coleman of Battle, Miller.
1690   Thomas Langley (Lingham).
1707   "To Joseph Lingham for eleven years, of Sedlescombe, Miller, of the messuage Watermill and other Buildings, Meadow and Pasture 12 acres in the Parishes of Battle and Sedlescombe lately in occupation of his father, Thomas."
1710   To John Lingham Miller of Battle, Lease for 8 years Meadow, Pasture and Cornmill late in occupancy of Joseph Lingham.

1713 John Lingham for Lord Montagu's mill.
1719 Antony Viscount Montagu, Lease for 21 years to John Lingham of Sedlescombe, Miller, Watermill with lands, building, meadows belonging, 12 acres in Sedlescombe and Battle, late in the occupation of Joseph Lingham.
1745 Widow Lingham.
1746 Samuel Butler, late Widow Lingham.
1748 John Langham at the Bridge.
1762 John Langham junior.

*Chapter Thirteen*

## THE CHURCH

We do not know when the first church was built in Sedlescombe or when the first inhabitant became Christian. We do know that many Romans brought Christianity with them and that, though it practically died out of the country during the chaotic centuries after their departure, Sussex became Christian again when Aella, King of Wessex, was converted.

At the time of Domesday in 1087, twenty-one years after the Conquest, there was a small church or chapel "ecclesiola", in the village. It is supposed that this small building was erected by the Saxons of wood, their usual building material, and that, though no traces of it can be seen, it was on the same site as the present one, standing commandingly like so many other churches round about (Bodiam, Sandhurst, Whatlington, Fairlight) on the top of the hill. Many people today ask why the church should be so far out of the village. The answer is that it is in the very centre of the parish where the ancient divisions, Footlands, Herst and the Street, meet. Had it been built in the Street, where many feel that they would like to see it, it would have been at the extreme edge of the parish and a long distance from the farmhouses of Swales and Bellatkins (now Strawberry Farm), Footlands, Jacobs and the large houses of Hancox and Sanders. Built where it is, no one in the parish would have had to walk more than a couple of miles to reach it.

When the Normans built a tiny church of stone to replace the wooden one it was never, as was Whatlington church, under the Abbots of Battle. There is nothing left of that church either, the last remaining part of it, the chancel arch, having been removed when the church was enlarged in the nineteenth century.

## The Thirteenth-century Church

The oldest part of the present church, all of which is made of local ironstone, is said to be of the first half of the thirteenth century. The second Rector, Ralph, was appointed in 1235, succeeding an earlier one, James, whose date is unknown. It is reasonable to assume that the church was either built or being built while James was in office. By this time most of Sedlescombe was part of the "feu of Basoc" (Chapter 11).

It appears by the MS Pleas of the King's Bench in Henry III's Reign that in 1225 the advowson of Sedlescombe was claimed from Robert Basoc by the Prior of the Hospital of Jerusalem to whose patron saint, St. John the Baptist, the church was dedicated. The verdict of the jury confirmed his right, inasmuch as the last "personae ecclesiae", Roger, now dead, who had become a monk at Lewes, had been admitted on the presentation of the said Prior, who had since rightfully presented John. (Neither Roger nor John are on the list of Rectors; they could perhaps be added.) So Robert Basoc lost.

By the end of the thirteenth century one quarter of this feu belonged to the Knights Hospitallers, who owned the advowson of the little church. (John's Cross Inn now bears the Maltese Cross in honour of them.) One quarter belonged to Battle Abbey (the southern part of the parish) and one quarter to Robertsbridge Abbey (the northern part of the parish) (Chapter 10).

In the fifteenth century the little church was enlarged. The perpendicular additions were made; the nave roof with its fine king-post, trusses with moulded tie-beams and wall-plates, the Tower arch and the Tower itself. Two arches of the north aisle, springing from octagonal pillars, are probably of the same period, but they have been much restored. One window in this aisle is of original fifteenth century work and two others of the same design, though principally of modern stonework, have old internal jambs. All are of two cinquefoiled lights in a square head. There is a clear line visible on the outside of the north wall, showing where the church at this date ended.

The font and its unique oak cover date from the early sixteenth century before the Reformation. The font itself is a plain octagonal limestone bowl, gathered in below to a round bead at the stem, which, together with the splayed base, is circular. The oak cover, octagonal like the font, is composed of beautifully carved linenfold panels surmounted by openwork tracery, the corner pieces being carried up to finials, in the centre of which the top rises in the form of a crocketted pinnacle. Whose hands, over 400 years ago, worked the wood into this beautiful treasure? Being now very delicate, it is fixed; hung on a rope and pulley. It is remarkable, too, in that it was made with doors to shut when the font is not in use. There are traces of an old lock, said to have been ordered by the Pope to protect the holy water, which had always to be in readiness, from profane use. The font was not in its present position by the Tower arch, but was much nearer the front and more in the centre of the little church.

With the dissolution of the monasteries under Henry VIII, later in the sixteenth century, the two parts of Sedlescombe which had belonged to the Abbeys of Robertsbridge and Battle respectively came into private hands and the gift of the living passed from the Knights Hospitallers, whose order was suppressed, to the Crown, where it has remained ever since. The Abbey of Robertsbridge passed to the Sidney family. Mrs. Brabazon Combe, in her last letter to Sir John Thorne,[1] shortly before her death, said, "We all thought Sir Philip Sidney had a hand in the building of Sedlescombe Church." Who can now tell? It is a romantic notion and tradition handed down by word of mouth is sometimes true, if often false.

*The Bells*

These are said to be unique in that, in spite of the difference in their dates—1595 to 1929—all were cast at the Whitechapel Foundry.

No. 6, the tenor and the largest, is also the oldest and is inscribed thus: "Robertus Mot me fecit 1595", with a medallion on which are three bells, one above and two below, the centre one being between the initials R.M.; between the two lower bells are the letters IHS. This medallion, Robert Mot's trademark, was first used when he established the Foundry in 1583 and it is still used, with slight modifications, by the same Foundry today.[2]

Robert Mot was a famous bell-caster. (He may well have cast guns too.) At least eighty of his bells were in existence until recent times, nearly half of them in Kent, where he was apparently well

[1] Thorne.
[2] D-Tyssen.

known. He may have been the son of Mot of Canterbury. "The inscribed letters are of a very high standard and, as similar letters vary slightly, the inscription could not have been stamped" writes G. P. Elphick in his book *Sussex Bells and Belfries*; "the letters appear to have been formed in wax, for their surface is very smooth compared with the brushed background on which they are set. It would be interesting," he goes on, "to know how Robert Mot stuck the letters to the metal with so little distortion."

In 1606 Robert Mot retired, selling his business to Joseph Carter, and Whitechapel register records "Robert Moate buried April 1st, 1608."

Bells 2, 3 and 4 (C, B and A) all bear the inscription: "Josephus Carter me fecit 1607" and Bell No. 5: "this Bell was made 1606" together with a medallion and the letters I and C one on either side. Joseph Carter was at Reading Foundry from 1578 to 1606, when he took over Whitechapel from Robert Mot, and the 1606 bell was cast there. There still remain about forty-five of his bells cast at Reading, the earliest known one in 1578 for his own parish church, St. Lawrence, where he desired to be buried when he died, in 1609. "He was not such a good designer of black letter as Mot nor such a scholar," writes Elphick, "but Sedlescombe's bell is inscribed in letters that are in a higher standard than his usual design. On the shoulder is the royal monogram."

Bell No. 2 bears the information: "John Darbie and William Dawe gave this bell", and we know that William Dawe lived at "late Carters", the house known today as Manor Cottages, the porch of which still bears his initials "W.D. 1611" (Chapter 14).

John Darby was living at Footlands in 1632 (Chapter 10). William Dawe is believed to have been himself an iron-master and, like others in this trade, his family had no doubt over the last fifty years prospered, and here is his thank-offering. It is natural to wonder if "late Carters" had any connection with the family of Joseph Carter, the bell-caster.

Bell No. 3(b) bears part of Mot's trademark, the crowned bell. Of 2, 3 and 4 Elphick writes: "These interesting bells are inscribed in rustic letters used by Thomas Kempe and they show that there were three alphabets, varying in size." On all three bells the letter S is reversed.

These five bells were taken down by the Whitechapel Bell Foundry in 1930, tuned and re-hung, together with a sixth; a new bell, cast by the same firm and given as a thank-offering by Mr. and Mrs. Ernest Kingdon, who lived and died at Castlemans and are buried in the churchyard. This bell is inscribed thus: "Mears and Steinbank made me 1929. A thank-offering, E. C. and A. Kingdon." It bears also a circle of leaves with three bells, the centre one crowned (Robert Mot's trademark), and the initials A.A.H. These stand for Albert A. Hughes, who joined his father in the Whitechapel Foundry. His son and grandson also entered the business. Albert died in 1964. Like his father before him, he was not only a Founder but also a practical ringer.

The bell-frame is constructed on a Burmese hardwood called Pynkadoe, an extremely hard and durable timber, which should, according to Mr. Hughes, have a considerably long life.

The bells were again cleaned and overhauled in 1963 by the same firm.

The Tower, where the bells are hung, is lighted by small rectangular windows, and the bell-chamber, on each side, by one trefoiled light. Above the doorway into the church is a three-light window with perpendicular tracery.

*Two Ancient Memorials* (disappeared some time since 1883)

In a floorstone by the Tower door was an inscription in small letters which E. A. W. Dunkin wrote down as follows:[1]

"Here lyeth buried the bodie of Richard Bisshop sonne of William Bisshopp who depted this mortal life the 12 day of Maye in the year of our lord and saviour jesus christ 1617."

---

[1] E.S.R.O.

No trace of this earliest memorial to a member of the family of Great Sanders now remains, though there are many others to Bishops in the church. Richard may have been a young son of the iron-master William Bishop who was living at Great Sanders in 1632 (Chapter 17).

*Ancient Glass in Window*

In 1619, two years after Richard Bisshop died, John Downton, who had lived at Hancox for years, farming the land and becoming prosperous, died. His daughter and only heir, Joan, had married John Sackville (Chapter 17). In memory of her father they had the Downton arms, formed in stained glass, put into a window where part of it, a shield with three goats, can still be seen.

*Another Old Memorial*

In the Tower, carved on the north wall and visible above the head of anyone walking in or out of the west door, is a memorial to "Mary", which reads:

"An humble and a lowly soul with graces many moe
Were found in her whose bones lie entombed here below.
Mary by name she called was and Mary-like her actions
Christe word in heart she lodged fast being patient in affliction
Dorcas for works of piety and Lydia for her care
To hear Christ's words attentively and love the Messenger.
A blessed and a joyful death succeeds the life of Grace,
In Virtue's school her life she spent, in peace ended her race."

This was Mary Waters, born in Brede, daughter of John Waters, and married in 1616 in Sedlescombe Church to the iron-master and churchwarden, Peter Farnden, by the Rector, John Ball. They lived at Brickwall. Among her "afflictions" was the loss of all her three sons in childhood. Her three daughters grew up and survived their mother (Chapter 17), who died in 1630.

*"The Re-edification of the Church" in 1632*

The first plan we have of the church is a rough one, not drawn to scale, dated 1632, a tracing of which hangs beside the south porch (Chapter 23). It shows the very small size of the church compared with its measurements today. The chancel was in what is now the nave and the east wall rose where the chancel steps are. There was no south aisle, but in the south wall, which stood where the arches are now, were two dormer windows and also two perpendicular two-lighted windows on either side of the old south porch, and a plain three-lighted window of the lancet type at its south-east corner. There was no vestry. The church was supported by a buttress on the north side. "Externally, the church had graceful proportions as shown in an eighteenth-century drawing made in December 1738 by S. H. Gammon, whose name is on a tombstone. It is a pity that more of its attractive features, in particular the dormer windows, were not preserved at the 19th century restoration."[1]

We have no details of what the "Re-edification" consisted, except for the fact that a gallery was built at the back across the whole width of the church. (The stones of the southern pillar of the Tower are noticeably rubbed smooth by the passage of people against it as they climbed the stairs, Sunday after Sunday, for over three hundred years). The big beam, now in the roof of the nave, with 1632 incised on it, was part of that new gallery, as were the carved panels now forming the backs of some of the pew seats. I have seen an old photograph of the interior of the church, showing the gallery still in place, with the date on the beam clearly visible.

Since each inhabitant of the parish had a place allotted, as seen in the Plan, it would not be difficult to check attendance; for at this time everyone was forced by law to attend church once every Sunday. It seems strange to us, perhaps, that it was the duty of the churchwardens (at this date Henry Frensham of Spilsteds, then called Slaughters, and James Grantham, Chapter 23) rather than the parson, Edward Barton, to visit the absentee and discover the cause and, if necessary, administer a reprimand.

The re-edifying had to be paid for. The churchwardens and others in the parish were responsible. The first List of Church-wardens' Assessments was made in 1611. The money was raised by assessing landowners at so many shillings in the pound on the value of their land, and the cess for the Great Charge was made in this way.

As is shown in the Plan, the maintenance of the churchyard fences was the duty of the parishioners, and lengths varying from eight to sixteen feet are allotted to the chief householders and to "the Street houses". Along the northern border of the Plan are written the words: "This hedge is anciently kept by the Parson of Sedlescombe from the East corner to the West rail", and along the

---

[1] Thorne.

southern border of the Plan are the words: "this hedge is anciently kept by Sir Thomas Sackville's house from the West rail to the stile in the East." Instead of the stile there is now the wicket-gate, known in some later records as Jacob's Gate because churchgoers from Jacob's Farm coming across the fields from the east of the parish used it. This maintenance of churchyard fences was a very ancient duty of parishioners, laid down in 1305 by the Archbishop of Canterbury, Robert de Winchelsey, and failure to keep a length in repair was an offence for which one could be called to account in the Archdeacon's Court. The fence was finally removed in 1950 because of the increasing cost of upkeep.

The ancient trees, Spanish chestnuts, still standing and still bearing fruit, are also marked on the plan.

*Iron Slab Memorial*

Seven years after the Re-edifying the William Bishop of the Plan lost his wife, Elisabeth. He himself died in 1664 and was followed five years later by his little great-granddaughter, Sarah. All this is recorded on the iron slab on the floor of the north aisle above the Bishop vaults and reads quaintly, owing to the odd way of dividing the words and the reversing of all the Ns. Only iron-masters were allowed these iron memorials and it was no doubt made in the Bishops' own Forge by local craftsmen whose illiteracy would explain the curious lay-out of the inscription:

> HERE LYETH THE BO
> DY OF WILLIAM SONN
> OF JOHN BISSHOPP G
> ENT BURYED NOVEM
> THE 14 ANNO
> DOM 1664
> ALSO ELIZABETH HIS
> WIFE DAUGHTER OF
> EDWARD HAUSE GEN
> T BURYED MAY THE
> 21 : 39
> AND SARAH THE
> DAUGHTER OF WILL
> IAM THEIR GRA
> NDSON BURYED
> DECEM THE 20 : 69

## Another Memorial

On the south wall to the west of the south door is a handsome marble tablet considerably older than the wall to which it is fixed. The inscription in Latin prose and verse was translated by Sir John Thorne felicitously as follows:

"Here lie the mortal remains of Mary Dyke, laid here in hope of eternity. She was the daughter of Peter Farnden esquire and the wife of Robert Dyke, Gentleman: and the mother of a son (her only child) named William Dyke, in bearing whom she perished.

"As maiden, bride and mother she hath paid
All Life's demands and every debt defrayed.
Death gave her quittance, saying let her rest,
For Earth's behoof she bore a child, then press'd
Onward to Heav'n; enriching Heav'n and Earth,
Herself she suffered thereby no dearth.
Believe not flesh nor spirit dies; for flesh
Lives in the child, spirit in Heav'n is fresh.

"This monument is placed here by her husband above-mentioned, Robert Dyke. While she lived he loved her most dearly; now he has paid to her dust this tribute, the last he can offer. She died April 5th 1642 in the 21st year of her age."

This Mary is the daughter of the other Mary, whose memorial in the Tower has already been described and, as Sir John remarked, the contrast between the handsome marble tablet of the daughter with the rough simplicity of the mother's only twelve years earlier is very noticeable. Robert Dyke married again but was himself buried in the churchyard only two years later, aged 24, leaving little William orphaned at two years old (Chapter 17).

## Restoration of 1693

The next restoration of the church took place sixty-one years later, while George Barnsley, Sedlescombe's most famous rector, was in office. Nothing new was added: it was a maintenance job. "The chancel of the church of Selscombe was well repaired, ye roof being wholly new, ye walls rough-cast in pannell, ye inside of ye roof cieled, ye walls whited. The tower took up almost 8,000 shingles at £1.10.0 a thousand; all which repairs were done by Colonel Sackville's Lady after his decease in pursuance of his order upon his deathbed that they should be done. The charge was about £48. The Communion Table and the doors into ye said chancel were given by another hand."

This Communion Table is without doubt the seventeenth-century central part of the one in use today; whose the hand that gave it we do not know. It was extended on either side in the nineteenth century.

Colonel Sackville was the cavalier Thomas, second son of Sir Thomas of the 1632 Plan, and he too was born at Hancox. His "Lady" was Margaret Compton, now widowed for the second time. Her mother was also a Sackville, a fact which she recorded on the memorial tablet which she put up to her husband over the Sackville vault in the south-east corner, but which was moved by Mr. Warner, Rector, to its present position on the west wall of the church, inside what is today the choir vestry. Carved in the marble stone above the tablet are the Sackville arms and below is a cherub's head. Hanging above the south door (but in earlier days above the lectern) is the Colonel's funeral helm, made especially to lay on his coffin, in the same way as a serving officer's cap is to this day. His sword, helmet and crest were first presented at the altar, having been carried in the funeral procession. He was buried with his ancestors in the Sackville vault (Chapter 17).

*Memorials*

In the Tower wall, above the stone already mentioned which commemorates Mary Farnden, is another whose lettering is so well-worn that most of it is impossible to decipher, but clearly visible are the words: "George Barnsley Eccl." and . . . "Olim Cathed magd." Barnsley we know was Rector of Sedlescombe for fifty years, from 1674 to 1724, and was Father of our Church School (Chapter 28).

There used to be a memorial to another eighteenth-century Rector, James Ingram, which must have been removed when the organ was first installed, for in 1883 there was still in the south-east corner of the chancel an altar tomb with three scallops on a shield carved on it with the words: "Here lyeth the body of James Ingram late Rector of this Parish and Vicar of Westfield who departed this life Sept. 3 1750 aged 64 years; also Ann the wife of the said James Ingram who died June 12th 1785 in the 86th year of her age." This is now outside in the churchyard (Chapter 51).

Hanging above one of the arches of the north aisle are the Royal Arms of George III, after the Union with Ireland.

## Restoration of 1838

The next restoration of the church took place about 150 years after the one paid for by the Colonel's widow. Recorded on a board in the vestry is the following statement: "This church was enlarged in the year 1838, by which means 100 additional sittings were obtained, and in consequence of a grant from the Incorporated Society for promoting the Enlargement and Repairing of Churches and Chapels 50 of that number are thereby declared to be free and unappropriated for ever, in addition to the 260 sittings previously provided, 90 of which are free. John Pratt, Minister; John Simes, James Byner, Churchwardens."

It is presumed that the enlargement thus recorded was the addition of the south aisle. Sir John Thorne writes: "An objection to this is that an article in the 1849 volume of the Sussex Archaeological Collections (Vol. 21, p. 275) gives Sedlescombe as one of the few churches of East Sussex which at that time had only a North aisle. On the whole, the grounds for attributing the South aisle to 1838 are sufficiently strong to warrant the surmise that the writer of the 1849 article was a few years out of date."

John Pratt holds the record at present for length of time as Rector of this parish; he was Rector for fifty-eight years and his family lived on in the village till after the first World War. The east window commemorates him and his wife, Mary, but it must have been put there after the next restoration in 1868, when the present chancel was built. There are many Pratt family graves in the churchyard (Chapter 51).

John Simes was the village butcher at this date and lived at what is now called Holmes House, where butchers carried on their trade for at least a hundred and fifty years, and which fittingly bears the name of the last one of all (Chapter 34). The other churchwarden, James Byner, was Parish Surveyor and was responsible for the building of the Turnpike road (Chapter 33).

The Hatchment with coat of arms at the back of the church, in "Oaklands" corner, was made at this date to commemorate Anne Mary, wife of Hercules Sharpe of Oaklands (Chapter 32), who died on July 12th of that year, 1838, aged 50, and was buried in the family vault under the north-west corner of the church. It has a black frame. The background is divided in two, the left half being white and the right black. If the whole were black it would indicate that the deceased was unmarried; the white half shows that her husband is still alive. In the middle is the shield, also divided into two halves, the left half having a black ground with a broad arrow (in heraldry called a pheon), which was the arms of the Sharpes of Northiam. The right half has a red ground with a gold band diagonally across it, on which are three swallows; this was the Brabazon arms. The fact that the shield is hanging by ribbons and at each corner is a cherub's head shows that the deceased is a woman. Had it been a man, his crest would have been shown over the shield.

*Enlargement of 1868*

In the porch, under the Tower, hangs a tablet recording yet another, and up to the date of writing, the last enlargement of the church, when a new chancel, vestry and porch were built. "Enlargement by voluntary contributions 1868. Richard Pratt, Boyce H. Combe, Churchwardens. Edward Owen, Rector. John Catt, Builder."

Edward Owen, Junior, succeeded to the living of Sedlescombe on the retirement of John Pratt; his father was buried in the churchyard in the north-east corner in a grave enclosed in iron railings which were removed in 1942 for use in the war effort. Richard Pratt was the third son of the previous Rector. Boyce Harvey Combe had married the sister of Hercules Brabazon, son of Hercules and Anne Sharpe, then owner of Oaklands and famous water-colour artist. It is good to see a builder putting his name to work; John Catt, son of the schoolmaster, also built the new bridge over the Brede (Chapter 1).

The enlargement consisted of the building again of a south porch, the old one having of course been pulled down in 1838 when the south aisle was built; and, much more important, the building of the present chancel and vestry. When the east wall was demolished a builder's apprentice-lad found an old leather bag beneath it in a hollowed stone. Great was his disappointment to find it full only of rusty nails. James Dengate, verger for very many years and himself a builder, nephew of John Catt and the son of one of two builder brothers, told me that all the stone was quarried from Whydown Hill, the stone-working and carving being done by the masons on the spot in the churchyard. The heads carved on either side of the chancel are, he said, portraits of local people but, disappointingly, he would never divulge who they were. The old east window was saved and put into the new east wall, the plain glass being removed from it and the present stained glass, showing the Crucifixion and the Last Supper, was put in to commemorate the late Rector and his wife, John and Mary Pratt.

The gallery of 1632 was at this date removed, the beam with the date incised on it being used in the enlargement and put in the central place where it now is.

The old acorn-shaped spire of oak, six foot high, was taken down in 1866 and burned as firewood. The birds, as Miss Tottie Flint, of Ivy Cottage, Brede Lane, would tell, used to drink out of the acorn cup, but she could not say when it had been erected. The weather-vane was put up eight years later, when the restoration was completed, for the date upon it is 1874. The old pulpit was replaced with the present Victorian one of stone and inlaid marble. The wrought-iron chancel screen is of more modern local craftsmanship. The Vestry also was built at this date. In the parish records is a letter to H. Arthur Pratt, Esq., dated March 22nd, 1874, from James Byner:

"Dear Sir,

I remember quite well all about the alterations where the Vestry Room now is. There were several remains taken up and tombstones removed, the bones of many others were buried in the corner of the Churchyard. I am almost certain that there are some graves under the Vestry Room that were not disturbed at all. John Dengate was at work for Mr. Catt at the time and knows all about it, in fact he helped to remove the remains of several persons. I quite think in excavating for the fire apparatus some remains will be found.

Yours faithfully,<br>James Byner."

*The Windows*

The east window of the north aisle, which depicts the Transfiguration and the Ascension, is in memory of the last of the Bishop family to live at Great Sanders, John, who died in 1870 leaving no heir. The window was presented by his two surviving daughters. Thus ended the importance of a land-owning family of the Bishops, whose records in Sedlescombe go back at least three hundred and fifty years; but there are still descendants of this family living in the village (Chapter 17).

Another window in the north aisle is dedicated "In honour of God and in memory of Thomas Stokes Salmon 1867." In the churchyard, in the enclosure devoted to the Pratt family graves, is one with flat stones engraved "In affectionate memory of Thomas Stokes Salmon . . . and in affectionate remembrance of Mary Salmon who died at Reading 23rd day of October 1853 in the 82nd year of her age." The Rev. John Pratt was born in 1772, Mary Salmon was born in 1771 and from her inclusion in the family graves it seems likely that they were brother and sister. In the central aisle a small brass square let into the floor is beautifully engraved with the words "Beneath lie the remains of Mary Frances wife of Capt. M. Andrews, only daughter of Dr. Salmon, M.D., born April 20th, 1800. Died March 7th, 1824." A child of three years old when her uncle, John Pratt, became Rector of Sedlescombe and only twenty-four when she died, her married life must have been very short.

On the opposite side of the church, east of the south porch, is a window in memory of William Mead Warner and his wife. Their son was Rector for twenty-nine years and is still spoken of with affection in the village.

On the north side of the chancel is a stained glass window of St. Peter, dedicated to the memory of Charles Woodroffe, who died at the age of 40 in 1888. Who he was is now unknown.

The reredos was erected in 1884 by Messrs. Earp, Son & Hobbs for £67 and was paid for by six members of the Pratt family, the Rector, Mr. Warner and Hercules Brabazon of Oaklands.

*Oaklands Corner*

This is at the west side of the south aisle and the memorials contained in it give the family connections of the Brabazon Combes of Oaklands House (now Pestalozzi Children's Village) beginning with Sarah, Baroness Teynham ("relict of the first Baron Teynham") who died at Oaklands, the home of her brother-in-law, Hercules Sharpe, of Northiam, widower of her sister Anne. Together Hercules and Anne had built Oaklands to the design of the famous architect, Decimus Burton, son of James Burton, designer of St. Leonards-on-Sea. It was Anne who brought the name Brabazon into the family and it was her daughter Anne who, by marrying Boyce Harvey Combe, introduced that name into the family. Anne and Boyce lived and died at Oaklands, the home also of Anne's bachelor brother, the famous Victorian water-colourist Hercules Brabazon

Brabazon, the owner of the initials H.B.B. seen on many cottages in the village (Chapter 32).

The last member of the family, Harvey Combe, known to all as "the Captain", great-grandson of the first owner of Oaklands, has no memorial in the church or churchyard, for his ashes were scattered in the park he loved.

*Brass Memorials to two Young Men*

"In loving memory of Henry, dearly loved son of Thomas and Susanna Weston of Guestling who died in Brazil and was interred in the European Cemetery at Rio de Janeiro on March 13th 1892 aged 23 years." The Westons were farmers in Sedlescombe in the nineteenth century, owning land between this village and Brede, including the Powdermill.

"Geoffrey Raywarde Parker, killed by accident at Boat Drill on H.M.S. Kenilworth Castle July 25th 1912 aged 29 years. So he bringeth them into the haven where they would be." The Parkers built and lived at Glebe House opposite Castleman's Triangle. Two tragedies are thus shortly recorded on brass tablets on the same wall a few yards apart, but separated by twenty years. Two years later, Mr. and Mrs. Parker lost a second son, John, in the Great War.

*War Memorials* (Chapters 43 and 47)

Twenty-six names are recorded killed in the first war and eleven in the second. James Dengate and his son Frank fashioned the memorial, which is on a plain oaken board with a triangular pediment and the words:

"Fratre Orate pro Nobis
The Great War 1914-1918

"To the undying memory of all dear to us in Sedlescombe who laid down their lives that we might live in Peace this tribute of love is reverently dedicated."

*The Organ*

There seems to be no record of the date when the organ was first installed. Musically it has contributed much to the services but architecturally it has destroyed the balance and beauty of the church. For years the bellows were operated by successive small boys hidden in the corner and when, in June 1947, the electric blower and a clarinet stop were added as an additional memorial to those killed in the war, some thousands of sweet papers came to light, the relics of sweets consumed by generations of small boys to while away the tedium of the morning.

On a ledge beside the organ stands a model of the church made out of gypsum by John Catt, the builder.

*The West Door*

This fine oak door was given by the Byner family in the early days of this century. Most of the Byner descendants live now in Australia, but some have returned at intervals, seeking out Asselton House where their forebears lived and visiting the church and the family graves beneath the Irish yews, cypress shaped, and noting the door. One member of the family complained after the second war that the wood badly needed oiling, a matter which was soon made good.

The brass ewer beside the font was given in 1900 by J. Woodcock and his mother, of the Manor House, to the Rector, Mr. Warner, "in remembrance of your kindness in preparing me for confirmation".

It was in 1930 that the church and the village were first lighted with electricity and in the previous year a new heating system had been installed.

*The Two Twentieth Century Memorials*

The first is to "Edward Barrington Crake, younger son of Vandaleur Crake of The Highlands, St. Leonards, died 1910 and buried in this churchyard. Placed by his wife Clara Alice." There are several graves of this family in the churchyard.

On a pillar of the Tower are two brass plates, one above the other. The top one is inscribed:

"In Memory of my beloved husband
General Sir John Eccles Nixon, G.C.M.G., K.C.B.
Grand Officier Legion d'Honneur
15th December 1921
And of my beloved Son Adrian Nixon
19th October 1918
'Heaven's morning breaks and earth's vain shadows
 flee'."

Sir John, who lived with his wife at the Manor Oast, was a general in the Great War and was at first blamed for the failure of the attack on the Turks at Baghdad by Townsend in November 1915 and the surrender in April 1916. He lived in Sedlescombe for the next years, during which he had the additional grief of losing one of his sons in the war. He was at last exonerated and made a G.C.M.G. in 1919 and died at the age of sixty-four two years later in the village (Chapter 43).

T. E. Lawrence, in the *Seven Pillars of Wisdom*, writes: "Had we published the promises made to the Sherif, or even the proclamation afterwards posted at Bagdad, and followed it up, enough local fighting men would have joined us to harry the Turkish line of communication between Bagdad and Kut. A few weeks of that and the enemy would either have been forced to raise the siege (of Bagdad) and retire, or have themselves suffered investment outside Kut nearly as stringent as the investment of Townshend within it. ... Had the British headquarters in Mesopotamia obtained from the War Office eight more aeroplanes to increase the daily carriage of food to the garrison of Kut, Townshend's resistance might have been indefinitely prolonged. His defence was Turkishly impregnable; and only blunders within and without forced surrender upon him."

In 1923 Lady Nixon received permission from the Parochial Church Council to erect the brass tablet to her husband and son. When she died four years later her surviving sons put up a twin brass tablet with a Latin inscription commemorating both their parents.

*The Side Chapel*

In the north aisle, it was dedicated in November 1960 by the Bishop of Chichester and was designed by Duncan Wilson, F.R.I.B.A. The oak altar with linenfold design was made by craftsmen of the firm of Paddon and Durrant of Bexhill, the iron screen by John Welfare, Blacksmith of Guestling, and the matching floor tiles came from Penhurst Church near Battle. The Rector, the Rev. Geoffrey Martin, was the one who inspired all this work. The oaken processional cross given at the same date was made in Ditchling.

*Chapter Fourteen*

## FOUR OF THE OLDEST HOUSES IN THE STREET

The little village of Sedlescombe needed virtually rebuilding after the devastation and desolation inflicted on it by the Normans, both before and after the battle. Nearly all its lands passed out of Saxon hands, the overlord in place of Harold being the Norman French-speaking Count of Eu. While he and his fellow barons were constructing themselves castles and strongholds of stone for protection against each other and against their countrymen across the Channel, their Norman tenants were busy building themselves timber-framed houses with central halls very much like those of their Saxon predecessors. The huts of the villagers, villeins and cottars, easy to burn down, were nearly as easy and quick to rebuild, with unlimited supplies of timber to be had for the cutting; for though the Normans made laws to preserve the sport in the forests they made none to preserve the trees.

The four-bayed Hall-house became the architectural pattern for all houses of any size in the Kent and Sussex Weald, until the chimney came into general use in the reign of Queen Elizabeth. The cottages were one-bayed or two-bayed versions of the same plan.

There are many such houses still standing in the Street today which have their origins in the early fifteenth century, and several of them had been enlarged before the close of that century, so that they were of some size and importance, and it is interesting to speculate why this building programme took place at that time for it was not general in all the neighbouring villages.

The reason is probably once again the presence of the river. The monks of Battle Abbey had built both corn-mill and a tannery on its banks and its Abbots had taken pains to acquire many of the near-by pastures. Sedlescombe could have been called the harbour

# FOUR OF THE OLDEST HOUSES IN THE STREET

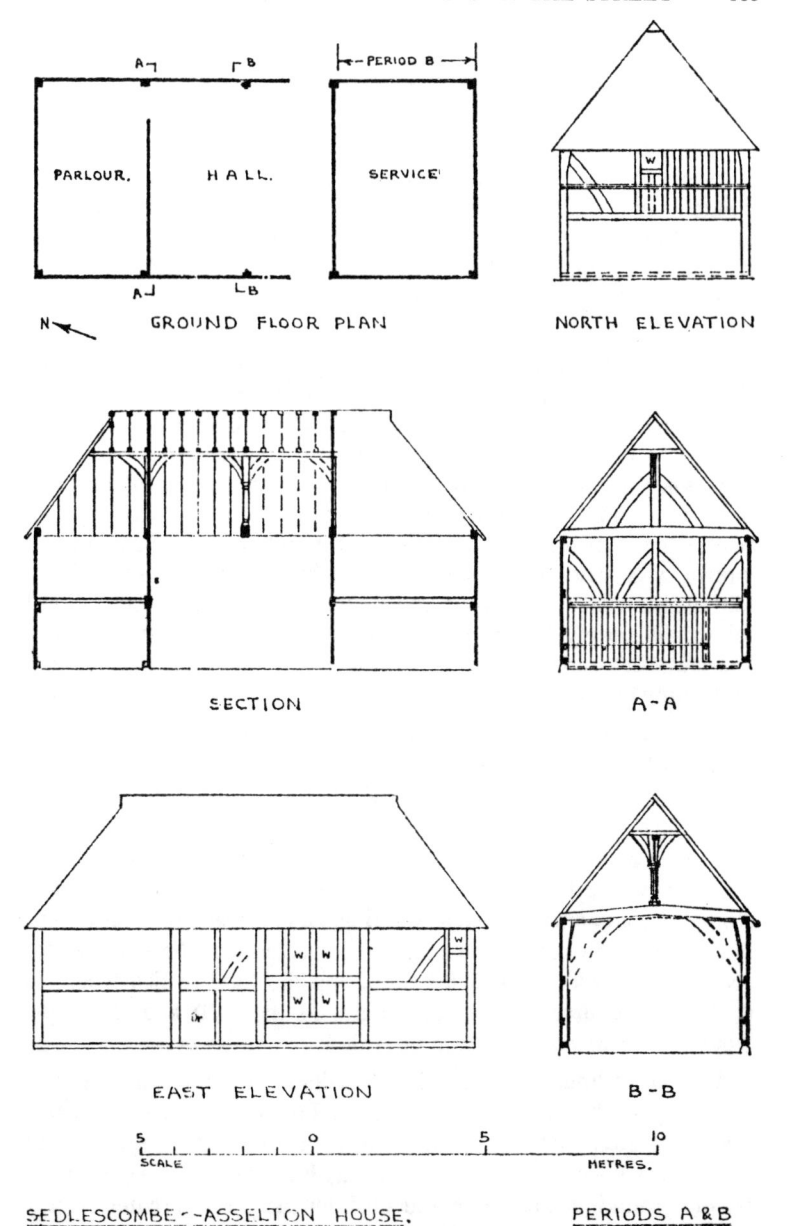

*Plan of Hall House by David Martin.*

of Battle and was therefore obviously an opportune place in which to build a house. Brede, the next village down-river, also has many old houses.

Of the ones still standing in the Street today, Asselton House, Barrack Cottage with Iltonsbath, Manor Cottages and The Old Thatch are probably the oldest. Though much changed and added to over the centuries, all are "Hall-houses" built on the same rectangular plan, with the central two-bayed hall open to the roof, and an additional bay at each end with a storey above.

In the centre of the Hall, the common meeting, eating and sleeping place, was the fire, the smoke from which found its way out through a vent in the roof. At one end of the Hall was a dais where stood the long table with central salt cellar. Behind it, and often pegged to the wall, was the settle, as at Asselton House, on which the owner of the house and his family sat. The beams at this more important end are often decorated with some form of carving. The rest of the floor may also have been of wood or just of beaten earth, strewn with straw or rushes mixed perhaps with wild sweet herbs like meadowsweet, woodruff and bedstraw. Once or twice a month all would simply be swept out and replaced. Usually there was a short wooden screen spurring from the wall beside the door to help in keeping out draughts.

The roof timbers were massive; in the centre the great crown-post, a squared-off tree trunk with diagonal beam from each face, supported the roof of thatch. This crown-post, too, often had its importance accentuated by carving.

The room, behind the wall where the lord sat, was usually called a Cellar, where his valuables were stored, and above on the upper storey was a chamber or solar offering some privacy for himself and his family. The bay at the other or lower end of the hall was the service-wing, with kitchen for preparing the food (which would be cooked, of course, at the central fire in the hall) and the larder where the meat was preserved or larded.

The whole house was built by the village carpenter and his men; there was no builder as we know him. Tree-trunks were cut with a double-handed saw, one man (known as the under-dog) standing below in a pit over which the tree was laid and the other standing on the ground, each pulling and pushing the saw alternately. Up to the time of the first World War there was still such a pit, where the two-handed saw was operated, in front of the wheelwright's shop adjoining the smithy at the lower end of the village (where the Bridge Garage now is) (Chapter 34). The great beam was sawn and squared and finally faced with an axe, leaving the surface surprisingly smooth. Naturally-curved branches were used frequently where diagonal supports were required. The rough planks remaining from these processes were used to cover the roof rafters, and the smallest waste pieces became wattle filling in between the beams in the walls.

When all was ready, the plan was set out on the land and a small foundation wall built into which the great timbers, eight or nine inches square, were fixed upright about 8 ft. apart, the corner ones being generally larger, often curving outwards at the top to carry the angle-posts of the upper storeys built at each end of the central hall. The main beams laid across these frequently projected a foot or more in front of the wall below, as can be seen at Barracks Cottage and Iltonsbath. When all the beams were in position, the house was a timber skeleton which in the early stages, until the most important tenon or mortice joints were made, had to be supported by stays. Sometimes the slots which received these stays can still be seen in the large timbers on the ground floor of such houses.

The next step was to fix the window-timbers about nine inches apart and to fill the spaces between the wall timbers with wattles or laths, chopped straw and clay and, finally, a roughly-smoothed finish of coarse plaster mixed with horsehair for strength, flush with the beams. This was frequently decorated with various simple designs by means of a "comb" and became known as "combing". The rooms in the upper storeys were low-ceilinged, and the roofs of these houses come noticeably well down, sheltering the walls as well as covering the building. In the course of the years, for additional weatherproofing, many of the old houses had their walls tile-hung or plastered.

### *The Old Thatch*[1]  (A)

This cottage, which stands at the foot of the village, has the distinction today of having the only thatched roof now left in the whole parish and also of being the smallest mediaeval house yet surveyed in the Rape of Hastings[2], measuring only 14 ft. from front to back. Built in the fifteenth century as a three bay hall-house, its

---
[1] The letters refer to Map 3.
[2] R.O.H.A.S.

fourth bay, a double one, was added at the South end at the close of the century. Its hall was one of the customary two bays and in the roof above can still be seen tufts of thatch smoke-blackened from the central fire, and the rafters and beams are still dark with its smoke.

On the ground floor in the North end are traces of a small room which seems to have been, right from the date of building, a shop.[1] Its large glassless window-opening, which can still be traced, had a shelf along it both inside and out at which the customer stood to be served. (It was in fact exactly like the butcher's window at Holmes House right up to the time of its closure in 1960. When the shop was shut, the window was covered by a shutter of trellis-work as it had been no doubt since the days of the first butcher.)

The chimney and floor over the hall were added towards the close of the sixteenth century, both fireplaces have a bake-oven. It is possible that it was at that time that the windows were first glazed.

In the same way that the houses on the East side of the Green were copyhold of Battle Abbey through gifts of mediaeval landowners, so those on the West side were part of the Manor of Bricklehurst in Ticehurst, held by Peter de Scotney (Chapters 11 & 35) as a knight's feu. A summary of "the Boundaries of certain lands in Sedlescombe holden of the Manor of Bricklehurst", dated 1543, shows that: "John Dawes holds in farm of John Hammond a messuage and garden", the boundaries of which were: "East: Highway Sedlescombe to Westfield; West and North: Bothurst Land; South: lands of Thomas Rodes' wife." The names Dawes and Hammonds appear many times in records of Sedlescombe and part of the Brooks was frequently known as Hamondsland.

All through the centuries, cottagers lived under the thatch, sometimes one family, sometimes two, tending the strip of garden. In 1830 it was James Pepper, the wheelwright and his family and, eleven years later, it was the home and shop of John Archer the Cobbler, (whose son later followed the same trade at the house, now the Post Office, which was known for so many years as "Archers".) Eighty years later it was described on the Auction Schedule as "A Pair of Old Plaster and Thatch Cottages dated 1590 with outbuildings in rear and capital gardens in front. Let on weekly ten-

[1] R.O.H.A.S.

ancies at 3/- and 2/-"; for, at some earlier date, it had like so many other cottages been bought up by the Combes of Oaklands. (Chapter 32)

For many years now The Old Thatch has been one dwelling house, under successive owners, cared for and modernised, its garden loved and neglected by turn.

*Manor Cottages. Once "Late Carters" and "Eliott's"* (B)

The beauty of this old house with its black and white gabled exterior, accentuated for many years by the topiary peacock and teapot in the garden now long neglected, was exceptional and struck the passer-by immediately, as do the initials W. D. and the date 1611 incised on a small panel on the central projecting wing. "It is probable," says the article in the V.C.H. "that the date refers to this wing and the main building is of earlier origin." This W.D. is William Dawes who, together with John Darby of Footlands, gave the church bell which still bears their names upon it. (Chapter 13). A fine old fire-back inscribed W.D. 1610 W.D. was found in the old barn behind the house, when it was sold in 1952.

The house was built as a 3-bay medieval hall in about the year 1420 and, at the end of that century or early in the sixteenth, a fourth bay was added, as with Asselton House and The Thatch.[1]

Like the latter house, it too was held of the Manor of Bricklehurst and in 1543 "Thomas Collway holds of the lease of Peter Easton ½ of Bothurst Tenement and a messuage, garden and 4 parcels" (about 8 acres) bounded by "the Highway Sed. to Westfield E.: lands of Ashburnham Esq called Ashbournehams W: lands of Peter Easton and John Buchellens N: and lands of Wm. Bothurst and Robert Waghornes S."

A hundred years later in about 1600, William Dawes started a massive re-building to the already old house which included the addition of a taller section on the Northern end and a large central porch. He intended too to rebuild the earlier house but this he never did. In order, therefore to lessen the differences between the roof-heights of the new and the old, he built another roof on top of the old one; and the two roofs, one under the other, can still be seen in the attics.[1] William Dawe had married Elizabeth Lawrer in 1607 and they lived at "Late Carters", the name by which the Manor

---

[1] R.O.H.A.S.

Cottages were then known. Did 'late Carter' have any connection with Joseph Carter who had made the church bells? (Chapter 13) Did he perhaps stay there while the three bells were being hung? This we shall never know but the fact remains that the house was known by that name for 200 years, till in a deed of 1813 it became 'formerly Carter's now Elliotts', and Elliotts it remained for much of the nineteenth century during which it became glorified to "Elliotts Manor House."

How did William Dawes become wealthy enough to give, with his neighbour, the church bell at a time when he was spending much money converting his house into a remarkably fine one? In 1665 John Daws is described as a tanner.[1] In view of the fact that the Elliotts, who followed the Dawes at Carters, were tanners at Iltonsbath, it is very possible that the Dawes may have been earlier proprietors of the same tannery; and, like the Bishops, have become highly prosperous in that trade.

*Thomas Dawes*

In 1632 Thomas Dawes, son of William, was living at 'late Carters' which his father had enlarged. It seems from the Sittings Plan (Chapter 23) that he owned also Austford House. How long the Daws family continued to live in Carters after 1632 there is no record but the name John Daws appears in a deed dated 1728, the earliest concerning this house, which it describes thus:

"All that Messuage or tenement, Barn, Stable-buildings, Garden, Orchard, Tanyard, and three parcels of land, meadow and pasture . . . containing by estimation 8 acres . . . and now in the tenure or occupation of John Elliott the Younger."

This deed was executed by "John Elliott, the Elder of Sedlescombe, Tanner" and his wife Martha, together with their son Richard, also a Tanner, in evidence of £500 lent by Richard to his parents. The boundaries of the property are shown: —

"On the North . . . the lands now or late of John Daws.

On the West . . . the lands now or late of John Everendon Gent. (Beech/Chapter 23)

on the South . . . the lands now or late of Harrison.

on the East . . . the King's Highway there leading between Sedlescombe Church and Westfield".

[1] Hearth Tax, E.S.R.O.

So John Daws was, nearly a hundred years after the date of Sittings Plan, still owning land close to Carters. Twenty years later, a Daws child was one of the first twelve to attend the newly opened Sedlescombe Church School. Today there are still Dawes living in the village.

The Elliott's Tanyard was the old Abbey Tannery beside the Bridge at Iltonsbath, opposite the mill installed also by the monks long years ago (Chapter 34). John Elliott, the Elder, was buried in Sedlescombe churchyard in June 1729 and his wife, Martha, followed him there a scarce two years later. Their son, Richard, married 'Constant' and mortgaged the house to Frances Grace, widow of Battle, for £200 just before his father's death. In a document of that year, he is described no longer as a tanner, but as 'of Ewhurst, farmer,' and he mortgaged the house "commonly called Carters" again, to his brother John, ("the Younger"). Millhouses are added to the buildings on his land; the mill-houses at Iltonsbath (Chapter 12). In the boundaries, John Reed succeeded to John Daws' land, and John Plummer to those of his brother-in-law, John Everendon, on the West.

This John Elliott, the Younger, made his will in 1760, "being weak in body but of sound and disposing Mind, Memory and Understanding, Thanks be given to Almighty God for the same, considering the uncertainty of this mortal life, and being desirous to settle my wordly Affairs so as to prevent any unhappy Disputes or Differences which may otherwise arise after my Decease . . ."

He left "the Barn, Buildings, Tanyards, Lands, Premises, and Appurtenances thereunto belonging, situate in or near a certain Street called Sedlescomb Street", and all his personal estate to "his loving son, William," (Baptised Dec. 4. 1730). William was to pay his sister, Elisabeth Elliott, (two years older) an annuity of £8. Among the witnesses of the will are Thomas Colbran, the schoolmaster and mapmaker (Chapter 28), and also a character called Thankful Butler, whose name appears in 1791 as an Overseer of Poor. In spite of the weakness of his body, John lived nine years and was buried in the churchyard on Oct. 22, 1769. His loving son William, died nearly 50 years later in 1813, having made his will a year earlier, which shows him to have acquired considerably more property than he had been left by his father, and he is described as "Gentleman". He seems never to have married and there is no mention of his sister, Elisabeth, in his will. He left Carters with

£225 to William Grace, the son, perhaps, of the widow, Frances; and on trust to him and to Robert Mercer of Hole Farm (Chapter 26) £1000, the interest to be paid to a cousin, described as the wife of a labourer; £10 on trust for the benefit of the poor persons of Sedlescombe; to Robert Mercer £25; and all the rest of his personal estate, with a farm of 80 acres, in Warbleton and Dallington, was to go to Kentish cousins who were farmers. William, a Trustee of Sedlescombe School and a churchwarden, was the last of the Elliotts to live at Carters. Henceforth it became 'late Elliotts', with William Grace, its owner.

*William and Henry Grace*

William Grace is described in William Elliott's will as Grocer and Draper of Sedlescombe. His shop was in the house now called Harriet (Chapter 34). Born in 1764, he died aged 72, and his grave is beside the path leading from the South porch of the church to the wicket gate, Jacob's Gate. He, too, was a trustee of the school, and was to have been the first secretary of a Society to be set up in Sedlescombe in 1795 for dealing with Thieves and Felons and Receivers of Stolen Goods. He died unmarried but in his will, dated 1835, he left all his landed property to "my reputed son Henry Grace of Sedlescombe"; and to his housekeeper, Ann Jempson, spinster, an annuity of £30 and "the Bed whereon she now sleeps" in Asselton House.

Among the baptisms in the Church Registers is the following entry: "25 October 1801 Henry, son of Ann Jameson "Base Born." So Henry Grace was the ilegitimate son of Ann Jameson (Jempson), housekeeper to William Grace, whose surname the boy took. Both Henry and his father were highly respected members of the village, trustees of the school and churchwardens, Henry was one of those who attended the fateful meeting at Battle on October 16th 1830, at which William Cobbett made his famous speech; and he signed the Declaration in defence of Cobbett (Chapter 31).

In the Tithe Map of 1841, Henry Grace is shown as owning several houses in Sedlescombe Street. As well as Elliott's and the grocers shop at Harriet House, occupied at that date by Edward Barber, he owned also Asselton House next door, where Ann and Jane Jempson, his mother and his aunt, lived.

In a book (the property of the late Mr. George Knight of Lyndhurst) wordily entitled: "Recollections of John Grace: for 29 years

## FOUR OF THE OLDEST HOUSES IN THE STREET

Minister of the Gospel at Brighton, being a review of his eventful life . . . his call by Grace and to the work of the Ministry . . . his remarkable success therein . . . and his peaceful end" (published in 1893), William Grace is described as:

"his bachelor uncle, who resided at Sedlescombe near Battle, besides hop growing and tanning, carried on a general business. He was a peculiar man, and lived to scrape together a considerable amount of property; yet, in his way, was kind and liberal, and shewed a good deal of kindness to John Grace and several members of his family . . . John Grace has cause to look far higher than to his uncle; for he once remarked to me across the shop counter, 'My uncle, you know, hated my religion and liked me none the better for it; . . . but you see the Lord it was who constrained him to will the property back to me.' . . . The reader can imagine that it was anything but gratifying to him to find that his uncle had left the bulk of his wealth to his reputed son."

John himself had been greatly in debt and was enabled by his uncle's legacy to pay off his creditors and thenceforth to prosper, as a successful preacher at Brighton.

By 1859, Elliotts had become divided into cottages as it is today, with seven occupiers; Leonora Davis, Dina Dinnett, the Widow Pankhurst, George Wise, Edgar Edwards, James Eldridge and Henry Cook. Pankhurst, Davis and Eldridge are all names of schoolchildren in the first school list of 1748, a hundred years earlier.

At the same date, Henry Grace, described as a farmer of Hurst Green, and his wife, Dinah, executed a comprehensive mortgage deed in favour of a Mrs. Carr of Tunbridge Wells, covering six items of property including "Carters now called Elliotts." The Tanyard is still mentioned as part of Elliotts, and also "the cottage formerly a mill-house". The other 5 items were 1) that "messuage or tenement in two dwellings, with the wheelwright's shop (formerly a barn), Blacksmith's Forge, stable, garden and one piece of land . . . one acre." (Chapter 34). This is now the Bridge Garage. 2) A property "formerly used as an Inn or Public House and then called by the name or sign of the King's Head" (Chapter 39);
and a grocer's shop with the ground adjoining "where there was a Fellmonger's yard and out-buildings which have now ceased to exist some years since . . . at or near a certain place now or formerly called Iltonsbath". The grocer's shop can be identified with the one

still occupying the same house, now called Tanyard Cottage opposite the Bridge Garage. The Inn, called the King's Head, may be the Coach and Horses (burned down in 1914), or it may have been an altogether earlier Inn close by the cottages now called Barracks Cottage and Iltonsbath, with a third beside them where the Old Chapel building now stands.

3) is a house and land, one acre, "now or formerly occupied by Felix Mitchell". These were all freehold.

The last two, 4) and 5) were Asselton Bath and one acre of land, "occupied by Ann Jempson" and an unidentified dwelling-house close by, occupied by William Webb. The mortgage amount for these six items was £1,500.

After he married, he and his wife, Dinah, moved to Wittersham where he had two sons who later became coal merchants of Wittersham and Rolvenden, but he was buried in Sedlescombe when he died in 1873, in the same grave as his 'reputed' father. In a document a year later, he is curiously described as "a Stranger in Blood of William Grace, the Predecessor from whom the said Property is derived".

The year after Henry Grace died, "Elliotts" was sold to John Catt, the builder, who was then living there (Chapter 34). He, too, was buried in the churchyard when he died in 1891. In his will made six years earlier, he left his property to his wife, Catherine, in trust.

At some time during the last decade of the nineteenth century, the oasthouse and outbuildings of Elliotts were converted by F. Thomas (who became F. Thomas and Sons) into a dwelling-house which took over the name of the Manor, omitting Elliotts, and the lovely old pre-Elizabethan house became "Manor Cottages". Now in 1977 when it is becoming two or three flats, how appropriate it would be if it could again be called Carters, or even Daws after the William Daws who so long ago put his initials on its face.

*Barrack Cottage and Iltonsbath* (a)

This is the only cottage left in the village with a jettied upper storey carried on carved brackets on the jutting ends of the wide floor joists, to overhang the lower storey, giving a most attractive and unspoilt exterior. Yet its history is strange.

It was built in the middle of the fifteenth century as a medieval Hall-house, of which only the Southern end now survives as Barracks Cottage. The hall-house was of Wealden type with North and South bays jutting forward beyond the front of the central hall. Before the end of the century another bay was added on the South end (now Iltonsbath) giving, it is possible, accommodation for a shop on the ground floor, for there was no access from it to the room above which could be reached only from the one beside it. In the sixteenth century an oriel window was inserted in Barracks Cottage, and a small rear wing extended it in the seventeenth century. It is not known at what date in the eighteenth or nineteenth century the Northern bays of the original hall house, which would have extended over the garden, were pulled down.[1]

The chimney, which was added, is rebated like many of its neighbours and stands sturdily above the steep-pitched roof.

The very old name, Iltonsbath, found in numerous records and deeds for hundreds of years, spelt in more than a dozen different ways, applied to a manor, which included the whole area of the bridge and the mill-pool and much of the east side of the Green and has been attached to this particular cottage only at some date since 1925 (Chapter 34).

In 1569 "William Lawrence holds by copy one messuage with one acre of land . . . between the garden of Rofes and Garrantay North, and the messuage of the heirs of Richard Johnson, South; and Blacklands, East. 18d."

It is very interesting that the garden of Rofes and Garrantay has been a garden ever since and is now the allotment gardens.

The name Barrack Cottage is said to refer to the days when a guard of soldiers was put to watch the Powdermill during the Napoleonic Wars when, although it was privately owned, it would have been subject to wartime regulations. The field of allotments behind is known as Barracks field; whether the soldiers were billetted in the house or whether there was a camp in the field is unknown. Apart from this name there seems no record of this guard, nor any reference whatever to it.

The first Deed (seen by the kindness of Mr. Ted Thomas) is dated 1792 and concerns "two messuages and tenements with the gardens, orchards, closes, stables, brewhouse, outhouses, at or near

[1] R.O.H.A.S.

a certain place called Iltons Bath, and an Inn commonly known by the sign of the King's Head with the stable-yard in the occupation of Mary Young, widow, in the tenure of Henry Martin and then of Richard Mercer." It was sold to Edmund Weekes by Richard Bishop of the family of Great Sanders, for the witnesses were William Bishop of Great Sanders and Daniel Goody. The innkeeper at that time was William Hudson.

Six years later Edmund Weekes sold the property which included "the Inn called the King's Head, a parcel of ground one acre, the cottage and garden situated behind or nearly adjoining the Inn heretofore in the tenure of William Hudson now untenanted."

A deed of 1803 describes how Richard Bishop "of Sedlescombe, Innholder with his wife Elizabeth" sold the whole property to Edward Ades, the younger of Sedlescombe, farmer of Hancox; the Bishops moved into the small cottage which was later converted into the bigger house now called The Cottage (Chapter 35).

Four years later, perhaps because the cottages included in the property of the Inn were then occupied independently of it, a great many Sedlescombe people were concerned in the Deed of Sale; the butcher, Waghorne, and Eldridge, the carpenter, were using parts of the land as a "fell monger's yard" (Chapter 34), a place for treating hides and skins. Two fellmongers from Westfield, James Dawes and William Bishop, were also concerned in the transaction, and these are clearly Sedlescombe names.

Five years later in 1813, the property was sold again and nine people were involved this time. The price was £422.10. Dawes and Bishop, fellmongers; Cruttenden, senior and junior, farmers; Tilden Smith, landowner and farmer; Henry Freeland, farmer of Homestall; William Thorpe and two others (see Tanyard House and Park View). In April 1817 the property was sold for £600 and William Eldridge, the late carpenter, became innkeeper.

The last deed, dated November 1842, shows John Catt, as one of the parties, Henry Grace, now of Ewhurst, and Horace Martin of Battle, gentleman, as the buyers. William Eldridge was still innkeeper, his son, Joseph, had followed him as carpenter, and the fellmonger's yard had become a carpenter's yard. For the cottages, Thomas Mallyon and others are named in the Tithe Map of 1841 as occupiers, the owner being an Eldridge, but the cottages had become quite separate from the Inn. The Southern-most pair were pulled down and the Wesleyan Chapel was built on its site (Chapter 40). Iltonsbath and Barrack Cottages were left housing two families for half century and more. Alfred Dawson and his wife brought up their many sons and daughters in the two bedroomed cottage, Iltonsbath, and there he lived, for many years a widower, until he died.

In 1925 both cottages were brought by Mrs. Thomas, widow of F. Thomas of the Sedlescombe firm of builders and it is her son, Mr. Ted Thomas, his wife and son who still live in Barrack Cottage. When Alfred Dawson died, Iltonsbath was sold as a separate property.

*Asselton House* (b)

"Asselton House", wrote in 1945 the late John Ray of Hastings, well-known for his study and knowledge of antiquities in this part of the world,

> "stands on the East side of the Street, lying back behind the line of buildings on each side of it, and from its frankly nineteenth century front does not indicate from the exterior any trace of its antiquity.
>
> "The name is probably derived from the family of Issoldun, one of whom, Ralf d'Issoldun, married Alice, Countess of Eu, in about 1200." (Chapter 9).

As described in Chapter 9, she gave land at Iltonsbath to the Monks of Battle Abbey "for the health of the soul of her dear Lord, the late Count of Eu". Strangely, until about 1925, Asselton house was known in its Deeds as Asselton Bath; and the similarity between the two names, Iltonsbath and Asselton Bath, is striking, especially as Asselton Bath is in the area described in old Deeds as 'the place called Iltonsbath'.

> John Ray continued, . . . "In the fifteenth century the Leat Courts for this part of the Rape of Hastings were held at Sedlescombe and it is tempting to suggest that they may have been so held because the Lords of the Rape had a country house there— a Hall—where such Courts could conveniently be held. There is however no proof of this . . . There are 4 bays in the length of the house, each being separated from the next by a pair of posts, one at the front and one at the back of the Hall. Bay 1. forming the private part, or parlour, at the North end: 2. and 3. the central hall; and 4. the service end."

This 4th bay was added later in the century, the earlier service area being probably some form of lean-to.[1]

The hall was entered by a wide spandrelheaded doorway at the Southern end of the Western wall, not where the door now is. The embattled, moulded dais beam is a feature of the Hall, with close vertical puncheons below it which are visible on both faces of the partition. Beside the door which led into the parlour-bay is a scar where protruded a short spur to protect from draughts the dais bench, the large peg-holes of which are clearly visible.

In the rear wall of the Northern hall-bay are the remains of one of the two groups of the hall windows, divided by a heavy central mullion on which still survive the rebates for hinged shutters; and, on the outer window jambs, the shanks of the shutter hinge rides.[1] The crown-post holding the roof has a square base, the shaft above being octagonal to the moulded cap from which branch the four-way struts. "This upper part of the Hall is preserved almost intact", wrote John Ray, "with at both ends its combed plaster work of alternating bands of straight and wavy lines".

Of the external walls, only those to the North and East are now partially exposed. The Northern wall is unusual in that only half of it, and that the Eastern end nearest the road, is close-studded. The existence of these makes it virtually certain that the front face of the house was originally of close vertical studding throughout, while the rear, which could not be seen, is of the cheaper large rectangular daub panel type.[1]

When the chimney and upper storey were inserted, the tie-beam at first-floor level which ran across the lower end of the hall was re-used as the mantel-beam for the chimney, and still retains its moulding at each end but the middle has been cut away. The lean-to forming the kitchen was also put in either at this date or later.

> "In the late nineteenth century a wing was built out at the north end", continued John Ray, "The front of the old part was bricked up to floor level and a bay window was inserted in the front of the lower end, the upper part being tile-hung covering the original plastering and timbers."

Under the floorboards at this time were found quantities of clay-pipes of the type known as churchwardens.

[1] R.O.H.A.S.

## FOUR OF THE OLDEST HOUSES IN THE STREET

In 1569 "William Broke holds by copy one messuage with one acre . . . and abuts on the lands called Blacklands East. rental 18d." He held also a cottage with two gardens of half acre each "between the meadow called Collywish North and East. and to a rivulet South . . . and abuts the lands called Blacklands."[1]

The first occupier of the house according to the Deeds was a man called Isaac Looch, but nothing beyond that is as yet known of him. In 1711 Thomas Cain and his wife, Ann, lived in the house with their children and when Thomas died eight years later it remained Ann's home until she died in 1733, when she left it to her grandson, Thomas Cooper. Six years later Joseph Mercer of Sedlescombe bought it and to Mercers, father, son and grandson, it belonged for the next ninety years.

"On the eighteenth day of November in the sixth year of the reign of our Sovereign Lord George the Fourth . . . in the year 1825 at this court . . . of the Manor of Battle before Thomas Barton, Gentleman, Steward of the said Manor, . . . comes Richard Mercer of Sedlescombe, Yeoman, one of the customary Tenants of the said Manor and Fanny his wife: she, the said Fanny, being first separately examined by the Steward apart from her said husband and freely and voluntarily consenting in consideration of the sum of one hundred and fifteen pounds of lawful money of Great Britain, to him the said Richard Mercer, in hand well and truly paid, by William Grace of Sedlescombe aforesaid, Yeoman, and Henry Grace of the same place, Yeoman, by the Rod each of them doth surrender into the hands of the Lord of the Manor . . . all that customary messuage . . . called Asseltons Bath . . . holden of the said Manor by the yearly rent of one shilling Heriot Relief and other Services . . . And the said William and Henry Grace being present in Court in their own proper persons desire to be admitted to the aforesaid . . . premises . . . to whom the Lord of the Manor by his said Steward granted seizin thereof by the Rod to them and their heirs for ever by Copy of the Court Roll at the Call of the Lord according to the Customs of the said Manor by the Rents, Customs and Services therefore due and of right accustomed, and they are admitted tenants thereof and pay to the Lord for a fine on such their admission Ten Pounds Ten Shillings have seizin thereof by the Rod and their fealties are respited."

[1] B.A.S. 1969.

Until as late as 1924 every time the house changed hands, the vendor and buyer had to attend the Manor Court at Battle and surrender and be admitted to it, for it was part of the feu of Basoc and Manor of Iltonsbath, given to the Monks of Battle Abbey long ago in the thirteenth century, and therefore still held copyhold of the Lords of the Manor of Battle Abbey, their successors. The Manor Courts, though presided over by the Steward, were by tradition democratic and decisions at the Court were binding on the Lord as well as on his tenants. The fact that Fanny Mercer was first separately examined by the Steward, to see if she agreed to the selling of the property seems surprising in days when wives had few privileges, but it was part of this old democratic system of the manorial courts, when all freeholders and tenants were bound to attend its meetings and all could speak. The system of Heriot had, for Asselton Bath, been commuted, as had the fealty to the lord.

William Grace died on the 24th day of March, 1836, leaving his "reputed" son Henry owner of the property. In accordance with his father's will, William's housekeeper, Ann Jempson, who was Henry's mother, continued to live in the house with her sister Jane. The will had left Ann an annuity of £30 and "the Bed whereon she now sleeps", together with all the bedding, and her sister Jane an annuity of £20 and "the other bed in the room where the said Ann Jempson now sleeps", with all the bedding. After Ann died a Charles Stapely shared the dwelling with Jane. It seems to have housed two or three tenants in the next few years, including Albert Blackpool and Walter French, followed by Phineas Paine and William Ball, blacksmiths.

In May 1841 came Dinah Grace, widow of Henry, and her sons, William and Thomas, and, in consideration of the sum of £40 paid to her and £60 to each of her two sons by John Catt, he was admitted to the tenancy, after they had surrendered it to the hands of the Lord of the Manor. Phineas Paine was at this time occupier.

"At a General Court Baron of Caroline Wilhelmina Duchess of Cleveland Lady of the Manor of Battle . . . before Charles Sheppard Gentleman Steward of the said Manor . . . the second proclamation was made after the death of John Catt . . . (1891) . . . who held . . . Asseltons Bath . . . now in two tenements or dwellings . . . comes Hercules Brabazon of Sedlescombe Esquire, by Robert Flint his attorney, and produce in open Court the probate of the last Will and Testament of John Catt . . . the said Hercules Brabazon Brabazon . . . and he is admitted tenant thereof in form aforesaid paid to the Lady for a fine . . . fifteen pounds hath seizin thereof by the delivery of the rod to his said attorney and his fealty was respited."

Up till this date Asseltons Bath had remained virtually unchanged since the sixteenth century, when the chimney was inserted and the floor across the hall joined the upper storeys on either side, making one complete upper floor. Now Hercules Brabazon, through Herbert Dengate, the builder, who lived next door at what is now Harriet House, undertook an enlargement of the old house which changed its face for ever. A plan was drawn up, which was recently kindly given to me by Miss Mercy Dengate, the builder's daughter, for a North wing extending to the West, thus making the house L-shaped. At the same time the windows of the old front were taken out and two bays made and the old plaster and timber front was hung with tiles. The house was thus enlarged by three rooms, and a bathroom was installed upstairs. A shield with Brabazon's coat of arms, was placed in the gable of the new wing.

It was then let to the Byner family, who owned what is now Miller's shop at this date. Many of the older villagers remember "Jimmy" Byner in his old age, with a laugh at the tricks they used, as children, to play on the old man; and describe how he lost on one occasion his false teeth and how they were eventually and "unaccountably" found up in the old apple-tree in the garden of Asselton; and how the boys would in the dark take the garden gate off its hinges and "make him mad". In the autumn the men used to bring the old hop poles on to the green and saw them up so everybody had their faggots. Jimmy Byner's were put on the lawn. When he saw them, "Damnanblast," he shouted, "the boys might have brought them round the back". So after nightfall the boys did bring them round the back and piled them up against the door so that in the morning he could not open it!

His old father died and was buried in the Byner plot among the Irish yews on the North side of the church door. Some years later his mother died and was to be buried in the same grave but by then there was some doubt as to which of two this was. "Never mind," said Jimmy, "open up that one and put her in there; her'll soon muddle around and find 'n".

Charles, the eldest son, after his father died emigrated to Australia, whence his descendants return from time to time and seek out the old house.

In 1924, on the death of Major Harvey Trewithen Brabazon Combe, nephew of Hercules Brabazon, who had inherited Oaklands estate on the death of his uncle in 1906, much of the property in the village was sold, including Asselton Bath, or House, which was sold for £810 to Lt. Col. and Mrs. Gaitskell. On the death of her Husband, Frances Amy Combe and her son Harvey, well known in the village as "the Captain", had been admitted by the Court of the Manor of Battle as tenants in the customary manner and had then (by virtue of Acts of Parliament passed during the years 1882 and 1890) in consideration of the sum of £172.3.2d. been admitted

"In fee simple as freehold, and discharged from all quit rents, fines, heriots, reliefs, suits and manorial services due to the Lord of the Manor of Battel for or in respect of the said premises . . . excepting and reserving to the Lords of the Manor all mines minerals quarries of coal, stone, slate, iron-stone and other ore mines and mineral substances . . . and all such ancient fisheries and rights of fishing and all such liberties of chase and free warren and killing of game if any as had theretofore anciently been used and enjoyed by the Lords or Ladies of the Manor . . ."

So in 1925, for the first time the ancient house was freehold and not copyhold of the Manor of Battell.

Ten years later Mrs. Gaitskell, who with her husband had moved to Eastbourne, sold the house to Mrs. Tomlins for £635, who two years later sold it for £900. The new owner never lived in the house, which was let during the war years to a mother and her young daughter. Its latest owner bought it just before the end of the war and has lived in it ever since.

*Chapter Fifteen*

REBELLION

Before and during the building of these old houses Sussex was in a pitiable state. The war with France, so heroic and successful under King Henry V, was going badly under his unwarlike and scholarly son. The glorious days of Agincourt were past; battles and territory were being continually lost; taxation was high and the drain on man-power had added to the poverty of a county where farming was always a struggle; the raids of the French were a constant and very real menace. The year 1366 had seen the well-nigh undefended Winchelsea viciously attacked. Eleven years later it was the Abbot of Battle, Hamo, who had organised the defence of that town with the result that, for the first time, the attacking French were successfully beaten off. Meanwhile, the French fleet had sailed to the equally undefended Hastings and burnt it. Hamo was a hero and when, in 1381, the attempt to collect a poll-tax finally put the match to the pile and caused the Peasant Revolt, there were no attacks on the Abbey. Had not monks, lords and peasants fought side by side against the French invaders, and shared in long watches on the hills?

After Hamo's death in 1383 the Abbey was still the centre of defence and his successor called on "all able-bodied men, both those who have wherewithal to arm themselves and those who have not" to array themselves in view of the imminent invasion by the French, and the "bodily feeble to contribute to arms and expenses." There was no central government for defence, all expense was borne locally. The depredations of deserters and wandering soldiers from the encampments of men waiting to sail to France were now additional threat and danger. The poor hid in the forests or took to the highway.

The ferment of discontent grew so that the Lollard doctrine of communal ownership fell on ready ground. This discontent was turned in enmity towards the King and his misgovernment, in contrast to the near hero-worship and loyalty felt for Richard II at the time of the earlier Peasants' Revolt.

Jack Cade, a servant of Thomas Dacre of Heathfield, organised action and the people of Kent and Sussex began to gather and elect captains and masters to depose the King, "proposing to hold all things in common". One John Climpsham, a carpenter, met with about a hundred others in a wood near Hastings for this purpose. Another Captain, John Cotyng, a yeoman, headed an attempt to break up the Abbot's Fair at Robertsbridge in September 1449.[1]

Holinshed describes Jack Cade as a "certain young man of goodly stature and pregnant wit," but this wit does not seem to have saved him from being used as a tool by the Yorkist faction who saw in the dissatisfaction of the common people an opportunity to depose the Lancastrian Henry VI. Cade therefore assumed the name of Mortimer, claiming descent from the Earl of March (which would give him kinship with the Duke of York), and put himself at the head of the populace of Kent, in opposition to royal authority.

As far as the rising in East Sussex was concerned, it had very much of the character of a military and duly authorised levy and array. In many Hundreds the musters were levied by the Constables; the Hundred of Staple, for instance, was under the leadership of its Constable, Richard Beche of Sedlescombe, yeoman. Small outbreaks of violence against the gentry erupted; the Leat Court being held at Sedlescombe was broken up, as was also the Sheriff's tourney at Battle. The rebels were rapidly increasing in number and kind, for their names include the Abbot of Battle and the prior of Lewes; the bailiffs of Seaford and Pevensey; the constables and inhabitants of eighteen parishes and all the men of eight parishes. This imposing array joined Jack Cade and his Kentish men, making an army of 20,000 men marching on London. The King, Henry VI, retired hurriedly to the safety of his castle at Kenilworth.

Lower writes of Cade: "How he encamped on Blackheath with his Kentish army, how he defeated the royal forces at Sevenoaks, how he beheaded the Lord Saye and Sele at Cheapside and proclaimed himself master of London and how he was finally routed

[1] S.A.C. 18.

by the King's forces and put to death by Alexander Iden are things so well known that further reference to them is unnecessary." Lord Saye and Sele was the owner of the famous Knole House at Sevenoaks at that time, a well-hated man, his neighbours being some of the strongest of Cade's supporters.

The feeling in favour of the rebels faded after looting took place in the city and they started, as a result, to quarrel among themselves. The citizens of London then rallied for the King and drove them out. Jack Cade fled to Lewes with a price on his head of one thousand marks, but a free pardon was offered to all of his followers who would return home. Among the pardons issued were over four hundred to Sussex men who availed themselves of the offer and went home. Among these were Richard, Abbot of St. Martin's Monastery at Battle, with all his monks and servants, Christopher Fynhawe of Westfield, Richard Oxenbridge of Peasmarsh and Richard Beche of Sedlescombe.

Jack Cade himself seems to have been the only one who suffered among the rebels. "As he was playing at Bowls", so tradition once again has it, "in the garden of an ale-house in Heathfield" (where no doubt he felt safe, since it was his home-land) "he was pierced by an arrow from Mr. Iden's well-strung bow",[1] on July 11th, 1450. His body was taken to London and, in the fashion of the time, dismembered and the parts exhibited in various well-chosen places, to have a chastening effect.

In the nineteenth century Francis Newbery, "the eminent druggist of St. Paul's Churchyard" and then owner of Heathfield Park, erected a stone to commemorate the event. It reads thus:

> "Near this spot was slain the notorious rebel, Jack Cade, by Alexander Iden, Sheriff of Kent A.D. 1450. His body was carried to London and his head fixed on London Bridge: 'This is the success of all rebels, and this fortune chanceth ever to traitors.' "[1]

Alexander Iden had pursued him from as far away as Rochester, so perhaps earned his triumph, and Jack himself was spared a far worse fate had he been captured alive.

---

[1] Lower.

Thus ended "one of the greatest insurrections that England has witnessed," and one can feel only astonishment at the extreme leniency and total pardon of all the rebels, save the one. Rebel he was, and long may there be such. The harsh name of traitor he earned when there were many of these, including he who eventually overturned King Henry, and made himself King Edward IV.

*Chapter Sixteen*

## BACK TO IRON: PROSPERITY FOR SEDLESCOMBE

After the Romans had left Britain the iron industry, like the roads, had declined all over Sussex, to become a small industry serving mainly agriculture, in what were almost entirely farming communities. But now, at the end of the fifteenth century in Tudor times, a new process of iron-smelting, discovered on the Continent, was brought to Britain and resulted very soon (in 1492) in the first iron cannon being made at Buxted in Sussex by Ralph Hogge, who cast the canon in one entire piece of bored metal instead of in separate wrought portions to be banded together. After this the industry grew rapidly. Men in East Sussex became quickly rich. Landowners on whose land iron was found, owners of the vast woodlands, merchants who financed the industry and who speculated in furnaces, the lesser gentry and skilled craftsmen who became ironmasters and ironworkers with the actual management in their hands, all shared in the unprecedented prosperity, helping to create an important and wealthy middle class.

An age of pollution and spoilation of the countryside followed. "The quietness of our beautiful Weald at the present day," says a writer in 1846, "offers a striking contrast to the ceaseless activity and bustle which characterised it in its Iron Age, the days of the Tudors and Stuarts." Camden, speaking of Sussex, says: "Full of iron mines it is in sundry places where for the making and founding thereof, there be furnaces on every side and a huge deal of wood is yearly burnt; to which purposes divers brooks in many places are brought to run in one channel, and sundry meadows turned in to pools and waters, that they might be of power to drive hammers, which beating upon the iron resound all over the places adjoining."

And in 1732: "A great deal of meadow ground is turned into ponds and pools for the driving of mills by the flashes which, beating with hammers upon the iron, fill the neighbourhood round about night and day with continual noise." Water power was used for driving the wheels which worked the bellows at the furnaces where the iron ore was cast into bars and pigs; the forges, where the cast-iron was converted by the hammers into wrought-iron, were usually located lower down the same stream (like Brede Furnace and Westfield Forge).

Trees by the hundred were cut down to feed the furnaces, and woods and forests which had flourished from time immemorial grew thinner very rapidly—the forests that the Romans had called Anderida, and the Saxons Andreadsweald, and which had gradually become generally known as the Weald.

At night the sky was red from the glare of the furnaces and by day the noise of the trip hammers was a natural accompaniment to living. Within a radius of five miles of Sedlescombe Green were more than thirty forges and furnaces. A look at the ordnance map shows numbers of place-names with Furnace, where the rich iron ore was converted by the heat of the charcoal-fed furnaces into lumps of iron; and Forges, where these were hammered into bars for export or into the cannons, cannon-balls, agricultural tools and iron firebacks for which Sussex became famous.

The whole basin of the Brede was a great centre of iron production, and iron was in ever greater quantities shipped down the river in barges from the iron store at Brede Harbour. An illicit trade in guns themselves arose. On some of the ships of the Spanish Armada, captured by the British, cannon were found which had been manufactured at Ashburnham Forge and bore its trade-mark, a Tudor rose.

*Brede Furnace* (Map A)

There was a furnace off Brede Lane, where the Powdermill reservoir now is. The first we hear of it is in 1578 when the valley was dammed to provide the water power for driving the great bellows of a blast furnace for smelting the iron, and the towns of Hastings, Rye and Winchelsea complained to the Privy Council of the waste of wood caused by the erection of the new iron-works by "three Kentish men".[1] In 1558 an Act had been passed prohibiting the cutting of wood, more than one foot square, for ironworks within fourteen miles of the sea, because the Sussex Ports had a considerable trade in wood fuel with French Ports; and Sussex oak was needed for the building of ships, and the speed with which the Sussex woods were being eaten up was causing intense concern. Hence the complaint by the three towns. In the records of Panningbridge Furnace, a subsidiary of Robertsbridge Furnace, kept from 1542-1549, out of 73 workmen employed, no less than 53 were woodcutters (paid 3d a cord for the wood). There were but two charcoal burners (paid 1/10 a load), two charcoal carriers (4d to 6d a load) and one founder (6/- for six days).[1]

The Sackville family of Sedlescombe owned Brede Furnace for many years in the later part of the 16th century until after the end of the Civil War. They were part, of course, of the great Kentish family of Knowle, of whom the head was the Earl of Dorset.

John Browne, gunmaster to the King, was the manager before the war and remained in control when Parliament took over at the beginning of hostilities. After the Restoration his family again provided the Royal Gunmaster. In 1676 Colonel Sackville sold the furnace. The master craftsman was Richard Lennard, son of the Lawrence Lennard whose family had worked there almost since its beginning. Richard lived close to his work in "Little Udimore" (a detached portion of that parish lying between those of Sedlescombe and Brede) and his children were baptised at Brede Church.

In Hastings Museum and in a bedroom at Bateman's, where Rudyard Kipling lived, can be seen the famous fireback which he made. Another is nearer at hand, built into the outer wall of the Bridge Garage in Sedlescombe. The initials R.L. and the date 1636 are in the bottom right-hand corner. "The central figure is Richard Lennard himself, a gallant one with well-trimmed beard and moustaches, and dressed in knee-breeches and flowing gown; his dog, however, has a lean and hungry look. Richard Lennard is grasping a hammer and round him are the tools of his trade."[2] Later in the seventeenth century members of the Lennard family migrated to America, where they prospered again as iron-masters.

During the Civil War 1642-53 a great number of the guns of the Parliamentary Army were cast in Brede Furnace, which must have been a hive of activity as it was, together with Horsmonden, their

[1] Wealdon Iron.
[2] Thorne.

chief supplier of ordnance. The fields on either side of the road still have an uneven surface and in November 1960, when Mr. Hamer of Bramshill Farm at Telham was ploughing, he turned up a piece of cannon 20 inches long by 8 inches wide and 4 inches thick, which weighed about 1 cwt.[2] It was identified by Colonel Lemmon as a 101-degree segment of the breech end of a Minnion, a gun which was 6 ft. 6 inches long, weighed 9 cwt. 1 qtr. 14 lb., had a calibre of $3\frac{1}{2}$ inches and fired shot weighing 5.2 lb. which had probably burst on testing, for they were fired from one side of the valley into the bank on the other side for this purpose. Bullets were also cast here and a block of lead found in the field near Mrs. Apps' cottage (now demolished) on the hillside was presented by her to the same Museum. "In size and shape it resembles," wrote Colonel Lemmon, "a cake of kitchen soap, which suggests that the lead was put up in this portable form for conveyance, possibly by pack-horse from the distant lead mines."[1]

During the eighteenth century quantities of iron were still being sent by land carriage, as well as by sea, to London, and guns were still being made at Brede Furnace as late as 1760, being brought down the Brede by barges to Winchelsea Gun Wharf; but the trade was fast dying, though the charcoal industry and the manufacture of gunpowder continued unabated.

*Westfield Forge*[2]   (Map A)

This was the forge run in conjunction with Brede Furnace, a little lower down the river, less than a mile west of Brede Bridge where the iron store was situated for storing cannon and shot pending shipment by barges to Rye, thence to be transferred to sea-going vessels for London and the Continent. In 1757 'Jockey' Gibbs drove six stallions belonging to Mr. Richardson of Powdermill Farm to the Furnace, where he loaded the guns and then drove the said team entirely by himself to the Wharf, where he unloaded them. "As the guns weighed 35 to 55 cwt. each, this must have been a wonderful feat."[3]

There was considerable trade in smuggling guns abroad and, apart from the evidence of those captured from the Spanish Armada, there is a record of a complaint in 1573 by Ralph Hogge,

---

[1] B.H.S. Museum.
[2] On R. Brede. South of Park Wood.
[3] Austen.

the Buxted iron-master, about the sale of cast-iron guns across the sea; he received only £8 apiece for his guns, whereas the smugglers got £12 to £13. It was very difficult to stop this smuggling, partly because the export of small-bore cannon was permitted and, once the guns had been exported, there was nothing to prevent the bore being enlarged.

So Sussex had become an industrial as well as a farming county and was the centre of armament making of England. The great Queen herself travelled through Sussex to Rye, resting at Northiam. Surely many a man, woman and child must have walked through the woods and meadows to see her as she passed on the road to Rye. The inn, beside the Green at Sedlescombe, was called after her.

In 1586 an Order in Council proclaimed that all guns specified for coastal defence should be made from Wealden, i.e. Sussex furnaces; a tremendous boost, if such were needed, to the industry. One of these early Sussex guns is still to be seen at Pevensey Castle with Queen Elizabeth's cipher and the Tudor rose trademark of Ashburnham Furnace. This Order was one of the signs that the increasing rivalry of Spain was causing the Queen's Government to look very seriously to its defences.

A year later all Sussex iron-founders, including presumably Sackville and Bishop from Sedlescombe, were summoned to London and their industry was placed under Government control (which has a modern sound!). So at the time of the Armada, 1588, the whole construction of English guns was in the hands of Sussex ironmasters; not only this, but there being as yet no navy (Queen Elizabeth owned only thirty ships), Sussex was the breeding-place of gunners. "It was in those days the invariable custom that the man who fought with the gun was the man who made it," surely a method of ensuring good quality.[1] (The Royal Marines were not formed until Charles II's reign.)

When Queen Elizabeth ordered the Cinque Ports to provide ships to fight the Armada, Hastings and Winchelsea subscribed one and Rye and Tenterden another, both of 60 tons with two guns which were, in fact, of brass, not iron. They were ordered to sea on May 6th "with plenty of salt meat on board", but it was not until July 25th that the defeat of the Armada took place. "It is interesting to

[1] S.C.M. 12, p. 740.

note that the mark on the ordnance is, to this day, the broad arrow drawn from the arms of the Sydneys, the Earls of Romney, one of the Cinque Ports."[1]

In a review of a book by Colin Martin called "Full Fathom Five", about wrecks of the Spanish Armada around the coast of Britain,[2] Ion Trewin wrote: "Philip II of Spain's Armada has held its mysteries for nearly 400 years. In particular, why were the Spanish guns so ineffective against the British? We can dismiss the fanciful musings of the historian, Camden, who suggested that Spanish ships were so tall that their shot hurtled above the smaller British vessels. Was it the cannon? The gunpowder? The shot? The quality of the Spanish gunners?"

It was not the gunpowder, nor the shot, nor the Spanish gunners. It was his first suggestion, the cannon, for Spanish guns were made of brass and bronze. Because of the nature of these two metals the guns had thick walls and a high specific heat and therefore, after firing, the Spanish artillerymen were forced to let their guns cool down sufficiently to be handled. The Sussex guns, with which practically all the English ships were armed, being, with a few exceptions, of cast-iron, had thinner walls of a low specific heat, and for this reason could be charged repeatedly and more continuously. This gunnery superiority proved, as is historically accepted, the decisive factor in the battle.[3]

For many decades after the defeat of the Armada, Sussex continued to be the only place in England where iron guns were made. Sussex landowners and craftsmen prospered. Bigger and more comfortable houses were being built, for the first time with chimneys. Bricks were more and more replacing timber. Sedlescombe was a growing village enjoying with all the country around a period of unusual prosperity.

There were already Durhamford, Little Castlemans, Hancox, Footlands, Great Sanders, the Queen's Head, the Manor Cottages (though not the porch) and in the Street, Asselton House, the Old Thatch, Iltonsbath and Barrack Cottage and possibly the Tithe Barn; further afield were Herst, Bellatkin (now Strawberry Farm), Jacobs and Chittlebirch.

[1] S.C.M. 12, p. 740.
[2] The Times, 12th June, 1975.
[3] S.C.M. 12, p. 140.

## Beckley Furnace and Forge

At this date (1599) the other great iron-master of Sedlescombe, Peter Farnden, who would later live at Brickwall with his family of seven daughters, was a child of seven years old. We do not know when he arrived in Sedlescombe, but he married Mary Waters of Brede in Sedlescombe Church in 1616.

On August 8th, 1653, a Thomas Newberry wrote to the Ordnance officers, describing a journey he had made to various forges in Sussex with the object of making contacts; "that Mr. Farrenden (Farnden), an iron-master, said he had no water at present but could make 100 tons by March, but would not deliver it further from his furnace than Hastings or Rye and his lowest price was £13.10s. per ton. Mr. Evernden of Lewes and some other mill-owners also wanted water."[1] Mr. Farnden is said to have leased Socknersh Furnace from 1673-76. But Beckley Furnace belonged to him. "A handsome pair of brand-irons ornamented with the Tudor rose and marked with the initials P.F. (formerly belonging to my ancestors) now stands in my old-fashioned fireplace. They were probably cast at Beckley Furnace.[2] Many of the cannon balls made there were found some years ago when ploughing and draining the field for hop-planting . . . the ironworks finally closed down in 1770 . . . A survey of 1787 states that the Furnace, now owned by Miss Gott" (who was a descendant of Peter Farnden) "might work again in case of war. In the Tillingham stream are still to be seen heavy timbers and the remains of the trough which carried the water to the wheel. When the Furnace House was enlarged recently, several cannon balls and a large iron ladle were discovered."

Thomas Fuller wrote in July 1741: "I take Robertsbridge Furnace and Beckley to be the only two furnaces that can supply guns in winter, the one being on a navigable river and the other very near to the sea."[1]

[1] Wealden Iron.
[2] Austen.

*Chapter Seventeen*

## THREE FAMILIES AND THEIR HOMES

These three families all had interests in the iron industry; the Bishops of Great Sanders, the Sackvilles of Hancox and the Farndens of Brickwall. The Bishops were the first to come and the last to leave, but of the Farndens, who were here for only the one generation, we know more personal details than of either of the other two families.

*The Bishops of Great Sanders* 1458-1858

This family, said to be of purely Sussex origin, has a longer residence in the village than any other. Four hundred years and more is a long time and, though Great Sanders passed into other hands over a hundred years ago, there are still descendants living in the village. Happy the family which has its roots for generations in the same few miles of soil and happy the village which has such a family or families in its midst, however vast or small their number of acres. The sense of belonging gave a security, whatever else may have been lacking, a knowledge of everybody being bound up together in "the bundle of life"[1] which is deeply, though often unconsciously, missed today.

Among the earliest Bishops traced in Sedlescombe is a John, who witnessed a grant in 1456. The last Bishop to live at Great Sanders was also John, who died in 1870.

"How did a man come to be called 'Bishop'?[2] According to the experts he could have been nicknamed 'Bishop' (and the name might pass to his descendants) if he had a bishop-like appearance or bearing or, as happened in medieval times, if he had been chosen

[1] I Samuel 25:v.29.
[2] Thorne.

as the boy-bishop for the pageant on St. Nicholas Day." A book, *Nichols' Topographer and Genealogist*, is said to give a pedigree of the Bishops beginning with an Alexander in the fifteenth century (who witnessed a document in 1483) and tracing it for thirteen generations to the last John Bishop; but the earliest mentions of the name occurring in records concerning Sedlescombe are: a Thomas who appeared in 1415 at a Court of the Hundred of Staple held at Michaelmas "at Setlyscombe".[1] In 1447 "The house of Simon Bishop over against Mordon" is mentioned; and at the same date appear William and Alexander who were tanners. Was Simon's house Spilsteads, known to have been built for a Bishop in about the middle of the fifteenth century? The family seems to have been a large one which prospered greatly—probably through their tanning —during that century to become increasingly owners of land. By 1528 John Bishop had built two fine houses, (Little) Castlemans and Durhamford, which was known, significantly, for at least 150 years, as The Tanhouse; and another beside the highway south of Combe Wood, called Jeffries. At the same time Richard Bishop had lands close by, called The Herst and Beche, still so named today, and also Regge which is not. Herst was surrounded by the lands of Austford or Alkysford, granted by the Abbot of Robertsbridge Abbey in 1483 to John Amyot of Sedlescombe in a document witnessed by Thomas and Alexander Byschoppe. After the Dissolution of the Abbey in 1539, all its lands were given by Henry VIII to Sir William Sidney of Penshurst in Kent. After his grandson, Sir Philip, was killed in 1586 all their lands in the north of the parish of Sedlescombe were acquired freehold by the Bishop family, but much also was still copyhold of the Robertsbridge Abbey Estate. In 1592 John Bishop, churchwarden, was living at Austford.

The first mention of a "Bishop of Great Sanders" seems to be the William Bishop of the 1632 Church Plan (Chapter 23). The family's prosperity had continued and it would seem that, like many another hereabouts, it had interests also in the flourishing iron industry. Today there is still an iron slab in the floor of the north aisle of the church to this William, who died in 1664, which identifies him as an iron-master, for it is said that only these were allowed such iron memorials (Chapter 13). Strangely there is no record discovered of where the Bishops' Furnace and Forge were.

[1] S.R.S. 37.

William's daughter, Mary, married into an iron-master's family, that of the Fowles of Wadhurst, who lived in the fine mansion, Riverhall, built by the family in 1591. Mary died at Wadhurst two years before her father.

In the time of the Civil War at least one Bishop seems to have been a Royalist and he was concerned in a plot against Cromwell's life during the Protectorate. A Captain Henry Mallory was one of the leaders in this abortive plot and a point of great interest emerges in the family when, a century later, William Bishop of Hurst named his first-born infant boy not the usual William, John or James, but Henry Mallory! Henry Mallory, the Cavalier and Jacobite, the plotter against Cromwell's life, was William Bishop's hero at a time when the "Forty-Five" was only a few years ahead. King George was on the throne and William Bishop was clearly of strong Jacobite sympathies. What else can the choice of that name indicate? William's second son was duly baptised John and it was he who in 1756 became Rector of Sedlescombe and for twenty-seven years lived in the Parsonage (the Old Rectory). His brother, Henry Mallory, died unmarried before him and John, in his will made in 1783, left Great Sanders, the "Mansion House", to his son James, including also Austford, Beech, Chittlebirch, Durhamford, Hurst and Little Castlemans.

Twenty years later this James made his will, which begins thus: "I desire to be buried in a leaden coffin in a respectful manner", which caused one to wonder if some funerals were conducted at that time in a disrespectful manner. To his sons, John, George and James, he left respectively Great Sanders, Austford and Beech; Hurst Farm and various woodland; land not in Sedlescombe. To his two daughters he left four thousand pounds when they were twenty-one.

So John, now the Squire, and George continued to live in Sedlescombe after their father died in 1805, but Hurst with its woodlands was henceforth for ever separated from Great Sanders.

John sold Durhamford, built by his ancestors long ago, to the Rector, John Pratt, ten years later. In 1829 his son, the last John, was born; not only the last John, but the last Bishop to live in Great Sanders. One-third of the parish belonged to the Bishops of Great Sanders and this was not their hey-day.[1] John seems to have died in

[1] Horsefield.

Hastings but he was buried in the Bishop vault below the north aisle with his forbears. To his memory the window at the east end of that aisle is dedicated by his two surviving sisters in 1870; and the Great Sanders estate, with its beautiful woodlands, passed into the hands of strangers. George's children lived on at Hurst and his children's children at Sackville Cottage in the Street. Still today there are his descendants in Sedlescombe.

Great Sanders was bought by William Rushton Adamson who, with his family continued to live there until 1919 when he sold the whole estate to E. H. Chambers who lived in Austford house, selling the "mansion house" to a William Mewburn. Chambers then cut down and sold much of the valuable timber on the estate before selling the land to the Hastings Corporation for the building of a reservoir (Chapter 46). The house was let to various tenants and in the war to a school evacuated from St. Leonards, which brought with it its name, Merrion House School. In the nineteen sixties, the school reverted to its old name and so it remains today. The house, though still a school, is once more privately owned.

*Great Sanders House* (Maps A, B and 2)

Sir John Thorne, in considering the name Sanders and finding nobody of that name after whom it could have been called, made the suggestion that it might have been after the early Alexander Bishop, who perhaps built the house in the fifteenth century. A highly romantic and certainly apocryphal story is sometimes heard locally of this Alexander, "a giant, red-haired and red-bearded, known as Sandy", from which Sanders!

However, among the cases heard at the Court of the Hundred of Staple held in Sedlescombe in 1345 was one concerning a debt owed by a John Sandre, whose cottage could, according to custom, well have been the first dwelling known as Sanders.

A house called Sanders was certainly in existence by 1550, for in a will of that year William Bishop apportioned the different rooms in the house to different members of his family; a curious arrangement.

The central section of the present-day house was timber-framed with lath and plaster filling. The owner, in carrying out restoration in 1975, found that the walls had been re-faced several times and, when these layers were removed, old vertical beams were disclosed and also a rather beautiful medieval oak door; thirty feet away from this were found two matching windows of the same period, which have had to be re-hidden again.

When it was converted to a "mansion house" by the bachelor, Henry Mallory Bishop, two wings were added and the handsome exterior was faced with "Mathematical tiles". These are traditional tiles laid in an unusual arrangement so that they lie flush with each other like bricks, instead of overlapping in the normal way. Until they had to be removed there was no reason, in fact, to suppose that they were other than normal bricks. Over the porticoed porch is the Bishop coat of arms. By 1783 it was "the mansion house", with great coach-house and stables built round a bricked yard and the garden laid out with yew hedges making bays round the central lawn. It still has some beautiful ornamental trees but the great elms and beeches have been laid low in recent years by disease and storm.

The extensive deterioration of the house over many years is gradually being repaired under the present ownership; a tremendous but rewarding undertaking.

*Some of the Bishop properties*   Hurst (Chapter 23)

*Castlemans (Little)*

This, the first known residence of the Bishops which is still able to be identified, is the long, low house which looks across Durhamford valley to Hancox from the top of Stream Lane, where it has sat for more than 450 years. Opposite is the triangular coppice in which once grew the tree known for at least a century as Castleman's Oak and marked thus on a map dated 1726.

A John Castleman was tithingman for Sedlescombe in 1447 (Chapter 4). It is not impossible that he lived in a cottage close to the oak tree—or even on the site of the present house—which thus became for ever associated with his name.

The first mention of the house by name is in a will of John Browne of Sedlescombe, dated 1528, showing that it belonged then to John Bishop who was probably living in it. The present Little Castlemans is certainly not the same building though the earlier house may well be incorporated in it. According to the Victoria County History of Sussex the house is of late sixteenth century "much altered externally" and with a seventeenth-century wing added, making the house L-shaped. By 1609 Little Castlemans had been bought from the Bishops by John Downton and so became Sackville property. When a bathroom was constructed in the house after the first World War, two fragments of wall-paintings were revealed, one of which bore the date 1658. So it would seem that during the Sackville's ownership it remained a 'gentleman's residence' to be beautified by such means. Only 12 acres of land went with it.

In 1632 Thomas Avory was tenant. He could not sign his name on the Plan and so 'made his mark' with a cross. Nevertheless, by 1648 Thomas Avory had become 'phisitian''; perhaps he was of the next generation but there is no mention of him being 'the younger'.

In 1715 John Cord was the tenant, but by 1729 the Sackvilles had sold it, for Richard Budgeon, in describing the Great Hurricane of that year, recorded that the "House at Castleman's Oak belonging to Mrs. Tomlins had a stack of chimneys turned down upon the house which in their Fall broke two or three rafters." John Russell was her tenant at the time (Chapter 27).

Thirty years later Isaac Baker was the tenant. In Thomas Colbran's Map of 1759, the house at the top of Stream Lane is clearly marked Castlemans, while the one south of the church which looks down the hill to the school and bears that name today was not yet built. In later maps it was at first called The Firs, but on the Tithe Map of 1841 (Chapter 37) it had become Castlemans Farm, owned by Mrs. Woodward and farmed, together with Beach opposite, by Spencer Crisford. The old Castlemans was from thenceforward Little Castlemans and for a time became the farm cottages. In the first twenty years of the twentieth century it was a farmhouse occupied and farmed by the Dallaway family and known often as "Dallaways", but when the Castlemans farm broke up between the wars it was sold with its garden and paddock to Dr. Hunnard who with his wife made the garden most beautiful and filled the paddock and orchard with thousands of daffodils. There, after several changes of ownership, they still blow every springtime.

*Beech Farm or "Crouchers"* (Map A)

The two Beech Farms in Sedlescombe—one opposite the church, the other less than a mile away northwards along the road to Cripps Corner—were probably in very early days all one; part of much wider lands around Battle belonging to the de Beche family. There is still yet another Beech on the other side of Battle which is sometimes described in records as West Beche, while the Sedlescombe property was East Beche.

In 1367 Thomas Beche held the farmstead, E. Beche in Sedlescombe, of Battle Abbey; he took up also some 50 acres near Durhamford, Wickham land.

In 1475 "John, Abbot of the monastery of Battle . . . did grant to Robert Oxenbridge and Robert Brown, to Robert Wayte ward and marriage of the said Robert who was seized of the ward of the lord of the lands called the Beche." There follows a note that "John Brown did homage to the Lord Abbot in his Great Chamber according to ancient custom for lands called Beche part of the Manor of Whatlington . . . in the 22nd year of the reign of King Henry VIII" (1531).

By the sixteenth century the more northerly of the two Sedlescombe Beeches was in the hands of Richard Bishop and its site is clearly pin-pointed in a record of 1569 of James Sluter's lands,[1] also called the Beche, and Clove Oxe "lying between the lands of Thomas Darby called Sinder Burrough W. and lands of Richard Bishop, the Beche E. and N. and to his own lands, S." James Sluter's lands were Spilsteads (for many years called Slaughters after him) (Chapter 23). Clove Ox is a field, now become Glorix, and Sinder Burroughs is Cinderbury.

A corridor of Whatlington parish stole into that of Sedlescombe across Hancox lands so that Beech Farm lay in both parishes until the boundary changes of 1960. It remained Bishop property until the break up of the Great Sanders estate in the nineteenth century; and was farmed by tenant farmers, one of whom, Croucher, 1770, gave his name to the farm for a period of years, for on a map of 1795 it appears as Crouchers and again in 1825. Strangely, as long ago as 1449 the wist was "Crouchers", later known as Wodelands. "The rent for Crouchers 8/-."[1]

The house is a handsome building, erected probably by the Bishop family in the late eighteenth century, and is now no longer a farmhouse. All its farm buildings have been themselves converted into attractive dwelling-houses. Like every other farm in the parish it had its oast-house, the hop-gardens once lying in the valley behind it.

---

[1] B.A.S. 1569.

## Austford Farm

The approach to Austford Farm was down a sunken track, now a footpath, which leads north off the elbow in Hurst Lane opposite the house called The Brambles. There were, until very recently, traces of an ancient hedge along the track which, sunken as it is, shows its long, long usage through the centuries by wagons, carts, oxen, horses, cattle and other farm traffic. The site of the farm in the warm, brook-watered valley is easily deciphered and looks idyllic today. Sheltered on the north by Austford Woods, its meadows climb towards Chittlebirch and Cripps Corner, paths leading from it in all directions, north, east, south and west; one, well-marked, follows the curve of the valley and then heads straight for Great Sanders. One of its fields, now afforested, was called Precious Field—one of two so-named in the parish. Sir John Thorne traced the origin of the romantic-sounding name to Priest haus (or house). The connection is easier to see with the other Precious field lying as it does along the north side of the churchyard.

As well as Austford Farm, there was also Austford House, sometimes called the White House, and identified on the 1632 Plan as "the other Alford" (Chapter 23). Another half mile or more past the farm, across the brook and up the other side of the valley, it was actually in Ewhurst parish, and the main approach to it was from the Cripps Corner to Rye road at a point very close to where the ancient Gallows of Horn had stood. Fine rhododendron still mark the site of the house and the foundations of the well-made drive which led to it still form a very solid ride.

Neither of these old houses exists today for both were demolished in 1924 by the Hastings Corporation when the Powdermill Reservoir was created (Chapter 46). They were part of the property of Robertsbridge Abbey (Chapter 10) and in 1483 William, the Abbot, granted "two tenements of Alkysford in Sedlyscombe containing by estimation 68 acres of arable and woodland" and two "parcels" called Hothlands, 24 acres, "to John Amyot of Sedlyscombe". (Hothland meant poor land covered with gorse or furze.) The yearly rent due to the Abbey was 10/8d and the witnesses were "Thomas Byschoppe, Alexander Byschoppe and Richard Schyppard". The only other mention of John Amyot observed in the records is in a Subsidy Roll of 1524 for the Hundred of Stapull, but the Robertsbridge Survey records in Par. 30: "Description of tenement 1 barn and 1 garden and xvl parcels of land and wood called Amyotts

Wood and sometimes Bourners, lying in Auxford in the parish of Sedlescombe."[1] A note says that it had been lately held by Robert Bourner. Among the boundaries given are:
"on the North, the highway leading from the Gallows of Horn" (Chapter 11) "to Sedlescombe: and on the South the lands of Richard Busshop called Herst."
The grantee was Ambrose Comporte of Battle. The lands of Herst still adjoin those that were Austford's.

In 1592, an entry in the Parish Registers says, "John Bishop of Austford Churchwarden", in 1619 its owner was William Bishop who eight years earlier had been "of the Tanhouse" (Durhamford) "where he dwelleth."[1] There seems to have been a Bishop living at Austford whenever there was an adult eldest son.

But in the eighteenth century it was occupied by tenant farmers; in turn Richard Pralls, Dan Crossew, Edward Jarrett and Nicholas Ashdown, and in the nineteenth century, Thomas Richardson. In 1846 James Vidler was living in the house and farming the land and the Vidlers remained there to the end. For a family who had lived in the old farmhouse and farmed its surrounding lands for nigh on 80 years, what a terrible experience it must have been to learn of, and gradually be forced to accept, the sentence of demolition of their beautiful sixteenth-century home, together with the oasthouse and all the old barns and farm-buildings which seemed to have been so rooted in the valley.

At least the Austford valley and lands remain most lovely and entirely unspoilt, a surprising and delightful fate in the present destructive days. Conifers have taken the place of most of the oaks that grew there but, in spite of that, the woods which surround the waters of the reservoir are full of beauty and of living creatures.

*The Sackville Family and Hancox* (Maps A and B)
This fine house, Hancox, is the largest medieval "hall-place" still in existence in the parishes of Sedlescombe and Whatlington, on the very boundaries of which it was built, so that until these were altered in 1960 the house was in both parishes.

The oldest part of the present house was probably built early in the fifteenth century for by 1433 Hancox existed. Made up of the usual four bays, the central two being the great hall open to the roof, a larger and more imposing one than at Asselton House,

[1] S.R.S. 47.

Manor Cottages or the Old Thatch. In 1492 the name John Hancocks occurs in records, so it is fair to conclude that, as with so many other local houses, the name derives from a surname and that perhaps of the earliest, or one of the earliest, owners.

The fine ornamental timbers of the old hall are still visible but the upper storey, added later, now hides the crown-post and roof timbers.

According to the 1569 Survey of Battle Abbey, Hancox was then "newly rebuilt", perhaps by John Downton who, as an Indenture relates, had purchased "one capital messuage and tenement situate . . . in Sedlescombe . . . and Whatlington called Hancokkes containing . . . 3 score and ten acres of land . . . of Edward Howden."

In 1589 John Sackville, son of Sir Christopher Sackville of Kent and Constance, daughter of Thomas Culpeper of Bedgebury, married John Downton's only daughter and sole heiress, Joan. Thus started the Sackville connection with Hancox which lasted over 300 years, though the family had ceased to live in it by the time the eighteenth century began. The Downton family was important enough to have a coat of arms, but there seems no record to tell from where John came. The Indenture of 1609 relates that he had bought "also 14 acres of land in Sedlescombe from John Ashburnham, one tenement called Bakers from George Shute Esq. 7 acres from 'one Martin', two tenements called Castlemans about 12 acres from John Byshopp" as well as nearly 500 acres of pasture, meadows and woods in the two villages and also in Mountfield.

John and Joan Sackville probably lived at Hancox after their marriage, for two major extensions had been made to the old house before 1593. Firstly, a central chimney and fireplace was installed and a ceiling inserted across the great hall, thus joining the upper storeys already in existence on either side of it. Next, what was virtually a second house was added which altered the original rectangular ground plan of the hall-place to one resembling the letter F. Hancox was thus transformed into a large house, which was comfortable, fashionable and imposing. With their four sons, John, Thomas, James and William, and two daughters, Joan and Mary, born to them over the years, John and Joan Sackville were content to go on living with John Downton. Perhaps as the family grew large they had doubts for, in 1599, ten years after their marriage, John Sackville began to build the house we know as Brickwall, as

*Signatures.*

his initials I.S. and the date on the chimney still bear witness. But they never lived there and he never finished building it.

By the year 1620 when his father died Thomas, the first-born, was married to Elizabeth, and she had borne their first child, a daughter, Joan, called after her grandmother, and had borne and lost her second, Mary. In the year that Thomas succeeded to Hancox his wife produced a son and heir, named John after his grandfather and great-grandfather. Two years later their second son, Thomas, was born—the Colonel Thomas Sackville of later years.

Thomas, who had also inherited from his father the flourishing Brede Furnace, was a man of growing importance. By 1626 he had been created Knight of the Bath and a J.P. Hancox was large enough to contain his household and growing family of four sons and five daughters (two more babies, a boy and a girl, having died in infancy). The house must now have been beautiful and colourful as well as comfortable, for the panelling and other woodwork was painted in designs with bright colours, traces of which can still be seen round a doorway leading into a wing which has now disappeared. Besides the central chimney another one, free standing, joined only at its base to the house, had been added. Two years later his wife, Elizabeth, died after giving birth to her sixth child, Samuel, who did not long survive her and who was buried with her in the Sackville vault on the south side of the church. He must have married again the following year for in 1630 another son, Edward, was baptised, followed in 1632, 1633 and 1635 by three daughters born to "Sir Thomas Sackville and Anne his Lady."

In 1630 it is also recorded in the Parish Register that a son, William, was born to Sir John Sackville and that in 1639 Sir John's son, Walter, was buried. This Sir John, one can only presume, was a brother of Sir Thomas.

Sir Thomas's two eldest sons, also John and Thomas, went to Oxford where young Thomas matriculated at Christ Church in 1637 when he was fifteen, not then as remarkable an age as it would be today. As befitted a younger son, he then joined the army, his elder brother John, on the death of their father two years later, succeeding to the property on the eve of the Civil War.

Sussex was predominantly pro-Parliament and, whatever the Sackville family's sympathies, their Forge and Furnace off Brede Lane were taken over by Parliamentarian forces.

There is no doubt that young Thomas fought for the Royalist cause in the early days of the war, for in 1645, after his brother had died without an heir, Thomas "applied to compound having been in arms for the King". He stated that "being a younger brother and a soldier of fortune he had thrice listed at the Guildhall for service in Ireland but was left out at the setting of the regiment". He had left the King's employ "when it was in its best condition" and went to France. He had stayed at Rouen, never joining the Court or seeing the Queen. He then returned to York where he stayed till his elder brother died, "which made him consider that he had an interest in this Kingdom, which he would not have to be within an arbitrary power; on the disposal of any man's will . . . he had done nothing against the State since his estate fell to him." He was fined £400, a large sum of money.[1]

So returned Colonel Thomas Sackville to Hancox and Sedlescombe and to his wife Margaret, who was herself a Sackville—grand-daughter of the fifth Earl of Dorset, a connection of which, it would seem, she was very proud, judging from the fact that the relationship looms largely in the epitaph she put up to her husband in the church after his death.

The Colonel busied himself with his new estate. He may have had financial difficulties in the early days of his return, after payment of the Fine, for Sir John Thorne saw a document in which he mortgaged all his Sedlescombe property for £1,000 in 1648 to a

[1] Stanford.

London money-lender. After the Restoration in 1660 he became a J.P. and by 1688 he was a Member of Parliament for East Grinstead. He had sold Brede Furnace and in 1676 he let Hancox for 13 years at £135 p.a. to Thomas Piers of Ewhurst and he lived thereafter in one of his other Sedlescombe houses. During this time he sold it to his cousin, Richard Sackville, who died sometime between 1708 and 1712, when the house was inherited by his elder brother, Charles Earl of Dorset.

Four years later the Colonel fell seriously ill and died, at the age of 70, in 1692, having left an order on his death-bed that Sedlescombe Church should be repaired at his expense. His funeral helm remains in the church as an additional memorial to him. The goat above is said to be his crest, but a goat figures nowhere in the Sackville arms, though it did appear in those of his great-grandfather, John Downton.

In 1708 Richard Sackville was paying the rates for Hancox but by 1712, when Margaret Sackville died, he appears no more and the dues were being paid by his brother, the seventh Earl of Dorset.

For the next 150 years Hancox became a farmhouse, occupied by tenant farmers. Nicholls, Igglesdon, Hook and Russell succeded each other rapidly; followed in 1734 for 19 years by Moses Cloke. For nearly 100 years the Ades, Thomas and his son and grandson, both Edward, farmed Hancox.

A picture dated 1785, entitled ' Sedlescombe Place", the identity of which has long been a mystery, is undoubtedly a drawing of Hancox showing the wings, the free-standing chimney and oriel windows and also the front door and windows in the north-west front. The drawing was made during the long occupation of the Ades family. In 1810, when the third generation of that family was living there, the two old Jacobean wings were pulled down and, as was becoming the fashion, the plastered walls were covered with hanging tiles and the front was faced with stucco. The Sackville crest over the front door, a coronet composed of fleur-de-lys with a star above, was covered by a porch, though the house still belonged to the Sackville family, represented by the Duke of Dorset and, in 1813, by the Earls de la Warr, when Lady Elizabeth Sackville, daughter of the third Duke, married the fifth Earl.

At some time during the late eighteenth or early nineteenth century Hancox became orientated to Whatlington rather than to Sedlescombe.

The Ades were followed in 1840 by John Symes for 19 years. Then came John Swift and in 1865 Albert Apps who by 1870 was in arrears with his rent.

Nineteen years later Milicent Ludlow bought Hancox from Lord de la Warr who, in some financial straits, had taken out twenty-three mortgages on the house. The farmer boasted to her that he had removed four wagon-loads of panelling which he had stripped out of it. She lived in Hancox for the next ten years, repairing it and building on a new wing, creating a fine lofty drawing-room and two extra bedrooms above it; and farming the land. During this time her sister and brother-in-law came and lived with her and off her, unwanted guests, until she could bear it no longer. One morning in 1900 she announced at breakfast that she had let the house for the next six years to the Church of England Inebriates' Society. This was not a joke. It was the sober truth; only so could she rid herself of her unwanted guests.

During their tenancy one of the inebriates fell against a wall, damaging the plaster and thus revealing ancient panelling behind.

In 1903, Dr. Norman Moore, senior physician at Barts, married Milicent as his second wife. Norman was a great collector of books, an Irish scholar, speaking the language, and a naturalist. He had learned natural history as a boy from Charles Waterton, the explorer of British Guiana, who also established the first bird sanctuary. Norman had, too, a great gift of friendship. Among his friends were Hillaire Belloc, who often stayed nearby at Crowham Manor in Westfield where relations of Norman's first wife lived; Henry James, Edmund Gosse, Charles Darwin, whom he attended as a doctor, Leslie Steven, Sir Richard Owen and Sir Evelyn Wood, the Crimean V.C., and also, of course, his neighbour Brabazon (Braby). Barbara Bodichon, founder of Girton, built a Victorian country cottage a few miles away, and there all the friends would forgather, Braby painting all their names on the chimney breast.

As soon as the six year lease was up and the inebriate inmates gone, Milicent returned to Hancox with Norman and his two sons, Alan and Gillachrist, and one daughter, Eithne. One of the first actions of the family was to continue stripping the plaster around the hole made by the inebriate, to discover more and more panelling, some of oak and some of pine. At one end of the dining-room, where it was worn beyond repair, they renewed it and round the top carved a quotation from the Psalms in Latin: "Except the Lord build the house, they labour in vain that build it." Certain of the beautifully proportioned letters were picked out in gold forming the initials of the couple and the date, thus: "Nisi doMinus sedifiCerit doMum in vanuM laboraVerunt quI aedifIcant eaM," making N.M. CMMVII. M.

They removed, too, the porch and discovered again the Sackville coat of arms over the door; and they found too a seventeenth-century fireback made in the Sackville's Brede Furnace, depicting the Garter, and two more firebacks on which were a shield, encircled by the Garter.

Then came the Great War and the loss, in its early months at the Battle of Ypres, of Gillachrist.

The farm, let to Caesar Winter in 1900, continued to be farmed by that family until 1970. In 1918 Norman became President of the Royal College of Physicians and in the following year received a baronetcy. Three years later he died. In 1934 Milicent decided that she would prefer to live in a smaller house and made over Hancox to Alan. He, invited to a dinner party at Oaklands, had had no eyes for anyone but Mary Burrows the beautiful daughter of the Bishop of Chichester and in due course they married.

Alan had always wanted to be a naval historian. Though persuaded to follow his father's profession, he was always in the Public Health Department, never in private practice. He is remembered with great affection locally. His national memorial is the National Maritime Museum, of which he was co-founder, and he was the author of *Last Days of Mast and Sail* and *Sailing Ships of War*. He and Mary had two sons and two daughters, and one of the sons, with his wife and family, continues to live in Hancox today.

*The Farndens of Brickwall* (Map 5)

Peter Farnden was the son of Robert Farnden, of Haslemere, by Margaret, daughter of Robert Boxall, also of Haslemere. He was born there in 1592 and was buried at Sedlescombe sixty years later. We do not know exactly when he came to live in Sedlescombe, but his signature is on a Sedlescombe Indenture dated 1612, and on June 18th four years later, when he would have been about twenty-four, he married in Sedlescombe Church Mary Waters, daughter of John Waters, of Brede. It was in the following year, tradition has it, that he first rented Brickwall from John Sackville and later bought it. Mary bore him three sons and four daughters and she died on

THREE FAMILIES AND THEIR HOMES 159

July 7th, 1630. On March 14th, two years later, he married a widow, Lucy Avory, who bore him two sons and seven daughters. She nevertheless outlived him by twenty-seven years, for she did not die till 1679.

Peter Farnden begot, therefore, by his two wives, five sons, none of whom survived to manhood, and eleven daughters, eight of whom grew up to marry into families well known in the East of Sussex.

*Mary Farnden, his first wife*

"According to the Burrell Manuscripts," wrote Sir John Thorne, "the tomb of Mary Farnden stood in the churchyard on the South side of the steeple and inscribed on its foot in capitals were the words: 'Here lieth the body of Mrs. Marie Farnden, wife of Peter Farnden, Gent., who died the 7th July 1630, and had issue three sons, Peter, John and Peter, who departed this life before her, and four daughters, Joane, Elizabeth, Mary and Martha, whom she left behind.' On the south side of the tomb, Burrell said, was the inscription" (quoted in Chapter 13) "which today can be seen built into the Tower wall about five feet from the ground, just inside the church door on the left." Sir John describes how he looked "on the south side of steeple" in the churchyard and found two large rectangular tombs lying close together East and West, the long (North) side of the Southern one being right up against the long (South) side of the Northern one. Each tomb had a flat slab on top. On examining the tombs "to see whether by good fortune either of them might prove to be the tomb of Mary Farnden, I saw," he wrote, "on the flat top of the southern tomb some faint lettering which, after cleaning, I found to be the following inscription:

'Here lyeth Interred the Body
Of Mr. Laurence Avery who
Departed this Life January
the 29th Anno Domini 1699...'

and a fifth line in which his age would have been given, but only the word 'years' is decipherable." As Peter Farnden's second wife was a widow, Mrs. Avery, when he married her, it is fair to assume that this may well have been her son and Peter's step-son, which would also explain the close proximity to his first wife's tomb.

Sir John then examined the northern tomb, which is smaller than the Avery tomb, and presently on the short Western end he discerned letters which, to his delight, proved to be the inscription recorded in the Burrell MSS quoted earlier, "Here Lyeth the Bodie of Mrs. Marie Farnden, etc. . . ." Once the Avery tomb was placed beside hers it would be impossible for anyone to read the inscription on the south side of it, but Burrell was not born till after Laurence Avery died, so the inference *must* be that this tomb was moved into its present position at some date after Burrell saw it, however impossible such an undertaking would seem, and at the same time the "Mary" inscription was moved from her tomb to the wall of the tower.

Sir John comments on the inscribed verse thus: "Dr. Johnson, who composed a number of epitaphs on his friends, said: 'In lapidary inscriptions a man is not upon oath,' and no doubt many old epitaphs do not speak the truth, but there seems a touch about this crude verse which allows us to believe that Mary Farnden was a good simple woman of the home-keeping kind."

Mary was married by John Bell, Rector of Sedlescombe, in 1616, when her husband was one of the two churchwardens. An entry in the Church Register for 1630 reads : "Mary ffarnden, the wife of Peter Farnden, was buried the 12th day of Julie", but she was buried not by the Rector, then Edward Barton, but "by John Browne, minister." Could this indicate a leaning towards Puritanism by Peter Farnden at a time when war between Cavaliers and Roundheads was not far distant?

*Mary's daughters, Mary, Elizabeth, Joan and Martha*
In 1632 the eldest of the girls sitting in the Farnden pew with their stepmother was Mary, then aged about eleven. Eight years later she married in Sedlescombe Church on the last day of the year Robert Dyke of Frant. Fifteen months later she died in childbirth, her baby, William, having been baptised two days earlier. Her husband placed a tablet to her memory in the church and there it is to this day—on the south wall to the west of the south door—a handsome marble tablet with an elegant inscription in Latin, a strong contrast to the rough stone and the simple English verse of her mother's memorial. Sir John translated the inscription which is quoted in Chapter 13.

Robert Dyke himself was little more than a boy at the time, for he was born on February 11th, 1620. After his wife's death, he married again, Frances Petter, but lived only a year or two, for he was buried at the age of nearly twenty-four on August 28th, 1644. As there is no record of what happened to little William, he perhaps did not grow out of childhood.

The Dykes were gentry. Robert's grandfather was Thomas Dyke of Pepembury (Pembury) and his father was William Dyke, Rector of Frant, the elder brother of whom was another Robert, who made his home in Yorkshire. That Robert had a son, Thomas (who thus was first cousin to the young Robert who married Mary Farnden) and Thomas married Mary's sister, Elizabeth. He also was short-lived, and after his death Elizabeth married Thomas Collins, J.P., of Brightling, a widower whose first wife, of the Cruttenden family of Burwash, had died childless in 1648. The Collins too were gentry and ironmasters, who owned Socknersh Manor, a beautiful old black and white house which still stands. The marriage was on April 23rd, 1650. Elizabeth also proved childless. Thomas died in 1667 and Elizabeth in 1676.

Joan, the third sister, married Samuel Gott, of Battle, in about 1644. They lived at Langton House, now Langton Hall. The Gotts also had interests in iron, both as ironmongers in London and as ironmasters in Sussex. Samuel had been "called" as a barrister (Gray's Inn); he was a J.P. and in 1645 M.P. for Winchelsea, for Sussex in 1656 and for Hastings three years later. He had been a Commissioner for "ejecting scandalous and insufficient Ministers". Altogether he was a good match for a Farnden girl. Joan had a son, born in 1653, who also became of Gray's Inn and a Member of Parliament, for Hastings 1690-1701, and for Lewes 1716, and in 1708 he was Knight of the Shire.[1] Joan was buried at Wadhurst on January 21st, 1680; and her husband in Battle nine years earlier. Their descendants continued to live in the area for many years to come and a Miss Gott was the last owner of Beckley Furnace.

Lastly Martha, Mary's youngest daughter who was baptised in Sedlescombe Church on May 4th, 1623, married on April 14th, twenty-three years later, Edward Polhill, of Burwash, who was only a few months older than she was. There were two daughters of the marriage. The Polhill home, Franchise, was one of the great houses of Burwash parish. Edward in 1662 was a J.P. and a barrister; he was buried in December 1689. "He was of Puritan tendencies and a great friend and supporter of the neighbouring clergy who for conscience sake resigned their livings in 1662."[2] (Chapter 21.)

The Polhills, too, were interested in iron and there was an iron-master of the name in the eighteenth century.

[1] For more concerning the Gott family. S.A.C. p. 151.
[2] Lower.

### Lucy, Peter Farnden's second wife

Lucy, or Lucie, born in 1602, fourth daughter of Thomas Godman, of Wivelsfield (a man of some position, apparently, because it is recorded that he built Ote House, Wivelsfield, in 1600) was thus thirty years old and a widow when she married Peter Farnden, who was then forty. Edward Avery, of Lamberhurst, her first husband, may be presumed to have died in 1624, as his will was proved on the 7th August in that year. As suggested earlier in this chapter, it may well be that she brought with her a young son, Laurence Avery. Her two Farnden sons seem to have died in infancy.

### Lucy's daughters, Sarah, Lucy, Mary and Ruth

The seven daughters she bore to Peter were called Ann, Jane, Sarah, Lucy, Margaret, Mary and Ruth. Ann was baptised in 1632, but she, Jane and Margaret died young. The other four daughters grew up and married.

The eldest, Sarah, was baptised in Sedlescombe Church on November 22nd, 1634, and in September twenty years later she married, in a London church, Walter Dobell of Street Manor, near Plumpton, who had been born five years before her. He came to live in Sedlescombe and resided there from the date of his marriage for seven years, perhaps in connection with his father-in-law's business. Walter became an important man and was High Sheriff in 1669-70, by which time Sarah had borne him nine children—four sons and five daughters. She was buried at Street on August 30th, 1686, and her husband was buried in the same place in December eight years later. In the east window of Street church is a stained glass memorial to him in which is pictured his coat of arms, which forms a pun on the name "doe-bell".

Lucy, the second surviving daughter, baptized in 1638, married Robert Fowle, J.P., of Salehurst, eighteen years later. In the floor of the tower of Salehurst church lies her husband's memorial—a flat, slaty stone, the inscription on which is partly covered by a modern partition—which reads: "Robert Fowle of Iridge Esq., son of Sir John Fowle of Sandhurst in ye County of Kent Knight by Anne daughter of Sir John Wildegoose of Iridge Knight. The said Robert married Lucy daughter of Peter Farnden of Selscombe Esq. and had issue Robert, Anne and Lucy. He departed this life the first of December 1681 and in the fifty and fourth year of his age." He was born, therefore, eleven years before Lucy. This was another "good" marriage, for the Fowles, like the Wildgooses, were of the aristocracy. Concerning the children, we know that little Lucy was baptised in June 1661 and that Anne died young (in 1662).

The third of Lucy Farnden's daughters was another Mary, born July 24th, 1642, more than twenty years after the first Mary, her half-sister. She, like her sister Sarah, married a Dobell—Barnham, the younger brother of Sarah's husband, Walter. She was unusually old (twenty-six) at the time of her marriage, which was in April 1668, and she died just a year later. Her husband, Barnham, was a doctor with a Padua degree. Was there some mystery and some unhappiness about this Mary? Only three months after her death Barnham married again and then her sisters, Lucy Fowle and Ruth Baker, started an action to upset the settlement of her property on him, the ground alleged being that she was insane. The suit failed, but the facts seem to amount to something sinister. "Here is a theme," thought Sir John, "for a story of avarice and intrigue."

The youngest of the Farnden girls was Ruth, baptised in 1646 by George Baker, Rector of Sedlescombe, and therefore only seventeen when, in 1663, she married John Baker. This again was a fine match, for her husband was of the Baker family which lived in the old Palace at Mayfield, bought in 1617 by the bridegroom's father, whose mother's father was a baronet. Ruth bore six sons and six daughters. Her husband was eighty when he died in 1723 and his monument can be seen in Mayfield church.

*Peter Farnden's property*

Of these eight daughters four—the issue of the first marriage—were wedded before their father died in 1652 and presumably he arranged the matches. The other four, daughters of his second marriage, were married after his death. "In those days," wrote Sir John, "a family of daughters was a great financial burden in England, as it may be in India, and for the same reason: bridegrooms had to be bought. To obtain husbands from the fine families into which these girls married—Dyke, Gott, Polhill, Fowle, Dobell and Baker—large dowries would have to be paid. Peter Farnden, therefore, must have amassed great wealth, for he invested in land property and forges and furnaces, as well as in sons-in-law." Some of these were:

1. Crowham Manor in Westfield (Map A), which by the time he bought it had been divided up; Peter's partner in the transaction was his son-in-law Samuel Gott (husband of Joan Farnden). The Farn-

den daughters and their husbands were involved in constant litigation over Crowham for many years. Eventually John Baker, husband of Ruth Farnden, acquired most of the estate.

2. Some lands in "Hollinton", which in 1628 Peter exchanged for another manor in Westfield, called Detcham (now unidentifiable, but perhaps De Cham Road in St. Leonards is a relic of it).

3. Conster in Brede parish (Map A), which figures in a book by Sheila Kaye Smith. "Peter Farnden held it in 1639 and it passed through the family of Gott to Edward Frewen about 1730."

4. Moorholm in Brede (or Coggers) (Map A). "In 1636 it was called the Well House and was held by Peter Farnden, from whose relative Elizabeth Coggers (1681) it passed to her son."

There seems to be no Coggers in the Farnden pedigree but there is the record of a marriage in Sedlescombe church in 1676 of William Coggers of Brede and Frances Munn of Sedlescombe.

*The end of the story*

We know more about Peter Farnden and his wives and children than we know about any other generation of a family in Sedlescombe, but we know of no sons born to him (or to his nephew, the other Peter Farnden) to carry on the name in the parish—though in Westfield the name survived, apparently in a much more humble social grade, into the nineteenth century. This then is the end of the Farnden story and the remarkable family of daughters, seven born between 1621 and 1646 and all married, by worldly standards, very well. One can picture them growing up at Brickwall, playing in the garden there, and on Sundays and Saints' days occupying with their parents the two big pews just below the pulpit, set apart for the family in the church. There must be many of their descendants in Sussex still.

His wife, Lucy, saw all her stepdaughters and daughters married and her husband, Peter, buried in Sedlescombe Churchyard, though his grave cannot now be identified. Lucy then left Brickwall and made her home at Salehurst with her daughter and son-in-law, Lucy and Robert Fowle, and her three grandchildren, Robert, Ann and yet another Lucy. There in 1679 she died, twenty-seven years after her husband. In the Salehurst Parish Registers is this entry: "Mrs. Lucy Farnden, widow, of ye Parish of Salehurst, was buried Jan. 21st 1679. I recd. no Affidavit but ye forfeitures were levied, according to the Act" (the Act of Charles II's reign which required that all dead should be buried in woollen shrouds and that parsons conducting burials must give an Affidavit that the bodies had been so wrapped, otherwise a fine had to be paid). Lucy Farnden presumably preferred to be buried in something finer than wool and her son-in-law paid the fine. Sir John Thorne commented on this: "There is a poem by Alexander Pope (*Moral Essays,* Epistle 1) which contains the following lines:

> 'Odious! in woollen, 'twould a saint provoke,
> (Were the last words that poor Narcissa spoke)
> No, let a charming chintz or Brussels lace
> Wrap my cold lips and shade my lifeless face,
> One would not, sure, be frightful when one's dead.'

This story is said to be founded on truth. 'Narcissa' was the actress, Ann Oldfield, who was buried in Westminster Abbey in 1730. The Act was finally repealed in 1804."

## The other Peter Farnden

In the Indenture of 1731 (now hanging in Sedlescombe School) the Deed preamble recites that in October 1652 Sir Thomas Pelham, great-grandfather of the Duke of Newcastle, had leased to Peter Farnden 'all that parcel of waste ground lying and being in the High Street within the Hundred of Staple beginning and extending from Sedlescombe Bridge all along up to Seddlescombe Church" for a hundred years at a yearly rent of sixpence. It was presumed that the Peter Farnden of the Indenture was this same Peter Farnden, but this is not so, for he had been buried several weeks earlier on August 29th, 1652, by Edmund Thorpe, Clerk and Rector of Sedlescombe. The Peter Farnden who obtained the lease of all the "waste ground" in Sedlescombe from the bridge up to the Church was this Peter's nephew. According to the pedigree in the "Visitation" Robert Farnden, of Haslemere, had had two sons, the younger being Tobias (shown in the pedigree as 'of Brede');[1] he had a son, also Peter, described as 'of Sedlescombe', born in 1623. Peter of Brickwall had been married seven years earlier. In December 1656 Peter (the nephew) married Ann, daughter of John Busbridge, of Etchingham, and was buried in September 1705. In Etchingham Church is a tablet to Samuel Farnden, son of the marriage. As he died on Nov-

[1] Vis. of Sus.

ember 16th, 1660, he must have been very young. The Busbridges were a family of good standing who lived for generations at Haremere (now Haremere Hall) just east of Etchingham Church.

Horsfield also confused the two Peter Farndens and the Victoria County History, following Horsfield, repeated the mistake.

*Brickwall* (Maps 3 and 5)

"Brickwall," says the Victoria County History, "faces the North end of the triangle of the Green and is an L-shaped building with a staircase wing in the inner angle. Said to have been built by Peter Farnden, ironfounder, but bears on a chimney stack in the South front the initials I.S. and the date 1599. The lower storey is of brick and the upper tile-hung . . . There are two gabled projecting bay windows to the upper storey of the South front. The three old chimney stacks are either square or of the local rebated type, containing wide fireplaces. . . ."

The stone "I.S. 1599" inscribed on the chimney bears evidence that that part of the house at least was built by John Sackville of Hancox at a date when Peter was a small boy of seven years and probably had not come to Sedlescombe, but the mention of Peter's house "newly built" in the 1632 Plan suggests that the larger part of that house was built by him. Half a century earlier "the heirs of Stephen Wystonden held by copy another messuage newly built"[1] which by the boundaries given is clearly Brickwall or the earliest beginnings of it.

Some time after Peter Farnden died his heirs sold Brickwall to Joseph Mercer (1658-1736) who, with his wife Susannah, lived in it for thirteen years, till in 1713 she died of smallpox (Chapter 26). The Mercers, father Joseph and son and grandson, both Thomas, owned the house during the whole of the eighteenth century, but no longer lived in it, having moved to Hole Farm across the Brede River. Thomas, the son, let Brickwall, therefore, in 1740 to William Weston for £11 p.a. and Thomas, the grandson, let it in tenements to three cottagers, Edward Butler, shoemaker, for £4.19.6d. p.a.; John Mills, carpenter, and John Rootes for £6 p.a., who were all still living there in 1769. (In a list of apprenticeships, 1710-1752, Edward Butler, to whom William Cooper was apprenticed in 1746 for seven years, is described as a cordwainer—i.e. "a worker in

[1] B.A.S. 1569.

cordwain — a shoemaker; cordwain is Spanish leather, goatskin tanned and dressed; originally a maker of shoes from leather from Cordova." William Cook, of Sedlescombe, was apprenticed four years earlier to Thomas Butler, of Sedlescombe, also cordwainer, for seven years.)

In 1807 Thomas Mercer and his brother, Robert, sold all their copyhold property in Sedlescombe, including Brickwall, for £2,000 to Moses Ades, farmer of Hancox, and at this time the Oast was built. It is possible that the Westons continued as tenant farmers, for by the date of the Tithe Map, 1841, Robert Weston was occupying the house. Hercules Sharpe, of Northiam, who had bought Hole Farm from the Mercers, soon began to acquire other property in the village. Brickwall was bought by his son, Hercules Brabazon, when it was described as "a spacious old mansion now let in tenements. A well-enclosed farmyard in which is a barn with Oak Floor, Cattle-sheds, Sheds, cart-sheds, wagon sheds, stabling for 4 horses, carpenter's shop and garden, oasthouse field and mill-field; orchard, ostan's croft, cottage and gardens." The Gorselands houses are now built on the mill-field. From then on it housed workers on the Oaklands Estate.

It is recorded that Mrs. Thomas Parsons (Anna) died at Brickwall, her residence, aged 86, on December 12th, 1896, and that she had been in the service of the family at Oaklands for 72 years. She must therefore have been a Northiam girl in the service of the Sharpe family in 1824 while they were still at Domans, and have come with them when they moved to Sedlescombe six years later. Her husband also died at Brickwall at an advanced age, having been farm bailiff to Major Combe for many years before Hercules Brabazon Brabazon died.

For the next years the house was let first to Lady Mallet, the wife of a distinguished diplomat and then to Mrs. Godman.

On July 21st, 1925, at 2.30 p.m., Brickwall and all the other Oaklands property in the Street was auctioned at the Castle Hotel, Hastings. Described as a "charming old house, standing high up and facing due South, looking over the prettiest part of the old-world village, its main structure is of mellow brick and tiled, with lattice windows and tall arrow-head chimneys", it was sold for a little under £3,000. Whether or not the buyer was Edward Patry, the painter, it is certain that he was its owner a few years later when, in 1932, the Viscountess Wolseley visited him and wrote a description and history of the old house for the *Sussex County Magazine* in the series "Historic Houses of Sussex" which she had long been contributing. Her description of the inside of the house is interesting but out of date since the fire of 1951. She adds: "Mr. Patry has secured for the oast-house a pair of handsome nail-studded oak doors that at one time hung at the entrance to the crypt of Chichester cathedral. They now lead into a shadow-house or summer-room that he has fitted up in the garden, and a picture of them is shown in the January number of the *Sussex County Magazine*."

During the last war a schoolmaster and his family from Hastings lived in it and after the war it became an hotel. It was then in 1951 that the terrible fire raged in the first hours of the morning of Thursday, October 6th, and practically destroyed it. The fire engines from Battle and Hastings quickly arrived but, in order to obtain any water, the hoses had to be unrolled right down the Green to the river at the bottom, giving the fire time to get full hold. Ironically all through the war there had been a large tank full of water just beside the house near the road, which had been removed only a few months earlier. The crackling of the flames penetrated sleep and could be heard a mile away, so that the road was soon full of people watching and ready to help. Escaping residents were looked after at the "Queen's Head".

The old descriptions of the outside of the house give a correct picture of it as it is today, so well was it rebuilt by the village building firm, F. Thomas & Sons.

*Chapter Eighteen*

## THE POOR

While prosperity was coming to iron-owning and iron-working families, and farmers and farmworkers could support themselves, there were of course people in Sedlescombe, as elsewhere, who were on and over the hardship line of poverty.

It was in Queen Elizabeth's reign that the first laws for the relief of the poor were enacted, partly as a result of the Dissolution of the Monasteries, which had been to a greater or lesser extent centres where the poor could expect food and relief. In 1563 an Act provided for the levy of poor rates and allowed children between the ages of 12 and 16 to be compelled to serve in husbandry. Overseers of the Poor were first appointed under an Act passed nine years later and, together with the Churchwardens, were elected yearly at the "Vestry" held in each village (as the Churchwardens still are today). The Churchwarden of one year often became the Overseer of the next, a fact not surprising since both had responsibilities towards the poor, the Overseers continuing the process begun by the Churchwardens and, in the matter of the Indentures binding pauper children to serve as apprentices, both officers were responsible.

The earliest of such documents among the Parish Records[1] is dated March 1612, and is a true Indenture in that, drawn up in duplicate, there is a zigzag line between the two halves so that when this was cut along, the Indenture could be proved by fitting the cut edges together. The document reads thus:

"Witnesseth that the churchwardens and overseers of the poore of the parish of Sedlescombe in the County of Sussex whose

[1] E.S.R.O.

names are hereunder written according to the statute made in the XLIII yere of the raigne of our soverayne Elizabeth late Queene of England . . with the assent and consent of John Sackville and George Shirley Esqrs. beinge two of His Majesty's Justices of Peace, have putt William Harte son of Richard Harte late of Sedlescombe deceased unto William Dawe of Sedlescombe aforesaid yeoman to be an apprentice, him to serve, and after the manner of an apprentice, with him to dwell, from the feaste day of the Annunciation of our Lady St. Marie the Vergine late past until he shall accomplish the full age of foure and twentie yeres, in all which terme the said William Harte as an apprentice the said William Dawe as his master well and faithfully shall serve, his secrets shall keep, his commandments lawful and honeste everywhere shall doe, fornication in the house of his said master nor without it he shall not comitt, hurte to his said master he shall not doe nor consente to be done to the value of XIId or above. Taverns of Custome he shall not haunte, at dice cards or any other unlawful games he shall not play, the goods of his said master ynordynately he shall not waste nor them to any man lend without his master's lycence. Matrimony with any woman within the said terme he shall not contract nor espouse, nor from his master's service neyther by day nor by night shall he absent or prolonge himselfe. But in all things as a true and faithful servant towards his said master and all his, both in words and Deeds he shall gently beare and behave himselfe. And the said William Dawe the said William Harte his apprentice well & orderly shall teach & bring him upp to husbandry or to some other worke or labour to gett his livinge, in the due manner of conversion or chastisement, findinge and allowing to his said apprentice meate, drinke, lynnen, woolen hose, shooes, beddinge, apparell, and all other things meete and necessary & conveniente for such an apprentice dureinge the terme aforesaid as well in sickness as in health. Giving and allowinge unto his said apprentice at the end of the full apprenticeshippe two sutes of apparell vis. one sute for the working dayes and one better sute for the holly dayes, meete necessary and conveniente for such an apprentice.

"In witness whereof the said parties to these present Indentures interchangeably have putt their hand & seales the nyne and twentieth day of March in the Tenth yere of the Raigne of oyr

Sovrayne Lord James by the grace of God of England France and Ireland King, Defender of the Faith, & xlvth of Scotland. 1612.
William Dawe

John Sackville
Gge Shirley
Seales & Delivered in the presence of
Rychard Byshopp
John    ?
Peter ffanden"

All these names are familiar: John Sackville of Hancox, the Sedlescombe J.P. George Shirley, also a J.P., of Battle; Richard Bishop of Great Sanders, Peter Farnden of Brickwall and William Dawe of Carters, or Manor Cottages which still bear his initials.

Though the name, Harte, figures in parish records of the eighteenth century and is perpetuated in Hart's Green, of Richard Harte of Sedlescombe, who had died leaving this boy orphaned, we know nothing save that he left at least two other children between the ages of 12 and 16; Constance, apprenticed on the same day as her brother, to the blacksmith and his wife, Thomas Fowle and "Beatris"; and "Ane", who about a fortnight later (perhaps she only then reached the age of 12), was apprenticed to John Everendon and Joane his wife (Chapter 17). Girls were always apprenticed to be trained as housewives till the age of 21 or till marriage, whichever happened first; while boys were apprenticed till the age of 24, marriage being forbidden. The blacksmith, Thomas Fowle, was illiterate and made his mark. John Everendon, of Beech House, was, the following year, one of the Overseers of the Poor and, as such, witnessed the Indenture when another orphan boy, James Damper, was apprenticed outside the village to Nicholas Baker, of Wadhurst. The Bakers were an important family of iron-masters, into which Peter Farnden's daughter had married, so it is easy to see his hand in the arrangement.

The Indentures which survive among the records seem to go in groups, the next group being dated between 1635 and 1640. Three orphaned children were apprenticed at the end of June 1635; Nicholas Oliver to Peter Farnden; Allin Foster to John Darby; and Edward Yorke to Sir Thomas Sackville. Again all the masters are well-known in Sedlescombe: John Darby being of Footlands. The name Foster appears in the parish records and that of Goddard Foster figures on the 1632 Plan.

The children in the next three Indentures all share the same surname, Kennett. Bennett Kennett (a girl), and Elizabeth Kennett were apprenticed on the same day in 1636, Bennett to Henry Barnes, yeoman (living at Gilds; Chapter 23), and her sister, Elizabeth, to Thomas Avory, "physition" of (Little) Castlemans. Three years later, their brother, John, was apprenticed to a John Kennett, senior, who lived at Stone, in Kent, and who was presumably a relative. One of these documents states that the child is to be instructed in the "trade, mystery or occupation of husbandry"; the word "mystery" being used also in documents relating to the "art" of housewifery.

The next group of the Indentures all belong to the year 1661; the first, dated April 11th, refers again to an Oliver, the child's name being Elizabeth, and her master's Thomas Sackville, of Hancox, the Colonel. There is a note at the bottom of this document saying, "given with this child nothing". The other four in this group are all dated four days later. The first relates to Grace Baker apprenticed, strangely, to two men, Richard Carpenter, glover, and George Bigg, tanner. These are the first masters named in these Indentures about whom we know nothing, except their occupations. Their crafts being closely connected, they probably worked and maybe lived together and so could share Grace's housewifery services. "Given with this Child three pounds." The next two concern a brother and sister, again of the Oliver family; the boy, Thomas, and the girl with the beautiful name, Argent. Thomas was apprenticed to Walter Everendon and "nothing was given with this Child"; and Argent to Thomas Frencham "physitian" of Slaughters (Spilsteds) and Janet Sole, a widow; "given with this child four pounds". The fact that money was given with her and not with her brother perhaps indicates that the Frenchams were not very well off, while the Everendons and Sackvilles were of course prosperous. The last of this group bound a child, John Stevens, to William Darby, of Footlands.

The next group of Indentures covers nearly thirty years. These are the first to be written on printed forms and so are much easier to read. They include also a new clause "that the master shall and will provide for the said apprentice that he be not any way a charge to the said parish or the Parishioners of the same but of and from all Charge shall & will save the P'sh or P'shioners harmless and indemnified during the said term". Three of the masters involved belonged to the families already mentioned in this chapter; Bishop, Darby and Barnes. The fourth was Richard Glazier, yeoman and carpenter, to whom John Willis was bound in 1687. In January 1691, Edward Jarrett was bound to George Burden, "colyer", to be brought up in the "art, traid or Mistery of a Colyer", that is, a charcoal burner. George was thus the only boy on record to be apprenticed to this calling so busy in these parts (the reason likely being that charcoal burners could not as a rule afford to keep an apprentice; most of the masters named in these documents being of notably well-to-do families).

The last Indenture is dated February 11th, 1707, and bears two sixpenny stamps. It is different also from the earlier ones in that the term was for only seven years and the apprentice received a quarterly payment of one shilling and fourpence. It was executed by John Lucas "with the consent and good liking of Thomas Lucas, his father" as apprentice to Thomas Newnham, malster of Jevington, to be brought up in that "Science or art".

This system of Apprenticeship was clearly, at best, most beneficial to both parties to the agreement and it was not confined to poor children; but, at a time when life was short and many children were orphaned early, it was a very positive way of taking responsibility for their security and training. It fell down only, where most plans fall, on human greed and cruelty. There were undoubtedly abuses, particularly in the industrial age of the nineteenth century. But as far as the children of the Oliver, Harte and Kennett families and all the others named from the village were concerned, it would seem that their situations on reaching the age of twelve were as good as those of any orphan could be and perhaps as good as some unorphaned. Almost all their masters have names well-known in Sedlescombe history, families of standing, of comfort and moderate prosperity; farmers, iron-masters, land-owners and physicians, and the tradesmen such as blacksmith, glover, tanner and charcoal-burner. Money was given with the child to the less prosperous masters, for the expense of having an apprentice was not inconsiderable, particularly with the commitment to provide the two suits at the end of the term.

So the children became members for perhaps eleven years of the Sackville, Everendon, Bishop or Darby families and benefited or suffered by all their individual human virtues and faults; and themselves learned and profited as much as in them lay from those families. Some could do very well indeed with such a start and have the chance to educate themselves. At worst they were taught a means of earning a living. No doubt in a village, where all is known, the most likely of the orphaned lads and lasses were sought by those who needed apprentices. The important thing was to see that they were not an expense to the parish, and towards this end to give them employment; some were doubtless given this without apprenticeship.

Professor Trevelyan wrote of the Poor Law of 1601, which lasted for two hundred years, that it made provision for the poor

"better than anything there had been in an older England, and better than anything there was to be for many generations to come in France and other European countries."

Complaint was made that

"the parish dole was often three times as much as a common labourer, having to maintain a wife and three children, could afford to expend on himself; and that persons receiving outdoor relief refuse to work, and seldom drink other than the strongest ale-house beer or eat any bread save what is made of the finest wheat flour."[1]

This sounds exaggerated and very similar to stories concerning national security relief of modern times. Laws and privileges are abused by human beings in all walks of life, a fact that perhaps needs to be remembered, and would make us all more tolerant if it were.

In 1696 it was made compulsory for a master, chosen by the Churchwardens and Overseers, to receive the pauper apprentice, which would perhaps immediately have made the system unpopular and the apprentice also. It was certainly a hard school even when not abused, or so it seems to us in these days when discipline is frowned upon and disapproved. Holidays were few but they were universal and the merrymaking totally shared.

There were of course many other poor in Sedlescombe who needed assistance besides the orphan children. In the Account Books, kept by the Churchwardens and Overseers from 1611 onwards individuals can be divided into four categories: 1. for taxes or for board, at home or in the Poorhouse; 2. for clothes provided; 3. for firewood; and 4. during sickness and death.

[1] Trevelyan. Chap. 6, v. ch. 9.

## THE POOR

Under category 1.:
"In 1699 Goody Bissenden 6/- for a month's pay."
In the early eighteenth century:
"Goody Oliver received her quarter's rent 4/-."
"1757 Widow Coleman and Sam Selmes their taxes 5/5" each were allowed.
"Young Frensham his board 10/-" and Stephen Crisford's taxes were allowed
"for keeping Mary Frensham 4/-."
"pd. Goodman Bird for keeping his mother 16/-."
"David Selmes his tax 9d."
1726 "Widow Gibbons tax 1/6." and "Hart's tax 4½d."
"Goodman Star 4 weeks at 4/6 per week, 3 and 20 weeks at 5/6."
Under category 2, the following payments are recorded over the years:
1722 "to John Elliott for cloth and stockens for Jack of Sedlescombe 6/7."
"to Jo Chapman for making Jack's clos 3/6."
"to Will Huckens for mending Jack's shoos 6d."
1728 "pair of breeches for John of Sedlescombe 1/6."
"a cap for John Frencham."
"stockens for John Frencham."
"shirt and woosted for Thomas Frencham."
"making clos, shoos and a payer of stockens for John Frencham."
Under category 3, sums were paid out for firing for the following:
"for faggots for Goody Glover."
"for faggots for Mary Cook."
"wood for the poor."
"wood for Goodman Star."
Under category 4, as would be expected, the largest total sum was paid out every year. The following are some of the entries:
"1716 hospital for Jo Star" (where, one wonders, was the "hospital"?).
"1718 doctor for curing Star's wife."
"for Goodman Star in his wife's sickness."
"Pd Goody Hunt for Mary Frensham's bleding 15/6."
"Given to Auld Andrews."

"1764. Pd. Master Pain for curing Hester Higgins of the Itch 1/-."

"5/- for curing Eliz. Langham."

"1769 Gave Elizabeth Thring a hop pocket to lodge upon; 1/-."

"Goody Cooper's Coffing 10/-."

"for Goody Glover's grave and wringing bell."

"pd. John Reed 2lbs wool and covering for Goody Glover."

"Goody Bennett for helping and laying forth Goody Glover."

John Reed was a farmer and it would seem that in order to satisfy the law that everyone must be buried in wool (Chapter 17) the 2 lb. of wool was just laid as it was over Goody Glover in her coffin.

"pd. for Widow Renals and ye alphy David 2/-" (an original spelling of "affidavit").

"For the clerk for ringing the nell and digging the grave, more for carrying her to the church, 2/6."

There was a fifth category of payment made to poor people who were passing through the village; tramps, wanderers and "travellers" or gypsies. These are most frequently listed as "passengers" or just "pass". Thus in 1730 appears the misleading entry,

"Gave to men with a Pass 2/-."

In 1726 money given to passengers is recorded as 15/-, 6/-, 11/- and 2/- and the next year from 2/- to 7/-, and in

"1728 paid to passengers and ye old woman 15/-."

"1625 given to two poore Eirishmen by Allen (churchwarden) 4d."

"1743 given to five poore men whose ship was burned 4d."

"1745 pd for the Wooll to bury the Woman Inn, that died at Mercer's 1/6"; being unnamed, she was presumably a passenger and not a villager: Mercer's was "Jacobs".

"for laying her forth and the Affidavit 1/6, for box 1/4."

"the Clark ringing the Bell and Diging the Grave 3/-."

"Coffin 10/-" (so what was "the box"?).

Because the poor were a charge on the parish, tramps must not be allowed to linger long and the sick were sometimes returned to their parish of origin for fear that they should die where they were.

A document[1] records the following:

---

[1] S.A.C.

# THE POOR

"1781 The Churchwardens and Overseers of the Parish of Battle in the County of Sussex: We whose names are here under written, Churchwardens and Overseers of the Poor in the Parish of Sedlescombe in the said County do hereby own and acknowledge John Crisford, Philadelfia his wife, and Philadelfia, Samuel, Edward, William and James, their children" (Chapter 38: The Cottage) "who now all reside in your said Parish of Battle, be our inhabitants legally settled in our said Parish of Seddlescombe and do hereby promise for ourselves and our successors to renew this acknowledgement when and as often as the Churchwardens and Overseers of the Poor in the said Parish shall require.

"Witness our hand this 19th day of March in the year of our Lord 1781

Churchwardens  John Baker
                     Wm. Cook
Overseer          George Mantle."

Many members of the Crisford family of bricklayers and farmers are buried in Sedlescombe churchyard, but none with these Christian names. They do, however, appear in the deeds of The Cottage in Sedlescombe Street. Perhaps they were the feckless ones of the family, for the owner of the Cottage turned them out. Clearly the Battle officers were making sure that the responsibility for them remained with their native village. In 1726 a Steven Crisford had house and land in the parish and seven years later his "taxes were allowed", proving that his affairs were, at least temporarily, in a bad way. A hundred years later, in 1839 a Steven Crisford was himself Overseer for the Poor in Sedlescombe.

The Overseers and Churchwardens, though prepared to accept responsibility for their own, were not however to be put upon to do this unnecessarily. Among the Parish Records are copies of Quarter Sessions Orders dated 1707 and 1708 concerning Adrian Spray's upkeep of his grandson, "a poor child chargeable to the parish of Sedlescombe"; Adrian Spray was ordered to pay "the sum of 18d. towards the relief of the said Samuel Wicks his grandson until further order of this Court".

In 1708 "The matter in question being Adrian Spray, Grandfather of Samuel Wicks and Thomas Wicks, poor children of the parish of Sedlescombe; and the parishioners of the said parish, touching Adrian Spray's contributing towards the relief of the grandchildren. It is ordered by this court that the former order for the said Adrian Spray to contribute 1/6 per week to the relief of . . . Samuel Wicks, one of his grandchildren, be discharged and by the Court it is discharged accordingly. And it is further ordered by the Court that the said Adrian Spray doth pay unto the churchwardens and overseers of the poor of . . . Sedlescombe the sum of four shillings per week for and towards the relief of Thomas Wicks, one of his grandchildren. But if Adrian Spray doth take . . . Thomas Wicks from the . . . parish and provide for and maintain him at his own charge then and so long . . . Adrian Spray shall be free from the payment of the . . . said summe of four shillings per week. And the parishioners of the parish of Sedlescombe agree to maintain and keep the said Samuel Wicks, the other grandchild, and provide for him all this charge; and . . . Adrian Spray is discharged from providing or maintaining Samuel Wicks his other grandchild."

Poor Samuel and Thomas. Did their grandfather live at the old farmhouse at the crossways, now called Spray's Farm, in Westfield parish, which bears his initials? (Chapter 30).

Other relief to the poor was paid half-yearly or annually "for maimed soldiers". This must have been a definite charge levied on all parishes after periods of war. Sums were paid, usually £2 per annum "for the poorhouse" and once, in 1770, is an entry, "gave to the poor in the workhouse for encouragement 15/-".

*The Poorhouse*

Where was the Poorhouse, for the upkeep of which these annual sums were paid? According to Sir John, the earliest one known was Guns, now Spilsted Cottages in Stream Lane (Chapter 23). Guns appears in the records for some years as the home of Jonathon Star and his wife (mentioned earlier in this Chapter). Evidence that it was at some date the Poorhouse comes from the fact that the Battle Board of Guardians sold it in 1839.

The change in name in 1770 from the Poorhouse to the Workhouse would seem to indicate a change of attitude to the poor, and a change somehow for the worse. The use of the word "pauper" in place of "the poor", in nineteenth-century records, increases the feeling that the condition of poverty is not just one of misfortune but of blame. He is no longer just poor; he has become a Pauper; no longer just a needy neighbour but, according to the dictionary, "a beggar", "a recipient of poor relief".

## THE POOR

Apart from Guns, there are indications in Deeds of three other cottages having been used for certain periods as Poorhouses or Workhouses. These are Magpie Cottage, the Brede Lane Cottages which were pulled down in the nineteenth century to make place for Ivy and Springfield Cottages, and Riverbridge Cottages. All show in their deeds that they belonged to, or were in the occupation of, the Churchwardens and Overseers of the Poor in the Parish. Magpie Cottage probably followed Guns as the Poorhouse,[1] for it was in 1736 that Thomas Reed sold it and it was before his ownership that it had been in the occupation of the Churchwardens and Overseers. Riverbridge Cottages[2] were probably the next to contain the Workhouse, and in 1836 the Churchwardens and Overseers sold the Brede Lane cottages[3] two years after the Sedlescombe Workhouse was closed; so it seems likely that these were the site of the last Workhouse (Chapter 35).

In 1771, the year after the Poorhouse became the Workhouse, the Workhouse accounts appear separately in the records for the first time. The first such, called "Workhouse Cashbook", to be seen among the parish records today is undated. Kept in a cheap notebook (the first page of which is adorned with a line drawing of a windmill and mill-house with a motto at top and bottom) by the Workhouse Matron, Mrs. Eldridge, the carpenter's wife, in a beautiful handwriting, it is entirely household accounts:

"1 gallon salt 4½d." sugar, butter, cheese, a pint of oatmeal, ginger, grease, thread needles, vinegar, peace tape, buckram, buttons, cloves, linen, tea, handkerchiefs (once only), candles and cloth, all bought in large quantities.

Book 2, dated 1806, begins with the statement:

"To weekly pay for the Poor."

This varies through the year between £2 9s. and £2 3s. 9d. until November when it becomes regularly £1 16s. 6d. Page 3 is headed:

"A/C of Flour delivered to the Workhouse by Mr. Jo Ades" (of Hancox Farm) and it consists of records of weekly deliveries of "a Bushel and a half flour; 2 Bran" and three times "2 Bran and ½ bushel Poland", and sometimes "½ bushel oats".

[1] Map 5. No. 16.
[2] Map 5. No. 23.
[3] Map 5. No. 22.

All the remaining pages contain records of "Work done by Paupers" for local people.

"*For the Rev. Mr. Pratt.*
"April 5 children a day @ 4d each.
"June 4 days haying, lobbetter and dearing" (Leadbetter and Dearing) "7/6
"Wooll carded for Mr. Prat 2/6"
Again later in the year:
"Ann Blackman and Hannah Leadbetter 1 day a week
"6 children 1 day 2/-.
"haying, Harry 6 days and Peter 5 days.
"4 child.
"3 child.
"October, Thom. Hook 5 days at 4d a day 1/8."

"*For Mr. Crisford.*
"August. 2 women harvesting 2 days. 4/-.
"Sept. 2 women haying 2 days 1/8, and Dame Garner ½ day 5d.
"Oct. James Wood 4½ days, 3 days and 4 days, total earned 3/10."
Among the women and girls who worked for the Matron, Mrs. Eldridge, were Leadbetter and Dearing again several times harvesting.
"Sept. Hannah Leadbetter tyed 1900 hops 17.0."
"July. Hannah and Mary Dearing haying 6d a day.
"Hannah Leadbetter tyed 1 cater and quarter of hops at 9d per cater. 11/3.
"Mary Dearing tyed 2 acres and a half of hops 12 pockets £1.10."

"*For Mr. Sellens.*
"Mary Dearing and Hannah Leadbetter 1 day."

"*For Saml. Cook. Pooling flax.*
"Dame Garner and Ann Blackman 1/4 a day, August and July 2 weeks."

"*For Mr. Mercer. Haying.*
"Mary Dearing and Hannah Leadbetter
"Dame Garner and Ann Blackman."

"*For Mr. Crisford.*" The four women hayed, hooked peas and harvested.

"*For Mr. Eldridge.*" 4 girls were picking up potatoes.

"*For Edward Young. Crapeing Bark.*" Thomas Hook in June was paid for 4 days' work.

Mr. Eldridge, tanner, employed girls through May and June up to five at a time; work unspecified, perhaps also scraping bark. New names appear in the course of 1807; Dame Gurner, Fanny Turner and Sall Spilsted worked for Mr. Ades, junior, and Mr. Crisford, both farmers; and for Mr. Moses Ades, of Hancox Farm, John Spilsted and his wife, Sarah, worked together.

Besides the named men and women are very many entries such as "2 girls weeding"; "2 women harvesting"; "2 children 2 days"; "5 children 1 day $\frac{1}{2}$".

Through that year there were 6 women mentioned by name frequently and 5 men infrequently, perhaps really too old and too infirm to work; 4 girls are the most mentioned together at one time and 6 children. So the number of "paupers" living in the workhouse in the year 1801 cannot have been less than 6 women, 5 men, 4 girls and 6 children. Twenty-one people in two cottages seem a lot to us who live in more spacious days of a bedroom for each 2 people or children. Older villagers, however, tell of their childhood in a small cottage with sometimes as many as 12 children and seldom less than 8. In richer families, too, in those days of many children, none would have had a bed to itself, let alone a room.

The people listed in this chapter as receiving poor relief in one form or another are clearly those who had fallen on hard times; widows who had lost the breadwinner, men who had known prosperity but who had become too old or infirm to continue to work; for most of their names can be found in lists of taxpayers in earlier years with a house and garden or a farm. The saddest to read of are the children, orphans presumably, living in the workhouse; and the girls—who were they whom no housewife snapped up to help her in her house? Surely the days of orphan apprenticeships were preferable to this.

In 1834 the Sedlescombe Workhouse in Brede Lane was closed; for the new Law had formed parishes into unions of 15 and the Union Workhouse was at Battle. Thither all the poor, aged or sick from Sedlescombe had to go, away from home and friends to be among strangers. Looked at from distant Battle, where husband was separated from wife, the Sedlescombe Workhouse, whatever its faults and discomforts, among friends or enemies, long-known, must have seemed a more desirable place in which to finish one's days. Today, that dreaded Workhouse in Battle is a hospital where one would be happy to do even that.[1] In April when its grey walls are thick with hanging trusses of the blossom of the old mauve wisteria, it is a most lovely sight. Perhaps, in the old days of hard misery, its beauty warmed the hearts in some old breasts.

[1] Map A.

*Chapter Nineteen*

## THE CHURCHWARDENS

Although the first of the Churchwardens' accounts among the Sedlescombe parish documents is dated 1611, the office of Churchwarden goes back further than that and the first such name recorded is that of John Bishop, of Austford, Churchwarden in 1592 (Chapter 17). It was a post of great responsibility and considerable work, covering not only the upkeep of the church and all that pertained to it but included the care of the poor, "maymed soldiers, charitable uses and the upkeep of the gaol", as well as the maintenance of the roads. To some extent too they were an early form of village policeman for they were responsible for the decent behaviour of the people. They could enter private and public houses even against the owners' wishes. They might also have to call to book those involved in sexual misdemeanours, whether married or single.

Among examples of presentations at the Archdeacon's Court at Lewes for 4 years of Charles II's reign: 1674-7, Sedlescombe does not figure in the first. In 1675 Mary, wife of John Thorpe, had acted as village midwife without episcopal licence. With the terrible examples of midwives pictured by nineteenth-century novelists, this necessity for a licence in the seventeenth comes as a surprise. Mr. Frencham (Chapter 23), who was already in a state of excommunication—probably because he was a dissenter—was accused of absence from church and from the Sacrament. Thomas Badox, a Churchwarden of the previous year, was also excommunicated. Further research into the reports of the Archdeacons' Courts could be interesting. Sedlescombe seems to have been well-behaved during these sample years.

Probably because it took up so much of a man's time, the term of office was usually only for a year, occasionally for two. Practically every man in the village took his turn and nearly everyone mentioned in this book whether landowner, farmer or tradesman appears among them, a fact which would prevent too much busybodying or harassment.

They were assisted by swornsmen or sidesmen (a corruption of synodsman) who were chosen with the two Churchwardens at the Vestry in Easter week "by ministers and parishioners from among the most respectable of the inhabitants of the village". When summoned by the Bishop to attend the Synods, one of their chief duties was to give information concerning the state of the morals and conduct of the clergy and people; and they were bound to bring forward all heretics and dissenters. There is no mention of these sidesmen, however, in the Sedlescombe Parish records.

The Churchwardens had also to levy taxes in the parish to provide money for the expenses they incurred and to present their accounts. The presentation of these opened each year with the words: "A sesse made by the said Churchwardens and Inhabitants of the Parish of Sedlescombe for the maymed soldiers", etc. and in 1726 and thereafter was added "repairing the Body of the Church and Steeple".[1] The sesse was a land rate. Among the entries under "Disbursements" over the years are the following:

Concerning the church itself:
"To Goodman Ffowle" (blacksmith) "for mending the bells 6d."
"For oiling the bells." "For new bell-ropes 15/-." "Sallerowls for Bells."
"Daies work about mending the bells 2/1."
"For mendinge a seat in ye church 6d."
"For work done about ye church." "For paveing part of the church."
"3 matts to lay around the Communion rails."
"Spade, 2 locks and a hasp for the gate of churchyard."
"¼ lb. of spicks for ye church 2/9. glasiar."
"Making ye tablecloth and watching" (washing) "ye linen cloth."

Concerning the services:
"Paying the bellringers." "Ringers 5th November." "King's Birthday" 1732-34. "The Prince's Birthday."
"Olteration of Prayers" probably when a new sovereign came to the throne. 1728.

[1] E.S.R.O.

## THE CHURCHWARDENS

"Communion bread and wine" 4 times a year; "1/6" and again "6/-".
"A Church Bible and Common Prayer Book £3.6.6."
"Washing the surplice." "A box to put ye books."
"Ffor a book of Homilies 6/-."
"Pd. Mr. Lord for Catrional" (occasional?) "prayers." 1728.
"For Sergt. Darnall's opinion." "Clerks wages for ritting the Book."
"For 1 year and ½ due at our lad: day 1625 13/2."
"Isaac Gostling" (schoolmaster) "for entering the a/c." 1730.
"More spent making the a/c." "Making the Book; 5/-."

In 1708 an assessment was made for "raising severall sum of sixteen shilling for the Reparation of ye house of Correction and four shillings for Lambrogg Bridge." The house of Correction was at Battle and the Bridge somewhere between the Northern boundary of the parish and Robertsbridge. There were also items concerning the repair of the road: "mending the road and fetching loads of iron waste from Robertsbridge furnace", but mostly the road repairs figured in the Constables' Accounts (Chapter 2). Money was paid out also for the killing of vermin: "for a fox"; "for killing hedgehogs and puly" (pole) "cats 9/4."

These old account books are fascinating and romantic to see. One of the earliest, dated 1618, is very frail with frayed edge and beautifully written in ink now faded to sepia; difficult to read because of the old-fashioned writing with many flourishes. The sums of money recorded, however, are very clear. The writing is either Thomas Sackville's or that of John Barron, the two Churchwardens for the year. The accounts of 1624 are written in beautiful, small neat letters, very clear and readable, when John Everendon and Allan Gibbon were the wardens. John Everendon was used to keeping his farm accounts and the hand-writings could be compared. The following year during the term of office of William Ledes and Henry Barnes, an inventory was made of "those goods belonginge to the p'ish as followeth:

Item one, Silver Chalice with a Silver cover,
One lether Glass Bottle of 3 quarts,
A Carpett for the Communion table of green Devonshire carsie fringed with green cruell. A linen cloth for the Communion table, A greene cushion for the Pulpitt garneshed with a silken frendge and 4 silken Tassells. One Bible, one booke of Common Prayer, a book of martyrs,

A booke of Homilies. Two ladders, one Joyned Chest with 3 Locks, one Shovle, one Spade with a mattock."

To a similar list made in 1726 are added: "One Pewter Flaggon and One Silver Salver for the Alms and a Silver Paten." They were described in 1870 as: "Hall-marked 1789" and "Patten on a foot hall-marked 1697." In 1714 had been added a silver Communion Cup inscribed: "W.D. TH. Churchwardens 1714."

From the middle of the nineteenth century onwards the duties of the Churchwardens gradually declined as, little by little, the State assumed responsibility for the affairs of the parishes conducted for so long by the Church. Now the only ones remaining to them are those confined to the upkeep of the Parish Church itself and all that pertains to it. Still they are elected as of yore at the Easter Vestry.

*Chapter Twenty*

## THE PARISH RECORDS

Before the Reformation the Registers of the births, marriages and burials of the members of great families were kept in the religious houses; but the people of the humbler classes were born, married and died unrecorded except, perhaps, by themselves, if they were able to write. At the Dissolution, registration was extended to all ranks of society. Stowe writes: "This month of Sept. 1538, Thomas Cromwell, Lord Privy Seal, vice-regent to the King's Highness, sent forth injunctions to all bishops and curates through the realm, charging them to see that in every Parish Church, the Byble, of the largest volume, printed in English, were placed for all men to reade in, and that a book of registers were also provided and kept in everie parish church; wherein shall be written every wedding, chrystening and burying, within the same parish for ever."

"Many of the clergy," wrote Strype, "would hum and hawke at the reading of the Bible and the king's injunctions, so that almost no man could understand them; and they blew abroad that, by means of the registers, the king intended to make new exactions at all chrystenings, weddings and burials."

No doubt this was looked upon as an invasion of individual privacy as well as being suspected as an excuse for more taxes.

The registers often open with a declaration of loyal wishes to the monarch, a necessary precaution at this time of religious party strife, and particularly in the diocese of Chichester, where the bishop, Dr. George Day, was a leader of those who opposed the Reformation.

The Sedlescombe Registers of Births, Deaths and Marriages in the County Record Office at Lewes begin in 1558 when Richard

Wheatley was rector. The first few pages are difficult to read, being in a neat but archaic hand with obscuring flourishes.

Here are to be found in the varying handwritings of succeeding rectors the names of most of the people of Sedlescombe mentioned in this book, together with many another. Among the unusual ones recorded are:

1625   Fearnot Foster who married in that year Edward Body.
1683   Faintnot Garret who married in that year John Hawkins.
1759   Thankful Butler (Chapter 35) and Thankful Bishop.

An unusual surname is Eightacre; Elizabeth married William Lawrence, yeoman of Sedlescombe; and Alice married John Ledes of Westfield. In 1619 Ralfe Little married Marie Benskynne, whose family may well have given its name to the old house called Benskyns in Westfield parish.

Francis Browne Wright, rector in 1730, who married Isabella Plumer of Beech House next door to the Rectory, made neat columns and James Ingram, who followed him, often gave a word of description of the ones he buried. Thus:

Jan. 27   1748   Jonathon Clout, travelling cobbler.
Dec. 31   1749   Soldier's girl, Mary Roberts.
Jan.      1749   Ann Kedwell, an old maiden. (Footlands, Chapter 10.)
Feb.      1749   David Selmes, old man. (Of Killigan, Chapter 18.)
Dec.      1753   Abraham Bodle, carpenter. (Chapters 35 and 51.)

John Bishop uses the word "base-born":

Sept.        1780   Cornelius son of Susanna Goby, baseborn.
Feb. 9       1780   Philly d. of Mary Beeny, baseborn.
Mar. 14      1783   Patty Pooley d. of Sarah Simmons, baseborn.

George Barnsley, 1674-1724, seems to have been asked to make "a register of the births of children of Dissenters within the parish. . . . The first I have notice of is a daughter of Mr. Samuel Frensham" (Chapter 23) "and Mary his wife, named Elizabeth, born April 11 1698." Another daughter born to the same couple, "Her name Sarah, June 11 1700." He recorded yet another daughter born to Samuel and Mary in 1702 named Martha, and another in the following year, Ann. There were two other children born to dissenters, one in 1700 and one in 1703.

## THE PARISH RECORDS

A great proportion of the Sedlescombe Parish Records consists of Assessments of Rates made by Churchwardens and Overseers of the poor over the two hundred-odd years between 1615 and 1844 and also items of expenditure of the money thus raised by those officials. In the Assessments, the names of the house owners are given, but by no means always the name of the house. Even so it is possible through these lists to trace something of the ownership of a given house over the years. There is also a copy of the 1841 Tithe Map (Scale: 3 chains to 1 inch) with every field and property numbered. The original is the property of the Incumbent. The accompanying list gives the name of every field and farm and the owner and occupier of every building at that date. Census returns for the years 1841 and 1851 also give the names of past householders.

Volumes of Deeds of properties of Lord Ashton of Hyde give much information concerning lands and properties in the north of the Parish which were earlier held of Robertsbridge Abbey. Research concerning Sedlescombe could go on almost indefinitely, for the more that is discovered the more scope for further knowledge opens up.

*Chapter Twenty-one*

## THE RECTORS

Painted on a piece of an old beam from the belfry, the list of Rectors of Sedlescombe hanging beside the south door of the church covers seven hundred and forty years, starting with "James", undated, followed by "Ralph" 1235, and finishing with "Dennis Prince 1973". The first three cover two hundred years, so presumably there were other rectors during that time whose names are now lost. Between James and Ralph came "Roger" and "John" (Chapter 13). In between the first and the last dates are the names of thirty-nine men. It is not surprising that of about half of these nothing is now known. They no doubt all did their work, christening, marrying and burying the people of Sedlescombe, comforting and advising them in troubles and helping them in numerous ways through the pains of living and dying; hearing their confessions and performing the Mass every Sunday and Saints Days, in the earliest years in Latin; blessing their crops and wells at Rogation-tide every Spring, when the Bounds of the Parish were beaten, and giving thanks when harvest was safely in.

Beating the Bounds (Chapter 44) was a most ancient ceremony dating from Saxon days and continued to be a necessary and practical custom in the days when maps were rare, so that everyone and, most particularly, the men should be absolutely familiar with the boundaries of the parish from their earliest years, in order that this clear knowledge should be passed on from generation to generation and the position of the boundary stones known with exactitude. So James, the priest, with his churchwardens and other men of the parish, followed by a crowd of boys armed with leafing branches, perambulated the periphery of the parish in the spring of every eighth year. At each boundary mark the procession halted and the stone or tree was cleared of any inroads of growth. Each boy then beat it with his branch. Sometimes, in order to strengthen the impression, the boys themselves were beaten with the boughs and sometimes they were bumped on the stone to make their memories doubly sure. James then blessed the lands for harvest.

While he was Rector the little old Norman church was extended, for the oldest parts of the present church are said to be of the first half of the thirteenth century.

By the time Thomas Illorn was Rector, in 1429, the advowson was owned by the Knights of St. John, or the Knights Hospitallers, as they were called, of the order of the Hospital of St. John of Jerusalem. This was founded in Jerusalem as a hospital to help poor and sick pilgrims. Alone among all the great Orders of Chivalry of the Middle Ages, it still does approximately the work for which it was formed, in the activities of the St. John Ambulance Brigade. Today this most venerable order runs in Jerusalem the great ophthalmic hospital, designed as a consulting centre for the whole of the Middle East, and it organises first aid and nursing services throughout the world. Its ancient Crusader emblem, the eight-pointed white cross, is a familiar badge at all disasters, great sporting occasions and wherever the modern descendants of the Hospitallers may be needed. In 1975 when the new Duke of Gloucester was installed as Grand Prior of the Order, the ceremonial used was of the time of the Crusades; fanfares of trumpets, elaborate oaths and liturgies, banner bearers and cross-bearers and a prodigious two-handed sword, the emblem of the temporal jurisdiction of the Grand Prior.

The fact that for over a hundred years the names of the Rectors came in pairs was for a long time puzzling. The explanation proved very simple. In the original version of the list in the East Sussex Record Office at Lewes, there is a small 'r' against the first name in each of those six pairs: that is, against Thomas Illory, James Fyndward, John Standon, Thomas Dalyson, John Parker and Richard Waters, signifying that that was the date on which each *retired* from the living, either by death or for some other reason. This date was also the date of the new appointment, and that is the second name in each pair. It has evidently not been possible to discover when the first man in each pair had been appointed.

In a deed dated 1528, William Livington is named "parson of the parish of Sedlescomb", though there is no sign of him in the list. William Moke is given for the year 1527-28 and his successor,

Richard Waters, is one of those whose date of appointment is unknown. It is possible therefore that William Livington did come in between the two.

Richard Waters was the parson in office at the time of the dissolution of the abbeys of Battle and Robertsbridge, and of all the monasteries. The advowson of Sedlescombe Church was taken away from the Knights Hospitallers by the King and reserved for the Crown which still holds it today.

John Lede followed Richard Walters for a span of eleven years. In 1547, two years after his appointment, the name Sir John Ledes of Sedlescombe figures as a witness to a Deed and in 1613 the name appears again in the parish records when Joan Leedes of Sedlescombe married John Yarrow; again, in 1632, in the Seating List, there is still Leedes House (Chapters 10 and 23). Sir John "Lade" appears as owner of Footlands and other land for several decades.

While John Ledes was parson came an alteration in the ceremonies of Beating the Bounds. An injunction of Queen Elizabeth prohibited the Blessing of the Crops, though the perambulation of the borders was ordered to continue. Was this blessing of their crops looked upon by the farmers and their workers as a superstitious practice smacking of Papism, as well as by the law-makers? Or did they regret this loss of blessing? Perhaps Sir John continued to bless them silently.

In 1560, Thomas Frensham became Rector and remained so for 47 years. His family continued to live on in the village for another hundred (Chapter 18). In 1632, twenty-five years after his death, a Henry Frensham was living down Stream Lane at Slaughters (now Spilsteds Farm) (Chapter 23) and in 1655 a Thomas Frensham, "Physitian", married in Sedlescombe Church a widow from Westfield, Elizabeth Saires. Half a century later, Samuel Frensham, living at Spilsteads, was one of four people in the village qualified to vote in the Parliamentary Elections. During Thomas Frensham's last years as Rector the first bell was hung in the tower.

In 1616 it was John Ball or Bell, the Rector, who married his churchwarden, the ironmaster Peter Farnden, to his young bride, Mary Waters, of Brede; but it was John Browne, minister, not Edward Barton (who according to the List became Rector in 1628), who buried that young bride when she died in 1630. Two years later, during Edward Barton's ministry, the "Re-edification" of the church was undertaken at some expense, in which all the inhabitants shared according to their means, in money and a few in materials (Chapter 23). A seating plan was drawn up with great care because by law now each member of the village must sit always in an allotted seat. One Sunday while the Rector, Edward Barton, was taking the morning service, not long before Christmas in 1639, a shocking incident took place, with Anna Clarke, widow of the Hancox Miller, shouting aloud at her neighbour in the pew in front: "Beggars' bratt, beggars' bratt," she bawled to the daughter of the widow Gatskole. It was the responsibility of the churchwardens to silence and rebuke her. The uproar must have been quite considerable and how they quelled it is not recorded; but they certainly reported her to the Archdeacon, to whose Court at Lewes she was eventually brought and charged with "brawling in church and living contentiously and maliciously with her neighbours." Her punishment is not stated in the parish records.

George Baker, evidently a man of education, the first M.A. (or A.M. anciently) in the list of Rectors, followed Edward Barton for ten years. This was a part of the country where Puritan sympathies predominated though, as everywhere, individuals opted for the King; a Bishop of Great Sanders, a Sackville of Hancox and an Everendon of Beech were among these. Four years after Baker was appointed, that is in 1645, the use of the Book of Common Prayer, edited by Cranmer and used in all Church services since 1558, was prohibited by law and no set form of prayer or service was thenceforth allowed. Whether George Baker was evicted from the living is uncertain but in 1651 the Puritan, Edmund Thorpe, was presented to the living by Cromwell. He was also a man of some learning, having entered Christ's College, Cambridge, at the tender age of fourteen, in 1635. This was the same age and about the same time as the young Thomas Sackville of Hancox and his elder brother, John, were entering Oxford University (Chapter 17). A note in the Parish records states that "Edmonde Thorpe was chosen by the parishioners in November 1653 as Register, according to the Act, and took oath before James Temple."

After the Restoration in 1660, the use of the Common Prayer Book was again introduced but Edmund Thorpe would have none of it and refused to take the oath required by the Act of Uniformity, which made every minister declare in the presence of his congregation "unfeigned assent and consent" to the Book of

Common Prayer, to repudiate the Solemn League and Covenant and to swear not to take up arms against the King. This Act was passed in May and the Ministers were given three months—till August 24th, the Feast of St. Bartholomew—to make up their minds. Over sixty ministers in Sussex (that is, about a quarter of the total in the County) came out, ejected for refusing to use the very book which their predecessors had been thrust out for using. The day soon became known as "Black Bartholomew"; the date added to their hardships because it meant the loss of Michaelmas dues. Refusal to conform meant hunger and want for themselves and their families, for all civil offices and the learned professions were closed to them and few had private means. Mark Antony Lower writes of Edmund Thorpe, "He was at the time very destitute having five children and only nineteen pounds a year for the sustenation of his family. Being much loved in his neighbourhood he found many friends and was enabled to open a school, which, though an illegal act, was connived at, and he had as his pupils the sons of many gentlemen both of Kent and Sussex. One of his pupils was Titus Oates, of plotting notoreity, who was connected with Hastings and, afterwards, a preacher there. Mr. Thorpe seems to have been a man of most admirable character, 'a good poet, no contemptible orator, well-skilled in polemical and practical divinity, and much applied to by his learned and pious friends for his opinion on difficult points.' He was very intimate with Mr. Polhill, the learned lay theologian of Burwash. He throve so well in spite of his ejection that he was enabled to give two of his sons a university education. He subsequently moved to Brenchley in Kent, where he constantly attended church twice every Sunday. His scruples against conformity must have been very mild as he lived on brotherly terms with Mr. Monkton, the incumbent of Brenchley who preached his funeral sermon in which he gave him 'a handsome character'." He died at Brenchley on March 17th, 1678, aged 57. Edward Polhill, Esq., 'the learned lay theologian of Burwash' had married Martha Farnden, daughter of Peter Farnden, of Brickwall. He became a barrister and J.P. and was a man of strong Puritan tendencies, a great friend and supporter of the neighbouring clergy who for conscience sake resigned their living in 1662. A namesake of his had been in 1634 Rector of nearby Etchingham.

In 1665 conditions for these dissenters was made yet harder under the Five Mile Act by which they were forbidden to be found within five miles of their former cure. This meant that Edmund Thorpe had for the time being to move his home to Hastings.

In 1672, Charles II published his Declaration of Indulgence which said, "We shall from time to time allow a sufficient number of places as shall be desired in all parts of our Kingdom for the use of such as do not conform to the Church of England to meet and assemble in, in order to make their public worship and devotion . . . Our Will is that none of our subjects do presume to meet in any Place, until such Place be allowed, and the Teacher of that Congregation approved by Us." The King immediately received applications for licences and he granted three thousand five hundred in the course of one short year of grace before he was forced to cancel his Indulgence by public opposition to it. Such was the fear of Papism that the news of the Withdrawal of the Declaration was greeted with the greatest joy; bells were rung and bonfires blazed up and down the land. From Sussex came twenty-six applications during the year, among them one from Edmund Thorpe: "Sedlescombe April 13th 1672. The house of Edmund Thorpe to be a Presbyterian meeting-house." In fact, he seems to have used his house just for family worship and not for meetings to which outsiders came.

There are many references over the years to Thorpes in Sedlescombe, both in deeds and in place-names of fields and woods. It could well be that at least one of his sons continued to live in the parish, providing descendants for some time to come. As late as 1894 there was a John Thorpe at Spilsteads Farm and in the twentieth century another member of the same family returned to live and die at Highfield and to own the same farm, Spilsteads.

Replacing Thorpe at the time of his ejection came Edward Natheley or Rathely. To him certainly fell the task of reintroducing the Book of Common Prayer to the people's worship. (In his diary, Pepys writes: "Nov. 4th (Lord's Day) In the morn to our own church where Mr. Mills did begin to nibble at the Common Prayer by saying 'Glory be to the Father, etc.' after he had read the two psalms, but the people had been so little used to it, that they could not tell what to answer." (He adds, "My wife seemed very pretty today, it being the first time I had given her leave to wear a black patch.") Nothing is known about this Rector, Natheley, but that when he died in Sedlescombe twelve years later he was buried not in Sedlescombe churchyard but at Crowhurst.

There then came to Sedlescombe perhaps its most famous and outstanding Rector, George Barnsley, who (but for one year's unexplained gap in 1706-7 when Thomas Bowes' name appears) was in office for half a century, for part of which time he was Rector also of Burwash, 1707-1724, and of Northiam 1676-1692. At no time therefore was he rector of more than two villages. In all three he left a name remembered to this day, for in his will he provided money for the education of poor children in each of them. During his first year as vicar of Northiam as well as Sedlescombe, there was a religious census to discover 'popish recusants" and 'other dissenters which either obstinately refuse or wholly absent themselves from the communion of the Church of England', that they were not so numerous that they could not be suppressed. The figures for Sedlescombe show no Papists and but five Nonconformists, perhaps Thorpe's followers.

George Barnsley was evidently admired also outside his parishes for in 1695, after he had given up Northiam and before he had taken on Burwash, he was chosen by his fellow-clergy to represent this archdeaconry in Convocation. "As for Convocation," wrote the Vicar of Cuckfield to the Bishop of Chichester, "is one Dr. Barnsley of Sedlescombe having near 50 for him, to 13 for Dr. Sanders of Buxted . . . Sir John Pelham sent us venison to express his respect to the sober clergy and particularly for Mr. Barnsley for whom he has a great kindness . . . As for Mr. Barnsley we chose him not only as a man of excellent piety, humility and learning, but also of known temper and moderation and by the relation of all that knew him."

When he was buried at Sedlescombe just before Christmas in 1723 George Barnsley was deeply mourned, having ministered to the people of the village during five reigns, those of Charles II, James II, William and Mary, Anne and George I. The unexplained gap of one year in the reign of Queen Anne remains a mystery. When he returned in the following year he was instituted too to the living of Burwash and he remained Rector of both until he died.

In both livings he was followed by Peter Pickering, who saw the beginning of the building of the schools for which his predecessor had provided, but not their opening; for this did not occur for a quarter of a century after their benefactor's death and after two more rectors had passed from the village. Perhaps the frustrations of the legal and building processes were not less then than now.

## THE RECTORS

Before Sedlescombe school was opened, Francis Browne Wright had become Rector for 16 years and had married 'the girl next door', Isabella Plummer, grand-daughter of John and Jane Everndon of Beech House (Chapter 23), beside the Parsonage. It was while his successor, James Ingram, was Rector that the teaching of the village children in the new school really got under way, with its first schoolmaster, Isaac Gostling. Five years later, the only person who could be found to replace this old man, now past his job, was his assistant, a lad of 17, Thomas Colbran (Chapter 28), who was to continue in this post for 61 years—all his life. James Ingram, who was also Rector of Westfield, died in 1750 and was buried in Sedlescombe church (Chapter 51).

The village seems for the next five years to have been without a rector, for it was not till 1756 that John Bishop was appointed; John Bishop, younger son of William Bishop of Hurst House and Great Sanders, and brother of Henry Mallory Bishop (named after a Jacobite plotter) (Chapter 17). John, born and bred in Sedlescombe, must have been a young man when appointed to the living and perhaps it was kept vacant for those five years awaiting him. For twenty-seven years, John Bishop lived at the Parsonage serving his fellow villagers. His whole life seems to have been bounded by Sedlescombe. Seldom can a rector have known his flock better. By the time he died in 1783 he had inherited from his elder brother, Henry Mallory, Great Sanders ("the Mansion-house"), Austford, Beech, Chittlebirch, Durhamford, Hurst and Little Castlemans. He was in fact a squire-parson, or "squarson". Some of the property passed to a later rector, John Pratt.

Between these two land-owning Rectors came John Alcock for twenty years. The notice of his death in the *London Chronicle* for Sept. 20th, 1803, is as follows: "On Saturday sennight, the Rev. G. Alcock, Archdeacon of Chichester and Rector of Seddlecomb. The vacant Rectory is in the gift of the Crown."

It was thus that in the year 1803, when he was a man of twenty-nine, came John Pratt to be Rector of Sedlescombe for over half a century, eight years longer than George Barnsley; and with his wife, Mary, brought up a family of six. These were hard times for farm labourers. The iron industry had moved North. Britain, during the early years of his ministry, was at war with France and then came the years of industrial revolution, with all its problems for the agricultural worker. He saw the troubled times of revolt in

Sussex with its often violent agitation for better wages and against tithes, in which many of his parishioners joined. He himself seems to have put all his savings into land and, as the Bishop family and the Smiths (Chapter 23) gradually had to sell their land, he bought it; first Durhamford (then known as Stream House). Later, when he retired, wishing to continue to live in the village, he built Highfield in a field on Beech Farm, which he also owned. One of his daughters married the owner of the new house beside the church, known as Castlemans but then The Firs. His son, Richard, and his grandson, Arthur, and Arthur's daughters all lived at Highfield in their turn and took a great part in the life of the village. His unmarried daughters, Sophia and Harriet (Chapter 41), lived in the village until they died and it was in memory of them and their married sister that, when the well was sunk on the village green in 1900, the Pump House was built over it. The east window in the church is a memorial to this Rector, John Pratt, and his wife Mary. When John Pratt retired in 1861 Edward Owen succeeded him. His father also lived here and is buried in the churchyard. It is recorded in 1883 that the gravestone from his grave had been removed to be repaired. There seems no trace of it today.

Nine years later came John Warner, M.A., to be Rector and it is he that so many old people remember lovingly today from their childhood. He taught them in the school, he prepared them for confirmation, he took the memorable May Day service and shared in the festivities that followed it (Chapter 42). With him they Beat the Bounds at Rogation tide. In the last few years he sought the help of a curate, and him too the older people of today well remember (Chapter 35).

The next three Rectors, Barry Browne (Chapter 43), Henry Percival and Ernest Reid, followed each other at five- to seven-year intervals, the latter becoming eventually Archdeacon of Hastings. A keen cricketer, he played in the village team and shared in many other activities. Years later he chose to be buried in Sedlescombe churchyard, and the Lychgate was erected in memory of him by his widow. It was during his time in 1922 that Sedlescombe and Whatlington were united under one Rector, after a Public Meeting had been held in Battle the previous year to discuss the proposed amalgamation; under his predecessor in 1926 the first Parochial Church Council was elected.

In 1929 came William Noble, to be Rector for twenty-three years, with his wife, Elizabeth, and their two daughters and one son, John, later to be killed on D-day. Next to Mr. Warner he was the most loved of the twentieth-century Rectors. Quiet, courteous and kindly, he seems now in his old-fashioned grey knickerbockers and stockings to belong to another age. Anybody, even only temporarily sick, would be visited on a Friday afternoon. Without fail he would look in, perhaps for a few minutes only, but the message came across that he cared. If something needed doing, he would do it if he could. He would light the fire or bring the medicines. During the war his comfort to mourners bore extra weight through the memory of how he had carried through all the Sunday services the day after he had received the news of the death of his only son. The grass of the churchyard was in these years mown by twelve church sheep, a custom that might again be revived. On January 1st, 1950, he retired, a very sick man, to nearby Hawkhurst Moor with his wife. Three weeks later came the news that he was dead. His work was done. Nearly all in the village felt they had lost a friend.

He was followed by Geoffrey Martin, the first Rector of the parish who had not been bred to the Ministry of the Church, having already had a full secular career. So although he was a man of middle age, this was his first parish. He it was who planned and carried through the erection of the side altar, and saw that all was well-made by Sussex craftsmen. He and his wife were the last to live in the large house, now the Old Rectory (Chapter 23) which was, at his retirement, sold.

For Philip Barry and his wife, Rosemary, and their three children a new small modern rectory was built in the kitchen garden of the old one. The old house that had been added to again and again over the centuries, with its sloping lawns around the ancient oak tree where the nuthatches nested every spring and hawfinches visited every autumn; the lawns that had seen so many parish activities, children's parties and tennis matches, with its orchards and its garden full of thick rows of daffodils and narcissi and long hedges of sweet peas, and its rooms that had seen so many parish meetings; all had now become too expensive to keep up, too expensive and difficult to heat, its gardens impossible to keep from neglect. With it went for ever a house that was a natural centre for hospitality and the business of the village. The new one was small and cramped with no room to spare for meetings, no room in the garden for tennis club or parties for the Sunday school and choir children. Philip Barry was perhaps the right man to begin the life of the new rectory, for he liked change and brought it all through the church so that every service was altered and many of the customs; all the time he was dogged by ill-health, faced indomitably. After nine years he moved to a smaller parish and was succeeded by Dennis Prince, the Rector of today.

Church-going being no longer either compulsory by law, or fashionable, the largest congregations are on Remembrance Sunday when the church is full again as the familiar names of those who died are read again and the faces of young men are before the eyes of their mates, now growing old; and at harvest, still a season of thanksgiving, come some of the farmers to give thanks. But the heaps of cabbages, potatoes and marrows, apples and tomatoes grow smaller, the piles of tins larger; still the hops are brought and the plaited loaf, carrying on the long custom of Gregory's, the local bakery, now but an arm of Betabake. Even at the Carol Service, once packed to the doors, there are vacant places. This too follows a cycle; an age of scepticism follows an age of faith, to be followed itself by a renewal of faith, as winter is followed by spring, and summer by winter.

*List of Rectors of St. John Baptist Church*

| | |
|---|---|
| James | |
| 1235 | Ralph |
| 1347 | John Waley |
| 1429 | Thomas Illorn |
| ,, | John Blood |
| 1440 | James Fyndward |
| ,, | Henry Wells |
| 1479 | John Standon |
| ,, | William Smyth, B.D. |
| 1486 | Thomas Dalyson |
| ,, | Oliver Edson |
| 1502 | John Parker |
| ,, | William Dandyson, B.D. |
| 1527-1528 | William Moke (1528 Deed cites William Lyvington "parson of parish of Sedlescombe") |
| 1545 | Richard Waters |
| ,, | John Lede (Sir John Leeds of Sedlescombe Witness to document 1547) |

## THE RECTORS

| | |
|---|---|
| 1556 | Richard Wheatley |
| 1560 | Thomas Frencheham |
| 1607 | Hamlet Marshall, A.M. |
| 1611-1612 | John Ball, L.L.B. |
| 1628 | Edward Barton |
| 1640-1641 | George Baker, A.M. |
| 1651 | Edward Thorpe (Turned out at Restoration) |
| 1662 | Edward Rathley, A.M. |
| 1674 | George Barnsley, A.M. |
| 1706-1707 | Thomas Bowers |
| ,, | George Barnsley, A.M. |
| 1724-1725 | Peter Pickering, A.M. |
| 1730 | Francis Browne Wright (*m.* Isabella Plummer of Beech House) |
| 1746 | James Ingram, M.A. |
| 1756 | John Bishop (of Great Sanders) |
| 1783 | John Alcock, L.L.B. |
| 1803 | John Pratt |
| 1861 | Edward Owen, M.A. |
| 1870 | John Warner, M.A. |
| 1909 | Barry Browne, B.A. |
| 1914 | Henry Charles Percival |
| 1921 | Ernest Gordon Reid, M.A. |
| 1927 | William Hatt Noble, M.A. |
| 1950 | Geoffrey Noel Martin |
| 1964 | Philip Maurice Barry |
| 1973 | Dennis Prince |

*Chapter Twenty-two*

## THE YEAR 1632

Why 1632? What is the importance for Sedlescombe of that particular year? The answer is that it was not of any particular importance at the time, but it is today, because it happens that we know a very great deal about the village and its inhabitants at that date.

We know, for instance, the names of twenty-three houses—fifteen of which are still standing—and the whereabouts of three more, though the buildings no longer exist. We know also the names, at least, of the people who lived in them, as well as those of a number of the poorer villagers.

The poor of Sedlescombe, together with a great many others all over the kingdom, but most especially in the East part of Sussex, had been suffering, because of two extremely bad Winters and Springs, from a great scarcity of grain caused by two appallingly bad harvests, which had resulted in the doubling of the price of corn. In many places plague had followed depression and unemployment. There is no evidence that this village was thus affected, but I was lately told that the reason that Westfield contains so very few old houses is that, after plague visited that village in the seventeenth century, every contaminated house was burnt.

King Charles I was ruling now without any constitutional check, having dismissed Parliament and refused to call another. Dissatisfaction was rife; rebellion was stirring and civil war was not far ahead. At a Council Meeting held at Whitehall in June 1630 the following letter had been directed to be sent to all magistrates in England and Wales: —[1]

[1] S.A.C. 16.

"Whereas it is generally observed that, in most parts of the Kingdome, all sorts of grayne doe this year prosper so ill as that there is just cause to fear a dearth to ensue: And we well knowing that those parts beyond the seas, from whence we were wonte to be supplyed with corne, are soe wasted and troubled by warres and otherwise as that we cannot reasonably expect that supply from thence as formerly: Have, therefore, by his My's express command (whose princely care and providence herein for the good of his people and Realmes we cannot but with comforte acknowledge), thought good, for the better husbanding and preserving of the Grayne within the Kingdome, to recommend unto you theise direccons following, viz: —Take especial care that no corn of any kind whatsoever be exported out of that county into forraigne parts.

"That all possible restraints be made of makeing of maulte (to the end that sorte of grayne may be the more preserved for bread corne) not onely by suppressing the number of maultsters, but by lymitting those that shall be allowed of, to convert only such a portion of barley into maulte as shall be needfull, and twoe or more of you the justices next adjoining, take a weekly account thereof from them.

"That the unnecessary nomber of alehouses be carefully supprest in all places within that county, and that the dependances of tenants or servants to gent: in the country (which is generally observed) give not any connivance therein.

"That the laws provided as well against brewing or spending of strong ale or beere in innes and alehouses be strictly put in execucon, as lykewyse against ingrossers, forestallers of corne &, and for the regulating of marketts in the prizes of grayne, and that you cause the graynaries of those to be visited who are noted for ingrossers, and see that they supply the marketts according to the lawes.

"And generally that you use all other fitt courses and remedies, either provided by law, or which you, by your experience, know best or can find out for the preservacon and well husbanding of the grayne within that county, in such manner as that there may be sufficient from tyme to tyme to supply the necessities of the county. Lastly we expect and require that you have an account of your doings and proceedings herein to the judges of assize, in their next circuite, unto whom his Maj.'s pleasure hath been alreadie signified, to call upon you for the same, and from whom his Majesty and this board will require an account at their retourn from the said circuites." etc. etc.

This letter had been followed by another in January of the next year.

"His Maj. in his princely care and love to the administracon of justice, takes notice that many disorders are growne in this kingdome through neglect or faint execucon of those lawes that tend to the releeving of impotent poore people, setting to worke those that are able, and punishing such as are idle or vagrant. And to stir up all others to activeness and diligence in theire places (for what greater motive can be than to see such zeale of justice in a King) hath pleased to express unto us what he dislykes and what he desires to be done for his own better informacon and the more due execucon of those laws. To which ende after mature deliberacon his Majesty with the advice of his privie Councill hath thought of a way which will appeare unto you by the tenor of commission and by orders and direccons which herewith wee send unto you put into bookes in print, that so the same may be better published, executed and obeyed, willing and requiring you, the Sheriff of that county presently upon receipt thereof, to make the same knowne to the Justices of the Peace of that County, and they to make divisions amongst themselves in such sorte that what is thereby required may be exactly performed. And of such theire divisions as shall be made, that you returne the severall names of the justices of each division unto us that so wee may the better discerne upon that your returne, the dilligence or negligence used in this service. Whereof his Majesty will require a good account at our hands, and so, etc."

Sir Thomas Sackville and his fellow Justice, Robert Foster (youngest son of Sir Thomas Foster, Justice, of Battle) replied with the following letter, written in April of the same year: —

"Hastings, Sussex.

"Accordinge to his Majesties orders in all obedience thereunto, wee have within this devision of Hastings rape caused the constables, churchwardens and overseers to give theire monthly accompt of the performance of theire severall offices, and wee have caused severall somes of money in the severall parishes to be raised by severall taxations of the inhabitants as well for providinge stocke to sett the poore to worke as for releife of impotent and disabled inhabitants, and have caused the said officers as much as in them lyeth to see the said poore inhabitants be dewly kept to worke and have fitting materials provided for them, and that the idle bee dewly punished and the impotent releived; and wee have hitherto found the said officers willinge to make theire presentments. And in this devision since the publishinge of his Maties said orders there hath bin putt out apprentices in the severall parishes in this devision, seaventeene persons, viz., in the parish of Ticehurst, six; Plaiden, one; Peasmarsh, one; Beckley, one; Montfield, one; Wartling, two; Heathfield, three; Salehurst, two.

"There hath also binn Apprehended as vagabonds in the severall hundreds within this devision three-score and tenn persons who have received correction and bin sent to the places by the statute in that case appointed.

"Such persons allsoe as by the lawe were to bee sent to the houses of correction have bin thither sent, where they have received punishment by the statute appointed, and have been sett to labour, and we have seene to the convenient maintenance, government, and well orderinge of this house of correction within this devision." (One was at Battle).

"And we have caused forfeitures to bee levied of tenn severall unlicensed ale-house keepers (beinge all have binn convicted) and that wee can take notice of; and the moneyes leavied upon them disposed of to the poore of the severall parishes where the said offences were committed.

"These have beinn the severall offenders, and these offences punished in this devision. For the other offences menconed in the said orders there hath beinn none presented to us, nor that wee can learne guilty of; but as the same shall be committed and presented to us, or that wee cannot take notice of, wee shall endeavor his Maties said orders bee dewly executed, and wee shall doe and performe what in us lyeth in the dewe execution of his Maties said command.

      Thomas Sackville,    R. Foster.
      of Sedlescombe. K.B.   of Battle".

A month later, these two justices wrote another letter to the Privy Council pleading for special treatment for the suffering poor in their hard-hit district.

"Rapa de Hastinge.—To the Right Honorable the Lords and other of his Majesties most honorable privie counsell.

"Whereas wee receaved letters from yor Lordshipps, for a searche and viewe of the quantity of corne within the countye of Sussex, we, whose names are hereunder subscribed, doe herby certefye that wee have accordingly performed the said service within the rape of Hastinge (being the place of our devision) with all dilligence, and wee finde, by the presentments of the viewers, that there is not sufficient quantetey of all manner of graines to suffice the inhabitants there, by a full third parte, by reason whereof our markets are not soe well stored as they ought; neither, as we conceive, is it altogether soe fitting for them, that have a little to spare, to bringe it to market to sell it at home to theire poore neighbours, whoe beinge very poore and farre from markett wilbe much disabled by losse of time; neither have they money to buy in time of the markett, but are constrained, by reason of theire necessity, to buye when they have money; besides wee find those, whoe have any corne to spare, sell it better cheape at home to theire poore neighbours than in the marketts, and in those parishes which have not wherewith to supplye the wants of the poore, we have, by our earnest investigations, perswaded the able men thereof to provide corne to be layde in at every several parishe for the poor; the which heitherto they have done, and are still willinge to doe the same, soe yt corne may be procured for money; Soe yt now we become peticioners unto your Lordshipps to give liberty unto us to have free passage by sea, to fet corne from those parts where it is more plenty full, otherwise it will be soe scarcie and deere that the poore will not be able to live. As for all things that are contained in his Majesty's booke of orders we have punctually observed, and, God willinge, intend to continew in the observation hereof, and shall be ever redy to fulfill whatsoever his Majesty or yr Lordshipps shall farther command us, Soe, leaving all to yr Lordshipp's consideracions, we rest

    Your Lordshipps' servants, to be commanded,
      Thomas Sackville, Ro. Foster
Dated this 9th May 1631."

On this application, the following satisfactory order was made by the council on the 13th May 1631: —

"Thier Lps. haveing been informed that within the Countie of Sussex at large, there is such plentie of corne, as it may serve to supply the wants of some places within the said Countie, where they have not sufficient to serve their tournes, and that if the poore that want should be forced to goe from place to place to buy their provision within the Rape of Hastings (where there is not sufficient to serve the inhabitants of all manner of graine by a full third parte), it would be very inconvenient and a great hindrance unto them. Their Lps., therefore, doe think fitte and order that corne may be provided in anie place within the Countie of Sussex, to supply the wants of the Rape of Hastings, and that the same may be carried by sea or land to anie place within the said Countie, provided that Sir Thomas Sackville, kt., and Robert Foster, Esquire, Deputie-Lieutenants of the said Countie and Justices of the Peace, who have certified the Board of the wants of the said Rape doe give their warrant for the carrying by sea or land of such provisions as shall be bought for the use of the Inhabitants of that Rape, and doe take good securitye that it shall not be transported out of the kingdom or to anie other place but to the Rape of Hastings."

A week later a letter was sent by the Council "to the Justices of the Peace in the Countie of Sussex, next adjoining the Towne of Hastings or anie two of them, and to any other Justices whom it might concern.

"We have bin informed by a peticon of the Jurats and Commonalty of the Towne and Port of Hastings, that whereas they have bin accustomed to buy such quantities of corne and graine within the countie of Sussex and elsewhere, as should be needfull for the necessarie supplie of their towne, and to transport the same by sea or otherwise to their said Towne of Hastings, that at this present their said towne is in great distress for want of corn, and they cannot be suffered to transport the same as they were wont by reason of the late published orders, forbidding the transporting of anie corne out of the said countie. Theise are therefore to signify unto you, that you or anie two of you may authorize anie pourveyor that the Towne of Hastings shall appoint, to buy within the said countie of Sussex, such a proportion or quantities of wheat or barley as shall be needfull and requisite for the sucre and relief of their said towne and to embarque the same at any of his Majesties Ports, provided that good security be given not to transport the same to anie other place but to the towne of Hastings, and that it be sold there in open markett, and not converted to the use or commoditie of any one private man. And in case they shall have occasion to provide any corne for the use aforesaid out of the said countie of Sussex, anie two of the Justices of the Peace next adjoyning to the place where the said corne shall be bought and transported, may by virtue hereof give the like license as aforesaid and upon the same condicons and the shewing of these our letter shall be to you and them sufficient warrant. And so, etc.

Signed.

Lo. Privie Seal (Earl of Manchester) Ea. Marshall (Earl of Arundel) Ea. of Suffolk, Lo. Visc. Dorchester. Lo. Visc. Wentworth. Lo. Visc. Falkland. Lo. Bishop of Winton (Rich. Neale) Mr. Trer, (Sir Thos. Edmondes). Mr. Comptroller (Sir Henry Vane) Mr. Sec. Coke. Mr. Chanc. of the Exchequer (Fras. Cottinton)."

The town of Rye was assisted in like manneer.

In the autumn and winter of this same year there took place an expensive restoration and enlargement of the church in Sedlescombe (Chapter 13). The village had clearly been growing in extent, its population increasing; and, though farming had been disastrous for the last two seasons and food therefore very expensive indeed, the iron industry was flourishing, giving employment to villagers and wealth to the Sackvilles, Farndens and Bishops. It seems that some work on the church was set in progress by Sir Thomas Sackville and the churchwardens, who were personally responsible for the welfare of the poor of the parish, with the idea of giving employment to the poverty-stricken and others without work, such as farm labourers. Though the carpenters and masons must have been skilled workmen, there was wide opportunity for unskilled labour as well. The year 1632 was promising better, the winter weather with alternating frosts, rains and sunshine having been more seasonable. The bill for the winter's work on the church had now to be paid. The framed plan hanging on the South wall of the church (Chapter 13) gives "A platforme of the Seats in the Parish Church of Sedlescombe" at the time of "the great Charge bestowed about the Re-edifying of the Same Anno Domini 1632"; that is, the heavy expense of the repairing and restoring of the church. From the churchwardens' accounts for that year we know how it was paid. On May 28th a "sesse" (cess of tax) was levied at "two shillings in the pound;" and so each land owner paid two shillings in the pound on the value of his land. The total thus collected was £54. 7s. William Bishop of Sanders paid the highest cess at £8. 4s., his land being assessed at £82. Sir Thomas was second, paying £7 (land valued at £70). John Everendon of Beech came third, assessed at £52 on which he paid £5.4s. Peter Farnden of Brickwall paid very much less, only £1. 4s. his land being assessed at only £12. John Darbie of Footlands paid £4. Thomas Avory of Castlemans, a farmer, paid 18s. Thomas Dawes and Thomas Frensham each paid £1 for Carters (Manor Cottage) and Slaughters (Spilsteads) respectively.

In addition, the sum of £39. 5s. was collected as "a benevolence from certain of the Inhabitants towards the new building of the church." As might be expected, Sir Thomas headed this list with a gift of £10, William Bishop and Peter Farnden followed with £8 each and half a dozen people contributed lesser sums.

A smaller cess was levied also on holdings of woodland. William Bishop and John Darbie (Sanders and Footlands) had each a hundred acres on which they paid £2. Sir Thomas had 50 acres and the others had smaller acreages on which they paid in shillings. A few people gave gifts in kind, some in timber and some in lead. The whole value received totalled £104, the amount paid out being £99. 19s. 5d., the "Carpenders" payments forming the largest single item at £17.

From the plan we know that a great many houses standing in Sedlescombe today were to be seen there in 1632. Close by the church were Beech, the home of the Everendon family; part of the Old Rectory, where was living the Rector, Edward Barton; (Little) Castlemans, where the Avory family lived; Durhamford with Thomas Pooke; Spilsteds—under the name of Slaughters—where the Frenshams lived; Great Sanders with the Bishops; Footlands with the Darbies; further afield Hancox with the Sackvilles; Swales with Henry Creasey and his family; and Bellatkins—now Strawberry Hill Farm—in Poppinghole Lane where the Skinners lived. In the Street was Brickwall, the home of the Farndens; and late "Carters" (now Manor Cottages) where dwelt Thomas Dawes.

It is noticeable that a large number of the houses were known by the names of their last occupier: "late Johnson's House" occupied by "Jo Atholl;" "late Bachelor's" by "Allan Gibbons' heirs;" and "late Weekes House" by "John Sheather," (a surname that has died out of the village only a year or two ago).

A curious fact about the Plan is the complete absence of the names of any houses in the Street, though many of those beside the Green today were standing there in 1632. They may well be represented in the list by "late Bachelor's," "late Brigden's" etc., for few of these houses had names even as recently as twenty-five years ago, and fewer still at the start of the century, when the exceptions were the Queen's Head, Asselton House, the Forge Cottages, the Coach and Horses, Homestall and the old Gun House. Another reason for the omission of the names of any of the Street houses may be that they were all landless save for a crofter's strip. All the houses named on the Plan have several acres, at least, of land around them.

So on a Sunday morning in the year 1632 under the azure sky of mid Summer, the villagers from the Street crowded up the hill between a field of green corn on their left hand and the flower-scattered meadows of ripe hay on their right, in quietly talking groups, the men in their Sunday-best roundfrocks, followed by their women-folk and children. Others passed them on horseback or in wheeled vehicles stirring clouds of white dust to settle on their shoes or even on their heads. Some, too, came riding or walking from the West up Stream Lane—already deeply sunken between high banks, its surface more like a bad farm track than a highway—or from the North of the parish down the Old Roman Road, unkempt now and deeply rutted, rough and dangerous with hidden pitfalls for the feet of both beasts and people, thickly shod though the latter were. All converged besides the steps of the church at the mounting block. The horses were put up in the stables of the nearby houses and farms or were tethered to the fence which then enclosed the churchyard and which was removed only some twenty-five years ago owing to the expense of keeping it in repair; a problem which was solved in 1632 (as can be seen on the Plan) by the allotment of fixed lengths of it to be the responsibility of different land-owning parishioners.

So all passed then as now between the furrowed trunks of the chestnut trees and beneath the green haze of their long leaves, along the path to the church door, the peal of five bells ringing out merrily above drowning the rivalling songs of the birds. All made their ways to their allotted seats, the wives separate from their husbands though often immediately behind them. Last of all entered Sir Thomas Sackville who strode up the aisle to his large pew in the front.

The Rev. Edward Barton conducted the service from the pulpit at the East end of the church, assisted by the parish clerk who sat in a seat beneath it.

There were psalms but no hymns, the service being all said in English, the Rector reading from the huge Bible which had by law to be chained in its place. He wore a black cassock and white surplice as today, as is proved by the entry in the churchwardens' accounts of the time, "paid to Goody Clarke" (the miller's wife) "for washing the surplice 1/6".

The long service over, Sir Thomas Sackville, followed by his family, led the way out and crossed the road to Beech House with the Everendons, who were connections by marriage. After them went also the Bishop family and the Farndens. There was much of serious import to discuss besides the likelihood of a better harvest and the consequent possibility of a lowering of prices, especially of corn; for trouble was brewing, with the country restive because of the King's refusal to call Parliament. Sir Thomas' opinion and knowledge of State affairs was anxiously awaited. The children could now escape notice and disappear into the fields to play and gather flowers from the hedgerows, leaving the garden with its warm scent of lavender and roses to their solemn parents.

Other friends and neighbours were foregathering at Castlemans; the Darbies of Footlands with the Avories, the Frenshams and the Pookes. Others grouped outside the church; the farming families from Swales and Bellatkins joined their neighbours at Castlemans before making their ways home to the borders of the parish. The servants of Sir Thomas stopped to talk with their cronies, news of State being sought, too, from them. The world of Sedlescombe on this Sunday morning was full of converse and the interchange of news and views. Perhaps some words of approval were spared for the new state of the church, mixed liberally, no doubt, with ones of criticism of the high cost, as is the way of human beings.

The Street families filled the road downhill with their chattering voices, the men making a halt at the Queen's Head for more discussion and to clear the dust from out of their throats. There were no shops then round the larger, rougher Green, only workshops and those, at this hour, closed. There were carpenter's and wheelwright's; smith"s, tailor's and cobbler's; stonemason's and miller; the brickyard and the tanyard; cordwainer's, too, which were high-class shoe makers. Anything thus not supplied that families needed, they made themselves and every Sunday afternoon they could take surplus wares to Battle market and, with the money obtained from their sales, could buy any other necessities; an arrangement that was only one step away from the original system of barter. The houses around the Green looked very much as they do today though there were more thatched roofs and one-storeyed cottages, more vegetables among the flowers in the gardens and no lawns.

*Chapter Twenty-three*

## THE HOUSES AND PEOPLE ON THE 1632 PLAN

In 1909 Percy Godman published an article in *Sussex Archaeological Collection* Volume 52 in which he wrote:

"By the courtesy of the Rev. J. Warner, late rector of Sedlescombe, I have been enabled to take the accompanying tracing of a Plan of the Parish Church—executed in 1632—showing the allotment of sittings as then arranged. I had the opportunity of comparing this plan with another (now in the possession of Harvey Combe) of the same date, from which I have been able to fill in some of the blanks left in the parish copy."

On the copy hanging in the church is the note: "This Plan was copied from a tracing presented to the Church by Mr. F. P. Gasson June 1936." It is said that Mr. Gasson found the original tracing in a bundle of old documents which he bought at an auction at Oaklands, the home of the Combes. So, while the original of the parish copy traced by Godman has disappeared, the tracing of Harvey Combe's, with which he compared it, has now become the Church copy (the original having also disappeared).

The two tracings are not identical. The variation in some of the names is mostly little more than of spelling, resulting from a different reading of a very faded original. Thus Higham becomes Lingham; Sun, Stunt; Koman, Sloman; Paris, Jarvis; Paris, Rens; Selden, Solden; Jasper, Jaques; "hiers" of Willm Van, heirs of Wenham; Thomas Dawes for Stone, Thomas Dawes Jo Stonham. Sometimes by reference to the names of wives it is clear which is the right interpretation.

Percy Godman's Plan shows a list of 26 signatures which is absent from the Church version. Eleven of these have "mk" beside them, showing that these had been unable to write their names and so had made their marks X. The pews in his copy are numbered 1-44 and, in that order, descriptions follow in this chapter of all that has so far been discovered about the individuals and their houses.

Pew 1. *John Everndon.* "*Fence; Jo Endon for Beach 9 foote.*"

Beech House[1] received its name (like Beech Farm: Chapter 17) from the de Beche family of whose estate both were, in early days, part.

A list of the Muster Roll of the Rape of Hastings for 1339, which shows the landlords who were liable to produce able-bodied men to serve as soldiers, with the names of them and their officers, for each Hundred. For the Hundred of Staple, 72 men are named: the Captain and four Lieutenants, one of whom was in charge of 13 archers, one of 19 halberdmen and two together of 35 men armed with staves and knives. The name of one of the thirteen archers is John de Beche, of one of the halberdmen Robert de Beche, and one of the lieutenants is Symon de Beche.[2] So the family was well-established in the Hundred in the fourteenth century and, little more than a hundred years later, it was still known in Sedlescombe for one of the two constables from the Hundred of Staple pardoned for their share in Jack Cade's rebellion, was Richard Beche of Sedlescombe, yeoman (Chapter 15).

The attractive tile-hung old house with its walled garden, opposite the church, is named in the 1632 Plan simply as Beach. It is not known exactly when it was built, the first evidence of its existence being in 1618. But a Walter Everndon was living in Sedlescombe in 1584, for he was engaged in a lawsuit against John Browne and his son (Chapter 24) concerning rents and tenements in Brede and Sedlescombe.

*John Everndon*

The earliest Deed yet discovered of the house by name and description is dated August 26th, 1667, when it belonged to Walter Everndon.[3] The lands of Beach had, however, been farmed by the Everndon family as early as 1618 for an article entitled "Extracts from Account Books of the Everendon and Frewen families in the XVIIth Century"[4] describes some kept by John Everndon from

[1] Map B.
[2] Dawson.
[3] Thorne.
[4] S.A.C. 4 and 22.

## THE HOUSES AND PEOPLE ON THE 1632 PLAN

March 1618-1660 which clearly relate to Beach Farm, "comprising 14 pieces of land totalling 84 acres," of which 5½ were woodland. In the "cess" for the Great Charge of 1632 this land is valued at £52.

John Everendon was a man of property and position as is shown by the contents of these accounts; and also by his marriage to Mary White, sister of William White who owned Brickwall, Northiam, before it passed to the Frewen family, and who himself married a sister of Sir Thomas Sackville of Hancox. In an Indenture dated 1612, a child, Ann Harte, was apprenticed to John Everendon and Joane, his wife; it is possible that these were John Everendon's father and mother.

In addition to Beach Farm, John rented 30 acres of marshland near Winchelsea where he kept his sheep in the summer-time. On March 16th, 1618, he set down the number and value of them as follows: 142 ewes worth £93 6s. 8d.; 59 wethers and rams, £40; 20 fatting wethers £2 2s. 0d.; 95 lambs £57; 12 old ewes £8; one ram 13/4. Total value £221. His other stock on that date was

| 4 oxen | £22 | 1 young mare | £10 |
|---|---|---|---|
| 6 kine | £24 | 6 hogs | £2.8 |
| 3 yearling | £8 | 1 Old Black | |
| 1 Bull | £4 | Mare | £4 |
| 2 Gelding | £16 | | |

6 acres of wheat £24. 7½ acres appointed for oats £10.

Total value £124 8s. So the total value of all his stock was £345 8s. which was a considerable amount in those days. By the next year it had risen to £411. In 1618 he had 24½ acres of grass mown and in the following year 21¾ acres of grass, 8 acres of wheat and 10 of oats, which was about half the area of Beach Farm, the other half was presumably pasture.

The Account Book gives interesting details of wages and costs:

| | |
|---|---|
| For hedging ... | 1¼d. a rod |
| For making a new hedge and ditch ... | 3d. a rod |
| For reaping 10 acres wheat ... | £1 18s. |
| For binding sheaves ... | 2s. a day |
| For mowing grass ... | 8d. an acre |
| Out-of-door labourer ... | 3s. a week |
| To his servant Elizabeth Coffin ... | 7s. 6d. a quarter |
| To his man John Farnham ... | £1 2s. a quarter |

| | |
|---|---:|
| For catching moles ... ... ... ... | 1d. apiece |
| Broom faggots to lay in the wheat for draining ... ... ... ... ... | 1s. 9d. for 9 score |
| Bricks ... ... ... ... ... | 16s. a thousand |
| Tiles ... ... ... ... ... | 13s. 4d. a thousand |
| To the Goodwife Sheather making a ruff and band ... ... ... ... ... | 18d. |
| And for schooling his children together ... | 2s. 2d. |

He paid £1 a year for the schooling of his daughter Elizabeth and £2 a year for his son, Walter.

Another item in the accounts is: "April 1626. Spent at London at St. George's Feast when I waited on the Earl of Dorset, £15 10s. 8d."

The Earl of Dorset was the head of the Sackville family of which the Sackvilles of Hancox were a branch, with whom John was connected by marriage. It seems to have been an expensive evening out.

In both copies of the Sittings Plan, John Everendon's seat is that of the Parish Clerk immediately in front of the reading-place by the pulpit. It may seem remarkable that the gentleman-farmer of Beach and friend of the Earl of Dorset should have been parish clerk; but it was then a very different post from that of more modern days. It was essential, for one thing, that he should be able to read and write. In the other copy of the Sittings Plan, part of Pew Twenty-three is reserved for "wife of Goddard ffoster Clarke of the parish", but there is no sign of Goddard ffoster himself, though his name appears in other parish records.

*Walter Everndon*

John died about 1660 and from that date the Beach Account Book was kept by his son, Walter, until 1678. One of Walter's daughters, Mary, returned to the home of her grandmother, for she married Thomas Frewen, Rector of Northiam. (Stephen Frewen, a prosperous skinner from London, had bought Brickwall, Northiam, from the Whites, Mary's ancestors). Mary brought the Everendon account books with her and the Frewen family, including Stephen, continued the entries.

Mary's sister, Jane, married her cousin, John Everndon, "Batchellor of Physick," of Cliffe near Lewes. It would seem that his father was a mill-owner for Thomas Newbury in 1653 mentions that "Mr. Everndon of Lewes and some other mill-owners are in want of water."

# THE HOUSES AND PEOPLE ON THE 1632 PLAN 217

*A platforme of the Seates in the Parish Church of Sedlescombe confirmed by consent unto all the Howses and Inhabitants within the same Parish upon the greate Charge bestowed about the rædifying of the same Anno D'ni 1632*

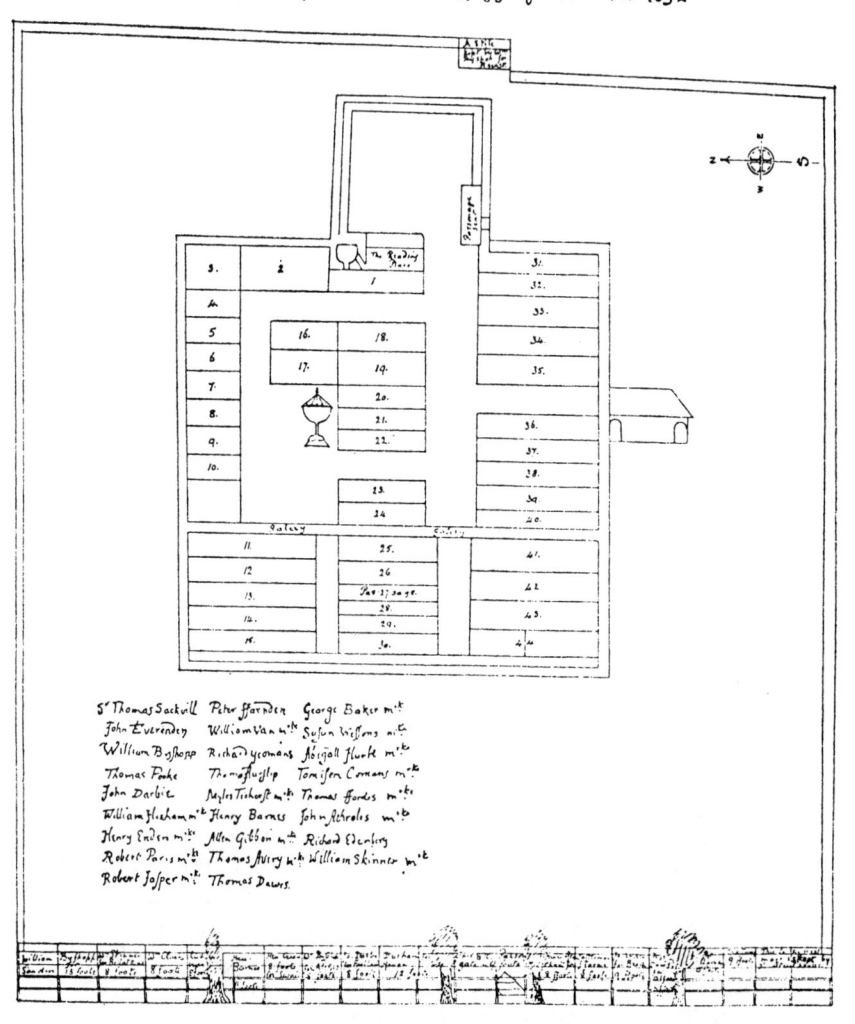

Plan of Church Sittings, 1632.

"For and in consideration of the marriage," states a deed drawn up in August 1667, Walter gave the young couple "the land messuage and tenement commonly called or known by the name of Beach; the land containing by estimation four score acres with boundaries as follows: East, the highway from Sedlescombe to Westfield" (the old Roman road), "and other land of Walter Everndon; East and South: land of the heirs of Thomas Dawes; West: lands of William Bishop Gent. of Great Sanders, Spilsteds; North: the Glebe lands of the Rectory or parsonage." During the lifetime of Walter the property was to be held for his "use and behoof" and, after his death, to be possessed by John and Jane and their heirs. The witnesses were Thomas Champion, John Everndon, Jane's brother, and John Eldred. John, the bridegroom, signed as John Everendon, though throughout the document his name is spelt Everndon. Another indenture, executed on the same day between the same parties and witnessed by the same three persons, records the matrimonial arrangements that led to the transaction.

Walter, who was a Justice of the Peace and therefore an important person, died in or after 1678. He is mentioned in a Deed of December 26th, 1670, relating to the purchase of 7 acres of land known as "Faggety Fields" in the Beach neighbourhood. He must certainly have died by May 20th, 1681, for on that date his son-in-law, John Everndon, mortgaged Beach and all other lands in Sedlescombe belonging to him for £200 to a William Pellatt, citizen and grocer of London. In September of the same year this was increased to £250. John is now described as "Doctor in Physick", a promotion from his previous rank of Bachelor. Among the witnesses is an Antony Everndon.

*The Plummer Family*

John died early in 1693 leaving no male heirs, so the property passed to his daughter, Martha, who married Samuel Plummer; and it remained in the Plummer family for fifty years. With the property Martha inherited also the mortgage and on March 20th, 1706, this was assigned to John Tilden of Brede. (This is the first mention of the name Tilden which became so familiar as a Christian name in this district. See Spilsteds). The mortgage was finally paid in full by Samuel Plummer in 1715. A deed of October 21st, 1706, between Samuel Plummer and Martha Plummer and Thomas Frewen Esq Northiam is the first of the deeds to bear a revenue stamp—two blue stamps of 6d. each. It gives more information on the Beach property; "one messuage (the dwelling-house), one barn, two stables, two gardens, two orchards, 50 acres of land (arable), 10 acres of meadow, 20 of pasture, 5 of wood;" the total thus being still 85 acres.

On January 2nd, 1726, Samuel Plummer made his will. He had two sons, John and Samuel; and five daughters, Jane, Mary, Elisabeth, Isabella and Lucy. Jane had married the Dean of Battle, Richard Nairn, but the other sisters were yet unmarried. Besides Beach, Samuel had land and houses in several parts of Kent. His will begins in the usual fashion by committing his soul into the hands of Almighty God and his body to the earth; he made his wife, Martha, sole executor and his principal legatee. She was to continue to live at Beach, "my mansion or dwelling-place wherein I now dwell", for one year after his death—after which she would live in one of the Kent houses. Beach was then to go to his son, John, and his son-in-law, Richard Nairn, to be sold with all convenient speed to the best purchaser, the proceeds to be invested and the interest to be paid to the four unmarried daughters "share and share alike" till the principal was paid. In due course this was to be paid in quarter shares to each of the daughters on their marriage "marrying with the consent of my wife and not otherwise"; if any of them married without her consent, or died before payment, that share was to go to the survivors and Jane Nairn equally; and provision was made in the event of them dying unmarried. This will was proved in 1731.

*John Plummer*

So in the autumn of 1731, John Plummer succeeded his father, Samuel, and he and his neighbour, Henry Bishop, of Great Sanders, were the first trustees of the school and the Rector, the Rev. Francis Browne-Wright, his next-door-neighbour, was also his brother-in-law, having married his fourth sister, Isabella. The youngest sister, Lucy, married a surgeon of Battle, Jeremiah Botting.

Three years later Beach had still not been sold and a deed of August 6th, 1734, relates that John Plummer himself bought it for £1,365, and this sum was divided between Elisabeth Plummer, Isabella Wright, Lucy Botting and Jane Nairn in accordance with their father's will. Mary, the other sister, had died.

George Tilden of Battle, gent, was a trustee of this deed. The property now included adjoining land, "woodbrooks, 11 acres", which was copyhold of Battle Abbey, not freehold like the rest.

Thus John Plummer, great grandson of John Everndon, the Parish Clerk, became owner of Beach where he had been reared, but he did not own it for long. On January 19th five years later he and his wife, Mary, together with George Tilden and his wife, mortgaged Beach to John Legas of the famous family of Wadhurst ironmasters, for £800. On April 27th of the same year John Plummer "for and in consideration of the love and affection which he hath and beareth unto Mary his wife" declared that during his own lifetime Beach should be for his own 'use and behoof'; after his death it should be for Mary (if she survived him) and after her death for her children. It is impossible to know the object of this declaration for John was already in great financial difficulties. In a deed of February 13th, 1740, his debts were recited as follows:

| | |
|---|---|
| To Jeremiah Botting on a judgement | £262.19s. |
| To Botting and Tilden jointly | £200 |
| To Tilden on a Bond | £173.16s. |
| To John Lingham, miller of Sedlescombe, mortgage on Beach | £200 |
| To John Legas the mortgage on Beach | £800 |

The total of £1,636 15s. together with the interest would be a heavy burden and John was unable to pay these debts, so he conveyed Beach to Botting and Tilden on trust, to be sold for discharging the debts 'as far as the money will go'. Thus Beach, the family home and farm of the Everendon and Plummer family, traced for a hundred and twenty years, and certainly going back earlier, passed to strangers.[1]

As far as Everndons in the village are concerned, the Marriage Registers show that in 1678 Thomas Russell of Ewhurst married Bennett Everndon and in 1722 Edward Drew married Elizabeth Everndon. Today the name Everndon has returned to the village.

In an affidavit dated July 22nd, 1740, sworn at Battle before George Worge, one of the 'masters extraordinary of the High Court of Chancery', John testified that the Beach property was worth a rent of £50 to a good tenant. He had himself lived on the farm six years, he said, his parents and sisters had lived there for more than

---

[1] Thanks to the researches into the Deeds by Sir John Thorne.

forty years and the farm had never been rented in their time, but he had heard that the last rent was £48 more than forty years ago. The statement that he had lived in the house for only six years is strange. He must have kept up his interest in Sedlescombe for, though he was now 'of Battle', he was still trustee of the school in 1748 and 1754 (Chapter 28).

Meanwhile, in March 1740, Botting and Tilden had paid off Lingham the miller of Iltonsbath's mortgage. Three years later the sum due to Legas of Wadhurst had mounted to over £900; and at this point Philadelphia Holmesby of Goudhurst contracted to buy the property for £970 and pay off the mortgage, and John Tassell of Sedlescombe became her tenant. Over the years other tenant farmers followed him. A hundred years later in the Tithe Map, Beach is called Street Farm, probably to differentiate from the other Beech Farm, then part of Great Sanders estate. Street Farm belonged to Edward Hussey but was farmed by Spencer Crisford, who farmed also Castlemans opposite, owned by Mrs. Woodward. The Crisford family had lived for many years in Sedlescombe and there are at least eleven of their tombs in the churchyard bearing eighteenth- and nineteenth-century dates. In addition, there is the tomb of Cordelia Butler, wife of Philip Butler and daughter of John and Martha Crisford (Chapter 35). The earliest grave is of John Crisford, born in 1716, died 1762. The family seems to have grown in importance in a quiet way; more than one of its members was overseer or Poor Law Officer.

Towards the end of the nineteenth century, Edward Hussey sold Beech and all its lands to John Pratt, the Rector who, after he retired, built a house for himself in one of its fields called High Field, and it, with Spilsteads, became the Highfields Estate. Beach was thus detached from its land and was let for many years and finally sold as house and garden, as it continues today, its old bricks and tiles rusty with age and its walled garden still adding great charm to the village and a comfortable home after more than 350 years.

*Pew* 2   Sir Thomas Sackville for Hancox (Chapter 17).
*Pew* 3   Lady Sackville and her children.
*Pew* 4   Her maid servants.
*Pew* 5   Four of Sir Thomas's men.
*Pew* 6   Thomas Avery and Richard Ellenbury or Ettenbury.

*Thomas Avery* had a seat allocated to him in both Pew 6 and Pew 32, the latter being specifically designated 'for Castlemans'.[1] His wife also had a place in each of two pews. Little is known of either Thomas or his wife. He was illiterate and signed his name with his mark (Chapter 17).

*Richard Ettenbury,* who shared Pew 6 with Thomas Avery, appears as Edenbury among the signatures and in other records as Ellenbury. No house is mentioned with his name but, as he was responsible for the upkeep of 8 ft. of the fence, he was presumably a man of some property, perhaps one of the larger houses in the Street, none of which are named on the Plan. His wife, Margery, has a place in Pew 36. In 1665 John Etonbury was a weaver.[2]

*Pew 7* Wife of Thomas Avery and Wife of William Langham.

Here is *Mrs. Avery's* other seat, immediately behind her husband. It is possible that she was born and married in a neighbouring parish for there is no record of her marriage in Sedlescombe church. The only Avery marriage is in 1637 when John Avery, perhaps her son, married 'Ruth' whose surname is not recorded.

*Bridget Langham* or Lingham had been born a Bishop and had married the miller of Iltonsbath in 1614 (Chapter 12).

*Pew 8* Wife of George Baker (or Barber) and Wife of Franc Grantham.

While there is no George Barber on the Sittings Plan, there is in Pew 35 a George Baker, so it can be assumed that this is his wife, but her name is unknown.

Franc, Francis or ffrancis Grantham's wife was Elizabeth Lullam, only two years married. While Thomas Grantham and his wife are both allotted seats, there is none set apart for Francis unless, as seems likely, he was in fact "Francis Grant Leedes House" in Pew 25.

*Pew 9* Wife of John Sheather and of Nicholas Goodman.

John Sheather sat in Pew 43. There seems no record of his marriage, nor does he appear in the tax lists. The only Sheather marriage is in 1701 when Mary Sheather married Will Huckstepp, the shoemaker. John Sheather sits in Pew 40 for 'Late Week's house'.

[1] Map 2.
[2] Hearth Tax. E.S.R.O.

Mrs. Sheather may well be the washerwoman and school "dame" mentioned in the Account Book of John Everndon of Beach (Pew 1).

Agnes Russell had been married to Nicholas Goodman at this date for 23 years. In one plan Nicholas is not mentioned. In the other he has a seat in the gallery in Pew 42.

*Pew* 10  Wife of Robert Jasper and of John Turner. Nothing is known.

*Pew* 11  is left blank.

*Pews* 12-16 the Gallery. For "Sir Sackville's sons" and "his men-servants".

The two eldest Sackville boys were John and Thomas aged 11 and 10, far too old to be classed as children to sit with their stepmother and sisters. No doubt the men-servants in the seat behind could keep some check on their behaviour and stop any 'larking'.

*Pew* 14  These three other seats are left: —

*Pews* 15 and 16  Common for Cottagers; Youths and Strangers.

*Pew* 17  Mr. Wm. Bishop for his house called Great Sanders (Chapter 17).

*Pew* 18  Mrs. Bishop and her Children.

Mrs. Bishop was Elizabeth, daughter of Edward Hause, and she died seven years later. They had several children.

*Pew* 19  Mr. ffarnden for his house and messuage lately built, Motkyns and Blacklands. Fence: Peter ffarnden  9 feet.

Because the 'house and messuage lately built' is in the singular and Motkyns and Blacklands are plural, it is thought that the lately built refers to a third house, Brickwall, since the Farndens are known to have lived in it. As with other houses the 'lately built' may refer to enlargements and re-building, for building on it had began thirty-three years earlier by John Sackville (Chapter 17).

*Motkyns* (Map 3)

This pleasantly named house seemed to have disappeared without trace, defying all efforts to identify its site, until in a summary of Deeds of Brickwall and Hurst House the name unexpectedly appeared: "and reciting that the copyhold messuages . . . were all held of the Manor of Battell and were part of those to which he William Brooks had been admitted under the description of 'all that tenement and lands called Waterlands and that other tenement called Motkyns'." William Brooks and John Palfrey Burrell were associated with the cousins, Hercules Sharpe and Sir William Brabazon in the purchase of Hurst Farm, Hole Farm (which became Oaklands) and other surrounding lands in 1830.

Since Motkyns was copyhold of Battle Abbey, a likely site for it was in the south of the village near Iltonsbath; and in 1569 there appears: "The heirs of Stephen Wystonden hold by copy one tenement with a Barn and three closes of Pasture containing 3 acres called MOTKYNS in the parish of Sedlescombe." The names of the owners of the messuages on the north and the south are named and the three of them "lye between the lands called Waterlands N. and to a lane leading between Tiltonsbathe and Brede S. . . ."[1] It can thus be deduced that Motkyns lay North of Brickwall as far as the North border of French's Engineering Works, and included also the field east of Brickwall where the Park Shaw houses stand. "It pays yearly 2/6 and gives heriot and the usual entry fine." This later became part of Joseph Mercer's land (Chapter 26), and was close to "land called Blacklands". Thus, as might be expected, Brickwall, Motkyns and Blacklands were near neighbours.[2]

Concerning the origin of the name, Motkyns, "in 1401 Thomas Wodeman was pardoned after having broken the close of the Abbot of Battle at Marley and stolen a cow with her calf and 2 heifers, 3 years old, of John Motekyn; 2 heifers of Peter Shedere; a bull of Thomas Beeche of Sedlescombe; 2 more heifers 2 years old; and a cow and calf at Battle belonging to the Abbot; and 1 bull and 2 cows besides. The pardon was requested by the Abbot because he was not a cattle thief but the outcome of local squabble and scandal"!

In a Subsidy Roll 1524-5 for the Hundred of Staple, the names William and Richard Mottyn appear.

*Blacklands* (Map 3)

"Lands called Blacklands" figure repeatedly in the records in most cases as an eastern boundary to lands whose ownership was being particularly described. In 1569: "The heirs of Lawrence Avann hold lands called Blacklands containing by estimation 34 acres, between lands of Rotes and Bartholomew Carraway called Blacklands west . . ." and "The heirs of Robert Avann hold by

[1] B.A.S. 1569.
[2] Map 8.

copy one parcel of Brookland containing 1 acre called Colesbrook alias Collyshe at the end of lands called Blacklands..."[1] Both these parcels of land were later the property of Joseph Mercer. They are referred to as "the excellent pasture of Blacklands" and "... the enclosed field with Blacklands 34 acres found ready tenants."

The Tithe Map for 1841 under the heading of Blacklands lists seven named fields, Broomfield, Barn meadow, Rye Grass field, Holly field, Lodge meadow and Lower and Upper Shaw fields. These were some time part of Mabbs Farm (Chapter 32). On one of these, the mill field, the council houses called Blacklands now stand.

Somewhere on these lands stood Peter Farnden's house called Blacklands. In 1713 Henry Barnes farmed both Hurst and Blacklands. He was followed by Thomas Snepp in 1726 and ten years later his widow 'Madam Snepp', was named as ratepayer. In 1745 it was 'John Crisford for Madam Snepp', in 1751 Dan Wood for Blacklands and, in 1774 'Widow Wood for her own and Blacklands' paid land tax £23 7s. 6d. By 1841 Blacklands Farm was owned by David Spencer and farmed by the Weston family, Robert, James and Thomas, who lived in part of Brickwall house. For the next ninety years the Blacklands lands were part of the Oakland estate. Today, once again, as in 1700, they form part of the Hurst estate, and belong to the Keeling family.

*Pew* 20  Mrs. ffarnden and her children.

This was Lucy, the second Mrs. Farnden, and her stepdaughters, Mary, aged 11, Elizabeth, Joan and Martha (Chapter 17).

*Pew* 21  Durhamford House and the wife of John Darby.

Thomas Pooke for Durhamford House had a seat in Pew 31. Mrs. Pooke sat in this one. John Darby of Footlands sat in Pew 31. The name of his wife is not known.

*Pew* 22  Wife of Thomas Dawes and of Thomas Avory and of Henry Eden.

Thomas Dawes of "Carters" sat in Pew 31 (Chapter 14). There seems no record of his marriage so it is possible that his wife was not a Sedlescombe girl and the marriage took place in another parish.

The wife of Thomas Avery has been described under Pew 4.

[1] B.A.S. 1569.

Henry Eden's wife was Ellen Eginford, whom he (Pew 33) had married in 1610 and they lived at "the other Alford" (Austford). In 1639 Henry Iden, their son, married Mary Jordan.

*Pew* 23   Wife of Thomas Grantham, of Henry Barnes and "hairs of Soan".

Thomas Grantham's wife was Willina Parrys or Paris, whom he had married in 1619. His pew is No. 26.

There is no record of Henry Barnes' (Pew 25) marriage so he too probably married a girl from a neighbouring parish.

Although Soan is a name still well represented in the village today, there is no record of them in the seventeenth century apart from this. The alternative copy of the Plan has in this Pew "Richard Van's heirs".

*Pew* 24   Widow Van, Widow Stunt, Widow Sloman and the Wife of Goddard Foster, Clark of the Parish.

If Percy Godman's copy of the Plan is correct, Widow Van is the widowed mother of the young unmarried women or girls who sat in Pew 23. The name Van and Avann is certainly to be found in local records of Street houses and others in the parish. In 1624 William Van was one of those fined a shilling for being absent from church on the Sabbath day. In 1634 he married Anne Bishop.

Widow Stunt's husband had been John Stunt who had paid cess 2/8 in 1624. Of Widow Sloman there is no record.

Here is the only wife among the four women in this pew and yet, curiously, there is no sign of Goddard Foster himself in any seat in either plan; in both, John Everndon's name is on that reserved for the parish clerk. Nor does Goddard's name appear among the signatures or among the tax lists, though that of Richard Forster does.

The first record concerning Goddard is in 1560 when he and his wife Agnes appeared as plaintiffs in a case concerning the rent of tenements in the manor of Iden near Rye, which they won. The next record is of 1638 when Goddard Foster married Thomasina Cresy in Sedlescombe Church, so she cannot be the wife named here. In 1666 a Goddard Foster married Joan Etenbury, perhaps the daughter of Richard and Margery—Pews 6 and 36.

*Pew* 25   Henry Frensham for Slaughters: Henry Frensham for Castleman's Farm. 8 ft. of fence.

Henry Barns for Gilds. 11 ft. of fence.
Thomas—or Francis Grant for Leedes House.

Slaughters is to be identified with the beautiful farmhouse with steep-pitched roof, now called Spilsteds,[1] which stands on the hillslope in Stream Lane, on the far side of the Rusty Brook which gave this 'highway to Battle' its name centuries ago. The date on a gable in the front of the house is 1604, but the house was built as a medieval hall by one of the Bishop family in the fifteenth century. The chimney was added in the sixteenth century and the moulding round it is identical with that round the chimney at Hancox. The porch was, as with the Manor cottages, a later addition.[2]

*The name "Slaughters"*

In the 1569 Survey the name James Sluter occurs several times.

"James Sluter doth hold freely by deed of agreement, one garden called Luckfish containing by est. ½ acre, lying in Sedlescombe . . . on the W. part of his own house lately burnt, and also doth hold the place of the messuage where the house was burnt and 13 acres of land called Welfeild, abutting to the King's Highway leading from Robertsbridge to Winchelsea N. and to a lane called Wickham Lane W. . . . and to the lands of the said James held by copy E., pays 11/9 and gives for heriot at every alienation of the messuage burnt and land, 6/8 for a relieve, and gives heriot for Luckfish." (Map 2.)

"James Sluter doth hold by knight's service certain lands in the parish of Sedlescombe . . . within the Hundred of Staple, called the Beche and Clove Oxe, containing by est. 41 acres lying between the lands of Thomas Darby called Sinder Burrough W, lands of Richard Bishop called the Beche E. and N. and to his own lands . . . S, and pays 4d for the castle Guard, rent 2/2, and the Lord shall have heriot, ward and marriage when they shall happen." (Chapter 17.)

Sluter's property was clearly beside Stream Lane; and Burnthouse meadows figures in the Deeds of Spilsteads alias Slaughters.

According to old Deeds of Highfield, in 1675 Thomas Sackville of Hancox sold to Thomas Frencham for £208 16 acres of land, identified as part of what is now Spilsteds farm, and described as 'all those 2 pieces or parcels of land called Burnthouse meadows . . .

---
[1] Map 2.
[2] R.O.H.A.S.

now sowed to wheat,' and held of the Manor of Battle.[1] The boundaries of this land were:

N. and E. 'the King's highway leading from Sedlescombe to Battle';

S. and E. other lands of Thomas Frensham 'adjoining to his now dwelling-house' (now Spilsteds);

S. and W. also his lands;

N. 'a field called Coneyberry field' which is the one where the Hancox Windmill stood, marked now by Windmill cottage.

So, the Burnthouse meadows ran along Stream Lane from the edge of Spilsteds farmhouse up to the edge of Coneyberry field, lying a couple of fields in depth from the lane and were the old "welfeild". "Where was the Burnt House?" asked Sir John. "It must have been," he concluded, "on or adjoining the 16 acres of land described as the Burnt house meadows, standing where the present Spilsteds farmhouse stands. The fire had perhaps only partially destroyed it, so that it could have been rebuilt in 1604 on to the remains of the older house using some of the old material; which would explain the mid-16th century date suggested by the *Victoria County History*."

David Martin's examination of the house, however, showed no trace of burnt timbers and every sign of having been built as a hall-place in the late fifteenth century. It must be, therefore, that the Burnt house, close by, was utterly burnt out and demolished.

By the purchase of these meadows, Thomas Frensham rounded off an estate which already included part of the present Spilsted farmlands, to the S.E. and S.W. of the Burnthouse meadows. He was a descendant—son or grandson—of Henry Frencham of the 1632 plan. (In 1623 one of those fined for non-attendance at church was "Jo ffrencham"). Thomas was styled 'gent' in the Sackville deed of 1675, and in his will made in January eighteen years later he is called 'phisitian' like his neighbours Thomas Avery of Castlemans and John Everndon of Beach.

The will was proved in June six years later. At the time of his death he was possessed of three copyhold properties and one freehold; the latter being "Burnthouse meadows or Well fields".

[1] Thorne.

The copyhold lands, all held of the Manor of Battle "in the Burrough of Mountjoy and Uckham", were, firstly, that "commonly known by the name of Slauters in Selscombe, a house, a barn and a maulhouse with one orchard, 2 gardens and 8 acres of land"; secondly, also in Sedlescombe, "Rowland" 18 acres of land adjoining Burnthouse meadows on the S.W., and thirdly, "Tanner's Wish" in Whatlington; the rest totals 48 acres. In 1538 in a grant made by Henry VIII to Sir Anthony Browne of Battle Abbey "Bowlands 18 acres" appears; and also "pasture, Huckam field 10 acres" (Uckham or Wickham) and "A meadow called Welland 20 acres." (Well fields.)

## The Frenshams
### Samuel Frensham

All these lands Thomas Frensham bequeathed to his eldest son, Samuel, on condition that he should pay "to my loving wife, Elizabeth" £5 a year. Elizabeth had been a widow from Westfield when he married her in 1655, so perhaps she had money of her own to supplement this tiny annuity. She was to live in the house for the rest of her life and have the use of any of the goods or household stuff. All the family, except Samuel, fared very poorly from their father's will. His two eldest daughters, Elizabeth, married to John Slany of Staplehurst, and Sarah, married to Henry Henly of Sedlescombe, received 5/- each! To his two younger sons, Henry and John, he left "3 silver spoons with knopps". Samuel, as well as all the land, received all his father's goods, chattels, linen, plate and household stuff.

Two years after he succeeded to his father's property, Samuel extended the farm to the south along the stream by buying "from William Bishopp, the younger, of Sedlescombe, Gent, all that one piece or parcel of land called Long Brook containing by estimation 10 acres." This deed dated June 24th, 1701, is the first of the Spilsted series to carry a stamp, two stamps, each VI pence; stamp duty having been imposed for the first time in England in 1694. The boundary to the east and south is "the land of Samuel Plummer Gent in right of his wife", Martha, daughter and heiress of John Everndon of Beach Farm.

A document dated June 5th, 1712, shows that Samuel Frensham mortgaged this same Long Brook for £60 to a spinster of Brighthelmstone (Brighton), Grace Cook, junior, the interest being £3 a year; and the following year he mortgaged Burnt house meadows or Wellfield to another Brighton spinster, Martha Harman, for £100, at 3%. The boundary, Stream Lane, was then described as the Queen's Highway since Queen Anne was on the throne.

Samuel died six years later, having enjoyed the property for nearly twenty years. His will directed that all his land should be sold and the proceeds, after payment of his debts, invested for the benefit of 'Mary, my loving wife'. After her death, his son, Thomas, was to receive £200 and the rest was to be equally divided among his other children (in marked contrast to the will of his father under which he had inherited virtually everything). Of his plate, Thomas received 'one Silver Tankard and one large silver spoone with a knobbe at the top', the rest to be divided among his daughters, leaving his wife the remaining household goods, linen and "Implements of Household".

### Thomas Frensham the Second

Though Samuel had directed that his lands should be sold at his death, this was not done. Endorsements on the Mortgage deeds of 1712 and 1713 show the interest to have been paid up to January 1724, six years after Samuel died; till 1719 'by the hands of John Duke', Samuel's Brighton friend; in April 1719, by his widow and then, until 1724, by John Duke in his capacity of executor. On April 15th, 1725, the mortgage of Long Brook was transferred to him by Grace Cooke, mother of "Grace Cooke junior, spinster of Brighton" (who had died) and an endorsement of January 11th, 1728, shows the mortgage terminated by the payment to John Duke by Thomas Frensham of the full amount of principal and interest. At the same time Thomas mortgaged the whole property to a farmer of Exceat by Cuckmere Haven and in the following year he sold it outright for £300. Thomas Frensham, up to this date described as "yeoman of Sedlescombe", has now become "tallow chandler of Brighthelmstone late of Sedlescombe" and the farm is in the occupation of William Duke.

So the Frensham family, who had lived in Sedlescombe since Thomas Frensham became Rector there in 1560, and at Spilsteds—or Slaughters—since before 1632, left the village for ever in 1727. But some off-shoots of the family still seem to have remained, perhaps the sons, Henry and John, who were left nothing in their father's will but "three silver spoons with knopps"; for in the disbursements to the Poor in the Churchwardens' Accounts for 1730 an entry reads, "for young Frencham's Board 10/-" and in 1735 "going to see Mary Frensham" and "for fetching Mary Frensham's goods" are items of expenditure; and in 1738 "Mary Frensham, bleding", "for keeping Mary Frensham 4/-, for moving Mary Frensham 1/-". Is this poor 'Mary, my loving wife'? Then there are items, "stockings for John Frensham", "for a pair of stockings for John Frensham", "a cap for John Frensham", "shirt and woosted for Thomas Frensham". In 1726 the Churchwardens Accounts had been signed by J. Frensham and Thos. Frensham. It would seem that these two old men (probably brothers of Samuel) and his widow had fallen on very hard times indeed, and may well have been living in the poor-house next door to their old family home. It is curious in view of the family's long occupation of it that the house never became "Frenshams" but remained Slaughters until it was called Spilsteds after a man who lived there for a very much shorter time.

*The Boys Family*

When in 1727 it was bought by William Boys and his son of the same name, of Ringmer, both described as 'gentlemen', they had also to pay the mortgage due to Stanford, the Exceat farmer. One of the witnesses to the document was George Worge, a name well-known in Battle, which occurs also in the stories of the Powdermill and of Beach, in Sedlescombe. The Boys family, though they owned the farm for the next 73 years, never lived there and it was occupied by tenant farmers, one of them being Stephen Spilstead. In 1800 he was "now or late under-tenant" and his name has been attached to the house ever since. Some of the Spilstead family too soon fell on hard times for the names "Sall and John Spilstead" figure in the Workhouse Accounts for the year 1807 as being employed at Hancox farm, Castleman's farm and by Mr. Pratt, the Rector, always at 4d. a day.

All this time the farm and its lands—apart from Burnthouse Meadows or Well field, and Long Brook—continued to be held of Battle Abbey and subject to its manorial customs. Thus when William Boys, the younger, died and was succeeded by his son John, a young man of 20, those rights were claimed. A document of June 7th, 1785, relates that, at the Court Baron of Sir Godfrey Webster before Charles Nairn, gent, steward (son of a Dean of Battle and Isabella Plummer of Beach House):

"It is Inrolled: On the third Proclamation after the death of William Boys, came John Boys, only son and heir of William Boys, and claimed to be admitted to the following copyhold lands: 1) the messuage or tenement and 8 acres; 2) Little Bowlands; 3) Bowlands alias Hamonds; 4) Wickhams; and 5) Ponders Land. To whom the Lord of the said Manor by his Steward granted thereof Seizin by the Rod—and he paid to the Lord for a Fine for such his estate sixty pounds and was admitted tenant thereof in form aforesaid and had Seizin thereof by the Rod, but his Fealty was respited."
So the lands were still the same, but Bowlands had become Hammonds.

Since John Boys was an 'infant' under the age of 21 "so that neither he nor the said premises could be taken care of and managed for himself, therefore the Lord of the said Manor by his Steward aforesaid doth commit and grant as well as the custody of the Body of the said John Boys as of the said premises" unto Samuel Boys of Ringmer until he attained the age of 21. It required that Samuel Boys should "well and honestly educate the said John Boys and find and provide for him competent cloaths and provisions as far as the rents and profits of the said premises should extend" and look after the property and render a full account when John came of age. The fine for this grant of guardianship by the Lord of the Manor was 6s. 8d. This shows the remarkable powers belonging to the Lord of the Manor even as late as the end of the eighteenth century.

*Tilden Smith and Richard Smith*

A Deed of October 1st, 1800, shows that John Boys, now 24 years old, together with his wife, Charlotte, both of Ashcombe, sold the property to Tilden Smith of Vinehall. It comprised the same freehold lands of Burnthouse meadow and Long Brook 26 acres and a new item, Leeford Wood 29 acres in Whatlington. John Boys also undertook to surrender the 5 copyhold lands including the farmstead to the Manor of Battle, the total acreage being 30 of arable, 20 meadow, 20 pasture, 30 wood, 10 furze, heath and common. The price paid for these 110 acres by Tilden Smith was £2,500, and on the same day he was admitted by the Manor as copyholder on payment of fine of £55. When John and Charlotte Boys surrendered the holding, she was "first and privately and apart from her husband examined by the steward and freely and voluntarily consented".

## THE HOUSES AND PEOPLE ON THE 1632 PLAN

The Lord of the Manor at this time was Sir Godfrey Webster 5th Baronet, a child of eleven years. Born on October 6th, 1789, he had succeeded to the Baronetcy eight months later; his guardian appointed by the High Court of Chancery being Thomas Chaplin, Esq.

Tilden Smith, by the time he died 34 years later, was a rich man, living at Vinehall and owning over a thousand acres and many houses in the parishes of Mountfield, Etchingham, Whatlington and Bodiam as well as in Sedlescombe. His estate was proved as under £45,000. He had four daughters to whom he left sums of money; and his lands he divided between his five sons, the youngest, Richard, succeeding to the Sedlescombe property which consisted of, besides Spilsteds, Footlands 96 acres and 12 acres of Pennygrove Wood close by, and also some houses in the Street. So he was in his turn admitted to the Manor as copyholder, by a document dated December 3rd, 1835, which stated that Tilden Smith had died since the last Court "whereupon there happened to the Lord for Heriots five horses which were seized and compounded for £61.6s.8d." It is startling to understand that as late in history as 1835 the best horses in the farm stables were seized by the officers of the Lord of the Manor at Battle. In addition, the fine for Richard Smith's admission was £120, twice that paid by his father. His residence is shown as Great Sanders though it was still owned by John Bishop.

During the next fourteen years Richard Smith, landowner in Sedlescombe, fell into financial difficulties and on March 10th 1849 several ominous documents were executed. By agreement, his elder brother, a banker of Hastings, called Tilden Smith after his father, undertook, as a preliminary to a mortgage, to keep safe the documents relating to the sale on October 1st 1800 so far as they covered the freehold lands of Burnthouse Meadow and Long Brook. The Mortgage given by Richard and Eliza, his wife, states that Richard needed a sum of £3,500 and had asked the Rev. John Pratt, Rector of Sedlescombe, to lend him that amount, interest to be at 5%. The property mortgaged is called for the first time Spilsted's Farm (a Thomas Spilsted was at this date occupier of Great Sanders house and garden in the Poor Rate lists). The copyhold land is described as in the old deeds; but the freehold land appears in a new fashion. For the first time the fields are numbered as well as named and for the first time hops are mentioned. So Burnthouse meadows are now prosaically, 393, 397; Long Brook is 381 and 382; and The Brook hop-gardens 379, for in 1836 the Tithe Commutation Act had been passed for which purpose all land had been surveyed and mapped. The area of the freehold land was now 27½ acres instead of 26 as of old.

The copyhold lands were surrendered on the same date by Richard Smith and Eliza his wife in favour of John Pratt, and because Eliza was a party to the transaction "it was required that it should be perfected with the solemnities for rendering the deeds of married women effectual to extinguish their interests in lands".

Eight years later on February 20th 1857 Richard Smith, described as a farmer of Salehurst, borrowed £116. 15s. 6d. from the Hastings firm of bankers, Smith, Hilder, Scrivens and Co., in which his brothers, Tilden and Francis were partners, pledging as security all his freehold and copyhold lands subject to the encumbrances existing on them. These must have included houses in the village and Poppinghole, Swales Green, Spilsteds and Footlands farms as well as others outside the parish. He seems to have ruined his brothers as well as himself for, four months later, petitions for adjudication of bankruptcy were presented against the bank, Smith, Hilder, Scrivens and Co., as well as against Richard, who was now called "butcher, dealer and chapman" of Salehurst. One of the chief claimants against him was the Rector of Sedlescombe, John Pratt, to whom he had mortgaged Spilsteds and Swales as well as land in Dallington. He claimed £3,458. 16s. 0d.

*The Auction* 1857

On Wednesday September 30th of the same year at the Mart opposite the Bank of England, London, the estate was put up for auction described as "about 109 acres of highly productive land, in a ring fence, in the parishes of Sedlescombe and Whatlington, with a comfortable farmhouse, a cottage adjoining, substantial brick-built oast house with good stowage and two circular kilns capable of drying 800 bushels in 24 hours, barn, stabling, cart hovels, etc. with sheltered stockyard in the rear, all plentifully supplied with good water. The soil is rich but light, easily worked loam well suited to the growth of barley, turnips and hops, and is in an excellent state of cultivation having been farmed by the owner for about 50 years. As at present cultivated 14½ acres are pasture and meadow, 58 arable and 30 hops, the remainder being orchard, garden and plantation, or occupied by roads and buildings." Also for sale were the Stream House (once Gunns and the Poorhouse: see Pew 27), now Spilsted Cottages, then let as two cottages at 4/6 a week, and 2 cottages on the other side of the Hastings road let at rents amounting to £15 p.a. These were Lot 1. "Of this Lot, the Farm Buildings and about 27 acres are freehold of the manor of Battell, subject to the annual quit rent of 11/8 and to heriot of the best beast on death, and a relief of a years quit rent on death and alienation and the remainder is copyhold of the said Manor at quit rents amounting to £1. 19. 10. per annum, and is subject to fine at will on admission and to six heriots of the best beast on death." The names of the fields have changed from Burnthouse meadows to Little Wood and Ten Acres. Long Brook has become Brook Upper and Brook Lower. Lot 2 is the freehold messuage in Sedlescombe Street, known as the Tanhouse (Chapter 34).

*The Pratts: Father and Son*

On April 10th the following year an immense document was executed and signed and sealed by no fewer than 11 people reciting the story of the bankruptcy and auction and showing that the Rev. John Pratt offered the best bid at £2,500 for Spilsteds farm and so was declared the purchaser, all parties agreeing that £500 should be considered the freehold part and the balance of £2,000 the price of the copyhold part. John Pratt obtained also the consent of all to the conveyance of the land to his son, Richard Frederick.

Another document executed a fortnight later completed the story. Richard Frederick "in consideration of the natural love and affection which he hath and beareth for his father" covenanted that during the old man's lifetime the property was to be held upon trust for the father's sole use and benefit; on his death it was to revert to Richard Frederick, the son.

Thus, thanks to the researches of Sir John Thorne, the ownership of Spilsteds, late Slaughters, has been traced from 1632.

1632–1727   The Frensham Family
1727–1800   The Boys family:   owners.   Spilsted family and others: occupiers
1800–1857   The Smiths
1857–1930   The Pratts

So, like Beach, Spilsteds, after the building of Highfield, became part of the estate. In the last decade of the nineteenth century John

Thorpe farmed it. He was the son of a shoemaker in Hastings, the ancester of Thorpe's of Battle. John's uncle was William Thorpe, who in 1844 had been "clerk to Mr. Bishop of Great Saunders". John's brother, Arthur, followed his uncle and became a solicitor, Thorpe's and Co., of Hastings. In 1930 he returned to Sedlescombe, buying Highfield where he lived for the rest of his days, thus becoming owner of the farm his brother had worked, Spilsteds. John Thorpe's two daughters, Nancy and Phyllis, returned also in late life, to live in Battle, like homing pigeons from far places.

The land is still farmed though the hop-gardens have disappeared that lay along the river, where generations of Sedlescombe women and children in September and October filled the air with their chatter as they went hop-picking there, breaking off by custom from any other work they might normally do, including house-work at the "big" houses. The Spilsted hop-gardens were the last ones close to the village to go, and they went after the Second World War. But kingfishers still streak along the bank of the brook, like a hallucination of colour, and the house still stands below Coneyberry field bordered by the steep banks of Stream Lane.

*Henry Barnes for Gilds*: 11 *ft. of fence*
Gilds is the only unidentified house of all those named on the Plan whose owners were responsible for the upkeep of part of the Fence, and to it and Henry Barnes is allotted the longest stretch of any, 11 feet.

In 1624 Henry Barnes paid cess 4d. and, 1625, "the sum of 14s. 3d. was payed over to William Leedes and Henry Barnes being chosen churchwardens for the year 1625 in the presents of divers of Parish; Follows money received when William Leedes and Henry Barnes were churchwardens, totalling £05.07 01."

Henry Barnes was again churchwarden in 1648 together with James Jones, and he signed his name as he had in 1632, James Jones making his mark. In the cess which follows made "for the maymed soldiers and charitable uses, the Goale and other Necessary about the Church", Henry Barnes paid 1/6 while Peter Farnden paid 13/-, W. Bishop 8/- and John Everndon 6/-. In 1646 Henry Barnes was Constable and kept the accounts "of the Survey for ye highways in the p/ish of Sedlescombe.
Recd. 08. 00. 10. Expenses 08. 13. 00."

# THE HOUSES AND PEOPLE ON THE 1632 PLAN 237

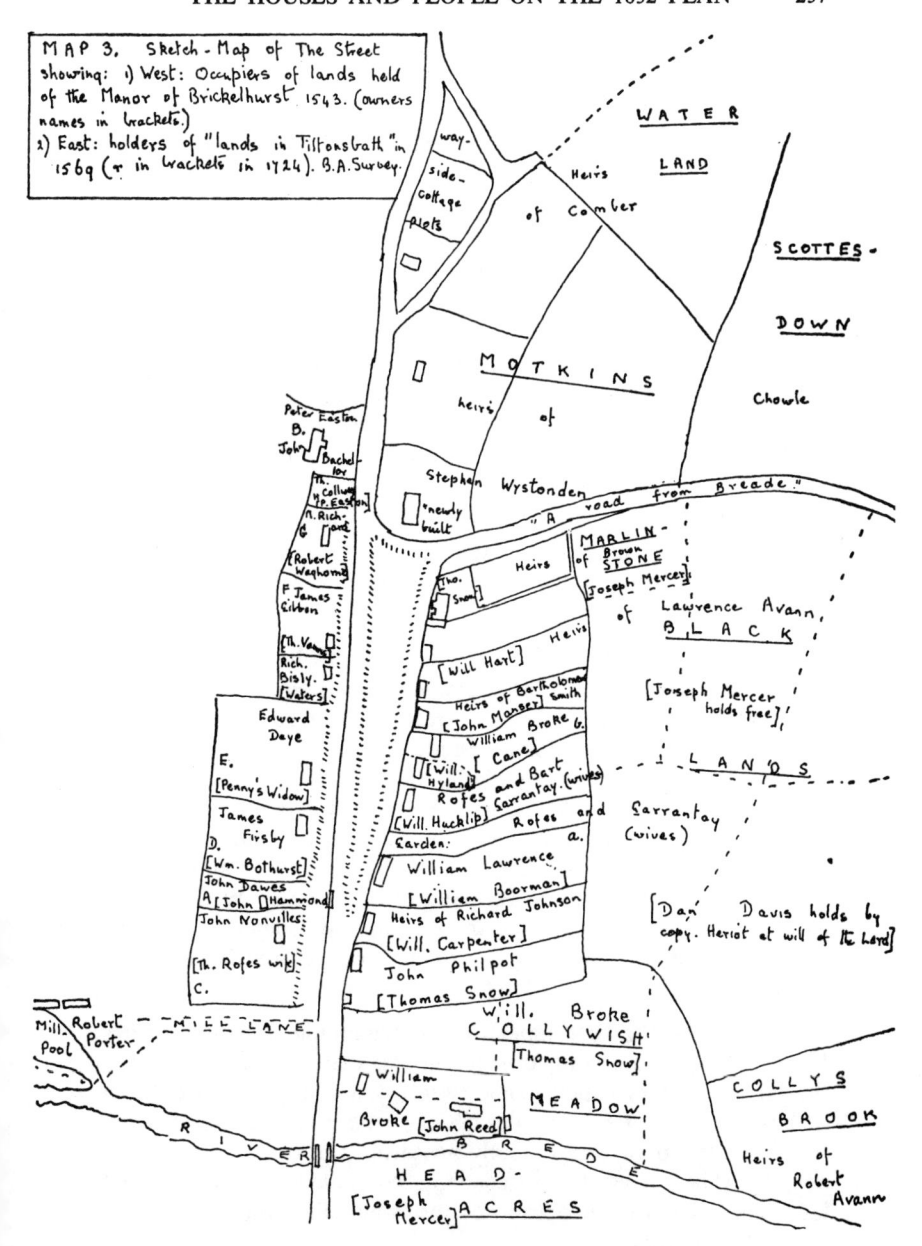

MAP 3. *Sketch Map showing Street houses in sixteenth century.*

In 1700, for the first time, the house and land for which a Henry Barnes paid taxes since at least 1624 until 1723 is named. "Hurst and Blacklands." It is feasible that Hurst could have been Gilds, for it is very surprising that Hurst, which we know to have been in existence in 1632, is not mentioned on the Plan. After 1723, there are no more records of a Barnes at Hurst or anywhere else. In 1726 it was Jasper Diamon paying tax for Hurst. He was churchwarden for that year and is named "Master Diamon."

*Hurst* (Map A)

Hurst, one of the three areas into which Sedlescombe was divided from earliest days, is the name of a lane, a wood and a house, whose lands are carved out of the woodland surrounding it. The Saxon, Ulwin, was dispossessed of it at the time of the Conquest and, most unusually, it was given to another Saxon, Ednod, one of the very few who held land in Sussex at the time of Domesday. It was quite a small property, having one acre of meadow, land for one plough but, strangely, no woodland. Its value, 10/- before the Conquest, remained unchanged.

Its next recorded owner was "Richard Bishop of Hurst and Regge" in 1528. As the Bishop family acquired more and more land in the North of the parish, Hurst became for several hundred years part of their estate of Great Sanders. In 1726 Jasper Diamon, churchwarden, was farming Hurst. In 1731 there was a William Bishop Esq. of Hurst but William Redhead was named as farmer. Five years later William Young was farming its lands until 1765, during which time he was Overseer of the Poor twice and Churchwarden three times. He was followed at the farm by William Cook for about ten years, who was also both Churchwarden and Overseer. In 1775 he moved to Alford, another house of the Bishops, and became Rates Assessor for the parish.

In 1805 for the first time, though remaining Bishop property, Hurst belonged to a younger son and was therefore separated from the Great Sanders Estate. Some twenty years later, George Bishop or his heirs sold it to Hercules Sharpe who was creating an estate for Oaklands park by gradually acquiring farm after farm in the neighbourhood. George's descendants continued to live in the village, until the present decade of the twentieth century, in one of Sackville Cottages.

While part of Oaklands estate Hurst again housed tenant farmers; in 1890 he was Fred Cheesman, but in 1900 it was modernised and let for long periods; in the nineteen-twenties, fashionable house-parties took place at which one of the ladies-in-waiting to Queen Alexandra was a frequent visitor. At the auction in 1924 Hurst Farmhouse was sold privately and in the next years changed hands several times. The Watson family is remembered because he, who was an author, and his wife rode two beautiful white horses (properly termed "grey") and his little daughters white ponies, making a very pleasing sight to meet in the lanes and fields.

The house was then bought, together with many of the Oaklands farms lying on the north side of the river, by Mr. (now Sir John) Keeling, since when it has given its name to an estate of which it was once only part. So the farms have changed very little all through their histories, based first on Great Sanders, then on Oaklands, and now on Hurst.

It is impossible to say when the earliest Hurst House was built. Today it stands, mellow, in the midst of fair gardens, having grown little by little over the years, as the original small farmhouse or cottage was enlarged time and again, on all sides, to become a rambling, comfortable family home.

*Pew* 25 (continued)    "Francis Grant for Leedes House" or "Thomas for Leeds House".

Leedes House no longer exists but a family called Leeds or Lades had a long connection with the parish over 200 years. The first to appear in the records was in the reign of Edward VI when Sir John Leeds of Sedlescombe witnessed in 1547 a Bishop document. At about the same time a John Lede was Rector of Sedlescombe until 1576 and it is difficult not to suppose that this was the same man. In 1624 and 1625 a William Leedes was churchwarden and in 1613 a John Yarrow had married Joan Leedes in Sedlescombe church. In 1671 Sir John Lade and his trustees were concerned with William Darby of Footlands in a mortgage on that estate and by 1726 Mr. Lade owned it. In May 1759 Sir John Lade died leaving his widow, Dame Ann, with child who was born three months after his father's death, becoming another Sir John Lade.

Of Francis Grant who lived in Leedes House nothing is known and no other Grants appear in any records so he could well be identified with Franc Grantham, whose wife, Elizabeth, to whom he had been married for two years, was allotted a seat in Pew 7.

*Pew* 26   Thos. Grantham. Henry Creasey for Swales.[1]

Thomas Grantham was churchwarden at this date but there is no indication of where he lived; perhaps it was at one of the houses in the Street. His signature does not appear on Plan 2.

1708   John Grantham paid rates on a house.
1726   Thomas Grantham was paid 2/- for "writing ye Books".[2]
1728   Thomas Grantham paid rates for "part of Hyland's House"

Mr. Will Hyland appears in the rates records of 1708 and in 1735, Henry Hyland, son of Will Hyland of Sedlescombe, shopkeeper, was apprenticed to Will Allen, shipwright of Rye. If he was a shopkeeper, it seems likely that "Hyland's House" would have been in the Street.

*Henry Creasey* was a farmer, his lands lying at the north of the parish, between those of Footlands and Bellatkins. The old farmhouse in which he lived still stands at the mouth of Poppinghole Lane at the crossroads of Swales Green, looking across the deep little valley to the Ewhurst woods of Morgay and Badlands.

In the eighteenth century the farm had become divided into Swales Green Farm and Little Swales Farm and the farmhouse of the latter is the farmhouse of Swales Farm today, the land of which has been farmed for very many years by the Hindes family. Henry Creasey's house is now detached from the farm and in other hands.

Swales Farm used to be, like so many other Sedlescombe farms, held of the Manor of Battell; in the eighteenth century in turn by Robert Mercer, and then William Grace followed by his son, Henry; and in the nineteenth century by Richard Mercer, senior, styled in his will of 1814, "of Swales Green, Gent", followed by Richard Mercer, junior, "of Swailes Green in Sedlescombe, farmer". By 1846 Swales had become, together with all the surrounding farms, part of the Vinehall Estate of Tilden Smith and later of Richard Smith who went bankrupt (see Pew 25). The Eldridge family who had farmed it since 1792 continued to do so.

By 1900 George Oliver had moved from Strawberry Hill farm to Swales and his grandchildren, Cecil and Ivy, remember being driven every Christmas in one of Charlie Thomas' broughams to spend the

[1] Map A.
[2] Churchwardens A/C. E.S.R.O.

day there. Hops were grown on the farm and when in September at the Bakery the children heard a beautiful jingle of bells they would rush out to watch their grandfather's horses tossing their heads with the great bells fixed well above their ears. They were on their way to Hastings station to pick up the Londoners for the hop-picking.

Following the Olivers, the Hindes moved into Swales farming Footlands too. After the war, the farmhouse was sold independently of the land and the Hindes continued to farm from Little Swales, and so it is today.

Little is known of the Creaseys though nearly a hundred years after the date of the Plan a Thomas Creasey was still farming in Sedlescombe.

*Pew* 27    Gunns.[1] Richard Yeoman's House: Thomas Dawes: Jo Stonham.

The house called Gunns does not appear in the Church copy of the Sittings Plan. As there certainly was a house of this name in Sedlescombe, it may be that by the time the Church copy was traced in 1934 the word may have become obliterated. Only the name "George Yeoman his house" appears on that Plan.

Was Richard Yeoman the owner or occupier? The only other mention of his name occurs in the Churchwardens' Accounts 1624: "Paied Rich. yeomans for paveinge part of the Church and for a bushell of Lime 2.6d."

Gunns is identified with the twin cottages lying on the roadside between Durhamford and Spilsteds farmhouse in Stream lane and, like Spilsteds, it was copyhold of Battle Abbey. They were built in the fifteenth century as a large but very plain Hall-house with a two-bay hall and a bay on either side. The usual floor and chimney were later inserted and in the eighteenth century the whole was re-roofed to a much lower pitch which gave the house a less fine appearance. In the nineteenth century it was extended on the east, given a second chimney and split into two cottages.[2]

In the fourteenth century, John Gunne, whose family had held of Battle Abbey a leuga service tenement since at least 1200, was, with Robert Hamond, one of the three largest holders of Marley demesne

[1] Map 2.
[2] R.O.H.A.S.

land. In 1367 he took up 3 demesne holdings with a total rent of £1 15s. 2d., and at his death in 1383 he held of the Abbot 42 acres of demesne lands of Wickham for 28s. 8d. He had meanwhile sold lands, dowered his daughter, Florence, who married Robert Hamond, and left his son, John, his demesne lands as well as a messuage and lands at Derhamford, that is Spilstead Cottages or Gunns. A heriot of one ox was paid at his death. Florence and Robert Hamond had one son, Simon, who became the father of John Hamond, the last Abbot of Battle Abbey, who died in 1546.[1]

By 1569 "John Bishop doth hold by copy one tenement and a barn in the parish of Sedlescombe . . . with a garden containing ½ acre called Gounes, lying on the backside of the same house, and pays yearly . . . 2d. and gives a heriot."[2]

At some period the Churchwardens and Overseers of the Poor in Sedlescombe became responsible for it, buying it perhaps from the Bishops, because the cottages were for a time the village Poorhouse. According to Sir John it was the earliest of these in the village. He must have had some evidence of this which I have not discovered.

In 1751 and 1752 Jonathan Star was paying tax "for Guns". He and his wife figure several times in the Churchwardens' Accounts:

"Hospital for Jo star"; "1718 doctor for curing Starr's wife";
"Goodman Star in his wife's sickness;"
"Goodman Star 4 weeks @ 1/6";
"Goodman Star 3 and 20 weeks at 5/6."

In the early years of the nineteenth century the cottages seem to have become the property of Walter Mason of Hellingly, for in March 1810 he sold them for £200 to Henry Freeland of Sedlescombe, who was admitted three months later by the Manor of Battell on payment of a fine of five guineas. In March 1839 it was sold by the Battle Board of Guardians to Richard Smith for £200 and James Freeland was to surrender the copyhold right to the Manor. The occupants at the date were James Harvey and Beney. The property is called "a tenement in two dwellings with a pig pound and also ¾ acre of garden and orchard ground".

The entry into the picture of the Battle Board of Guardians is evidence of use as a Poorhouse for they were the successors to the Churchwardens and Overseers in responsibility for the Poor, and

[1] Searle.
[2] B.A.S. 1569.

the Workhouse was by this time at Battle. Had the cottages for years been the property of the Churchwardens and Overseers? How did poor James Freeland fare in the transaction which seems somewhat confused?

In the auction of Spilsteds Farm 18 years later, the two cottages were named Stream House and became part of the property of John Pratt, the Rector.

On the north side of the churchyard a gravestone records that Edward Honeystreet was

"born at Sedlescombe Stream 1787 and died there in 1867." (Chapter 51.) Is this to be identified with Stream House, once the Poorhouse?

Ever since the two cottages have housed workers on the Spilsteds Farm.

*Thomas Dawes.* See Pew 31.

*Pew* 28   Jo Stonham for Killingham's House and Weston's.

The Pew for this house was right at the back of the church in the gallery beside the large pew set aside "for youths and strangers". In one of the two plans it is connected with the name of Jo Stonham. All we know of him is that in 1611 John Stoneham married Triphena Potter in Sedlescombe church.

Killingham's or Killigan's Wood still climbs the hill slope across the valley from the church, some of its trees hedging Hurst Lane, but Killingham's House has long since disappeared. The first mention of the name is in 1528 in a will made by John Browne, in which he left to his son, Richard, "the land called Bartlets and Killingham in Selliscombe". Bartletts Wood is close beside Killinghams and also borders part of Hurst Lane. Together with a copse called Row Shaw they surround Row field, beside which was the Brick Kiln in the eighteenth and nineteenth centuries (Chapter 34.)

Killingham's House figures in the Evendon Accounts (Pew 1), which show that in 1622 it and its 10 acres were leased by Walter Evenden to Edmund Grigg for 13 years. Yet 10 years later it is coupled with the name of Jo Stonham. In 1661 Walter Everndon was paying Tithes for it. In 1713 David Selmes was paying tax for it and sixteen years later, when he was perhaps getting too old for work or was sick, the Churchwardens' Accounts show "Discount for David Selmes' tax 9d." Later in the same year tax was paid for "late David Selmes viz Kidingham", showing the old man to have died or gone to the Poorhouse. The last mention of the house in the records is in 1750 "Edward Alexander for Chittenden".

The site of the house is thought to have been in front of the brick kilns where Littlehurst now stands. The Tithe Map 1841 shows that the earlier house stood parallel with the lane, not at right-angles as it was re-built by Hercules Brabazon in the late nineteenth century. The present outbuildings are of an older date. In 1841 the Brick Kiln, owned by Mary Woodward of Castlemans, was being worked by Spencer Crisford and the house was two cottages occupied by several of his workmen [and known as Brickyard Cottages].

It is probable that, like so many other local names, Killingham preserves for ever that of some long dead, long forgotten family. The trees of its wood, mainly birches and oaks, are today of no great age, nearly all the old ones having been felled during World War I. In the earliest days of spring, its floor is of wind-flowers, pure white, blush pink and some few plum-coloured. Before these are blown they are hidden by a deep mist of bluebells which floods the whole wood down to Strawberry Field in the valley, where the primroses grow thickly among great cushions of vivid moss. In June the air is full of bird song, particularly of the warblers, including the blackcap and nightingale.

Weston's house was at the time empty, Weston having died and his widow moved to a cottage. There is no mention of "hairs" and there is nothing to identify the house which may well later on have taken the name of another occupier. In the nineteenth century there were many members of a Weston family who were farmers in the village.

*Pews* 29 *and* 30    These two seats for Sir Thomas Sackville's House called Hancox.

*Pew* 31    John Darby (Chapter 10): Durhamford: Thos. Dawes for late Carters (Chapter 14).

*Durhamford*   (Map 2.)

This lovely cross-winged house, with its beautiful black and white exterior of closely set timber-framing was built all at one date by one of the Bishop family early in the sixteenth century though its name is a great deal older, coming from the words "deorr", meaning a deer, and "hamm" a water meadow. No doubt the ford at the water-meadow of the deer, known as early as 1296, was where the little bridge now is, and when the house was built beside it it was natural to call it by the familiar name. It was not a hall-place and has no crown-part; but was one of the first houses in Sedlescombe to be built with an original chimney, possibly the present central stack which is built of old thin bricks with a wide fireplace under.[1]

In 1611 Mr. William Bishop paid tax "for the Tan house where he dwelleth, 30 acres,[2] this was Durhamford; but in 1632 Thomas Pooke, described as yeoman, was living in the house. We know nothing of him, but in the Church Register nine years later a Francis Pooke is recorded as having married Abigail Craddock at Whatlington Church, so one can conclude she was a Whatlington girl, and perhaps Francis was Thomas's son.

Over a hundred years later, it still belonged to the Bishops of Great Sanders, and was still occupied by the tanner, who was Simon Watson. The land, consisting of about 35 acres, was farmed. Described as "all that messuage and tenement with backside garden, orchard, barn, close and several pieces or parcels of land, meadow and pasture", it was known by the name of "Durhamford alias Tanhouse". Thomas Colbran, schoolmaster of Sedlescombe, drew a map of "the lands called the Tanhouse Farm, situate in Sedlescombe in Sussex, being part of the Estate of Wm. Bishop Esq. Made in 1759 by me Thomas Colbran."[3] This map,[4] drawn when he was 22, is one of the earliest made by him for local landowners. It shows Durhamford house and homestall, the house plot, garden, orchard, the closes and the yard, but there is no sign of the tannery. The land (area "rough and plain 58 ac. 3 r. 23p., plain only 38 ac. 2 r. 0.5p.") included Combe Wood on the north and was bordered on the west by the Rusty brook which flows south under the road.

By 1803 Richard Eldridge, the Tanner, who had followed Simon Watson, had died and in 1815 it was again Durhamford Farm, but by 1856 when the Rector, the Rev. John Pratt, bought it from John Bishop, it was known as Stream Farm, and in a book by Galsworthy Davie, published in 1900, called *Cottages in Kent and Sussex* there is a picture of it. In the Tithe Map of 1841 John Pratt is listed as the occupier as well as the owner, but during this time it housed

[1] R.O.H.A.S.
[2] Tax 1611. Frewen MSS 520.
[3] Thorne.
[4] E.S.R.O.

five families, tenants of his. When his daughter, Bessie, married he removed the old linenfold panelling from the Durhamford cottages to beautify the dining-room of her married home at Beech house next to the Rectory; and there it remains to this day.

Durhamford continued to be cottages till just before World War II, when it once again became a single house. It was after it was bought in 1950 by Colonel Swan, who lived there with his wife and three children for nine years, that the word Manor was added grandiosely to its name. It would be pleasant if it could revert again to the simple, unpretentious Durhamford, as of yore.

Set in a hollow beside the Brook, it remains a lovely example of an ancient yeoman's house, built with a natural eye to beauty of proportion and a sense of fitness that seems lost to our own contemporaries.

*Pew* 32   Thomas Avery for Castlemans (see Pew 5); Will Skinner for Bellatones (or Bellatkins); Will Higham for Alford (Chapter 10); William Bishop: Fence for Alford 8 ft.

*Pew* 33   Henry Eider for other Alford: Wm. Clarke for the Mill: George Baker.

This house, with its agreeable name, Bellatkins, defeated all attempts to identify it and the conclusion was that, like Killingham and Leedes House and others named on the Plan, it had ceased to exist. One day, however, during a casual look through Sedlescombe deeds in the Record Office at Lewes, the name Bellatkins stood out from all other words on the page.

"1811.   Tenements called BELLATKINS and Yorkhill in the borough of Streatfield, later called Strawberry Hill and Poppinghole Farms."

Strawberry Hill[1] is an old farmhouse as beautiful as its name standing beside the road in Poppinghole lane. Built in 1500 as a "smoke-bay"—i.e. of one very narrow bay, before chimneys were inbuilt but after the days of the open hall one end of the bay was floored over to give a tiny room upstairs. In 1600 this end was demolished and re-built, a chimney being inserted in the old smoke-bay.[2] A sixteenth-century record tells of "Inkpens and Bellatkins; lands of John Darby called Hogmans divided with lane leading to

[1] Map A.
[2] R.O.H.A.S.

Yorkeshill", so at that date it was part of Footlands whose lands it still adjoins. A 1528 record speaks of "Richard Inkpyns and before him Henry Inkpyns" and so once again, unlikely as it might seem, the curious name of Inkpens farm is derived from that of a local family. On the Ordnance Map of 1813 it was still Inkpin Farm. Why it became Strawberry Hill there is as yet no indication.

William Skinner was living at the farm as early as 1612 and perhaps before that; in 1619 and 1624 he was churchwarden together with John Hollman. In 1632 he was one of those responsible for keeping part of the churchyard fence in repair. By 1653 it was Andrew Skinner who signed his name as churchwarden for the year. Thirty-two years later another Andrew Skinner was born. Eighty-three years later he died and on his gravestone in the churchyard is the inscription:

"In Memory of Andrew Skinner, late of Worthing, Gent.
Who departed this Life 1768 aged 83."

Sixteen years earlier, in a list of occupiers of land in Sedlescombe appears Thomas Leadbetter "for Skinner's Farm"; so, after about a century and a half, the last Andrew Skinner of Bellatkins had left house and farmlands when he was nearly 70 years old to live in his old age at Worthing, perhaps with a son or daughter.

Though Thomas Leadbetter appears at "Skinner's Farm" only in 1756, a John Leadbetter had been farming in the parish at least 20 years earlier on "Leadbetter's land". In 1774 he is listed under "Outdwellers". By the nineteenth century one of the family had become "a pauper" for, in the workhouse accounts of 1806, "Lobbetter and dearing' were paid 7/6 on June 23rd for 4½ days haying for the Rector, John Pratt, and in the same month Leadbetter and Dearing were paid for working for Mrs. Eldridge, the workhouse matron. In September, Hannah Leadbetter "tyed nineteen hundred hops" and was paid 17/-. This was clearly work to which she had been accustomed and one hopes was happy in. No mention is made of how long it took her, but the princely sum earned indicates some good length of time. The following year she was haying for 2 days for Mr. Mercer with "Dearing" when they earned 3/4, and the next year again for Mr. Crisford in the meadows of Beech and Castlemans. In July she "tyde 1 caker and quater of hops at 9d per caker" and thus earned 11/3. Her companion was nearly always Mary Dearing who was as good at tying hops as she was, for Mary earned £1 10s. for "tying 2 acres of hops 12 pockets" at Spilsteds.

After the day of the Skinners was over it seems that John Fuller, M.P., the famous squire of Rosehill at Brightling, held both Strawberry Hill and Poppinghole farms which were still copyhold of Robertsbridge Abbey Estate. In 1834 Sir Peregrine Acland "was admitted to the customary tenancy of Bellatkin" and in 1866 he sold it and the farm called Yorkshill (Poppinghole farm) to W. R. Adamson of Vinehall (later of Great Sanders); the cottage and lands being now called Strawberry Hill. For many years it was farmed by George Oliver, a relative of many families in Sedlescombe (Chapter 34). When he sold it and moved to Swales Green Farmhouse, the new owner, Mr. Holmes "made the house more elaborate and up to date". When the estate was sold in the nineteen-twenties by Lord Ashton of Hyde, it became an independent farm, free for the first time of the copyhold of Robertsbridge Abbey Estate, and has been farmed by the Smith family, father and son.

*Austford Farm* (Chapter 17) or "Alford", known locally also as Horsford, was always part of the Bishop estate of Great Sanders held of Robertsbridge Abbey: the "other Alford" of the Plan (Pew 33) was also some time Bishop property. Two houses of the same name and four men named in connection with them is very confusing. Two of the men, William Bishop and Thomas Dawes, are presumed the owners and William Higham and Henry Eider or Iden the occupiers or tenants.

In the parish copy of the plan, there is no seat allotted to William Higham's wife but Percy Godman's has her in Pew 7 in place of William Lingham's wife; the two names could easily be confused in writing though not in speech. As William Lingham, the Miller, is not mentioned in either Plan it may well be that Higham is the true reading of the name in Pew 7. The earliest record, however, of a Higham marriage is nine years later, when, in 1641, Edmund Higham married Ann Everendon. In 1654 George Daw married Ann Higham and four years later Edward Yorke of Brede married Martha Higham.

The '*other Alford*' for which Henry Eider had a seat in Pew 33, and for which Thomas Dawes of Carters was responsible for 9 foot of the fence, was Austford House, another half mile or more past the farm of that name, across the brook and up the other side of the valley (Chapter 17).

The register of marriages for 1610 shows that Henry Iden married in that year Ellen Elinford; and also William Bishop married

## THE HOUSES AND PEOPLE ON THE 1632 PLAN

Elizabeth Hawes and his brother, John, married their cousin, Mary Bisshoppe. Twenty-nine years later another Henry Iden, in all probability the son of Henry and Ellen, married Mary Jordan. Neither Henry Iden, nor his neighbour at the farm, could write his name; each made 'his mark' among the signatures on the Plan.

It is very surprising to find Thomas Dawes' name "for his Alford 9 ft. of fence", for there is no other record connecting the owner of 'late Carters' in the Street with Alford.

*The Mill* where Will Clarke, following in his father, Robert's, footsteps, lived and worked is not the Watermill at Iltonsbath (Chapter 12) though, like that one, it has now ceased to exist. Will Clarke's mill was a Windmill; and the mound that remains whereon it stood shows it to have been a post mill (Chapter 34). Known as Hancox Mill, it stood for at least two centuries on the high land at the north-westerly corner of the Spilsteds lands where Stream Lane crosses into Riccards lane. Seen from the Brooks it was silhouetted against the sky and the creak of its sails was seldom silent, for on that hill which slopes up from Coneyburrow field there is nearly always a breeze blowing across the valley from the high woods round Battle, or from the water meadows by the Brooks when the wind is from the south.

Will Clarke and the millers before and after him ground the corn for the farms of Hancox, Spilsteds, Footlands and many another.

In church, Will sat in a pew on a level with Mrs. Farnden and her children. Some three pews behind him sat his wife, Anna, with the wives of two other men. She was probably a washer woman, for the Churchwardens' Accounts for 1625 show that she was paid 1/6 for washing the Rector's surplice—obviously a series of washings, not just one. A shrew of a woman she seems to have been for at the Archdeacon's Court at Lewes a few years later she was accused (Chapter 13) of living 'contentiously and maliciously' with her neighbours. She must have been sometimes a painful embarrassment to Will. By 1648 Will of the Mill had died and Anna was a widow.

In 1708 John and Thomas Clarke were living in Sedlescombe; John "on Mr. Bishop's land", so he may well have succeeded as Hancox Miller, for that mill was on Bishop land. In 1841 when the Tithe Map was made, William Bates, farmer of Riccards, was the mill-owner and James Dengate, the miller's man. In 1849 both were still there. Bates owned also Whatlington Mill only a mile away and it was probably there that he lived in the larger and better house, letting the cottage of Hancox Mill to his assistant, James Dengate. In 1873 the Mill was still on the map but today both the windmill and the watermills have gone and we are the losers, for a windmill with its working contract with the wind and the constant movement of its sail has a lively personality which is not merely picturesque. None seem now to remember the date when Hancox Mill was demolished. The cottage on its site bears witness to its memory for it is still named Windmill Cottage.

Perhaps *George Baker*, with others whose names are not attached to any house, lived in one of the Street houses, few of which had any land other than a strip of garden measuring an acre or less. In 1624 Jo, George and Stephen Baker were all paying cess. Jo was one of those who had been fined three years earlier for "being absent from Church on the Sabbath Day". He was married in 1619 to Elizabeth Alyfe. In 1640-1641 George Baker, M.A., was Rector of Sedlescombe. Since the George Baker of Pew 33 could not write his name but made his mark, this could hardly have been the same man. The name Baker remained for many years in Sedlescombe (see Magpie Cottage, Chapter 34) but it is not, of course, a very distinctive name. A cottage named Bakers figures in Sackville and Bishop properties.

*Pew* 34   Mrs. Everndon and her children.

Mrs. Everndon (see Pew 1) had been Mary White of Brickwall, Northiam, whose brother, William, had married the sister of Thomas Sackville of Hancox. Mary's children in the pew with her were Walter and Elizabeth.

*Pew* 35   The Wife of Henry Frensham; the Wife of Andrew Skinner; the Wife of Robert Jarvis; "Widdow" Gibbons.

Although the Frenshams had already lived for over 70 years (Pew 25) in the parish, the name of Henry's wife is unknown.

There is no record of the marriage of *Andrew Skinner* of Bellatkins so he may well have married a girl from one of the neighbouring parishes.

Godman has the name Robert Paris instead of Jarvis and his 'mark' also appears but nothing is known of him. Robert Rens of late Brigden's house could well be a mis-spelling for Robert Paris. The husband of "Widdow" Gibbons had been Allen Gibbons, churchwarden in 1624 with John Everndon, and had paid in that year 6d. cess. Their sons were adult in 1632 for they were allotted seats of their own in Pew 42.

*Pew* 36   Wife of Wm. Clarke (see Pew 33); Wife of Thomas Hucksted (see Pew 38); Wife of Richard Embury (see Pew 6); Wife of John Athrone (see Pew 38).

The wife of Wm. Clarke was Anna, the termagant wife of the Hancox Miller.

Thomas Hucksted's wife was Elizabeth and her maiden name Laurence and she was married to Thomas in 1617.

Margery Lewis had been married to Richard Elmbury in Sedlescombe church in 1609.

Nothing is known of the wife of John Athrone (or Athroll, see Pew 38).

*Pew* 37   The Wife of Moses Tyshurst (see Pew 39); the Widow Gutsal; the Widow Hunt; Widow Weston.

Nothing is known of the wife of Moses Tyshurst. Mr. Goodsale had been one of those fined for non-attendance at church one Sunday in 1629. The following year he was paying cess. Sometime during the next eight years he had died and, from the fact that Anna Clarke four years later was shouting "Beggar's Bratt" at their daughter, Elizabeth, it would look as though their circumstances had not been easy since, though there is no record of her having parish relief. The Widow Hunt had adult sons who sat in Pew 39. Her name was Abigail and she signed the plan with her 'mark'.

Widow Weston's name was Susan and she also signed her 'mark'. These were the only two women whose signatures appear on the Plan. When her husband was alive they had presumably lived at "Weston's House" named for Pew 28, where her sons were entitled to sit.

*Pew* 38   *Gallery*   Robert Rens for late Brigden's House; Giles Summers for Middlesborough; Thos. Hucksted for Marlings Town; Jn. Athrole for late Johnson's House.

Widow Brigden in 1624 paid 1/4 cess. In 1607 John Brigden, aged 60 years or thereabouts, had applied for a marriage licence to marry Agnes Holliman of Brede, widow. Rens may be a misspelling for Paris (Pew 35). No information has been discovered concerning either Giles Summers or his house, Middlesborough.

There were Huckstepps, spelt in many varying ways, in Sedlescombe for at least 120 years. Where was their house? "The lands called Marlynstone" (Map 3) are recorded close to Iltonsbath (Chapter 14). "It pays . . . 18d. and gives heriot and the heirs shall make a fine at the will of the lord";[1] "A close of pasture" held by copy "containing by estimation one acre, called Marlynstone" lay close to Blacklands.[1] Marlingstown and Marlynstone look fairly similar; spoken they are identical. In the same survey William Huckstepe has lands called the Wick, "holden of the late College of Hastings" (suppressed with the monasteries some thirty years earlier). He held also by copy a meadow in Whatlington called Waller's Wish, 2 acres and 3 roods.

In 1624 Thomas Huckstepp paid cess and his signature is on the Plan. In 1708 both John and William Huckstepp owned houses in Sedlescombe and later both were churchwardens, John in 1713 and Will 2 years later. Will was a shoemaker for in 1726 the Churchwardens' Accounts show items "pd for ½ a back for shoemaker Huckstepp", bought no doubt from the Tannery at Iltonsbath, "B. Huckstepp's Bill 3/3" and in 1730 "for signing Huckstepps certicate 2/-." In 1734 and 1735 W. Huckstepp senior was churchwarden and again in 1738. Three years later his grandson, Thomas, was apprentioctree for seven years to the butcher of Wadhurst, Thomas Vigor.

In 1617 Thomas Huckstep had married Elizabeth Lawrence.
In 1657 John Hucksteppe married Anne Oxenbridge.
In 1687 John Huckstep married Elizabeth Hider.
In 1701 William Huckstep married Mary Sheather.

*Jo. Athroll* in 1624 paid cess 4d. and on the 1632 Plan he signed his name.

*Pew* 39   Nicholas Goodman for late Batchellor's House; The hairs of Allen Gibons (see Pew 35); The hairs of Widow Hunt (see Pew 37); Moses Tyshurst for ye House late Brigden's (see Pew 38).

In 1609 Nicholas married Agnes Russell and in 1624 he was paying 2/4 cess, a largish amount. Of anybody named Batchellor or of a house of that name there is no trace.

This is the second mention of "Late Brigden's". Four years after old John Brigden married a widow from Brede, another John Brigden "of Brede", his son perhaps, married Martha Freeman or

[1] B.A.S. 1569

# THE HOUSES AND PEOPLE ON THE 1632 PLAN

Fryman in Sedlescombe Church. In 1624 Agnes Brigden was a widow again. There is no hint as to where Brigden's was.

Although Moses Tyshurst's wife had a seat in Pew 37, he himself figures only in Percy Godman's copy. In the parish records his name appears once in 1623 in a list of "Outdwellers" as paying 8d. cess. In 1664 a John Tyshurst married Mary Huckstepp.

*Pew* 40 John Sheather for late Week's House; Thos. Solden; Robert Jaques; John Cox. *Pews* 41 *and* 42 Empty.

There is no record of any "Weeks" who could have left his name to this house nor is there any clue to its site. In 1723 John Sheather was listed under "Outdwellers" by the Overseers of the Poor, as having paid 2/- cess, a larger sum than that paid by any other of the six outdwellers, including Andrew Sackville, Gent, who paid 1/8. The other five paid less than 1/- each, among them Laurence Chaderton, "Parson of Whatlington", who paid 9d. There seems no other record of John Sheather or his family, though the name has only very recently died out of the village.

Thomas Solden is listed in 1624 as having paid 4d. cess. He may well have occupied one of the Street Houses but he appears in no more records.

Jaques may be a misspelling for Robert Jasper, whose wife had a seat in Pew 10, and whose 'mark' appears on Percy Godman's copy of the Plan in the list of signatures. Nothing is recorded of John Cox.

So here are the names of some seventy people who attended church every Sunday together with those, unnamed, who lived in the Street. Of the personal lives, even of those about whom most is recorded, little can be told; yet to learn even so much concerning them and the houses they lived in those long years ago, is an unusual treasure for a village to have of its history. To know of these people, dead 350 years, who lived in the same houses in which we ourselves live today, is to keep them alive. The Darbys of Footlands and the Dawes of Carters who gave two of the church bells; the Everndons, the Farndens, the Bishops, the Skinners, Creasies and Avories and all the others lived among the same beams, bricks and hearth-places as we do. They, too, in spring-time brought in primroses from among the damp ferns, bluebells from Killigan woods, wild roses and honeysuckle from the hedges and meadowsweet from the river banks to brighten and scent the same rooms. They, too, lived through troublous times, when nothing seemed secure. Through it all they made love, gave birth, worked and grew tired, suffered agonies of pain, laughed and cried, were kind or crafty, lazy or industrious, generous or mean, ill-tempered or sweet, in just the same measures and mixtures as we are. They, whom we envy sometimes for what seems to us the security of their days, would most certainly envy us; at least for our freedom from so much sickness and premature death, and from the poor-house, and surely too for our leisure; for the easy water in our taps and for the warmth and comfort of those same houses.

They died and were buried close to each other in the churchyard, and were gradually forgotten; and others followed them in ownership of their houses or land, as can be read in these chapters; family after family came and went until at last we came and we, too, will go. Some, even though few, of our sons and daughters will, like them, carry on a family name for varying lengths of years. The houses on the 1632 Plan which still stand have nearly all been restored, refurbished and modernised. Far into the twenty-first century they will stand, may we hope, cherished and lived in by many more generations of families adding to the long history of the village.

*Chapter Twenty-Four*

## THE CIVIL WAR

When inexorably the long-threatened Civil War at last broke out, the east part of Sussex saw no fighting at all on its lands, a great part of which were still covered with forests. The deeply rutted roads were so appallingly muddy that they were often impassable for many months in the year, a fact which would have made military operations impossible. So when it was proposed to demolish certain of the great Sussex houses whose families were known to be Royalist in sympathy, Parliament declined on the grounds that their being situated in the difficult environs of Sussex would be the best defence against their offensive use.

The dividing line between Royalist and Puritan sympathy was certainly not a social one. The gentry of the county were fairly equally divided between the two causes, the majority of the yeoman and townsfolk were for Parliament. Sussex had become very Puritan, a proof perhaps of the truth of the saying, "The blood of the martyrs is the seed of the Church", for its people had suffered a very heavy toll of victims under the persecutions of Queen Mary's reign. Thirty-three men and women were burnt at the stake, an eighth of the total number in the whole of England. This is evidence that Puritanism was already very strong in the county, but the burnings at Lewes were perhaps calculated to encourage rather than diminish militant protestantism in the hard heads of the stubbornly independent Anglo-Saxons. The slackness and inefficiency of some of the clergy played into the hands of the Puritans.

There were at the time 27 furnaces in Sussex, at most of which guns and shot were being made; and 42 forges or iron-mills. Together these, with all the subsidiary employments involved, gave work, it is said, to at least fifty thousand men. Practically all these iron-works were in the hands of Parliament, including the Sackville Furnace off Brede Lane, which, as well as the Kentish one at Horsmonden, was still in the management of John Browne, who had in happier days been the King's gunfounder. The loss to the Royalist cause of all these ordnance factories must have been dire. There are many references to John Browne in records concerning Sedlescombe the first being in the probate of a will (1528) of John Browne giving "direction for burial in the churchyard of Sellescombe Parish Church", etc. (Chapter 2), leaving legacies to his wife Margaret, his son William with his children, and his son Thomas who also inherited land "called Combe and Beche in Selliscombe and Whatlington". His son Richard inherited land called Bertlots and Kyllingham in Selliscombe and also lands called Hormans in Whatlington; (all these names are still on the Ordnance map). In 1584 John Browne with his son, also John Browne, was plaintiff in a successful action against John Asheburneham esq. concerning the Manor of Beche and tenements in Sedlescombe. It is curious that the will of 1528 mentions no son "John". In 1630 a John Browne, minister, buried Mary Farnden, Peter's first wife. Were the family name involved Wildegoose or even Bishop, It would be fair to assume the connection but with a name like Browne—though it is consistently spelt with an E which is odd at a time when the spelling of names varied almost on each writing—the relationship can be suspected but not taken for granted.

The Sackvilles and Bishops were, at least partly, of Royalist sympathies. Certainly one Bishop and one Sackville figured on the list of "active Cavaliers" in Sussex though the Bishops suffered no confiscation of their land in Sedlescombe. After his brother, John, died in 1645, Col. Thomas Sackville had had to appear before the Sequestration Committee and pay a fine before he could inherit the Hancox estates (Chapter 17). His neighbour, John Everendon of Beech, was a member of this committee, as also was Peter Farnden's son-in-law, John Baker of Mayfield, Ruth Farnden's husband.

After the war was over, during the Commonwealth, one of the Bishops was involved in a plot against the life of Cromwell which the father-in-law of Peter Farnden's daughter, Mary, was invited to join. Most of Peter's daughters had married pronounced Parliamentarians; Sarah's husband, Walter Dobell, was Captain of a Trained Band in the Rape of Hastings, and Joan was the wife of a Puritan Member of the Long Parliament, Samuel Gott (Chapter 17).

Whatever their sympathies the three furnace-owning families in Sedlescombe must have been prospering financially through the war. John Browne was very busy making guns and ammunition for both army and fleet. In 1645 provision was made for him to supply for next summer's fleet the following iron ordnance and shot: [1]

| | |
|---|---|
| 16 demo-culverin and sakers | £428 15 0 |
| 20 sakers and 4 demi-culverin cuts | 416 0 0 |
| 10 minion cuts | 115 10 0 |
| Round shot for several pieces of ordinance | 1,392 17 2 |
| Bars of Iron | 29 17 0 |
| Hand grenades for demi-culverins and sakers | 125 0 0 |

He too seems to have been suspected of plotting for the King, for "in June a letter from Thomas Walsingham of Kent to Lord Digby fell into the hands of Parliament. Walsingham strongly urged a Royal advance into Sussex and Kent. 'Be assured of the people there, especially Mr. Browne, the King's gunfounder, who makes all the cannon and bullet for Parliament's service. My advice is that H.M. march thither with 41,000 horse and foot, and 10 days before to send intelligence to Mr. Browne, so that he may come from London into Kent where his works are, and against the King's coming he will provide cannon and bullet so that his Majesty need not bring any with him. The rebels have no guns or bullets but for him, and that from hand to mouth there being none in the Tower, which he is forced to provide . . .' ".[1]

This would seem to need some powers of explanation on John Browne's part, when

"The House ordered the examination of Mr. Browne and his son before a committee. John Browne senior said he dwelt in Martin's Lane by Old Swan and had recently come out of Kent. He knew none of Walsingham save Sir Thomas and did not know he had a son. He denied all. John Browne junior knew none of the Walsinghams. He lived at Horsmonden where his father had three furnaces for casting culverin, etc., and all kinds of round shot. His father by letter gave directions every week what should be cast. A former workman of Browne said he sent in 1643 to the King 4 men to cast ordnance and a servant was called to testify that John Browne was with the King when he went to the Houses of Parliament to arrest the five members."[1]

---

[1] Stanford.

John Browne seems to have cleared himself for, later, Commissioners of the Navy "peruse proposals made by John Browne senior, gunfounder, for furnishing ordnance for 3 frigates intended to be built, confer with him and report on prices he asked or what others should be given". No doubt John Browne was indispensable to Parliament. No doubt also he was carefully watched. From the fact that Charles II appointed his family once again to be his gunfounders on his Restoration one would suspect that John Browne had helped the Royal family surreptitiously when he could, or maybe he was just an indispensable gunfounder.

The iron furnaces and their subsidiary trades were flourishing, but this was all. The war was draining the country of both ablebodied men and riches. Taxes levied on practically all goods, including food, pressed heavily upon everybody. Plundering troops added to the poverty and dissatisfaction. The King, who had through the long years of strife exasperated even his own followers, became on January 30th, 1648, at one fell swoop a national hero or a martyr. The world outside also was horrified and stupefied at the execution of a king whom even his worst enemies would agree was a good man. Life under the Commonwealth for all but fanatical Puritans was colourless and dull at a time when labour was heavy and exhausting; for the people were now deprived of all their natural amusements, cock-fighting and merrymaking; dancing and fairs at spring, mid-summer, harvest and saints' days. Holy days were no longer holidays, but serious and forbidding and full of prohibitions.

The Royalists though crushed were not idle. A thriving business grew up in Hastings and Rye and other sea-port towns in the smuggling of passengers and letters secretly to and from the Continent.

Race meetings, though not altogether prohibited, were frequently forbidden because they were said to give a cloak to meetings of seditious Cavaliers. Certain it is that in 1658 John Stapley, George Hutchinson of Cuckfield, and Captain Henry Mallory met at Hangleton Races and discussed the details of a plot in which Stapley and his brother Antony, who lived at Lewes, were involved. John Stapley seemed a valuable recruit to the Royalist cause for he was an influential and moderate man whom, it was thought, many would follow who would not normally follow the Cavaliers, for he came of a well-known Puritan family. He sounded out others of his friends, besides his brother; Captain Henry Mallory was offered a commission. Stapley said he had 200 arms and had kept 14 horses in his stable all winter. It was at Hangleton Races that he reported to his comrades that he had been in London and had seen Cromwell "who had given him a severe look at first, but they parted on good terms". Spies learnt of the plot and sent a list of "active cavaliers" in Sussex including the names of Mr. Mallory, Mr. Bishop and Mr. Sackville. John Stapley was summoned about the end of March to attend Cromwell at Whitehall. At first he denied all knowledge of the plot but, finding how much was known, broke down and confessed all, telling details of the plot and the names of all his associates. Anthony also turned informer and bore witness against his own brother. Numerous arrests were made, but the remaining conspirators still planned a rising in the city of London. Active among them was "an ancient man in grey clothes" who was Guy Carleton, ex-Fellow of Queen's College, Oxford; and his son, Henry Carleton of Guyson's, Fairlight, a Captain of Horse in the Parliamentary Army and one of the Sequestrators for the County of Sussex. The rising, fixed for May 15th, was abortive.[1]

The chief witnesses at the trial of John Mordaunt, son of the Earl of Peterborough, who had control of the Surrey branch of the plot, were John Stapley and Henry Mallory. The latter escaped the night before the trial (proving himself thereby a more honourable friend that many of his fellow plotters). Mordaunt was therefore acquitted on insufficient evidence. Mallory was recaptured on June 5th and condemned to death but was reprieved and imprisoned. The Stapley brothers were pardoned, partly for the value of their information and partly out of respect for the memory of their father, Colonel Anthony Stapley of Framfield, an aggressively Puritan Parliamentarian.

William Dyke, father-in-law and uncle-in-law, respectively to Peter Farnden's daughters, Mary and Elizabeth, and rector of Frant, was questioned about the plot, and

"deposed that towards the end of March . . . he walked with Capt. Anthony Stapley, who told him there was a design for Charles Stuart coming to England, and proposed to him that he should be of his party. Dyke replied that he did not believe he could come in . . . About a fortnight later, Stapley came to his home at Frant

Stanford.

and stayed a few days. He said the landing would shortly take place and asked what horses and arms Dyke had. Dyke replied, 2 geldings and no arms."[1]

There is some evidence that Henry Mallory had property in Sedlescombe, for in 1662 the following case is recorded "Henry Mallory Esq.—Richard Chatsworth L.L.D. plaintiffs: and Henry English Esq. and Lucy his wife deforciants. The Manor of Montfield and tenements in . . . and Whatlington and Sedlescombe, quitclaim".[2] The plaintiffs and heirs of Henry Mallory won their case. As described in Chapter 17 a later Bishop of Great Sanders gave his eldest son the names, Henry Mallory, in baptism.

The Royalist plot had failed but there were, thus exposed, signs of trouble in the Parliamentarians' own ranks. Two years later the bells of all the villages were ringing out with joy of the Restoration. At Hastings the Corporation's accounts record "payments to the Musketeers on the Proclamation of the King £1.0.9d. Moreupon them in white wine the same day, 10s. For half a barrel of beer and bread to the ringers 5s.2d. More to the ringers upon the Thanksgiving Day 2s.".

The institution of an Order of the Royal Oak to commemorate Charles' escape after Worcester, was contemplated but never carried out.[3] The knights, six hundred and seventeen in all, were to wear a silver medal with a device of the King in the oak at Boscobel. The scheme was laid aside as likely to revive animosities. Among the nine Sussex men, intended to be made knights, were Walter Dobell (Sarah Farnden's husband, whose estate was valued at £1,000). This is very surprising since he was a Captain of a Trained Band in the Rape of Hastings and presumably a Roundhead. The Inn at Whatlington, a few hundred yards away from the Sackville's house Hancox, bears perhaps tellingly the sign "The Royal Oak".

John Evelyn records in his diary on June 30th. "The Sussex gentlemen presented their address, to which my hand was put. I went with it and kissed his Majesty's hand, who was pleased to own me more particularly by calling me his old acquaintance and speaking very graciously to me."

---

[1] Stanford.
[2] F. of F. Dunkin.
[3] S.A.C. 5.

*Chapter Twenty-five*

SMUGGLING: A SUSSEX INDUSTRY

The subject of smuggling seems to be of perennial interest, sympathy going almost invariably to the smugglers. In nearly all tales they are the heroes and excisemen the villains.

In Sussex practically everyone was involved in it; landowners as well as tradesmen and labourers; magistrates and clergy too (though not necessarily active) were frequently in sympathy. The trade was highly organised and hide-outs numerous and varied. Even if caught, smugglers were very infrequently convicted, and escape was often connived at. Many followed in the day-time law-abiding and respected trades.

The smugglers of Kent and Sussex—known as "owlers" since they operated at night, and also as "free-traders"—were more numerous and more formidable than anywhere else in the country, owing to the narrowness of the Channel and the close proximity of France. The Sussex coast was more ideal even than that of Kent because, with the few extra miles width of the Channel, there was an invaluable stretch of water which was invisible from either side.

Organised smuggling is said to have started in England in Edward III's reign when he tried to prevent the export of wool; for wherever there are import or export duties on commodities there is likely to be smuggling either in or out of the country. At that time England produced the finest wool in Europe and as Flemish weavers were the best in the world there was a continuous drain of wool from England to the Continent. In order to prevent this and to help the wool trade, the King encouraged Flemish weavers to come to England and practise their craft and teach it to the English people. Furthermore, he not only put a heavy duty on the export of wool, but also only allowed its export, under licence, from certain ports (of which Winchelsea was one). The Sussex "free-traders" defied these laws and sometimes, sure of public sympathy and with a well-organised 'early warning' system, openly brought down the wool-packs on horseback to the seashore and loaded French vessels with them. It was estimated that in the first years of James I's reign though 16,000 sheep were said to have been shorn on the Rye marshes not one ounce of that wool saw the English market, and that in two years in the mid-seventeenth century no less than 40,000 packs were shipped from the coasts of Kent and Sussex to Calais alone.[1]

So once again the Government acted, and the sale of wool within fifteen miles of the coast was prohibited; and later on in 1698 a law, prescribing that everyone must be buried in wool, showed that the position was still very serious. Clergy had to make an affidavit that there was no material other than wool in the coffin. If the affidavit were not made, a fine had to be paid (Chapter 17). In the Parish registers is an entry for 1745: "paid for the Wooll to bury the Woman Inn, that died at Mercer's" (now Jacob's); and in the Whatlington registers in 1710 it is recorded that "Joan Diamond, a traveller" (tramp or gipsy) "was buried on July 2nd, and because not buried in wool, then taken up again and reburied." As related in Chapter 17, Lucy Farnden, widow of Peter Farnden, disdained to be buried in wool and "ye forfeitures were levied according to the Act". In 1680, in order to raise revenue for the Dutch war, an import duty was put on five luxury articles. These were the ones made famous in Kipling's "Smugglers' Song", silk and laces "for the Lady", tea and spirits, and "baccy for the parson".

So smuggling took an even more prosperous turn, the ships that smuggled out the wool brought back a cargo of any or all of these goods. With this, smuggling started to get out of hand. The ordinary life of the countryside, especially at harvest-time, began to be adversely affected. The farm labourer's wage being about 9/- to 12/- a week, he was naturally happy to work at nights for the smugglers' gangs who paid as much as 10/6 a night with a bonus once a quarter of a dollop of tea. It is not surprising that even the poorest cottages had plenty of tea in those days for a dollop was not the thimbleful of one's imagination but was an old Saxon word meaning a stone, or 14 lb. of tea! As a result of the night's

[1] S.A.C.X.

activities, farm labourers' work was less than good and in some places harvests could not be got in, for smuggling was hard work. First, there was the landing of the cargoes, and the possibility of violence with the preventative men; then the carrying of the goods inland to be hidden until they could be put on the market. There are many stories of underground passages to various houses in Sedlescombe; to Homestall, the Manor, the Old Gun Cottage, and between Beech House and the Churchyard. The only authenticated one is that at Beech House leading out of the bottom of the well. Though it is now bricked up and impossible to explore, the steps down the side of the well can still be discovered by a careful eye. This passage may have connected with a vault in the churchyard. Were the respectable families of Everndens and their descendants involved in the trade? Tales of long underground passages are unlikely to be true, but short ones are more than probable. Family vaults inside the church and under gravestones outside were more than likely used as hidingplaces and there is certainly one at the top of a flight of stairs in the Gun Cottage (Chapter 35); the whole floor of the tiny landing lifts up to show a deep place below, probably more suitable for hiding quantities of tobacco or tea but which would also take a few barrels of brandy. A hollow haystack in the field near the cottage is said to have been another local hiding-place. As thieves today change the number plates of cars during their getaway, so the owlers and their assistants changed the tail-boards of carts at every village on their routes inland from the coast. Many a load of hay or mangel-wurzels travelling the road on a farm-cart hid a cargo that would have interested the "preventive" men, and many a barge bringing coal or grain on the tide up the River Brede from Rye brought too a hidden commodity more welcome still to the villages through which it passed. How many of the respected people described in these pages obtained their luxury goods as a matter of natural custom in this method, free of tax? A local tradition says that smuggled gin was stored in the Sackville cottages where the washerwoman lived, whence it was retailed to customers in pennyworths. Warned one day of an immediate inspection by the Custom's men she, with quick inspiration, tipped the barrel of gin into her wash-tub and pretended it was bleach!

In 1721 there was a much greater number of soldiers stationed in Sussex than in any other county; 77 dragoons and 36 soldiers billeted in 43 places in towns and villages inland and along the coast. It is possible that a few of these, billeted in one of the cottages near Sedlescombe Bridge, left it the permanent name, Barracks Cottage.

In this same year the Customs Officers were blithe because they captured Stephenson, a master smuggler of Rochester, who was fined £2,100 for smuggling tea off Hastings. Lacking the money to pay, he was committed to Horsham gaol, from which he was not slow to escape. It was said that setting soldiers to catch smugglers was something like setting elephants to catch eels. However, Lieut. Burnett of General Grove's Regiment, in a Memorial to the Lord of the Treasury, stated that he "had the good fortune to apprehend and take Jacob Walters the chief and most notorious of ye gang of smugglers and brought him to London under guard of twenty men when they designed to have him rescued again . . . and that your memorialist was at great expense in having him and all ye men quartered in one room every night from Battle to London." Lieut. Burnett received, instead of the usual reward of £100, £200 for his successful exertions. Was this Jacob the famous Smuggler Jacob who is said to have given his name to Jacobs Farm? (Chapter 32).

A letter written from Horsham on August 17th, 1749, after describing various social occasions, continues thus, "there was another sight at church not so agreable . . . the six smugglers that are to be executed in a few days; they come to church every time there is a service, their melancholy looks and the clanking of their chains make it so disaggreable that I wonder the people can bear it. For they stand in the middle Isle where it is impossible to avoid looking at them. They say great application has been made to save their Captain but in vain. And indeed I think it would be hard upon the others to suffer, sho'd he escape."[1] These smugglers were members of the notorious Hawkhurst Gang which had terrorised the whole of the counties of Kent and Sussex. Another record says that they were hanged in the respective parishes from which they came and one was hanged at Ninfield. Led by a Kentish man of great violence called Kingsmill, this gang was composed mostly of Sussex men. Notoriously cruel, they stopped at neither torture nor murder of anyone who in any way opposed them or refused to help. This was no longer a life of adventure, people were terrorised and terrified. Sedlescombe was on their route from the coast to Hawkhurst and Cranbrook. Years ago among the great quantity of ancient papers and deeds belonging to Miss "Tottie" Flint, of Ivy Cottage, in Brede Lane, there was a paper, drawn up in the eighteenth

[1] S.C.M. 8, p. 562.

*The Village from Chapel Hill*

*Sedlescombe Church in 1738 from the drawing by S. Gammon* (page 103)

(by kind permission of Neil Farrow)

*The Lennard Fireback (S.A.C. Vol. 46)* (page 139)

*The Old Thatch (with the Smithy, now Brookfield)* (page 118)

(David Martin)

*"Seddlescombe Place"* 1738 *(an old drawing of Hancox)* (page 156)

(by kind permission of Neil Farrow)

*Spilsteds* (page 227)

(David Martin)

*Linenfold Panelling (now in Beach House)* (page 246)
(David Martin)

*Durhamford* (page 246) (David Martin)

*Hercules Brabazon Brabazon by William Rothenstein*, 1893 (page 326)

(by kind permission of the British Museum)

*Gregory's Bakery* (page 365)

(Mrs. Gregory)

*The Interior of Gregory's Bakery* (page 365)

(Mrs. Gregory)

*The Village Green, showing the first garage, and Byner's, the first post office* (page 365)

*The Charcoal Burner: Jim Smith, brother of "Bangy"* (page 438)

(Mrs. Lottie Wilson)

*Charcoal Burning: The Pet* (page 435)     (Mrs. Lottie Wilson)

*The Oast-house at **Luff's** Farm (with hop pockets)* (pages 322 and 434)

(Neil Farrow)

*The Oast-house at Brook Lodge showing men with Scovets* (page 436)
*Jesse Hall (second from left) dug the well on the Green.* (Lewis Knight)

*Hop-picking at Luff's Farm* (page 435) (Neil Farrow)

*Bark Flaying for the Tannery* (pages 180 and 357)

(Lewis Knight)

*The Queens Head* (page 439)

*"Carters": Manor Cottages* (page 119)     (David Martin)

*A detailed view of the front of Manor Cottages* (page 119)     (David Martin)

*Brickwall before the fire* (page 166)

*The Coach and Horses after the fire* (page 442)

century, calling for people of Sedlescombe to join together and support each other against the smugglers. It was signed with four or five names which, alas, meant nothing to me then. Over the years the inhabitants of Sedlescombe would have helped the smugglers and benefitted thereby, but this Hawkhurst gang was quite another matter; and eventually the people of Goudhurst decided to unite themselves and oppose the smugglers by force if necessary. The story of how, led by a young soldier named Sturt, they fought a pitched battle round the church and routed the gang is famous.

At the "Red Lion" at Hooe, can be seen a double space behind some of the bedrooms where smugglers' ropes were unravelled. These consisted of two strands of hemp and one of tobacco, "money for old rope". At the "Lamb Inn" there is also a hiding-place for smuggled tobacco. Little smuggling took place within the actual boundaries of Hastings and Rye because any such activity if discovered would have lost for these towns their prized Cinque Port privileges.

In the days when everyone was on the side of the smugglers, many were the methods used to warn them of presence of the customs men. For this purpose the sails of Windmills (including the ones at Hancox and Staplecross), which were landmarks visible for miles around, were utilised by being turned in a different direction. If a shepherd carried his crook pointing forward, the Customs men were about, but were it facing back over the shepherd's shoulder all was well. All smugglers benefited, too, from the fear of haunted houses, ghosts and witches. When smugglers became too old to take an active part in this hard life they could still be helpful and keep danger at bay by acting the part of a ghost, dressed in a white sheet at night, haunting the houses and churchyards used as hiding-places.

There are no local stories describing the activities of particular smugglers, but there is mention of one called Lowry, said to operate from Hancox, whose deeds were so nefarious that when he came to his end his final resting-place was *outside* the churchyard hedge. Jacob has already been mentioned. There was also Joseph Mercer fined in 1741 for "running uncustomed goods" (Chapter 26).

"I knew an old man," Jim recalled, "who in his younger days worked in the Powder mills as a powder-monkey, and he told many tales of smuggling there. One day the Customs Men called to make a search and as they approached one particular barrel someone suddenly shouted with great presence of mind, 'For God's sake, don't touch that or you'll blow us all up!' The men were so scared they left at the double without searching any further. The barrel was of course full of spirits. There used to be," Jim added, "an underground passage from the Powder mill to Homestall."

Old George Kenward, the bricklayer, would tell how his grandfather had been a smuggler and that there was a well, hidden in gorse bushes up the hill beyond Long Lane, which could tell many a tale of his smuggled contraband.

Smuggling continues, of course, to this day and is perhaps regarded still as something of a sport; but the organised smuggling of human beings or narcotic drugs on to the beaches of Sussex and Kent is quite another story, and one of the most unsavoury of crimes committed today.

*Chapter Twenty-six*

## THE MERCERS OF SEDLESCOMBE

While the Bishop family gradually came to own most of the land in the north of the parish, the Mercers seem to have been the first family to own much of the land in the south of it for more than one generation. Peter Farnden had bought up many local estates in the seventeenth century, but at his death they were divided between his daughters or sold. The Mercer family was large and widely spread in Sussex and beyond, in Kent.

*Joseph and Susannah*
The first to live in Sedlescombe was Joseph who came with his wife, Susannah, and their children in 1700 and bought Brickwall from the Farnden heirs; and the last of their descendants died in the parish 250 years later: Miss Sarah (Tottie) Flint on August 27th, 1951, at the age of 86, in Ivy Cottage, Brede Lane. At the same time that he bought Brickwall, Joseph bought also three nearby farms on either side of the river; Hole Farm (later Oaklands Park), Field Farm (Brede Barn Farm) and White Down (Why Down), in all, 273 acres.

It was an unbaptised child of Joseph and Susannah who was the first Mercer to be buried in the churchyard, on April 27th, six years after they had come to Brickwall; and seven years later its mother followed. Susannah died at Brickwall, according to the Mercer family Bible "of smallpox in 1713 and was buried in a railed grave on the south side of the churchyard", not now identifiable. Other Mercer graves are perhaps the most noticeable in the whole churchyard; massive table-type tombs, they stand on raised ground on the left of the path that leads up to the church door, so that the eyes of those walking into church can hardly miss one of the inscriptions largely cut: "Robert Mercer, Gent."

*The first Robert Mercer and his sons, Joseph and Thomas*

Sir John Thorne saw a number of the family records, one of them being a pamphlet, "Some Members of the Mercer Family", by Sir William Collins, a Baptist, who received most of his information from Miss "Tottie". He writes: "In the late seventeenth century, many of the Mercers . . . became associated with the General Baptist Movement and ardent supporters of that liberal form of dissent from the Anglican Church."[1] He particularly mentions *Robert* (1687-1740) and his sons, *Joseph and Thomas,* as active in the community and marrying wives of the same faith. Robert was one of two elder brothers of the "unbaptised child", buried in 1706 (the lack of baptism is explained by the family adherence to the Baptist faith). The parson, George Barnsley, for a while entered births of the children of dissenters separately; and among these is Robert's brother, "Thomas, the son of Joseph Mercer and Susannah, his wife, born July 7th, 1703" when Robert was 16. Later, the Sedlescombe Mercers, as distinct from those in other parts of Sussex, followed the practice of the Church of England, and the Parish Registers contain many entries of their baptisms and marriages as well as burials.

A year before he died in 1740 at the age of 52, Robert wrote a letter to his eldest son, *Joseph,* then aged about 28, thus:

"To my son, Joseph Mercer . . . I have now lately put a Great Trust into your Care and management when it shall please God to take me out of this difficult world. I have left the execution of my Will to you Joyntly with your Mother in trust and Confidence that my small Estate may be carefully preserved and administered to you joyntly to ye support of yourselves and the Rest of my Dear Children. And therefore I begg of you as the most Earnest and sincere Request of a loving Father, that you always be kind and Dutiful to your Mother; and also kind and just to your Brother and sisters, and in these and all other cases Let it be your greatest Care to Exercise a Conscience void of offence Both to God and man." The letter continues: "And also I most Earnestly desire you to beware of vain and evil Company, & the prevailing love of pleasure, & Pride. For these things will corrupt good manners if they be allowed to prevail and Delighted in . . . You may remember that I have spent much time and pains in the Publick Service of Religion;

---

[1] Transactions of Baptist Historical Society.

and I do assure you that I never found anything so truly satisfying as such labours: Especially when I have most solidly weighed and considered the just and certain ground of that Religion which I have professed; and when I have been most aprehensive of my leaving this World and giving an account of myselfe in the next, this has been my Comfort." He died a few months later and Joseph lived only seven years longer. His brother, Thomas, now a Surgeon of Lewes, provided for the fatherless family.

*Joseph Mercer of Jacobs and Hole Farm*

One of these was yet another Joseph, less than a year old when his father died, who grew up to marry when he was 32, in 1779, a Sedlescombe girl of only fifteen years old called Mary, daughter of William Cook (Churchwarden in 1781) and his wife Ann, and they lived together at Jacobs (Chapter 32). Poor Mary's first baby, like so many another, died in infancy, but she had six other children before she, who was but 25, died of childbirth on October 17th, 1778. On the day of her burial in the earliest of the Mercer tombs still visible, where her first-born had been buried eight years earlier, her last infant was baptised.

"Her virtues" reads the inscription on her gravestone, "need not here be enumerated, having left a lasting impression on the minds of those who knew her and are better known to Him who alone is able to reward her." It brings to remembrance the inscriptions to two other Sedlescombe Marys: Mary Farnden and Mary Dyke (Chapter 17).

Joseph, the widower, left Jacobs and removed with his children across the river to Hole Farm, one of the three bought by his grandfather nearly a hundred years earlier.

*The Mercer Flints*

This infant daughter, another Mary after her dead mother, grew up to marry James Flint, of Kingston Manor near Lewes, and these were the grandparents of Miss Tottie Flint; for their son, Robert Mercer Flint, returned to Sedlescombe to marry Mary Mercer, his first cousin and to set up a Mercer household again at Jacobs, where Miss Tottie's brother was born in 1861 and she herself four years later: Mercers on both their father's and mother's sides.

*Robert Mercer, Gent. and Joseph: the two Brothers*

Two of the other children of Joseph and Mary Mercer, Robert, aged eight, and Joseph, a year old when their mother died, lived together all their lives; and until 1830 at Hole Farm with their father. In that year they sold it and all its land to Hercules Sharpe of Domons, Northiam, who set about transforming it into Oaklands Park (Chapter 32). In the sale, it was stipulated that an annuity of £60 was payable out of the estate "for and during the life of a Gentleman (a widower), aged 79 in November next, at whose Decease this valuable property will absolutely belong to the Purchaser". This old gentleman was Joseph, the father of the two brothers, and widower for 46 years of Mary Cook. He died four years later aged 87, according to the inscription on the large and impressive grave of his wife in which he too was buried, and where her father and mother, William and Ann Cook had also been buried. Joseph left a will, made twenty-five years earlier, bequeathing to his sons and daughters sums amounting to £13,800, together with land in Wivelsfield and Hurstpierpoint, as well as in the Sedlescombe neighbourhood. William Cook had made a will at the same time leaving £5,200 to his Mercer grandsons: to other relations, including a "natural daughter", smaller legacies; and all the rest of his estate to his grandson, Robert Mercer, who thus with the two legacies became a wealthy man.

Robert was a man of exceptional character. After leaving Hole Farm, he and his brother, Joseph, returned to Jacobs where they had been born, and there they lived, two bachelors, until they died. Miss Tottie, his great-niece, said that he was reputed to have the best library of anyone in the neighbourhood—great volumes about birds and birds' eggs, flowers and all country matters, together with cases of butterflies. He would give anything, she said, for an old book. He was prominent in local affairs. When he died he was buried beside his father and mother in a similar large grave with the inscription: "Robert Mercer Gent. of the parish of Brede died 1861 aged 80." His brother Joseph lived on for another twenty-two years until he was 95 when he was buried in his brother's grave. "Joseph Mercer late of Jacobs, Brede."

Although the Mercers were so much a Sedlescombe family, of the brothers' two homes, Hole Farm was at that time just in the Parish of Westfield and Jacobs within that of Brede.

*Richard Mercer of Swales Green*
Between Robert Mercer Gent. and Joseph came a third brother, Richard. In 1814, when he was barely thirty, he, "Richard Mercer

of Swales Green, Gent", on the northern boundary of the parish, made a will making a bequest of "two leasehold cottages, garden and premises in Sed, held of the Earl of Chichester to son Richard Mercer. To daughter Betty Lina Mercer £1,500. Residue of personal estate given between son and daughter, Richard and Betty Lina Mercer, Son Richard to pay testator's wife, Ada Lina Mercer, such sums of money as testator had become bound to her on their late separation. Executors: Robert Mercer and Joseph Mercer younger brother of said Richard, both of Westfield, Gents."[1] The reason for the early will is clear, Richard's legal separation from his wife, Ada Lina. His son, Richard, then only a child, grew up to marry Fanny and lived for several years at Asselton House, which had been bought by his great-grandfather, Joseph, in 1739. But in 1825 he sold it to William Grace and he and his wife moved to Swales Green, perhaps to the cottages his father had left him. For some eighteen years he lived in Swales Green, styling himself farmer or sometimes yeoman. In 1843 he sold the leasehold of his property for £950 and no more is known of him or his family.

*Joseph Mercer, The Smuggler, and Elizabeth, his Wife*

Where did the Smuggler come in the Mercer family tree? Prosecuted in 1741 (that is the year after the first Robert died) for "unshipping or Running uncustomed goods", a "victualler" of Sedlescombe, he too was Joseph. Among the Mercers already described are five other Josephs. One suspects him of being a "black sheep" brother of Robert who wrote the long letter to his son, Joseph, shortly before he died, warning him "to beware of vain and evil company, and the prevailing love of pleasure". This may have been the ordinary advice of a serious and religious-minded father, but it could perhaps have been a particular warning because of the bad example of Uncle Joseph. Though smuggling was hardly considered wrong-doing in Sussex in the eighteenth century, it may well have been so counted by the non-conformist consciences of Robert and his sons. Though the process against Smuggler Joseph did not take place till after Robert died, it is not unlikely that he would have known of his brother's errant ways.

Joseph had married Elizabeth Cook in Sedlescombe Church on November 8th, 1736, and in the following seven years they had five children, three sons, Thomas, Joseph and Richard, and two daugh-

[1] Sed. P. R. E.S.R.O.

ters. Neither Joseph nor his wife were literate, for both signed the deed of 1741 with "their marks", a curious thing in itself in this very educated family.

In 1771, the year that Elizabeth died, Joseph transferred to his three sons "all his movable property" in return for £6 per annum to be paid him by each one of them. In this document he is called a "yeoman" and it appears that he possessed a quantity of household goods and farm animals. His sons all signed their names, though their spelling of these is variable. Their father still made his mark.

Joseph, when prosecuted for "unshipping or running" smuggled goods, was described as "a victualler" of Sedlescombe. Did he therefore run an ale-house or inn in the village? In the Deeds of Barracks Cottage, which stands at the foot of the Street close to the "Coach and Horses", is the following statement:

"October 1792 Two items. Two Messuages and Tenements . . . at or near a certain place called Iltonsbath *and an Inn* commonly known by the sign of the King's Head, with the stable yard in the occupation of Mary Young, widow, *in the tenure of* Henry Martin and then of Richard Mercer, sold to Edmund Weekes."

So here is Richard Mercer, son of Smuggler Joseph, clearly connected with the "King's Head Inn" (now the "Coach and Horses") at some time before 1792. It is therefore tempting to suggest that this was where his father before him had been "a victualler". How well-placed he would have been, so close beside the river, to collect his "uncustomed goods" from their hidden place in the river barges; and to sell them "at the sign of the King's Head'"; until he was caught in 1741.

Joseph died in 1776, five years after his wife, and his family fade into oblivion.

*The Last of the Mercer Family*

Miss Tottie's father and mother lived at Jacobs with their infant son. She herself, born four years after her great-uncle Robert's death, never knew him whose memory she so greatly revered and kept so fresh. Her father, who was attorney to Hercules Brabazon of Oaklands, was in the fashion of the time a stern disciplinarian though a loving father. She remembered the long walk over the field from Jacobs to church every Sunday from her youngest years. After the service she and her brother would wait by the little gate on the east of the churchyard while their father talked with the other men. On one occasion he firmly bid them wait by Jacobs gate till he returned for them. Two hours later they were still there, their father having remembered them only after he had returned home, to his wife's horror, without them. She was sixteen when he died and Jacobs was sold, and they went with their mother to live at Ivy Cottage in Brede Lane which had been re-built four years earlier by Hercules Brabazon. There she looked after her mother until she died and then cared for Joseph, her brother, who suffered from epilepsy. She never left Ivy Cottage, which was filled with chests crammed with yellow deeds relating to old Mercer properties all over Sussex and Kent, and with shelves of great-uncle Robert's beautiful books. But where had all that wealth gone which he had inherited from his two grandfathers?

In 1926, when much of the Brabazon Combe property was for sale, including Ivy Cottage, the then Rector, Ernest Reid, made her future secure by buying the cottage in the name of the Church. There she lived, crippled with rheumatism, the walls dripping with damp, for another quarter century. A character of great independence, intelligence and pride, gaunt and upright, a beloved Sunday School teacher and sick visitor, she was the last of a large family of great standing and repute in the village.

*Chapter Twenty-seven*

## THE GREAT HURRICANE

The weather, we know, is a subject of inexhaustible fascination to the inhabitants of these islands, with its infinite variety from day to day. There are records of great storms in the past, in particular those two in the thirteenth century which damaged and finally drowned Old Winchelsea. These were sea storms but the Brede, being a tidal river, must have been affected by the extraordinary double tidal flow that caused an enormous rush and flood of waters along its whole valley. A contemporary account describes the second storm, which happened on October 1st, 1250, thus:

"The moon being in her prime, the sea passed its accustomed bounds, flowing twice without ebb, and made so horrible a noise that it was heard a great distance inland, not without the astonishment of the oldest man that heard it. Besides this, at dark night the sea seemed to be a light fire and to burn, and the waves to beat with one another, in so much that it was past the mariner's skill to save their ships; and to omit other examples, at a place called Eastbourne three noble and famous ships were swallowed up by the violent rising of the waves and were drowned. And at Winchelsea, a certain haven to the eastward, besides cottages for salt, fishermen's huts, bridges and mills, above 300 houses by the violent rising of the waves were drowned."[1]

We can imagine something of the wildness of that noisy, tempestuous night, the river flowing up and up, rushing more and more strongly with the never-ebbing tides, till the banks could no longer contain it.

---

[1] Lower.

The most famous storm in this neighbourhood, however, was a land storm, a tornado, which occurred in 1729 on May 20th. "The odd thing," wrote Colonel Lemmon, "about tornadoes is that they apparently take a course of about thirty miles and that they accomplish this course in about an hour. The speed of the wind is of course very much more than that, because the wind goes round and round and it is said to attain a velocity of about 80 miles an hour. This tornado struck the Sussex coast very near to where the meridian of Greenwich cuts the coast, an easily identifiable point, and it took a NNE course. The tornado revolved rapidly in an anti-clockwise direction and had a course of about twelve miles, which it accomplished in 20 minutes; that is a speed of thirty-six miles an hour or thereabouts, so we can imagine that it possibly started as a waterspout about 18 miles out at sea. It proceeded in the NNE direction passing over the northern part of Sidley Green and then on to Cole Wood and Henniker Wood, where it laid low some 200 trees. Passing half a mile west of Crowhurst Church, it then came to Loose Farm" (on the Hastings-Battle road) "and did a lot of damage to the farm, as well as destroying a malt-house and a barn. All the apple trees in the orchard were not only uplifted, but blown over the hedges and scattered among the surrounding fields. The tornado then went on, crossing the Hastings-Battle road close by where Telham Mill now is and made for Battle Great Wood (unpoling a hop-garden on the way) following the course of the stream, that rises there, all the way through the wood. Here it was of great breadth and levelled most of the trees in the wood. On the Battle Abbey Estate it was estimated some 1400 trees were uprooted. The tornado went on down the stream until it came out of the wood by Marley House, which escaped damage being just outside the lefthand edge of the storm. A very strongly built barn on the other side of the road was, however, destroyed. Going on down the stream (Brede River) it had a breadth of some 200-300 yards; in Battle Wood they say it was 450 yards broad. . . . It turned a bit to the left going through Felons Wood, and headed over towards Sedlescombe."[1]

As it storms its way to Sedlescombe, a contemporary writer, Richard Budgeon, takes up the tale:[2]

[1] Trans. B.H.S.
[2] S.A.C. 36.

MAP 4. Map of Hurricane by Richard Budgeon, 1729.

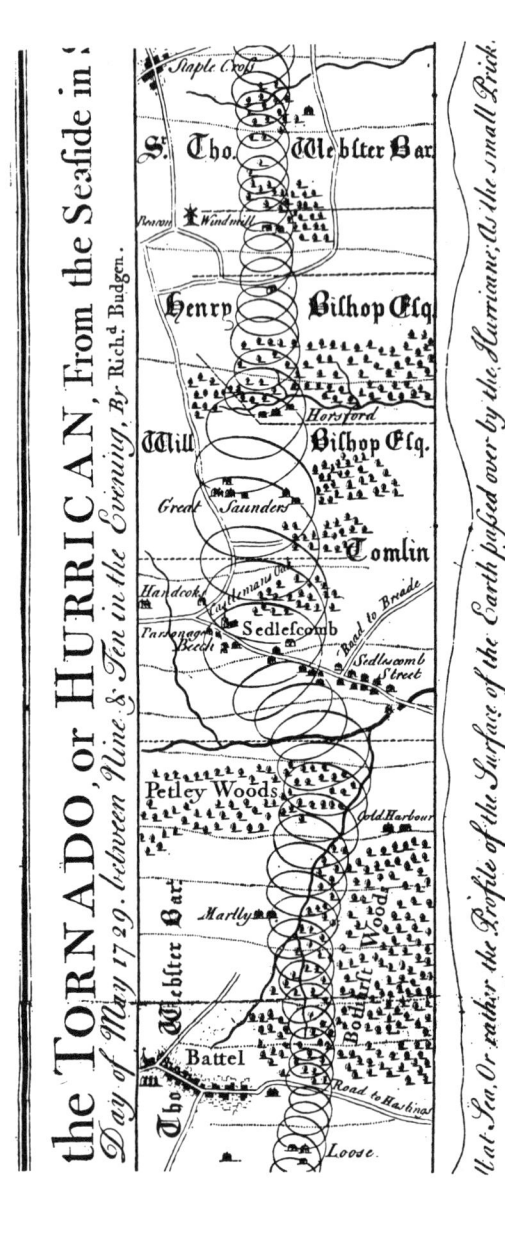

"After it had slaughtered down the timber in Bathurst Woods" (part of Great Wood) "near a mile in length, and at some places half a mile in breadth, it forced a Glade through Petly Woods, likewise very thick-set with Timber; which is either torn up by the Roots, twisted and shook in pieces, or the Tops cropped off and demolished. . . . From the Woods it crossed the Brooks, and no more Woodlands or Buildings lying in the way till it reaches Sedlescombe Street; . . . only the Hedges disordered and drove out of their Places, Stems turned up by the Roots, and the Earth of some sowed Land drove into the Hedges with such Violence and Quantities, as intirely to cover the Wood and Leaves of the Hedges.

"Richard Elliot, the South Side of Sedlescomb-Street" (he lived at the house now called Manor Cottages, for many years known as 'Ellliots') "had two Barns down; . . . his House somewhat damaged in the Tileing; down lower in the Street the Thatch is a little damaged in some places, but the damage is inconsiderable (Chapter 14).

"The next House to the Westward belongs to John Reed, who had a Corner of an Out-building down, and his House pretty much uncovered. William Wallis's House stood in a piece of Ground inclosed by the Highway" (the Gun Cottage) "the Occasion of his House's falling seems partly owing to a large Apple-tree brought out of a Neighbour's Orchard, over three Hedges, with the Roots and Earth about them, that fell upon his House; he had the Misfortune to have his Thigh broke in the Fall. Over against Wallis's House, Mrs. Tomlin had a House and Barn blowed down. Over against the Church, Samuel Plummer Gent" (Beech House) "had the Roof of a large Out-building taken off; some rafters out of his Barn, and his House pretty much damaged in the Tileing. The Parsonage House had the Ridge and Corners uncovered, and a Barn by the Way-Side blowed down."

"The House by Castleman's Oak" (Little Castleman's) "belonging to Mrs. Tomlin aforesaid, had a Stack of Chimneys turned down upon the House, which in their Fall broke two or three Rafters.

"From Sedlescomb-Street it bore up a small Valley between two Woods (pretty much damaging the Timber of the said Mrs. Tomlin, on the Western Side of its Passage, and some Woodlands belonging to William Bishop Esq. on the East) to Great Sanders, where out of five it beat down three stacks of Chimneys; a Barn and Lodge by the House, and a Malt-House very much shook and damaged in the Covering. And above two hundred Yards in Length of Brick Wall, of which some was little more than three Feet high, and appeared by the Situation as well as Height to have been secure from the utmost Violence of the Wind.

"Mrs. Tomlin had another House and Barn blowed down about two Furlongs East by South of Great Sanders" (Hurst?) "the Woman, her Tenant, with the Fright and some Hurt received by the Fall of the House, is dangerously ill." (This, five months after the storm.)

"About three Furlongs from Great Sanders, in a Gill, it passed through more Woodlands of the said Mr. Bishop's, very full of fine Timber, where it raged with great Violence, sparing scarce anything in its way; and about a Furlong down the Gill at Horsford belonging to Henry Bishop Esq."; (Austford House, Chapters 23 and 46) "demolished one Barn and Lodge and took off the Corner of another Barn, from thence ascending through Woodlands of the said Mr. Henry Bishop, where it not only tore the Trees up by the Roots, but took the Earth which was rent up in prodigious Flitches, with such Violence, that it covered the Bodies, Boughs and Leaves of the Trees. And in the next Field, blowed up a Barn, and scattered the Timber to the North and West at three or four score Rods distance.

"The next Building in its way belonged to Thomas Holman who had the Roofs of his House and Barn taken off, and the Chimney down to the middle. A Man in Bed slept out the Storm, and knew not the Conveniency he had for Star-gazing, till awakened by the rest of the Family."

It blew on to half a mile east of Staplecross cross-roads, half a mile east of Ewhurst church, down to Newenden Levels and blew itself out at another easily defined point where the Kent Ditch runs into the River Rother. According to Budgeon: "about two Miles further, in the East Part of Benenden Parish, it had pretty well recovered its former Violence" . . . then, "Ent'ring a large Vale (at crossing the Eastern Branch of the Medway) under the Ridge of the Kentish Hills, the Force visibly abated and if the Matter was not exhausted, yet so far diminished or chilled, as to have no Appearance of its Passage through the other Part of Kent."

Richard Budgeon, who was a famous map-maker, wrote this description of the Hurricane in a pamphlet dedicated to "the Honourable Sir Hans Sloane Bart, the President, and to the Council and Fellows of the Royal Society" (it was he who gave his name to Sloane Square and Hans Place in London).

The Pamphlet consists of: (1) A Particular Account of the Damage and Devastations to the Buildings, Timber etc. that stood in the way of its Course; (2) An Account of the Weather and Bearings of the Wind that preceded the Hurricane, etc.; (3) Some Observations on the Way and Manner of its Course; and (4) By Way of Enquiry some Account attempted of the Cause of Tempests, Whirlwinds and Hurricanes together with "An Exact Plan describing the Passage of the Tornado or Hurricane from the Seaside in Sussex to Newenden Level."[1]

He describes the weather thus on the day of May 20th, "A slight flying Tempest in the Morning with a little scattering Rain; the rest of the Day very clear, and extreme Hot and Sultry. Wind South till about five in the Afternoon, when there began to appear a Haziness in the South which by degrees, with a Vanishing Edge, arrived at our Zenith about seven; when there began to appear plain symptoms of a Tempest. We distinctly heard the Thunder at Eight, and had a prospect of Two different Tempests. . . . About Nine these Tempests were passed over us to the North, and made an opening in the South-East, where we had the surprising Horror of seeing (at about twenty miles distance at Frant) such intermitting Coruscations together with such dreadful Darting and breaking forth of liquid Fire, at every Flash of Lightning (in the way of the Hurricane from the Sea-side in to Kent) as perhaps has not been seen in this Climate for many Ages. . . . The Inhabitants that live by the Sea-side in Bexhill, where this hurricane landed, give but a very imperfect Account of the Appearance of the Clouds at that time; which might be owing partly to several Tempests about, almost covering the Face of the Heavens, and in some measure to the approaching Duskiness of the Evening, and the Dread and Terror of facing such prodigious Flashes of Lightning; nor could I hear of any Sea-faring Men that happened to be off at Sea anywhere near that Evening. At Battel, it was observed as, and compared to a prodigious Smoak rolling from a Limekiln; at Ewhurst, a Brightness was observed in the Clouds, approaching about the Breadth that afterwards appeared to be taken in by the Hurricane, and such a strong Light during the time of the greatest Violence of the Storm,

---

[1] S.A.C. 36. p. 119.

as far exceeded any of the preceding Flashes of Lightning. By the best Account I could collect, it came ashore about nine o'clock in the Evening, or somewhat before, and entered Newenden Level at twenty minutes after. The whole Duration of this Hurricane at every particular place it passed over, was computed at three Minutes; but of that violent Part which did Damage to the Buildings and Timber, all agreed did not exceed a Minute; some affirmed half a Minute to be the full time it lasted . . . which, if it be considered, how little for the most part the Duration of a Minute is understood by the Persons from whom we are obliged to collect this Account, and the unspeakable Horror and Surprise they were in while their Houses were shook and torn in pieces over their Heads; perhaps few People in such Circumstances would guess twenty Seconds, much less than half, if not a whole Minute."

We must be grateful to Richard Budgeon for so complete a description of a terrifying experience and occasion, which would otherwise by now be completely forgotten.

*Chapter Twenty-eight*

## THE SCHOOL

At about the date of the hurricane, steps were being taken to provide free education for the children of the village (Chapter 21). "We are apt to forget," wrote Sir John Thorne, "how new a thing education in England is . . . education, that is, of the many as distinct from the few. Dr. G. M. Trevellyan, in his *English Social History*, says: 'No attempt was made to teach reading and writing to the mass of people until the 18th century brought the Charity Schools. . . . In the reign of Anne, these were founded by hundreds all over England, to educate the children of the poor in reading, writing, moral discipline, and the principles of the Church of England. They were much needed, for the State did nothing for the education of the poor, and the ordinary parish had no sort of endowed school, though in many villages "dames" and other unofficial persons taught rustics their letters in return for small fees; and, here and there, an endowed Grammar School gave secondary education to the middle class.' "

John Everendon (Chapter 23), in the first quarter of the seventeenth century, paid £1 a year for the schooling of his daughter, Elizabeth, and £2 a year for that of his son, Walter.[1] Earlier when the two children were younger he had "paid to the good-wife Sheather . . . for schooling his children together 2s. 2d." She was perhaps the wife of Thomas Sheather living, according to the 1632 Plan, at "late Weekes House". She was clearly "Dame" Sheather. Sir Thomas Sackville's two elder sons rode away from Hancox to Oxford University at the tender age of thirteen and may well have gone to Eton or Winchester before that, after they left the village

[1] S.A.C. 4, p. 22-24.

"dame". Alternatively they may have had a tutor. In days of large families this was often the answer, tutoring being sometimes supplied by the rector of the parish. Certainly in 1662 Edmund Thorpe, the Puritan Rector of Sedlescombe, evicted at the Restoration, started a private school for a time in the village, but later in Hastings, where a Grammar School had been founded in 1619 as the result of a legacy from the will of William Parker. Twenty years later a legacy from Thomas Peacock started the Grammar School in Rye which still bears his name. It was to this school that middle class lads from Sedlescombe, not tutored at home, went.

It was left to George Barnsley, Rector of Sedlescombe, to do the same for the village. He was Rector for 49 years and also of Northiam and Burwash for parts of that time (Chapter 13). Before he died in 1723 he made a will leaving £500 "for the education of poor children", in the three parishes, "whose parents are not of ability to pay for their learning, in the knowledge and practice of the Christian religion as professed and taught in the Church of England in the best manner of the Charity Schools now in use in this Kingdom". He named as executors, "the Right Reverend and Father in God, Thomas, Bishop of Chichester", the Rev. Robert Pain, the Rev. Stephen Frewen (Rector of Northiam) and the Rev. Richard Thornton (Vicar of Dallington).

After Barnsley's death (the Bishop having predeceased him), the three remaining executors "did make a disposition of the above Summe of Five Hundred Pounds in such manner as they thought would best answer the charitable and pious intention of the Testator". Under this arrangement Sedlescombe was allotted £150, but it was not till six years after their benefactor's death that the money was actually received by "the Churchwardens, Overseers and Principall Inhabitants of the said Parish of Sedlescombe being now met together in a Vestry," (the name of the gathering, not of the place of meeting, which became in course of time the Vestry Room). The deed, dated August 11th, 1729, is signed by the two churchwardens, Jno. Rupell and Jno. Henstey, and five parishioners, Thos. Snepp, Wm. Hyland, Thos. Snow and Henry Snow, all of whom were farmers, and Wm. Huckstep, shoemaker. It was witnessed by the Rector, Peter Pickering, Samuel Plumer (of Beech), Henry Bishop (Great Sanders) and Wm. Duke, overseer (Spilsteds). The other two villages in the bequest received £100 each, making a total of £350, which left a balance of £150 unaccounted.

Hanging in the school building today is a framed and decorative document, the first two words with their ornamental curving scrolls being the easiest to read: "THIS INDENTURE", the cross-piece of the capital T embracing the Royal Arms. "Just beneath, on the left margin, are three blue stamps each embossed with the rose of England surrounded by the Garter motto and with the phrase VI PENCE. The writing of the document is good and clear. At the foot is the signature of the Duke (as Lord of the Rape) and his seal, the Pelham Buckle (won at Poitiers when a Pelham took the surrender of the French King) within the Garter ribbon and motto. The Preamble is worth quoting:[1]

"This Indenture made the twenty eighth day of December in the Fifth Year of the Reign of our Sovereign Lord George the Second by the Grace of God King over Great Britain ffrance and Ireland Defender of the ffaith anno dni 1731 between the Most Noble Lord Thomas Holles Duke of Newcastle Marquis and Earl of Clare Viscount Houghton Baron Pelham of Laughton Knight of the Most Noble Order of the Garter One of His Majesty's Principal Secretarys of State Vice Admiral of the County of Sussex and Lord of the Honour Barony Castle and Rape of Hastings in the said County of the One Part and the Reverend Richard Thornton Vicar of the Parish and Parish Church of Dallington in the said County Clerk the Reverend Francis Brown Wright Rector of the Parish and Parish Church of Seddlescombe in the said County Clerk The Reverend Robert Pain Rector of Saltwood in the County of Kent Clerk Henry Bishop of Seddlescombe aforesaid Gentleman and John Plummer of Seddlescombe aforesaid Gentleman of the other Part.

"Note that France was still named among the territories of the King of England. The substance of the document is as follows: In October 1652 the Duke's grandfather, Sir Thomas Pelham, Bart., (Chapter 8) had leased to Peter Farnden all that parcell of Wastground lying and being in the High Street within the Hundred of Staple beginning and extending from Seddlescombe Bridge all along up to Seddlescombe Church for 100 years at a yearly rent of 6d.

Joseph Mercer of Maidstone Gentleman, 1658-1736 (Chapter 26), held the lease for the remainder of the ten-year term and, by assignment, the date of which is left blank but must have been shortly

[1] Thorne.

before the date of the document, demised to Richard Thornton and the four other Trustees a piece of the said "Wastground" containing by estimation three-quarters of an acre; the boundaries were West: highway and Street; South: leasehold cottage and wastground in possession of John Cooper (now occupied by the school and lately by the schoolmistress); East: footway. The purpose was the building of a 'Schoolhouse and other necessary and convenient buildings for the poor children of the Parish'; the Duke 'for and on Consideration of the good Will and Favour he beareth to the said Trustees . . . and for the promoting and encouraging of so good and pious an undertaking' demised that piece of the property to the said Trustees for a term of 99 years from the expiry of the 100-year term; the rent was to be 'one Penny of good and lawful money of Great Britain.' "

From Norman days all wasteland in the village had belonged to the Lord of the Rape. By 1652 most of it in the Street below Brickwall had been built on, but even so Peter Farnden's nephew did very well to get all the waste ground left from the bridge right up to the church on a 100-year lease for 6d. a year (Chapter 17).

There seems to be no record of any new agreement being made after the 199 years, covered by the two leases, expired in 1851. The Trustees purchased an estate in Westfield Parish, called Darbies, which brought in £20 a year to pay for the Headmaster's salary and any repairs to the School buildings. Presumably the £150 balance, unaccounted for, was used for this. Its site is unidentified.

We know nothing of the actual process of building or when this was started. George Barnsley would surely have been very disappointed that so many children grew up in the 25 years after his death without the schooling he had provided for them in his will. For any others who cared about seeing the provision of his will implemented they must have been frustrating and infuriating years, not least for the Rectors, Peter Pickering, Barnsley's successor, and Francis Browne Wright who followed him. It fell to the lot of James Ingram to be the first Rector of Sedlescombe to teach in the new village school.[1] It was perhaps he who wrote on the outside of a parchment-covered book "Sedlescombe School 1748" and inside the first entry:

[1] Map 5.

"Memorandum June 23rd. 1748:"
which recorded a scheme of ten clauses agreed upon by the Trustees, John Ingram, Henry Bishop and John Plummer, now of Battle. Clause 5 said: "the number of scholars not to exceed twenty, every writer to be reckoned as 2." This curious rule seems to have been based on the idea that every scholar who could write as well as read needed twice as much attention as one who could not.

Clause 3 required the parents to keep the scholars "sweet and clean that they be not a nuisance to the rest of the school," and Clause 2 required them not to keep the children from school "except at such times of the year when the children may earn something towards the maintenance of the rest of the family", and then by consent of a Trustee. These were mostly early in the summer at grain harvest and late in the summer at hop harvest. This clause continued to regulate the date for the start of the autumn term until some years after the end of World War II, when for the first time the school opened on the date fixed for the rest of the country and all pupils were expected to attend, hop-picking regardless.

The first list of scholars of June 23rd, 1748, consists of 14 names, 8 boys and 6 girls, the surnames being: Pankhurst, Weston, Mercer, Watson (2), Hook (2), Redhead, Richardson, Pain, Eldridge, Davis and Burgis. The first five were all farmers, and there were many families of Eldridges practising a variety of trades.

Isaac Gostling was already an old man when he became the first headmaster and had more than probably been teaching Sedlescombe children long before the new school building was ready, for it was only seven years later that Thomas Colbran, a lad of 18 who had been assisting him, was appointed to succeed him, the vacancy arising "through the incapacity by reason of old age of Isaac Gostling". Colbran was to be "allowed use of the school house to teach therein the poor children committed to his care and others who may come to him for instruction". These others he could charge a fee.

*Thomas Colbran* 1737-1816
Thomas proved to be a remarkable man, holding the appointment for 61 years until his death at the age of 80. He is said to have been born at Ninfield but he may have been of a local family for a William Colbran was paying rates for his farm in Sedlescombe in 1708.

His first entry in the School Book is:

"I, Thomas Colbran, was appointed Master of the Free School at Sedlescombe at Ladytide 1755."

This is followed by another written 57 years later:

"1812
1755
___
                57
aged    18 when appointed
___
        75 my age at Ladytide 1812"

The salary of the schoolmaster was not fixed. It depended on how much of the rent money from Darbies had to be spent on repairs to that cottage, and no record was kept until 1805 when he received the full amount of ten guineas. The following year the sum was only £5 6s. 7d. and nearly every year following some deduction was made. In 1771 the following agreement had been made with him:

"The Trustees promise to pay Thomas Colbran 40s. per year in case he should by sickness or any other accident be rendered incapable of managing the said school or die, for each and every year of the said term of twenty years next ensuing the date hereof, that may happen to be unexpired at the time of his becoming incapable or Death, out of the salary due and payable to his successor by two equal payments in the year ... the first payment to be made out of the first half year's salary that becomes due next after his inability or death and in consideration of the sum of Forty pounds laid out and expended by the said Thomas Colbran in making an addition to the school house at the southeast end thereof."

Apart from getting better quarters at his own expense it seems difficult to see how this agreement benefited him. By 1800 he had increased the very small proportion of those who could write to three-quarters of his pupils.

He left his name not only on the school but also on many a map, still in existence, often with the signature, "by me, Thomas Colbran". Map-making of their estates for local landowners was an occupation by which he augmented the living he received as a schoolmaster, and which perhaps also made it possible for him to pay for the building additions to the school-house. There are plans

THE SCHOOL 287

or maps of Mabbs Farm, Crowham Manor Farm in Westfield, Huntly's belonging to Henry Mallory Bishop (Bourne Farm), "The lands called Hurst part of the estate of William Bishop, Esq.", and others still to be seen, which show his skill in drawing and measuring.

It seems that by the time he died he was receiving entrance money not only from the paying scholars but also from those children who should have been free ones for, when his successor, Charles Winter or Winser, a Northiam man, was appointed, it was laid down that "inasmuch as it is understood that Entrance Money has been demanded by the late Thomas Colbran on the admittance of free scholars" this was not to continue.

The next recorded appointment was 47 years later; John Barber of Tring in 1863. Charles Winter did not reign, however, for all those 47 years for the *Kelly's Directory for Hastings* 1855 names Henry Kinchett headmaster of Sedlescombe School. In proof of this is a school bill still in existence in the hands of the descendants of the family it concerns; a younger branch of the Bishops of Great Sanders living at the time at Sackville Cottage (Chapter 35). Furthermore, from 1801 John Catt taught the Sedlescombe children for thirty years as his gravestone in the churchyard records. Born in 1760, when Thomas Colbran was 17, he must have received all his education from him, and himself became an assistant teacher before his master died. It is passing strange that this statement on the gravestone is the only record of this village schoolmaster. He was a careful and faithful teacher, making his own copybooks in beautiful copper-plate handwriting. His descendants, the Dengates, still live in the village; and his son was John Catt, the builder.

Soon after John Barber's arrival, the school was restored in 1864 at a cost of £39 raised by public subscription. This headmaster must have been a very different character from his predecessors for, after five years, he was discharged for inefficiency and a Sedlescombe man, Joseph Hefford, was appointed in his place. He had the help of a pupil teacher, who had the familiar name of Eldridge; A. Eldridge.

On October 10th, 1877, when Joseph Hefford had been headmaster for nine years, the following entry was made in the School Record:

"The School Master received notice that owing to the decrease in the number of scholars, consequent on the opening of Westfield Board School, we should not be able to continue with him after 31st January 1878."

Whether this was an excuse for getting rid of an unsatisfactory schoolmaster or whether it was an economy with the pupil teacher carrying on at his lesser wage, it is impossible to be sure; but it is certain that only three years later, in 1881, the Boys' Department of Sedlescombe School was enlarged at a cost of about £140, by the building of an extension at the north end, paid for once again by voluntary donations; Miss Pratt gave £10, her father the late Rector £5, Mr. Warner, the Rector, £20, Hercules Brabazon £20, and Mr. Sutton of Castlemans, John Pratt's brother-in-law, £20. A Reading and Musical Entertainment raised a further £3 10s. and a collection in church a little under £6. Mr. Catt's contract to build was for £112; he also donated £2 2s. The blacksmith, Mr. Tuppenny, made the iron fence which still surrounds the playground, and Mr. Colman, the carpenter, made the desks and tables. The builder, John Catt, was, like the others, an old pupil.

The school was growing. There were 119 children on the books. Clearly the opening of the Board School at Westfield had not had the expected effect of withdrawing the children who lived in that parish just across the River Brede; for even in wet weather when the river was often flooded and the bridge completely submerged, it was very much easier to push the children in handcarts across it and so to Sedlescombe school than to face the long three-mile walk to Westfield and back.

Miss Florence Martin, a retired missionary from Korea, was appointed to teach the girls and later, in 1884, became the first teacher of the newly-opened Infants' Department, Miss Durrant then teaching the girls. According to *Kelly's Directory* the Headmaster in 1890 was Mr. Charles Field.

*The Infants' School*
By the following year there were already 65 infants on Miss Martin's register. The records which she so meticulously kept show not only her curricula but also the many interruptions, some caused by casual holidays but many more by the epidemics of children's diseases, and in the winter by the terrible chilblains, often badly

broken, on the swollen and inflamed little hands; sufferings requiring too much endurance from tiny children and, mercifully, practically unknown today.

In spite of these and many other difficulties and the fact that her sole assistant was an elder girl or monitress, she managed to provide a varied curriculum which was instructive and interesting. Besides the three Rs she taught Nature Study and Object lessons studying one selected example, a lion maybe, or a spider, or a flower, a knife, a watch, the blacksmith, the sun or water. Every aspect of it was discussed. She taught also handwork, again making the subject very varied, teaching how to make wool balls, plaited mats, paper flowers and many another practical craft. She also taught them songs to sing and verses to learn by heart.

The day-to-day log kept by her gives a clear picture:

"1885 May 1st. The attendance is very poor today; children are away carrying May Garlands; only 27 present, and 25 this afternoon. The children have not yet recovered from the chicken-pox.

May 8th. The Master's sister who is a school mistress under the Local Board has assisted with the Infants this week. The registers have been marked by myself. I have had charge of the Boys' School again this week as the Master is still very ill.

June 5th. Have commenced this week with two fresh varied occupations: viz. block-building and stick-laying.

Dec. 2nd. A holiday was given on Wednesday for the 'Polling Station' for the election.

1886 Jan. 29th. A great many of the younger children away with bad colds and chilblains.

March 1st. There are only 29 children present this afternoon; a snow-storm has prevented them from coming.

March 5th. The attendance this week has not been so good, a great many of the children are absent with broken chilblains.

May 3rd. A holiday given on Monday.

May 21st. The attendance this week has not been at all satisfactory. Some of the children have been away with mumps and others have been kept from school to go with their mothers hop-tying.

August. Half-holiday for Flower Show.

Sept. Six weeks holiday for hop-picking till Oct. 10th.

Nov. 19th. I have taken cork modelling as a fresh varied occupation this week."

1887 was a very snowy winter with bronchitis, colds, measles and mumps afflicting the children; and in June there was whooping cough; and cases of ringworm had to be sent home.

The winter of 1889 was again a very cold one and the children had to walk to school through deep snow, too deep for the smaller ones; intensely severe weather, Miss Martin called it, and the children suffered bronchitis, measles and croup and, in March, whooping cough, and still the snow continued so that on the 13th only one child came to school. A week later two of the children had died, John Nightingale, whose father was landlord of the "Queen's Head", and David Brett. John's brother, Alfred, was very ill too and was away for thirteen weeks.

In 1892 on July 15th "By Managers' request a half-holiday was given, there being a grand wedding in the village." The bride was the daughter of the Adamsons of Great Sanders.

In 1895 on May 3rd "Frank Carrick (8) admitted. He has been a very delicate child. Doctor's certificate that he would only be able to attend school occasionally even now." Many still remember Frank who lived at Riverbridge Cottages and was a frail wisp of a man and tiny.

The following winter was harsh again and the school was closed for a month in January when 40 children were away with measles.

"1900 March 1st. A half-holiday was given this afternoon in commemoration of the relief of Ladysmith."

On March 30th new desks were received and found a great improvement.

In July "many little ones very unwell with the excessive heat."

Miss Martin continued to teach in spite of ill-health till 1908 when it forced her retirement.

*Horace Martin, Headmaster*

Florence Martin's brother, Horace, had joined her at the school in 1891 as head of the Boys' Department and, when the amalgamation took place in 1905 of the Boys' and Girls' Departments, he became headmaster and remained so until 1923. He is still remembered by many a man who was taught by him and sometimes caned

THE SCHOOL

by him. One boy, unnamed, is described as having fought back when being caned, biting the schoolmaster in the leg and, in his struggles, pulling his tie askew and tearing his collar.

Under Mr. Martin, the boys learned gardening every Friday morning besides their ordinary curricula. Each one of eight strips in the allotments at Balcombe Green was in the care of two boys who bought the seeds for their plot and shared the produce of it, sometimes selling to Rowland Dann who bought their purple-sprouting broccoli and other vegetables to sell in his shop. The elder girls learned cooking at Battle in a room beside the "Chequers Inn", the trip there and back once a week in Robert Thomas' van making a delightful weekly break from ordinary lessons. They were joined there by girls from the other villages round Battle.

In 1893 the Inspector's report says:

"Boys' School—the boys are soundly taught, and have an intelligent knowledge of all their subjects. They are much interested in their work, and in very good order. Under the unfavorable circumstances of prevailing sickness, the efficiency is very much to Mr. Martin's credit.

Girls' School—"(This was, at the time, with the Infants' School opposite) "considering the prevalence of sickness, I can report very well of the instruction, which is both intelligent and thorough. The girls are well drilled, much interested in their work and in very good order. Miss Durrant deserves much credit for the efficiency. The room should be more thoroughly warmed, and more suitable arrangements should be made for hats and cloaks. A map of the world is required.

Infants' School—it is real proof of the thoroughness of both discipline and instruction in this department that, except in the number of absentees, the late prevalent sickness is scarcely noticeable. As Miss Martin has, owing to ill-health, been unable lately to give personal attention to her school, the efficiency has been once again severely tested. Better provision should be made for hats and cloaks.

All the departments therefore have passed an 'excellent' examination, and have earned the highest grant allowed, that for Boys being 20s. 6d. per child: Girls, 20s.: Infants 16s. 6d.: total on average of 154, £146 15s., besides the Fee Grant of £177."

The Grant was absolutely dependent on the result of this examination. The cost of running the school in the previous year was a few shillings under £300, the grants were lower by £16, and the Fee Grant by £100. £70 8s. was raised by voluntary contributions and the names of contributors included all those who had given to the enlargement ten years earlier, with the addition of Mr. Adamson, now of Great Sanders, Mr. Alchin the grocer, Mr. and Mrs. Bucknill (Pratts), Mr. Mullens of Westfield Place, Mrs. Sellens and Mr. Cramp, the other grocers, and Mr. Nightingale of the "Queen's Head".

In the summer the children ate their lunches in the fields or spinneys close by the school; those who lived within half-an-hour's walking distance returning home for their mid-day meal, but in winter, muddy conditions made walking across the fields too slow and wet, so they too brought their lunches to school.

The following extracts from the Records of the Boys' Department present a clear impression of those schooldays.

"1898—Feb. 2   Boys allowed to remain in playground till 9.45 as school was full of smoke.

Feb. 28   Cottage gardening omitted, the ground being frozen hard. Taken next afternoon.

March 17   A. Bryant received a sharp punishment for repeated inattention and carelessness.

Military drill has been introduced. Hope to find more suitable desks next year of a modern type. Inspector.

Aug. 17   At yesterday's Flower Show Ten Prizes out of 12 were taken with produce which the Cottage Garden Class has assisted with the cultivation of.

1899   Three new desks supplied in March.

July 9   Owing to the number of applications for children to come out before the usual time in the afternoon for sundry purposes—tea-parties, pea-picking, haying, etc.—school will commence and close one half-hour earlier.

July 17   Tea and Sports in Rectory grounds.

July 27   An effort of the boys and myself to form a Cricket Club for the school resulted in generous subscriptions amounting to £2. 15. 7d.

## THE SCHOOL

March 6   William Reed leaves today to become gardener's boy. Fred Eldridge leaves today.

June 23   Budding began with the Cottage Gardening Class.

Aug. 16   Notwithstanding the drought 100% of the briars budded during C.G. lessons have been a success.

Aug. 22   A half-holiday was given to enable the boys to visit Sanger's Circus at Battle.

1902—June 25   School was closed this afternoon for the Coronation (postponed) festivities.

July 8   Registers marked ½ hour earlier to allow children to attend a menagerie at Battle.

July 11   Ditto for haying for next fortnight.

July 25   Good attendance continues to be spoiled by frequent parties.

Aug. 19   For repeated slovenliness and inattention in arithmetic Victor Stubberfield received two sharp strokes of the cane.

Aug. 21   21 prizes out of 26 exhibits won from our produce.

Nov.   Diphtheria.

1903—Jan. 14   The school most unpleasant to work in through smoke. Whenever the wind is E. or N.E. the only remedy is to have the door continuously open."

"It is difficult to say anything new about this admirable school. The boys have been taught with great care and their singing deserves very high praise. Inspector's report."

1903—Nov.   Smoke trouble again.

1904—Apr. 19   Re. Fire Drill, at the usual orders the boys had quitted the school carrying with them their hats, coats, dinner-bags etc. and had assembled in lines in exactly one minute.

May 2   A whole holiday today being the annual festival of the village Friendly Society.

July 6   Ernest Jenner admitted from Mountfield School.

July 7   Ernest Jenner was so convinced of the fact that we work here that he has returned to Mountfield School.

July 29   100% budded briars successful.

Aug.   Absentees through parties, S.S. and other societies.

Aug. 25   Fire Drill down to $\frac{3}{4}$ minute.

Nov. 16   School closed $\frac{1}{4}$ hour earlier this morning to admit of distribution of presents by Mrs. Adamson" (Great Sanders), "in the form of sweaters, cloaks and tam-o-shanters to the most regular and deserving children.

1905—Jan. 16   School smoking like a kiln every time fresh coals are put on; the fireplace is much too shallow and the combustible stove still in unworkable condition.

April 1   Coughs and sneezes through smoke.

April 7   Standards 1 and 2 in the Old Girls' school; 3 and 4 in Boys' school; the former, under assistant and monitor; the other under Master and monitress, on trial. There being two separate schools supervision of the whole by Master is extremely awkward.

April 27   Three 'travelling' boys were admitted" (i.e. gipsies).

"Aug. 18   The children are working on specimens of needlework for exhibition at the local Flower show, on Monday next.

Oct. 17   School so full of smoke, singing and any work requiring the voice impossible.

Oct. 20   A new stove has been substituted for the old combustible stove. At the present it works well but an easterly wind will test it.

1906—May 24   This day the upper classes were transferred to the Infants' Room.

June 26   Master absent for Miss Martin's wedding.

1909—May 17   A school rifle Cadet Corps has recently been formed, but the practice will take place outside school hours in Oaklands Park.

May 24   The afternoon was devoted to Empire Day festivities."[1]

Horace Martin, an ex-sailor, was a man of great personality, a master for ever remembered by his pupils. A strict disciplinarian, he possessed too a great sense of fun. When the temperature was freezing, for instance, he would hose the playground to form an ice rink, and the whole school led by him would then slide from one end to the other. Any youth in the village who threw a snowball

[1] Sed. School Records.

remotely near him received a well-aimed double-sized one in return. On Empire Day he would in true Navy style swarm up the flag-staff and raise the Union Jack.

He took endless trouble in the preparation of lessons using methods of his own to ensure that they would be remembered, and sometimes he delivered them in rhyme, as for instance,
>"Where clods prevail
>Onions fail,"

one of his maxims which memories still hold. His enthusiasm for gardening was injected into many of his pupils for life.

There were few, if any, village activities in which he was not interested, or committees of which he was not a member. For years he was on the Parish Council; he was church organist, choir-master, and Sunday School teacher, too. In his later years he suffered sudden attacks of cramp, sometimes when playing the organ. Rather than interrupt the service, he relieved the pain by sitting on the cold tiles continuing to play with his hands on the lower keyboard.

At last, in 1923, he had to retire through ill-health. It is difficult to find anyone who went to school in his day who does not speak of him with the highest praise.

*Mr. Brandish, Headmaster*

A difficult man to follow, he was succeeded by Mr. Becherwaise and he by Mr. Bowyers, who resigned in 1926. It was then that Mr. Brandish was appointed, a man deeply concerned over the comfort of his pupils while in school. In particular he tried in vain to persuade the caretaker to raise the level of heating, which he constantly measured on the classroom thermometer. Finally, he asked the School Managers to intervene with the caretaker over the matter. After eight years he too had to resign through ill-health, and was replaced for four years by Mr. Hitchen.

During part of this time Mr. Greengrass was an assistant teacher. "Do you remember when we was in the choir, Harry," chuckled Tom, many many years later, "and old 'Greeny' was the choirmaster and teacher at the school? Well, he had been sort of sharp with us and we was riled. So, one Sunday, we tore out of church and, by luck, he was the only one left inside. So we up and locked him in and hid in the Rectory shrubbery to see him get out. He got out, too, but my, did he look wild? And next day at school we fair copped it. In those days anyone could thrash us and we had our fair share."

## Miss Gibbs

As the men of today remember Mr. Martin, so the women remember Miss Gibbs who came in 1908 to teach the girls. She lived at Cherrytree Cottage beside the school, where the house called Tudor Rose stands today. She too was a disciplinarian. A rap on the shoulder from her ruler for correction is still remembered but with no rancour.

"She was our beloved school teacher and took a real interest in the village. She started a stool-ball and cricket team. The cricket team were very smart in white blouses and blue skirts and went to all the villages around in a brake to play; and Miss Gibbs never forgot the bottle of brandy to revive our drooping spirits or our bodies if a ball knocked us out. Those matches were real fun and sometimes we challenged the men who had to play left-handed with sticks."

## The War Years 1939-1945

Mr. Edmund Leigh came as headmaster in 1938 but in the following year was called up for active service with the 7th Battalion, the Royal Sussex Regiment. In 1940 he was wounded in France with the British Expeditionary Force and discharged from the Army, and was allowed to resume his appointment as Headmaster of the school. During his absence, his assistant, Edith Wright, had carried on, taking temporary charge of the school. She had the problem of an influx of children evacuated from London, who, too numerous to be fitted into the school classrooms, had to be taught separately in the village hall. With the fall of France and the resulting threat of invasion, this problem was solved by the removal of the 'evacuees' to a safer place further from the coast.

The threat and warning of air-raids, very frequently of the tip-and-run variety, caused constant disruption to teaching; and later the further distraction of aerial dog-fights which occurred in this part of the country throughout the Battle of Britain. The younger children could not be expected to walk the long distances to and from school under these conditions and the Rector, Mr. Noble, often took them there and back in his car.

The influence of the entry of America into the war showed in the school when, on November 26th, 1941, special lessons were given and American songs were sung to commemorate Thanksgiving Day. A greeting was cabled to the Center School, Hingham, Massachusetts, U.S.A., and the following reply was received:

"Greetings to Sedlescombe School Sussex from Center School Hingham Mass. Who could foresee on the first Thanksgiving that its celebration 321 years later would bring two great nations even closer."

After danger from the dog-fights in the air had passed, there came the screaming racket of the flying bombs with their flaming tails, more shocking and terrifying to the young children than anything else to which they had been subjected.

At last, on May 26th, 1945, the whole school celebrated V.E. Day at a Sports Meeting organised by the local members of the Home Guard and Observer Corps, followed by a tea in the village hall provided by the bakery of W. Gregory and Son.

Mr. Leigh was shortly replaced as headmaster by Mr. A. L. James who remained for 27 years. He too had an enthusiasm, and this was for cricket. Many were the matches organised by him and played on the cricket pitch across the Brooks. Mrs. Norton was appointed at about the same time to teach the infants and she lived with her husband and son in the little old school-house adjoining the school building. A new school-house was built at Balcombe Green just behind the school.

## The School Buildings

The amenities of the now very old school buildings were appallingly bad. The health authorities had continually complained before the war about the state of the lavatories and, eventually, chemical closets were installed, for it must be remembered that no main water was yet laid on to the village. Even after the war the only water available to the school was from the draw-well in the yard; and in 1953 this became contaminated so, for a while, all water had to be brought to the school from Battle, three miles away. An electric water-pump was next installed so that water-closets could be built to replace the chemical ones. At last in 1958 main water was supplied to the village, benefiting the school with all the other inhabitants, but the lavatories remained far below the standard by then required.

The classrooms too were proving inadequate by modern standards for the 97 pupils and the small kitchen had very limited storage space. The playground too was not large enough. By 1973 plans were prepared for a new school to be built in Gate field off Brede Lane, behind the houses on the Green. As in the first days, year after year passed, one headmaster, Paul Furley, gave place to another, David Marshall, and still, by 1977, the school was not started because of the economies in public expenditure made necessary by the inflation and long economic crisis in Britain.

When at long last it shall be built, may it give as good service as has the now outdated one, provided all those years ago by George Barnsley, Rector of Sedlescombe.

*The Dame Schools*

Through the years there were often 'cottage schools' taught by a 'dame' for a charge of a few pence a week.

There once were six cottages on the slope of Church Hill, three under one roof on the east side of the road and two at right-angles to each other on the west side, with a bungalow some few yards to the north of them. One of the two on the west side, slate-roofed, was for an unknown number of years a small school. It was not free; payment of, perhaps, 1d. a day was charged for attendance and an exercise book had to be provided. In order to avoid this extra expense pupils usually brought slates.

Naomi Dengate, mother of the Dengates of The Haven and wife of the last verger and sexton, James Dengate, had been a pupil. The 'Dame' of her day had a blind husband; sometimes she would go out and leave him in charge of the children, with a very long stick to keep them in order, which could penetrate to all parts of the cottage room. Was she, perhaps, the Susan Martin whose gravestone in the churchyard states that she kept the Infants' School in this parish for upwards of thirty years and gave her services also as "Nurse and Friend in the hour of sickness" and who died in 1881? (Chapter 51). Her work as a nurse would explain her absences from school when her blind husband managed as best he could. This school is said to have been started by the Rector, John Pratt. Later, Naomi with her brothers and sisters joined the Church school at the bottom of the hill. It might be possible to pay for one child but to pay for several on the wages of the late nineteenth century would have been out of the question.

Later there was a Dame School at Rose Cottage—known then as Broom Cottage—where Roselands now stands—for infants only; later still, during the Second World War, another such was carried on close by at the Presbytery by a woman teacher who was fol-

THE SCHOOL 299

lowed later in the War by two sisters of great personality, Connie and Margaret Locke, daughters of a doctor. After the war they retired to a house at the corner of Hurst Lane and finally to St. Leonards.

*Eighteenth- and Nineteenth-century Schoolmasters*
(not all in the School Records)

Isaac Gostling 1748-1755
Charles Winter 1817
Henry Kinchett 1851-1855
Joseph Hefford 1868-1878
Horace Martin 1890-1923

Thomas Colbran 1755-1816
John Catt 1821-1851
James Barber 1863-1868
Charles Field 1878-1890

*Chapter Twenty-nine*

## THE POWDERMILLS

In 1750 a tremendous change took place at the Water Mill beside the River Brede at Iltonsbath, where for over 500 years miller after miller and his men had ground the local grain into their fine dust of flour. For the last several generations the millers had all borne the surname Linghams or Langham and had rented the mill lands from Lord Montagu, the owner of Battle Abbey, to which the mill had belonged in the days when it was a monastery (Chapter 12).

Gunpowder had been made in and around Battle since 1676 when John Hammond of that town had leased for 21 years "the 4 parcels of brook-land and upland called Peppering-Eye with permission to erect a powder mill." By 1750 the reputation of the Battle Gunpowder Works (of which Peppering-Eye was but one of several) was very high; it was not only the leading factory in Sussex but was said by Defoe to make the best gunpowder in Europe.

In that year on April 11th "George Mathews of Battle late officer in the excise etc. bond to Sir Thomas Webster" (who had bought the Battle Abbey Estate from Lord Montagu), "George Worge of Battle Gent and William Gilmore gunpowder maker in the penal sum of £50 as security for his trust in the conducting of the Powder works of the said partner in the parish of Sedlescombe."[1] So the corn mill became a powder mill.

It is difficult to imagine ourselves and all our neighbours in The Street living quietly in such close proximity to so dangerous an industry; and dangerous it certainly proved to be.

From grinding corn to grinding powder was perhaps a sign of the times, for the middle of the eighteenth century was filled by three great wars in which Britain took part; the wars of the Austrian suc-

[1] Thorpe, p. 179. Map 5.

cession 1739-1748, the Seven Years War 1756-1763 and the American War 1775-1783, which were all part of Britain's struggle with France, under the two Pitts, which continued right on until Napoleon's final defeat.

"One cannot say when gunpowder was invented," wrote Colonel Lemmon in 1950. "We were taught at school that it was discovered by Schwartz, a German monk in 1320: but there is evidence that it was made in England 100 years earlier, and there seems little doubt that the Chinese had used it for thousands of years . . . Gunpowder was used for all purposes—firing guns, bursting shells, and for demolition. Its composition is quite simple: six parts of saltpetre, which exists in beds in the East, and can be produced synthetically anywhere without much trouble; one part of charcoal, universally available; and one part of sulphur which is found free in volcanic districts, and can also be obtained from Gypsum and other substances. If intimately mixed and fire applied, the ingredients are transformed into a large volume of gas (nitrogen and carbon dioxide) and a white powder (Potassium monosulphide), the latter making the characteristic white smoke."[1]

The saltpetre and sulphur were imported; the charcoal for ordinary gunpowder was made from alder wood burnt in pits in the way that had been practised locally, in Petley Woods in particular (Chapter 36), from time immemorial. For the finer or sporting powder, dogwood was used. Both of these woods are still very plentiful in our countryside. When the underwood in the district was being cut, the dogwood was carefully reserved, peeled and tied into bundles. The grandfather of the late Herbert Blackman of Battle worked at Battle gunpowder mill and in 1923 Herbert wrote an article giving the recipe for gunpowder and the following description of powder-making.[2]

"These works at Sedlescombe consisted of several buildings, some of which were still lately standing. The largest was called the *Refining House* where the crude saltpetre was put with water into cast-iron furnace-pans and boiled for several hours, the water being later drawn off leaving beautiful white crystals of the refined saltpetre. This was later heated in smaller pans to a liquid state and poured into moulds to cool, ready for grinding. This grinding was done of course in the Mill itself which was made of a stout frame-

[1] Trans. B.H.S. 1958.
[2] S.A.C. 54.

work but with light roof and panelled sides so as to offer very slight resistance in the event of an explosion. The grindstones known as runners can still be seen in the garden and were about six feet in diameter and 16 inches thick weighing about 6 ton. There were two pairs of these revolving vertically in pans, or beds some 3 or 4 feet wider than the runners, one pair in each bed. The power was transmitted from the water-wheels by overhead gearing. Eighty pounds of saltpetre was put under each pair of stones and took ten hours to grind, during which time it was broken up by the mill-man at regular intervals and kept slightly damp by the automatic sprinkling of water.

"The *Presses,* where the next process took place, were situated well away from any other buildings." There was a brick building until a few years ago at the far end of the Powdermill garden, where the path across the Brook passes alongside, which was perhaps used for this purpose. "The dust powder, damped, was spread evenly about 2 in. deep on sheets of copper 3½ ft. square which were placed above each other until half a ton was in position. The pressure was produced by a screw press, the long wooden arm to increase the pressure being manipulated by hand. The powder was thus reduced to a thickness of about ¾ inch and looked like slate.

"The next process was of *granulation or 'corning'*. As they came from the press the cakes of powder passed between zinc-cogged rollers and were reduced to the size of marbles, and so through plain brass rollers for the different sizes required. Finally, they were sifted through meshes of various sizes from coarsest, for blasting purposes, down to the finest grain for sporting powder. It was in the *Sifting-house,* where was a ton of powder, that the terrible explosion took place in 1764. After it had been sifted, the powder went to the *Glazing House,* a large building with a wooden shaft running its entire length on which were fixed wooden cases, shaped like barrels, into which the powder was put together with a small portion of plumbago. The barrels were slowly revolved by water power; and the powder, sliding round the barrels continually, gradually assumed its characteristic shiny blackness.

"After passing through the *'dusters'* to extract all fine dust powder it was taken to the *Drying house* or stove. The drying house at Sedlescombe, the furnace and chimney under the same roof as the drying chamber and separated only by a brick wall, were in 1923 still standing." It is hair-raisingly said that workmen in the powdermill in Battle used to take powder home to dry in their mother's or wife's oven.

The last processes were *grading and testing*. Two of the instruments used for testing at Battle can be seen in the Hastings museum. Finally, the powder was packed in kegs holding 28 or 56 lb., and the sporting powder in 1-lb. canisters, both of which were made locally. The packing was mostly done by women. The soldiers, originally perhaps installed in Barracks Cottage opposite as part of the war against smugglers, remained to guard the kegs. Magazine Farm, about a mile away, built in 1910, is said to be definitely the site where the gunpowder was stored, following the principle of keeping all the buildings well separated.

The river was still navigable by barge to Sedlescombe bridge and so the gunpowder made at the Gilmore mill went easily down to Rye in this way, to be shipped thence to London or to the Continent. The barges returned up-river laden with fodder and other merchandise, in which, in this the hey-day of smuggling, were frequently concealed brandy and other contraband.

It was in 1764 early in December "before breakfast" as the story still tells, that an explosion burst in the Sifting House and four men were killed, including James and Thomas, the only sons of the proprietor, William Gilmore. The Burial Register of Battle Church records "In 1764 Dec. 5th. James Gilmore and Thomas Gilmore, both buried in one grave who were accidently killed by the blowing up of the Sifting House at Sedlescombe Gunpowder Mills; in which house there was computed to be a Ton of Gunpowder; at which time and place there was two other men killed which were buried at Sedlescombe;"; John Watson and James Coldgate.

William Gilmore had one surviving child, his daughter Jane, who had married eight years earlier Lester Harvey (probably her father's assistant) and she thus became his heir, and, on his death, his son-in-law succeeded to the management of the works in both Battle and Sedlescombe, and, in due course, it passed to their son, William Gilmore Harvey, who lived at Powdermill House, Battle. His daughter, Mary, painted a picture of that house (which still hangs in the drawing-room) in about 1815 after her father had made additions to it. The initials W.G.H. and the date 1806 can still be seen in the bricks of a bay in the Sedlescombe mill-pool below the waterfall. Another terrible tragedy took place in the family of the proprietor while the Gunpowder Works at Battle were at the height of their prosperity, for two sons and a daughter were drowned in Powdermill Lake, before the eyes of their parents who were powerless to help. (Shortly afterwards, a Mr. Curtis joined the firm which, as Curtis and Harvey, moved to Hownslow and was, until it became part of ICI, probably the largest manufacturers of sporting cartridges in the country.)

Meanwhile, the Battle Powdermills, together with those at Sedlescombe came under the management of Charles Laurence who had been in charge of the manufacture of gunpowder at *Crowhurst and Peppering-Eye*.[1] Under him and his son, Charles, the powder-mills continued to work until as late as 1874. Charles' daughter married George Till to whom the business in Battle (but not the Sedlescombe powdermill) passed. The closing of the Battle mill was due to the refusal of the Duke of Cleveland (owner at that time of the Battle Abbey Estate) to renew the lease because the frequent explosions caused by testing and blow-ups frightened the duchess. The output of the seven mills totalled 22 cwt. a day. The height of their prosperity was during the wars with France 1793-1815. The firm was finally incorporated with Messrs. Pigon and Wilkes and moved to Dartford.

The Powdermill at the foot of the Street was not the only one in the vicinity of Sedlescombe. When the Brede Furnace (Chapter 16) closed in 1766 a gunpowder-mill took its place and became the seventh in the Battle area.[1] Here too explosions burst, in 1778, 1787 and 1808. An extract from the *Sussex Weekly Advertiser* for July 16th, 1787, describes that explosion with terrible vividness: "On Wednesday last between 10 and 11 o'clock in the forenoon, Brede Powdermill belonging to Messrs. Brooke, Jenkins and Company, blew up, by which accident two men that were in it at the time, were most miserably burnt, one of whom named James Gutsel languished until next day and then died in great agony, and the other lives with little hope of recovery. The deceased, though he had the presence of mind to strip himself of his clothes immediately after the accident was scorched from head to foot, and in that miserable condition ran home to his family who lived about a quarter of a mile off. The other in some degree lessened his sufferings by jumping into a pond and extinguishing the fire about him. Had they been at the other end of the Mill, where the powder was

[1] Map A.

running they must have been blown to atoms. The explosion was felt at Westfield, a few miles distant, like the shock of an earthquake. The accident was occasioned by driving a large iron bolt from the troughs. A Powdermill at the same place blew up some years ago, when one man was blown to pieces, whose limbs were afterwards found scattered a great distance from each other. Another man, named Henley, was seriously injured at the same time." He survived to experience the explosion of 1808 which broke all the windows in Brede parish. "Old Mr. Henry Smith, formerly of Brook Lodge, used to relate that he was a schoolboy at the time. He was eating his dinner in front of the fire at the old boarding-school at Brede Hill when the explosion occurred. It threw his basket into the fire and he was pitched out of his chair. Portions of brick and stone from the building were found scattered in Rafters Wood. A few years ago when an oak tree was being sawn into planks, a brick was discovered which had been embedded in the tree by the explosion."[1]

In March 1808, "The attention of many persons here (Lewes) was attracted by a noise that resembled the report of a very heavy cannon. It was attributed to some distant disastrous explosion, which proved to be the fact as intelligence was received of the blowing up of the Powder-Works at Brede, a distance of at least 25 miles from the town. It was effected by three distinct explosions in quick succession—the first of these took place in the sifting house; the second in the running house; and the third in the magazine that contained 150 barrels of powder; which at a distance exhibited a very grand sight, being in appearance like a huge rock ascending majestically to the clouds. Not a vestige of the buildings in the manufactury was to be seen standing after the accident, and unhappily two men and an infant boy lost their lives. One of the men named Sinden, at work in the sifting house, had his head and limbs separated from his body and carried in different directions to a neighbouring wood wherein they were collected and placed together and presented a shocking spectacle. The other, named Harrod, it is supposed was killed crossing a small bridge with a barrel of powder to deposit in the magazine, as his left shoulder and part of his head were blown off. The child was killed in an adjacent cottage, that was much shattered by the explosion, either by the fall of the chimney or from the stroke of a piece of iron which came in contact with his bowels

---

[1] Austen.

and tore them out; he nevertheless survived the injury a few hours. By the violence of the explosion, large pieces of timber were forced into the earth and driven to the distance of a quarter of a mile. The town of Battle was strewn with brown paper and some portions of it were picked up at Boreham, distant more than 12 miles, in about fifteen minutes after the magazine exploded. The cause of the accident cannot be ascertained, nor is the amount of the loss yet known, but some have estimated it is between three and four hundred pounds. An old man named Henley, who thirty years ago received considerable bodily hurt from a similar accident and occupied a wooden building about a stone's cast away from the mill, this time escaped without injury, although the building was shivered about his ears. The unfortunate sufferers have both left widows with families to lament their dreadful catastrophe, and Mrs. Sinden who has six children, is far advanced in her pregnancy."[1] William Sinden was buried at Salehurst Church on March 7th: "cause of death: blown into 5 parts, his head, his leg and thigh, body and other leg, thigh and arm, and other arm from sudden explosure of Brede Gunpowder Works". The Mill buildings were rebuilt and continued to be used for the production of gunpowder until they finally closed down in 1825 without any further tragedies. But it was another half-century before the creak of the turning mill-wheel and the splash of the water in the mill-pool at Iltonsbath, which had filled the air for more than 600 years beside the Brooks, at last fell silent for ever; though the Mill cottage close to the smithy and wheelwright remained inhabited for many years longer before at last it was pulled down.

[1] S.W.A. 14. 3. 1808.

*Chapter Thirty*

## BEAUPORT PARK[1]

The ordnance map shows a very green area stretching from Rye to Heathfield, with Battle in about the centre of this very wooded piece of country. Battle Great Wood still remains a great wood. It includes Bathurst Wood[2] which in the old maps extended as far as Hollington, covering what is now Beauport and spreading across the present A.21 road to include the wooded lands which became Baldslow Place (now Claremont School).

*The Story of Beauport*
In the eighteenth century a family of hop growers, with a good eye for a site, built a house which they called Beacon Hill on the high ground at the southernmost end of Bathurst Wood, and there they lived.

It was in 1767 that it acquired its present name, Beauport, in the following manner. James Murray, who had been one of Wolfe's three commanders in the expedition against Quebec in 1759, became, the following year, Governor of Quebec, and in 1763 Govenor of Canada[3]. When the British settlers accused him of partiality to the French Canadians, he had to retire from his post and, in 1766, returned to England. There he bought Beacon Hill and a large part of Bathurst Wood, rebuilding the house in classical style. Beauport was the name of the house near Quebec which had been the headquarters of the French general, Montcalm, before the Battle for the Heights of Abraham in which Murray had commanded the left wing against him. Beauport, the newly-built mansion became and Beauport Park took over from Bathurst Wood.

[1] Map A.
[2] Map B.
[3] Enc. Brit.

After a House of Lords' enquiry, Murray was exonerated from the charges brought against him in Canada and in 1774 was made Governor of Minorca[1]. Here he fell in love with Anne Witham, the young daughter of the British Consul, and married her as his second wife while she was still in her teens and he was nearly sixty. He seems to have been born to trouble for, besieged by a large force of French and Spaniards in 1781, he was obliged eventually to surrender after resisting a siege for more than half a year. Court-martialled on his return to England, he was once again acquitted and was made a general a year later. He enjoyed Beauport for about another ten years and died there in the early summer of 1794, four months after his infant son, George. Both were buried at St. Helens, Ore, where a mural monument commemorates him and other members of his family. His surviving son, James, was eleven when his father died and became a General too and also an M.P.

In the following year, Beauport was bought by Sir James Burges, recently retired from politics, having been Under Secretary of State for Foreign Affairs. As well as being given a baronetcy on his retirement, he had received also the appointment of Knight-Marshall of the Royal Household, a romantic post which gave him a part in the medieval ceremonies at the Coronation, with the right to ride in the royal procession and also to manage the Ceremony of the Champion in Westminster Hall after the Banquet. He was in fact the Earl Marshall's deputy. The appointment carried also a salary of £2,000 a year and gave him precedence over all other baronets in the Kingdom.

Sir James married a French girl, Anne Montolieu, and their child was duly christened Charles Montolieu Burges. On receiving an inheritance from a friend named John Lamb, Sir James changed his name by Royal Licence to Lamb and thus became the first of the Lambs of Beauport, a dynasty which was to last until 1921.

Charles Montolieu duly inherited and became Sir Charles Lamb of Beauport in the County of Sussex. He married the widow of Lord Montgomerie, whose son, Lord Eglinton, was therefore half-brother to young Charlie Montgomerie Lamb, born at Beauport in 1816 and christened by the Rector of Hollington. How these two, Lord Eglinton and Charles Lamb, were involved in the Last Tournament to be held in Britain in 1839 is described in a fascinating

[1] Horsefield: 1.

book *The Knight and the Umbrella* by Ian Anstruther. Knights and fair ladies had always exerted a strong fascination on Charlie from his earliest youth and he built a tilt-yard at Beauport and also made a collection of armour. Romantic circumstances surrounded also his marriage to Charlotte Gray, by whom he had several children, the eldest being Archibald, who inherited from his grandfather, Sir Charles, in 1879, his father, Charlie Lamb, having already died.

Sir Archibald was Baronet of Beauport for forty-two years, the fourth and last generation of a colourful family who had inhabited it, loved it and beautified it over a hundred and twenty-seven years, planting in the park, it was said, a specimen of practically every known tree. When he was thirty he married a young widow, Louisa Fenwick, but she gave him no heir. He lived richly and many are the stories still current about him. He died at last in 1921 and the son of his sister, who had married a Singleton, inherited Beauport.

The trees remained unique and, with public footpaths crossing it, the park was a beautiful place in which to wander until, in 1939, it became a testing ground for Canadians for their mortars; and a forbidden area. Accidents occurred when this rule was flouted, and one lad who picked up something that looked to him interesting lost a hand and an eye.

After the war the mansion was run as an hotel and the stables, which had been used as Riding Stables before the War, continued again as such. In 1969 a small golf course was constructed in part of the park by Hastings Corporation and some archaeological enthusiasts did some excavating while the chance offered.

*Bathurst Wood*

Beauport had been carved out of Bathurst Wood (now Battle Great Wood) in the midst of which, tradition says, stood a castle called Bathurst Castle which was destroyed in the conflicts of the Wars of the Roses.[1] Interested people are still seeking its site; but history in Bathurst Wood started long, long before that.

It began, like other sites in Sedlescombe, with the finding and smelting of iron by the Romans in the early first century or, very possibly before they came, by the early Britons. These bloomeries were very extensive ones leaving behind a huge cinderbank described by James Rock as "a wooded knoll, with heavy timber upon it, presenting but little to indicate that it was the handiwork of

[1] Horsfield.

man. It covered the space of two acres or more, and at the highest part had an elevation of 50 feet above the surrounding land."[1] First recorded by a Rector of Hollington, S. Arnott, in 1862, it was noted by James Byner, the Parish Surveyor, as a storehouse of material for use in road-metalling. Eight years later, after the cinder-pile at Oaklands (Chapters 2 and 33) had been exhausted, he set his workmen to open the heap and to start removing from it load upon load of iron slag thus using up 2,000 to 3,000 cubic yards per annum.[2] Amateur archaeologists kept a watch for antiquities and paid the workmen for any particular discoveries. These included two Roman coins, one of Trajan (A.D. 53-117) and one of his successor, Hadrian; some pottery remains and a bronze ring; but the most interesting object found was "a small beautifully modelled statuette of cast iron, much corroded" which can be seen with the other discoveries in the Hastings Museum today.

Charles Dawson (now of Piltdown Skull fame) described how the statuette had been discovered in about 1877 by William Merritt of Kent Street, one of the workmen employed in digging in Beauport for road metal and how he, Charles Dawson, had acquired it from him some six years later.[3] "If we may speculate," he wrote, "upon the discovery of one isolated specimen, it would seem that the Romans, or Romano-British, who smelted iron at Beauport, had already attained the art of casting iron to a great degree of perfection". This was news indeed, for the Romans were thought to have been unable to make cast-iron, so there was much discussion over the find among the learned. The Keeper of the Roman Antiquities at the British Museum pronounced it to be of Roman form. Sent to the Royal Arsenal at Woolwich for analysis, a portion of metal removed from inside one of the leg stumps of the statuette was reported to be, without the slightest doubt, cast-iron. Charles Dawson, therefore, triumphantly claimed the statuette to be "the earliest known example of cast-iron in Europe at least".

Straker, writing in 1931, many years before the Piltdown Skull (also found by Charles Dawson) was discovered to be a cunning piece of forgery, says shrewdly:

"Notwithstanding Mr. Dawson's belief in the authenticity of his find, there are some doubts on the matter. The sale of the objects found was a valuable source of income to the diggers, and

[1] S.A.C. 29.
[2] Wealden Iron.
[3] S.A.C. 46.

it is possible that deception may have been practised. From the context it is evident that similar bronze figures have been produced, and a replica in modern cast-iron would not be difficult to cast and to corrode by burial."[1]

There is little need to forge finds of antiquity, for the whole of this area shows indisputable and intensive Roman occupation. The name Kent Street for that small stretch of road, which was an ancient parish track still easy to trace long before the Turnpike road was built, has always seemed to indicate a Roman origin and a habitation site has now been discovered. A five-metre square of it was completely excavated to show walls standing unusually high suggesting "parts of six different rooms. One of the two largest has a hypocaust and the other is well-paved with tiles and has painted wall-plaster. Here was found a fine so-called chimney lamp."[2] More and more secrets will undoubtedly be brought to light when money is available for further excavation of this, "the most extensive of all the Roman iron sites of the Weald."[2] Roman-British iron-workings were found too when Baldslow Place (now Claremont School) was built by the Ebdens in the woods beside the new Turnpike road, before the turn of the century; and the cinder-remains from them were used in local time-honoured fashion for metalling drives and paths through its grounds.

The length and breadth of Bathurst Woods must have been an intensely-worked industrial area in those far-off days when Britain was an occupied country.

*Farms on the Beauport Estate*

The estate covered in an unbroken stretch all the land of small farms between the Hastings-Battle road on the west, Bluemans Lane and Westfield Lane on the east and south and New England Lane on the north. These included Norton's, Carpenter's Barn, Gotways, Irelands, Bluemans, Buckhurst, Moat Farm and Spray's. It was not for about thirty years that the Turnpike road, now A.21, was built, cutting the whole estate in two. By the end of the nineteenth century most of that part of it lying on the east of that road had been bought from the Lambs by the Sayer family of Fairlight, and it was Carlile Sayer who in 1928 sold to the Hastings Corporation the parcel of land at Kent Street where the artesian well and pumping station now stand.

[1] Wealden Iron.
[2] Trans. B.H.S. 1968-9.

*Norton's* (Map A): In 1569 this farmhouse belonged to a member of the Bishop family: George Bishop doth hold . . . land called Colyscroft . . . and lands called Manning belonging to his tenement called Nortons."[1] In 1433 it had been held "lately by John Norton and formerly by Robert Cole".[2]

A Ewhurst Deed describes its sale in 1628:

"Norton's. 1 messuage 1 barn, 1 garden 1 orchard, and 6 pieces of land, meadow and pasture together with Colles als Collescroft and Mannyngs 18 acres in the parishes of Battle and Westfield, messuages lately purchased by Nicholas Catt, yeoman of Ewhurst, from Thankful Bishop."[3]

Today, more than 350 years later, it stands there still well settled among great elm trees, its fields sloping up from Kent Street, with an old track to Battle running through them. One of its barns was built at the very end of the same century. At an early period it was, as might be supposed, farmed by a family called Norton's but, for many generations in the nineteenth and twentieth centuries, it was farmed continuously by members of the large Eldridge family. The main farm of the Beauport Estate, it was often at that time known as Eldridges. The farmworkers served, man and boy, generation after generation. One of the family remembers a steam-plough at each end of a field with coils of wire pulling the great four-breasted plough across and back. It was surprising to read in the farm accounts that as late as 1886 a field was twice ox-harrowed. It proved to be, however, that an ox-harrow had been used drawn by four horses; a horse harrow used only two horses. An ancient cottage on the farm, the home of a labourer pulled down in living memory, was nothing more than a hovel with earthen floor.

After many earlier alterations, a modern wing was added to the old farmhouse in the late nineteenth century. Bert Eldridge, farmer and hop-grower, was the last member of the family to live in it, with his two sisters, Rose and Margaret. Rose, an L.R.A.M., was a lady of great presence, who delighted to try to continue to live in the grand old style. During the 2nd war, she organised rifle practice on the lawn, fully determined to deal with any invading Germans. A German aircraft did, in fact, crash on the farmland and canisters of incendiaries fell around the cowsheds. This was just what Rose

[1] B.A.S. 1569.
[2] B.A.S. 1433.
[3] E.S.R.O. Tufton MSS. U. 455. T 113.

had been preparing for, and all was ready for the event, with stirrup pumps, sandbags and fire-drill. A landmine too fell nearby in Beauport Park; and Buckhurst Farm across the road was machine-gunned, so she was happy to be proved right to be well prepared.

She died in 1961 and the following year the lease was up and the farm was sold; so Bert and Madge had to leave their old home, thankful perhaps that Rose had not lived to see the day. Madge died five years later.

The farm is now one of many where fruit and vegetables can be bought, ready picked, or picked by the customer. In its barn is a museum of old farm tools, carts and bygones; and a nature-trail, part of the ancient track from Sprays Bridge which went through the farm, takes walkers past Wet Woods and Burnt Chimneys, once a smallholding, through the woods to Battle. Close by is Stonehouse, of old a Keeper's cottage, where once a Swedish sculptor lived and for long crumbling to ruin, but now restored and inhabited.

Horses are again drawing the plough across its fields and the farmer's wife wins the ploughing match.

*Irelands Farm*

Irelands Farmhouse dates from the late sixteenth or early seventeenth century and has, like most old houses, been added to in the course of the centuries. Its attic, reached by a short steep flight of stairs from the first storey, is interesting in two ways. There is a secret room below it with a trap door into the kitchen; and in the kitchen floor immediately beneath is another trap-door leading down into the cellar below the house. The secret room is large enough to hold a person and was used by smugglers as a hiding-place, when hard-pressed, and for their contraband spirits and tobacco. In this connection the other interesting item in the attic is a Snuff-mill clamped to one of the sloping joists in the roof. It was only when the present owners, who were born in the house, happened to see a photograph of a snuff-mill in a journal that they discovered what the strange contraption in their attic was. Set back on a lonely hidden lane the farmhouse would have been a most useful smugglers' hide.

After the building of Beauport, it became with all the neighbouring farms part of that estate; a mixed family farm, composed of sheep, cattle and corn. Passing from the Lambs to the Sayers, it became independent again in 1933 when the latter estate was sold.

*Buckhurst* (Map A)

This is a traditional farmhouse of the late sixteenth or early seventeenth century. The date 1684 can be seen on a beam inside. The bricks on the front of the house are red and slate-blue alternately, making thus an unusual chequered pattern not often seen. Built at a time, I am told, when the west wind was thought to be an "evil wind" responsible for bringing with it the sick humours of life, including rheumatism, it faces east; and the low roof comes protectively down on the west side in a "cat's slide" to within six feet of the ground giving the fullest amount of shelter that was possible to all within.

In the garden is a yew tree old enough to have been useful in providing wood for bows and arrows for defence and for hunting. The farm road, which joins Moat Lane and once crossed from the farm over into Beauport Park and so to the Battle road, is said to be part of an old coaching road.

*Carpenters Barn*

It is a surprise, perhaps, to discover that this modern house of fair size, which stands on the edge of Beauport and close to the A.21 on its western side, began its life as a tiny two-roomed thatched cottage complete with bake oven which can still be identified at the northern end of the building. Here, too, is an unusual window, long, narrow and of two lights; the northerly one being protected with two vertical bars of twisted iron. On the central division of the window are two gate-irons which could have held a shutter. Why did only half the window need such particular protection?

A tradition says that here was a toll-gate and this was the pay-window, but it is difficult to relate it to the Turnpike road of the eighteen-thirties; though certainly this crossed close to—but not close enough—the ancient coach-way running from the Battle ridge to join the old Roman road at Sprays Green near Westfield.

The tiny cottage was added to in the later nineteenth century, probably by one of the Lambs of Beauport for their labourers. When the Beauport estate was sold it became an independent smallholding and has recently been once again enlarged.

Whether it took its name from a one-time occupier or whether it was the workshop barn of a carpenter has not so far appeared.

*Spray's Green* (Map B)[1]

Spray's Bridge, spanning a stream which rises in Beauport Park and flows southwards into the River Brede, is in Westfield parish. A few yards east of it beside the crossways, where Blueman's lane joins the old Roman road from Sedlescombe to Westfield, stands the beautiful old house of mellowed brick, its roof crowned with a tall pair of ornamental chimneys. The curved head of the central porch is reminiscent of Dutch architecture and bears the date 1699 and the initials A.S.E., surely those of Adrian Spray (and his wife, Elizabeth) "of Sedlescombe" who figures in the records of 1707 and 1708 as a recalcitrant grandfather of "Samuel and Thomas Wicks, poor children of the parish of Sedlescombe" (Chapter 18.)

It is possible that the date refers only to the building of the porch, part of an enlargement of an earlier house; for Horsfield states that the Sprays Green estate was "formerly the property of a family of that name the last of whom, Adrian Spray, died at the beginning of the eighteenth century, when it passed to the Rev. Dr. Lamb of Iden", thus becoming for a time part of the Westfield Place estate, bought by Dr. Lamb's father, Thomas Lamb, Esq., of Rye. Dr. Lamb aliened Westfield Place to Sir Charles Montalieu Lamb, of Beauport; and Sprays Green figures in the will of Charlie Lamb, Sir Charles's son, who died in 1856. By the end of the nineteenth century Sprays, with Buckhurst and Irelands, had passed to the Sayer family of Fairlight and so it remained for over half a century. When that estate in turn was sold, Sprays Green House was bought independently of the farm, in the fields of which it is so happily set.

The house is beautiful inside, too, with fine oak beams and doors, and the spacious kitchen is typical of the farmhouse of old-fashioned children's stories. A map of 1740 shows a watermill standing close by Spray's Bridge, a cornmill.

The house from which the farmer now farms his 92 acres stands a few hundred yards away, up Spray's Lane.

*Gotways*

In 1433 Thomas Wodeman held "lands called Goteway" of Battle Abbey.[2] In 1569 the same lands were held by Nicholas Dobson in the right of his wife, daughter and heir of George Batchelor."[2] The old farmhouse stood beside the old parish way which climbed down

---

[1] Marked 6 Old Mill Bridge.
[2] B.A.S. 1433.

Whydown Hill to meander through Kent Street past Carpenters Barn uphill to the Harrow. For centuries a small farm, it, held of Battle Abbey, became in the nineteenth century part of the Sayer estate. Young Raymond Hook had his first job there, helping his father with his four-horse team, ploughing, carting and shifting for George Dann, the tenant farmer. At 14 you had to be a man, carrying sacks of beans weighing $2\frac{1}{2}$ cwt. At 16, when his father died, he took over the team.

In 1920, Major Sayer, back from the war, sold Gotways to Mr. Green, whom tragedy soon overtook. As his pedigree Jersey herd were crossing the road for milking, an unaccustomed car speeded down the road. In trying to save his show cow, he was himself knocked down and dragged along. By the time he reached hospital he was dead. His son carried on the dairy farm. The house has since been modernised and, after World War II, the farm has been sold more than once.

As Major Sayer sold plots of land at Kent Street, bungalows and houses sprang up one after another between the wars. He himself built Suntrap. Dickerbosch was set up by the British Legion as a general store for Reg Sellens who, blown up on Hill 60 in War 1, returned home minus a leg and plus a metal plate inside his head. Named by him from a war-time memory he might have wished to forget, it remained a shop, known as Dickie Bush, run later for years by a well-remembered character, Mrs. Floyd. It is now Yew Tree Cottage.

*Chapter Thirty-one*

## THE LAST LABOURERS' REVOLT

The years after the Napoleonic Wars were some of the hardest that the country people in England had ever known. Till the turn of the century there had been few villages where they did not derive a regular income from the work of their hands in their own homes or in some small mill or factory; this, together with the produce from their strips of land, and their cow and pig which grazed on common land, gave the villagers freedom from complete dependence on their wages. The Enclosures, very gradual in East Sussex though they had been, had taken this away by depriving them of their land. In Sedlescombe there seems little sign of any enclosures; each of the houses in the Street still had its acre strip or a little less; but Taxes were extremely heavy even from today's point of view, the Poor Law was unaltered since Elizabeth's reign, unemployment was high and farm wages below subsistence level.

All over Kent and Sussex protest was once again spreading. Men of the villages were gathering, as they had in the fourteenth and fifteenth centuries, choosing a leader and marching determinedly, but without violence, to the houses of the parson or the squire, where they demanded a decent wage, a reduction of tithes, a lowering of rents, more humane poor relief, and often the destruction of the new mechanical threshing machines which were depriving them of their work. The only violence was the occasional wrecking of a workhouse or the ducking of an unpopular overseer.

Many of the smaller farmers and a few of the clergy and gentry sympathised with them and showed concern over their poor conditions.

On October 16th, 1830, a meeting was held at Battle which Cobbett, the political reformer, and famous author of *Rural Rides*, addressed. Speaking for two hours, he advocated an alliance between all countrymen—aristocracy, farmers and labourers. He condemned violence, arson and destruction but rejoiced at the improved wages which had resulted. Having aroused his audience in turn to great bursts of applause, laughter and fierce anger, Cobbett concluded:[1]

"Here is a petition ready, let us all sign it; and then we shall be restored to the happy state in which our forefathers lived."

He reported the meeting in his "Political Register":

"At Battle, last night . . . a stage made with faggots and boards for me to stand on; a chair for me to sit on before I began; an audience consisting of about 500 persons, chiefly from the villages around the town, and some from a distance of 15 miles, about a third part of the audience in smock-frocks, about a twentieth of it consisting of women, mostly young; and, while the rest of the auditory had to stand all the while, seats had been provided for a row of these pretty Sussex women (always admired by me), who were thus ranged directly before me. I was really at home here; here were assembled a sample part of this honest, sincere, kind and once free and happy people, amongst whom I was born and bred up, and towards whom my affections have increased with my age."

A week or so later, fires were raging in the district and barns and ricks were being destroyed, actions that were sometimes preceded by a warning or threatening letter to the farmer which concluded with some such phrase, as "Beware of the fatal daggar", and signed "Swing". Who Captain Swing was, and whether he ever existed, has never been discovered but he was certainly a very real and frightening bogey all over the country. Two Battle labourers, Bushby, and Goodman, a young cooper, were charged with burning a barn belonging to a farmer named Alderton. They were tried at the Winter Assizes held at Lewes in December and were found guilty, chiefly upon the evidence of a woman whose husband had instigated them to the crime. Arson was a capital offence though there had been no case of such a punishment for it in Sussex for over forty years. Thomas Goodman was persuaded to write a confession in which he said that he never "should of thought of douing aney Sutch thing if Mr. Cobet had never given aney lactures. I

[1] Trans. B.H.S. 1954. 1961. 1962.

believe that their never would bean aney fires or mob in Battell nor maney other places if he had never given aney lactures at all."

Goodman was pardoned but transported. Bushby was hanged on Saturday, New Year's Day, 1831.

"Long before daylight large numbers of labourers might have been seen trudging to Horsham to witness Bushby's execution which was to take place at noon. . . . A few minutes before twelve o'clock the big gateway of the gaol was thrown open and the unhappy victim, accompanied by the executioner, the chaplain and the gaoler, walked out in full view of the crowd which numbered over a thousand. Immediately surrounding the gallows stood eight or ten javelin men attending the Sheriff, who was present; and inside the prison walls a troop of Life Guards and two companies of Foot Guards were drawn up ready for an emergency. Bushby was a strong good-looking young man, 26 years of age, six foot high and full of vigour, but meanly-dressed in a short round-frock, packing-trousers and half-boots. Three or four privileged persons approached and shook hands with him, saying 'God bless you', to which he heartily responded. After he was pinioned he mounted the scaffold with a firm step; and when the rope was put round his neck and the end put over the beam, his demeanour was resigned and even dignified. In answer to the question if he wished to address the crowd, he said: 'I hope none of my friends will share my unhappy fate. Lord have mercy on my soul.' The crowd on this occasion was very patient and decorous and in a quite different frame of mind from that with which it would witness the execution of a hardened criminal. It was felt that a victim of hardtimes, and not a felon, had suffered, and many an eye shed tears. 'God bless him' and 'Lord have mercy on him' were the expressions to be heard."[1]

*The Times* of the day before had had a leading article on the Sussex Assizes strongly criticising the Judge and the attitude of the magistracy towards the labourers.

Meanwhile, early in November, some three weeks after Cobbett's meeting at Battle, the first organised mob in Sussex appeared at Brede. The assistant overseer of the poor, a man named Abel, had long made himself deeply disliked by his poor neighbours through his hard and unsympathetic, though strictly legal, attitude towards

[1] S.C.M. Feb. 1937.

them. All normal efforts to secure his removal having failed, the Brede labourers gathered at the Hundred Pound on the evening of November 4th and again on the following day, at the "Red Lion Inn", to discuss what could now be done. Here they were met by several sympathetic farmers who were themselves in a state of dissatisfaction over taxation; unable to get the tax or rate reduced they had turned to an attack on the tithes, demanding of their Rector a deduction of 25 per cent. When he had refused, a crowd of his parishioners had met outside the Rectory to support the farmers till eventually they won their case and the Rector voluntarily reduced the tithes.

At the meeting at the "Red Lion" "to discuss the present distress of the poor", some said "they would not mind being poor if they received civility". At the end of the meeting it was resolved

"that the gentlemen agree to give every able-bodied labourer with wife and two children 2s. 3d. per day from this day to the 1st March next, and from the 1st March to the 1st October 2s. 6d. per day and to have 1s. 6d. per week with three children and so on according to their family. (2) the poor are determined to take the present (assistant) Overseer, Mr. Abel, out of the Parish to any adjoining parish and to use him with civility. Signed C. S. Hill, Minister; William Coleman (Chitcombe) Francis Bourne, J. Bourne and J. Bourne junior" (these may well have given their name to Bourne Cottage along Brede Lane), "J. Ades, David Smith senior and junior, David and T. Noakes, T. Henley and Joseph Bryant."[1]

They proceeded without delay to carry out the resolution, though Abel threatened to shoot any who laid hands on him. The farmers then agreed to persuade him to submit peaceably and the labourers put him in a small dung-cart he had had made, which carried also stone and gravel. Asked where he would go outside the parish he chose Vinehall, so accompanied by 300 people he was pushed by women along Pottery Lane. Some sort of brake must have been applied down the sharp slope of Steephill; and they took turns in pushing as they all happily flocked along the narrow lane up and down the hills to Sedlescombe, where they stopped outside the "Queen's Head" to quench their thirsts on the Green before tackling the long pull up Church Hill. By the time they had negotiated the hills of Stream Lane they were thirsty enough to halt again outside

[1] S.C.M. xi, p. 103.

the "Royal Oak". All the time they were increasing in numbers till at last they arrived at Vinehall where they left Abel and his cart; themselves to return merrily, arriving back in the evening tired but happier still. There were more rejoicings at the "Red Lion" in Brede.

On the same day, the labourers at Battle on parish pay demanded of the Assistant Overseer there that their wages should immediately be raised or they would help themselves. Sir Godfrey Webster, informed, granted as magistrate a warrant for arrest of the ringleader who was brought before him, accompanied by hundreds of sympathisers. He defiantly declared that he would not be committed or detained, whereupon Sir Godfrey amid cheers from the whole crowd set him free. The Assistant Overseer abruptly left Battle.

The authorities were tracing all these disturbances to Cobbett's meeting at Battle. Sir Godfrey wrote:

"The feelings of the lower orders hereabouts is that they have only to commit a great number of acts of arson and plead Cobbett to escape punishment—so that Cobbett is looked upon as a guardian angel and his admirers, too numerous already, multiply fast."

He considered it was Cobbett, not Bushby, who should have been prosecuted. The Battle people, however, got up a Declaration in Cobbett's favour. One hundred and three farmers, craftsmen, artisans and labourers of Battle and 14 surrounding parishes, who had attended the meeting, signed it to prove that Cobbett had counselled nothing stronger than peaceful petitioning, denying that he had incited to such crimes as arson. Forty-one of the signatures were from Battle. About eighteen were from Sedlescombe. They were all men of solid worth and standing, not easily to be roused, sober-minded: John Austin; Spencer Ades (of Hancox); Philip Butler (The Cottage, now the doctor's house); Samuel Cook (the Thatched Cottage up Church Hill); John Crisford, brother-in-law of Butler (bricklayer of Castlemans); James and John Dennett, blacksmiths (the Gun Cottage); and Thomas Dennet, blacksmith, of Forge Cottage; Cornelius Golby in one of Henry Grace's cottages; Henry Grace, yeoman, of (now) Manor Cottages; Henry Noakes, carpenter; and John Nash, tailor; James Pepper, himself Overseer in 1839, wheelwright living at the Old Thatch; William Reed, farmer, Brede High Farm (now under the Reservoir); Henry Spears, tanner; Stephen Swadling, Thomas Wrench and Stephen

Young. Many of these names are to be seen on gravestones in the churchyard. There were also 6 signatures from Westfield, 5 from Ewhurst, 14 from Burwash, 11 from Dallington and 1 each from six other villages. The last signature is that of Henry Alderton, the farmer, whose farm was burnt by Bushby and Goodman. The fact that he, the victim, testified to Cobbett's innocence gives good support to the suspicion that Goodman's confession was false.

Nevertheless Cobbett was prosecuted because, in his "Political Register" he had written congratulations to the labourers on the concessions they had gained. He was charged with publishing a libel calculated to incite labourers to acts of violence, and was tried in July in London Guildhall. Lord Melbourne, Home Secretary, and Brougham, the Lord Chancellor, and four other ministers were subpoenaed. After defending himself in an eloquent speech in which he told the story of Goodman, he was acquitted. The proceedings developed into a trial rather of the Government than of Cobbett. Although the Judge's summing-up was unfavourable, the Jury disagreed and Cobbett was free. James Gutsell, the Battle tailor who had organised the declaration, was promptly appointed to be Cobbett's private Secretary and the Overseer of his farm in Surrey, a strange transformation for a tailor.

*Chapter Thirty-two*

## OAKLANDS AND THE COMBES

It was at about the time of Cobbett's meeting at Battle that Hercules Sharpe left the home of his fathers at Northiam and moved to Sedlescombe. He had been born at the end of the eighteenth century at Domons, where his family had lived for many generations and which it continued to own until 1924. As a young man he went on the fashionable Grand Tour and while he was in Rome fell in love with Anne Mary, the nineteen-year-old daughter of Sir Anthony Brabazon, an Irish Baronet. After their marriage in Rome in 1819, Hercules and Ann Sharpe stayed on in Europe where two sons were born to them. Soon after the birth of the second, another Hercules, they returned to England to Domons, the picturesque old house near Dixter which still bears the Sharpe arms; and here two more children were born to them, a son who did not outlive infancy and a daughter named after her mother, Anne.

So Anne was seven years old and her brothers, William and Hercules, ten and nine, when their father came to Sedlescombe and bought Hole Farm (Chapter 26), together with 300 acres lying on both sides of the River Brede, from the Mercer family who had owned it for at least a hundred and thirty years. The farm included "an excellent farmhouse, 3 barns, an oast-house and other outbuildings." Among the 300 acres were 30 of Whydown and 112 of Brede Farm.

The name Hole aptly described the farm, for its buildings were comfortably settled halfway up the hill-slope from the River Brede, alongside which all its farmlands and meadows lay across the valley from Sedlescombe.

Hercules Sharpe immediately gained the services of the famous architect, Decimus Burton, son of a famous father, James Burton, who had created St. Leonards-on-Sea with its several battlemented buildings rising romantically among the plainer façades of the more orthodox nineteenth-century houses. Decimus, born in 1800, had already designed Hyde Park and Hyde Park Arch for the Government.

So Hole Farm disappeared, Oaklands House and Park arising around it. Decimus retained the great chimney of the farmhouse, which can still be seen in the library; and the kitchen demesne also shows itself to have been part of the old farm.

Here the children, William, Hercules and Anne grew and played, learning to love dearly the fields and woods around their new home; watching the copper beeches, horse chestnuts and other trees, which their father planted in the park, growing as they grew; learning to know the fish in the river and the birds in the woods, the butterflies and the flowers. All three loved it throughout their lives and two of them died in Sedlescombe, full of years.

But most particularly did Hercules, a gentle and friendly boy, come to know every part of it and, with his ready pencil, soon began to try to draw the farm animals and the trees and flowers in the curving fields through which he wandered. In bad weather he was never at a loss for occupation, drawing and painting for hours on end. He developed early, too, a great love of music, enjoying increasingly learning to play the piano.

The brothers were sent away to school, first to Dr. Hooker's private school and then to Harrow, where Hercules' name ensured that he would be expected to show attributes and fighting strength entirely foreign to his artistic nature. Gentle he may have been but he had plenty of sturdy independence. From there he went on to Trinity College, Cambridge, where he read Mathematics, and thus acquired through geometry a skilled understanding of the laws of perspective to add to his artist's equipment. It was at this time that his brother, William, on the death of their childless uncle, Sir William Brabazon, inherited his estate and Brabazon Park in Co. Mayo. By the terms of their grandparents' will, both grandsons assumed the name of Brabazon in place of Sharpe. Thus Hercules who had been baptised with his mother's surname for his second name became impressively, Hercules Brabazon Brabazon. Their sister, Anne, at about this time married Boyce Harvey Combe, thus introducing those names into Sedlescombe, where she continued to live after her marriage, and Boyce, the eldest grandson of Harvey Christian Combe of Cobham Park, Surrey, not born a Sussex man, became one by adoption.

After taking his degree, Hercules was expected to follow family tradition and read for the Bar but, not surprisingly, he refused, determining to study art and music in Rome. Skill in painting pictures was considered a most desirable accomplishment for a gentleman but certainly not a full-time occupation, and his father hopefully curtailed his allowance in an effort to bring him to heel; so for three years he lived in Rome, short of money but rich in artistic experience.

It was then that he and his family suffered a great loss when his brother, William, died suddenly in Malta at the age of only 26. Hercules, inheriting then the Brabazon estates in Mayo, became assured of a steady if modest income which enabled him to be independent of his father and so to devote his life from henceforth to painting and the study of art and music. Eleven years later, on the death of his father, he became squire of Oaklands and a wealthy man, free to paint as he willed without any necessity to sell his work.

*Hercules Brabazon, Water-colourist*
His name is still well-known in the world of art, for his impressionist water-colours remain amazingly modern in style.

He spent three years studying under d'Egville and Alfred Fripp, and he worked in France with Ruskin, more than once sketching the same subject. He travelled in Spain where he was fascinated by Velasquez who was still little appreciated in England; and month after month of winter he spent among the luminous colourings of the Riviera. As the *Manchester Guardian* expressed it at the time of his death, "In the more active part of his long life he moved about Europe from one beautiful place to another, like the English lords of his youth, on a never-ending Grand Tour." At a time when travel was difficult, he would pack a light bag with one spare suit and a few shirts, together with his box of water-colours and bottles of Chinese white, and travel to far-off places; Egypt and Algeria, India and Istanbul, Jerusalem and Baalbeck. For many years he was content to paint always in water-colour but later he turned increasingly to the use of pastels, often using both in the same picture.

Turner was his great inspiration; Ruskin considered him Turner's successor. Again and again he is compared with that master-painter. The description of "the perfect amateur" was applied to him while Turner was "the perfect professional".

He was nearly seventy years old before he ever exhibited but, on being elected in 1890 a member of the New English Art Club, he was duty bound to exhibit at its shows; and finally Sargent, who felt for him great admiration as well as gratitude, persuaded him to agree to a one-man show. This was held in 1892 at the Goupil Gallery, New Bond Street, and received universal acclaim. "Water colours such as Mr. B.'s," wrote one critic, "would lose nothing of their own power if placed next to Mr. Turner's beautiful drawings. The crispness and sincerity of his work as well as its exquisite simplicity enchant the eye"; and another noted "that impressionism can be exquisitely beautiful, as Mr. Whistler and Mr. Brabazon have taught us." Another declared, "Mr. Brabazon is perhaps at his best in pastel. . . . Beauty and character of place are the two things that concern this fine artist." Brabazon gave all the proceeds to charity, thus carefully maintaining his amateur status.

The painter, Augustus Hare, his neighbour at Holmhurst on the Ridge (now St. Mary's School, Baldslow), however, alluded to his sketches as "inspired smudges" and to his impression of the Coliseum as a "decayed sponge". H.B.B. was too courteous to reply.

In 1893 when he was 72, Sargent painted his portrait in oil and it now belongs to the National Museum of Wales; two years later Sir William Rothenstein made a charcoal drawing of him, now in the British Museum.

Throughout his life, H.B.B. had fed his love of music and had become a highly skilled pianist. Advanced music was his delight and at his London flat in Morpeth Street he would hold afternoon parties at which serious musicians of the day would play. His intense joy in fine performances, whether with brush, instrument or pen, was infectious in its enthusiasm. The comment repeatedly made was that his artistic and intellectual vision never grew middle-aged or old.

*H.B.B. as a Country Landlord*

It might well be thought that in such a life there would be no time in it for Sedlescombe, but though he travelled so much during his long life, he cared well for the Oaklands estate during the near half-century of his ownership, and added continually to it, so that by the time he died he owned nearly all the Street houses and many of the surrounding farms, including Hurst and Jacobs. The initials H.B.B., a familiar sight still today on cottages, are proof of the truth of Admiral Chambers' description of him as an "excellent landlord", for they mark ones which he restored or built. They include Tanyard House, Brede Barn Cottages, Little Hurst in Hurst Lane, Ivy Cottage and Springfield in Brede Lane, The Cottage, the new wing to Asselton House and many more.

As a landowner he was, it is said, beloved of his tenantry, and many a struggling worker received assistance at his hands. He was, too, a generous supporter of village affairs, the joint Horticultural Society of Sedlescombe, Westfield and Whatlington held its show yearly in the grounds of the Park, a field was set aside for the Cricket Club, the same which is still the cricket field today, by kind permission of the present owners.

Though he never married, being perhaps "wedded to his art", he was devoted to his family, his sister Anne, Boyce her husband, who died before his brother-in-law, and their children, Harvey and Mary, and his great nephews and nieces, Harvey and Boyce Combe and Harry von Roemer (for Mary had married Baron von Roemer). What happened to Harry, one wonders, in the First World War?

So the young grew up in the great day of the country house and in the most prosperous years of Oaklands, with a round of balls and parties; but none of the Combes inherited the gifts and purpose in life of their relative, though the younger Harvey had, at least, the same love of Oaklands and the village, knowing every tenant and villager.

## The Death and Funeral of H.B.B.

H.B.B. was growing very old; his ebullient vitality was beginning to fail and in 1904 he became seriously ill. He gave up his London flat and returned to Oaklands where he was still able to enjoy sketching and playing the piano for two more years; till, on May 15th, 1906, he died peacefully in his sleep, aged 84.

The funeral which took place a few days later must have been the most impressive and widely attended ever to be held in Sedlescombe church; more so even than that of the village's other famous inhabitant, Sir Thomas Sackville, Knight of the Bath, though perhaps not quite so sartorially colourful.

The coffin was borne in a glass car, with the bearers in white "round frocks" walking on either side, closely followed by a long procession of horsedrawn carriages bringing the family mourners and the gentry from all the neighbouring country houses, and also many of his numerous London friends. The horses were decked in the custom of the day with black plumes on their bridles and the shining beaver hat of each coachman was hung with black drapes. So the long procession moved, with bits and harness jangling and wheels creaking, slowly down the drive and out through the Oaklands Gates, over the bridge and up the dusty Street where the lilacs and horse chestnut trees were blooming but where the blinds were drawn over every cottage window. There stood quietly, with caps off, all who could not attend the service. At the top of the long slope of Church hill, under the ancient Spanish chestnut trees, waited the Rector, Mr. Warner, with his curate the Rev. P. C. Drury, at the churchyard gate.

The coffin was carried into church by the four smock-frocked tenants, "The scene", says the newspaper account[1], "as all those assembled outside the churchyard bared their heads and followed was extremely impressive." The quietness of the churchyard was filled with the slow sound of the footfalls, the songs of the birds and the movements of the waiting horses punctuated by the sorrowful toll of the bell.

All the family were there. There too were Sir Augustus Webster of Battle Abbey, Sir Archibald Lamb from Beauport and his neighbour from Baldslow Place, Mr. Ebden; Mr. Egerton from Mountfield Court, the Brasseys from Normanhurst, and Dean Currie from Battle; Mr. Mullens from Westfield Place, the Adamsons from Great Sanders, the Pratts from Highfield, from Hurst came Mr. Vivian and from the village the grocer, James Byner, the postmaster, Mr. Hilder, Mr. Eldridge the carpenter, and George Simmons, the blacksmith, Herbert Dengate the builder and Holmes the butcher; George Kenward and the doctor, Dr. Kendall, and his wife and many another villager, unnamed in the report.

Mr. William Shakespeare, an old friend of H.B.B., played the organ; "I know that my Redeemer Liveth" before the service began and, at the close, the Dead March from Saul. The great congregation followed the coffin, still borne on the shoulders of the white-frocked tenants out into the sunlit day to the corner of the churchyard where the hawthorn hedges overflowed with blossom and the mild blue of violets and bluebells on the banks beneath contrasted with the brilliant blooms of the numberless wreaths widely carpeting the grass.

[1] H. & St. L. Ob. May 1906.

Till the restoration of the church in 1870, the Oaklands family had buried their dead in a vault under the church below their memorial tablets, as had the Bishops and Sackvilles. So Boyce Harvey Combe had been the first to be buried in the churchyard. H.B.B.'s grave, lined with moss and flowers, was close beside it. On that grave lies now a cross of Irish granite surrounded by a curb on which is the following inscription, composed by his nephew, Harvey T. B. Combe:

"In Memory of Hercules Brabazon Brabazon of Oaklands, late of Brabazon Park, Co. Mayo. He died at Oaklands 14th May 1906 aged 84. Loved and Respected."

Thus passed H.B.B., probably the greatest of all the people described in these pages, and his funeral, the like of which will in the village never be seen again.

*Harvey Trewythen Brabazon Combe and Florence Amy, his wife*

His heir was Harvey Combe, son of his sister, Anne, who during his uncle's lifetime had lived with his wife at Jacob's Farm in Powdermill Lane where the two sons, Harvey Alexander and Boyce Anthony had been born. Both were young men when their father inherited, Harvey being 22 and Boyce 17.

In the year following H.B.B.'s death an exhibition of his works was held in Hastings Museum where still can be seen about a dozen of his paintings, which he himself presented. A Memorial Gallery was set up in the great Barn then on the Oaklands estate, now known as the Tithe Barn, where Mrs. Harvey Brabazon Combe arranged a permanent exhibition of his paintings. On a gate-legged table in the centre of the barn were displayed books connected with the artist's life, together with a bulky volume of appreciative press cuttings. In a little adjoining room, in ill-assorted contrast, was exhibited a collection of fearsome relics in the shape of iron-toothed man-traps strongly sprung for the purpose of catching and holding fast the legs of poachers.

Among all the pictures of foreign scenes were several of Sedlescombe; of Oaklands; "Brede Lane in Autumn"; Brickwall; "A Cottage in Sedlescombe"; and "Sedlescombe from Street Farm". These are all untraced today.

"The artist had made her," wrote Mrs. Combe, "the custodian of his life's work, which I am now, through the generosity of my husband, able to incarcerate in so worthy a gallery. It was to me, the wife of his nephew, that Brabazon bequeathed his folios of exquisite work, and my desire to share all that is beautiful and pleasant with my fellow-beings has prompted me to establish a gallery in his own village."

There were two thousand of these pictures.

The first World War brought tragedy to the Combe family as to so many others in the village and in the world when, at the Battle of Ypres on November 11th, 1914, Boyce was killed at the age of 24. Harvey had most dearly loved his younger brother and mourned his loss to the end of his life.

His father had been an invalid for many years and it was his wife who kept in touch with the tenants, and she is still remembered for her kindness. Edgar, an oldish man now, says,

"I'll never forget her for her kindness to my father, who came back from the 1914 war with his heart damaged for ever. She used to come and look after him and bring him brandy to help him."

That was not 'charity' to be despised as is the fashion to talk about it today. That was genuine caring as in fact was very much of the so-called 'charity'.

Nine years later his father died at the age of 71, having been "squire" of Oaklands for seventeen years. The local paper described the funeral thus:

"The village of Sedlescombe united in mourning the loss of a respected and beloved 'squire' on Saturday when the funeral of Major Brabazon Combe of Oaklands took place. The coffin was borne on a farm wagon, on each side of which walked bearers in their old Sussex white smocks with black gloves. The procession was met at the church gate by the Rector, the Rev. Ernest Reid, and the Rev. C. Morgan of Westfield. A large number of people were gathered in the road and the church was crowded. There was a pathetic incident when Mr. F. Woods, an old family servant was helped up the steps to the church."[1]

Major Combe was buried beside his father and uncle. Among the wealth of wreaths were those from the Parish Council, the Sedlescombe Village Men's Club, the Oaklands Staff and the Estate and farm employees.

[1] H. & St. L. Ob. 1923.

So "Har" Combe, "the Captain", now aged 39, married and father of a small daughter, Eileen, moved out of The Cottage and into Oaklands, succeeding to his great grandfather's estate at a time when it was encumbered with debt.

So it was that the great Auction took place of all the Combe property in the Street and of all their surrounding farms. Harvey retained only Oaklands House and Park itself.

At about the same time in an effort to help the financial situation, Mrs. Brabazon Combe, Harvey's mother, dealt a disastrous blow to the value of H.B.B.'s pictures and to his reputation as a painter by selling his pictures unrestrainedly and without reference to the catalogue he had carefully made in his last years. The London art market was, by this action of hers, flooded with over three thousand of his water-colours, pastels and drawings, and the prices obtained for them, at first extremely good, dropped on the third day of the sale to £15 apiece and lower.

In the nineteen-seventies, three exhibitions of his work have been held in London, a sign perhaps that his reputation is at last beginning to recover. His lovely paintings are greatly appreciated in America.

Harvey was to have two more wives but no more children and he soon knew himself to be the last 'squire' of Oaklands. In many ways he was a sad and lonely man but he loved every stick and stone, every tree and flower of Oaklands. Always he was short of money. The Second World War came and he was instrumental in obtaining the Bofors guns from Sweden for use in it, an achievement for which he vainly hoped to be financially rewarded and so save his estate. But in 1947 he reached the sad decision that Oaklands itself must be sold, one hundred and seventeen years after his great grandfather had built it. So the Brabazon Combes had owned for a few years less than their predecessors, the Mercers, its lands before they passed again into the hands of strangers.

The first purchasers, Lord and Lady Swaythling, never lived in it; but the next family, the Pritchard Jones, enjoyed it for a few years before it was on the market again. Purchased this time by the Trustees of the Pestalozzi Children's Village Trust in 1952 it had a completely new and busy life ahead; a life that still continues.

Harvey remained to live in the village among the friends of his youth until he died in 1955. No great funeral took place in Sedlescombe church for him. Gone were most of the landowning families from their old homes. Beauport was a hotel, Battle Abbey, Baldslow Place, Great Sanders and Vinehall were schools, and Normanhurst was demolished. Mountfield Court alone remained in the same ownership. Harvey has no grave even, beside those of his forebears. His ashes were scattered as he wished in his beloved Oaklands Park.

*Farms on the Oaklands Estate*
*Luff's Farm*
In 1830, Hercules Sharpe had bought beside Hole Farm itself "30 acres of Whydown and 112 of Brede Farm". Six years later the branch of the Turnpike road "through Sedlescombe to Cripps Corner" cut round Whydown Hill "through the lands of Hercules Sharpe to Sedlescombe bridge", thus putting the sloping fields of Luff's farm into an island.

The present house of Luff's with its oast was built some years later by John Catt, the Sedlescombe builder, for Hercules Brabazon, whose shield with coat of arms it bears. The farm buildings are very much older so there well may have been an earlier house on the site, though such does not appear on old maps nor, apparently, in the old records. Known as both "Westfield Barn Farm" and "Lutmans", it would seem to have had some earlier connection with Westfield Place, for a William Lutman of Hastings owned that house, according to Horsfield, from 1760 to 1787.

A small farm of some twenty acres now, it has the benefit of the water meadows, once covered by the river. When Mr. Hadley rented it from Hercules Brabazon, he farmed it together with the fields of Lower Marley, the old farmhouse where his mother lived. Part of the pastures of the dairy farm were, like those of every farm for miles around, given over in those years to hops. The water meadows round the old Powdermill were a small holding held by Jim Roberts who worked, too, for Hadley; and in the early twentieth century, Dallaway. Mr. Farrow took over Luffs and Lower Marley in 1913 and his family grew up there; but some years after he died, his son moved to Lower Marley, and the farm like the rest of Oaklands Estate was sold; since when it has remained an independent dairy farm.

*Mabbs Farm* (*now Brede Barn Farm*)  (Map A)
Hurst Farm, Blacklands Farm, and some of Brickwall Farm, were all part of Hercules Sharpe's 112 acres of Brede Farm, some

of which are now covered with the Council houses; the remaining fields belong to Mabbs.

In 1715 a Thomas Mabbs was paying rates on house and land in Sedlescombe. On the Tithe Map 1841 Mabbs Farm belonged to Hercules Sharpe of Oaklands as part of Hurst Farm, and its homestead was bordered by Brede Lane on the south and Hurst Lane on the east. Little more than a smallholding, it consisted of only six small fields, a narrow piece of woodland and three very small shaws, one of which, Park Shaw, has given its name to the estate of bugalows built in about 1960, westwards along Brede Lane close to the village.

After Hercules Brabazon succeeded his father as squire of Oaklands he rebuilt the homestead, making a pair of cottages which still bear the Oaklands heraldic shield. Today they are one cottage known as Brede Barn Farm.

The field path which continues southwards as an extension of Hurst Lane was the parish boundary with Brede.

Westwards of this path was another smallholding in the same ownership and called at that time, Field Farm. The pair of cottages which its fields surround was in 1841 still the property of the Mercer family (Chapter 26). Later it housed the Oaklands bee-man.

*Jacobs* (Map A)

There has been a house or cottage on the site of Jacobs since the thirteenth century, for a chimney of that date was incorporated in the later house and still remains. The name Jacobs is said to be another relic of that century and to have belonged to a smuggler of the name reputed to have lived in the cottage. Within a mile of the river Brede and secluded in its woodlands, it would have been a handy place for his smuggling activities, made the more secret by the alleged (but unlikely) building of a tunnel from it to a small cove on the river bank.

By the sixteenth century it was part of the Bishops' estate of Great Sanders and was known for some years as Henly's after the farmer who was leasing it. (In the seventeenth century Sarah Frensham married Henry Henly of Sedlescombe; in 1733 John Henly was paying tax for "Jacob's field" and Sam Henly in 1771.)

It belonged too for many years to the Mercer family (Chapter 26) and it was perhaps they who rebuilt and enlarged it in Queen Anne's reign giving it the façade which it bears today. A plan by

John Bowra made in 1777 shows that Mrs. Ann Davis, widow perhaps of Dan Davis, farmer, was the occupier and possibly owner of the house and its farmlands. In the nineteenth century, after they sold Hole Farm to Hercules Sharpe, the Mercers certainly lived in it for many years and Miss Tottie Flint and her brother were born there.

In about 1880 it was rented by Admiral Adeane who, when not in London, lived in it with his wife, Lady Edith, and their son, Henry Robert Augustus. The Admiral loved the place and found it not too far from his work at Chatham and in London. Henry spent much of his childhood and youth there and in 1909 married Victoria Bigge, daughter of Lord Stamfordham, who in the following year bore him a son, Michael. Four years later, before the war had been raging for many months, Henry was dead, killed at the Battle of Ypres (Chapter 43), like his neighbours Boyce Combe and Gillachrist Moore. Michael, then five years old, grew up to become Sir Michael Adeane (now Lord Adeane) private secretary to King George VI, as his maternal great uncle had been to King George V.

Jacobs was sold to Claud Bell but at the time of the second World War it belonged to Colonel King who was Captain of the Home Guard, "and a proper tartar he was" (Chapter 47). When the plan for the Reservoir was first being suggested, Col. King had, guilefully, spread it about that he was starting a pig farm in the rough field overlooking the Powdermill Valley which would of course pollute the proposed reservoir. In the negotiations with the Hastings Corporation, he was given in exchange for the 'pig field' a lovely pasture right in front of the house on the opposite side of the road. All the 'locals' knew that he had never had the slightest intentions of having pigs. Jacobs farm has benefited by his cunning.

After the war came Sir James Doak who built up a herd of Sedlescombe Golden Guernseys and a flock of Jacob sheep. This breed is so called from the fact that they are speckled and "ringstraked" like the ones described in the Bible story as promised to Jacob from the flock of his father-in-law, Laban; and increased by Jacob's mysterious trick with streaky rods at breeding-time.[1] The Doaks modernised the house to have five bedrooms and four bathrooms. Tragedy came to them when the elder of their two sons was killed in a car accident in his twentieth year.

[1] Genesis. 30. v. 31-43.

Sold to Sir John Keeling in 1971, Jacobs is now the home of his second son with his wife and their eight sons.

At the easterly end of the parish, unchanged outwardly, it is in much quieter surroundings today than it was in the seventeenth and eighteenth centuries, when the clang of the hammers and the roar of Brede Furnace was an accompaniment to living; and safer than when the powdermill was operating and several explosions rent the air (Chapter 16). Now a beautiful stretch of water covers the old hammer ponds, the home of waterbirds of many varieties and of trout and other fish (Chapter 46).

*Lower Jacobs Farm*

This used to be known as Beggar's Farm, nobody knows why today. Perhaps, they say, it was a place where beggars knew they would never be refused a crust of bread or, maybe, it was at one time yet another poorhouse, ill-named.

*Brook Lodge* (Map A)

Brook Lodge (Brook Farm on early maps) is another handsome roomy old farmhouse, with large well-proportioned rooms unusual in so old a house, standing within the bounds of Brede Parish but part of the Hurst estate of Sedlescombe. For years it was an independent small farm, one of the very few with flat fields, from which it took its name for, in Sussex, Brook is a water meadow; and all its meadows lie beside the river Brede.

Like neighbouring Jacobs, it is connected by tradition with the smuggling trade for which it had a perfect position, with a hedged path like a tunnel running dead straight to the river bank now a few hundred yards away but in earlier days, before the river shrank, the boats could tie up close to the house. Equipped too with a large cellar, the house seems to cry aloud for a rollicking tale of the eighteenth century; for in the corner of the cellar is a large well-like hole with steps in the bricks down its side. It may have been a well, for the water rises at high-water in winter time and floods the cellar; it would without doubt have made a good hiding-place for kegs of smuggled spirits.

Like practically every other farm in the parish, it has its oasthouse; an old villager remembers weeding the 'hills' round each hop plant while his mother 'tied'. He remembers the brimstone, used to help the hops to the primrose colour required, and the boxes of samples piled in the corner for the hop sampler. In his day 'scovets' were used for pushing the hops into the pocket and for pressing them down, but in his father's days they trod them. There were two great coppers where they used to make the beer. The old stable buildings, where the carters lived above their horses, stand close by with chimney and fireplace where the men could boil water and cook a hot meal. The same villager remembers his father sleeping above the stables. He wore hob-nailed boots, called 'water-tights', and long tanned leggings, while others wore trousers with a calf-strap below the knee.

In the woods close by, there was built in the nineteenth century the Isolation Hospital where Mr. and Mrs. Brown lived as caretaker and matron, with their young son and daughter. A single-storey shed with corrugated iron roof, it sounds a comfortless place and certainly was a dreaded one. Often it was empty, but a black flag on the flag-staff showed when there were small-pox or scarlet fever cases inside. It was pulled down only very recently in the second half of the twentieth century.

Brook Lodge, standing warm in its hollow, with clear traces of a once well-kept garden around it, is being restored again. Who knows how many times this has happened in its long life?

All the Oaklands farms, with the exception of Luffs, are now part of the Hurst Estate.

*Chapter Thirty-three*

## THE NEW ROAD

Until 1840 the only way to the "Royal Oak Inn" at Whatlington from Sedlescombe was by field path or by way of Church Hill and Stream Lane and then right, past Hancox. There was no road at all other than a parish track, from Black brooks; and travellers to Hollington from Sedlescombe must go round by Spray's Bridge on the old Roman road to Westfield and turn right at the crossroads there to Moat Lane, whence a "parish road" through Beauport led up to the Harrow and the road leading south to the sea.

The designing and founding of the new and fashionable town of St. Leonards by James Burton in 1828 brought an immediate demand for road improvement, for the St. Leonards coach had to make its way along the coast to Hastings and then inland to Ore in order to get on to the road through Battle to London.

In 1836, all this was changed by the passing of an Act for making and maintaining a Turnpike road from St. Leonards and St. Mary Magdalen to the "Royal Oak Inn" at Whatlington.

"Whereas," said the Act,[1] "it would be of great public utility if Powers were given to make a Turnpike Road or roads, commencing at North Lodge, St. Leonards," (where the Maze Hill archway now is) "and at South Saxon Hotel in the parish of St. Mary Magdalen, proceeding to and uniting at the Point of Junction of the Hastings, St. Leonards and Hollington roads at Hollington Lane in the parish of St. Leonards, to Blackbrooks in the Parish of Westfield; and from thence proceeding in two directions; one toward London up to and terminating at the "Royal Oak Inn" at Whatlington; (and the other towards Kent up to and

---

[1] S.A.C. 29. p. 168.

terminating at Cripps Corner in the Parish of Ewhurst;) (Chapter 2), together with a branch, leading out of such road commencing about a furlong on the South-West side of the Harrow Inn . . . and terminating at the Turnpike Road leading from Hollington to Battle to the West of the Harrow Inn . . . passing under such last-mentioned road near Harrow Inn by means of an archway, and from thence across certain lands of Sir Charles Lamb, Baronet, to and across a parish-road leading to Westfield 'Westfield Lane' through Baldsloe Wood and Moat Lane past the Yew Tree Cottage . . . crossing the present road leading from the Harrow Inn to Sedlescombe and to proceed from thence through the other part of the Moat Farm . . . whence the said intended Turnpike Road is to follow, for the distance of ½ mile, the road which at present leads from the Yew Tree Cottage to Carpenter's Barn; and proceed from thence through Norton's Farm to and along the road, which now leads from Kent Street to Whydown Hill, to Black Brooks from which place the road will proceed in two directions, one towards the Royal Oak at Whatlington leading through Brick Brook, Marley Farm and Petley Wood, over the stream near the corner of Petley Wood, through Spilstead Farm; in the Parish of Sedlescombe, and across the road leading from Sedlescombe to Whatlington[1] near Mr. Bates' Windmill[2] and from thence past Handcock's Farm to the Royal Oak at Whatlington and terminate in front of the cottage near the Royal Oak. . . ."

the other direction went to Cripps Corner through Sedlescombe (Chapter 2). Yew Tree Cottage, which no longer exists, stood just inside the field gate into Beauport, opposite Moat Lane, through which the old lane went up to the Harrow.

The portion of road between Black Brooks and the Royal Oak, still known as the New Road, was the only completely new stretch to be constructed where no kind of road existed before; for the portion from Black Brooks to the Harrow connected up and re-aligned short stretches of tracks or parish roads long in use for foot travellers and farm vehicles. All these old tracks where they diverge from the main road can still be traced; and it is noticeable that where a lane joins this new main road on its west side, there is without exception a clear indication of its continuation eastwards

---

[1] Stream Lane.
[2] Windmill Cottage.

on the other side of the road, making for Battle, the market town, to which practically all the old roads and tracks from Sedlescombe led.

The "New Road" was built with exactly the same material as the Romans had used for their road through Sedlescombe more than nineteen centuries earlier. James Byner, the Parish Highway Surveyor for Sedlescombe, having to find the material, had not far to look, for at the bottom of Oaklands Drive was a heap, thirty foot high, of iron-slag and iron-waste from the iron-workings described in Chapter Two. "Thousands of tons of cinder from this site," wrote Straker,[1] "were used when the New Road from the Harrow Inn to Whatlington was made in 1838-40" (Chapter 2).

The Act appointed Trustees for this Turnpike Trust, consisting of "all His Majesty's Justices of the Peace acting for the County of Sussex", together with every owner of land through which the roads would pass, "and their successors duly gratified," these included very many familiar Sedlescombe names including Bishops, Crisford, Duke, Daws, Henry Grace, Hilder, Laurance, Mercer, Pratt, William Read, Hercules Sharpe, Tilden Smith and Richard Smith, Selmes, Thorpe, Thomas and Winchester. Included also were James Burton, Architect of St. Leonards, and his four sons (one being Decimus, the designer, of Oaklands House, Sedlescombe), and also Sir William Ashburnham, and his son John, Sir Howard Elphinstone who owned land in the north of the parish, Charles Frewen, and Sir Charles Lamb of Beauport. Sir Charles, who was not only a Trustee of the Turnpike Trust but also a member of the Committee formed to bring the road into effect, served notices of action for trespass and ejectment on the Clerk of the Trust! This was to enable him to recover possession of land taken from his estate for the road, and to claim compensation for damage in the making of it. Two years later he put a proposal before the Trustees:

> "Payment for my land according to the valuation of Mr. Thomas including damage by severance or otherwise at £65 per acre—the slip of wood to be taken by me at the same rate—interest to be added to the price from the time the land was taken possession of—fencing to be paid for at the rate proposed by Mr. Bellingham and the land to be re-measured if I wish it. The Suit

[1] Wealden Iron.

in Chancery to be dropped, each party paying their own expenses. If this be agreed I will take a Bond for the money."
This was agreed, letters of Settlement being read to the Trustees at their meeting on December 4th, 1840. The Trustees had to pay Sir Charles £267 8s. 6d. in settlement. There is no record of any other land-owner acting similarly; the road did, however, cut his large estate in two.

The Act further pronounced:
"It shall be lawful for the said Trustees to erect or build upon each of the said roads or any part there-of or upon the sides thereof . . . when and where as they shall judge proper Toll Gates or Toll Bars, Toll Houses and Weighing Machines with Outhouses and Buildings thereto, and take and enclose suitable garden spots for such Toll Houses not exceeding One Eighth Part of a statute Acre as they shall think necessary."

There was already a turnpike system round Battle, and the road from Mount Street through Whatlington to Cripps Corner, where there had been a Toll-gate for many years, was part of it. Toll-gates on the new Turnpike road were erected at North Lodge in Maze Hill, St. Leonards where the Paygate Cottage still stands; and at Black Brooks (still known as Paygate though the cottage was demolished in 1956) for the branch road of Sedlescombe.

"Tolls to be taken by virtue of this Act shall not exceed the following: —

"For every Horse, Ass, or Mule or other Beast or Cattle drawing any Coach, Stage Coach, Landau, Berlin, Barouche, Sociable, Chariot, Calash, Hearse, Litter, Break, Chaise, Curricle, Gig or any other such Carriage; the sum of Fourpence.

"For every Horse, Ass, Mule etc. drawing any Wagon, Wain, Cart, Vans, Caravan or other such-like Carriage, having the Fellies of the wheels thereof the Breadth of 6 inches upwards at the Bottom or Sole thereof, the sum of Twopence. And in the Case of Fellies of the Wheels thereof are of less Breadth than 6 inches and not less than 4 inches and a half, sum of 3 pence; and in the case of the Fellies of the Wheels thereof are of less Breadth than 4 and a half inches the sum of 4d." (The narrower the felly of the Wheel, the more damage it was said to do to the Road.)

"For every Horse Ass Mule or other Beast or Cattle drawing any Carriage laden with Fish only, the Sum of 1d. and the same Toll on returning with such Carriage Empty on Another Day.

## THE NEW ROAD

"For Every Horse, Ass, Mule or other Beast or Cattle, Laden or Unladen, and not Drawing, the sum of 1½d.

"For Every Ass, Laden or Unladen, and not Drawing, the Sum of 1d.

"For every score of Oxen, Cows or Neat Cattle, the Sum of 10d. and so, in proportion, for any less number than a Score.

"For Every Score of Calves, Swine, Sheep or Lambs, except Calves, Lambs and pigs, not having been weaned and passing with their Dams, the sum of 5d. and so in proportion etc.

"And for every Coach, Waggon, Vehicle or other Carriage of Whatsoever Description, Propelled or Drawn Wholly, or in Part, by Steam, Gas, or any such-like means, or by Machinery or Otherwise than by Animal Power, the Sum of 2/-.

"And for Every dog, Goat or Other Such-like Animal drawing any Low Cart Truck, or other Carriage there shall be Paid the Sum of 1d.

"Such respective Tolls to be Paid before any such Horse, Mule, Ass, Cattle or Beast or such Carriage or Dog drawing as aforesaid shall be Entitled to Pass Through any Turnpike or Toll Gate to be erected on the said Roads.

"Return Journey Free on Same Day unless Drawing a Different Carriage.

"Steam Carriages to Pay every time.

"The Whole of the Works to be done and Performed at the Expense of the Trustees of this Act in such manner as shall be agreed upon between the Engineer and Surveyor, for the time being, of the Road intended to be made . . . and the Engineer or Surveyor etc. of the said Flimwell and Hastings Turnpike Road" (which was the continuation of the road at the Royal Oak northwards).

At the First General Annual Meeting recorded, held in 1836 at the South Saxon Hotel, St. Leonards, under the Chairmanship of Sir William Lamb, there were only seven Trustees present to hear the statement of Accounts which showed that a sum of £1,577 10s. had been borrowed on the security of the forthcoming tolls. Eleven hundred pounds of this was spent on the roads and £364 in salary to the Surveyor, Stephen Putland, of St. Leonards. In the following year, 1837, £2,208 was borrowed on security of the Tolls and £3 9s.

was brought forward from the past year. £1,616 of this was spent on the roads and £544 on buying land. The Surveyor received £30 and the Treasurer £10. 1838 saw part of the road finished, for £60 was received from tolls. £4,741 was borrowed and there was a balance in hand of £242. Only 5 Trustees were present at that A.G.M. In the following year the revenue from Tolls was £387, and "for Incidental receipt" £1,750. The last 3 A.G.M.'s had been held at the "Queen's Head Inn", Sedlescombe, under the chairmanships respectively of Sir Howard Elphinstone; the Treasurer, Joseph Jeffries; and John Bishop of Great Sanders. The debt had increased from £600 in 1837 to £19,758 in 1842.

It was one thing to make a new road it was another thing, as is well appreciated today, to keep the surface good, and there were as yet no steam rollers. So in 1870, James Byner, the parish surveyor, as described in Chapter 30, ordered the opening of the great pile of iron slag in Beauport Park, as a seemingly inexhaustible supply of road-mending material. The work on this and other of the turnpike roads provided some local employment at a time when work was very scarce. It is difficult to find the origin of a local tradition that prisoners from the Crimean War were employed on the New Road.

There were toll-gates wherever a by-road came in; at Blackbrooks, at the bottom of Chapel Hill, at Compasses Lane close to the saw mills and at Cripps Corner. Three of these cottages still stand. The name Gate Farm very frequently marks the site of one. They were as familiar as the level-crossing gates across the railway in the twentieth century but the time was long past when pikes, stuck in the ground, formed the barrier till the toll was paid, and gave the road system its name. Older men, slightly disabled perhaps, were glad of the job with its cottage and small garden and plenty of spare time to cultivate it.

The year 1880 saw the end of the tolls on the New Road; the Trust was wound up because the upkeep of roads was taken over by the Local Highway Boards.

The New Road, now over a hundred years old, still bears locally that name though it is today the A.21 to London, with firm macadamised surface and thousands of cars speeding daily along it throughout the summer to the sea.

Paygate at Blackbrooks became Mrs. Harriet Willard's sweetshop, whose fat pin-striped bulls-eyes are still remembered today by many who were children then. The cottage was built exactly at the junction of three parish boundaries, and she used to say that she went to bed in Battle, had breakfast in Sedlescombe and of an evening sat by her fire in Westfield. The Edwards family were the last to live in it until it was demolished in 1965. The corner is still known always as **Paygate**.

*Chapter Thirty-four*

## THE HOUSES OF THE STREET AND THE GREEN

*The Village Tradesmen and their Trades*
Sedlescombe Street it has been named on maps for hundreds of years, bearing record that it is a Roman road. Alongside it from the river northwards, through the centuries, the villagers have lived; and their cottages with low protective roofs, in earlier days of thatch, still stand beside it and around the village green, once common land where their goats and geese could graze, their straying hens peck and their toddling children play. Here was the very heart of the village and between the cottages stood the busy workshops of blacksmiths, carpenters, wheelwrights and coachbuilders, cobblers and saddlemakers, tanners and fell-mongers, the butcher's shop and the slaughter-house, the carrier's yard and the mill. Here too were the ale-houses, at the top and bottom. The noises coming from those workshops were part of the village itself, part of its pulsing life. A villager could go into them and discuss the creation of a tool or utensil, an article of clothing or furniture to be made to his own specification of materials chosen by himself.

From cock-crow to nightfall a multitude of sounds filled the ears of all; the first clip-clop of the horses' hooves and jangle of harness as they were led out to the fields; the clang of the hammer on iron and the thud of it on wood; the up-and-down notes of the saw; the ring and crunch of hooves on the road; the squeak of leather and the creak of cart wheels; the splash of the mill wheel; the chatter of voices and the laughter of children; and in the background all the different noises of the farm animals. Odours too in great variety assailed the villagers' noses; many which would not be tolerated today, but were then accepted as part of the business of living and of making a living. The stinking smell of skins and the scent of

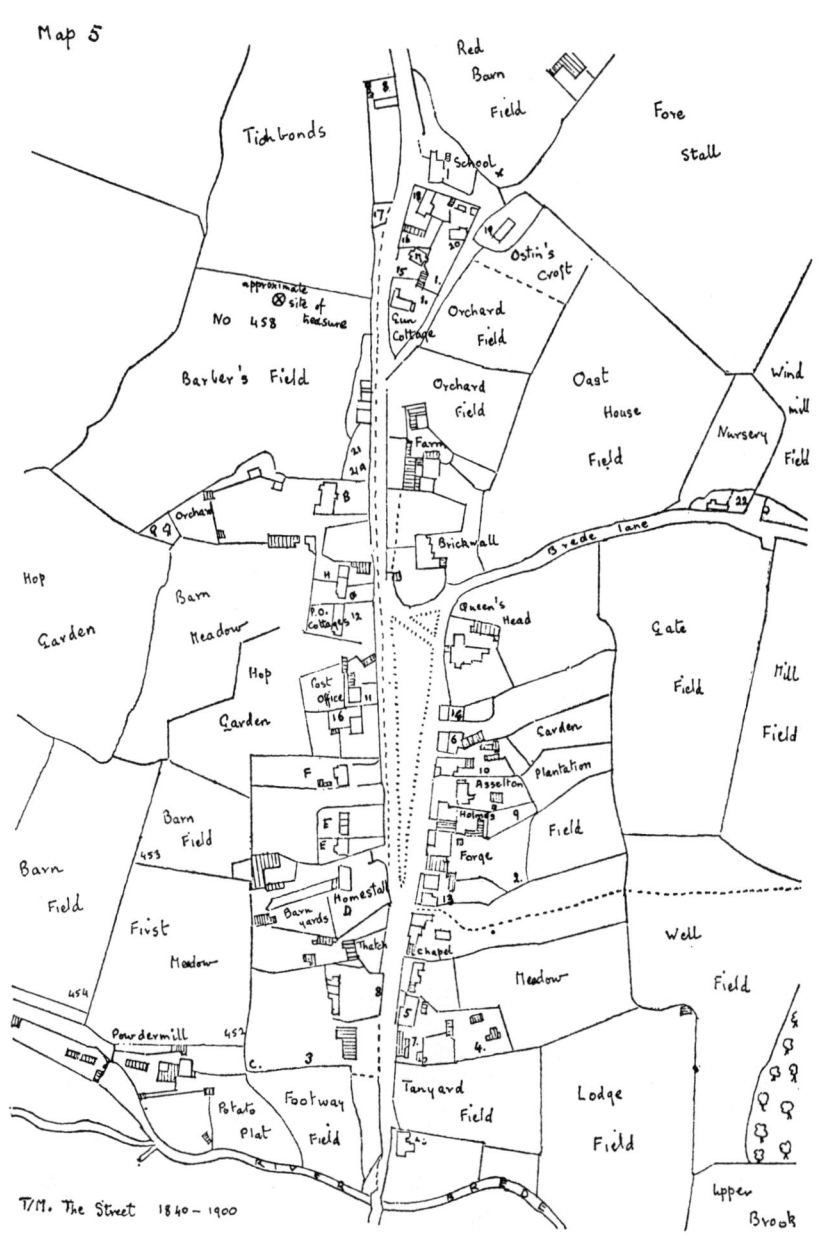

MAP 5. *Sketch Map of Street showing houses in nineteenth century.*

leather, the pungent smell of smoke and burning, and the fresh ones of wood shavings and of sweet baking bread; all mingled with the aroma of hops and the warm smells of horses, cows and pigs and their variously-odoured dung.

All through the centuries until the twentieth, the pace of the village was very busy but it was the pace of a man, unchanging. Now the pace and the noise are those of the machine. The workshops are gone, absorbed into the dwelling-house or converted into its garage; and, though the background noises of cows, sheep and bird-song remain, the noisiest sounds in the village are made by outsiders, passing motorists, motor cyclists and pilots of aircraft.

It was in the second half of the nineteenth century that gradually the work of the craftsmen became less and less in demand and one by one the workshops closed. In 1880 there were still three blacksmiths, a wheelwright, a carpenter's yard, a bootmaker and a bakery, besides two grocers-and-drapers, a toy shop and a builder's yard. Even after the second war there remained the bakery, the blacksmith, the butcher and the builder's and undertaker's, as well as the newsagent-post office and two grocers-and-greengrocers of today. The bakery and builder's are both now antique shops.

Something of what the parish records discover about the tradesmen of Sedlescombe, their trades and their homes over the centuries, is written in the following pages.

*The Blacksmith*

Away back in the earliest days of the iron-workings beside the rivers and all through the hundreds of years that followed, it was the blacksmith who made nearly every tool that was used; spears for fighting and for hunting, picks, forks, hooks and ploughs for agriculture; pans, knives and tools for home use. He made the first iron plough, he shod the horses, he repaired the implements and the cooking pots, he made the rings for the cottagers' pigs; hinges, staples and hasps for gates and doors; nails and tools for the carpenters; iron tyres for the wheels of carts, wagons and coaches; and pilts and studs for country boots. There was work for many smiths in the farms, cottages and houses all round the parish. It is no wonder that Smith is the most common name in the land.

It is no wonder either that there were several forges at work in the village; one at Balcombe Green where for over a decade at the

## THE HOUSES OF THE STREET AND THE GREEN

end of the nineteenth century Mr. Tuppenny swung his hammer up Long Lane; another beside the Green, where Claytons now stands with the Forge Cottages beside it; and a third was at the tail of the village close to the Bridge and the Mill.

The earliest blacksmiths whose names can still be found in the records are the "ffowles"; Thomas ffowle, to whose wife, Beatris, the orphan child, Constance Harte, was apprenticed in housewifery in 1612; and Richard Fowle, their son who, according to the Churchwardens' Accounts of 41 years later, was "paied 4d for mending a spade". (Chapter 18). A hundred years on, the blacksmith was Thomas Dennet.

*The Forge at Balcombe Green*[1]  1.

Here it was that the Dennets worked as blacksmiths for many generations, at the forge behind the Old Gun Cottage where they lived. In 1743 the lad, Stephen Clifford, was apprenticed to Thomas Dennet, blacksmith, of Sedlescombe, for seven years, and the following year Thomas' son, also Thomas, married Jane Hucstep of Sedlescombe. By 1841 a Thomas Dennet owned the Green Forge in the centre of the village and the cottages beside it, but he called himself "Coal dealer". Another Dennet was living still in the Gun Cottage, but by 1881 Tuppenny was at work at the Balcombe Green Forge. There he made the iron railings which still stand between the school playground and the dangerous main road.

When the forge closed is not now remembered; but it continued to be used for many years after as a workshop and when it was pulled down in 1974 hundreds, if not thousands, of horse-shoes in great variety of sizes were discovered bedded in the earth. It is perhaps a pity that the bungalow built on its site was not given an appropriate name, such as Horseshoe Bungalow or even Tuppenny's, rather than the meaningless Monkebo, as it is today.

*The Forge by the Green*  2.

It is possible that, though the Thomas Dennet of 1841 described himself as a coal dealer, a member of the family was still working at this forge on the east side of the village green; but in the last quarter of the century, Phineas Paine, the smith, worked there

---

[1] Numbers refer to Map 5.

though he lived not at the Forge cottages but in one of the two into which Asselton House was then divided. When the Tanyard at the bottom of the village closed, he moved down to these more spacious workshops and lived at the Smithy, now Brookfield, and William Ball, smith, took over his quarters both at the Forge and at Asselton House. When Phineas ceased work, William Ball moved down to the Bridge, using workshops on both sides of the road, and described himself as "coachbuilder, blacksmith and ironmonger". He was perhaps the last of the Green Forge smiths. There is no record of the closing down of that Forge, but it was pulled down in 1890.

*Claytons*

In the gap in 1900 a man called Clayton, an agent for the Prudential Insurance Company in Sedlescombe, built a red brick villa for himself and his wife, which they called, perhaps for some personal reason, Vale Marlowe. She was a local girl of the Oliver family. There they lived, worthy people, pillars of the Chapel, till they died not long after the end of the second war.

Norman Beyfus, who was living at Brickwall at the time of the fire, composing verses about the village from time to time, bought Vale Marlowe and lived in it, blind, with his wife, Beryl, till he died. Not thinking the name appropriate, he followed the pleasant habit of calling it by the name of its latest (and in this case also first) owner and renamed it Claytons and so it, happily, remains.

*Forge House*

On the south side of Claytons, separated by a narrow passage, stands Forge House. Originally two or more cottages, built in the late seventeenth or early eighteenth century, it was occupied through the years by a series of village families. At the beginning of the twentieth it was the Barwicks. He was gardener at Castlemans and their son, Edward, was one of those who were killed in the First World War. The Buttons bought the house and Mrs. Button's sister, Mrs. Chantler, and her husband lived there for some years, and the cottage was known as Green View. Then came Charlie Taylor, the blacksmith, and his family, and Charlie had a bicycle shop and workshop in the northern end. After the Taylors moved in their old age to Roselands, Dennis Thomas, builder, bought it to alter and beautifully renovate for his mother. There she ran a wool shop, and the bicycle shop at the back was incorporated in the house. A handsome shop window was put in and a lamp post on the flags outside gave the cottage its new name, The Lamp Post.

In the nineteen-seventies it became a tea-shop with a new name, Forge House, and now in summer days it looks cheerful and continental with small tables beside the lamp post, under rainbow-coloured umbrellas.

### Forge Cottages

These four cottages on the north side of Claytons are seventeenth century and have housed numberless cottage families. In No. 1, the ground floor of which was converted into a garage for Claytons, lived the great grandmother of Dennis Thomas, the builder. At the time of the Tithe Map all the cottages were owned by the blacksmith, Thomas Dennet, who had become a coal dealer. No. 3 is the only one still today owned and occupied by a native Sedlescombe family. All have been renovated and modernised unostentatiously.

### The Bridge Smithy 3.

In 1841 the barns and buildings on the west side of the road at Iltons Bath (now the Bridge Garage) were called "waste plat", for the Powdermill close by was still at work. But at the cottage next door, now Brookfield, and at the old Thatch, wheelwrights and smiths had lived and worked in small workshops adjoining.

But at the turn of the century, opposite in the old tannery buildings, the smiths and wheelwrights set up shop in a big way. Here it was that George Simmons served his apprenticeship to William Ball before taking over at last as Master Smith and wheelwright. Here stood his forge, its litter of iron of all shapes and sizes lying like a gigantic game of spillikins all over and around the large dark interior, where blinked the flickering light which at intervals flared like a magnesium flash as the bellows blew. It was this Rembrandtesque obscurity, whose secrets were revealed here and there by the whim of the flames, which made the forge so enticing, and the silhouetted figure of the blacksmith an almost legendary character.

George did all the smith's and wheelwright's work on Marley and Beanford farms on the Battle Abbey Estate and in 1893 had mended the iron-work on the churchyard fence at the time that the churchyard was enlarged. George's elder brother, Albert, worked as a manservant at Oaklands for the Combes.

In due course George Simmons' son took over from his father, and in May 1914 the *Hastings and St. Leornards Observer* recorded:

"VILLAGE BLACKSMITH MARRIED"

"George Simmons, second son of the late Mr. and Mrs. George Simmons of Tanyard House, Sedlescombe,[1] to Miss Crawley, who has been teacher at Sedlescombe Infants' School for the past 6 years. Mr. Simmons is well-known as the village blacksmith, the family having carried on the business as blacksmith and wheelwright for 37 years. The bride was given away by Mr. W. L. Gregory; and Mr. W. Button was best man."

They were baker and grocer respectively.

In the Auction Schedule of the Combe's property in 1924, the "Smithy's Holdings" included

"a comfortable Old-fashioned Cottage"[2] on the *East* side of the road, as well as an "extensive range of Brick and Tile buildings on the *West* side of the road, comprising Paint Shop, Wheelwright's Shop and Shoeing Forge, above which is a large Timber Store. In front, close to the road is a Brick and Tile Cart-shed[3] and a small One-Storey Red Brick-and-tile Cottage of Two Bedrooms and a Living Room.[4] In the rear is a useful small Paddock with a slip of garden running to the Bridge alongside the Public Road,[5] the entirety comprising an Area of about 1 acre, 1 rod, 14 perches. The Whole was let to Mr. George Simmons, wheelwright and blacksmith on a yearly (Michaelmas) tenancy at a rent of £100 per annum."

George Simmons bought the whole property for £600.

[1] Now Park View.
[2] Now Tanyard House.
[3] Now demolished.
[4] Now demolished.
[5] Now Tithe Barn Car Park.

## THE HOUSES OF THE STREET AND THE GREEN

*Brookfield*

Standing well back on the west side of the Street this cottage, which acquired its present name only in the second quarter of the twentieth century, was originally single-storeyed. It is described in its deeds as "all that messuage . . . in two dwellings with the cottage, Wheelwright's shop (formerly a barn) blacksmith forge and one piece of land thereto belonging with the appurtenances". Since the barn at least had once been part of the mill buildings of Iltonsbath (Chapter 12), it is not surprising to read that it had been "formerly in the occupation of Jeremiah Lingham", a member of the family which had worked the mill for the whole of the eighteenth century.

The occupants following Jeremiah Lingham were in turn Thomas Clarke and John Morley; Spencer William Taylor and William Richardson; "and then lately Phineas Paine, William Ball, George Spears; William Hylands and Edward Edwards (or their undertenants)". Phineas Paine and William Ball were blacksmiths in the eighteen-eighties and eighteen-nineties and so the cottage was known as The Smithy.

The Deed goes on to give the boundaries of the property as "abutting to the Queen's Highway (there leading between Sedlescombe and Westfield) East: to the Common Way called the Mill Lane, South: to the lands late of Edward Ades,[1] West: and to the lands then or late of Thomas Stace, North". The drive into the Waterfall House was once the Mill Lane, leading to the Powder Mill buildings and branching off, across the river and the Brooks, to join Marley Lane.

The "piece of land" was, between the years 1928 and 1939, divided into two, one becoming the back garden of the Old Thatch and the other the garden behind Brookfield. The "messuage with two dwellings" was The Smithy, now Brookfield. "The Cottage" is the one referred to in several old deeds as the Mill Cottage and was later demolished.

In Brookfield had lived sometimes a wheelwright and sometimes a blacksmith who worked in the nineteenth and twentieth centuries for the two generations of Simmons, master smiths and wheelwrights. Weekes, the shoeing smith, was a short, round-shouldered little man in great contrast with Charlie Taylor, the smith who followed him in his cottage and workshop.

[1] Hancox and Spilsteds.

In 1925 Gregory bought all the Smithy property on the west side of the road from George Simmons. He enlarged the cottage, adding an extra storey and there his daughter and son-in-law lived. She it was who gave it the name Brookfield.

So Charlie Taylor and his family moved up the hill to the cottage now called Forge House, where they lived for around forty years.

During the Second World War, Miss Margaret Walford bought Brookfield and lived happily in it for twenty years with her minute poodle, Bella, which in the estimation of her many friends she closely resembled, being herself as tiny for a lady as the poodle was for a dog; so diminutive was she that she could only just be seen above the steering wheel of her car. Moreover, she wore a curly fringe on her forehead not unlike that on Bella's. Eventually she retired to a flat over the border in Kent and Mrs. Woodhams from Battle became Brookfield's new owner, living there for the next fifteen years.

*The Last Smith, Charlie Taylor*
Charlie and his wife, Alice, lived in the house, Green View, and there the last two of their seven children were born; three sons they had and four daughters. The other children had been born at Brookfield when he worked for George Simmons; and among the earliest memories of his eldest son is the sound through the wall of the hammer ringing on the anvil. When George Simmons grew old, Charlie worked for himself in the old tannery buildings behind the Tithe Barn and later in what are now the Garage buildings. Always, as the years went by and the machine age took over more and more, his quarters grew smaller with each move.

He had learned the trade from his uncle in Hawkhurst, starting in 1901 when he was 13 years old. He then worked for a blacksmith, first at Beckley Forge (Chapter 17) and then at Headcorn. The 1914-18 war intervened and after it he came to Sedlescombe.

"The day I retire will be the end of blacksmiths in this country," Charlie was wont to say, and at 75 he was still working! "Standing in the cramped tin-roofed workshop," wrote a reporter in 1962, "which barely withstood the rigours of the beating rain outside, he explained that his wife had suffered a serious stroke a year ago. So now he could work only when either his daughter or kind neighbours could sit with her.

" 'I usually manage two full days a week and a couple of extra afternoons here,' he said as he surveyed the piles of iron-work and bits of bicycles which all but hid the wooden walls which he himself had built 30 years ago. It was raining too hard for him to walk that day to the other end of the village to shoe five fine Arab horses, so he was, he said, catching up on a long-standing order of sharpening 40 pick-axe heads for a local contractor. He showed no sign of exertion as he methodically pumped the furnace bellows, gaily chatting at the same time. Only when the two pick-axe points had reached white hot in the roaring fire, did he pause from the near-monologue, deftly to swing the heads from the blaze on to the ancient pock-marked anvil. During the pause before he attacked the glowing pick-axe heads, Charlie, giving an extra vigorous suck to his scraggy moustache that through years of training curled round his upper lip into the corners of his mouth, spoke of the days when most of his time was taken up making complete ploughs for local farmers."[1]

"Are you sorry," the reporter asked, "that none of your three sons have chosen to follow in your footsteps and wear the vast leather apron that is your trademark?"

"In a way, but there would have been less work for me if they had done," he replied with a twinkle in his eye.

His middle son had been fascinated by the forge and used to go there in every spare moment from school. Sometimes he was called upon to help; the most difficult job for an eleven-year-old was when he had to hold fast the juddering wheel with all the strength he could summon, while his father hammered the iron tyre into place.

Charlie was a broad man of great strength, but his son remembers his amazing gentleness, and repeatedly alludes to him as "truly a gentle giant". He wonders too how he earned a living for he was so generous, and careless of sending out bills. A "roader" (tramp) brought his bicycle to be mended. "I'll pay you when I come by again in three weeks." "That's all right," says Charlie. "Will it be all right?" asks his son anxiously, "will he pay?" "Not he," replies Charlie cheerfully.

The reporter finished his article thus:

"So, although you will not find Charlie there every day, he is scotching the rumours in the village that his final retirement is

[1] Sus. Ex.

imminent by spending as much time as he possibly can in his untidy but charming workshop. And, although the sizzle of rain coming through the leaking roof into the fire is not the only sign of wear and tear in the workshop, the warmth in Charlie's heart is still equal to the roaring blaze in the furnace."

Charlie finally retired in 1964 and he and his wife were the first to move into the newly-opened flatlets at Roselands, where they lived happily till they died.

*The Bridge Garage*

All the Smithy buildings on the west side of the Street were bought by Mr. Gregory of the Bakery, who had always been fascinated by things mechanical. In 1911 he had bought a Darracq car and later the very first Ford car sold by the Hollingsworth Garage in Hastings. He had started the first commercial garage in the village in the old builder's and carpenter's workshop at the house now Sherralds but then Wisteria Cottage. He planned to move the Garage to the Smithy buildings and his son-in-law, T. R. Hilder, bought himself out of the R.A.F. in order to manage it. There, as a boy of fourteen, Ken Stubberfield was first employed. The Garage ran also a Taxi Service and Cecil Gregory would be called out of the Bakery to drive perhaps to Major Mullens at Westfield Place, or to the Kingdons at Castlemans, and sometimes to Mrs. Godman at Brickwall. She would require to be driven by the most secluded lanes through depths of woods, where she would get out and walk away down the woodland path. Sitting on a tree-stump hidden, as she hoped, from prying eyes, she would count her money! In course of time, the Bridge Garage had a fleet of Austin cars for weddings, funerals and other taxi services.

In the Deeds was a clause "reserving unto the Vendors the Four Old Firebacks attached to the said Wheelwright's and Blacksmith's Shop and the right at all times hereafter to remove the same, making good any damage caused by such removal". One of these firebacks was the famous Lennard one (Chapter 16), used perhaps for a Trade Sign by Sedlescombe blacksmiths for untold years and remaining still today fixed to the wall as a fine memorial to them. Below it a scar can clearly be seen where another was once fixed. One more is still on the Garage premises.

Hilder ran the garage for many years, but eventually gave up in 1936 because he was so deeply distressed by the accidents at Paygate, the noise of which he could hear and to which he was more and more frequently called. He could, too, sometimes predict them by the sound and pace of the cars he could hear rushing along the New Road.

After the war, that same Ken Stubberfield managed the Garage where he had started work so long ago. So it remains, under different management now, in the old brick-and-tile buildings and barns to this day.

*The Wheelwright*
All through the years since the first wheel was invented, the town streets and the country roads were busy and noisy with the sound of the creaking, groaning and squeaking of the hand-made wheel; and the ancient and highly-skilled craft of the wheelwright had from time immemorial been practised in nearly every village in England. The Wheelwright and Smith worked in close association, the wooden wheel being usually shod with iron.

In Sedlescombe, in living memory they occupied adjoining buildings in the old barns of the Mill, the wheelwright's being the more southerly of the two and so nearer the bridge. In front was the saw-pit where the two sawyers, top-dog and under-dog, sawed the timber into sizes which the wheelwright could handle. When woodsmen had cut the trees and carters had carted it, the wheelwright examined it for shape with a skilled eye, so that any curve or crookedness could be used to advantage. The top-dog stood on a smoothed surface of the tree which was to be cut; for he it was who must keep the pace and watch the line of the saw so that no deviation should spoil the timber. He, too, must skilfully sharpen at intervals the intricate teeth of the saw, while the underdog, white now with saw-dust, could cross the road to cool himself and wet his dry throat with a drink at the Bottom-house. Up and down, up and down for hours they pushed and pulled the saw, interrupted only by the need to oil it or to move the tree. In the country round can still be seen an inn with the sign, "The Two Sawyers".

Always from the wheelwright's shop came the clean sharp scent of wood, and always it was filled with timber seasoning, sometimes for as long as ten years. Here was ash, elm and beech, sawn and roughly shaped into cylinders for the fellies, which the wheelwright would cut to pattern. Here were stacks of spokes of heart-of-oak, bought by the hundred from the woodsmen, who had cleft (never sawn) them in the woods, to be chopped, dressed and finished by the wheelwright's spokeshave; here were planks of long-seasoned elm from which he made the central hub, to be morticed with his spoke-dog to take the heart-of-oak spokes. All these numerous parts waited to be fitted aptly together to make the perfect round wheel for farm wagon, pony trap, coach, carrier's van, chaise or dung cart. All must run smoothly and sweetly or the wheelwright could shut up shop.

Here too were stacks of his wood chips to be sold to the neighbours for fire-lighting, and heaps of saw-dust for bacon-drying.

In 1830 at the time of Cobbett's meeting at Battle, James Pepper, living at the Old Thatch, was the Bridge Wheelwright, and he was probably not the only one in the village. In 1852 Reuben Weller, wheelwright, was living at the cottage now called Magpie. In the twentieth century, gradually the smith combined the skills of wheelwright too, as iron wheels superseded wooden ones; and the carpenters repaired the wooden ones.

George Simmons, the younger, remembered as a man with a slight moustache and small pince-nez, named himself Master Smith and Wheelwright and he had both a smith and a wheelwright working for him. For George Simmons, senior, Ashley Cooper, living at the cottage which is now Brookfield, had worked as wheelwright, whose grand-daughter still lives in the village. He was followed in the twentieth century for a while by Tedham, who lived in one of the cottages opposite, now Tanyard House, and later moved to Staplecross where he set up on his own as wheelwright and undertaker. George Hook, who lived in what is now Park View, is well remembered making great wagon wheels. Gwen, his little daughter, went to the village school and she and her friends would come home and watch him at work. One of the girls, Fanny Barnes, fell down into the saw-pit and George Simmons had to be fetched to get her out. When old Mrs. Simmons, wife and mother of a blacksmith, lay sorely ill unto death, straw was flung over the road to quieten the noise and clang which the milk carts made.

Strangely, the landlord of the "Coach and Horses", Fairhall, also worked opposite as wheelwright. He was a man gifted to pick up any tune and play it beautifully on the pub piano.

*The Brickwall Workshops*

Here was set up in the nineteenth and twentieth centuries the estate yard of Oaklands, where worked wheelwright, Chandler, who lived at Belle Vue (now Wendy Mill House) up Chapel Hill; and the carpenter, asthmatic Robert Southerden, moved down from his private workshop further up the village beside Battle View to work on the estate. His wife, too, during the First World War, worked for the Combes, outside in the garden. Fred and Charlie Soan were painters too for them. Labour in plenty was to be found on the Oaklands estate.

## The Tanyard  4.

This part of Sussex was particularly suited to the development of the tanning industry because of the great store of oak trees, the bark of which was the best material for the process. The industry was hedged around with restrictions and legislation and it was remarkable in how many ways the law could be broken.

Old deeds record several houses in Sedlescombe being called the Tanhouse for short periods. Certainly the present Tanyard House has a proven right to the name for without any doubt a tannery for several hundred years filled the space between it and the house now called Park View. It was set up there alongside the river Brede at Iltonsbath, a short distance from the corn mill, by the monks of Battle Abbey in the late thirteenth or early fourteenth century.[1] It is possible that the water power which worked the corn mill was used also for a mill to crush the bark; for in 1570 an indenture records "two mills under one roof at Tiltonsbath".[2]

A ditch spanned by a wooden bridge surrounded the tannery with water (in Deeds "the Rivulet") and the site, though some few miles from the Abbey, gave easy access to the ports of Winchelsea and Rye by barge, and also to Hastings by road cartage. (The Abbey had also a Tannery at Marley.)

Of the two processes of leather-making, tanning and tawing, the former was the much more expensive and lengthy, and took several years to produce the leather, using very large quantities of crushed oak-bark and lime, which the Abbey from its forests and lime-pits could easily supply. The timber felled for ship-building, for the iron furnaces and for charcoal-burning, could all have the bark first scraped; and there were lime-burners too on the Abbey's pay-roll. Skins were easily supplied by the Abbey cellarer from the animals consumed in the refectory and guest-house.[3] Butchers and mercers

[1] Searle.
[2] B.A.S. 1569.
[3] S.R.S. 65.

were by law forbidden to tan, and butchers were not allowed to sell skins secretly or bring skinned meat to sell at market; nor were shoemakers allowed to sell skins. The crust leather, the tannery's product, was sold either to travelling leather-middlemen, or direct to the cobbler, or to the currier who worked it to the required suppleness and thickness for the craftsmen. Repairs and running expenses of the tannery were quite heavy; in the year 1384-5 they amounted to over £6, but net profits could be as high as £20.

Battle became the hub of a local leather industry where cobblers and cordwainers, glovers and saddlers all made the skins into articles necessary to daily life and tailors fashioned jerkins, hoods and cloaks. Leather-brokers from as far afield as the Continent would come to Battle weekly market.

Between 1358 and 1364, the Abbey's tannery at Iltonsbath was leased to an independent tanner, and from the Dissolution till the tannery's closure towards the end of the nineteenth century, independent tanners followed each other.

Park View was known as Tanyard House until 1924 when it became Street Farm, and the present Tanyard House (then Iltons Bath) took over the name. Durhamford in Stream Lane was called The Tanhouse for years, owned and worked by the Bishops. Pump House was the Tanhouse in deeds of 1857; in the deeds of Manor Cottages, where the Elliotts lived who were tanners for several generations, a tanhouse is recorded. All of which is exceedingly confusing. It is possible that the Pump House bore the name only while the Tanner lived in it and that he always worked in the Tanyard at Iltons Bath. The records suggest that this was where the Elliott's tannery was. Moreover, there was beside it a fellmongers' yard, where in 1807 James Dawes and William Bishop worked as fellmongers. Fellmongering is a method of removing the wool from sheepskins, a trade which could well be carried on in association with the business of tanning, where the denuded skins could then be processed into leather. In the deeds of Brookfield opposite, which concern property "on the east side of the Hastings-Hawkhurst road, all that messuage and cottage with *wool-drying rooms stoves drying sheds*" is described as "situate and being in Ilton Bath". By 1812, William Bishop was in dire financial trouble owing money not only to his partner, Dawes, but also to three local farmers and two bankers from Hastings. It was then that a half part of the premises was sold for the benefit of the creditors and Henry Freeland bought it and built the Wesleyan Chapel (Chapter 40).

In 1870 William Piper, Fellmonger, and Eliza, his wife, lived in the Tanhouse (Park View). The wool-drying rooms, etc., were perhaps the old tile-roofed sheds which lie alongside the entrance drive to that house.

Here was still a busy tanning industry providing for very many years skilled and semi-skilled work for several men; though dirty, odiferous and discolouring to the skin. From the butcher's slaughter house, a few hundred yards up the Street, would come a continuous supply of hides; ox and heifer, cow and bull; those chiefly used in the making of heavy tanned leathers; and also sheepskin for the lighter ones. A good supply of water was available from both river and spring, and it is noteworthy that the water on this side of the Street is soft, a most necessary condition for use with skins, while the water on the west side is hard and would be disastrous to them.

The fresh hides, brought straight in from the slaughter-house to be cleaned of their dirt and blood, were then spread out in the yard to one side of the tanning pits with their various brews. Piles of bark, too, awaited crushing in a grinding machine before being soaked in pits of cold water to extract the tan. The hides went into the lime-bath for a fortnight to loosen the hair and to plump up the fibres of the skin to absorb the tan. Two men with carrying-poles with special hooks on the ends then drew the skins from the bath so that hair and flesh could be scraped away before they were ready for the tan-baths. Of these there were several in the yard, each containing a stronger solution, the last being the strongest of all. After this long process—it could take anything up to one year to tan one hide—the leather skins were hung up to dry, before the final action of oiling by hand.

The smells arising from the skins in all their stages of conversion into leather, mingled with the aroma from the mixtures in the pits, must have made the area at the foot of the village into a somewhat noisome place. A messy work and a smelly work, but work to satisfy a man when a skin could be so easily spoiled or, with infinite skill, patience and care, be converted into leather; hard-wearing, beautiful and vitally useful for the village saddler, cobbler, carpenter, glove-maker and many another craftsman who would come in and choose the skin most suitable to his purpose.

In the early nineteenth century one of the jobs done by the poor in the village and recorded in the Poorhouse Accounts was "crapeing Bark for Ed. Young and Mr. Eldridge, Tanner" (Chapter 18).

By the last decade of the nineteenth century, the tanyard had closed down; all the work and the local skins went to the Tannery beside the railway bridge at Battle, which worked on until after the Second World War, when it too closed down. In a few years the great barns were demolished and the Battle Hill Garage built on the site.

*The Tanyard Houses—Park View* 4.

Today Park View is a neat two-storeyed house surrounded on three sides by its flower and vegetable garden and on the fourth by the old tanning sheds and an orchard. Until after World War One, it was known as The Tanyard House. There the tanners had lived, when it was a considerably smaller cottage.

Like most of the houses in Iltonsbath, it was held copyhold of Battle Abbey and in 1826 William Eldridge and his wife, Elizabeth, were admitted to

(1) "all that customary messuage or tenement . . . in Iltonsbath, Sedlescombe, late Mosley's, holden of the Manor of Battel by the yearly rent of 1/6 heriot relief and other services (in occupation of William Piper, fellmonger) and also that piece or parcel of ground and orchard together with all and singular, the buildings standing . . . thereon, by estimate 3 roods more or less . . .

(2) "part and parcel of a customary tenement called Greens and Iltonsbath (as the same were fenced off and separated from the said tenement) formerly in the occupation of Elizabeth Eldridge, late of Robert Monk and then of William Piper (better known by the description 'all that messuage and cottage with wool-drying rooms stoves drying sheds etc.')

(3) "together with that . . . parcel of meadow or pasture land and garden adjoining the last described premises . . . containing altogether 2 acres or thereabouts."

Elizabeth Eldridge and Robert Monk had been connected with the King's Head (Chapter 39).

This "orchard or garden ground well-stocked with fruit trees" figured in the Combe auction of 1924, together with "a full right of way for all purposes, and cartway leading to the public road". It is difficult to identify with certainty Greens and Iltonsbath, but it is possible that these, "fenced off", were the building behind Tanyard Grocery Stores, described in the Auction Schedule of 1924 as a "red brick and tile Granary of Two Floors". Although dilapidated now, it could very well have been occupied as two cottages a hundred years ago.

After the tanyard closed down, the house and yard were used by the Wheelwright, George Hook, and later by Simmons, the Blacksmith and Wheelwright. At the auction the house, sold separately, was bought by Thomas and Alexander Gammon, farmers of Street Farm, Sedlescombe, and it became the Street Farmhouse until Frank Gammon took over the farm and lived in the bungalow beside Brede Lane which then became the Street Farmhouse; and the old Tanyard had another change of name, becoming Park View.

So it remains. The Gammons' two daughters continued to live in it after their parents died. Today it has passed to their nephew and his family.

*Tanyard House* 5.

This old house with its wide chimneys dates from the early seventeenth century and in the schedule for the 1924 auction, where it is listed as part of the Smithy's Holding, Lot 12, it was described as: —

"a comfortable Old-fashioned Cottage, Ilton Bath, of red brick and tile construction, at the lower end of the Village close to the Coach and Horses P.H.; containing six Bed Rooms on the Upper Floors, Shop or Living Room with Two Other Rooms on the Ground Floor, Wash-house, Kitchen, Scullery and Pantry. In the rear is a Red Brick and Tile Granary of Two Floors."

The Plan accompanying the Schedule clearly shows Lot 12 as standing *south* of the "Coach and Horses". The cottage adjoining the old Methodist Chapel *north* of that Public House, which now bears the name Iltonsbath, was not for sale in 1924 under that name or any other. Both houses have a right to that name since both are in the area known by it from eariest times. Tanyard House had also a right to its present name since the Tanyard was just behind it.

The deeds concerning the three houses, the present Tanyard House, Park View and Barracks Cottage with Iltonsbath, are most confusing with their interchange of names, including as they do the cottages called "late Mosley's and Greens". The Mosley family provided several generations of tanners in the eighteenth and nineteenth centuries, but whether they had occupied the "red brick and tile Granary on two floors" or whether the present Tanyard House, it is now impossible to tell. Alternatively, Tanyard house may have been "Mosley's and Greens".

At the end of the nineteenth century the cottages, now Tanyard House, were restored by Hercules Brabazon and the porch was added. Later, in the twentieth century, the shop window was constructed by the same landlords and Fred Phillips, once bailiff to the Combes, was installed in it as Postmaster and Grocer. Grocer it has remained ever since, though the Post Office moved away up to the Newsagent's shop in the centre of the village.

*Pump House* 6.

Lot 2 in the Auction of Richard Smith's Estate (Chapter 23) held at The Mart opposite the Bank of England on Wednesday, September 30th, 1857, is described as "a freehold messuage and premises in Sedlescombe Street known as The Tanhouse". The accompanying plan shows that this is not the house known today as The Tanyard House, nor is it Park View, earlier called by that name. It is clearly Pump House with Pump Cottage, opposite to the Pump on the Green, with Thomas's yard behind it. At that date there was, of course, neither pump nor well on the village green. Richard Smith had inherited the Tanhouse under the will of his father, Tilden Smith, in 1834, when it had been described as "the messuage, tanyard and premises, formerly Brooks", situated close by Waghorne's the butcher. In the Tithe Map of seven years later, the occupier of house, garden and buildings was Albert Weston. The Westons had long been farmers in and around Sedlescombe and at that date farmed Homestall and Brickwall Farm among others.

In 1900, after the well was dug on the Green and the roof erected over with seats beneath it, "Tanhouse", already renamed in delightful contrast "Rose Cottage", now became Pump House, housing the family of Robert Thomas, milk-roundsman and carrier. Since then the premises behind it have always been Thomas's, but not of the same family. They became in turn "Charlie Thomas's, Steam Haulage Contractor and Coal and Coke Merchant", and Thomas and Sons, Builders; Thomas Transport; and now Dennis Thomas, Builder.

Between the wars, Mrs. Aldridge bought the house with other cottages in the village and it was she who divided it into two, making the southern part into a small cottage expressly for the District

Nurse, who after all never lived in it. The building with the yard passed to the Thomas family, some of whom lived in the house until, after many years, it was sold to become an antique shop; the cottage being later sold separately when its occupant, Mrs. Read, now a widow (see Holmes House) moved to the Roselands flats for Old People.

*Some of the Iltonsbath Tanners and Fellmongers*
| | | | |
|---|---|---|---|
| 1661 | George Bigg | 1807 | William Bishop |
| 1700 | John Elliot; died 1721 | | and James Dawes |
| | John Elliot the younger | 1870 | William Bishop |
| 1736 | Henry Snow of Magpie (now) Cottage | | |
| 1743 | Simon Watson of Durhamford, the Tanhouse | | |
| 1747 | William Twort, the younger | | |
| 1754 | Robert Mosley | | |
| 1786 | Robert Mosley, junior | | |
| 1801 | Mr. Eldridge | | |
| 1812 | Spencer Mosley | | |
| 1830 | Henry Spears of the Old Thatch | | |
| 1870 | William Piper, Park View (now) | | |

*The Tithe Barn* 7.

This is an old and attractive barn but there is no evidence at all that it was ever a Tithe Barn. On the 1831 Tithe Map, it is marked as one of the Tanyard buildings, and after the Tanyard closed it was used firstly by the wheelwright and then by the blacksmith, and later for farm purposes. In living memory it had become a cart-shed with farmyard behind it where villagers still remember playing as children among the wagons belonging to the two Edwards brothers who lived up the hill in Whydown cottages. Wood-merchants, they took faggots and firewood around for sale in their pony-carts.

It was four years after the death of Hercules Brabazon in the spring of 1906 that Mrs. Harvey Brabazon Combe turned the Barn into a Memorial Gallery to hold a permanent exhibition of his paintings (Chapter 32); and installed as caretaker, Mrs. Boxall, whose husband worked on the estate. For them she fitted up a cosy kitchen with bedrooms above it in the north end of the barn, and there they lived for about a quarter of a century. Mr. Boxall became blind and in 1930 he died, but not before he was able to have his desire and feel his infant great-grandson, Bill, born to Mr. and Mrs.

Edgar Boxall, now of Fir-Tree Cottage. Mrs. Boxall remained caretaker till she died three years later. The exhibition was then closed and the Barn sold. Mrs. Combe, as described in Chapter 32, had written a pamphlet for the use of visitors to the exhibition, and in it describes the Tithe Barn imaginatively as having been "used by Abbot Athelstan of Sedlescombe for the service of Battle Abbey retainers early in the 16th Century". Search in the records for Abbot Athelstan has not been rewarded.

The Barn re-opened shortly before World War Two as The Tithe Barn Tea-shop and a very popular place it became, with the shortage of petrol, for people in the nearby towns. It was directly after the war that the gallery, made by Thomas and Sons, was installed.

A tea-place, and sometimes a lunch-place too, it has remained ever since, changing hands innumerable times.

*The Bakery* 8.

Every cottage and house in the village had a bake-oven built in beside the hearth and on the weekly baking day each one was heated with faggots to the right temperature before the fire was scraped out and the bread, scones, buns, cakes and pies were put in in ordered turn, filling the air with the warm, tasty smell which brought the children quickly round with watering mouths and hands held out.

With the closing down in the late nineteenth century of Hancox Mill, the last of the village corn-mills, the immediate local supply of flour was gone, though the Staplecross Mill was still working. Perhaps this was why the first known baker, George Stapely, is recorded in the village in *Kelly's Directory* of 1890. His bakery was opposite the school, in a four-gabled building beside the hairdresser, now mostly pulled down.

Meanwhile, young Wallace Gregory had been born, one of a large family, in Brighton in 1870. At the age of eleven, he left home on his own initiative to work for a baker in the town for 6d. a week. Three years later he came to Staplecross where his uncle, Mr. Moon, owned the Mill and there he learned both milling and baking. So when he fell in love with and married in 1895 Annie Laura Oliver, the farmer's daughter from Strawberry Hill in Poppinghole Lane, he was ready to take over the bakery from Stapely. On his wedding morning there was great concern on finding out that he had no clean white shirt to wear, so he bicycled from Staplecross to Battle to buy one and arrived back in time for his wedding.

The Bakery building was "pleasing to the eye" and consisted as his daughter, Ivy, remembers, "of four bedrooms and a flour storeroom on the first floor, and three living rooms, and a very nice bay window with four or five long panes for the shop, where stood rows of glass jars containing sweets, cakes, boxes of strip Spanish (liquorice) and a few sundries such as cheap coloured beads. The Bakehouse was alongside, under the flour store to which sacks were hauled up on a wheel-pulley from the delivery cart below, which was drawn by a pair of huge cart-horses. The oven was heated by large stacks of wood and all the dough was of course made by hand". Both Ivy and her brother, Cecil, were born in the house, and there they lived for ten years. Meanwhile, a dispute had arisen between Alchin, the grocer who owned the property, and Gregory. There were no less than thirteen bakers coming through Sedlescombe from all the villages around and Alchin wanted to set his son up in the Bakery and therefore gave Gregory notice—a real body blow for him. Mrs. Combe and Squire Combe came to the rescue and allowed him some ground on which to build himself a Bakery and house. At the bottom of the village beside The Old Thatch stand two cottages empty these many years but lived in then by Albert Soan and his family; and it was on the long gardens, which stretched in front of them to the roadside hedge, that the new Bakery was built. While F. Thomas and Sons were building it, the father fell off a ladder and broke his arm. Till the house was ready the Gregory children stayed at Vale Marlowe, for Mrs. Clayton too was an Oliver and a cousin of Mrs. Gregory.

So the new Bakery started and, winning very quickly a reputation for its bread, it prospered giving employment to more and more villagers. In 1905 the first of very many gold medals was won.

In 1924 both Cecil and Ivy married and Cecil became a partner. An automatic oven bought from the Continent was installed, the only one at that time in Sussex. Forty or fifty local men and women were working in bakery, shop and tea-garden, and others in the shop at Battle. Wallace had already, with his superfluity of energy and interests, started a small garage at Sherralds and at this time he moved it down to become the Bridge Garage.

During the Second World War, the bread somehow remained good and after the war visitors unfailingly remarked upon its unusual excellence. In the summer of 1945 there was a great celebration amongst their numberless friends when Wallace and Annie had their golden wedding.

When electric ovens were installed in 1950, however, some of the particular goodness of that bread was lost for ever. Cecil's son, Terry, was growing up to earn a reputation as a most skilful cake-maker, much sought after at weddings, birthdays and christenings and many were the awards he won. It was a very sad day when the Bakery was sold to Betabake and the work buildings became stores from which the delivery vans set out before dawn every morning; and there is no longer any local employment. The shop sells antiques. Eventually Terry left the village. Cecil and his wife continued to live close by in the bungalow they had built beside the river behind the Bakery.

*The Butcher at Holmes House* 9.

This house, nameless until but a few years ago, was built in the early sixteenth century on Asselton House land as some sort of adjunct to that house, as a shop, warehouse with barn, perhaps.[1] At the end of the century it was converted into a dwelling-house in its own right, and the wide chimney stack was built in. Some hundred or more years later another bay was added at its south end and it thus became two cottages. At its first building it must have had some importance for it was jettied at its northern end, an unusual architectural ornamentation for a minor building. Today the long roof, originally of thatch, slopes still right down over the back wall, where the old timber-framing is still visible though, as with most of the old houses in the village, the front is now tile-hung in the upper storey.[2]

The first record of the house yet discovered is in a will of William Wood, of Vinehall, dated 1809: "Devise to William Waghorne of Sedlescombe, butcher, of the messuage or tenement where the testator was living." William Waghorne, Butcher! So this house is known to have been a butcher's shop for at least 150 years and who knows for how many years before that? Now there is no village butcher at all.

William Waghorne, the butcher, died in 1835 and was buried not in Sedlescombe churchyard but in that of St. Mary in the Castle, Hastings, in which parish he had lived for the last few years of his life, leaving his son, John, to manage the butcher's shop.

[1] See Map 5.
[2] R.O.H.A.S.

In 1834 Tilden Smith's will (Chapter 23) in favour of his son, Richard, includes " a copyhold messuage in Iltonsbath late Waghorne's with the butcher shop and premises, holden of the Manor of Battel, to which John Symes was admitted in trust for the testator." John Symes, Churchwarden of Sedlescombe and Overseer of the Poor, son of John Symes, the farmer, was now the village butcher. He was followed three years later by Robert Weston. In 1852 the butcher was William Turner and then in turn James Dawes and Robert Bishop, who rented the shop on quarterly terms at £4 a year. Robert was of the family of Great Sanders and his descendants still live in the village. The fathers of both had in 1807 been fell-mongers at Iltonsbath.

In about 1870 Edmund Martin became butcher and lived in the house with his wife and family. The ground floor north of the front door was still given over to the butcher's shop and adjoining the south wall of the house was the slaughter-house (now the house garage). Martin died young in the eighteen-eighties, leaving his wife with at least four daughters and two sons, all young. For several years with great courage and determination she carried on the butcher's business and shop; but not surprisingly it proved beyond her powers. She then, with the help of her daughter, Florence, became a washerwoman in Forge Cottage next door; very laborious and skilled work; and at the same time they looked after Florence's young invalid sister. Florence, herself stone-deaf through a childhood illness, married Edgar Read, gardener, and they lived in various cottages in the village, bringing up their only son, Henry, who was to be killed in the 1939 war in his early manhood. Edgar died in Pump Cottage, gardener to the doctor, and she lived on in it for many years till she moved in her old age to Roselands flats, remaining there until she died at the age of 95, in full command of her clear intelligence, though failing sight made it impossible for her any longer to lip-read, thus increasing her loneliness. She would tell how she and her brothers and sisters would hide high up in the beams above the slaughter-house when an animal was to be killed and watch in fearful and excited secrecy. Children of other families used to take the same fascinated interest when the family pig was killed. Not so many years earlier, public executions had drawn large audiences of adults. Perhaps it was the wholesale slaughter of the two World Wars that has made us so squeamish about death today, so that we try to hide it from our children and ourselves till we can barely use the word, preferring euphemisms such as "passing away" or "when something happens to me". It is death, however, which gives an edge to the delight of living.

After Mrs. Martin gave up, William Holmes, tall and gaunt, came from Kent to be butcher, living in the old house with his wife, and son and daughter, Will and Frances. Still the slaughter-house was in use and the old custom of tying up a bullock outside the shop some weeks before Christmas so that all could see the prime meat which they would be eating at the festival. Holmes would go to Ashford market every week and was very particular and proud about his meat. In old age, during the Second World War, his fallen standards grieved and irked that pride and he would grumble fiercely of the "rubbish" he was forced to sell, becoming a rather awesome character as he served customers, sometimes grumpily as they stood outside the age-old shop-window and he opened the latticed shutter.

When Holmes died in 1956 his son and daughter soon moved back to Kent, near Ashford, from whence the family had come, and the house and shop were sold, first as a private dwelling and then as a restaurant. Having no name but The Butcher's it was, in the good old custom, advertised by the Estate Agents as "Holmes' House", and Holmes' House it has fittingly remained, a memorial to the last butcher in Sedlescombe and, through him, to all the butchers who carried on their trade in it through the centuries. Today the butcher's shop itself is, not inappropriately, the dining-room where night after night customers are fed.

*Ditch's the Grocer at Harriet House* 10.

This house, also nameless until very recently, was built in the early sixteenth century. Built of only two bays it was very narrow, ending where the front door now is, and, in comparison, tall.[1] It has "a 17th century chimney stack of cross-shaped plan and, above the tiled roof, a weather vane pierced with the initials IME and the date 1697."[2] It was at this date that the extension southwards with its very fine brickwork was built.[1]

"Even in the case of church vanes," wrote V. J. Torr in an old Sedlescombe parish magazine, "anything before 1700 is highly noteworthy and valuable. Not very far away from Sedlescombe,

[1] R.O.H.A.S.
[2] V.C.H.

the 'fretty' vane on the tower of the remarkable church of Etchingham, which depicts the arms of that family, is very probably the most ancient 14th century weather-cock now in use anywhere in England."

The first known owners of the house were the Mansers in the eighteenth century, first John and then Robert, so it is not impossible that the M stands for this surname and the initials I and E for, perhaps, John and his wife.[1]

The house was first recorded as in the copyhold of Battle Abbey, like all the houses in this area from the Green to the Bridge; part of the Manor of Iltonsbath from earliest days until as late as Victorian times. In 1746 Robert Manser surrendered the house to the Lord of the Manor, Sir Thomas Webster, in favour of John Grace, a cabinet maker of Battle, and with his descendants it remained for close on a hundred and thirty years. It is probable that John carried on his cabinet-making and carpentering from the premises; and his widow, Frances, continued to live there after his death until her own in 1771. The house then became the home and shop of a mercer, Henry Hyland, the Grace's son-in-law. A record of 1735 names Harry Hyland "shopkeeper", the first such mention in the village. History does not tell where Harry Hyland sold, or what; but it was no doubt anything that his neighbours needed, which they could not make themselves; matches, ribbons, tapes, cottons and the like. As described in Chapter 37, Lizzie Hyland was a shop-keeper at Cripps Corner in the late nineteenth and early twentieth century.

In 1795 Henry Hyland (perhaps Harry's son) and his wife were granted the freehold for £48 3s., rather unusual in the Battle Abbey properties in Sedlescombe, so that four years later when Elizabeth Hyland died, the house passed to her sister Martha's son, William Grace, of Sedlescombe, who carried on a grocer's as well as the draper's business in the house for 37 years. When he died in 1836, his "reputed" son, Henry Grace, inherited it and all his other property in Sedlescombe, including Asselton House next door (Chapter 14), where his mother, Ann Jempson, lived with her sister, Jane. Soon after he married his wife, Dinah, Henry moved from the house and it was let again as a shop and dwelling-house first to Edward Barber, then to George Bex, described also as grocer and

[1] Map 5.

draper; then in 1859 to Felix Mitchell and, finally, in 1871 to John Ditch, grocer and draper; and "Ditch's" it was right into this century, "a very useful shop for the villagers".

"I remember little Mr. Ditch," said Lizzie. "Whenever a child went into his shop, he would clear his throat and ask, 'What can I get for you, my little maid?' There was an orange box turned up on its side and in it was an immense Dutch cheese wrapped in muslin. He had a two-wheeled trap he used to take his goods around in. After the well was dug, he used to sit on the pump seat outside his shop and discuss things."

The Ditches christened their daughter, Gertie, and she, poor girl, was re-christened at school, Dirtie Ditch. Thankful she must have been to become Mrs. Fred Newble, of Frymans, destroyed in World War II by a landmine. They then moved to Chitcombe which passed on Fred's death to their son, Bob.

"Ditch's" was bought by a son of the late rector of Sedlescombe, also a parson, the Rev. Joseph John Pratt, for £375, who, when he died unmarried six years later, left it to his sister, Harriet Catherine Pratt. The grocer and draper's shop gave place to that of a builder, the occupier being Mr. Herbert Dengate and his family. Ten years later, when Harriett Pratt was 81, she gave it to her nephew, Samuel Bucknill, of Castlemans and shortly before the First World War, Herbert Dengate, the builder, who had lived in it by then for at least 33 years, bought it from him. When he died in 1925 his wife and daughter continued to live there till Mrs. Dengate died eleven years later and her daughter, Mercy, moved to Scotch Down in Brede Lane, selling the old house to two ladies, Miss Brightman and Miss Harding, for £1,100. Under the name "The Workbox", Ditch's became once again something in the way of a draper's shop selling at least some of the articles it had sold a hundred years earlier. So it continued all through the war years until in 1948 it was bought by a Mr. Geddes, who for two years sold antique furniture in it. In 1950 Norman Duncan from Otham in Kent, father of the late Sir Val Duncan of Rio Tinto fame, bought it for £7,000 and lived there for the next eleven years until, on Easter Day 1961, Mrs. Duncan died very suddenly of heart failure after influenza.

So once again the house was sold; this time to a Mrs. Gamble or Hamilton, who lived there for two years with her husband and little pug dog, Harriet. It was during the two short years of their ownership that the house, whose address since the closing of The Workbox had been simply The Green, gained the name of Harriet House, commemorating as is written in the deeds, its one-time owner, Harriet Pratt, who together with others of her family did so much for the village and in whose memory the village pump opposite the house had been built. As the name on the door was at first spelt Harriet's House, it was locally held that the first inspiration for the name was the little pug dog!

Two years later it had a new owner for four years and it was then bought by Colonel Sir Frederick and Lady Pile, who have lived in it ever since. It still retains the shop window front and the fine old fireplace beneath the big chimney with the remarkable weather-vane beside it.

*The Post Office*
Until 1780, the Mail was carried to the different parts of Britain by postboys who were hard riding, active men mounted on cobs which they changed along the way at special inns, which became known as post-houses. Their landlords were called Postmasters and their duties were to provide the changes of mounts for the postboys and to distribute the letters in their own districts. They had, too, the monopoly of hiring out horses to the public.

When this privilege and monopoly were abolished in 1780, anyone was free to establish a posting-house business; and inn-keepers everywhere were quick to take advantage of this opportunity, so that very soon every town had at least one posting-house. The post-chaises, almost always painted yellow, carried not only the mail but passengers and armed guard as well, as every reader of historical novels well knows. They were expensive, most uncomfortable and, not seldom, dangerous too for springs were negligible if not unknown, and the pair of horses was expected to gallop over roads which were full of every kind of pitfall and hazard even for pedestrians. The system was also inconvenient in that the passenger's luggage had, at the end of each stage, to be transferred to another chaise.

By 1784, Mail coaches had come into being, better horsed and better manned. They too also carried passengers. The arrival of the mail coach at the inn in Sedlescombe was a bustling occasion, heralded by the sound of the distant post-horn.

*Durud The First Post Office* 11.

The first recorded Postmaster in Sedlescombe was Philip Butler, the tailor, in 1855. The first Post Office in the village was set up (soon after the opening of the railway from London to Robertsbridge which henceforth carried the mail) in the top cottage of a row which stood beside the Roman road at the head of the Green, and had started life as a very small one of two storeys with a room, top and bottom, on either side of a central chimney, between 1540 and 1650. In the eighteenth century it had been extended at both ends.[1] Its posting box can still be discovered between window and drain-pipe at the North end of those cottages, now the house called Durud. Here Alchin, Postmaster, had too a grocer's and draper's shop; he was followed by James Byner, still very well remembered (Chapter 14). By 1880 the Post Office was transferred to the grand new solid Victorian shop which he had built on to the cottage Post Office, and "Byner's" had become also Grocer, Draper, Hardware and Furniture Stores. Soon it was possible to buy almost anything you could need at the Post Office and Stores, including a ready-made dress, the first such garment in the history of the village. The name BYNER can still be faintly deciphered below the swallows' nests on the north wall of the building.

When James Byner retired, Mr. Hilder became postmaster and general storekeeper, and there his family were born and grew up. At this time the Green was cut but once a year, by the scythe of Bangy Smith (Chapter 50); and it was the village playground, where the north football team (above the Pump) played the south team (below the Pump). Here too the boys played "kick-can": a ring was drawn and a can set in the midst, and all but one child scattered into hiding-places. The aim of the game was to get back to the can without being seen, and to kick it as hard and as far as possible, for the single seeker to go after and bring back.

Hilder gave up the Stores and William Button, from what is now Farthing Cottage, took it over; Hilder went to Farthing Cottage, taking the Post Office with him. Button's Stores, the old Byner's remained, until 1964, when Colonel Miller bought it and it became henceforward Millers. Who converted the cottages into one house and named it Durud, and why, remains to be discovered.

[1] R.O.H.A.S.

*Postboys* 12.

These were three cottages which at the date of the Tithe Map, 1841, were in the occupation of Samuel Watson "and others". It is impossible to say when they were built, but the beams are old and thick and numerous. On a chimney breast is carved the date 1816 with the initials J. W. The W could possibly stand for Watson, Samuel's father.

With the opening of the Post Office next door, they became known as Post Office Cottages, and so remained long after the Post Office had moved away down the village. In the first half of the twentieth century No. 1 was in the occupation of Fred Soan, who worked with his son, Charlie, as painter for the Oaklands estate. When Charlie's wife was killed during the Second World War, his sister, Fanny, her parents dead, made a home for her motherless nephews and niece until their father married again.

Percy Wilton, returned from the war, started, with the help of the British Legion, a tiny paper shop and tobacconist in the small northernmost cottage, borrowing a bicycle to deliver the papers when they were brought by the Carrier early every morning. Wilton did well and in 1928 moved his shop to the opposite side of the road. Bert Smith, now on his own, moved into the erstwhile paper shop and Fred Cooper (son of the wheelwright, Ashley Cooper), moved in from School Terrace with his wife, their son (also Ashley) and daughter. Fred worked close by at Buttons Stores and after his wife died, his daughter, Ivy, looked after him. He was for very many years in the village band. Soon after his death Ivy Cooper moved down to Riverbridge cottages and the row of Post Office cottages was bought by Paul Salkeld who converted two of them into one house to live in with his wife and two daughters, calling it Postboys. Bert Smith continued to live in the remaining cottage, playing his accordion and digging his garden and at opening time walking across to the Queen's Head, there to spend the evening. When he died the whole row became one house, Postboys, a permanent reminder that once upon a time the first Post Office in the village had been next door.

*Farthing Cottage   The Second Post Office*   13.

Hilder brought the Post Office with him to this cottage when he and William Button exchanged dwellings and here it remained until about 1924. The date of this cottage is mid-eighteenth century, and was perhaps part of the Forge buildings, for it was not at first a dwelling-house.[1] Like most of its neighbours it has, however, been a workshop and dwelling-house long before living memory. In 1841, owned by Robert Flint, it was occupied by Henry Selmes; by 1890 it was "Sellens and Cramp, Grocers and Drapers"; both of these surnames were well-known in the village for very many years and Cramp is among those on the memorial of 1914-18. When the Post Office moved down to the bottom of the village, the cottage and workshop were bought by F. Thomas and Sons, the local builder. Mrs. Thomas called the cottage Savernake, in nostalgia for the home in Wiltshire which she had, as a girl, left.

Soon after their eldest son, Will, died very suddenly in 1958, the premises were sold to the building firm, Eldridge and Cruttenden, who occupied them for the next ten years, when they were bought by Molly Campbell and became an antique shop, the cottage being renamed, for personal reasons, Farthing Cottage; and so it remains.

## The Third Post Office at Tanyard House   5.

On the retirement of Hilder from the office of Postmaster at about the time of the big sale of Oaklands property in 1924, Fred Phillips, an employee and protegé of Capt. Combe, applied for the job and was installed as Postmaster, grocer and greengrocer at the bottom of the village at what had then become Tanyard House, the old quarters of the smith. For forty years it remained the Post Office, with two more postmasters following Fred Phillips for short periods. Fred took a large part in village affairs, being Clerk to the Parish Council and a member of most committees: his wife, Pat, was a gay and lively member of the Dramatic Club, the W.I. and all social affairs.

## The Fourth Post Office   14.

In 1965 it moved again, this time back to the centre of the village almost exactly opposite where it started. There it has stayed under successive Postmasters in the old quarters of Archer, the Snob.

## The Postman

In the eighteenth century when it was the obligation of the Postmaster-landlord of the local posting-inn to deliver letters in his parish, he must have employed a man to do this for him; the first

---

[1] R.O.H.A.S.

postman. Memory cannot say who this was in the village. A postman Veness is remembered going round with a horse and cart, but for the late nineteenth century and much of the twentieth it has been a Smith, grandfather and grandson. George Smith, the grandfather, walked to Battle to pick up the mail, distributed it and came home. Will Smith, the grandson, postman for thirty-six years till he retired in 1960, fetched and delivered it on a bicycle. Today the postman has a van.

*The Cobblers and Cordwainers*
One of the customers for leather at Elliott's tanyard in the second decade of the eighteenth century was William Huckens, the shoemaker who, as recorded in 1722 "made shoes for Jack of Sedlescombe" at the Parish expense (Chapter 18). Probably there was more than one shoemaker's workshop in the village. Some who appear in cottage deeds are called cordwainers and made "high-class" shoes and boots; some, less skilled, concentrated on working boots, like Will Huckens. A true craftsman, whether high-class or not, had it in his hands to make life a lot more comfortable for his customers or a lot less so. A comfortable boot for the ploughman or any labourer who was on his feet from morning till night was a friend, a boot that allowed for the vagaries of a particular foot. The human race is not mass-produced; each member is hand-made and so are his feet.

After Will came the Butlers, Thomas and then Edward, for thirty years or more, followed by John Weston in 1768, at Magpie Cottage.

*Archer's, the Snob: Now the Post Office* 14.
This cottage, close to the "Queen's Head", was for a long time a pair known as Archer's, for here by 1890 lived and worked for more than a quarter of a century the cobbler, or snob, Thomas Archer, son of John Archer, the village cobbler before him, whose cottage and workshop had been lower down the village at the Old Thatch. At Archer's, he could be seen working at his last, his rubbery face below his bowler hat turned up attentively to welcome the customer. His son, George, became a carpenter, not a cobbler. Here with him once lodged Warwick Deeping, son of a well-known Hastings doctor, seeking refuge from the medical career that he did not wish to follow. He wrote one of his lesser-known novels, Uther and Igraine,

there and, from the proceeds, started to build the house in Whatlington Road called Green Gore, where he afterwards lived, moving later to Gate House nearer Battle.

After Archer gave up, Fred Newble lived in the cottage and married Gertie Ditch next door. Wilton from Chestnut Tree Cottage then bought it and turned it into one house with shop front, where he established his tobacconist and newsagent, substantially grown from their small beginnings over the road at the Post Office cottage. An example of the impermanence of cottage names in the village, Archer's has been during the last thirty years known successively as Wilton's, Ferraro's, Dadswell's, Atkinson's, Drury's—though by then officially the Post Office—and now Robinson's.

*The Cobbler's Shop*  15.

So after the First World War, the Cobbler's shop moved again further up the village to the tiny workshop just beyond the Gun Cottage; there from 1918 Fred Carter worked as a shoemaker. While a Naval Petty Officer during the war he had received an injury to his spine from which creeping paralysis resulted. Thus, working became increasingly difficult for him as time went by. Nevertheless he carried on for 16 years till he died aged 48 in 1934.

In 1929 an Agreement was signed between A. E. Johnson (a descendant of John Pratt), owner, and Frederick Carter, Shoemaker, to a workshop and shoemaker's shop on a yearly tenancy of £10. When Harold Cheshire bought the Old Gun House in 1930, the carpenter's shop of Robert Southerden (called the Minor Hall) and the bootmaker's shop of Fred Carter were included in the sale.

*The Last Shoemaker*

A man named Ballard followed poor Fred Carter, working in the same tiny workshop. He too was an old sailor, and during World War II he walked every morning from Battle and every evening, after work, he walked back there again. He mended rather than made shoes and children used to love taking him their worn ones, for he made them welcome and talked with them, showing them his leather and his tools and telling them stories about his life at sea, so that they took home with them much besides their shoes. The smell of leather is to many of them still nostalgic today.

In 1955 he, the last Sedlescombe Cobbler, shut shop and walked home for the last time, from Sedlescombe to Battle, where his daughter still lives today.

## THE HOUSES OF THE STREET AND THE GREEN

*The Miller*

The water-mill at Iltonsbath, which ground the village corn for at least five hundred years, and the Lingham family, which gave it several generations of millers, have been described in Chapter 12; and its transformation into a gunpowder mill in Chapter 29; but this was not the only mill in the village; there were also windmills.

The working hours of these millers were often unorthodox, ruled by the presence of a wind more capricious than water. In its absence no grain could be ground. Though there was other work that the miller could then do, it must have been a frustrating trade when work piled up waiting and the wind was wanting. If there was a long windless spell, the price of bread could rise, flour becoming scarce.

Hancox Mill, which was standing at the top of Stream Lane in 1632 with Will Clarke, the Miller (Chapter 23), living with his wife, Anna, in the adjoining cottage, was a Post Mill, as the mound still to be seen beside Windmill Cottage shows. This was the earliest and simplest type of mill, the post on which the mill pivoted being originally a large oak-tree, firmly fixed upright. To manipulate it to face the wind, a long bar was pushed round by hand. Hancox Mill was still being worked in 1848, with William Bates, who owned also Whatlington Watermill, as miller. His assistant, James Dengate, lived in the adjoining cottage.

At about this time iron rollers began to supersede the traditional stone ones. Mills were being built in the big towns to grind the foreign grain which, by the repeal of the Corn Laws, was being allowed into the country. By 1875 nearly half the wheat consumed in Britain was imported, and the bad harvests of that decade increased this to 70%. Moreover, people liked the finer white flour which the iron rollers produced; so the tolling-bell for the little country windmills and watermills of time immemorial was sounding and very many, including Hancox Mill, were silent and motionless by the turn of the century. How long it had stood there before 1632 is unlikely now to be known and the date of its demolishing too seems to be forgotten. The cottage in which the millers lived, generation after generation, has been rebuilt and modernised and so is, happily, still in use.

There must have been another windmill in the village, standing in Windmill field, half-covered now by the houses of Gorselands, but no trace remains of it either in the field or in old records.

Between Cripps Corner and Staplecross, close by Beacon House, stood the Beacon Windmill, owned in mid-nineteenth century by Gilbey Cullen and worked by Aaron Cloke, the son of Moses Cloke, once farmer of Hancox. On November 5th in the eighteen-seventies, it was burned down—as some say, accidentally on purpose. The story goes that a fire was started and the miller, instead of trying to save what he knew to be a doomed mill, turned the sails so that they were on the side of his house, in order that when they fell the destruction would be complete. Some brave lads rushed out to turn them round again so, though the mill was destroyed, it did not fall on the house. The miller cursed.

It must have been a large and important mill in its day for the Tithe Assessment of 1858 rated it at 16/- while the Staplecross mill, no small one, was rated at 10/6, and Hancox at only 5/-. The Staplecross mill is marked on a map dated 1783, but the mill remembered today was built in 1815 by Martin, the millwright. Thirty-three years later it was owned by Thomas Martin and worked by Henry Richardson, later by Mr. Moon (Chapter 37). It continued to work until the close of the First World War. It then remained standing idle, until 1952 when it was demolished as unsafe; for on both sides of it were adjoining buildings. An octagonal smock mill, it differed from a post mill in that only the cap at the top of the mill had to be manipulated to turn the sails into the wind.

The miller was a man of importance in the village; and the mill, too, had a personality; the creak of its sails increasing to a roar when the wind was strong, and the grumbling of its timbers spoke a comfortable converse to the passer-by, and its silhouetted sails were a landmark for countless people for miles around, till the day came when there was only silence and an empty space.

*The Tailor*

In days when no article of clothing could be ready-made, there was always work for a tailor; to make breeches and corduroy trousers, caps, hats and stockings. In 1722 John Elliot is recorded as doing this and, twenty years later, Henry Martin. In 1830 John Nash, Tailor, was one of those from Sedlescombe who attended Cobbett's meeting at Battle. It is not apparent at which cottage he lived and had his workshop. In 1855 Philip Butler of The Cottage was Tailor and also Postmaster.

In 1900 the first ready-made dress was bought at Byner's Stores and men's "ready-mades" were soon available there also. Henceforward, if a tailor were needed, Battle was where you would find him.

## The Glover

Richard Carpenter (Chapter 18) in 1661 is the only recorded glove-maker in the village.

## The Carpenters and some of their Cottages

In early days when the houses were made of wood and plaster, the carpenters were, as described in Chapter 14, the only builders; and many carpenters there must have been in the village, with workshops adjoining their cottages. The first to be recorded by name was Richard Glazier who was doing jobs about the church in 1687. The names of "the carpenders", whose bill for making the new gallery in the church (Chapter 22) "was paied in 1632", were not given, but various sums of £3 and more figure in the church accounts as paid to Croft and Turner, who were more than likely carpenters.

William Weston and Thomas Reed of (now) Magpie Cottage, John Chapman of Sackville Cottage, and John Mills of Brickwall, all worked as carpenters in the eighteenth century. In the second half of that century and in the nineteenth many of the Eldridge family, one after the other, were carpenters and some were bricklayers too, the first on record being Will Eldridge in 1773. Another Eldridge, Richard, is recorded in 1778 as "glazier", so the family must have made a good building team. Joseph Eldridge who died in 1885 was the first to call himself "Builder".

## Sherralds, or Wisteria Cottage. 16.

The nucleus of this longish house beside the Street was two single-storeyed cottages of the eighteenth century which were, in the first half of the nineteenth, in the occupation of John Bishop, Ann Mosley and her son, Spencer, the tanner, and were owned by Mary Ades of Magpie Cottage, who owned also several others in the village. On her death in 1852, it was bought at an auction held at the Queen's Head by the builder, John Catt, whose home and workshop it became. It housed, too, the yard of a wheelwright and carriage-maker, later to become partly a bicycle shop. It was probably John Catt who added the additional storey as he had to the neighbouring cottages.

According to the Oaklands deeds, by 1874 the house belonged to Hercules Brabazon (Chapter 32) and was rented by a clergyman of the name of Marshall. The workshops remained the Builder's Yard, occupied by Herbert Dengate after John Catt died. Wallace Gregory, the Baker, lived in it with his wife who called it, because she so loved the flowers, Wisteria Cottage, and her husband established there the first garage beside the wheelwright and bicycle shop.

When he moved the garage down to the wheelwright and smithy's shop, Mrs. Aldridge bought the house and promptly changed its name again; to Sherrald. "Mrs. Aldridge," wrote Sir John Thorne, whose home it was for some years, "who built several houses in the neighbourhood, had a fondness for names beginning with Sher. I know of no other reason for the name." Her fondness for names beginning with Sher was because these were the first four letters of her maiden name, "Sheriff". Combining these with the first three of her married name, she created "Sherrald". In the same way, she named Shercot, and also "Ridge Flats", which are not so called, as one might conjecture, because they are in fact on a ridge, but because she used her name again, this time the second half of her married name, Aldridge.

She extended Sherralds by building on to it on the north side and, by demolishing the front of the workshops, she formed a garage for the house. So when Miss Edith Savill of the Manor House bought it in 1938, it had assumed its present commodious appearance.

In 1949 came Sir John Thorne, retired from the government in India, where he had been Home Minister under Lord Wavell. A widower, he lived with his sister, Jane, in the house till he died, interesting himself in the village and doing much research into the history of the Farndens of Brickwall and becoming one of the first chairmen of the newly formed Battle and District Historical Society. Soon after he died his sister moved to the Brickwall Hotel and the house was bought by Mr. Victor Best, whose widow still lives in it.

*Battle View: Carpenter and Wheelwright* 17.
This house began life as a dwelling which housed two cottagers. Though small, it was built from its beginnings with an upper storey.

The earliest record among the deeds is an Indenture of Release between three parties; two outside landowners (of Willingdon and Hamsey), the Lord of the Rape the Earl of Chichester, and two local men, James Weston, yeoman of Sedlescombe, and James Martin, Gent. of Battle. Two years later the cottage was sold to Henry Cook of Sedlescombe, husbandman, who was perhaps a son of William Cook, Churchwarden in 1781, and so brother-in-law to Joseph Mercer of Hole Farm (Chapter 26). Since, when Henry Cook died in 1848, he left his real estate to Robert and Joseph Mercer, this seems a likely deduction. The tenants of the cottage at this date were George Tolhurst and Robert Stapley and two years later, when the Mercers sold, the tenants were Samuel Polhill and Robert Stapley's widow. Henry Hicks, the younger, a cordwainer from Northiam, was the buyer. Whether he continued to let it to the tenants or whether he had a cobbler's shop there is not now known but when Edward, often called Edwin Eldridge, carpenter, bought it from him he certainly worked there and built himself workshops. His father was Joseph Eldridge, builder, who died in 1885, whereupon the following year Edwin described himself no longer as carpenter, but as builder. His mother, Harriet Eldridge, was at that date still alive.

In 1890 Edwin insured for £100 his "workshop brick-built and tiled . . . the lower part used as a Wheelwright's Shop having one Bench therein, and the upper part as his Carpenter's Shop having two Benches and a common fire place for heating glue and iron therein and Forty Pounds on Utensils and Stock in trade therein. Warranted that there be no Stove for drying Timber, nor any German or Pipe Stove on the Premises." William Cruttenden of Battle was the Agent for "The Corporation of the Royal-Exchange Assurance for Assuring Houses and other Buildings, Goods, and Ships from Fire; and also for the Assurance of Lives." Clearly the building was now all workshop. Edwin lived opposite at what is now called Magpie Cottage (Chapter 35).

Carpenters and wheelwrights often worked together and were sometimes one and the same man. It was said that a good carpenter might make a bad wheelwright but a bad wheelwright would make a good carpenter. Workshop it still remained when like many another it was bought in 1899 by the Combes, for it was let by them as cottage and workshop to the carpenter, Southerden, and Thomas Podmore, his son-in-law who, when it was up for auction in 1924, bought it privately. It had been enlarged by the Combes, for it was described as "a freehold five-roomed cottage of red brick-and-tile construction with outhouses". Later the Podmores enlarged it again and in 1960 it was once again added to, so that it would be difficult today for Edwin Eldridge to recognise his old workshop.

*The Builders*

It was only in the nineteenth century that Joseph Eldridge, one of the family who had provided carpenters and bricklayers for several generations, began to call himself "Carpenter and Builder". His carpenter son followed suit. Before that, though obviously the house-builders, they had always designated themselves carpenter or bricklayer. The Kenwards, father, son and grandson, William, Reuben and George, all followed this trade, but only George thought of himself as a builder.

*John Catt*

John Catt was, however, the first to use the word builder by itself to describe himself. The son of John Catt, the schoolmaster (Chapters 28 and 51), he was a man of honest skill and considerable ability, a fact noted by Hercules Brabazon who early employed him to improve and rebuild cottages on the Oaklands estate. Soon he was doing all the big jobs in the village, enlarging the Church and building the new bridge. In 1852 he bought the house now Sherralds which became his home and workshops. His grandson, James Dengate, served some of his apprenticeship under him.

*The Dengates*

When John Catt died, his son-in-law, Herbert Dengate, with his brother, John took over his work, and his nephew, James, worked for him as he had for his grandfather. Herbert Dengate took over "Ditch's" as his home but still had his father-in-law's workshop.

James set up for himself as joiner, builder and undertaker, with his son, Frank, in The Haven, the house they had built for the family beside the road, north of Little Castlemans. With workshop beside it and surrounded by a garden filled with flowers, vegetables and fruit, planted by the green fingers of Frank, it was a haven indeed, for the family had been turned out of one of the Brickyard Cottages (Chapter 23) where they had lived for twenty-five years when it was wanted for the Oaklands pigman. James was verger

## THE HOUSES OF THE STREET AND THE GREEN

(Chapter 51) and grave-digger too for very many years. In course of time "Young Frank" carried on single-handed as carpenter and painter rather than builder.

### F. Thomas and Sons

Meanwhile, Frank Thomas, son of Mrs. Thomas, of 1 Forge Cottages, had begun to work as a builder, living in 1920 at Powdermill House beside the Brooks. When work was scarce in the years before the First World War, he worked as gardener at the Rectory for the Rev. Barry Browne (Chapters 21 and 43). Returning from the war before his eldest son, he and his second son, Ted, worked as builders for the Battle Abbey Estate. They moved to Cherry Tree Cottage with its workshop and began to do more building work in the village. One of their first jobs was to build Red Barn Cottages for Ernest Kingdon, of Castlemans, under the architect, Nathaniel Lloyd of Great Dixter. Later they moved to Savernake[1] with more extensive workshops and bought too the Battle business of Jempson, the undertaker, who worked then for them. There were now four brothers in the firm and three of these went to the Second World War, while Will, the eldest, who had been in the First War, carried on till they all returned after 1945 to continue working together. In 1958 Will died very suddenly. Savernake and the business was sold to Eldridge and Cruttenden; and Will's son, Dennis, started up on his own, the third generation of builders in Sedlescombe, who had given employment to carpenters, plumbers, bricklayers and many another in the village.

### Dennis Thomas, Builder

Since then Dennis Thomas had done much of the major building work in the village, new houses in Gorselands stand to his credit. Where many a village has been spoiled by modern buildings these, though close to its centre, have detracted nothing from its beauty, and have provided convenient homes for its many incomers.

### The Brickyards

There were two at least of these in the village where bricks, tiles and land drains were made for untold years.

---

[1] Now Farthing Cottage.

One was behind Littlehurst (once Brickyard Cottages, Chapter 23), just past the elbow of Hurst Lane where the path from Austford crosses it to pass behind the brickyard site to lead down to the village. It was originally largely worked as the estate brickyard for Great Sanders from clay dug from the nearby fields, Great and Little Claypits. By 1830 it had become part of Castlemans Farm belonging to Mary Woodward and farmed, together with Beech opposite, by Spencer Crisford, farmer and bricklayer. The Brickyard cottages were then occupied by George Apps and another man from the brickyard. It was perhaps here that Will Eldridge worked in 1773. When work was slack the brickyard labourer would become a stone breaker; wagon loads would be deposited beside the road for the stone breaker to hammer into pieces for use on the road. This brickyard closed during the First World War.

## The Carricks: Brickmakers at Neatenden Brickyard off New England Lane

The other brickyard lay at the other end of the village in the middle of Share Wood a few yards east of Neatenden farmhouse, skirted by the footpath through Harts Green Farm. It is long forgotten now when the first clay and brick-earth were dug from the field past the little shaw; but for the last hundred years the master brickmaker had been a Carrick, grandfather, father and son. The father, remembered today as "old Carrick", lived in a cottage at Kent Street next to "Dickie Bush" and travelled to and from the brickyard on a tricycle. Pushing it up Whydown Hill, he steered it by means of a string attached to the handle-bars.

The brickmakers worked with brick-earth, and the tilemakers worked with better quality clay. The Carricks made both bricks and tiles. Carrick's elder son, Carlos, eventually took over but his brother, Charlie, was "not quite sharp" and could do only simple jobs.

The clay was dug in the winter and left in a great heap as high as a house to mellow. Young Raymond Hook, with his four-horse team and cart, would carry it later in loads across to the brickyard where it must be turned again to weather. In the spring it was well soaked before going into the pugmill which was operated by a horse whose continual tread wore a hard bare ring around it. The clay, cut off, was rolled in sand and put into moulds for ridge tiles, plain tiles, corners, pipes or gutters. Taken out, they were carefully dried so as not to warp or twist. At dinner-time on Thursdays a small fire was started in the kiln to warm it up. The tiles would then be stacked inside and before midnight burning would start; to continue, carefully watched, till Saturday morning. The shift-watchers would have for company lizards, adders and grass snakes drawn plentifully to the warmth. Sleep could easily take, unaware, the weary man on night-shift where he watched lulled by the heat of the kiln; so he would seat himself on a single wall of loose bricks, sure in the knowledge that if he nodded off he would over-balance and wake; for a drop in the temperature would ruin the load. A man's shoes would become so dried up that the hob nails would all drop out.

Arthur Edwards was a brickmaker. The brick-earth was a darkish loam and the first process when it came out of the pugmill was to make a "loaf" which was a job poor Charlie could do. Thirty-two of these would be loaded on a barrow and wheeled up a narrow plank to the moulder. Charlie was made to do this one day to give the men a laugh but the laugh was on them for to their surprise he negotiated it with ease without a spill.

Throwing the loaf into the mould called for skill and had to be done with sufficient force for the corners to be well-filled with clay before the surface was struck level with a wooden strike. Firing had to be done at a higher temperature, and every 20 minutes five or six shovelfuls of coal must be thrown into the kiln.

It is of these Neatenden bricks that Red Barn Cottages are built, specially made to the specification of the architect in varied colour, some being "blue".

In wet weather work would continue on pipes and ridge tiles in a great long shed where they were put on a board to dry. In winter the men would cut hop poles and thatch-wood in the woods; and Carrick would chip stones, too, for road-making, sitting by the nut orchard at the bottom of Crazy Lane. In their spare time the men would sometimes make garden pots for themselves, which they would decorate making notched patterns around the sides with a stick, sign their name and the date on the bottom and fire them in the kiln.

Carlos Carrick was a most conscientious and devoted Chapel man who would tolerate no bad work and turned out first-class stuff, anything flawed being used for road-making. When asked once by his men for more money, he replied with an invitation to "come into the office and we'll see what we can do about it". What he did was to give a welcome increase of 6d. a day.

In 1936 the last load of bricks was burned and the yard closed down. Many a brick has since been used from the piles that were left scattered around (one is built into a Gorselands house by Dennis Thomas, the builder), but today all that remain are the over-burned ones from broken-down kilns, useful only as rubble, and the site, deserted and overgrown, is hard to find.

*The Carrier at Pump House* 6.

A Carrier cart, with man and horse, had travelled on certain days of the week along the Roman road from the village to Hastings and along the steep "highroad to Battle" down Stream Lane on others, from time immemorial. Another from Cripps Corner linked the village with those north of its boundaries. This was the only public transport available between the villages and the market towns and was an important service, even more for goods than for passengers.

The names of only the last of the long line of these men are still remembered, Nelson Baker of Cripps Corner, and Robert Thomas of Sedlescombe.

Robert had been born at Breadsall Farm but after he married Emily Veness in 1895, he and his wife lived in one of the two cottages which stood below Castlemans on the slope of Church Hill, long demolished. A rectangular bank at the edge of the meadow, filled with long grass and nettles which have never been cleared by succeeding farmers, shows clearly their site. Robert kept his horses in Castlemans stables and bought hay for their feed from Homestall Farm in the Street.

A son was born to them and he remembers how, as soon as he was old enough, he was sent to the Infants' School at the bottom of the hill, dragged unwillingly there, for the first time, by older friends who passed by the cottage on their way. By mid-morning he was back home and in hiding between the double row of peas in his mother's garden. During the lunch hour he tried to hold his breath as he heard her with Miss Martin, his teacher, searching and calling for him. When at last hunger brought him out, his mother fed him and then cut a bunch of her roses for Miss Martin and sent him down to afternoon school with them. Later, when he was old enough to join the Headmaster's class, he became one of the "gardening boys" (Chapter 28), and Hubert, Claude and Ron Martin, the headmaster's sons, were his particular friends.

Twice a day at 5.30 a.m. and 1.00 p.m. his father's van took milk from the farms to St. Leonards dairies and for 3d. each way passengers could go too, sitting among the clanking churns. Once a week he went to Battle, often taking skins from the butcher's slaughter-house to the Tannery where they were weighed. The smell was horrible.

He was tremendously proud of his horses and it was a sore thing when in 1914 they were all requisitioned, but, nothing daunted, he bought a "Tin Lizzie" Ford engine and had a van built on the back to his own specifications. The family moved then from Church Hill cottage down to the house beside the Green, which was then Street Farm (now Pump House and Pump Cottage), and the buildings behind became his stables and yard. His dairy cattle grazed the fields of Street Farm, once Blacklands, behind the Street houses, where the new school will soon be built, and he ran his own dairy business. He also let out ponies and traps. In 1915 his son left school and would help him to drive the cattle into the slaughterhouse at Holmes. Sometimes the doomed animal would get wind of what was awaiting it and would jump over the wall into the gardens of Forge Cottages in a wild attempt to escape.

Soon a further blow shook Robert when Capt. Harvey Combe, returning from the war, let all the grazing fields behind the Street Houses to the new farmer living at what is now Park View, but which then became Street Farm. So Robert had to sell his dairy cattle and his sheep, but the horses he kept for there was still stabling for them and an acre of ground; and so he continued to deliver the milk though it was no longer from his own cattle; and to hire out his horses, wagons and traps. He bought the house from Harvey Combe and renamed it Rose Cottage. After he died in 1932, his wife and son continued to carry on the business for a while. They then sold the house to Mrs. Aldridge of Sherralds, who renamed it Pump House. By a coincidence Robert's son, now retired, lives in another Rose Cottage in the village.

*The Village Policemen*

It seems to be impossible now to discover when the first village constable was appointed to Sedlescombe. The East Sussex Constabulary was founded in 1840 and the first three Superintendents appointed had all had experience in London with the Metropolitan Police. The *Sussex County Advertiser* stated in April 1841 that

" 'watch and ward' is not yet perfect, and it is even less so than we could wish it to be, owing to the reluctance with which local constables join the police and the difficulty of finding parties calculated to fulfil the duties of local constables". The first uniform was a top hat and frock coat and the constable could carry a cutlass if he could persuade two local Justices of the Peace that his beat was particularly dangerous. Boots were shapeless so that they could be worn on either foot and constables were recommended to wear them on each foot alternately, and never to wash their feet but to rub them each evening with sweet oil!

The first village policeman remembered today was a constable called Knight, who lodged at Riverbridge Cottages; and after him Constables Harry Bateman and Baldy, both of whom lodged at Battle View. During the war came Sergeant Goodsell who lodged up Chapel Hill with Chandler, the Wheelwright, at Belle Vue (now Wendy Mill), which later became the Police Station. Sergeant Osborne is well remembered as a great footballer for Sedlescombe.

The first to inhabit the Police Station in an official capacity was Sergeant Dallaway, followed in about 1935 by Sergeant Gearing who a few years later, being involved in a serious car accident at Kent Street, had both his legs so badly broken that he was on sick leave for a very long time. Thus it was that young Constable Graves came to the village and lodged at Springfield in Brede Lane with the Will Thomases. Now, for some time a burglar had been troubling the country round, breaking into country houses as well as into others in Hastings and Bexhill. He would often carry a ladder for perhaps half-a-mile from a farm and put it up against a window of the chosen house so that he could get in easily and ransack. His name was known to be Thurston.

Constable Graves, seeing a photo of Thurston in the *Police Gazette*, was sure that he recognised in him a man who was living under another name, in Midhurst Cottage along Hurst Lane close to the Churchlands lane. Detective-sergeants from Hastings and Bexhill, together with Detective-sergeant Field from Battle, met Constable Graves and they all went round to the cottage. Graves being "the boy" had to stay outside while his superiors went in to talk to the suspect, who of course denied that he was Thurston. While they were talking, the suspect's girl-friend manoeuvred a pram between him and the police, whereupon he made a bolt for it and went charging out of the back door. There the "boy" laid him low with a Rugby tackle and the detectives, not far behind, fell upon him too in a big pile-up. Thousands of pounds worth of goods were found in the bungalow by the police; and Thurston received five years' prison sentence and five years' preventive detention.

Years later, when Constable Graves was serving at Crowborough, he was vividly reminded of Thurston and wondered if he was up to his old tricks, when he was called to a break-in where the burglar had carried a ladder half-a-mile to assist his entry. Thurston was a clever criminal who always wore gloves and never left a fingerprint behind.

When at last Sergeant Gearing recovered he never walked again without a bad limp and his legs were very crooked. Graves left and another young constable lodged with the Thomases and worked with Gearing.

Soon after the end of World War II a new Police Station was built at the end of the Blacklands Council houses and since then Sedlescombe has never been without a resident policeman. The present one has fame as a horticulturist and is a specialist on pinks and carnations, as well as on matters of crime and law.

*The District Nurse*

There must have been many nurses in the village in the past. In particular there was Susan Martin who died in 1881 and to whom a stone was erected in the churchyard "by voluntary subscriptions from those who knew and valued her great services as Nurse and Friend in the hour of sickness"; and who had also kept the Infants' School in the parish (Chapters 28 and 51).

The first trained District Nurse, though, was Nurse Laker, most dearly loved, who bicycled round the parish wearing a little straw bonnet with ribbons tied under her chin. Many were the babies she brought into the world, one being, rather unexpectedly, the first child of the Chief Scout, Baden Powell; for Lady Baden Powell was living at nearby Ewhurst Place when her first baby arrived a fortnight early. She stayed there through the war and her other two children were also born there.

Nurse Laker lived in one of the three cottages on the east side of Church Hill, since demolished. Mrs. Aldridge who bought many cottages in Sedlescombe, divided Pump House into two, so that the District Nurse could live in part of it. Nurse Laker, however, married George Kenward, builder and bricklayer of Sackville Cottage, and so after all she never lived in the Pump Cottage.

Other District Nurses have served the village well, but none have since lived in it.

*Chapter Thirty-five*

OTHER HOUSES IN SEDLESCOMBE

The land on the east side of the Village Green—copyhold of Battle Abbey in the Manor of Iltonsbath—had been divided, as a look at the map shows, into long narrow strips of roughly an acre each. The land on the west side, between Manor Cottages and the Bridge, held of the Manor of Bricklehurst in Ticehurst,[1] was divided into eight holdings, wider and larger than those. The Summary of their Boundaries in 1543[2] shows the owners and tenants of each of the eight plots. It is noticeable that none were owner occupied.

*Homestall* D

No. 8 in the Summary, next to The Old Thatch, seems to be on Homestall land.

"James Firsby holds in farme. Parcell of Bothurst land and messuage, garden and 2 pieces called Bothurst; c. 12 acres.

Boundaries: Highway Sedlescombe to Bodiam, East:

Peter Easton, wood late Bothurst, West:

Mill dike belonging to the mill called Abbey Mills, south."

Nothing is so far known of James Firsby. The name Easton figures in records periodically.

The next mention of Homestall in parish records is 200 years later in 1732 when Henry Bishop of Great Sanders was paying rates for "part of the Homestall". Thirty-six years later William Bishop was the ratepayer and a Mr. Lulham for the "other part of Homestall and for Dial field". Dial field is a part of the Great Sanders estate close to the house and this raises the doubt that "the Homestall" refers to the Home Farm there, rather than to the house

[1] Lower.
[2] Letters refer to Maps 3 & 5.

known as Homestall today. Moreover, at the date of the Tithe Map, 1841, this house was listed simply as "late Freelands" suggesting that, like many another cottage and farm in the parish, it had no fixed name but was known by the name of its farmer, which in a few cases stuck permanently. Freeland had been farmer of Homestall in 1813.

Robert Weston, farmer, was later owner-occupier of this small independent farm which consisted of the farmhouse, now Homestall, the oast house and farm buildings on the further side of the farmyard, and six fields lying behind it, two being hop-fields alongside the river. Besides this, Robert rented all the meadows behind the houses on the east side of the Street which were bordered by Brede Lane on the north and by the Brede River on the south. These were David Spencer's Blacklands Farm and part of Hercules Sharpe's Brickwall Farm. The East View houses now mark the eastern end of the former farm and the Blacklands council houses perpetuate its name. Robert rented also, from his father or brother, James, the "Street Field", No. 458, opposite the School, together with cottages, known as School Terrace, and their gardens which are now replaced by the gravel drive. Another of the family, Albert, rented from Richard Smith the house beside the Green, now Pump House and Pump Cottage, with its yard and buildings which backed on to Brickwall Farm. The Westons had owned and farmed also other land between Sedlescombe and Brede including Powdermill Farm, but the family seems to have died out in the village. Thomas Weston moved to Guestling but when his son, Henry, died far away in Brazil at the age of 23 in 1892, it was in Sedlescombe Church that the parents put a memorial (Chapter 51).

Robert Weston was followed by John Barber at Homestall and as tenant farmer of Brickwall and Blacklands farms and also of the Street Field. It was in this field, No. 458 T.M., known often as "Barber's field", that the hidden treasure of Saxon coins was discovered in 1876 (Chapter 6). John Barber was then described as "of Homestall", a suitable name for either him or Robert Weston to choose for their home farm, meaning as it does "the homestead", a house with outbuildings and farm.

The next farmer of Homestall was a man called Leigh (Chapter 43), who came some few years before the First World War and remained till about 1920. It became a poultry farm and he used to run the International Poultry Tests. All the breeders would send him their samples, which he registered and tested. He was also Rector's Warden.

In 1925 came John Busbridge and farmed for the next 24 years just Homestall's own six fields. When he died, that was the end of the farm as such, and in 1960 the oast and barn were converted into a house in its own right. Gregory of the Bakery had bought already the field beside the road on the south of the house.

In the chimney of Homestall are two bricks laid on edge; on the upper one are illegible initials, and on the lower date 1738 when the house, quite a large building with a small rear wing, was built. A rafter in the roof with a curved scroll thought to have been an old ship's timber proved on closer inspection to be a piece of moulded wood used from an ancient bedstead or other piece of furniture. Though built with an original chimney, the traditional plan of all the medieval houses is still followed, though it never had any exposed framing, but was always tile-hung. The brickwork was built in later. Undoubtedly, it replaced an earlier pair of cottages.[1]

*Fir-Tree Cottage* E.

No. 7 on the Summary shows a large plot which includes that on which the Sackville Cottages stand.

"Edward Daye holds. Lands of Penny's Widdow.
Boundary, east. Highway. west and south, lands of Wm. Bathurst.
North, lands of Widdow Waters."

Nothing more is known of these.

Fir-Tree Cottage, timber-framed with plaster front bearing the date 1737, stands between Homestall and Sackville Cottages. From the size of the old beams in its interior, it is probably older than that date indicates, which is simply that of its oldest existing deed, which states that it was then owned by Abraham Bodle, a carpenter, and his wife, Mercy. It may be that old beams were re-used in the building of Fir-Tree Cottage for in 1748 (Chapter 12) Widow Lingham moved from the Mill at Iltonsbath to "Abraham Bodle's new House". An Abraham Bodle was a tenant of one of the Sackville Cottages next door from 1800 to 1837 a hundred years later. The earlier Abraham Bodle is buried in the churchyard.

[1] R.O.H.A.S.

In 1751, two years before he died, Abraham sold his "new house" for £151 to a family called Rutley of whom nothing is now known; and thirty-four years later, Richard Eldridge, the bricklayer, bought it. This well-known family in and around the village produced bricklayers, a tanner, carpenters and farmers who did well enough to buy small properties in the village by way of investment. In 1732 "Goody Eldridge" had been the washerwoman and had washed the Rector's surplices. By 1890 Edwin Eldridge is listed in *Kelly's Directory* as a Builder in Sedlescombe (Chapter 34). Many of the family have found their resting-place in the churchyard.

In 1838 Eldridge sold the cottage to Mrs. Harriet Crisford, wife or mother of Spencer Crisford, living at Castlemans, a brickmaker who owned the two brickyards (Chapter 34), and she let it to two or three tenants. In 1841 "widow Hilder" was one of the occupants; another name very familiar still in the village today.

Over the years it has remained two cottages and for the last years one was occupied by Miss Kate Furner and the other by Mr. and Mrs. Edgar Boxall, whose cottage garden is famous in the village for its wealth of flowers, and most particularly for its beautiful sweet peas, delphiniums and pansies.

*Notes from the Records concerning Abraham Bodle's New House*
1745   Rates:  A. Bodle . . . new occupier. Part of his new house empty.
1751      ,,       Thomas Longley for A. Bodle's new house.
1752      ,,       Thomas Martin part of A. Bodle's new house.
              Thomas Weston the other part of A. Bodle's new house.

*Sackville Cottages*   E.

Though these cottages beside the Street overlooking the Green bear the date 1697, they are certainly older than this for behind their brick façade is a timber-framed building of three or four bays, which may have been built as a medieval open-hall in the fifteenth century or later at the beginning of the sixteenth. In the early eighteenth century it was re-fronted with brick and later in that century it was extended to the south.

The earliest deed relating to them is dated 1749 and concerns "Mr. Chapman of Sedlescombe, carpenter, and Thomas Jenner of Guestling, wheelwright." John Chapman conveyed "one freehold tenement, one stable and about $\frac{3}{4}$ acre in Sedlescombe Street", the estate of his father, a staymaker, "for fourscore pounds" to Thomas Jenner who had "full liberty to let the house". John Chapman acknowledged the payment to him of £1 in part payment of the fourscore pounds. The document is signed "Thomas Ginner" and is witnessed by "James Ingram" who was Rector of Sedlescombe at the time.

Thirty years later the cottages were owned by Thomas Easton of Hawkhurst, yeoman, and Mary his wife, and they sold it in 1778 to Richard Eldridge, glazier, of Sedlescombe, with a "parcel of land called Ellin's Acre". There is no mention of the stable, but there were now three cottages, whose occupants were Edward Hayler, Thomas Freeman and David Noakes. Richard Eldridge, the glazier, was married to Elizabeth and they had two sons, William and Richard. Richard, the father, died in 1808 when the occupants of the cottages were William Wood, John Durrant and Abraham Bodle (Fir-Tree Cottage). Richard Eldridge, buying Fir-Tree Cottage seven years later, called himself bricklayer. Perhaps he was the son.

When William, the elder son, died in 1837, his son Richard, yeoman, sold to William Pocock, farmer of Hollington, for £130, "these three cottages" says the deed, "are the very same as sold in 1778 by Thomas Easton and Mary his wife". Included in the sale is "that parcel of land in occupation of Thomas Byner". Was this still "Ellin's Acre"? The occupants were then Ann Hayler, Widow Swadling, and still Abraham Bodle. They were followed by William Turner and Robert Weston, butcher at the shop opposite.

The next deed describes the sale in 1852 by the farmer, William Pocock, to Arthur Ades, of the Ades family of Hancox, and butler to the Rt. Hon. Earl Clanwilliam of 32 Belgrave Square, for £180; and once again specifically included "the parcel of land late in the occupation of Thomas Byner and now of Richard Smith". It also says that "Arthur Ades' widow shall not be entitled to a dower in or out of the said hereditament". The occupants were then William Spencer Turner, butcher, and Mr. Tutt.

Eighteen years later, Arthur Ades, the butler, had become "Arthur Ades, Gentleman, of 73 Cambridge Terrace, Hyde Park Gardens", and he sold his property in Sedlescombe to Mrs. Elizabeth Saunders of Kilwin, Middlesex, for £100: "a messuage with three tenements and garden occupied lately by William Spencer Turner, butcher, and Mr. Tutt, and now Dennett; also the land adjoining, late in the occupation of Thomas Byner, then Richard Smith and now Dennett". Mrs. Saunders sold it again in two years' time, 1872, to John Catt, builder of Sedlescombe, for £265, making thereby a nice little profit of £165. Still described as "three tenements with garden, bakehouse and wash-house", lately occupied by the butcher and Tutt, together with Thomas Byner's parcel of land, "late Dennett's", the occupants were Reuben Kenward, Betsy Dengate, Mrs. Stephenson and Frank Bishop, who was a descendant of one of the Bishops of Great Sanders. His descendants remained in two of the three cottages until the nineteen-sixties.

John Catt had built a fourth cottage joining on to the most northerly of the three, hence the four occupants. It was he who gave them the name Sackville Cottages, commemorating thereby a branch of that great family which lived for nearly 100 years in Sedlescombe (Chapter 17).

In the 1872 deed, John Catt's widow also was "not entitled to dower". This was to guard the tenancies of the occupants on his death. At this date a portion of ground measuring 35 perches was made over "for the use of Hercules Brabazon and his heirs for ever", in order to extend his next-door property, "The Cottage".

John Catt lived opposite at Harriet House until he died, in February 1891. He was buried in the churchyard near other members of his family. He left a widow, Catherine, a son, John Robert Hyland Catt, and a daughter, Bertha. His trustees were these members of his family together with Edmund Linton Alchin, grocer and draper of Sedlescombe. An auction of the property which included the "land occupied by Byner, then Smith, then Dennett" was held at 12 Claremont, Hastings, and Alchin's wife, Mary, was the highest bidder at £380. The Bakehouse remained, the washhouse was converted into a privy and shed.

During the next few years, No. 4 Sackville Cottages was made into a separate house, taking in extra land on the north for a garden. (See Linton House.) Was this Thomas Byner's parcel, perhaps Ellin's Acre?

So once again there were only three Sackville Cottages, and here lived George and Nurse Kenward for many years. In 1964 the Alchin family sold them to Paul Salkeld of Sedlescombe; the occupants were then Mrs. Sheather, who had been born a Bishop, and her sister-in-law, Mrs. Minnie Bishop, daughter-in-law of Frank. The other cottage was empty since Mrs. Hilder had died. Paul

Salkeld sold to Peter Jackson, Mrs. Sheather died and Mrs. Bishop moved to a flat at Roselands, and the Jacksons converted the three cottages into two. The bakehouse still stands behind with its old chimney and bake-oven, and the garden which was in three strips is now one, stretching behind Fir-Tree Cottage to join the Homestall fences.

*Linton House* (See also Sackville Cottages)
 Linton House, a house with two gables facing the Green, was built over the one-storeyed No. 4 Sackville Cottage by Edmund Linton Alchin, the Sedlescombe grocer, after the purchase of the four cottages by his wife, Mary, in 1891. He took in some extra land on the north to make the garden, perhaps Ellin's Acre mentioned in the deeds of Sackville Cottage. The Alchins called their new house Linton House, from his own middle name. In 1919 his widow sold it to Mr. A. J. Jenner, Inspector of Nuisances and Rural District Surveyor, for £575. There must have been only one well for all four cottages, for rights to draw water from it are mentioned. The Jenner family, which included a son and daughter, lived there for the next thirty years, during which tragedy overtook them when the son, Reg, was killed in a motor-cycle accident. Eventually, Mrs. Jenner, now a widow, and her daughter moved to Battle and the house was sold to become a guest house, where the old or delicate were looked after and wonderfully fed by Mrs. Pick, who had been for some years hotelier at Brickwall. When she herself became too infirm to do this work she sold the house, which has passed into different ownership several times since.

*The Cottage* F.
 This house, like many others on the west side of the Green, began its life as a pair of single-storeyed cottages in the late seventeenth or early eighteenth century. The earliest document concerning it is an Indenture of Lease and Release of 1768 between John Crisford, a carpenter of Northiam, and John Russell, victualler, who in the following year were fighting each other in a legal battle; John Russell (possibly junior, as the case seemed to concern the will of a John Russell) being the plaintiff, and John and Philadelphia Crisford and Thomas and Biddy Johnson—no doubt occupying tenants —the "deforciants" who lost their case and presumably their homes. Twelve years later this same John and Philadelphia Crisford and their five children were living, somewhat unwelcome, in Battle, and

the Overseers and Churchwardens of Sedlescombe in a signed document made themselves and their successors responsible that the family were legally inhabitants of the parish of Sedlescombe and not of Battle (Chapter 18).

During the next twelve years, Stephen and Elisabeth Selmes and their children occupied the pair of cottages and, in 1791, were followed by George Brook, possibly the tanner, and Ann, his wife, and their family. In 1806 Robert Weston and Richard Bishop, the late innkeeper owned and lived in it. By 1821 it had passed into the ownership of the Butlers, Philip, whose wife Cordelia Crisford died there two years later, and Thankful, his brother. In the Sussex Archaeological Museum at Lewes can be seen a canister of red ware made in the form of an old-fashioned hand-churn or washing dolly. It is ornamented with five bands top and bottom, filled with slip, and in the space between is an inscription, bordered with minute stars, that reads,

"Jane Butler; Sedlescombe, Sussex. August 20. 1815."

In the Post Office Directory of 1855 Philip Butler is recorded as Tailor and Postmaster of Sedlescombe.

In 1843 the cottages were bought by Hercules Brabazon who set John Catt, the builder, to work on them to transform them into a house which was to be, virtually, the Dower-house to Oaklands. It bears, like others, a shield with the Brabazon coat of arms. An Indenture of 1874 between Brabazon and John Catt names it *The Cottage* for the first time. John Catt sold "a parcel of ground . . . by assessment 3 perches . . . bounded on the north by a messuage and garden belonging to the said H.B.B. and in the occupation of the Rev. J. Marshall" (now Sherralds) and thus the carriage drive for The Cottage was made. The designing and enlargement by John Catt was so successful that in the schedule for the 1924 auction it could be described in the following terms:

"The Cottage is practically in the centre of the village of Sedlescombe . . . with a Pleasant Front Garden Large Lawn and Well-Laid Flower Beds Enclosed by Fine Old Yew Hedges 9 ft. high with Gateway Entrance at the side, giving access to the Brick-built and Tiled House through Tiled-floored Entrance Porch and Hall, fitted with Anthracite Stove, off which A Quaint Drawing Room about 20ft 10in. by 16ft 8in. with pillared support to oak-beamed ceiling, open brick fireplace with brick hearth and sides. On the opposite side is Dining Room with bay window, modern fireplace and mantelpiece, and a door to a small conservatory. On the Upper Floor are Six Principal Bedrooms and Dressing Rooms all fitted with good stoves. Capital Bathroom fitted with bath (hot and cold) Lavatory (hot and cold) W.C. Two Staircases and Three Maids Bed Rooms each with stove." etc.

. . . "The Outbuildings around Paved Yard a Two-stall Stable, Harness-room, Wood and Coal-house, Lamp and Oil Room, Garage for large Car, Large Potting-shed and closet. Well-planted Kitchen Garden in the rear. . . ."

It had been let to a Major Prendergast for two years in 1906 after Hercules Brabazon died, but it was marked on the Estate Map as the Agent's House and it was here that Harvey Combe lived after his marriage and here his daughter, Eileen, was born.

In the Auction it was bought by a Doctor, who set up his practice there, and the Doctor's House it has remained ever since, but it is still *The* Cottage.

*The Doctors in Sedlescombe*

It was not until after World War One that Sedlescombe had a doctor and surgery in the village, though in the records of Deeds of houses, surgeons and physicians are mentioned. In 1648, Thomas Avory of Castlemans (Little) described himself as "phisitian"; and in 1740 Stephen Robinson, "Surgeon of Sedlescombe", built himself a cottage, the most southerly of the three opposite Battle View (Chapter 34).

Early in the twentieth century it was Dr. Kendall of Battle who would come in pony and trap driven by his coachman (in later years the coachman became chaffeur) at any hour of day or night and not a penny would he charge anyone whom he thought could not afford it. And so he died, not rich as he could have been, but a poor man. An old man called Edwards would walk from Battle with a basketful of medicines, subscribed by Dr. Kendall, for a delivery fee of three pennies to the cottages of patients.

Dr. Johnson was the first to take up residence in Sedlescombe. The drive at The Cottage was at the time narrow and overgrown and the drivers of the furniture van complained that it was impossible to get it up to the house. After some altercation, Mrs. Johnson asked the driver to vacate his seat, whereupon she took over and drove the van up to the door of the house. She had been an ambulance driver in the war! The doctor too had been in the war and had as a result a crippling wound. He was followed after some years by a young Scotsman, Dr. Gordon, who did not stay very long. Then came Dr. King, well-remembered and well-liked; Dr. Hollins, an Irishman who had been a ship's doctor; and for the last 30 and more years, Dr. Wright. Sedlescombe has been very well served by its doctors.

*Chestnut Tree Cottage   G.*
This cottage would seem to be No. 4 on the Summary.

"Markes Richard holds the lease of Robt. Waghorne. Messuage and garden, c. ½ acre. Boundaries; east, the highway: West and North, lands of Peter Easton: South, lands of Thomas Vanns."

"A Rentall gathered Out of the Manor of Brickelhurst remaid A.D. 1609" shows "Johana Avann, Widdow, for a messuage sometime Waghornes", paying 8d. The name Vann seems interchangeable in many records with Avann. The name Widow Van appears in the 1632 Sittings Plan for Pew 24. The name Waghorne was still familiar in the village in the nineteenth century (Holmes House, Chapter 34).

When the father of the present owner bought this cottage it had for some years been a pair, and he immediately converted it back into one. In the course of the alterations, the floor was taken up and lowered in order to give more head-room under the low ceilings. In the earth below, a number of graves of new-born babies were found, some with little headstones and a date. One of these, bearing a rough drawing of a baby's head incised on it, was preserved and can be seen today built into the outside wall between door and window. On its reverse side, now hidden, are the words "Baby Mary" and the date, now unfortunately forgotten.

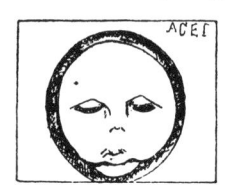

The explanation of this little burial place could be that the babies being still-born were unbaptised and therefore could not be buried in the consecrated ground of the churchyard, and perhaps were buried by a sympathetic mid-wife to whom sometimes a bereaved parent gave a little home-carved memorial. At the same time, one would suppose that the graveyard must pre-date the house, which would make it very old indeed; ignorance of the dates on the gravestones is very hampering. In 1675 Mary Thorpe had acted as village mid-wife without episcopal licence (Chapter 19).

At the date of the Tithe Map, 1841, the cottage is listed as "House, Shop and garden" owned and occupied by Edgar Eldridge. As far back as living memory goes, it housed two cottages in which lived Mrs. Hazel and Mrs. Bryant until after the First World War.

The present owner's father started a tiny paper shop in the most northerly of the Post Office Cottages next door, before moving over the road to set up a newsagent's at the late shop of Archer's, the Snob.

*The Manor Oast*

This house was converted from the Oast-house and Barn belonging to Elliot's Farm-house or "Manor-house" (alias "Carters"), the first of the oasts in the parish to be turned into a house. During and after the First World War it was the home of General Nixon and his wife and family. Their daughter married one of the earliest radio personalities, Christopher Stone, who was thus prevailed upon to open or appear at fetes and other village festivities.

The General, like that earlier one at Beauport, was for a time under a cloud, since his strategy or tactics at Kut in 1915 were criticised by higher authority. He was however cleared of blame and knighted a few years before he died.

The Savills were the next owners of the Oast; a bachelor brother, Cecil, and a spinster sister, Edith; uncle and aunt of Sir Eric Savill, who for King George VI created the Savill Gardens at Windsor. It is not surprising, therefore, that they too were both the keenest of gardeners, filling their garden with unusual plants, shrubs and trees which flourish still today in the smaller ones of the bungalows or houses which have since been built in the grounds.

*Manorside*

This cottage, which stands at right angles to the road, was built by the Savills on a small parcel of their land, for the use of their resident gardener, who in fact lived in it not much more than a year before leaving the village; and thereafter they had a daily one, so the cottage was sold and has passed to several different owners in succession since.

*Ringfold*
This attractive house, built by its present owner in the gardens of Manor Cottages several years after the end of World War II, has settled superbly well and looks as though it had stood there many years longer.

*The Presbytery* H.
This cottage, with its front of white Sussex slats, was a nameless pair where lived in 1841 "Henry Eldridge and others". Not till towards the end of the century did it acquire a name, when it housed the Rev. W. Drury who was employed by the Rector, Mr. Warner, in his old age, as an assistant curate to help him by taking some of the services, teaching the village children scripture in school and looking after some of "the flock". The cottage where he lived with his sister thus became known, rather grandly, as the Presbytery and so has remained ever since.

The curate is still remembered by the children he taught, most particularly for his habit, which mesmerised their eyes, of twisting unceasingly his golden watch-chain round and round, round and round, during his lessons. His small black-coated figure with round curate's hat was a familiar figure in the Street.

He was followed by Mr. Slade, an artist. After World War I came a doctor and his two daughters who ran a little infants' school in the room which adjoins it at right-angles and which has now become its garage, and during the second war another young woman took over the school for a while, until she became ill when a bank manager and his wife, evacuated from Hastings, took over the cottage. After they died another retired couple bought it and improved both it and the garden.

The Triangle of land which is enclosed by Short and Long Lane and the main road near the school has eleven dwelling-houses packed into its small area. Part of the waste land leased to Peter Farnden's nephew in 1652 by the Lord of the Rape, the stretch beside the main road had been divided into three "wayside" plots on each of which a cottage could be built.

*The Old Gun Cottage*[1] 1.
The Gun Cottage was the first of these, but the exact date of its building is not known. An article in *Sussex County Magazine* in 1952 suggests that it was used in the seventeenth century by Peter Farnden, the ironmaster of Brickwall, to store the guns and shot made in his forge and furnace, and that it was thus that it acquired its name.

An old tradition says too that it was once an inn, the "Dog and Gun", and that the origin of the name Balcombe Green just behind and above the cottage is from the word "balking", meaning "throwing out", an operation sometimes necessary for inn-keepers on their customers. It is possible that both these traditions are true. Compasses in the north of the parish, said also to have been an inn, is surrounded, too, by three lanes. Perhaps it was while it was an inn that the smugglers' hiding-place at the top of the flight of stairs was arranged and used (Chapter 25).

An old Indenture dated 1815, lent to me by the present owner of the house, was made out between the Rt. Hon. Thomas Earl of Chichester Lord of the Rape, of the one part, and Mary Stace, Widow of Westfield of the other part, and refers to two earlier Indentures of 1814, one of lease and one of appointment and release, made between six people, one of whom was John Bishop, gentleman, of Great Sanders (Chapter 17). The others were the Earl of Chichester of the first part, George Shiffner Esq. of the second part; George William Frederick, Duke of Leeds and John Lord Sheffield of the third part, and Thomas Partington of the fourth part. It was inrolled in H.M. High Court of Chancery 1818. Mary Stace contracted for the absolute purchase of this parcel of the Rape of Hastings at the price of £20. It measured 1 rod and 9 perches and included the cottage or tenement and all other buildings in her occupation at the time. It was bounded on the north by premises occupied by William Eldridge and the document was witnessed by William Shadwell and William Thorpe.

By 1841 the house was still owned by a Stace, Charles; perhaps the widow's son, but it was occupied by the blacksmith, James Dennet, whose forge was just behind it. Several generations of Blacksmith Dennets followed each other in cottage and forge. Charles Stace owned also the cottage behind the Forge, now Wood-

---
[1] Nos. refer to Map 5.

man's Cottage, but he did not, according to the Tithe Map, live in the village himself. So the Gun Cottage remained the home of the blacksmith until the forge was given up early in the twentieth century (Blacksmith, Chapter 34), when it became a pair of cottages owned by one of the Pratts. It continued to house villagers until 1930, when it was bought from a Pratt descendant by Commander Harold Cheshire, who lived in it with his wife for many years. Since then it has had two other owners who have improved and modernised it. It is unusual in having two floors above the ground floor.

*Magpie Cottage* 1, 2 *and* 3 *School Hill Cottages* 16.

The middle one of the three white-slatted cottages which stand on the north side of the Minor Hall has recently been named Magpie Cottage.

Built probably in the beginning of the eighteenth century, its earliest deed is dated 1736 when Thomas Reed, a carpenter, sold it to another carpenter, William Weston. As noted in Chapter 18, it had previously been the Poorhouse, for the deeds record that, before Thomas Reed bought it, it had been "late in the occupation of churchwardens and overseers of the Poor in Sedlescombe".

In 1740 William Weston sold a little over a quarter-acre of orchard beside his cottage to Stephen Robinson, "surgeon of Sedlescombe", who on it built himself a cottage, now the most southerly of the three.

After William Weston died his widow, Mary, married Edward Butler, cordwainer, or shoemaker, and her son, John, followed in the footsteps of his stepfather in that trade, rather than in those of his carpenter father.

So for a time it became the Snob's Cottage, with John practising his trade there until 1768, when he sold the cottage and workshop to Isaac Baker. Whether he was also a shoemaker is not apparent, but when he died in 1786, his grandson, also Isaac Baker, inherited the cottage which was then called "Montreal". Was this name chosen in honour of the battle for the Heights of Abraham, fought not long before grandfather Isaac had bought the cottage, as the grander house a few miles south had been named Beauport? (Chapter 30.)

The young Isaac sold it again four years later to John Watts and in 1798 he sold it in his turn to Edward Ades, farmer of Hancox, whose son, also Edward, had taken over the farm. Edward senior and his wife, Mary, lived in the cottage together for the next twenty years, and she as a widow till she died in 1852. After that for the next twelve years it became again a carpenter's cottage when Edwin Eldridge and Reuben Weller, wheelwright, occupied it, their workshops being opposite (see Battle View, Chapter 34). Edwin was still living there when in 1895 F. A. Langham bought it at the George Hotel, Battle, for £335 and sold it the following day to Edwin at a profit of £5. Four years later Edwin, the carpenter, retired and sold the cottage where he had lived for 47 years, inevitably to H. T. B. Combe. Part of it was soon converted into a third cottage, which was occupied by Widow Noakes, Magpie Cottage, by Relf, and the third, the surgeon's cottage, by an unnamed villager.

Today all three cottages, modernised, make comfortable little homes; No. 1 is Cherry Tree, after the next-door cottages, demolished; and No. 3 is Thimble Cottage.

*Myrtle Cottage* 17.

This cottage, tucked away behind the Minor Hall, and between the Gun Cottage, Monkebo and Woodmans, is invisible from any road and, moreover, the brick path leading up to it is so tiny that a passerby may never even notice its existence close beside him.

Myrtle Cottage has stood there for several centuries, housing two or three families. In 1841 it was owned, like the Gun Cottage, by Charles Stace and was "occupied by Henry Bird and Others". Early in this century a member of the Pratt family bought it and converted it to house one of their old retainers, Miss Fanny Bishop, who lived there until she died a few years after World War II. Recently it has been modernised by successive owners.

*Tudor Rose and West Wind*

Beside the School Hill Cottages, 1, 2 and 3, but on a higher level there used to stand three more with the same white frontage of Sussex slats, called Cherry Tree Cottages from the tree in the garden which was hung with foaming blossom every spring. In 1841 they housed the family and workshop of William Eldridge, carpenter and builder, father of Edwin (Chapter 34).

Some years after the end of World War II, the cottages were pulled down and replaced with the corner-house of two dwellings, one called West Wind and the other, Tudor Rose. The small retaining wall beside the pavement, which supported its garden, still stands but is no longer cushioned every summer by the gentian-blue blooms of the herbaceous plumbago.

*Balcombe Green*

At the time of the Tithe Map, 1841, Balcombe Green at the top of the triangle consisted of Balcombe House, Balcombe Cottages (now Woodmans), The Forge (now Monkebo), and the two small bungalows in Short Lane. Across it, at the entrance to the track that leads over the fields to Hurst Lane there was, at that time and within living memory, a gate which once a year was shut and locked in order to preserve the right of way, perhaps to Castlemans whose farmlands it cut across. Some say, however, that it belonged to the Church, a possibility since it leads to the lands called Churchlands. It may in fact have passed from the latter to the former when the Castlemans Farm was made and may have been lost when that farm was sold up between the wars.

*Balcombe House* 19.

A row of cottages is marked on the Tithe Map, but these were either pulled down and re-built by Hercules Sharpe, or were enlarged by the addition of a first storey. They were part of Brickwall Farm.

*Woodmans Cottage.* 20.

The nucleus of this cottage is a tiny building of two storeys with one room, top and bottom, on either side of the central chimney and a lean-to at the rear, built in the first half of the eighteenth century. It was extended in the nineteenth century at the east end, but on the inside the timber of the earlier outside wall is still visible.[1] The west end, like the front, is weather-boarded. By 1841 it had become three cottages owned by Spencer Crisford, tenant farmer of Castlemans farm, and was occupied by Thomas Hyland and others, no doubt labourers on that farm. Cottagers succeeded cottagers in each of the three until 1964 when they were converted into one dwelling-house and given the present name.

*The Bungalow and Montalet*

These two little bungalows are both shown on the Tithe Map. Today they have been modernised and, maybe, altogether rebuilt.

[1] R.O.H.A.S.

They too at that time housed farm labourers who worked for Spencer Crisford.

## Elthorne

All the land on the south side of Long Lane belonged in earlier days to Brickwall. The field in which this house was built in 1959 by Veness, the builder, was called Ostin's Croft.

Since the farmlands of Castlemans were sold after the first war, one house after another has been built alongside the path on the western edge of the Great Field. From their superb site on this ridge they look right across the meadows of Castlemans and Highfield to the high woods round Battle.

## The Old School House  X.

In spite of its name this is a new house, built for the schoolmaster just after the end of World War II to take the place of the tiny cottage now almost too dilapidated to be used as part of the school, but then occupied by the Infants' School mistress, her husband and son.

## Rose Cottages  21.

There used to be a row of four cottages beside the Village Hall, which stood by the footpath which was at that point a good step above the road, with a small sustaining wall of brick. In earlier days, in living memory, they were known as Broom Row and there was always a broom fixed to the wall of No. 1. The cottages were demolished in 1964, two were rebuilt and the Roselands flats (Chapter 48) were built on the site and the gardens of the others.

## Meadow Cottages

These four cottages, built on land bought from the Pratts of Highfield, were the first council houses to be built in the village. Until the building of Roselands they had small gardens in front as well as at the back.

## The Cottages up Church Hill

There were three on each side of the road, those on the east being in one row. Robert Thomas, the Carrier, lived with his wife and son in the top two and Tom Drury in the lower one. When he moved out, Nurse Laker, the District Nurse, moved in.

On the other side of the road in the bungalow at the foot of Beech House lived two old ladies who had earlier run an Infants' School in it; Miss Phoebe Coggers and Miss Chiffany, whose names have a Cranford ring.

The pair of cottages lower down the road were set at right-angles to each other, with old "Lady" White in one and the Postman Smith in the other.

Between the bungalow and the cottages was a spring of sparkling water which supplied the three households. A delightful story is told how one hot summer's day a travelling circus came through the village with three elephants among the animals which walked between the caravans. They, being thirsty and smelling water, stopped by the spring on Church Hill and began to drink. They drank and they drank while the rooks cawed overhead, and they splashed the cooling water over themselves, standing ankle-deep in the cool lace of the wild parsley blooms. They drank at the spring till they drank it dry; and dry it has remained until this very day! All the cottages were demolished in 1930, but their sites are very evident still.

*Highfield*  Map A.

John Pratt, while he was Rector of Sedlescombe, bought land; first, Durhamford from the Bishops, which then housed cottagers; next, as Richard Smith fell ever deeper into debt, Spilsteds; and, finally, Beech. All these lands closely surrounded his Rectory and its glebe where for 58 years he lived with his large family of four sons and three daughters and ever-increasing number of grandchildren. It was not surprising, therefore, that he planned to continue living in the village after he retired and, to that end, chose with care a site on his land on which to build a house for himself and his family after him.

The field he chose was one called the High field and there, facing south and looking down upon the village he loved, where he had spent the whole of his ministry, a spacious house was built just after the middle of the nineteenth century. One of his daughters married the owner of Castlemans and lived opposite, and another on her marriage was installed by her father at Beech; so many of his grandchildren too were reared in Sedlescombe and his spinster daughters never left it, contributing much to its life, and well-loved.

His son Richard died at the age of 56, so Arthur, his only grandson, inherited while he was still barely twenty-one. He became chairman of the Parish Council, and Churchwarden. Crippled in later years, he was pushed in a wheelchair to church and back. His two daughters, Violet and Cicely, grew up and married and went away, so he was the last Pratt to live at Highfield, for when he died not long before World War II, the house was sold, after having been the home of the Pratts for over seventy years.

But Arthur Thorpe, solicitor, who bought it was no real stranger, for his brother, John, had farmed Spilsteds at the turn of the century; and his cousins owned the shoe shop at Battle. When his invalid wife died, he married the Matron of the Buchanan Hospital, who was to live on at Highfield for twenty years after he died. Marrying again and outliving her second husband too, she was proud of the house, lands and garden and delighted to entertain. On her death they passed to a Thorpe relative, who sold it separately from its farmlands of Spilsteds. So all the three lands that John Pratt had bought are now separate again, but Highfield remains as a permanent memorial to him, as the Pump-house over the well on the Green stands to his daughters.

*Glebe House*

This house was built on Glebe land opposite the Castlemans triangle, purchased from the Rector before World War I, by William Parker, who had been living down the hill in one of the cottages on the north bank of Stream Lane. A brass tablet in the church commemorates his son, Geoffrey, killed accidentally in 1912; another son, John, was killed a few years later in World War I; both had grown up in Sedlescombe and had taught in the Bible Class. His sister, a dearly loved Sunday School teacher, had married a Mr. Elton and they too lived in the village. Her son, John, was killed in the first war. After the Parkers died, Mrs. Godman, wishing for a smaller house, moved up from Brickwall with her daughter, who lived there after her mother died until 1937, when it was bought by a Mrs. Benson Cooke, who enlarged and greatly improved it, and let it during the war.

After the war came Arthur and Barbara Acott, who beautified the garden. Today the south face of the house is thickly hung every springtime with mauve wisteria blossom, which attracts the nesting fly-catchers year after year to hatch out their young in a nest, well-hidden among its rope-like stems.

*Springfield Cottage and Ivy Cottage in Brede Lane* 22.

These two brick cottages with slated roofs were built by Hercules Brabazon in 1873, replacing earlier cottages which in 1839 his father had bought, soon after Oaklands was built, from the Guardians of Battle Union. This suggests that, before the union of the parishes under the Poor Law, it was one of the cottages used as a Poorhouse for the village (Chapter 18). They were called, simply, Brede Lane Cottages.

The wash-house around the yard at the back was part of the original cottages which had in 1860 been occupied by Frank Ellman and Mary Pankhurst respectively. Perhaps it was after they had both died and the cottages were empty that they were pulled down and rebuilt, each with three bedrooms, kitchen and larder and sitting-room, for workers on Oaklands estate. In 1900 Mrs. Justice (called "Justy") Eldridge and her husband, the carpenter, whose workshop was at Sherralds, lived at Ivy Cottage and did all the laundry-work for the Combes.

By 1924, when the Auction of Oaklands property in the village took place, Miss Sarah Flint, whose father had been attorney to the Brabazons, lived in one of them and James Dengate, builder, in the other. "These cottages," says the brochure, "occupy a charming position with old Yew Hedges, just out of the Village with Grand South Views, and with Gardens and small matured Orchard comprise an Area of nearly One Acre."

Miss Flint lived in the cottage, named thereafter Ivy Cottage, until she died. For very many years of her life she had been a devoted Sunday School teacher. The other cottage, bought by the firm of builders, Thomas and Son, was named by them, Springfield Cottage. It has since passed to other ownership. Both cottages have been vastly improved, but the yew hedges and orchard still surround them and the initials H.B.B. bear witness to their inclusion in the past in the Oaklands Estate.

*Chapel Hill*

Before the Chapel or any houses were built on it, this hill must have had another name. A spur of Whydown Hill, it was climbed on its north-east side from time immemorial by the Roman road from Sedlescombe to Westfield and on its south by Crazy Lane, which linked with the old way through Beanford from Battle. New England Lane stretched across the top of Whydown Hill, making also for Battle across the parish path which wound up and down it from Blackbrooks to the Harrow (later re-aligned to form part of the Turnpike road, now the A.21). The name figures in old records also as Whitedown (Chapter 32) and Way down, sometimes spelt Wey. Today on the ordnance map there are still Waydown Wood, Whitefield Wood and Whydown Poultry Farm (built in 1917), Whydown House and Whydown Cottages. The contrast between Blackbrooks at the foot of White Down may be chance, for the origin of the variably spelt Whydown is now lost, as is that of the name New England for the lane which crosses its ridge.

*Orchard Cottage*

This cottage was originally the toll-gate, built when the Turnpike road was made from Blackbrooks round the bottom of the hill to join the old road to Staplecross, which became part of the Turnpike system (Chapter 34). After the turnpikes ceased, the cottage was bought by Hercules Brabazon and enlarged to make a pair, to house estate workers. For many years these were the Hylands, father and son. Both had been inveterate poachers, the father having got shot in the leg for his pains, so that he walked lame ever after. George, the son, followed his father's example so expertly that Squire Combe decided that the only way to cure him was to make him his gamekeeper. Thus Orchard Cottage became the Gamekeeper's. To walk past it on Mrs. Hyland's baking day was a mouth-watering experience, for she was famed in the village as a most perfect baker. Their sons were all expert at sports and one played for his county. The only one to remain in Sedlescombe returned there badly gassed after the First World War, but he still managed to play cricket for many a year. Another one of the family was the last smith to work the forge at Whatlington.

Today the pair of cottages has been swallowed up in the modern extensions which have resulted in a large L-shaped house, still called Orchard Cottage.

Most of the other houses have been built up the hill between it and the Chapel since the end of World War II.

*Crazy Lane*

No-one seems to know when or why this lane first received its name. Twists and turns it has, but not in such over-abundance as to earn the name Crazy. Whydown Poultry Farm was built beside it in 1916 and most of the other houses between the wars or later. The narrow path between two of them down to the main road below is known as the "twytten", a Sussex word. The houses bordering that road are all of a similar date.

*Chapter Thirty-Six*

## CHARCOAL-BURNING IN PETLEY WOODS

Seldom is it that there is no blue-grey smoke of burning-charcoal hanging over the chestnuts, oak and birches of Petley Wood, which lies alongside Marley Lane and spreads northward nearly to Whatlington Church and westward not far short of Gate Farm, near Battle (Map A). When the westerly wind blows, the acrid smell of the smoke stings the nostrils of Sedlescombe householders; which is no cause for complaint for, sharp though it be, it is a clean smell, and one that has pervaded the air round these woods for at least five hundred years. A record says "for the charcoal burners hired for making charcoal in Pettele Woods 6/8d; in the 8th year of the reign of King Henry, the Fifth after the Conquest."[1] The method used by those charcoal burners of 1424 remains virtually unchanged today. The collier, as he was called, acquired his skill by long experience and also by inheritance, for it was frequently passed down from father to son.

The collier and his mate would begin operations by clearing the hearth upon which the mound or pit (pronounced pet) was to be set, and driving a stump into the centre of it as an axis round which the pit would be built up. They would then lay three billets, (a billet being a length of wood of about 3ft. 3in.) on the ground round the stump in a triangle with ends overlapping, building up the triangle with more and more billets until a chimney or "hole" about 3ft. high was formed. They then laid more billets against the chimney in successive rings until the pit reached its full diameter. The upper course was then started but it was laid in a different way, shorter billets being laid horizontally round the hole, radially; the inner

[1] S.R.S. 65.

edges of succeeding layers being more and more raised until, by the time the upper course was completed, the billets were inclining at the same angle as the course below. The chimney in the upper course was circular, not triangular.

Next, the men covered the mound completely with used stable straw, brushings of wood or sometimes grass, beating all down firmly with a "staff shovel" till it was about three inches thick. They then soaked it well with water and finally covered it with a coat of sand mixed with the dust of old ashes. A space at the base of the mound was left to allow for a draught. The "staff shovel" had an iron spike on its handle which was used for pushing air-holes in the pit.

Firing was started in the daytime; shovelfuls of red-hot charcoal, which had been heated nearby, being poured down the hole, from which the central post had first been removed. As the billets at the bottom caught the burning charcoal's heat, unlighted charcoal was shovelled in until the hole was full, when a round turf was placed on top. As the burning proceeded and the charcoal in the chimney sank, it was filled up again. Finally the whole was covered with layers of litter and sand.

An average sized pit of seven cords burnt from 36-40 hours, according to the weather; burning being slower in hot, dry weather. During all this time the pits had to be closely watched by master-craftsmen of long experience who could tell the progress of the fire by reading the smoke. This was first a dark bluish colour which gradually during the burning became lighter and lighter until at last it passed into an almost invisible vapour.

When the charcoal was judged to be ready the dust and litter were raked off with a large square-bladed hoe called "the Rebel", and when sufficiently cool the charcoal was raked out with long-pronged rakes, each cord of wood yielding about forty bushels of charcoal.

The uses of charcoal were numerous. As described in Chapter One, it was the sole fuel used in iron smelting in the early bloomeries, as also in the later furnaces. It was used for gunpowder making (Chapter 29) and, until the general use of pit coal in the middle of the seventeenth century, was indispensable also to the cutlery trade of Sheffield, where it was used for carbonising steel and in the manufacture of knives and edge-tools. As well as being the fuel for household cooking it was, after the introduction of hops to this country, used entirely for drying them (Chapter 38). In the larger farms the charcoal burners would do their burning on the spot, using up the old hop poles for their billets. They would move on from farm to farm, covering a wide area and being employed, perhaps, from April to November. While the colliers were at work, the farmers would keep them generously supplied with home-brewed ale. The smaller farmers bought their charcoal straight from the burners who worked on fixed sites like the ones in Petley Woods. The artist, Patry, while living at Brickwall painted a picture, The Charcoal Burner, which was exhibited at the Royal Academy, and was a portrait of Jim Smith, a local charcoal burner, and brother of Bangy (Chapter 50).

Jane, an old-age pensioner of Sedlescombe, remembered how she left working on a farm for 2/- a week, to try her hand at charcoal burning:

"and it was good, once one got the hang of it," she said. "Annie and I got taken on and I remember now, as if it were yesterday, how we did it. It was like this; you start by making the ground quite even and then draw a large ring, and in the centre stick a pole. Round this pole you put the wood cords and build it right up to the top of the pole. Then you pile grass to cover the wood all over and on that put dust. Take out the pole and drop into the centre, where the pole was, red-hot charcoal to light the pile; fill the hole with wood, then shut the top in. Let it burn five days and nights with someone there all the time to watch it and see it burns all right. After five days, open it and water it, let it be for two hours, take off stuff and draw it out, pull charcoal out, lay it round in a ring; leave it laying for two hours, then pick it up and take it away. Yes, Annie and I enjoyed that work and it paid us well; near on £5 a week. But one day I got a scare when I was watching the fire; an army of rats came out of the wood, but I got up on a gate, safe, till one of the men came and chased 'em away."

It must have been rather unusual for women to do charcoal burning.

Today the uses of charcoal are still numerous: for medicinal purposes, for decolourising, for purifying and for giving a polish to metals. The workers of Blackman and Pavie Ltd. carry on in Petley Woods today "the art, traid or Mistery of a Colyer"' as it was called in 1691, when a Sedlescombe boy, Edward Jarrett, was bound apprentice to George Burden, colyer (Chapter 18).

*Traces of Another Industry in Petley Woods*
One cannot walk far in Petley Wood without coming across numbers of round pits.

"The central portion of the wood consists almost entirely of pits and there is no natural surface, a fact which may have caused the locality to be called Pyttlegh or 'pit clearing'," says a report concerning some excavations carried out in 1952.[1] "There are two kinds of pits," the report continues, "large ones, fifteen to twenty yards across and about fifteen feet deep; and small ones now showing as shallow indentations 12 feet in diameter. There is a complete and notable absence of spoil-banks and iron cinder heaps. The large pits have been worked down to the underlying sandstone, and the whole contents carted away, the iron-ore for eventual smelting and the clay for marling. The small pits have been worked for iron-ore only, and the marl was found to have been spread on the surface. These two methods of mining are mentioned in 'Wealden Iron'. Small pits are found close to the brink of large ones, which suggests that the small pit system was the earlier ... The conclusions reached from the excavations," which are fully reported in the Transactions, "were that the centre of what is now Petley Wood was a place where in the early Third Century iron ore was dug from small mine pits and then roasted on flat stone floors to render it brittle; that the prepared ore was then stacked, and subsequently removed to another place for smelting; and that later the area continued to be mined for ore and marl, dug from large pits."

The excavations were started because some years earlier a member of the Society had found there some ancient pottery fragments. A total of 147 shards of pottery was found during the excavating, all dating from the second or early third century. "Of these, 56 pieces, including 42 of rims and 8 of bases, were listed. There were 5 pieces of rather inferior Samian, and 5 of patterned thin black New Forest ware (introduced in about A.D. 230). The remainder were portions of dishes, platters, porringers, and cooking-pots in grey-fumed or buff coloured native ware."

Much still remains to be discovered in these woods.

[1] Trans. B.H.S. 1953.

So, in Petley Wood, as well as at Footlands and beside the river at Sedlescombe Street, people were living and working iron nearly twenty centuries ago, sending the roasted ore down the river or up the river to be smelted. Maybe miners were working other woods in the parish too for iron is very plentiful for miles around. But Petley Wood is the only site that still provides industry for workers today.

*Chapter Thirty-Seven*

## FARMS AND FARMHOUSES

The acreage of the village is 2,061,[1] all of which (Chapters 1 & 2) was in early days covered by the wide-spread forest of Anderida, so that every field for cultivation had to be carved out and liberated from that forest. In the course of time a number of fields became a farm with woodland attached. The number of farms increased over the years and all were well-wooded, as they still are today. Many are traced back to the sixteenth century and perhaps earlier (Chapter 23), and their fields were hedged long before the enclosures. All the farms are small, averaging 40 to 50 acres, for their size was defined by the amount of work a man could do in a year with whatever help was available, and the undulating nature of the ground in this parish made the work slower for himself, his men and his horses than it would have been on wide, level acres. The only flat fields to be seen are the water-meadows beside the River Brede. Every other field in the parish is on a curve, gentle or steep. After the first war a one-legged man bought Battle Barn Farm and eighteen months later he moved away to Hertfordshire where the land was flatter. The hilly fields had been too hard on his leg, but he was able to work the farm near Tring for many years.

In the nineteenth century many of the farms were bought up by local land-owners and leased to the farmers; so there were groups of farms in the estates of Vinehall and Great Sanders in the north of the parish, and Oaklands and Battle Abbey in the south and west. In the twentieth century with the break-up of these estates, the farms became independent once again.

[1] Horsfield.

There was skilled labour in plenty; the proud carter with his team of horses, with the graduated bells on their frame above each horse's collar tinkling musically as they worked; the ploughman whose work stood for all to see in the straightness of his furrows, the thatcher, ditcher and hedger, as well as the casual worker at harvest.

All wore the round-frock, or smock-frock, the traditional wear of the Sussex labourer for untold years. William Cobbett, writing of the meeting which he held at Battle in 1830, said that many of his audience were so dressed, though he wrongly called it a smock. The name "round-frock" was applied because, the back and the front of the garment being made identical, it could be worn back-to-front without altering its appearance. Perhaps this quality in it gave rise to the phrase "presenting a new front". The editor of the Sussex County magazine wrote in 1928, "In Sussex a white round-frock was worn as a mourning garment, though I have one in my possession that was worn by its original owner at his wedding". Following this tradition, white round-frocks were worn by the bearers at the funeral of Brabazon, the artist, in 1906; and again, for the last time in Sedlescombe, at that of his nephew, Harvey T. B. Combe, in 1923 (Chapter 32). The white one was worn often on Sundays; a plainer one of dark colour, black, slate-blue, grey or olive green, according to the district, on weekdays, over corduroy trousers tied under the knees with string or with a calf-strap. It was, like the kilt, one of the most sensible garments designed by man, warm in winter and cool in summer, as the thatched roof. Roomy, light and free, it could be worn over several layers of warm clothes, like a pullover. Cleaner than a coat because it was washable, it was made of coarsely woven calico which was dustproof and thornproof and, impregnated with linseed oil, it became also waterproof. The gathering of the material over shoulders, chest and back provided protection where the body most needs it. The large pocket on either side could hold nearly all that a man might require; and, if necessary, the front of it could be lifted to form a carrying bag for a pile of small articles. Edmund Austen of Brede said that his father and his father's uncles, the Colemans, always wore green round-frocks as the most practical garment at their shooting parties. One reads that in some districts different coloured round-frocks were worn by the different tradesmen and craftsmen. The embroidery, known as gauging, honey-combing and sometimes smocking, on chest, back and shoulders and often also at the wrists, varied naturally according to the ability and fancy of the woman who worked it. Often, especially if designed to be worn at a wedding, it was both elaborate and beautiful and sometimes had a special motif, such as a heart, worked into the design. It would later be worn proudly on feast days and holidays, like the Harvest feast, with the traditional red handkerchief round the neck. The invention of the rubberized mackintosh in the late nineteenth century slowly killed this most practical, comfortable and tidy workaday dress.

In the early days when the farms were independent, the farmer's wife fed the labourers as part of her own family in her capacious kitchen, but when they became part of the bigger estates this custom fell out of use and the labourers brought their own mid-day meal and went home to the evening one, which must have made a considerable difference to the family income; but old people today, who were children in the hard days of the late nineteenth and early twentieth centuries, still remember those flavoursome meals.

"The meat was home-killed and fresh from the butcher; and wonderful were the meat puddings made by Mother on a Sunday, great big puddings with a real suet crust and boiled in a cloth; she did not use a basin. And the gravy! If you have only had the gravy of these days you would not know what a real gravy, made from the meat with nothing added, tasted like. It had a real rich flavour. That Sunday meat lasted several days; then we bought 2d. worth of liver and that did for seven people for two days. When we were children we had half an egg each and sometimes for a great treat when eggs were really cheap, maybe 9d. a dozen, we were allowed a whole one each. Everyone kept a pig and cured and dried their own hams and bacon and made sausages, but if ever we children asked for a sausage, we were told they were not ripe yet! A pennyworth of skimmed milk made a large rice pudding and butter was but 9d. a lb. The food was good, but not with much variety like there is nowadays. I remember my Mother's baking day and didn't we run home from school that day to have something hot out of the oven! We had a big old-fashioned oven and into it she popped the faggots which Father had got ready for her, and she lit them. Her bread was on top of the stove and rising while the oven hotted up just right. When the faggots had gone out the oven was ready for the bread, which had risen, to be put in to bake.

While it was baking she prepared her tarts and cakes and buns and they were then cooked all in turn. Then came the best moment of the day when we children all had our 'Tasty'. Once a week we had our baking day because on most other days, likely as not, Mother was out working in the fields along of Father or the other women. Sometimes Father or Mother made ginger beer or nettle or parsnip wines and they took drinks out into the fields when they had to stay out all day. We went to work young in those days. The boys went on the farms and the girls went into service, some on to the farms where maybe you were the only girl and at the beck and call of all on the farm inside and out. It was a hard life that."

Another elderly villager recalls how she used to cycle to work on the Vinehall estate, changing into clogs at the farm before setting to work to spread manure or thin mangolds and turnips. During the First World War, the German prisoners and their guards would march up from the camp in Granny Bishop's Lane at Robertsbridge to help with the farm work. One day they were "breaking" through a field of swedes and she was leading the horse, Punch, which drew the little plough between the lines, when one of the guards thinking that Punch was not moving fast enough threw a "clad'" (clod) at him, hitting her instead of the horse. "Hit the horse that won't go," she cried, "not the one that will." She remembers too the cold winters of her childhood when the winters seemed to be longer than they are today and the ground was frozen for at least fourteen weeks every year and the snow lay about and it was cold. "But we had our red petticoats and chest protectors and if I had a cold or cough, Mother put brown paper smeared with tallow grease on my chest; and every Friday night we had brimstone and treacle. There was a doctor, yes, but we never saw one."

## The Farmhouses

Nearly all of these stand well away from the central village, in the midst of their own quiet fields for, by the time they were built, peace and law and order were secure over the land. In many parts of Germany their counterparts can be seen clustering closely round the village for safety from the attacks of the marauding barons and princelings who plagued the country for centuries.

The names of the fields are mostly commonplace descriptive; brick-kiln field, orchard and minepit field, turnip plat, tanyard field, mill, well, warren and gate field; hollow, rough, banky, spring, hilly and shooter's field; great claypits and little claypits; and nearly all the farms have a marlpit field. These are relics of the very old practice of marling customary in Roman days and revived in the sixteenth century to be widely practised until the end of the nineteenth, when it ceased suddenly, with the heavy cost of labour and transport. The effects of marling, a process of digging sub-soil, rich in minerals and humus, and top-dressing the fields with it, were said to last a life-time. The treatment of a cricket pitch was the last survival of marling and sometimes the grass grew almost too luxuriantly.

Amongst more unusual field names are Tichbonds, Stumbletts, Pennygrove, Lavix and Dallox, Mirgy Shaw and Great Murgy, Haw-haw field, Scotch Down and Yorkshire field, Badlands, Dial meadow, Tory Wood, Precious Field, and Pinnocks Pitt. Among the parsonage glebe fields was Devil's Brook and the Wood in Devil's Brook. Does it, perhaps, mark the place where some long dead parson met that antagonist in right vivid form?

Many of the farmhouses have already been described (Chapters 17 and 23); the remainder now follow.

*Battle Barn Farm* (Map A)

This farm, which stretches steeply up from Black Brooks and nudges into that part of Bathurst Great Wood called Whitefield Wood, alongside Beanford, does not appear on any map until the Tithe Map (1841), where it is marked large and clear, "RAT'S CASTLE". A later nineteenth century map renames it Battle Barn, placing Rat's Castle on the old lane between Paygate and Beanford. Although actually in Battle parish, it was naturally based on the nearer village of Sedlescombe, but nobody has any recollection of it under that name. The present Rat's Castle stands a mile out of Battle on the north side of the Hastings road, its back windows looking straight across the woods north-eastwards to this farm, not much more than a mile away and once bearing the same name. This is hardly likely to be a coincidence. Though the farm is now called Battle Barn, one of its fields is still Rat's Castle.

It was never, like Beanford and its neighbours, held of Battle Abbey, though the 2 cottages at the bottom of the drive were. At the date of the Tithe Map, it belonged to Hercules Brabazon, whose father, Hercules Sharpe, owner and builder of Oaklands Park, was still alive. The farmer-occupier was John Banister, but six of its fields were let to Stephen Jewry of Beanford Farm. Built probably early in the eighteenth century, it had like every other farm in the parish, an oast house.

At the auction at the George Hotel, Battle, in 1924 after the death of Major Combe, the farm was sold as an independent unit "with 48 acres; Comfortable house, Arable, Pasture, Wood, Hoplands and Two Cottages. Freehold except Battle Barn Cottages which are Copyhold of the Manor of Battle. Quit Rent 10d. p.a."

Though it still retained some cattle, it became then largely a poultry farm. There were three wells; the house-well, another which was also close to the house, and a third at the bottom of the drive for use by the cottages as well as the farm. The house-well had a hand-pump and in all spare moments, it was a hand to the pump; counting seemed compulsive—735, 736, 737; it became a mania, you had to count as you pulled and pushed.

Early in the second half of this century Battle Barn was planted like many of its neighbours with fruit, both hard and soft. Main water became available and it began a different, more modern style of life.

*Castlemans*

This house standing on the hill on the south side of the churchyard among the attractive farm buildings, oast houses, stables and barns, looks down the valley to the village across its own fields, once the "waste ground" bought by Peter Farnden in 1652 (Chapter 17). Enlarged at the beginning of the nineteenth century, its date is unknown. Its name is confusing. By 1841 it had become Castlemans Farm, owned by Mrs Woodward and farmed by Spencer Crisford, but on an earlier map it was The Firs (Chapter 23, Beech). Its farmlands and woodlands consisted of all those enclosed in the rectangle formed by the old Roman road (become the turnpike road from Hastings to Cripps Corner) on the east; Hurst Lane on the north and west, and Brede Lane on the south; so, besides Peter Farnden's waste land, it included Killingan Wood and the Brickyard in Hurst Lane and also the fields now covered by the houses of Gorselands and Park Shaw. The original old farmhouse became "Little" Castlemans and was turned into two cottages, housing farm workers.

Towards the end of the nineteenth century, Castlemans became the home of one of John Pratt's daughters, who had married a Major Blake. After his death she and her sister lived together in the house until they died. During this time Little Castlemans had again become the farmhouse.

After the Pratts, came Mr. Mills to own house and farm. An old villager, whose father, working for Mills, lived at Little Castlemans, remembers how every morning at 6 a.m. water had to be pumped to the big house. In the middle of the 8 acre field across the little valley from Castlemans is a fenced square around a small hut. It was to this tiny pump-house that the carter brought his horse every morning and harnessed it to the pump-shaft, and for half-an-hour or more the cart-horse trod round and round and round. Thus was the day's water supply forced to the house and farm. Perhaps only a certain amount could be drawn each day, for there was constant friction between Mills and his men; Mills wanted most of the water for the house and the men wanted it for the beasts. This led to constant quitting and change of tenant farmer in Little Castlemans. Eventually, in 1923 Mills himself left and for five years a man named Cottingham farmed. After that the house was again sold and some of the farm lands separately, many along the roadside, for building plots to speculators and individuals. Thus came the crop of tiny bungalows along Hurst Lane and in Churchlands. Some of the farm land was bought by Mr. Keeling, now Sir John, and so became part of Hurst Farm. Little Castlemans too was sold and Castlemans Farm had left to it only Peter Farnden's "waste ground" and the meadows around the church and between the road and Killingan Wood; it was bought by Ernest Kingdon, a retired eye surgeon, and let by him to a local farmer. He and his wife concentrated their attention on the house and garden and their only daughter, Eleanor. He it was who pulled down the two cottages on Church hill, just below his garden, and employed the architect, Nathaniel Lloyd of Great Dixter, to design at the bottom of the hill in Red Barn field two more to replace them in a manner which would show that cottages could be dignified and beautiful; so there stand today Red Barn Cottages 1 and 2, with their rather grand Georgian façade.

After Ernest Kingdon died, Eleanor sold the place and a few years later John Cumming bought it, bringing to the stables his beautiful Arab horses; and for many years the pure-bred creatures were a lovely sight galloping across the hillside, showing their superb action with curved necks and graceful high carriage of their tails. Aaron had won many prizes and Irex, then 26 years old and retired from stud, was still famous for his perfect head. All round the world his progeny were scattered. Often beside the peacefully grazing mares were beauteous foals frisking playfully. John Cumming's sister, Margaret, an artist, painted many a portrait of the lovely creatures.

On John Cumming's death the property passed from one hand to another. The barns were converted into dwelling-houses and, in 1976 the house itself was redesigned, part of it being pulled down and the rest modernised; but the stables are still used—for the horses of a riding school.

*Chittlebirch Farm*
Chittlebirch, which stands in the north of the parish beside the old road just beyond its junction with Compasses Lane, was not the original farmhouse. This, in earlier days was Compasses, the house in the Compass triangle which later became Compasses Inn. The present Chittlebirch, dignified though it may look today, started as a "wayside cottage", as I am informed by David Martin. They were so called because they were built on the waste land of road verges in the late sixteenth century when there was a rapid increase in population, and houses were very scarce indeed. They were almost "squatters houses".

Sir John Thorne traced the history of Chittlebirch back to the fourteenth century but the article, one of a series contributed to the Parish Magazine in the nineteen-fifties, seems to have disappeared.

In land held of Robertsbridge Abbey by Richard Bishop in 1567 one of the boundaries is "the land of John Tufton Esq. called Chittleberche".[1] There well may be other references to it in the same volume. In 1611 "John Freebody hath lands called Kettlebirch containing 36 acres".[1]

"Our family," writes Miss Hindes, "came to live at Chittlebirch farm from 1911-1919. The back part of the house is very old indeed and consists of three rooms downstairs and three upstairs, all dark and low-pitched with beamed ceilings. Downstairs we used the middle room for a kitchen, one of the side rooms was

[1] S.R.S. 47.

the dairy and the other side room, always designated the 'backplace' was a store room and work place for cleaning knives or boots and shoes. The staircase was one of the oldest and quaintest I have ever seen; the first step was so high that it was difficult to step up it, and the second had a hole where most of the step would come, but the stair never gave way under our feet. It was little used except by us children when we chased each other through and round the house. In one of the bedrooms was a quaint little cupboard in the wall.

"The front part of the house had been added at a later date, two rooms downstairs and two bedrooms upstairs with a staircase built to connect the back with the front. Even so the newer rooms were old and there was in one of them an old-fashioned fire-place known as a 'duck's nest' where long logs of wood could be burnt.

"There was no water laid on, no indoor sanitation and no bathroom; and after living in a modern house on the Webster estate at Battle it must have seemed to my mother a step back into the dark ages as she entered it for the first time; but she was a woman of great resource and fortitude. Lamps and candles were of course the only sources of light for all my childhood.

"The long school holidays were a delight for there was so much to see and do in the busy life of the farm. The house next door had a large pond and in winter we slid on the thick ice. In spring and summer we fished for the roach and searched for the eggs of the farm ducks which sometimes nested round the edge, and once we saw a dead carp which had floated to the surface. We picked up the shiny black flints and found orchids in the wood behind the pool.

"It was a very useful pond. Mr. Aylett, who ran a small private laundry at Cripps Corner close by, always fetched water from it on a Monday morning, his push-cart supporting a large barrel in which to carry it. We ourselves used its water for the farm and for some household purposes.

"Although there were few motor cars on the road, we saw other kinds of traffic; huge steam engines travelled it, sometimes pulling threshing machines to thresh the corn in the farmers' stacks in autumn. Threshing time was exciting for us but hard and dusty work for the men, and the women folk were kept busy providing great mugs of tea. These steam engines too used to fill up with water from our pond. Timber tugs used to pass along carrying great tree trunks to the nearby saw-mills, drawn by four shire horses with bells on their harness; and they too were sometimes watered at it.

"In those days when the animals were not transported by lorry but were driven along the roads, flocks of sheep came by from the marshes to winter in the higher land, and both cattle and sheep passed by to Battle market. Circus and fair people also travelled the road. Rag-and-bone men came round with horse and cart to collect rags; and the scissor-grinder with his little push-cart with grinding-stone attached which he worked with his foot. More frequent were the gipsies who camped by the roadside and came to the door with laces, pins, cotton and buttons to sell, but also to beg for food or old clothes, and they were accompanied by many bare-footed children. When we heard the owls hooting down the Junction Road, my mother would say that it was the gipsies calling to each other; but I never knew whether it was owls or gipsies. Irishmen, too, used to come round the farm at hay-time and harvest looking for work and, if given any, they would 'sleep rough' in the farm buildings. Tramps came with a small billie-can and little else. One came asking for 'pudding or cake' and my mother cut him a very thick slice of bread saying, 'If he is hungry he can eat that.'

"In the first World War we could hear the guns from France and we saw the German Zeppelin pass along the coast.

"My father was a very busy man. He drew our water from the drinking well, milked the cows, ploughed the fields with a horse plough, cut the grass and corn with reaper and binder drawn by horses; and sowed the corn by hand. Putting it into his Sussex trug, he walked up and down the field scattering the seed in methodical fashion. At harvest time the sheaves of corn had to be stood up to dry before being stacked to await the arrival of the threshing machine. Once a week he made butter in the big wooden churn by turning for about twenty minutes or half-an-hour the handle which revolved it. Sometimes he killed a pig for our own use and we children watched with interest all the various processes as nearly every bit of it was used in one way or another. He undertook the cutting up of it, the curing of the bacon and making the sausages. My mother cleaned the chidlings for the skins for the sausages; she refined the flead into lard and made scrap pie, which resembled mince pie, from the scraps left from this process combined with dried fruit. She made flead cakes—a sort of rich pastry—trotter pie from the pig's feet; she fried the liver and crow and made a stew with various other parts of the offal.

"She was also responsible for the final processes of the butter-making, working the butter on a board with special pats to squeeze out all the moisture, and then shaping it into half-pound pats and little rolls. Some she sold locally and some she salted down in large crocks for the winter to be eaten on toast for tea, or for cooking. Before the butter could be made the cream had to be saved each day. She poured the milk into a container at the top of the separator and when the handle of the machine was turned cream came out of one spout and skim milk from the other, which was used for cooking and to feed the pigs. All the parts of the machine had then to be washed.

"My grandmother lived with us much of the time and this was a great help to my mother. When she went out she wore a black bonnet and black cape—a lace one in summer—and black felt boots and she walked to Sedlescombe church one-and-a-half miles away until she was quite old. A gentle old lady, she always strove to pour oil on troubled waters of our turbulent household, with its seven children.

"My mother kept chicken, ducks and turkeys most of which she sold and the eggs too, but we had our share. The 'gobbler' was rather a ferocious but handsome bird with his red wattle, strutting gait and tail spread like a fan. We were well fed because practically everything we ate was home produced. The sausages were a hundred per cent meat, the only additions being the seasoning of salt, pepper and sage. Rabbits shot by my father were made by my mother into delicious rabbit pies and casseroles. She made all our cakes, jams and pickles, she bottled fruit and salted down runner beans for winter use, she preserved eggs in isinglass in crocks, she made wines from various roots, flowers and fruits, especially elderberry and parsnip, both of which made very stimulating drinks with hot water and sugar. One of our customs was to eat plain suet pudding with our roast on Saturdays, although the true Sussex custom is to eat the pudding as a first course before the meat. During the first war my mother made cheese as well as butter and local people were anxious to buy any she could spare to help the meagre rations.

"Shop goods were very cheap but people had little money to buy them. We would buy an ounce of sweets for a halfpenny, a sherbet sucker for a farthing and my father's tobacco cost about fivepence-halfpenny an ounce. Mr. Caistor kept a general shop at Cripps Corner opposite the old forge, but the shop and house are gone now. He journeyed once a week to Hastings in his trap to stock up with groceries and to take in produce to sell. We used to pick blackberries for him in the autumn. There was also a butcher's shop at the corner with Junction Road, and also a very little old-fashioned shop (now a private house) between the Inn and the bridge on the Robertsbridge Road. This was a fascinating shop to a child, first because of the clanging bell when you opened the door and then because of the smell of paraffin mixed with a great variety of other smells that greeted your nostrils. The shop was known as 'Lizzie Hylands', and besides paraffin she kept cheese, tea, biscuits, sweets, candles, flour, bread, sherbet suckers, many other groceries, and strips of 'Spanish', The scents all mingled together with the paraffin predominating. She made her own sweet bags from grease-proof paper and her sugar bags from blue paper. Her goods, stored in tins, bags, sacks and canisters, she weighed out as required. A very honest old lady, she always weighed a loaf of bread before selling it and if it did not come up to the right weight she would add an extra slice from another loaf. After dusk the shop was lit by a paraffin lamp.

"Sometimes in the summer holidays for a treat we would go in Mr. Caistor's trap to Hastings for shopping and a day by the sea. Mother bought the boys' suits and boots at Mr. Apps' shop at Silverhill, still there today. After the shopping we had fried fish and chips and then went on the beach and paddled. The large wooden breakwaters stretching out into the sea were good hunting grounds for shells and seaweeds and little fish. We watched the Punch and Judy shows and we had donkey rides on the sand.

"In the winter we made our own amusements indoors; we played card games, snap, whist, beggar-my-neighbour, and Happy Families; and ludo, dominoes and draughts. We made scrap albums of old Christmas cards and cracker decorations. Books were few and poorly illustrated but my mother read us stories like Kingsley's The Heroes and what would today be called 'Westerns', our two favourites being 'The Redman's Revenge' and 'Lost in the Wilds'. We collected cigarette cards which we exchanged with each other till we had a complete set. Who would have guessed how valuable they would be fifty years later? We arranged the wild birds' eggs we had collected in the summer. I used to crochet, working with fine cotton and hook. Our glass cake stand was adorned with my crocheted doyley and my white pinafore had my crocheted insertion down the middle of its front, and the bottom frill, finely whipped on by my mother, was finished too with a small edging of my crocheted lace.

"After the war our family of ten, seven children and my father, mother and grandma, moved to Swailes Green Farm, not far away and life went on much as before; but not for me, for I was by then a weekly boarder at Rye Grammar School, eleven years old, my childhood virtually over. Every Monday morning I cycled the ten miles to Rye where I stayed in lodgings all the week and cycled home again on Friday evenings or Saturday mornings. Although I was only home for the weekends and holidays the countryside around it was a part of my life, the song of the nightingale in the woods on a May evening and the twopence pocket money which my grandmother gave me on a Monday morning were still as welcome to me as ever."

When the Ashtons of Vinehall sold up, the farm became part of Swales and farm labourers lived at Chittlebirch. After the war the house was sold and was quickly modernised to become a most attractive home. Chittlebirch Oast too was sold to the Kents who were working in London and hoped to retire to it. At weekends they used to cycle all the way down there and work on it. After the war they realised their dream and lived with their daughter, Daphne, most happily for many years in the beautifully converted oast. Now they are all dead and it has passed into other hands.

*Farms on the Westfield Place Estate* (Map A)
In Domesday Westfield Manor was held of Wenestan, like Sedlescombe. In the 8th year of the Reign of Queen Elizabeth, Richard Sackville (Chapter 17) bequeathed to his son, Thomas, his manor and lands in Westfield. According to Horsfield, the manor and seat of Westfield Place was "sold by Sir George Piers in whose name and family it had been for generations". In 1759 Sir John Lade's posthumous son (Chapter 23) aliened it when he came of age to Mr. William Lutman of Hastings, whose heirs sold it to Thomas Lamb of Rye, whence it passed to the Lambs of Beauport

# FARMS AND FARMHOUSES 431

(Chapter 30) Horsfield adds that the "Manor house is very near the church on the south of it" which is not a description of the present Westfield Place.

For many years this belonged to the Mullens family and Major Mullens is well remembered by many a Sedlescombe man and woman whom he employed on his farms of Harts Green and Randalls on the west end, or Sedlescombe side of his estate. Lying halfway between the two villages, it was a long walk to either church and he it was who, therefore, had the "iron church" built on the estate. Besides services, a Sunday School was held in it, and once a year the Sunday School races were held in a field on the farm. He also captained a cricket team of his estate workers.

*Randalls Farm*  (Map A)

Bangy Smith's daughter, Lottie (Chapter 48), was born at Ashdown Cottage, at the junction of Cottage Lane beside the top entrance to Oaklands, when it was part of Westfield estate. She remembers the two cottage pigs her father kept there and how they were killed by "sticking", after which boiling water was poured over the dead animal to loosen the skin. The house, sometimes known as Ash-tree house, was held to be haunted. Three misers had lived there and were said to have buried their gold under the stairs, where Bangy hunted in vain. He never heard or saw any sign of the ghost, which both his wife and sister heard. Ashdown Cottage, now an independent house, had perhaps some connection with Nicholas Ashdown who appears often in the parish records as paying rates.

Bangy and his family moved from it to Randalls farm. His daughter remembers there another incident concerning a pig, which fell into a pond, now filled in, and nearly cut its own throat with its trotters in its struggles to get to dry land. Bangy's other daughter, Bessie, married a gamekeeper on the estate, Edward Howard, who used to bring home ducklings to be reared under the chick-hen, an old broody, and they were taught to swim in the water-butts. There was an old yew-tree on the west side of the road which was supposed to be magic and if you ran round it three times something would jump out at you, but no-one dared run round it more than $2\frac{1}{2}$ times.

Now Randalls is an independent small farm.

*Harts Green*

Harts Green is a farmhouse of the seventeenth century which stands on the south side of the old Roman road between Sedlescombe and Westfield, surrounded by many outbuildings and stables of some age. In the Church-wardens' accounts of rate-payers there appears under "Outdwellers"

"1726 Joseph Hart for part of Rose Farm"
"1735 Harts Farm and Rose Farm"
"1736 John Sims for part of Harts."

So it would seem that Joseph Hart left his name to Rose Farm. The other part of the farms was no doubt listed in Westfield parish records. The farm was bounded on the north by New England Lane; today it includes land on Whydown Hill down to Paygate and is entirely a fruit farm.

The farmhouse has now been sold independently and the new farmhouse is built in New England Lane beside Share Wood whose name it bears.

*Chapter Thirty-eight*

## HOPS

The cultivation—the stringing, tying, picking and drying—of hops played a tremendous part in the life of this village and its economy for probably around three hundred years, but most particularly in the nineteenth and twentieth centuries when every farm had its hop-garden in a valley, were it only of eight acres. In 1833, there were 111 acres of hops in the parish, when the population numbered 732. In 1890 the chief crops in the parish were wheat and hops.[1] In the scant mile between Luff's and Little Castlemans there are six oast-houses. In the whole parish nearly every farm had its oast and nearly all are now converted into dwelling-houses. The only hops to be seen are the wild descendants in the hedgerows of those cultivated ones, that help to discover the whereabouts of the old hop gardens.

Picture the hop garden across the Brooks; what an interest it must have added to the landscape; and again, in the meadows on each side of the New Road (the A.21), between Marley Lane and Riccards Lane, where many a wild hop-bine still twists in the hawthorn hedges. The village must have nestled in Hop gardens, and the lives of very many of the villagers were extensively bound up with them from birth to death, and few there must have been who did not in one way or another work among these aromatic plants. For winter employment, there was the fuel to prepare for later use in the drying kilns, by the burning of hornbeam wood to charcoal —a hardwood plentiful locally which was used for making gear wheels for mills and other wooden parts of machinery. There was the cutting and preparing of sweet chestnut poles so excellently

---

[1] Kelly's Directory.

straight, which had to be shaved, and their ends sharpened and dipped into tanks of boiling pitch before being finally erected in row after row. Then came the planting and feeding of the bines for which manure from the "fattening pits" was used. These deep pits were in the sheds in which cattle were put to fatten. When the manure reached the top of the pit, the beasts were considered ready for market and the manure was carried out and put on to the hops. Fed so well by this manure the ground remains the most fertile in the parish. Later there was the stringing, tying and training of the plants and finally the picking, drying, packing and marketing. Tying and picking was women's work and very quick and skilful they were.

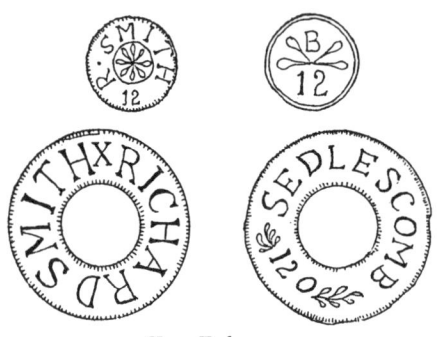

*Hop Tokens.*

The picking season was the annual holiday and way of life for most families in Sedlescombe for three weeks in September, looked forward to by young, middle-aged or old with jolly anticipation of holiday mood happiness and, hopefully, weather. Picking was hard work; some there were who hated and dreaded it but for most it was enjoyable with whole families sharing a bin, which was a large receptacle of sacking or canvas, on a light wooden frame about ten feet long by $2\frac{1}{2}$-3 feet wide, on legs a little over two foot high. In Kent, wicker baskets holding 5 bushels were used in place of the Sussex bins. Some were quick pickers and some were slow but all had to pick cleanly—no leaves. It must have been a grim, uncomfortable job in wet weather, but in sunshine under the blue dome of the warm sky one can imagine the laughter and shouting, the gossiping and fun; the family and communal happiness in a shared occupation; and when the hops were all gathered and safely drying in the oasts, the merry-making and dancing, the feasting off potatoes baked in the ashes, washed down with home brewed beer; all the unselfconscious happiness of the sun-baked tired bodies and the sense of achievement, with money earned to pay for comforts through the winter. What memories the aroma of hops must arouse in all who have known these experiences.

There were no London pickers in these small hop-gardens though some from Hastings swelled the ranks of local hands; there was therefore no need for huts and camps, for all would return home every night to sleep, tired and happy with the breath of the hops strong upon their hands and clothes, a very sleeping potion itself without the influence of the toil, the weather and the air. In September 1915, wounded soldiers in their hospital blue came out to watch the hop-picking.

An average picker would pick about 15 bushels a day (though very expert ones would nearly double this) and, at that rate, about six to eight pickers were needed per acre in order to complete the picking in three weeks. The Fuggle (discovered by a man named Richard Fuggle, in a flower bed in Horsmonden), an easy hop to pick by hand, was the variety mostly grown in Sedlescombe in latter years.

The bin-men would cut the hop-bines close to the ground, uproot the poles and bring them to the pickers round the bins. The gathered hops were removed three or four times a day by the measurer who scooped them lightly out of the bin into an eight-gallon or bushel basket to empty into the pokes, holding ten or twelve bushels, to be transported to the oast house. Sometimes there could be a "hard" measurer who would press down the light hops, making a fuller measure. The number of bushels gathered by each picker was kept from time immemorial by means of wooden "tallies"; strips of numbered wood about 12 inches long cut into

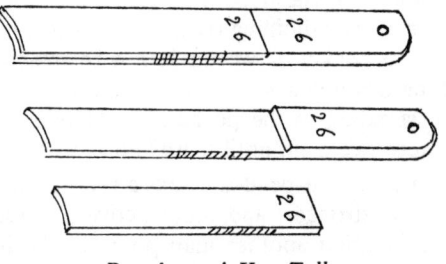

*Drawings of Hop Tally*

half, logitudinally, for about three-quarters of their length, the tallyman keeping the longer piece and the picker the shorter. When required for recording the amount picked, the two similarly numbered pieces were put together again and a narrow groove filed across both at once, for every 5 bushels picked. In later years metal tokens were used for tallies, locally made of various shapes and designs, often in the form of coin-like discs, having the grower's numbers and initials. It was this similarity to coins of the realm that allowed the treasure of Saxon coins, found in 1876 in a field opposite the school, to be mistaken for a heap of hop tokens.

The pokes were taken as soon as possible to the kilns in the oasthouses, and the green hops were spread in a layer at least six inches deep on the slatted floor, which was about 12 to 15 ft. above the ground. On the ground floor below was the furnace, fed largely with charcoal, a smokeless fuel and wood and turf. It was of the utmost importance to produce as much heat as possible with as little smoke, for smoke imparted an unpleasant flavour; and also that the heat obtained should be equal all over the drying floor, and condensation reduced to an absolute minimum. It was to help to carry off any such moisture that the familiar white cowl, which moved with the varying wind, was introduced towards the end of the eighteenth century.

The value of the hops could easily be decreased by careless drying; they needed above all to keep their natural colour of primrose, and the seeds to become dry and hard, the stalks brittle.

In about 1840, round kilns became fashionable on the assumption, which proved false, that on a circular floor a more even distribution of heat would be obtained. Modern oasts, like the early ones, are rectangular, being less expensive to build and more convenient than the familiar and perhaps more picturesque round ones.

As they became dry, the hops were raked into the cooling room on the first floor of the adjoining barn. There was a hole in the floor of this to which a pocket of woven jute with treads inside, would be fixed, to hang down below to receive the cooled hops. Originally a man or lad, standing in the pocket, would press down the light hops as they were raked in, until it was filled with 1½ cwt.

"Into the bag thus suspended," says a report, "a man descends; the heavier and stronger, and more active so much the better: while in this situation another man pours in the hops upon him into the bag (the top of which being for some time usually above his head): the man in the bag treads round and round with his back to the sides thrusting down his heels with all his might; going his circuit incessantly, and the hops by a weighty and dexterous fellow are so compressed together that when the bag is completely full it is comparative as round and hard as a timber tree"

The pocket was then closed and marked with the familiar shield charged with six martlets (the Sussex stamp); and so to the hop-market where all hops had to be brought before being sold. This was one of the firm rules that governed the buying and selling of hops; and, until 1862, when the heavy excise duty on them was removed, the whole operation of drying, weighing and packing had to take place under the eye of an Excise man.

Ale, a non-keeping sweetish drink, had been the popular drink of the Middle Ages. Beer is 'hopped ale'. The use of hops as a preservative in brewing was introduced into this country, perhaps, by the Flemish weavers brought over by Edward III to help the wool trade, but it was not until 1542 that their cultivation began to be seriously undertaken, and the bitter flavour and aroma imparted to the ale by the preserving hops was acquired and appreciated, and the 'foreign' drink became naturalised.

Stories and memories of hop-picking are easily revived among the older villagers. While hops were grown across the Brooks, there was no great flooding there it is said, as there often is in winter and spring today, for the plants need plenty of moisture during growth. After picking was finished, there used to be an annual party in the barn of Luff's oast. One year, when the merrymakers were doing "the gallop", an arch supporting the floor of the barn collapsed and cries of "Help! help!" were heard from the two men who were below looking after the drying of the hops. The buried men were, in the course of time, extricated, but one of them had to be taken to hospital. So that was the last of the yearly parties to be held in Luff's oast.

Hops were grown also at Powdermill Farm where the reservoir now is. The old furnace and the powdermill buildings were pulled down and the extensive ponds drained, leaving the moist basin of reclaimed land ideal soil for a hop-garden. Fifty-five acres were planted.

Picking machines, introduced first in the nineteen-fifties, revolutionised the industry, and every year less and less hand-picking took place. In 1955 the children in the hop-picking districts had for the first time to attend school on the same opening day as those in the rest of the country. To be absent in the hop-gardens was no longer an allowed excuse.

The last hop-gardens in Sedlescombe were at Spilsteds Farm but they too are now no more, but the cones of the oast-houses still stand in and about the village, nearly every one now marking a dwelling-house.

*Chapter Thirty-nine*

## THE TWO INNS

There are two inns in the village; one at the head of the Green, known as the Tophouse, and one at the foot of it, the Bottomhouse.

*"The Queen's Head"*   (Maps 3 and 5)
The Tophouse, an old gabled building with the picturesque quality which people delight to see in a village inn, has had many alterations and additions over the long years of its life. Its original fifteenth-century plan was rectangular, with three bays and an overhanging upper storey. Roof trusses divide the three bays but "there is," says the *Victoria County History,* "an extra truss only a few inches away from the northernmost, suggesting that two separate buildings have been thrown into one."

Inns and alehouses were subject from earliest days to many legal restrictions which kept a firm limit on the number allowed in each district (Chapter 8) but it is likely that an alehouse was very early established in Sedlescombe to allay the thirst and hunger, both human and animal, of those who attended the Court Leat held on the Green every six weeks. Whether the fifteenth century inn was in the northern or southern end of the present building, it was warmed and lit by a central fire whose smoke, before being drawn up through a vent in the roof, lay curled and grey in the many crannies in walls and beams.

In the reign of Good Queen Bess, the large cross-shaped central chimney stack was built, with a very wide fireplace in the northerly room having corner seats where customers could toast themselves while drinking the good home brew. Perhaps it was at this time that the two buildings were joined and soon after given the sign of the Queen's Head to celebrate Elizabeth's journey through Sussex to Rye.

Over a hundred years later, when William and Mary were newly crowned, the inn was lengthened at the south end by the addition of a cross-wing with its own chimney stack.

Most inn-keepers did their own brewing until well into the nineteenth century, but there were also licensed maltsters whose numbers were prescribed by law. Most of the bigger houses and farmhouses had their own brew-houses and malt-houses, the liquor from which could not, of course, be sold. The restrictions on brewing were many and in years of bad harvest the use of grain for the purpose was not only restricted but sometimes altogether prohibited (Chapter 22).

It must be that very few of the men whose names appear in this book did not at some time in their lives, if not every day, drink a pint within these mellow brick walls. In early days the only closing hours were when the last customer had finally made his perhaps uncertain way out into the dark night to find his path home as best he might.

On one night in the eighteenth century, it was the scene of a very serious gathering of some five or six local farmers who, after discussion, drew up a small document which they all signed, promising to support each other against the growing demands of the smugglers whose wild ways were getting out of hand and threatening violence to all who did not obey their orders. These dangerous men may well have been the members of the notorious Hawkhurst Gang on whose direct route from the coast Sedlescombe lay. This document was among Miss Flint's papers and is now unfortunately lost (Chapter 25).

The names of the long line of independent landlords have also disappeared in the mists of time. In 1841 James Breeds was the owner and Stephen Turner inn-keeper, followed later by his son, Thomas. At some time during the next years, the inn was bought by a brewery and thereafter the landlords were always its tenants. Like many another of the very old houses in the village its face has been altered by brick-and-tile-hanging over the original beams and plaster, for additional weather-proofing.

On May Day, the "Queen's Head" and the Green had been from time immemorial the centre of gay festivities (Chapter 42) and it continued to be so when the Men's Friendly Society was formed in the late nineteenth century and took over the May Day holiday and the Green was transformed into a wonderland, and puddings were boiled in the great coppers of the "Queen's Head".

In the cheerless days of cold November, the waste ground on the north side of the Inn would become the scene of the great woodpile of the Guy Fawkes bonfire (Chapter 42).

Inn-sign gives place to inn-sign, each one less attractive and less flattering to its royal subject than the last, but still the Tophouse remains the happy place of hospitality and foregathering that it has always been, and many now come from well outside the parish to taste its pleasures.

*The Coach and Horses* (Map A)

The "Bottomhouse" was, until the unfortunate fire in 1914, as charming in outward appearance as the "Tophouse". Old photographs show a rambling building of attractive proportions, ivy-covered, with an inviting seat beside the entrance.

How long it had stood there is impossible to say. The earliest mention of the Inn is in some deeds of 1792, concerning the neighbouring Iltonsbath and Barrack Cottage (Chapter 14). They refer to "a certain place called Iltons Bath, and an Inn commonly known by the sign of the King's Head, with the stable-yard, in the occupation of Mary Young, widow . . ." The Inn and the cottages were sold at that date to Edmund Weekes, and William Hudson became the inn-keeper.

The "Queen's Head" at the top and the "King's Head" at the bottom of the village made a fine royal double, though which king's head was on the sign cannot now be discovered. Eight years later the Inn, sold again together with the cottages, was untenanted and the cottages deserted. The buyer, Richard Bishop, yeoman of Westfield parish, just across the river, became the inn-keeper for three years with his wife, Elizabeth. They then sold it, still known as the "King's Head", to Edward Ades, younger, farmer of Sedlescombe. William Eldridge retired from his carpenter's shop at Cherry Tree Cottages and became the landlord for nearly forty years. A deed of 1842 names him still as inn-keeper though the Tithe Map of 1841 gives Robert Monk as both owner and occupier of, not an inn, but a house and shop.

In a deed of 1859, the building is referred to as "a messuage or tenement formerly used as an Inn or Public House and then called . . . the King's Head". In 1866 the *Post Office Directory* named the

Landlord of the "Coach and Horses" as Thomas Cronk; so at some time during the intervening seven years while Robert Monk was inn-keeper the name had been changed, fittingly enough, for Sedlescombe Street, now part of the Turnpike system, was used by stage coaches bringing passengers to the smart new town of St. Leonards.

"It seems likely," say the Brewers who now own it, "that the name was an appropriate choice when Victorian and Edwardian coaches would choose it as a baiting stop before the long pull up into the Hastings ridge. But this is, of course, conjecture."

So landlord gave place to landlord, until one Sunday afternoon in 1914 when Mr. and Mrs. Field were taking their Sunday walk with their small child, fire broke out in their absence and the "Coach and Horses" burned, and burned rapidly. The air was filled with the crackling of flames and above the roar of them could be heard the high screeching of the terror-stricken parrot. As the onlookers watched, the flames burning blue and orange began to turn every brilliant colour of the rainbow as they reached the store of spirits; and the beauty of the terrible blaze of vivid blues, purples and greens, as well as red and orange, was fascinating as a nightmare. The blacksmith who lived next door was also, like the parrot, in mortal fear, lest his cottage adjoining be engulfed in the blaze; and he added to the destruction and nightmarish scene by taking up an axe in his powerful arm and smashing away at the part of the building nearest to his habitation.

Sadly, the Bottomhouse was re-built in less attractive style than the old building, but inside its warmth and hospitality never, over the next half century and more, failed to attract its flow of regular customers.

*Chapter Forty*

## THE CHAPELS

*The Wesleyan Methodist Chapel* (Map 5)
The Deeds of this Chapel, like those of the cottage called Barrack Cottage beside it, are intricately involved with transactions concerning "the Inn known by the sign of the King's Head, the fellmonger's yard and two messuages and one acre of ground".

From 1737 to 1812 "the two messuages, gardens, closes, orchard, stable, brewhouse, outhouses and buildings at Iltons Bath" were sold many times and with each sale more and more people became involved until in 1812, when Henry Freeland, farmer of Poppinghole, bought the piece of land, there were no fewer than nine people concerned which included trustees and a banker.

Henry Freeland then built the Chapel or meeting-place on the piece of land. There was at this time a great expansion of Methodism all over the country; large mission halls were being built in the big towns and the villages shared in this renewal, many of their services being held in the open air.

On his death in 1817 he left his farms in Poppinghole Lane in trust to John and William Grace of Sedlescombe and John Needham of Whatlington until his son, Samuel, should come of age. William Eldridge, carpenter, still owned the two cottages and, since the deeds were all together, it was agreed that he should hold them and the Trustees should have access to them when they wished.

There were nine Trustees, all but one of whom were from Ewhurst: Thomas Boots, Spencer Parks and William Neve, all yeomen; John and Thomas Richardson, the Staplecross millers; James Goodsell, cordwainer; James Eldridge and William Hollis, a leather rutter from Rye. They covenanted with Joseph Entwistle, of Middlesex, Minister of Gospel, and all other future members of "the yearly conference of the people called Methodists" to permit only those appointed by that conference "and no others to have the use and benefit of the chapel". Those appointed to "preach and expound God's Holy Word" must preach no other "than that which is contained in certain notes upon the new testament and the first four volumes of sermons published by the Reverend John Wesley". It was also ordained that no preacher should be sent to the said chapel for more than two years successively. If no preacher were appointed then the Trustees should nominate one or more of their number to expound and preach as described already and "shall be moral in conduct and of sufficient ability".

That the Trustees were nearly all from Ewhurst is perhaps not surprising since Henry Freeland lived on the borders of Sedlescombe and Ewhurst and they were no doubt his friends and the nucleus of the congregation.

By 1871 all the original Trustees had died, except Thomas Richardson, and new ones were appointed. This time there was only William Richardson, miller, William Cook, grocer, from Ewhurst, and Samuel Leach, schoolmaster, from Staplecross. From Sedlescombe there were William and Reuben Kenward, bricklayers, George Carrick, brickmaker (Chapter 34), and John Sellens, a farmer from Mountfield. Their signatures were witnessed by Frank Bishop, James Eldridge, Walter Boots and Henry Richardson. The regular minister at this date was the Rev. John Lewis of Sandhurst, but the lay preacher still remembered today is old Edward Blundell of Spilsteads farm down Stream Lane. The congregation sat facing south. Mr. Blundell would often begin thus, "Before I speak, I will say a few words." There was very good feeling between the church and the chapel and Edward and his wife always attended evening service in the church and she belonged to its Mothers' Meeting.

The emigration of the Hook family after the First World War must have been a blow to this chapel for the wheelwright's family had always been great Methodists. It was in 1924 that the agreement to terminate the use of the building as a Methodist Chapel was made, and the building was bought by Daggett, a draper, of Whydown Poultry Farm. For a short time the chapel became a draper's shop. In 1943 planning permission was given for its use as a cinema and during the war it was well patronised; but, as transport improved after the war, it could not for long compete with the better programmes of the town cinemas. For many years it was then used as a store or workshop by Thomas and Sons and then by Eldridge and Cruttenden. In 1966 it became an engineering workshop and so remains today.

*The Congregational Chapel*

Just over 100 years ago in 1876 the minister of the Robertson Street Congregational Chapel in Hastings, Mr. Charles New, suggested to his Young Men's Union that they should go out into the villages around and hold services. Sedlescombe was chosen as their first venture and they began to hold regular services on the village green in the summer of that year. During the winter months they rented a barn of one of the farms. In the following year the minister appealed for subscriptions to help with their expenses; 9/- every Sunday for the hire of a horse made heavy demands on the young men's pockets, especially as they had already raised £6 for a harmonium and they paid regularly for the oil for the winter lamps. In 1878, unaided, they bought and paid for a plot of land on the hill at Sedlescombe for the erection of a Chapel. Built by John Catt, the builder, Reuben Kenward and E. Jewhurst, bricklayers, and E. Hayler, carpenter, all of whom inscribed their names on the topmost beam, it was completed and opened by October of the following year. The Sunday School Superintendent had the familiar name of Avann. Other well-known names among the officers were Gregory, Sellens, Fred Cooper, Eldridge and Dawson. Minnie Bishop and Lottie Smith were among the children taught by Miss Carrick. There was a large swivel chair in the vestry where they attended and any child who answered the questions correctly was allowed to "have a ride" in the chair.

Some time during the next ten years a disagreement split the congregation in two, the Tuppenneyites following Mr. Tuppenney and the others supporting still Mr. New. Separate meetings were held and the Tuppenneyites built a new Chapel beside the old in which to hold their services. Two Carricks, Charles and Thomas, were treasurer and vestry secretary, and John Ditch, the grocer, was the business secretary. By 1900 attempts were being made to heal the breach and reunite the two churches and congregations; and eventually it was agreed that the Tuppenneyites would unite with Mr. New's congregation on Sunday evenings if Mr. New's would unite with them for morning service. So the fracture was gradually healed, though the two congregations continued to have a separate existence until, in April 1907, "The United Committee of the two Churches are of opinion that the time is ripe for unity" and by August this had been effected. Mr. Elliott, Evangelist, of Wistaria Cottage (now Sherralds) had taken a large part in the diplomacy.

Tuppenney's Church therefore became redundant and was a few years later converted into two cottages. In 1910 it became the Police Station, housing the village policeman and his family until 1949. The new Police Station was then built at Blacklands, and the old one became once again two cottages and so remains.

The Chapel throve and has ever since been a quiet power in the village.

*Chapter Forty-one*

## THE WELL ON THE VILLAGE GREEN

It might be imagined that the well on the Green had been there from time immemorial, providing the inhabitants with a central water supply, but this is not so. Through all its long history, Sedlescombe has been entirely dependent for its water on river, springs and private wells.

Under the manorial system, a draw-well could be dug only after permission was obtained from the lord; and there are many records through the years of frequent applications at the Courts Baron. In the course of time every one of the bigger houses in the parish had its own well, sometimes a draw-well and sometimes wells operated by hand pumps. As far as the cottages round the Green were concerned it was usual for two or more to share the use of one well, and in the heat of the summer water became very scarce and some of the wells dried up altogether. There was, however, always the river, and washing could be done beside it.

The well opposite the school served it and all the surrounding cottages that were not otherwise provided. With what admiration we can regard these cottage women, most of whom kept themselves and their children spotless, in shining white aprons and clean pinafores; and the washer-women with baskets of sheets and other linen to return spotless for a tiny charge, how was it for them when water ran short?

It was not until the final year of the nineteenth century that the Minutes of the Parish Council for July recorded action: "Permission to sink well on the village Green: It would be very desirable, in consequence of the v. bad and insufficient supply of water in the village—for owners of property to become voluntary subscribers if permission be given by this Council to sink a well and erect a pump on the V.G. for the free use of the villagers. Proposed by Mr. Pratt," (of Highfield, son of the late Rector) "seconded Mr. Alchin" (grocer and postmaster) "that this council do give and sanction permission of the said owners of property to dig a well and erect pump as proposed. Carried unanimously."

Accordingly, the well-digger, Jess Hall, who lived in Goatham Lane on the eastern edge of the parish, was sent for and soon began his operations, watched with interest by all who could find reason to pass by. An old photograph is still to be seen showing the Green without the familiar pump roof in its centre.

Jess Hall dug his well and found water and a fine leaden pump was erected over it. Then came the builders to build the pillared shelter, and finally the carpenters with the two high-backed seats. On the north and south sides of the beautifully designed leaden pump the following words are inscribed in handsome lettering:

1900
IN LOVING MEMORY OF
SOPHIA ELIZABETH AND
HARRIET CATHERINE PRATT
AND THEIR SISTER
MARY ANNE BUCKNELL.

The three sisters thus remembered were the aunts of the chairman of the Parish Council, Arthur Pratt. All their lives Sophia, Harriet and Mary Anne had lived in Sedlescombe; first at the Rectory, where their father, the Rector, had lived for 57 years, and then at Highfield, till Mary Anne had left in 1847 to marry Dr. Bucknell of Castlemans and so to live for the first time on the other side of the road. Sophia died in 1878.

For a hundred and twenty-five years and more the Pratt family, father, son, grandson and great-grandchildren lived in the village and many were their benefactions. Harriet is immortalised too in Harriet House, close beside the pump.

On June 26th, 1902, the Minutes of the Parish Council recorded:

"The Parish Council gave permission for well to be sunk and a cover, pump, with seats on either side, placed on the Green for the use of the public; that in November last in consequence of wilful damage to the Pump, Notice Boards were put up on the Green with an intimation that persons committing damage should be prosecuted; and the sum of 12/6 was expended thereon. A sum of 6/- was paid for removing and storing for the winter the two seats (and putting them back again last month, March, the same amount)."

[This removal of the seats every winter continued for several years.]

In 1903 complaints were received by the Parish Council of "improper use of water from the village pump". It was proving its value, however, for it was recorded that thirty-three houses were using its water. In April of the same year it was proposed that an iron dog-trough be fixed to take the surface water from the pump, and also that a drinking cup be attached to the pump with a chain. These two have long since gone.

It was not long before the village pump gave its name to the cottage nearest to it, and so Rose Cottage, divided in two for the first time, became Pump House and Pump Cottage.

For more than half a century the pump was used regularly by all who had no well of their own and it never in all those years failed. It was a familiar sight to see them pass up and down the road with well-fitting shoulder yokes from which hung an empty bucket squeaking and rattling on either side, and to return with each one filled and splashing over.

At last in 1956 a main water system was provided and all at once the water drunk for half-a-century was judged "unfit for human consumption" and the well was sealed so that it could not even be used for refreshing the gardens. How extraordinary and mysterious and not infrequently infuriating are the ways of those who govern us. How invaluable could the water from that unfailing supply be in times of drought.

In 1965 the old oak seats, quite worn out, were replaced as a memorial to Major Haddon who had lived with his wife at the north end of the village at Beach Farm-house, opposite Great Sanders. On the south-facing seat are inscribed the following words:

In Memory of
1899   Major John H. Haddon   1965
Royal Marines
Per Mare     Per Terram

and on the north side:

In Memory of
1899   John H. Haddon   1965
'Write me as one who loves his fellow men.'

Certainly this could be truly said of Major Haddon, who had a smile and a helping hand for all. He could be seen at every "occasion" giving ready assistance in putting up stalls or stage scenery, and wherever a strong arm was needed.

So the unused Pump with its high-backed seats remains a happy and decorative memorial to four people who loved the village and who served it in their own ways; a pleasant place to idle on a summer's day and often too on a winter one, sheltered from the wind and warmed by the pale sun.

*Chapter Forty-two*

## SPORTS AND FESTIVALS

*Sports*
The old recreations of the country people, bear-baiting, bull-baiting, cock-fighting, trials of skill with quarter-staffs, quintains, boxing and archery were gradually brought to an end in the solemn days of the Commonwealth. Some were prohibited and most were frowned on, but the annual fairs at Hawkhurst, Battle and Roberts-bridge, of which they were a part, continued to be a time for merry-making on their allotted dates, until the First World War brought them too to a halt.

Archery was not just a sport; it was a necessity for the defence of the realm that all males should be well-taught and practised in the art, and compulsory practice had taken place regularly every Sunday in the fenced churchyard, where yew-trees, so poisonous to beasts, were safely grown for use in making the bows. With the invention of iron cannon, this too fell into disuse; the old men continuing still the customary Sunday practice and bemoaning the modern times when the young refused to take an interest in the old-fashioned skill.

Charles II, the Merry Monarch, tried to revive the sports and dances of Merrie England but, as in modern experience, such efforts tended to be successful only in rare instances. Perhaps it was then that team games, such as cricket, long the traditional village game, became so popular; and also stoolball, the Sussex cross between cricket and rounders.

From a time further away than living memories can reach, the pitches were always on the flat water-meadow on the east side of the road at the foot of the village, where many an inter-village match took place and village patriotism was strong and local heroes proudly supported. Many are the photographs of winning village teams still to be seen hanging on the walls of the Village Hall.

Perhaps surprisingly, stoolball still survives in the village today. A team sprang up again almost directly the war was over and played beside the road where the tennis courts are now. "It is a sort of feminine edition of cricket," says Marcus Woodward. Tradition has it that it was invented by milkmaids; the wicket is called the 'stool', said to have been originally the milking-stool.

At some sad date between the wars, freedom to use the traditional football and cricket field was withdrawn after some unfortunate incident at a fete held in Oaklands Park. So a cricket pitch was carved out of the often flooded water meadows of the Brooks on the west side of the road, and a football field on a far from flat one behind the Street houses on the east side of the Green. Both were played on with bitter hearts until the Combes departed from Oaklands a few years after World War II. With the coming of the Pestalozzi Children's Village Trust the hearts of the sportsmen lifted and they took steps to have what, rightly or wrongly, they considered "their rights" restored. At last after two or three years of negotiations and setbacks, a working arrangement assured that the Oaklands meadow should be the Sports Field for all; and there all the village matches, as well as the school games of the Children's Village, take place. There too is held the annual Flower Show and Fete. Thus did the International Village live up to its name and restore a lost harmony.

Tennis too became popular again. The Tennis Club had of old played on the Rectory Court. After the war a great money-making effort made it possible for two courts to be made on the old Powdermill land on the Brooks alongside the Mill lane; and, later, beside them the children's playground with swings and merry-go-rounds was created.

*Festivals*

*May Day*

The May Day Festival, held on the first Monday in May—which was also the right and proper day for planting runner beans—was, from time immemorial, a holiday for all the village as it was for the rest of England.

Winter was over, with all its numberless discomforts, discomforts utterly forgotten today and difficult to recapture in imagination; the freezing chill of the bedroom; the ice on the water for washing; the poor and uncertain light of candle and lamp; the chilblains and rheumatism and the worse ills of bronchitis and the fatal pneumonia. No wonder in memory "the winters seemed to be longer and the ground frozen for at least 14 weeks every year and the snow lay about and it was COLD".

Rejoicing, therefore, was very real indeed in the hearts of all when the countryside started to bud and the days to grow lighter and longer. The young trooped off merrily at break of day on the May morning to gather garlands with which to decorate themselves and their homes.

Through the years the sports, trials of skill, rejoicings and entertainments took varied forms, changing as fashions change, but the garland-gathering was still traditional in the village in the last quarter of the nineteenth century, although the day was no longer a school holiday; the School Log for May 1st, 1885, records that "the attendance is very poor today, children are away carrying May garlands" (Chapter 28).

With the formation in the following year of the Men's Friendly Society to provide sick-pay for its members and their families in return for 6d. a week subscription, the day became again a school holiday; for the men took over the old May Day for the Club Festival and Annual Dinner. "The whole village made a day—and a night—of it," remembers a villager today. "It started in the morning with all the men, dressed in their smocks, processing through the village. . . . On the village green, booths were set up where you could buy almost anything. There were swings, whirlygigs, sideshows and tests of skill and a huge marquee outside the 'Queen's Head' where everyone had a free dinner; there had to be two sittings but it was 'some' dinner. In 1904 there was an awful gale and everything was blown down and the marquee flattened but we got our dinner in the 'Coach and Horses'." Another villager remembers it a few years later also as a gala day: "The school was closed and everyone had a holiday. It began with the church bells ringing and in mid-morning the Club members in their Sunday suits, gay with the sashes of their Society across their chests and rosettes in their button-holes, assembled on the Green. With band playing and banners flying, they marched up the long hill to the church and after the service they marched down again to a large marquee erected on the Green. With the Rector, the Rev. J. Warner, presiding, all sat down to a grand feast, and afterwards dispersed to join their womenfolk and children in the field adjoining the 'Queen's Head', where the Fair was held with roundabouts, swings, Aunt Sally, coconut shies, gingerbread stalls, and all the fun of the fair. The band played all the time and dancing would begin; many a romance started on the fair-ground. The shy young man would ask the girl of his choice to 'have a ride on the Roundabout'; or 'How about a swing?' another would ask. Laughter and merriment went on to a late hour until everyone, happily tired, went home. It was the children's day too. All saved up their halfpennies and farthings for many a week, small coins in those days had big value. Tradition had it that the old horse chestnut tree at Brickwall should always be in bloom on Club Day. The old portrait of Queen Elizabeth in 'Ruffs and Ringlets' hung outside the 'Queen's Head' and she seemed to look down on this scene of gaiety, so like the revels in her day, with approval." "In the big tent set up opposite the 'Queen's Head'," remembers another, "roast beef and plum pudding were laid on the tables by the womenfolk." The plum puddings, she said, were boiled by the wife of the inn-keeper, Mrs. Nightingale, and later, Mrs. Hilder, in the 'Queen's Head' coppers which alone were big enough. "Children would buy a shilling's-worth of meat and some plum pudding to go with it. The Green was transformed into a wonderland with the cheerful tinny music of the merry-go-round dominating all the noise and laughter, and the shouting and squeals of those on the roundabout. A crowd of men was gathered around the weight-jumping, making bets on whose pull on the great pole, the size of a telegraph post, would send the weight highest. The blacksmith, George Simmons, was a near certainty." These different descriptions show how the celebrations developed over the years, potted music eventually taking the place of the band. "It were a sad day," said one, pensively, "when that Club closed because the young men would not join when they could get sick-pay through the National Insurance; and there were no more May Festivals."

For a year or two after the end of World War II a travelling fair halted for a night or two in the "Queen's Head" field with merry-go-rounds and chalk-faced clowns and sideshows.

The Young Wives, newly formed, held the first Fair on the Village Green after the war, to celebrate the Coronation. There was a little pageant by the children and the crowning of a May Queen. There were sideshows and stalls, dancing round the maypole and free

Elizabethan refreshments for all—cider together with what is today called a Ploughman's lunch. The cider from the barrel was more potent than was suspected by several respectable ladies who drank freely only to discover to their chagrin when they attempted to stand up that their balance seemed to have deserted them. It was a happy and colourful affair with all the stallholders dressed in bygone fashion.

## The Flower Show

Living memory does not go back to the first Flower Show. As far as memories and records do go into the nineteenth century it was another Gala Day when the three villages—Sedlescombe, Westfield and Whatlington—all combined and held a joint show. All roads led to Sedlescombe on that day at the end of July; in the morning they were filled with horses and carts and ponies and traps bringing produce from the villages; and gay with walkers carrying basketfuls of flowers and vegetables; everybody converging on Oaklands Park where the show was held. Tents were set up and the judges soon were busy. In the afternoon there were coconut shies and Aunt Sallies and bowling for the pig. There was rivalry between the villages and criticism, as ever, over the allotment of the prizes, given away always by Mrs. Brabazon Combe. It was a precious holiday too for the school children, some of whom competed, winning many prizes, for they had been well taught by that enthusiastic gardener, their headmaster, Horace Martin. There were, too, sewing and embroidery exhibits from the girls. After a great tea, some of the exhibits were auctioned. Sometimes before the end there was dancing and, afterwards, the long job of clearing away before the Park was empty again of the very last person.

After each war, the Flower show was revived, but Westfield and Whatlington began to hold their own. For some years the Sedlescombe one took place in the grounds of the Manor, by invitation of Mr. Cecil Savill and his sister, Miss Edith, keen gardeners themselves as befitted the uncle and aunt of him who was to create the famous Savill Gardens at Windsor.

Now the Flower Show, combined with a Fete, is held on the Sports Field and once again part, at least, of Oaklands Drive is busy with the arrival of competitors with car-loads of produce and armfuls of flowers, to make into lovely arrangements. No coconut shies today, but there are many other sideshows; stalls and competitions, fancy dress and Festival Queens. And still there is cheerful criticism of the Judges' choices.

*Harvest Feasts and Festivals*
These were held in the barns of the various farms when the grain was safely in; for all who had worked together to this end shared in the sense of satisfaction, completion and relief. So rejoicing was natural, with feasting, dancing and singing, as it was, too, when the hops were all picked and slowly drying in the kilns. A natural custom it had been too, for generations, to bring some of the fruits of those harvests to the church with a sense of thankfulness, for the harvest meant a supply of food for the winter and for the year ahead. So the pews were full, as every farmer and farm worker, every cottager and householder brought of their produce an offering of fruit, vegetable and flowers. Today the harvest does not bring that sense of achievement and relief, for there are apples from Canada all the year round and tins of fruit; peas in the deep freeze and packaged bread, and when the potato crop fails there is always pasta in packets. When there is no cause for anxiety, there is no reason for joy. Security is what we all long for and yet it is the sense of insecurity that adds spice to life as the war-years showed. That spice comes from harvest won with some difficulty, the suite of furniture saved for laboriously, not the one bought with a credit card; the washing machine which had to be patiently awaited till the money was in the kitty and then bought with great pride and joy. Each such achievement became a small festival, almost unknown today.

*The Bonfire Boys*
"This," Harry remembers, "was another great day—or evening, maybe. Nothing like it nowadays, we knew how to do things proper. Have you heard tell of our band? We had 18 instruments and we used to practice in Rose Cottage. One day when we were practising, the trombone which, because of the crush in the small room, had to be half out of the window, began to make the strangest noises, muffled-like. At last we found the cause, passing boys had quietly stuffed it with rags.

"On Guy Fawkes Day we processed with the Band all round the village, though we did not play all the time. We started up Church Hill from the Green and went down the Stream to Home Place in

Whatlington where we had a little refreshment, and then on to the Royal Oak, Great Sanders, Castlemans and Highfield. Then there was a long trek up to Westfield Place and back to the village by Oaklands—it must have been nigh on eight miles. Having drunk a little somewhat at most of the houses we were not really in such good shape when we got back to the village and the Band had wellnigh exhausted itself. The last of the fireworks were let off as we left Oaklands and the bonfire was lit on the Green. It was a good evening's work and we collected a large sum of money which we spent on hospital tickets, so that the poor folk could go there when they needed."

After the First World War the Bonfire Boys again went to work with a will; treacle tins were saved and sticks, provided by the woodsmen, were nailed into them and the tins were on the day filled with paraffin-soaked rags, to be topped up at intervals. Fireworks were still home-made, Gotways being the work-place for this; Raymond Hook used 7 lb. of gunpowder. The 'Bonfire Jumpers' were specialities. The Day was very well supported by Battle and Rye as well as by Sedlescombe and it was a most successful money-raiser. All the funds were used for financing village gaieties, parties for the school children, for the Clinic and for the older people.

Jim's memory describes it thus: "Bines and hedge-brushings were collected for six weeks to two months before Guy Fawkes Day and we pulled a wagon with a tar barrel up the road to replenish the torches. Everyone met at the top pub at six o'clock sharp together with the village band. We went up the hill to Highfield and there we did the Ribbon Dance, six boys and six girls, and Bangy played the tune on his concertina. Then we crossed the road to Major Blake at Castlemans; on to Sir John Adamson at Great Sanders, and Lady Mallet at Hurst; then to the Newbles at their farm (Brede Barn), down the field to Oaklands and then up to Major Mullens at Westfield Place. Each time we did the Ribbon Dance and each time we had refreshments. We were back in the village to light the fire at 10 o'clock. George Simmons, the blacksmith, used to lead the procession all the way, dressed in a hired hat and curled wig. We were mostly all in fancy dress. The Ribbon Dance? oh! it was pretty. Each pair of dancers carried a long coloured ribbon decorated with bells. There were usually six pairs but you could have as many dancers as you wished." Clothes were sometimes hired by the ambitious from a firm in Maidstone. Potatoes and roast chestnuts were sold from a trolley. They had been baked in the big ovens at Gregory's.

After World War II, the Bonfire Boys went to work in Sedlescombe again and torches set up round the Green on November 5th shone bright in the cold night as the procession set forth. Some were in fancy dress and others were well wrapped up in their ordinary coats and scarves but all carried torches with flames and smoke that wavered in the night wind. Others were gathering at the "Queen's Head" field beside the great bonfire, with Guy Fawkes atop, waiting the return of the procession. At last the bonfire was lit and great was the primitive joy of thrusting the lighted torches into the heart of it to add to the blaze, and of dancing round in its light and warmth, the face ruddy and warm and the back cold and black, while the sparkling fireworks shot up and joined the stars.

Money was still lavishly collected which all went back into the village and thus the Darby and Joan Club was enabled to start, and the Christmas parties financed.

Gradually with the increase of private transport, the rival claims of the more spectacular shows in Battle and Rye killed the local effort and for many years now the only local bonfires have been private ones.

*Jubilees and Coronations*

Other less regular festivals have been the patriotic ones, starting with the Victorian Diamond Jubilee, which is further than memories reach today, but which the clock on the grocer's stores commemorates, put there by Public subscription. Empire Day was regularly celebrated for the first quarter of the century with an invitation to the schoolchildren to tea and games at Oaklands Park. For the younger ones it was a long walk up and a long walk back and there were many tired little legs; but this troubled none, for many walked further than that to school and back every day.

A Jubilee Oak, Memorial to the 25th anniversary of King George V, stands on the Green under the gaze of the Jubilee Clock and opposite the "Queen's Head". Sports were held on that day in Windmill Field, now covered with the houses of Gorselands, and a beacon fire was lit in the evening and all the village danced and the band played.

On V.E. Day the bells rang out joyfully as they had in November 1918, their glad sound adding to the pain of many aching hearts.

Celebrations at the Queen's Coronation had nothing to dim them and they filled the whole of a long week; and a rapid harvest of television aerials sprouted like beanstalks on the old lichened roofs around the Green. Twenty-five years later, the results of that Coronation were sincerely and lovingly celebrated; some of the same decorations adorned the same houses, the Green blossomed with loyal banners and scarlet and blue flowers; the children made merry again with sports between the heavy showers; and in the evening beacon fires shone on all the high places as in earlier days they had for the victories against the Armada and Napoleon.

*Chapter Forty-three*

## THE FIRST WORLD WAR

In August 1914, soon after the fire at the "Coach and Horses", came the outbreak of war, the war which would be over by Christmas, and which at first seemed the great opportunity for adventure and glory to many young men in going to fight for the country they loved; but which all too soon turned into an unimaginable horror that was to kill millions of them and to change for ever the face of the world, of this island and of practically every place within it. Sedlescombe, too, was, of course, never to be the same again.

There had always been Sedlescombe men through the years who, in search of adventure or freedom, had 'gone to be a soldier' or, with a love of the sea in their bones, had joined the seafarers; and others in time of threatened invasion had been ready staunchly to defend their country and, with whatever weapon came to hand, to repel every enemy foreigner who attempted to land on it. But now, for the first time in history, every grown man was called on not just to leave his home and his job but to leave also his country and to go across the sea and from foreign shores to defend his native land; and in thousands upon thousands to destroy and be destroyed with the terrible new nerve-shattering weapons.

It happened that on August 4th the Rector was leaving Sedlescombe for good to take up a new job at Brighton and, on the evening before, he and his wife went for their last meal to the Leighs at Homestall. As they started homewards in the summer night, the reservists were collecting on the Green, for the policeman had knocked on their doors. The Rector gathered them all around the Pump and, under the brilliant moonlight, they prayed a short prayer together, with the scent of honeysuckle, jasmine, stocks and roses from the rows of gardens, homely in the air and the shadows of the horse chestnut trees dark across the way. It is probable that the Rector's wife was not the only one who never forgot that scene.

George, a driver in the Field Coy. of the R.E., came home on leave and went into the pub at Broad Oak. "What's it like out there?" an old man queried. "I've come home on leave and I haven't left there anything that I want but if you like to go out and get it for me you're welcome," was all the answer he received. But remembering now, George says, "The worst of anything was the old Grans, sweethearts and wives and their last kiss before the train doors were locked. That hurt. And the second worst thing was the refugees in France, with their little children and the push-carts and push-chairs piled up with their homely belongings, fleeing away from the Germans."

At home the worst job of all was the postman's when a War Office telegram had to be delivered, but the Postmaster himself would do this, and he always told the Rector immediately. Wounded soldiers in their distinctive blue coming out from Hastings to watch the work in the fields could often be seen, and German prisoners too from the camp at Robertsbridge, and when the wind was right the noise of the guns could be a chilling background rumble and vibration. Farming continued as usual with more help than ever from women and girls, withdrawn from domestic work in the private house.

Three of the first houses to be visited by the fatal telegrams were Hancox, Jacobs and Oaklands Park, when Gillachrist Moore, Henry Adeane and Boyce Combe were all killed at the Battle of Ypres. Telegrams followed at intervals during the next four years to

Brickwall, home of Walter Godman, Lieut. K.R.R. 60th Regiment.;

The cottage (now The Lamp Post), where Edward Barwick lived, whose father was gardener at Castlemans;

Cherry Tree Cottage, where Bert Bateup lived, whose father, Tom, worked for Phil Thomas and was later killed on his push-bike;

Brickyard Cottage (now Littlehurst), where Jim Dengate lived, son of James Dengate, builder and verger;

Barracks Cottage, to newly married Mrs. Harris, for Edward was killed;

Linton House twice when Edward and then Malcolm Macdougall were killed, whose father had retired from the Council;

Forge Cottages, where Mrs. Morris lived with her small son, Jack, and when the war was nearly over her husband, Percy, was killed;

The Presbytery, for Sydney Weller, who ran the Sedlescombe village band, was dead;

Footlands, when Wilfred Richens was killed

and the School Cottages, for Percival Relfe, who had worked a market garden, was gone; Magazine Farm when the only son, Walter Williams, a private in the Machine Gun Corps, was killed; Bourne Farm for Ernest Watson. To Great Sanders, too, came sad news when the butler to the Adamsons, William Hobbs, was killed. To Westfield Place and Glebe Cottage came the news that Cyril Mullens and John Parker were killed, and to the Boxall family that Harry was dead. The Bryants, the Cramps, the Cruttendens and Dawsons all had the fatal telegrams announcing that Charlie, Len, Frank and Reg were fatal casualties. There followed Albert Soan, brother of Jim and Charlie, and Charlie Johnson. The long list closed with John Rushton Moore and Christopher Hodgson.

So there were few houses or cottages which did not hold mourners, for relationships were closely interwreathed.

Those who did come back had shared not only terrible and appalling sights and experiences which they could never forget, but also a widening of their lives, a knowledge of new lands, new ways, new friends, new independence, which left them new men. Some could settle contentedly and with relief back into the life of the village again, into the old job; some found no job awaiting them; some wanted a more exciting life than the old village could give them; some had a disabling wound.

But village life was changing, too, and farming. Horses were fewer, tractors were appearing and some of the men who returned brought with them a welcome knowledge of the workings of machinery. Cars too began to be seen on the roads. Jim Soan, coachman to the Adamsons at Great Sanders, was sent by his employers to the Wolseley firm to learn to drive their newly-purchased car. George Hook, the wheelwright by the Bridge, became less and less busy and at last retired altogether, the smith moving into his old quarters; while Gregory, the baker, installed a garage with petrol pumps in the old smithy building.

A Men's Club met nightly in Gregory's tea-rooms and General Nixon started a Boys' Club in the Minor Hall beside the Old Gun Cottage, and the Village Hall opened. This was something the village had never known before and plans for it had included a reading room with comfortable armchairs, but the war had intervened and the higher prices made it impossible. Till then, the school had been used for any indoor entertainment and the Rectory, usually, for meetings. Leisure time in the past had been scarce but now working hours were ordained by law and, in the winter particularly, there was time to spare from life's task of earning a living.

*Chapter Forty-four*

BEATING THE BOUNDS FOR THE LAST TIME

This ceremony (Chapter 13), traditionally carried out every seven years with the object of impressing the boundaries of the parish unforgettably on the minds of the rising generation of males, fell out of use in Sedlescombe after the publication of Tithe Maps in 1841 fixed most clearly on paper those boundaries.

On May 30th 1914, the *Hastings and St. Leonards Observer* wrote: —

"After a lapse of over 70 years the ancient custom of 'Beating the bounds' was observed in Sedlescombe on Wednesday... Only one man now living can remember the event taking place 70 years ago; "General" Hayler, now living in Westfield. Mr. Byner (vice-chairman of Parish Council), who is 76 years of age can remember being told how the 'bounds were beaten'.

"On Wednesday at about 10 o'clock quite a large company was present at the bridge at the bottom of the village, from where it was proposed to make a start. There were Mr. Arthur Pratt (chairman of the P.C.), James Byner, G. Parker, W. Button, L. Dallaway, E. W. Hilder, all members of the P.C. and Mr. T. Hilder, clerk; Harvey Combe and Boyce Combe, A. Molyneaux, J. Leigh, C. R. H. Thomas, H. Dengate, C. Farrow, W. Holmes and W. Wood; with the Misses Fanler, Oliver, Miller, and Molyneaux. William Hyland, aged 92, one of the oldest men in the village, and Mr. Jim Eldridge aged 84, carpenter, watched the beaters commence what proved to be an arduous journey. About 14 of the older boys attending the day school accompanied the party.

"After Arthur Pratt had addressed the boys on the subject of beating the bounds, the Brede river at the bottom of the village was followed in the direction of Brede, this forming the boundary on the South side. About half a mile from the start, Mr. Byner, who constituted himself the leader of the party, was at fault, and a large wall survey-map, which was pluckily carried by various members of the company throughout the long perambulation, had to be consulted. The way led through a farm and various fields into Brede Lane which was traversed for some distance, and it was curious to note that a detached portion of Udimore parish was on the right hand and Sedlescombe on the left. After following a footpath through Jacob's Farm, a long journey was made through Moon's Wood. At one point here the map had to be consulted to confirm the boundary line but, of course, the custodian of this (which proved to be a very necessary and useful article) was not to be found; he had gone round the wood and not through it! En route the trees of the boundary line were 'blazed' by Mr. Dallaway with the letters S.P.B. 1914, or some other sign.

"The farm road from Powdermill was then encountered and this was followed for some distance. At the top of this lane a gate, where the parish of Brede boundary and that of Sedlescombe met, had to be crossed and some of the boys were "bumped"; but throughout the day they seemed to object to this very necessary procedure when 'beating the bounds'. Down over another field and Brede High Wood was encountered and after going through Horseford Farm there was a long climb through Greenden Wood into the road from Sedlescombe to Staplecross, about 300 yds south of Cripps Corner.

"Here to the delight of everyone, refreshment liquid and otherwise had been provided in a barn kindly lent by Mr. Hindes of Chittlebirch Farm (Chapter 37). Having regard to the way the viands disappeared, it seemed as though everyone had been longing for this welcome luncheon interval for some time. Credit is due to the three ladies who pluckily stuck to the party up to this point, defying the hedges, fences and woods to keep them back . . .

"The members of the party stepped out again like 'giants refreshed with wine' . . . but were quickly in difficulty in Hazel Wood where they lost themselves for a while. The road at Swales

Green was crossed and the boundary then led the walkers down in the direction of Poppinghole Lane where the map again could not be found when wanted! Returning to the main road the boundary then went through the middle of a pond, but this being too deep to be waded through, the boundary beaters had to be content with walking round the edge. A halt was then called for more refreshments the elder members having something from a bottle, and the boys slaked their thirst from a bucket of water. The road was followed for a short distance till a spile fence was climbed into Dorrell's Farm. The borders of Footland Wood and Beech Wood were skirted; those who followed the boundary as marked on the map and did not take the shortest cut to the refreshment house found themselves on the main road from Sedlescombe to Staplecross only a few hundred yards from the luncheon barn. After a visit to Great Sanders the road was again crossed and the route, which lay through the cow-yard of Beech Farm, was faithfully followed. A small wood here was like a jungle and many were the amusing incidents recounted when the party arrived on the other side. The course of the stream at the bottom of Windmill Hill formed the boundary and after a walk up the hill Hancox's barn was entered by the front door and left by the back, part of the building being in Whatlington parish and part in Sedlescombe parish. The same state of affairs existed in regard to Hancox House, the residence of Dr. Norman Moore; but, owing to the house being shut up, the party had to be content with going round the walls. Riccards Lane and Spilsteads Farm were included and a pleasant journey across the Brooks brought the weary party to the Bridge at the bottom of the village where they had started in the early morning.

"The journey had occupied nine hours from 10.30 in the morning to 7.30 at night with about an hour for lunch. Many were the estimates as to the distance covered but it was probably about $14\frac{1}{2}$ miles. There had been numerous amusing incidents en route, including tumbles and crawls through gaps in hedges; spile fences and hedges were climbed or got through, ditches jumped and waded and no obstacles proved insurmountable. With Mr. Byner's knowledge of the country and Mr. T. G. Hilder's study of the map, a true course was kept. Mr. W. Button was a valuable assistant.

"Mr. Arthur Pratt presided at the subsequent supper at the Queen's Head and after the very welcome repast expressed the hope that no one had suffered from the long perambulation. Mr. Byner thanked Mr. Pratt for the trouble that he, as head of the Parish, had taken in the matter; to which Mr. Pratt replied that although he had been unable to accompany them all the way round, he had watched them from several high points as they went from place to place."

The wall survey-map mentioned as being carried was the one that hangs in the Village Hall, a cumbersome item with which to crawl through hedges or to carry for 14-odd miles! When rolled up it is over 6 ft. long.

Mr. Edgar Boxall of Fir-Tree Cottage remembers the beating of the bounds taking place again nine years later in 1923, by the Parish Council. He remembers the start along the path by the river over what is now the Sports field, and across the second of the two brick-and-earth bridges which then spanned it leading to Brede Barn Farm where the cows used to drink through a hole in the wall which was the parish boundary. At Bourne Farm further along Brede Lane, a willow stump was blazed by old James Byner, 85 years old and chairman of the Parish Council, backed by the clerk, Tom Hilder. At Jacobs they turned through Brede High Woods, very soon to be lost under the reservoir, and so to Cripps. They had lunch at Swailes Farm again provided by Mr. Hindes; and returned at last to the Bridge via Hancox and the Bowlings. Mr. Boxall remembers old Jim Byner carrying a bottle of gin for sustainment.

In 1959 the Parish Boundaries were altered to remove, by exchange, odd isolated areas of another parish where it lay pointlessly now in the middle. Thus Sedlescombe gained Battle Barn Farm and Beech Farm from Battle and Whatlington, respectively; and gave to Whatlington part of Footlands Wood; and Battle, Brede and Sedlescombe also exchanged pieces of land, to the advantage of each. The new boundaries were never beaten since they were known to all by being shown clearly on maps. However, "No one can understand a village or see it properly until he has walked the parish bounds. The village lands are the thing itself; and how the village lies in relation to them".[1]

---

[1] Pakington.

*Chapter Forty-five*

## THE VILLAGE GROWS

Up till the end of the First War most of the building in the village had been re-building; cottages pulled down and re-built, often with much of the same materials, by individual owners and, latterly by the Combes of Oaklands to house members of their own family or workers on the estate. The Battle Abbey Estate, too, had re-built the old Powdermill house, the Bowlings across the Brooks, Horsmans and Magazine Farm, all in the south of the village.

The first building to be erected after the war was the Village Hall, which was to have been built in 1914 on a parcel of land given by the Combes, and with money raised almost entirely by the efforts of the villagers. One such, which took place a few months before the war started, was described in the Hastings and St. Leonards Observer thus:

"Owing to the individual efforts of Mr. W. G. Parker" (of Glebe House), "the services of the Ore Male Voice Choir were secured for a Concert which was given in the Schoolroom on New Year's evening in aid of the fund for the proposed Village Hall. The room was full, the numerous items were much appreciated and many of the artistes were encored. The choruses by the Choir included; 'Music, All Powerful'; 'Christian Martyrs'; 'Hallelujah Chorus'; 'Soldiers Chorus'; 'Peace to the Souls'; etc. and were capitally rendered. Worthy of mention were the songs, 'Mountain Lovers' and 'Tommy Lad', by Miss Ada Pattenden whose contralto voice was heard to splendid advantage. There were other contributors and the programme concluded with the part song, 'The Long Day Closes'. Mr. Fred Shoesmith conducted and the accompanist was Miss Pankhurst. The Rector (the Rev. B. M. C. S. Browne) at the close proposed a vote of thanks."

This was only one of many concerts, sales of work and varying entertainments arranged to raise the necessary money.

As usual after a war materials were scarce and expensive so that the plans, which had included a rest room and a reading room for the men, had to be pruned, and the building which arose and was officially opened in 1920 by Mrs. Brabazon Combe was ugly and ill-proportioned, like the newly re-built Pub, and regrettably different from the original intention (Map 5. 21A).

But now houses were proving insufficient. The standard of living was slowly rising and the overcrowding of large families into tiny cottages was no longer acceptable. Young men returning from the war with a longing to set up a home and start a family had more difficulty in finding a cottage than in finding work. Gregory, at the Bakery, employed 40 to 50 villagers; Thomas and Son, builders, nearly the same number; and there was still work for farm labourers on the surrounding farms and fruit farms; and on the estates hedging, ditching and thatching; and some could find work in the building of the reservoir or in the Gypsum Mines at Mountfield. Work of a domestic kind too was still available in all the big houses as gardener, chauffeur or butler. Only the age-old call for the work of the individual craftsman, wheelwright, blacksmith and carpenter was steadily diminishing.

Mr. Cecil Savill of the Manor, a member of the Parish Council, pressed for the building of Council Houses to meet the need, with the result that in Barns Field on Mabbs Farm a row of twelve were built facing east; and in 1924 the first young couple, Mr. and Mrs. Edgar Boxall, now of Fir-Tree Cottage, moved in and in the following year their son, Bill, was born—the first baby in East View Terrace. In the same year another row of twelve houses facing the earlier ones was built by the Council, thus creating for the first time, half a mile from the centre of the village, a settlement of families all of similar status and mostly of similar age. These were built not a moment too soon for, with the auction of the Combe property in the same year, more cottages, rented for years by villagers, were removed by individual purchase into the hands of strangers.

Four years later, when Castlemans and Beech Farms were sold, building plots alongside the main road and in Hurst Lane and Churchlands came on the market. Many a bungalow thus sprang up, and huts of fragile build, some little more than caravans or old army huts, to give secluded refuges away from the troublesome and disillusioning world, either for holidays and week-ends or for permanent living by individuals searching for peace and a better life in country places. Many bore unusual or quaint names, speaking of the nostalgia or fantasies of the refuge-seeking owners.

In the nineteen-thirties, members of the Women's Institute, seeing that the number of cottages available for renting was getting smaller and smaller, conceived the idea of building a cottage or two semi-detached houses to be let to Sedlescombe residents at strictly economic rents. To this end the great sum, as it seemed then, of £2,600 was raised, but once again, as for the Village Hall a quarter of a century earlier, plans for buying a site and starting building were brought to a halt by the outbreak of war, and the money was invested to await happier days.

*Chapter Forty-six*

## THE POWDERMILL RESERVOIR (Map A)

In the year 1926, the new owner of Great Sanders House, E. H. Chambers (Chapter 17), approached the Hastings Borough Council suggesting that his land might be examined with a view to its water possibilities. This was an imaginative and practical suggestion, for the estate was a natural basin and coincided almost exactly with the watershed of Powdermill Stream, which rises where the Gallows of Horne stood near Cripps Corner and runs through the estate to join the River Brede as one of its tributaries. This basin had, since before the days of the Armada, held two large ponds, the water of which had driven the great bellows of the Brede Furnace (Chapter 16) and, in the eighteenth century, the large edge-runner grindstones of the Gunpowder Mill (Chapter 29).

The Council welcomed Mr. Chambers' suggestion, for their water problem was increasing every year as the demand grew greater and existing supplies proved more and more inadequate. So in July 1927 the new Borough Water Engineer, Sidney Little, prepared a scheme for the formation of an impounding reservoir of 186.5 million gallons capacity by constructing a dam across the Powdermill valley at a cost of £80,000; with gravity-main in cast-iron to No. 10 Station beside the River Brede (Chapter 1) to carry 950,000 gallons in 24 hours; and a duplicate 134 hp pumping plant and buildings to raise 1,400,000 gallons per day to Baldslow or to Fairlight if required at an estimated cost of £31,000.[1]

Preparations were put in hand for the inclusion of this scheme in a Parliamentary Bill to be presented in 1928 and in due course, in spite of serious opposition, the water provisions were successfully

---

[1] Coleman.

obtained in the Hastings Corporation Act 1928, which included the acquisition of the necessary land, the construction of the reservoir and all ancillary works at a total cost of £220,000, and the making of bye-laws to protect the catchment area from pollution. In advancement of this latter aim, the old sixteenth century Austford Farmhouse and its neighbour across the Powdermill Stream, the "other Austford", were demolished (Chapters 17 and 23). The land to be flooded consisted of two more farmhouses, Brede High and Powdermill, with keepers' cottages, 130 acres of orchards, 286 acres of pasture, 55 acres of hopland, 484 acres of woodland, together with miscellaneous land, totalling 1,035 acres. Only one small keeper's cottage, where lived Mrs. Apps, whom many of us still remember, was left standing and after her death it also went. The 484 acres of woodland, which included the lower half of Brede High Wood, part of Coney Wood, Sandpit Wood and Ward's Wood, consisted of much oak but Mr. Chambers had been selling nearly all marketable timber for felling before he actually sold the estate. Great Sanders House itself remained, the house that had been for over 350 years the home of the Bishop family of Sedlescombe and which, from its beginnings as an Elizabethan farmhouse, had grown through the years, with additions in Queen Anne's and other reigns, into a 23-roomed mansion (Chapter 17).

In August 1929 work began on construction of the reservoir with about 80 men, half of whom were local and half unemployed from the distressed areas. As work progressed the number of men employed was doubled and reached eventually about 170, giving in those lean days much needed employment over three years. One can however understand so well the opposition of those whose homes and farm work were lost.

The old Powdermill dam was demolished, the material from it being used for filling purposes. The new earth dam with clay puddle core is 1,105 ft long and 40 ft high, its thickness being 12 ft at the top and 280 ft at the bottom. A total of 188.3 million gallons can be impounded and the lake has a surface area of 57 acres, just two acres larger than the old Hop-garden on the Powdermill farm.

On November 5th 1931 the filling of the reservoir began and a little over four months later, on March 17th 1932, top-water level was reached. Mr. Charlie Smith and his family have lived in the new water-bailiff's cottage ever since. There is not much about the reservoir and its surrounding woodlands that he does not know.

Much iron dross from the days of the iron furnace is still to be found in the bed of Powdermill Stream, and he himself unearthed a cannon-ball and iron-scoop.

At the request of the Hastings Borough Council a "Working Plan and Scheme for Afforestation of the Great Sanders Estate", covering 473 acres, was prepared by Leslie Wood F.S.L. which provided for planting with larch, chestnut, beech, ash, sitka spruce and Douglas fir in fixed programme.

Forty years later, the reservoir has been described as the most beautiful in Sussex. There are birds in great variety to be seen upon it and stocks of trout live in its water. Public footpaths through parts of the woodlands surrounding it give opportunity for walking several miles amongst great beauty in complete solitude. It is not often in these days that such a beautiful and happy fate overtakes an old estate. One of the old grinding stones of the Powdermill is set up on the bank behind the outflow system.

While Sedlescombe had the benefit of all this beauty, its people continued for years longer to be dependent on their wells, for it was Hastings that received the benefit of all the water.

*Chapter Forty-seven*

## THE SECOND WORLD WAR

Once again, in 1939-45, the young men left the village for foreign lands, there to fight for their country, and this time it was eleven who never returned alive. Some of the girls went too, and some to join the Land Army. The older men were happy to be needed in the Local Defence Volunteers, the Home Guard. On duty these slept at Jacobs in the early years, where Colonel King, their Captain, lived; later their sleeping quarters were transferred to Sherralds, the war-time home of Colonel Langton, and later still to Brickwall. Edgar Boxall, at Jacobs Cottage, gardener to Colonel King, was air-raid warden, together with Bill Monk, who was a tiny man, not much more than five feet high.

In the first year of the war, Sedlescombe was in the "safe" area so houses and cottages received children evacuated from London, and the Village Hall became an extension of the school for them. Old people too came looking for sanctuary and many were taken in at Great Sanders, where the Merrion House School for Boys had retreated from St. Leonards. After the fall of Dunkirk the whole of the situation changed and all were sent off again, away from the threatening danger of invasion.

It was then that Colonel King of the Home Guard, to the amusement of many, called for iron bedsteads and any other old iron or wooden obstacles with which to erect a barricade in Brede Lane. Among the stuff brought along was a pair of stag-horns which reared themselves protectively above it, threatening any incoming Nazis.

There were many 'incidents'. A land-mine fell one September night at ten o'clock when the rain was tumbling down, and Old George remembers how from East View Terrace he saw the great flash and, stretching forward his arms with his two palms together, he pin-pointed the direction. It had come down on Frymans, Mr. Newble's farmhouse opposite Brook Lodge on the corner of Brede Lane where Frymans lane joins it. There in the cottage lived Charlie Beaney with his family. He and his wife got down into their own dug-out just in time. Their son, meanwhile, was in the oast drying the hops and a big beam came down with the blast and protected him where he was jammed into a corner. He extricated himself from all the ruin and tended his father, who had escaped with a cut face, and his mother before he himself collapsed. All that remains now of the shattered farmhouse cottages and barns is a rectangle on each side of the lane full of nettles and roses where the gardens grew.

Other land-mines crashed down in Beauport Park and in Oaklands, neither bringing any damage to house or people. Strings of bombs fell round Jacobs Farm and the reservoir and the cottagers had to find shelter in the village, but again no one was hurt. Enemy aircraft machine-gunned the village and a young nurse from the hospital at Hastings, riding on her bicycle up the Street on her half-day, saw with mesmerised horror an aeroplane above her, the black cross on its wings looming larger and larger, till she was pulled off her machine and crammed into a hedge by the Warden. The shots went through the roof of one of the Manor Cottages and knocked holes in the back door of another. Buckhurst Farm, too, was machine-gunned. Mrs. Beeching, in Plumtree Cottage near Spray's Green, was working at her kitchen sink leaving her infant son, Basil, in his cot upstairs. A machine-gun bullet from an enemy aircraft pierced through her roof and hit her in the neck. It was some time before the child's crying was heard and she was found. Too late, for she died from loss of blood in the ambulance.

One spring morning there was a great scare. German parachutes were seen sailing down the sky northwards of the village. Old Tom shouted, "The Germans are coming, the Germans are coming." All the bakery workers came out to stare. Young Louis blubbered an echo to Old Tom: "The Germans are coming." The church bells too began to peal out the same warning. The parachutes were seen to land near the saw-mills and the two Germans escaping from their doomed machine were quickly captured and the church bells, and everybody, became quiet again.

At the end of May and the beginning of June the countryside seemed suddenly secretly alive, stirring everywhere with hidden life and the roads were busy as never before, teeming with grey-green transport; and the day called D-day dawned.

Then came the flying bombs, the doodlebugs, a searing terror to children with their uncanny screech and fiery tail. One fell in Oaklands Park after midnight, its hot breath killing only a tree, the tree which still stands today stark and dead as though struck by lightning. The warning had gone and there was a general hollering of "under the beds". All were safe though some were blown across their rooms and many doors and windows were driven out. Another fell in daylight in Poppinghole Farm where Harold Anstey and a German prisoner were working with a tractor, the noise of which masked the noise of the doodlebug, and both men were killed. Nineteen days earlier the Parish Magazine had recorded that the Rector's only son had been killed in France on the day after D-Day.

"He was made for love and laughter," wrote Patience Strong, living then in Whatlington,
"Useful work and happy life—
Not for hate and violence,
The battle and bitter strife.
He was made to play the game
And walk the countryside—
Free to take the morning road
With merry heart and swinging stride.

Yet he did not reap the harvest of the fields of Time
Not for him the fruit of manhood ripening to golden prime
Fate upon that clear young brow had drawn the mark of destiny
He was of the generation born to save humanity."

Another message of sympathy went "to Mrs. Barber whose husband was recently killed in action. Mrs. Barber will be well known and affectionately remembered to many in Sedlescombe as Miss Eileen Combe." (Chapter 32.)

Other doodlebugs fell before the war was over; one at the back of Highfield and another further up the hill at Sandrocks, shot down by the R.A.F. Memory brings back too the aerial dog-fights in the blue sky over the wide Brede valley when the thrill and anxiety as to the outcome was almost too great to bear.

So at last came June 1945 and the paragraph in the Parish Magazine:

"There was a full church on the evening of Victory-in-Europe Day at 7.30 as people from every part of the parish flocked to the house of God. . . . It was a short service but had the one underlying essential of real devotion and deep thankfulness. . . . On the following Sunday . . . in the evening a fine body of men and women who had done special service during the war came on parade and helped to make the act of thanksgiving all the more impressive. We may all hope that it will not be long before we are called upon to meet and thank God for the completion of all hostilities with the defeat of Japan, when I shall desire to express our corporate thanks to all those men and women of this parish who, disdaining the more lucrative and less exacting tasks, have given their all for their country and its great cause of justice and freedom. . . . The collection for Christian Reconstruction in Europe amounted to £17 6s. 8d."

The future remained and once again the life of the village was changed for ever, but most especially for the families and loved ones of the following:

Jack Crump, born at Brook Lodge; Private, the Hampshire Regiment.

Harold Farrow, Luff's Farm; Sergeant, the Royal Signals (30).

Jimmy Franklin, Powdermill; Lieutenant, The Queen's Bays.

Harold Hinde, Swailes Farm; Corporal, the Royal Air Force.

John Noble, Sedlescombe Rectory; Captain, Royal Horse Artillery.

Horace Shambrook, East View Terrace; Gunner, Royal Artillery (20).

Henry Read, Pump Cottage; Leading Aircraftman, the Royal Air Force (25).

Jim Smith, son of 'Strawberry' Smith, Woodman's Cottage; Aircraftman, the Royal Air Force.

Thomas Swanson, of Dell View, Hawkhurst Road; Gunner, Royal Artillery.

Marcus Williams, of The Bowlings; Queen's Commandos, Sergeant.

George Anstey, Poppinghole Farm; and Mrs. Beeching, Plumtree Cottage.

The following verses called "Sedlescombe Heritage" were published in the Parish Magazine "with thanks to Lieut. E. Hinds, the Platoon Commander, 24 Platoon, 22nd Bn. Sussex Home Guard, whose actual words, on a day in June 1940, are quoted in the first verse."

" 'They can't beat us,' the Home Guard said
When France had fallen and hope seemed dead.
'As long as there's one of us left alive,
They can't beat us,' he said.

'They can't beat us,' the Briton said
When the Romans tramped through their lanes.
'They can seize our iron and forge our chains,
But chained we can live and chained we can sing,
And they can't beat us,' he said.
The iron was seized for the Empire's might,
The Street was made to carry the spoil.
The Briton was chained and the Briton slaved,
And sad were the songs he sang at his toil.
'But they can't beat us,' he said.

'They can't beat us,' the Roman said
As the Saxons surged up the river.
'They can tear down our walls but not our pride,
Nor shake the faith that is our sure guide.
And they can't beat us,' he said.

The Saxon slew and the Saxon burnt,
He cleared the forest and ploughed the fields.
The Roman groaned and the Roman bled
And little he saw of the earth's rich yields.
'But they can't beat us,' he said.

'They can't beat us,' the Saxon said
As he crossed the Brooks on his way to battle.
The battle was lost and the Saxon fled
Back to his farm and his fruitful soil.
'But they can't beat us,' he said.

The Norman seized his farm and his hall;
The Saxon thane was an English thrall;
His wealth was gone and his King was dead.
'But, while there's a Saxon in the land,
They can't beat us,' he said.

Briton and Roman have left their trace
With Saxons and Normans in our race.
The roads we tread, the village we share
Are as they are because they were.
Battles they lost, but not their pride;
Conquered they lived and unbeaten died.

'They can't beat us,' the Home Guard said
When France had fallen and hope seemed dead.
'As long as there's one of us left alive;
We could only beat ourselves,' he said.

AUTHOR UNKNOWN."

*Chapter Forty-eight*

## THE VILLAGE GROWS AGAIN

As the second World War drew to its close, houses were once again in desperate demand. Many of the cottages and houses sold at the date of the Combe Auction came on the market again and were sold at greatly increased prices. Delay, even for an architect's or surveyor's report, meant the loss of the chance to purchase. Once again new houses were built, chiefly along the road between Hurst Lane and Beech farmhouse, and up Chapel Hill and Crazy Lane, and a few more council houses along Brede Lane. Oast houses and farm outbuildings were converted into dwellings, one after another, so that it is hard to find an oast house in the parish today that has not become a private house.

For twenty years longer, however, the lack of main water and drainage systems was still a limiting factor; but with the introduction of these services (in 1957 and 1962), building could go ahead. The estate called Gorselands was built in Windmill field off Brede Lane by the local builder and provided a variety of attractive houses and bungalows close to the centre of the village without in any way spoiling it. In 1966 a second housing estate was built along Brede Lane even closer to the centre of the village. Looked upon at first as expensive "dog-kennels", these bungalows very soon mellowed into the landscape and into the village life, with the help of their quickly maturing gardens and the strong neighbourly feeling which developed at an even more rapid pace in the new community, and the people in the two estates pulled their weight invaluably in all village affairs.

In 1964 the long-cherished dream of the Sedlescombe Women's Institute was realised, though the £2,500 raised for the purpose before the War had become, with the explosion of prices, hopelessly

## THE VILLAGE GROWS AGAIN

inadequate. The Battle Rural District Council, therefore, took charge of the scheme and bought Rose Cottages beside the Village Hall and the land behind them. One and Two Rose Cottages were re-built and, beside them, Roselands, with fourteen flatlets to house elderly people of Sedlescombe and neighbouring villages. Each flat contained bedroom, sitting-room, bathroom and kitchen; and a Warden was installed in one of them. The W.I. money was used to furnish completely the communal television room.

At first the flats were looked upon with distaste and suspicion, but when Charlie Taylor, the retired blacksmith (Chapter 34) and his invalid wife took the plunge and moved in and were seen to be happy, comfortable and independent, the distaste and disapproval evaporated and the flatlets became sought after by any who began to grow too aged or infirm to cope with all the work of house or cottage.

With the building of more council houses and flats in the field below East View Terrace, it was felt that the village's population had increased enough and that any more building would endanger the sense of community.

A few more houses were built along the Street, infilling among the age-old ones, with tact and care and neither 'ye-olde' mockery nor shock-modernity. Goose-Gate is one of these, so called because the family of geese which lived beside Brickwall pond had used its gateway always as their exit and entrance when wishing to visit the other side of the Street.

Will the architecture of the new school to be built beside Brede Lane and behind the houses of the Green add to or detract from the beauty of the village? Will it fit comfortably in with the clustering roofs of the houses which have grown up through so many centuries? When the roof of one of those old houses by the Green had to be replaced in 1968, the Battle Rural District Council insisted that hand-made tiles be put on the back of the house as well as on the front "so that any building that may later rise in the field behind may have a pleasant sight to look at"! Those house-owners would dearly like that thought reciprocated when the school is built.

*Chapter Forty-nine*

## THE INTERNATIONAL CHILDREN'S VILLAGE
(Map A)

Oaklands (Chapter 32), like so many of its neighbours, ceased in 1952 to be the home of a private family. During its occupation by the Brabazons and the Combes it had given hospitality to many interesting and famous people; its future was to extend and continue this hospitality beyond all imagining.

"At the end of the World War 2," wrote Mrs. Mary Buchanan in the Sedlescombe Parish Magazine in 1957, "it is said that some thirteen million European children had to face life without parents or home. . . . A young Swiss Editor, Walter Corti, was the first to speak out what many people in this country felt. He published an article in which he urged Switzerland to do more than thank heaven for having escaped the terrors of war, by giving a helping hand to those victims of war, homeless orphans, and provide them with food, shelter, education and, above all, love . . . By bringing children of many races together they would sow the seeds of tolerance and understanding among men, and . . . help the children to help themselves.

"The response . . . was immediate and widespread as was only to be expected in the Home Country of the Red Cross and of Heinrich Pestalozzi, the great humanitarian and educational reformer.

"In the spring of 1946 . . . the Pestalozzi Children's Village was founded at Trogen, Switzerland, by a small circle of far-seeing enthusiasts . . . practical idealists, that rare combination which is, perhaps more than anywhere else, to be found in two countries: Britain and Switzerland. Some 230 needy children are now being educated there, from Austria, Britain, Finland, Germany, Greece, Italy, Switzerland and Hungary. Soon . . . the village began to develop from a war relief scheme into a pioneer centre of international education. During the first eleven years of its existence it has been visited by educationalists, sociologists and many others . . . interested in this unique venture."

She goes on to say that the village had fully justified its existence for
"amongst those 150 boys and girls who have gone out into the world from it, over one quarter have taken up occupations which mean helping others through welfare and education; and another half are in jobs based on personal contacts with people. Some have already proved that they take a courageous stand against prejudice and superficial judgements on others in an adverse environment."

In 1948 the British Pestalozzi Children's Village Association was founded to enable British war orphans to take part in the life of the Swiss Village and to select and maintain those children and their house parents and teachers there. Encouraged by the success of the Swiss Village, the Association decided to go ahead with its second object: the founding in Britain of the second International Children's Village. In 1958 the Association's work was taken over by the Pestalozzi Children's Village Trust formed by a small group of professional men and women in London. It was this Trust which in 1952 bought Oaklands with its 174 acres to be the home of this second village, with the object of bringing together children from different countries and, by giving them the best education suitable to their abilities in an atmosphere of calm security and affection, to develop a spirit of tolerance and understanding of others irrespective of colour, class or creed and to make them into useful citizens. The Chairman, Dr. Alexander, and his wife spent several weeks touring the displaced persons camps in Germany to select boys and girls to become the first occupants of the Village together with two needy British children. All but the two latter spoke German as well as their native Latvian, Ukrainian, or Polish. As far as was possible they went back to their homes in Germany for the summer holidays.

The year 1959 was pronounced World Refugee Year and by the end of it all the camps were cleared, so the ideas of the Trust had to be altered. The aim became to provide education for children of developing countries who would benefit by such education but could not get it in their own countries and who would eventually go back to those countries with the benefits of that education.

In 1962, Colonel Freddy Spencer Chapman, D.S.O., war hero and late headmaster of a school in South Africa, was appointed to succeed Dr. Alexander as the first Warden. The following year, after the invasion by China of their homeland, 22 Tibetan children arrived at the village bringing with them their cheerful attitude to life, their picturesque dances and their amazing athleticism.

In 1966 the Swiss Hall was opened as a central meeting place for all the children of the Village, a gift from the Swiss Community. In the same year Mr. Gale was appointed Warden in succession to Spencer Chapman and during the next years came 12 Jordanians, 12 Indians, who proved to be brilliant academically, Nigerians, Vietnamese and Thai: Muslims, Christians, Buddhists of three persuasions, and Hindus. The emphasis apart from school work is on practical craft-work, farming, vehicle repair, carpentering and metal work; nursing, cooking and sewing. The original International House was built at vast expense to the designs of the architect, Sir Hugh Casson, who gave his services; and during the years houses for each nationality have been built. Today all the building is done by the members of the Village themselves under the tuition of a carpenter from Sedlescombe, Peter Corps, son of a Sedlescombe carpenter. Even the steel girders are welded on the estate under the training of a metal worker. On the farm barley and maize are the chief crops; fodder for the cattle.

In 1971, 24 South Vietnamese arrived, everyone of whom had lost a father in the long, long war. In 1977 the Communist Vietnamese Ambassador visited the Village and approved of all that the children were being taught.

When new children arrive with a language unknown to the others, this seems to prove little barrier. Information concerning the number of brothers and sisters each has is very soon discovered and some method of communication established.

Half the children who have finished their education and left the Village have returned to their own communities in other lands, though not necessarily to their homelands which, in some cases, are closed to them.

The Village has provoked an enormous and continued interest in this country and large sums were raised over the years to support it and its pioneering work.

*Chapter Fifty*

## THE LAST OF THE OLD-TIME LABOURERS: "BANGY" SMITH

He was born on January 10th, 1862, in one of the Little Footlands Cottages, a son of Spencer and Hannah Smith. Baptised Spencer by the Rev. Edward Owen, then Rector of Sedlescombe, he earned from his schooldays the nickname "Bangy" and was never known for the rest of his life by any other name. Bangy he became through his eager protection with his fists of his younger brother who was being bullied when he first started school.

His father was a farm labourer and Bangy followed the same occupation and talked with honest pride of his proficiency, especially in hedging (he could use a hook in either hand) and in hay-trussing. He had a great regard for his parents of whom in his latter years he often spoke; of his mother who was never too busy to help her neighbours and was much loved; of his father who was a noted step-dancer. Bangy loved music and was himself a well-known performer as well as step-dancer, to be seen at all festive occasions playing his German accordion which he treasured to the end of his life though his fingers were too knotted to be able to play it any longer "I remember," wrote Sir John Thorne, "his vital air as he sang to me, in his clear true voice, ballads of his youth." At the age of 63 he fell off a ladder while working at Glebe House on a frosty day, and broke a knee cap which kept him in hospital for many long weeks and left him permanently lame but he continued to work till the age of 87 and had several masters. These included the Combes at Oaklands, the Adamsons at Great Sanders, the Woodwards at Pork Lane (now Park Lane!), Whatlington, and Major Mullens at Westfield Place. He had therefore lived in many different cottages in the parish during his long life; Swailes Green Cottages where his daughter, Lottie, was born; Ashdown Cottage in Cottage Lane; Blackbrooks and Littlehurst; but his home for forty-five years was at Manor Cottages where his daughter, Lottie Wilson, still lives.

His wife, whom he had married in Battle Church, bore him two sons and three daughters. She died in 1916 and was buried in Sedlescombe churchyard and his own grave adjoins hers.

On fine days, after he had retired, his slight, small figure was to be seen seated at the Pump, where he was always happy to talk to his many friends, and to feed the birds and children that gathered round him; for in his left-hand pocket he always had a piece of damp bread rolled up in a ball, and in his right-hand pocket a bag of sweets. He grew rather deaf in one ear but his sight was very good till the end and he wore no glasses All Sedlescombe knew him and he was loved by all; serene and cheerful, with a smiling courtesy which warmed the heart of each with whom he spoke.

On October 10th, 1969, "he was sitting in his chair by the fire in his home in Manor Cottages, listening to the daily radio service; at the end his head dropped back and he was dead. "So, painlessly and peacefully," wrote Sir John Thorne in the Parish Magazine, "died our oldest inhabitant three months before his 97th birthday. Now he is gone Sedlescombe is very much the poorer but all who knew him will treasure their memories of him."

Nearly twenty years have passed but those who remember delight still to talk of Bangy and his pride and happiness in his work. The two attributes which a man shares with God are to love and to create and therefore it is in these that he finds his greatest happiness.

*Chapter Fifty-one*

## THE CHURCHYARD

Encircling the hill-top church, the village graveyard lies. Bordered on the north by the Precious field, on the south and east by the house and sloping meadows of Castlemans, it is entered on the west from the Queen's highroad by a few old stone steps beside the time-worn mounting block. The four guardian sweet chestnut trees scatter in the autumn their spiny husks like green hedgehogs over the path to the church door, for the feet of children and others to stamp and crush to discover the size of the contents. These vary from disappointing flatness to plump nuts with sweet white flesh inside skins that are glossy as a racehorse's rump.

A brick path also encircles the church, and three side-ones branch off from it between the graves one to the east leading to Jacob's gate, and two to the north which join yet another which comes up eastwards from the lych-gate beside the road. Over against all the paths, in comfortable rows lie those who have lived and died in the village and nearly all the people with whom these pages have been concerned, together in death as they were in life. Here, too, we or our ashes shall lie one day, not between strangers in a huge cemetery, white with tombstones standing up like dentures; but peacefully bedded under the swaying grasses which, if left uncut, will be scattered year after year with white moon daisies and sorrel spears red with clustering crumbs.

The oldest graves are on the south side of the church beneath grey-barked hollies and pyracantha trees, scarlet-berried every winter. Many of the names on these ochre-lichened headstones have been obliterated by time, and others can be deciphered only with great difficulty. The oldest, still identifiable, are probably the Farnden and Avory table-type graves close to the south porch (Chapter

17). The Sackvilles and the Bishops, their contemporaries and neighbours, are not to be seen in the churchyard, for their family vaults lie beneath the church itself, under the south and north aisles. There seems no trace of any inscription to the families who lived at Beech House opposite the church; The Everndons and Plummers. Nor are any Elliott graves visible. But all around are the familiar names of Lingham, 3; Eldridges, 13; Catts; Dengates; Mercers; Crisfords, 9; Bishops, Thomas, 3; Pratts; Bryants, Hindes; Ades, 8; Byners, who lie among Irish yews which stand above them dark like cypresses; Dennets, 5; Sellens; Nightingales; Spears; and Combes. Here lie William Grace and his 'reputed' son, Henry; and here five Rectors. Here they all are, each with his wife and children close by, or in the same grave.

Among the graves on the south side of the church are those of four notable school teachers. Firstly, the grave of Thomas Colbran (see Chapter 28) lies in a row with four others of his family. The headstone does not record the fact that he was a teacher at the village school from the age of 18 until he was 79, but merely states:

"THOMAS COLBRAN
WHO DIED NOV. 22 1816
AGED 79 YEARS"

The next gravestone records:

"ELIZABETH COLBRAN
SPINSTER WHO DIED
DEC. 1816"

There is no gravestone to Thomas's wife, Elizabeth. The word 'spinster' seems to indicate a younger sister who died but a few weeks after him. A third stone tells of:

"THOMAS COLBRAN
WHO DIED NOV. 1778
AGED 37 YEARS"

He is difficult to relate. Born four years after teacher Thomas, he can hardly be his brother, bearing as he does the same Christian name. The next in the row has the following inscription, quaintly abbreviated:

> "THOM. AND ELIZ. SON AND
> DAUGHTER OF THOM AND ELIZ
> COLBRAN. HE DIED
> 17 NOV. 1771 AGED
> 1 YEAR 8 MONTHS AND SHE DIED
> 16 OCT. 1774 AGED
> 1 YEAR AND 3 MONTHS"

These two children, named after their parents, died as infants. A third, who also died before his parents, is remembered on yet another tombstone:

> "WILLIAM SON OF THOMAS
> AND ELIZA COLBRAN HE
> DIED JAN. 2 1808
> AGED 32 YEARS"

It is not known if any other children outlived them.

Another headstone, a few yards eastwards of this row of five Colbrans, is graven thus:

> "IN
> MEMORY OF
> JOHN CATT
> For upwards of 30 years a schoolmaster
> In this Parish
> He died the 3rd day of July 1831
> Aged 65 years
> Also of
> MARY CATT
> wife of the above
> who died the 18th day of Feb. 1852
> aged 63 years"

Born in 1760 when Thomas Colbran was 23, John Catt must have received all his education from him, and himself became a teacher before his master died. It is a very strange occurrence that this statement on his gravestone is the only record of this schoolmaster in the village school. His son, John Catt, the builder, lies with his wife, Catherine, not close beside him, but some few yards away. His grandson, John Robert Catt, with his wife Kate, again lies separated by a few yards.

The third teacher's gravestone stands close against the southerly hedge of the churchyard, bordering Castlemans, and not far away from the road. At the top of the stone is carved a flying angel with the words "REST WEARY TRAVELLER" above it. Below the angel is engraved the following:

"In affectionate
Remembrance of
SUSAN MARTIN
who kept the Infants' School in this Parish
for upwards of 30 years
died November 29th 1881
aged 75 years
This stone was erected by voluntary
subscriptions from those who knew and
Valued her Great Services as Nurse and
Friend in the Hour of Sickness
Also
JOHN MARTIN
husband of the above
who died . . . 25th 1880
Aged 80 years
'Blessed are those servants of the Lord
............................cometh.' "

So Susan Martin was nurse as well as teacher of the infants. Was she, perhaps, the one who kept the little slate-roofed school up Church Hill on the west side of the road, whose husband was blind? (Chapter 28). It is told that she had to go out sometimes leaving him in charge to control the children with a very long stick which would reach out to find them. Why should she have to go out in school hours but for the reason that she was called to the sick?

Among the newer graves is one surrounded by a granite curb which bears along one side the following inscription:
"CHRISTINE MARY GIBBS DIED 30th AUG. 1944
AGED 56 YEARS"
and along the other:
"FOR 37 YEARS A DEVOTED TEACHER IN
SEDLESCOMBE SCHOOLS"
This was 'our beloved Miss Gibbs', remembered today by many whom she taught. Teaching in the school from the age of 19 she spent her whole career in Sedlescombe and became deeply involved

in all aspects of life in the village of her adoption. She had lost the man she loved in World War I.

Of all the forty-one Rectors of Sedlescombe, how many died in the village? The tomb of James Ingram (1746-1756) which E. A. W. Dunkin in 1883 described as being inside the church in the south-east corner, now stands outside in the churchyard close to the south porch. It had to be removed when alterations were being made and the organ was installed.

John Pratt lies in the centre of the churchyard with the graves of his large family of sons, daughters, grandchildren, sisters and brother-in-law clustered around him, surrounded by bushes of rhododendrons and box, all enclosed by iron railings until these were removed in 1942 to aid the war effort. His successor, Edward Owen (1861-1870) lies not far off; and John Warner (1870-1901), too, with his wife and father, is close by. The grave of William Noble (1927-1950) is in the new part of the churchyard, taken in from the Precious field in 1948. In the same grave lie his wife, Elizabeth, and the ashes of his daughter, Patience. He once said that priests are buried facing west, the opposite way from their parishioners, so that they may watch over their flock in death as in life.

The ages of the named dead are recorded more often than not on the tombstone. Of those who reached the age of 90, four stand out clearly:

"JAMES PANKHURST
who died in 1865 aged 93
and
ESTHER HIS WIFE
aged 85"

Born in 1772, he may well have been the son of the Pankhurst who was one of the first fourteen children who attended the village school when it was newly opened in 1748.

"GEORGE HOOK
who died in 1919
aged 93

was of the family of wheelwrights who shortly after that date emigrated to Australia.

"EDWARD BLUNDELL (Chapter 40)
who died in 1960
aged 91"

and "Bangy" (Chapter 50):

"SPENCER SMITH
WHO DIED IN 1959
AGED 96"

Close to the path on the north side of the church stands a grave with the following inscription:

"EDWARD HONEYSTREET
BORN AT SEDLESCOMBE STREAM in the parish of Whatlington 1787 and died there 1867 aged 80.

The family of Thomas D'Oyly in whose service he spent more than half his life desire here to record their respect and esteem for their old and valued servant."

Thomas D'Oyley, Esq., Sergeant-at-Law, lived in "one of the best residences in the one street in Rottingdean."[1]

Today, it is held that to serve is to demean oneself; but in the past, men of all classes "served" in their chosen method of earning a living; and here lies one among thousands who did so, gaining rather than losing in dignity and worth. One day it will become again an honourable condition to serve. Durhamford was Stream Farm, in the will of John Pratt, separated into five cottages, so one would guess that this, or next door at Spilstead Cottages (the old Poorhouse) was where Edward Honeystreet was born and returned so many years later.

Many are the young children and infants whose deaths are sadly recorded, very frequently on the tombstones of their parents, but there are a few who have memorial stones of their own. In the northwest of the churchyard is one such with the figure of an angel standing above it. On her skirts is carved a ribbon on which is the word BABY. The inscription below the angel reads:

"IN LOVING MEMORY
OF
GEORGINA EILEEN LOUISE
THOMAS
Aged 1 year and 8 months
SADLY MISSED"

---

[1] Horsfield.

She was the little daughter of Charlie Thomas, haulage contractor and coal merchant, who lived in turn at The Presbytery, Pump House and the "Coach and Horses", and he sorrowed for her for the rest of his life.

Not far away another inscription records:

"IN
LOVING MEMORY OF
Geoffrey Gammon
'LITTLE GEOFF'
died 23 Nov. 1936
aged 17 months"

He was one of the first to be known as a 'blue baby' through a fatal defect in the heart. His sister, Sheila, was able to survive a similar defect, triumphantly surmounting the limitations it imposed upon her, gallantly ignoring them to the best of her ability. Their brother and his family still live in the village.

Noticeable among all the stones which are so varied in shape and size stand six of identical form; those which were set up by the War Graves Commission. Two of these are of the First World War:

"PRIVATE F. C. BRYANT N.Z: Canterbury Regt. 20th Nov. 1918
A loving Husband and Son
Gone but not forgotten"

So he died nine days after the fighting had ceased.

"JOHN PARKER Capt. R.F.A. 1918"

was the son of Parker of Glebe Cottage and brother of Geoffrey of the Royal Navy, commemorated by a brass inside the church. Close beside John Parker lies his nephew:

"Sub Lieutenant G. W. ELTON R.N.V.R.
H.M.M.T.B. 30
7th June 1942"

Three other stones commemorate in turn:

"Aircraftsman J. P. SMITH R.A.F. 9th May 1942"
"H. E. READ R.A.F. 25. 1941"

both with the insignia of the R.A.F. engraved above; and

"Gunner H. SHAMBROOK R.A. 7th Aug. 1942 20"

with the insignia of the Royal Artillery.

A seat is placed beside the path at the back of the church, a pleasant place to rest the limbs and loiter, looking east to Jacob's wicket gate and across the valley to Killigan Wood sloping up from the Strawberry Fields. A plaque on the seat states:

"In Memoriam
Sir John Anderson Thorne
1888-1964"

commemorating him who spent many quiet hours in the churchyard seeking out the inscriptions on old graves and contemplating, no doubt, mortality. No morbid exercise this but a most necessary part of life, for it is the consciousness of death which sharpens the commonplace to beauty and the joy of daily living. Do we not remember how in the war years the real closeness of the threat of death enriched the very act of living? It is the joy of peril, too, that sets the adventurer climbing or sailing or seeking speed.

Beside the seat are two of the oldest graves; the inscription on one has been all but effaced by time, leaving only the name "Ann daughter of Edward" legible. The other can still be deciphered, though with difficulty, to bear the legend:

"Abraham Bodle
who departed
this Life Dec. Ye
..................... 1753
Aged 64"

"Abraham Bodle's new house" figures several times in records and his unusual name is not easily forgotten (Chapter 35).

So one can sit on the seat and ponder on the lives of all those who have over the centuries lived in our houses and walked our lanes and field paths; and not least over those who dug the graves. Only the last two grave-diggers are still remembered; Dick Guy and James Dengate.

Dick, son of Alfred Guy, gamekeeper to the Combes, worked as a carter for Mr. Mewburn at Great Sanders and lived at Compasses Cottages, so he had the best part of a mile to walk to the church. He had a good singing voice and always led the choir. Once when he had opened a grave in which there was to be a burial on the following day, a storm developed in the evening after darkness had fallen and the rain came down in sheets. Listening to it hour after hour, he began to be more and more concerned that the sides of the grave would cave in, till at last nothing would serve but to leave his fireside and hurry along to the churchyard and look. Arrived there he got down into the grave and set it to rights as best he could. Hearing footsteps coming by on the path to Jacob's gate and recognising them as belonging to Mr. Jones, the farmer of Austford, he put his head up out of the grave and asked him the time. The farmer let out a yell and ran for his life. Dick went after him, chasing him to the corner of Killigan Wood, where he gave up. The following evening Dick went down to the Queen's Head and there was Farmer Jones telling the story: "You won't believe me but old . . . got up out of his grave last night and chased me . . ." "Don't be silly," laughed Dick, " 'Twas me and the more I hollered the more you run!" Later, with his wife and young son, Tom, he moved to Rose Cottages, then called Broom Cottages. Down at the bottom was the sewage pit. One day Tom said to a friend, "Let's have a race", and away they went. Tom knew when to stop but his friend did not! Tom was put to bed in disgrace but it was the night of the Confirmation and, when all the people went by together with the Bishop, there was young Tom Guy waving to them from the roof of the cottage, clad in nakedness.

After Dick Guy gave up, James Dengate took over. For some months there had been no grave-digger. James' eldest son, Jim, had died as the result of the War in far-away India and he was broken-hearted. It was in an effort to succour him that the Rector, Mr. Percival, suggested he should assist him now and again. It was not long before James took over the job of grave-digger and sexton. He was also builder and undertaker. Continuing for over thirty years he was the last grave-digger in the village. Thereafter undertakers provided their own. He died in 1962 aged 89, his thatch of black hair still barely streaked with grey.

One last stone among all the others is worth quoting:
"In Memory of Mary
Wife of John Smith
of Warbleton who
dying left her with
three small Daugh
who she Carefully and
Proudly Brought up
She lived a Widow 30
Years and died April 26
1752 Aged 68 years"

From the fading lettering emerges the vanished memory of this ordinary villager with the more than ordinary name, Mary Smith, born in the reign of James II, wife of John Smith. Over-proud and over-careful she may have been, but here she is, transformed by this miniature biography into the living person that she was, out of the finality of time.

# BIBLIOGRAPHY AND SOURCES

|  | Abbreviations |
|---|---|
| Accounts of the Cellarers of Battle Abbey 1275-1513. Searle and Ross. | S.R.S. 65 |
| A History of Hastings Castle. Dawson, 1909. | Dawson |
| Anglo-Saxon Chronicle. | A/S Chr. |
| Articles in Sedlescombe Parish Magazine, 1950-53. Sir John Thorne. | Thorne |
| A Rental Gathered out of the Manor of Bricklehurst remaid 1609. E.S.R.O. Frewen 520. II. | Br. 1609 |
| Battle Abbey Survey 1569. Tiltonsbath in the Parish of Sedlescombe. E.S.R.O. Battle MS/42. | B.A.S. 1569 |
| Battle of Hastings. Lemmon. | Lemmon |
| Boundaries of certain lands in Sedlescombe holden of the Manor of Brickelhurst 35 Hen. VIII. E.S.R.O. Frewen 520 ii. | Br. 1543 |
| Battle Abbey Survey of the Borough of Uckham. E.S.R.O. trans. A. Moore. Frewen. 520. | B.A.S. 1433 |
| Brede. Edmund Austen. | Austen |
| Beach House and Spilsted. MS. Sir John Thorne. | Thorne |
| Carmen de Haestingae Proelio. Guy of Amiens. Edited Morton and Muntz. | |
| Catalogue of the Rents and Muniments of Battle Abbey. Thorpe. 1835. | Thorpe |
| Chronicle of Battle Abbey. | Chr. B.A. |
| Church Bells of Sussex. A. Daniel-Tyssen. | D-Tyssen |
| Courts of the Frank Pledge. | S.R.S. 37 |
| Domesday Book. Edited for the S.A.S. 1886. | S.R.S. 65 |
| East Sussex Record Office at Lewes. | E.S.R.O. |
| East Sussex Churches. MS. Notebook. E. H. W. Dunkin. E.S.R.O. | Dunkin |
| Encyclopaedia Britannica. 11th edition. | Enc. Brit. |
| English Hops. A. H. Burgess, D.Sc.(Lon.), pub. Leonard Hill, 1964. | Burgess |
| English Villages and Hamlets. Humphrey Pakington. | Pakington |
| Hastings & St. Leonards Observer. | H. & St. L. Obs. |
| Hastings & St. Leonards Waterworks, 1830-1970. G. D. Coleman. | Coleman |
| History of the Norman Conquest. E. A. Freeman. Clarendon Press. | Freeman |
| History of Sussex. Mark Antony Lower. | Lower |
| History of the County of Sussex. Horsfield, 1835. | Horsfield |
| Hops. George Clinch. McCorquodale & Co., 1919. | Clinch |
| Local Historian's Encyclopaedia. John Richardson. | L. Hist. Enc. |
| Lordship and Community. Battle Abbey and its Banlieu. 1066-1538. Elinor Searle 1974. | Searle |

## BIBLIOGRAPHY AND SOURCES

| | |
|---|---|
| Parish Records of Sedlescombe. E.S.R.O. | Sed. P.R. |
| Place Names of Sussex. Mawer and Stenton. | Pl. N. of Sx. |
| Rape of Hastings Architectural Survey: Timber-framed Houses. David Martin. | R.O.H.A.S. |
| Roman de Rou. Wace, Canon of Bayeux. | Wace |
| Roman Ways in the Weald. I. Margary. | Margary |
| Sedlescombe Tithe Map 1841. The Property of the Incumbent, the Rev. D. Prince. | T. Map |
| Survey of the Manor of Robertsbridge, 1568-86. S.R.S. Vol. 47. | S.R.S. 47 |
| Sussex Archaeological Collection Volumes. | S.A.C. |
| Sussex Bells and Belfries. G. P. Elphick, 1970. | Elphick |
| Sussex Manors in the Feet of Fines 1509-1883. Arr. E. H. W. Dunkin. | Dunkin |
| Sussex County Magazine. | S.C.M. |
| Sussex Express. | Sus. Ex. |
| Social History of England. Trevelyan. | Trevelyan |
| Sussex in the Great Civil War 1642-1660. Sir C. Thomas Stanford 1910. | Stanford |
| Sussex Record Society Volumes. | S.R.S. |
| Sussex Weekly Advertiser. | S.W.A. |
| Tax for the Sedlescombe Borough 1611. E.S.R.O. Frewen MS. 520. | Tax 1611 |
| The Golden Warrior. Hope Muntz. | |
| The Knight and the Umbrella. Ian Anstruther. | |
| The Norman Conquest. D. Whitelock & Others. 1966. | |
| Transactions of Battle and District Historical Society. | B.H.S. Trans. |
| Victoria County History of Sussex. | V.C.H. |
| Visitation of Sussex 1530-1630. Harleian Society. Bannerman 1905. | |
| Wealden Iron. Straker. | Wealden Iron |

# INDEX

## A

Abbey:
  Token: 24
  Shoots: 71
Abbots of Battle: 43, 44, 60-65, 79, 84, 134, 224
  Hamo: 133
  John Hammond: 64
  John de Whatlington: 63, 65, 150
  Ralph: 62
  Walter de Luci: 63
Abbots of Robertsbridge: 84, 145, 151
Abel: 319-321
Act of Uniformity: 193
Adamsons: 290, 328, 462, 485
  William Rushton: 89, 147, 248, 292
  Mrs.: 294
Adeane:
  Admiral: 334
  Lady Edith: 334
  Henry Augustus: 334, 461
  Victoria (Bigge): 334
Sir Michael (Lord Adeane): 334
Ades: 157, 320, 488
  Arthur: 395
  Edward: 126, 351, 404
  Edward (2): 156, 441
  Mary: 379, 405
  Moses: 167, 181
  Mr. Ades (Junior): 181
  Spencer: 321
  Thomas: 156
Aella: 35, 97
  and his sons, Cymen, Wlencing and Cissa: 35

Alchin:
  Edmund Linton: 292, 365, 372, 396, 397, 448
  Mary: 396, 397
Alder Shaw: 22, 24
Alderton, Henry: 318, 322
Aldridge:
  Mrs.: 362, 380, 387, 389
Alehouses: 204, 205
Alfred The Great: 27, 35
Alured de St. Martin: 74, 83, 87
  his brother, Geoffrey: 87
Amyot:
  John: 151
Amyot's Wood: 151
Anderida (Andreadsweald) see also Pevensey
  Forest of: 20, 21, 138, 418
  Fort of: 26, 35
Anglo-Saxon Chronicle: 35, 46, 49, 80
Anscitel: 82, 87
Anstruther, Ian:
  The Knight and the umbrella: 309
Apprentices: 169-174
Archdeacon's Court: 104, 183, 193, 249
Archer:
  John, cobbler: 118, 374
Archer's: 374, 375, 376, 401
Armada: 31, 140-142, 459, 471
Ashburnham:
  John: 153, 256
  Sir William: 339
Ashdown:
  Nicholas: 152, 431
Ashdown Cottage: 431, 486

*

Ashton: 430
Lord of Hyde: 89, 189, 248
　his daughter: Hon. Mrs.
　Whistler: 89
Asselton House: 115-131, 142, 152, 210, 327, 347, 369
Austen:
　of Brede: 140, 143, 419
Austford (Horsford, Alkysford): 145, 150-152, 197, 238, 246-249, 465, 495
Austford House (the other Austford): 152, 225, 246, 248, 249, 472
Avann (Van): 445
　Johanna: 400
　Laurence: 69, 224
　Thomas: 400
　Widow Van: 226
　William Van: 226
Avory: 211, 487
　Edward: 162
　Laurence: 159-162, 487
　Lucy (see Farnden)
　Thomas: 149, 172, 209, 211, 222, 228, 246
　Thomas's wife: 225

B

"Baby Mary": 400, 401
Badlands: 240, 422
Bake-oven: 118, 314, 364
Baker:
　George: 222, 250
　Rev. George: 163, 193, 250
　Isaac 1: 149, 404
　　　2: 404
　Jo: 29, 30, 250
　John: 163, 177, 256
　Nelson, carrier: 32, 386
　Nicholas: 171
　Ruth (see Farnden)
　Samuel: 89
　Stephen: 250
Baker's: 153
Bakery (see Gregory)

Balcombe:
　Cottages (see Woodman's): 406
　Forge (see Forge): 347, 406
　Green: 291, 346, 347, 403, 406
　House: 406
　Lane: 34
Baldslow:
　Place: 33, 307, 311, 328, 332
　Woods: 338, 339
Ball:
　William (blacksmith): 130, 348, 349, 351
Ballard: 376
Barber:
　Edward: 369
　John (farmer): 392
　　(schoolmaster): 287
Barber's Field: 56, 392
Barbican House:
　Museum: 11, 56, 59
Barges: 15, 16, 263, 303
Barns:
　Henry: 29, 172, 173, 185, 225, 226, 227, 236
Barnsley:
　Rev. George: 105, 106, 188, 196, 197, 268, 282, 284, 298
Barrack Cottage: 93, 116, 124, 125-127, 142, 264, 303, 361, 441, 443, 461
Barry:
　Rev. Philip: 199, 200
Bartelot:
　Richard: 44
　Woods: 243
Barton:
　Rev. Edward: 192, 193, 211
Basok:
　Adam: 91
　feu of: 92, 98
　John: 92
　Laurence: 92
　Milisent: 91
　Robert: 62, 65, 91, 92, 94
　Wysse or Ysse: 44
Bates:
　William: 249, 250

Bathurst (Botehurst): 70
  Castle: 309
  John: 44
  Woods: 25, 65, 307, 309, 311, 422

Battle Abbey: 43, 60-72, 79, 83, 87, 91, 98, 114, 118, 224, 229, 300, 316, 332, 357
  Abbots of (see Abbots)
  Chronicles of: 53, 60
  Courts of: 69, 77, 129-132, 231
  Estate: 86, 94, 129, 130, 275, 350, 383, 418, 426
  Leuga: 60-64, 72, 75
  Liberties of: 75
  Manor of: 92, 132, 229-241
  Monks of: 94, 130, 357
  Survey of (BAS): 69, 129, 150, 153, 166, 224, 225, 242, 252, 312, 315, 357
  Tannery: 360

Battle: 297, 306, 413
  Church: 60, 303
  Fair: 45
  Great Wood: 18, 275, 277, 309
  Market: 212, 358
  Mount Street: 17
  Rural District of: 53
  Town: 64, 279

Battle Barn Farm: 418, 422, 423, 468

Battle Historical Society: 22, 54
  Museum of: 11, 24, 25, 59, 140
  Transactions of: 22, 275, 301, 311, 318, 416

Battle View: 380-382, 405

Bayeux Tapestry: 46-55

Beanford: 66, 68, 69, 350, 422, 433

Beating the Bounds: 190, 191, 192, 198, 464-467

Beauport Park: 11, 18, 25, 31, 307, 316, 331, 337-339, 475

Beckley:
  Forge (see Forge)
  Furnace: 28, 161

Beech (Beach, Beche): 145, 149, 150, 197, 198, 227, 231, 256
  John de Beche: 214
  Richard Beche: 27, 44, 134, 135, 214
  Robert Beche: 214
  Simon Beche: 214
  Thomas Beche: 42, 150, 224
Beech:
  Farm-house: 67, 149, 221, 263, 449, 466, 469
  House: 24, 28, 171, 209, 211, 214-217, 277
  Wood: 22, 466

Beggar's Farm (see Lower Jacobs)

Bellatkins (Strawberry Hill Farm): 97, 142, 209, 240, 246-248

Benskins (Benskynne): 188
  Mary: 188

Bigg:
  George (tanner): 28, 172
Bishop (Bisshoppe, etc.): 110, 141, 145-152, 193, 198, 208, 245, 248, 267, 329, 472, 488
  Alexander and William (tanners): 44, 145, 147, 151
  Alexander and Thomas: 145
  George: 146, 283, 312
  George of Hurst: 146, 147
  Elizabeth: 104, 126, 223
  Frank: 396
  Henry Mallory: 146, 148, 197, 260, 278, 282-285, 287
  James: 146
  his sons, John, George and James: 146, 147
  John (1528) of Castlemans and the Tanhouse: 145
  John of Austford: 183
  John: 85, 144, 146, 152, 233, 242
  Rev. John: 146, 188, 197
  Laurence: 85
  Miss Fanny: 405
  Mary: 145, 249
  Minnie: 445
  Richard (1528) of the Herst and Beche: 145, 425
  Richard: 29, 69, 85, 101, 102, 126, 150, 152, 171, 227, 238

Bishop (Bisshoppe, etc.)—cont.
  Richard the Innkeeper: 441
  Robert: 367
  Simon: 44, 145
  Thomas (1415): 145
  Thankful: 188, 312
  William of Hurst: 146, 238, 287
  William of Great Sanders: 145, 146
    his daughter Mary: 146
  William: 29, 44, 45, 86, 101-104, 126, 145, 147, 209, 218, 245-248
  William "the younger": 229, 277
  William, the fellmonger: 358
Black Bartholomew: 194
Black brooks: 17, 31, 32, 66, 69, 86, 337, 422, 486
Black Death: 63, 65
Blacklands: 69, 91, 125, 129, 223, 224, 225, 238
  Council houses: 388, 446
  Farm: 332
Blacksmith: 11, 212, 344-354, 403, 404
Bloomeries: 11, 20, 21, 22, 24, 25, 89
Blundell:
  Edward: 444, 491
Bodiam: 39, 40, 42, 62, 82, 97, 233
  Castle: 42, 72
  Harbour: 21
Bodle:
  Abraham: 95, 188, 393, 395, 494
  Mercy: 393
Book of Common Prayer: 193, 194, 195
Botting:
  Jeremiah: 219, 220, 221
The Bowlings (Bowlands): 17, 62, 63, 66, 67, 229, 232, 468, 477
  Rough: 67
  Smooth: 67
Boxall:
  Bill: 363, 469
  Edgar: 364, 394, 467, 469
  Harry: 462, 474
  Mrs.: 363, 469
  Mr.: 363

Boys:
  Charlotte: 232
  John: 232,
  William: 231
Brabazon: (see also Sharpe & Combe): 482
  Anne (see Combe)
  Hercules (H.B.B.): 108-111, 130-132, 167, 244, 324-332, 364, 380, 382, 406, 419, 422
  William: 324, 325
  Sir William: 324
  Mrs. Brabazon Combe (see Combe)
Bras:
  Thomas of Ewhurst: 44
  Martyn Brasses: 86
Brasses Farm: 44, 86
Brede: 305, 319, 320, 335
  Barn Farm (Field Farm): 66, 267, 323, 333, 467
  Bridge: 12, 14, 16, 18
  Estuary: 12, 13, 15
  Forge (see Westfield)
  Furnace: 14, 15, 28, 30, 154, 155, 156, 158, 304, 335, 471
  Harbour: 21, 138
  High (Eye or Hithe): 85, 86
  Powdermill: 14, 15
  Pumping Station: 16-18
  River: 9, 14, 15, 17, 18, 21, 28, 36, 65, 82, 138, 140, 263, 275, 288, 300, 323, 333, 357, 418, 464, 471
  Valley: 21, 138, 476
  Village: 79, 85, 116, 139, 165
  Wharf: 140
Brede Lane: 297
  Cottages: 179, 327
    Ivy Cottage and Springfield: 264, 267, 327, 410
Brickyard: 244, 384
  Cottages: 382 (see also Littlehurst)
Bricklehurst, Manor of: 118, 119, 391, 400
Brickwall: 17, 102, 158-168, 223, 224, 267
  Farm: 332, 392, 406, 415

Bridge Garage: 117, 123, 354, 355, 365
Brigden:
  John: 251
  Widow: 251
Brigdens: 251-253
Broad Oak: 40, 85, 86
Broke (or Brook):
  William: 129
Brookfield: 348-358
Brook Lodge: 18, 305, 335, 475, 477
The Brooks: 16, 17, 19, 21, 63, 225, 249, 277, 281, 301, 306, 433, 452
Broom Cottage (see Rose Cottages)
Brown, Mr. and Mrs. (see also Isolation Hospital): 336
Browne:
  Sir Anthony: 64, 66, 229
  (Lord Montague): 300
  Rev. Barry: 198, 383, 468
  John, minister: 160, 192, 256
  John: 27, 30, 139, 148, 149, 243
  John, gun-founder: 256-258
  Margaret: 256
  Richard: 256
  Robert: 150
  Thomas: 256
Browne-Wright:
  Rev. Francis: 188, 283, 284
Buckhurst Farm: 314, 475
Bucknill (see Pratts)
Budgeon, Richard: 149, 275-280
Bungalow, The: 406, 407
Burden, George (charcoal burner): 173, 415
Burges (see also Lamb):
  Sir James: 308
Burglar:
  Thurston: 388, 389
Burnt House: 228
  Meadows: 227, 231, 232, 233, 235
Burrell Manuscripts: 159
Burton: 339
  Decimus: 110, 323, 324, 339
  James: 110, 323, 337, 339
Burwash: 196
Bushby: 318, 319, 321

Butler:
  Cordelia: 221, 398
  Edward: 166, 375
  Jane: 398
  Philip: 221, 321, 372, 378, 398
  Thankful: 121, 187, 398
  Thomas, cordwainer: 167, 375
Button (see Millers and Byners):
  William: 350
Buxted: 137
Byner: 488
  Charles: 132
  James 1: 32, 107, 109, 238-242, 272, 464, 467
  James 2: 131
  Thomas: 395
Byner's Stores: 131, 372, 379, 395

C

Cade:
  Jack: 77, 84, 134-136, 214
  Revolt: 27, 134-136
Cain:
  Thomas: 129
  Ann: 129
Caldbec Hill: 48, 54
California:
  Huntingdon University: 93
Camden: 137, 138, 142
Carpenter:
  Richard (glover): 172, 379
Carpenters: 116, 208, 209, 212, 380, 381, 382
  John Chapman: 379, 394
  Joseph Elridge: 379, 381
  Edwin Eldridge: 381
  John Mills: 166, 379
  Thomas Reed: 379
  Robert Southerden
  William Weston: 379
Carpenter's Barn: 314, 316
Carrick:
  Carlos: 384, 385, 445
  Charlie: 384
  Frank: 290
  George: 444
  Miss: 445
  Thomas: 445
  "Old Carrick": 384, 385

Carrier: 32, 373, 386, 407
"Carters" (see Manor Cottages):
Carter:
  Fred: 376
  Joseph: 100
Castlemans: 28, 44, 101, 149, 153, 197, 209, 211, 221, 222, 231, 244, 246, 277, 386, 406, 423-425, 433, 448, 469, 487
  Farm: 226, 384
  Oak: 31, 149, 277
  Triangle: 31, 111
  Little: 68, 90, 142, 145-149, 424
  John (tithingman): 44, 148, 149
Catt: 488
  John (builder): 16, 32, 108, 109, 112, 126, 130, 288, 332, 379, 380, 382, 396-8, 445
  John (schoolmaster): 287, 489
  Kate: 488
  Mary: 489
  Nicholas: 312
  Robert: 396
Cattle: 340, 341
Catts Green Farm: 86
Cavaliers: 160, 256-259
Cellar: 116, 335
Cesse (Sesse): 184, 208-209; 236
Chambers, E. H.: 147, 471
Chapel:
  Hill: 31, 342, 358, 410, 480
  Congregational: 445-446
  Wesleyan: 127, 443-445
Charcoal:
  Burners: 11, 139, 173, 413, 414, 415
  Burning: 26, 301, 357, 413-414, 416
Cherrytree Cottages: 296, 383, 405, 441, 461
Chestnut Tree Cottage: 376, 400, 401
Chestnut trees: 104, 210, 328
Chevallier, Mr.: 53, 54
Chevalier's Farm (see Horsmans)
Chichester (see also Lord of the Rape):
  Earl of: 381, 403
Chitcombe: 11, 18, 40, 42, 370
  furnace: 28

Chittlebirch: 197, 425-429, 465
  House: 142, 151
  Oast: 430
Chown, Eileen: 24
Church lands: 388, 406
Church of England's Inebriate Society: 157
Church: 81, 92, 97-144, 162, 165, 185, 186, 208
  Bells: 88, 99, 100, 184, 210, 475
  Font: 98, 99, 109
  Gallery: 103
  "Re-edification of": 102, 103, 192
  Spire: 109
  Tower: 98, 101
  Communion table: 105, 106, 185, 186
Church of St. Mary-in-the Castle, Hastings: 73, 82
Church Hill: 33, 34, 386, 387, 389
  Cottages: 407, 408, 424, 490
Church lands: 424, 469
Churchwardens: 183-186, 204, 208-209, 236, 251-252
  Accounts: 174, 183, 208, 211, 230, 243, 249, 252, 347
  Assessments: 103, 188, 241
  and Overseers: 169, 174-179, 188, 204, 238, 242, 282
Churchyard: 108, 112, 121, 124, 151, 254, 263, 268, 328, 487-496
  fence: 213, 235
Cinderbury (Sinder Burroughs): 90, 150, 227
Civil War: 30, 139, 146, 155, 255
Claremont School (see Baldslow Place)
Clarke:
  Anna: 193, 211, 249, 251, 377
  John: 249
  Robert (miller): 249
  Thomas: 249
  Will (miller): 193, 249, 377
Claytons: 348, 365
Cleveland, Duchess of: 130
  Duke: 304
Cloke:
  Aaron: 378
  Moses: 378

Clove-Ox (see Lavix)
Coaches: 31, 32, 340, 341, 346, 442
  Mail coaches: 371
Coach and Horses: 16, 31, 123, 124, 272, 355, 356, 360
  (and King's Head): 441, 442, 443, 453, 460
Cobbett, William: 122, 317-323, 355, 419
Cobbett's Political Register: 322
Cobbler: 212, 358
  Archer: 375, 376
  Ballard: 376
  Fred Carter: 376
  Huckens: 375
  Huckstep: 375
Coins (see also Roman):
  of Edward the Confessor: 56-59, 392
Colbran:
  Elizabeth: 488
  William: 489
  Thomas 1: 121, 149, 197, 245, 285-287, 488
  Thomas 2: 488
Coldharbour: 14
Coleman:
  Stephen: 95
  William: 319
  Widow: 175
Collier (Colyer) (see Charcoal burning):
Collins:
  Thomas of Brightling: 161
  Sir William (Baptist): 268-269
  William: 89
Collywishe: 129, 225
Combe (see also Brabazon): 324-336, 350, 452, 468, 480, 482, 485, 488, 494
  Boyce: 327-330, 461, 464
  Boyce Harvey: 56, 108, 110, 324, 327, 329
  Harvey, "The Captain": 111, 132, 213, 327-332, 374, 387
  Harvey, T., the Major: 132, 327, 330, 365, 419, 423, 464
  Harry (von Roemer): 327
  Mary (von Roemer): 327

Combe—cont.
  Miss Eileen (Barber): 331, 399, 476
  Mrs. Brabazon (Florence Amy): 14, 99, 132, 329-331, 364, 365, 455, 468
Combe:
  Cottage: 124
  Wood: 10, 24, 145, 245, 256
Compasses: 21, 494
  Inn: 22, 425
  Lane: 24, 31, 342, 425
Coneybury Field: 228, 236, 249
Constables: 204, 236
  Accounts: 185, 236
Conster Manor: 164
Cook:
  Ann: 269
  Henry: 381
  Mary (Mercer): 175, 269
  Samuel: 70, 180, 321
  William (cordwainer): 167, 177, 238, 269, 387
  William (grocer): 444
Cooper:
  Ashley: 356, 373
  Fred: 373, 445
  Ivy: 373
  William (shoemaker): 166
Copyholds: 65, 70, 232, 233, 241, 391
Corn-mill: 15, 114
Corps, Peter: 484
Cottage, The: 126, 331, 397-400
Cottage Gardening Class: 292-295
Court:
  Baron: 447
  Hundred: 41, 43
  Leat: 73, 75-78, 134, 439
  of Frank Pledge: 41, 42, 44, 45, 75
Craftsmen: 345-356
Crazy Lane: 31, 68, 69, 410, 411, 480
Creasey:
  Henry: 209, 240, 241
Cricket: 451
  Club: 292
  Pitch: 451-452

Cripps Corner: 21, 22, 31, 77, 85 86, 88, 89, 151, 338, 342, 378, 386, 426, 465, 471
Crips:
  Walter: 83
Crisford: 488
  Harriet: 394
  John: 42, 177, 221, 225, 321, 397
  Martha: 221
  Mr.: 180-181
  Philadelphia: 177, 397
  Spencer: 149, 221, 244, 384, 394, 406-407
  Stephen: 177
Cromwell: 30, 146, 193, 256-258
Crouch:
  John Pollard: 69, 70, 71
Croucher (Crouchers): 150
Crowham Manor: 157, 163, 287
Crowhurst: 39, 275
Crown-post: 68
Cumming:
  John: 424, 425
  Margaret: 425
Curwen, Dr.: 9

D
Dallaways:
  family: 68, 90, 149, 332, 464
  Sergeant: 388
Dame schools: 298, 299
Danes: 26
"Darbies": 284, 286
Darby of Footlands: 85, 86, 150, 173, 209, 211
  Elizabeth: 88
  John: 30, 88, 100, 119, 171, 225, 244, 246
  Laurence: 88
  Susannah: 88
  Thomas: 227
  William: 88, 89, 172
Darby and Joan Club: 458
Darvel or Derfold (see also Netherfield): 75, 77

Dawes: 213, 339
  James: 126, 358, 367
  John: 100, 118
  Thomas: 209, 218, 225, 241-244, 248
  William: 119, 120, 170-171
Dawson, Charles: 310
Declaration of Indulgence: 195
Deeping, Warwick: 135, 376
Dengate: 287, 298, 488
  Frank: 11, 382, 393
  Herbert: 131, 328, 370, 380, 382, 464
  James (miller): 108, 249, 377
  James (builder): 111, 298, 382-383, 410, 495
  John: 109
  Jim: 461, 495
  Mercy: 131, 370
  Naomi: 298
Dennet: 396, 403, 488
  James: 321, 403
  John: 321
  Thomas: 321, 347, 349
Diamon(d):
  Jasper: 238
  Joan "a traveller": 262
  "Master"
Dickie Bush (Dickerbosch): 316, 384
Ditch:
  Gertie: 370
  John: 370, 445
Ditch's: 368-370
Dissenters: 188
Dissolution of the Monasteries: 27, 64, 99, 169
  of Battle Abbey: 64, 99
  of Robertsbridge Abbey: 64, 99, 145
Doak:
  Sir James: 334
Dobell:
  Barnhem: 163
  Mary (Farnden): 163
  Sarah (Farnden): 162
  Walter: 162, 256-258

Doctors:
　Thomas Avory, "phisitian"
　Dr. Hollins: 400
　Dr. Johnson, 399
　Dr. Kendall: 399
　Dr. King: 400
　Stephen Robinson "surgeon of Selliscombe": 399, 404
　Dr. Wright: 400
Domesday Book: 46, 73, 77-82, 91, 97, 238, 430
Domons, Northiam: 167, 270, 323
Dorset (see also Sackville):
　Earl of: 156, 216
　Duke of: 156
Downton, John: 102, 149, 153, 156
　Joan (Sackville): 102, 153
Dury, The Rev. P.: 328, 402
Duke: 339
　John: 230
　William: 230, 282
Duncan:
　Norman: 370
　Mrs.: 370
　Sir Val: 370
Durhamford (see also Tanhouse): 62, 142, 145, 146, 149, 152, 197, 198, 209, 225, 241, 242, 244-246, 358, 408
Durrant:
　Miss: 291
Durud (see also Byner's and Miller's): 372
Dyke:
　(Elizabeth (see Farnden)
　Mary (Farnden): 105, 269
　Robert of Frant: 105, 160
　Robert of Yorkshire: 161
　Thomas: 161
　Thomas of Pembury: 161
　William: 160
　Rev. William: 161, 259

E

East Sussex:
　Record Office (ESRO): 120, 169, 184, 191, 222, 227, 240, 245, 246
　County Advertiser: 387

East View: 469, 474, 477, 481
Ebden's Hill: 32
　Mr. and Mrs.: 32, 311, 328
Edith Swan neck: 54, 56
Ednod, the Saxon: 82, 238
Edward the Confessor (see Kings):
Edwards, Arthur (brickmaker): 385
Eider (or Iden):
　Henry: 248, 249
Eldridge: 285, 287, 293, 312, 328, 402, 445, 488
　and Cruttenden: 374, 383, 445
　Bert: 312-313
　Edgar: 401
　Edwin (Edward): 381, 394
　Elizabeth: 360
　"Goody": 394
　Harriet: 381
　James: 123, 444, 464
　Joseph: 126, 381-382
　Justy (Mrs.): 410
　Madge: 312-313
　Richard (bricklayer): 394
　Richard (glazier): 395
　Rose: 312-313
　William: 126, 384, 441
　William (tanner): 360, 405
　William (carpenter): 443
Ellin's Acre: 395, 397
Elliott: 120, 358, 488
　Elizabeth: 121
　John, elder (tanner): 120, 121
　John, younger (tanner): 121
　John (tailor): 175
　Richard: 120, 277
　William: 121
Elliotts (see Manor Cottages)
Elphinstone:
　Sir Howard: 339
Elthorne: 407
Enclosures: 317
Etchingham Church: 165, 166, 194, 233
Ettenbury (Etonbury):
　Richard: 222
　John (a weaver)
Eu, Counts of: 41, 72-75, 91, 114
　Alicia (widow of 4th Count): 62
　Alicia (daughter of 6th Count): 74, 83, 94, 127

Eu, Counts of—cont.
  John (6th Count): 74
  Henry (5th Count): 74
  Henry (7th Count): 74, 83
  Ralf of Issoltun: 94, 127
  Robert (2nd Count): 72, 73, 75, 82
  William (3rd Count): 73
  William of Issoltun: 74, 94
Eustace of Boulogne: 54
Evelyn:
  John: 260
Everndon: 143, 193, 214-220, 228, 263, 488
  Ann: 248
  Elizabeth: 250
  Jane: 216, 218
  Joane: 171, 215
  John, senior: 95, 121, 171, 185, 214-218, 226, 229, 281
  John, junior: 29, 30, 218, 236, 251
  John: 215
  Martha (Plummer): 218, 229
  Mary: 216, 250
  Mr Everndon of Lewes: 216
  Walter, senior: 172, 173, 214, 216, 243
  Walter, junior: 250
  Account books: 214-216, 243
Ewhurst (Werste): 32, 40, 42, 43, 74, 82, 85, 151, 240, 278, 312, 322, 443, 444
  Place: 389
  Execution: 264, 319

F

Faggety Fields: 218
Farms: 420-432
Farm-labourers: 263
Farnden: 158-168, 208, 211, 487
  Elizabeth (Dyke) (Collins): 161, 225, 259
  Joan (Gott): 159, 161, 225
  Lucy Farnden: 159, 162, 164, 165, 225, 262
  Lucy (Fowle): 162, 164
  Martha (Polhill): 159, 161, 194, 225

Farnden—cont.
  Mary (Waters): 102, 143, 158-160, 225, 269
  Mary (Dyke): 159, 160
  Mary (Dobell): 162, 163
  Peter: 29, 102, 105, 143, 158-160, 166, 171, 192, 194, 209, 223, 225, 236, 259, 262, 267, 283, 424
  Peter (the nephew): 164, 165, 402
  Robert: 158, 165
  Ruth (Baker): 163, 256
  Samuel, son of Tobias: 166
  Samuel: 165
  Sarah (Dobell): 162, 256
  Tobias: 165
Farrow: 332
  Harold: 477
Farthing Cottage: 372
Fellies: 355
Fell-mongers: 123, 126, 358, 367
  yard: 358, 443
Felon Wood: 17, 65, 275
Field Farm (see Brede Barn):
Fir-tree Cottage: 364, 393, 394
Five Mile Act: 194
Flint:
  James of Kingston Manor: 269
  Miss Sarah (Tottie): 109, 264, 267-273, 334, 410, 440
  Robert: 130, 269, 374
Flints: 10
Flower Show: 290, 292, 294, 455, 456
Flying bombs: 297, 476
Fodilant (see Footlands)
Footlands (Foda's lands): 10, 18, 22, 24, 25, 36, 38, 82, 84, 87-89, 97, 142, 209, 233, 234, 240, 241, 249, 416, 462, 466, 467
Forge:
  at Ashburnham
    Beckley: 352
    Westfield: 14, 16, 138, 140
    Balcombe Green: 347
    the Bridge: 123, 349-356
    the Green: 347, 348, 375
  Cottages: 210, 347, 349, 367, 462
  House: 348, 349

Foster:
  Agnes: 226
  Goddard: 171, 216, 326
  wife of: 226
  Robert, J.P.: 204-206
Ffowle:
  Beatris: 171, 347
  Richard: 347
  Will: 30, 171, 184, 347
Fowles (of Wadhurst and Salehurst): 146
  Anne: 162
  Sir John
  Lucy (Farnden): 162
  Lucy: 162
  Robert 1: 162
  Robert 2: 162, 164
Freeland:
  Henry: 126, 359, 392, 443, 444
  James: 243
Freeman: 35
Frensham: 211, 235
  Elizabeth: 188, 229
  Henry: 103, 192, 226, 229, 250
  John: 175, 229, 230, 231
  Jo: 228
  Martha: 188
  Mary: 188, 230
  Samuel: 188, 229-231
  Thomas 1: 172, 175, 195, 209, 227-230
  Thomas 2: 230, 231
  Rev. Thomas: 192
  William: 42
  "Young": 175
Frewen: 214-218
  Charles: 339
  Mary: 216
  Stephen: 216
  Rev. Stephen: 282
  Rev. Thomas: 216
Friendly Society (Men's) (see May Day)
Fuller of Rosehill:
  Thomas: 143
Furnaces: 258, 357
  Ashburnham: 138, 141
  Beckley: 143
  Brede: 138-143, 256-258

Furnaces—cont.
  Panningbridge: 86, 139
  Robertsbridge: 139, 143
  Socknersh: 143
  Wealden: 28, 137-143
Fyrd:
  Select (see also House Carls): 47-55
  Ordinary: 47

G

Gale, Mr.: 484
Gallows of Horn: 85, 86, 151, 152, 471
Gammon:
  Alexander: 360
  Frank: 360
  Little Geoff: 493
  Thomas: 360
  S.H.: 103
Gasson:
  F.P.: 213
Geoffrey, the Canon: 73, 81
Gibbons:
  Alan: 250
  heirs of: 252
  widow: 175, 250
Gibbs, Miss: 296, 490
Gilds (see also Hurst): 227, 236
Gilmore:
  Jane: 303
  James: 15, 303
  Thomas: 15, 303
  William: 15, 300
Gilmore Harvey: 303
  William: 303
Glazier:
  Richard (carpenter): 172, 379
Glebe:
  Cottage: 111, 409, 462, 468
  lands: 409
Glorix (also Clove-ox. See Lavix)
Goatham Green: 18, 448
Goda, Countess: 80
Godman:
  Mrs.: 167, 354, 409
  Miss: 409
  Percy: 213, 226, 248, 250, 253

Golby:
  Cornelius: 188, 321
Goodman:
  Nicholas: 222, 252
  Thomas: 318, 319
Goodsell:
  James (cordwainer): 443
Goose-gate: 481
Gorselands: 167, 377, 383, 480
Gostling, Isaac: 197, 285
Gott:
  Joan (Farnden): 161
  Miss: 143
  Samuel: 161, 163, 164, 256
Gotways: 315, 316, 457
Grace:
  Dinah: 123, 124, 130, 369
  Frances: 121
  Henry: 122, 123, 126, 129, 130, 321, 339, 369, 488
  John: 122, 123, 369, 443
  Martha
  Thomas: 130
  William: 122, 124, 129, 130, 240, 369, 443, 488
Grant (see Grantham)
Grantham:
  Francis: 239
  James: 103
  Jo: 29, 30
  Thomas: 222, 225, 239, 240
  Willina (Paris): 225
Great charge: 103, 215
Great Sanders: 21 28, 30, 31, 77-97, 102, 142, 144-152, 233, 238, 277, 278, 292, 294, 332, 418, 449, 462, 470-473
Greens: 360, 361
Green View (see Forge House)
Gregory: 95, 200, 297, 364, 445, 462, 469
  Cecil: 240, 254, 365, 366
  Ivy: 240, 265
  Terry: 366
  Wallace: 350, 354, 364-366, 380
Gun Cottage: 210, 263, 277, 347, 403, 404

Gunpowder: 142, 300-306, 377 (see also Powdermills), 414, 457
  Explosion: 303, 305, 306
  Mill: 15
Gunns (Gounes):
  Florence: 242
  John: 241
Gunns, The Poorhouse: 178, 179, 235, 241
Guns: 141, 142, 257, 258
Gutsell (Gutsale), Elizabeth:
  James: 304, 322
  Widow: 251
Guy:
  Alfred: 494
  Dick: 495
  Tom: 495
Guy Fawkes: 456
  Bonfire: 441
  Bonfire boys: 456-458
  "Bonfire jumpers": 457
Gypsum: 301
Gypsum mines: 17, 469

H

Haddon:
  Major: 449, 450
Haesta: 37
Hall:
  Jesse (well-digger): 448
Hall-place: 76, 114-132, 152, 153, 241
Hammond: 65, 66
  Florence (Gunne): 66
  John: 66, 118, 300
  John, the Abbot: 66, 242
  Richard: 66
  Robert: 66, 241-242
Hancox (Handcocks): 14, 28, 97, 142, 149-158, 171, 227, 337, 338, 378, 404
  Mill: 227, 249, 250, 338, 364, 377
  John Handcocks: 153
Hare:
  Augustus: 326
Harold: 39, 46, 47-55, 58, 59, 61, 82
  Army of: 27, 47-55

Harriet House: 63, 122, 131, 368-371, 396, 448
Harrow Inn: 31, 337
Harte:
    "Ane": 171
    Constance: 171
    Joseph: 432
    Richard: 171
    William: 170
Harts Green: 21, 171
    Farm, 384, 432
Harvest: 456
    festival: 456
    feasts: 420, 456
Hastings: 207, 208, 265
    Castle: 41, 72, 73
    Corporation: 334
    Museum: 329
    Waterworks Department: 16
    and "St. Leonard's Observer": 330, 350, 464, 468
Hawkhurst Gang: 264, 265, 440
Heathfield: 133, 136
Henley: 305, 306
    John: 333
    Henry: 229, 333
    Sam: 333
    T.: 320
Henly's (see Jacobs): 333
Heriot: 63, 70, 86, 129, 130, 227, 233, 235, 242
Highfield: 221, 227, 236, 408, 448, 476
Hilder: 328, 339, 372, 373, 374
    T.R.: 354
    (of the Queen's Head): 454
Hindes: 241, 425-430, 465, 467, 479, 488
Hoar Apple-tree: 46, 48
Hogge, Ralph: 137, 140
Hole Farm: 166, 267, 270, 323, 324
Holmes: (the butcher): 33, 107, 118, 328, 366-368
    House: 107, 118, 366-368
Home Guard: 297, 474

Homestall: 56, 210, 263, 266, 386, 391-393, 460
Honeystreet:
    Edward: 243, 492
Hoo, Sir Thomas: 75
Hook: 444
    George: 356, 360, 444, 462, 491
    Raymond: 316, 384, 457
Hops: 16, 123, 143, 150, 180, 233, 235, 312, 335, 433-438, 456
    gardens: 233, 236, 433-438, 472
    picking: 289, 434-438
Horsmans: 70, 468
    Farm: 66, 70, 71
    Henry: 70
Horsmonden: 257
Horticultural Society: 327
House Carls: 47-55, 56
House of Correction: 185, 205
Huckens:
    Will: 175, 375
Huckstepp (also Hucksted):
    Elizabeth: 251, 252
    Jane: 347
    Mary: 222
    Thomas: 251, 252
    Will: 222, 252, 282
Hundreds: 40, 60, 72, 76, 79, 80, 82
    Court: 40, 41
    House: 41
    House Lane: 41
    land: 91
    man: 40, 41
    of Baldlow: 41
        Battle: 41
        Godstow: 41
        Staple: 39, 40-45, 134, 145, 147, 165, 214, 224, 227
Hurricane: 274-280, 282
Hurst (Herst): 38, 82, 97, 142, 145, 152, 197, 225, 238-239, 287, 326, 328, 336
    Farm: 332
    House: 278
    Lane: 18, 21, 25, 31, 151, 243, 298, 406, 424, 480

Hussey:
  Edward: 221
Hyland: 411
  Elizabeth: 369
  George: 411
  Harry: 369
  Henry: 240, 369
  Lizzie: 369, 429
  Thomas: 406
  Will: 240, 282, 464
Hyland's house: 240

I

Iltonsbath (Tyltonsbath, etc.): 43, 62, 92, 127, 294, 300, 306, 349, 357, 360, 369, 391
  Bridge: 15, 93
  Corn Mill: 15, 62, 93-95, 377
  Cottage: 124, 125, 142, 361, 441
  Manor of: 94, 130
  Millers of: 94-96
  Watermill: 69, 94, 95, 377
Iden, Alexander: 135
  Henry: 225
Indentures: 169-174
Inglegram de Freisenville: 87
Ingram:
  Rev. James: 106, 188, 197, 284, 285, 395, 491
Inkpens (Inkpyn): 247
  Richard: 247
  Henry: 247
  Farm: 247
Irelands Farm: 313
Iron:
  bloomeries: 22, 24, 414
  Furnaces (see Furnace)
  masters: 137-143, 161, 166, 220
  smelting: 413
  workings: 21, 26, 137, 344
Issoldon (Yssolden) (see Eu)
Isolation Hospital: 336
Ivy Cottage (see Brede Lane Cottages)

J

Jack of Sedlescombe: 175, 375
Jacobs: 97, 104, 176, 264, 269, 270, 271, 326, 329, 333-336, 464, 475
  field: 333
  Cottage: 474
  Gate: 104, 122, 495
  House: 142
  sheep: 334
Jacobs, Lower: 335
Jeffrays: 145
  John (the tithingman): 42
Jeffray's: 44, 77
Jempson:
  Ann: 122, 124, 130, 369
  Jane: 130, 369
John's Cross Inn: 98
Jubilee:
  Clock: 458
  Oak: 458

K

Kedwell:
  Ann: 188
  Elizabeth: 89
  Thomas: 89
Keeling: 225
  Sir John: 239, 335, 424
Kemps Wood: 22, 24
Kendal (see Doctors)
Kennett:
  Bennett: 172
  Elizabeth: 172
  John: 172
Kent Street: 311, 312, 316, 338
Kenward:
  George: 266, 328, 382, 390
  Nurse: 389, 390
  Reuben: 382, 396, 444, 445
  William: 382, 444
Killingham (Killigan):
  House: 243, 244
  Wood: 243, 244, 253, 424, 495
Kinchett, Henry: 287
Kingdon:
  Ernest: 101, 383, 424
  Eleanor: 424

Kings:
  Charles I: 155, 202-208, 211, 256-260
  Charles II: 195, 196, 451
  Edward I: 27
  Edward III: 262
  George I: 146, 193
  George III: 106
  George V: 334, 458
  George VI: 334
  Henry I: 62, 74
  Henry II: 75
  Henry III: 74, 83, 94
  Henry V: 133, 413
  Henry VI: 134
  Henry VIII: 84, 99, 150
  James II: 496
  Richard I: 74
  Richard II: 135
  William & Mary: 440
King's Head (see Coach & Horses)
Kirk:
  Christine: 24
Knights:
  feu: 72, 76, 91, 118
  Hospitallers: 92, 98, 99, 191, 192
Krips (see Cripps)

## L

Lambrogg Bridge: 185
Lambs of Beauport: 308-315, 430
  Anne Montolieu: 308
  Archibald (Sir): 309, 328
  Charles (Sir): 308, 315, 338-340
  Charlie: 308, 315
  Charlotte: 309
  James (Sir): 308
  John: 308, 315
  Louisa (Fenwick): 309
  Rev. Dr. of Iden: 315
  Thomas: 315, 430
Lamp-post (see Forge House)
Langton House (Hall): 161
Land-mine: 313
Laurence: 329
  Charles: 304
  William: 125
Lavix field (Glorix, Clove-Ox): 22, 150, 227

Leadbetter:
  Hannah: 179, 180, 247
  John: 247
  Thomas: 247
Leeds (or Lade):
  Dame Ann: 239
  Joan: 239
  Sir John (1): 89, 192, 239, 430
  Sir John (2): 239, 430
  William: 185, 336, 239
Leeds House: 239
Leeford Wood: 232
Lefsi, the Saxon: 80
Legas, of Wadhurst:
  John: 220, 221
Lemmon, Lt.-Col: 47, 48, 51, 140, 275, 301
Lennard:
  Lawrence: 139
  Richard: 139, 354
Lingham (or Langham) (see also Millers of Iltonsbath): 95, 213, 214, 300, 377, 488
  Bridget: 222
  Elizabeth: 176
  Jeremiah: 351
  John 1: 95, 220
  John 2: 95
  John, junior: 95
  Joseph: 95
  Thomas: 95
  Widow: 96, 393
  William: 222, 248
Linton House: 397, 462
Little Castlemans (see also Castlemans): 22
Little Hides Wood: 21
Littlehurst: 244, 327, 384, 461, 486
Lloyd, Nathaniel of Great Dixter: 383, 424
Long Lane: 266, 347, 402
Lower, Mark Anthony: 135, 161, 194
Luckfish: 227
Ludlow, Milicent (see Moore)
Luff's Farm: 14, 31, 332, 336, 433, 437, 477
Lutman:
  William: 332, 430
Lutman's: 332

# M

Mabbs Farm: (see also Brede Barn Farm): 225, 287, 332, 469
  Thomas: 333
Machine-gunning: 313
Magazine Farm: 66, 69, 70, 303, 462, 468
Magpie Cottage: 179, 250, 356, 375, 404, 405
Malfosse: 53, 54, 58
Mallet, Lady: 167
Mallory, Captain Henry: 146, 258-260
Manor:
  Cottages: 101, 116, 119-124, 142, 152, 171, 209, 263, 277, 358, 475, 486
  Oast: 401
Manser:
  John: 369
  Robert: 369
Margary:
  Ivan: 21, 22
Marley: 69, 224
  demesne: 241
  Farm: 65, 66, 69, 275, 338, 350
  Lane: 65, 351, 413, 433
  Lower: 14, 66, 69, 332
  Manor of
  Tannery: 357
Marling: 416, 422
Marlingstone (Marlynstone, Marling's town): 251, 252
Martin:
  David (R.O.H.A.S.): 115, 228, 425
  Edmund (butcher): 367
  Mrs.: 368
  Florence (Read): 367
  Henry (tailor): 378
  Horace (schoolmaster): 290-295, 386, 455
  Miss (schoolmistress): 288-291, 386
  Millwright: 113, 199, 378
  Rev. Geoffrey
  Susan and John: 389, 488, 490

Mathematical tiles: 148
May Day:
  Festival: 198, 293, 440, 441, 450
  Garlands: 389, 453
Mayfield: 163
Meadow Cottages: 407
Meiniers:
  Matilda de: 87
  Reginald de (or Rainald): 87
Men's Society: 330, 440, 441, 453, 454
Mercer: 180, 247, 267-273, 323, 333, 339, 488
  Fanny: 129, 130
  Joseph and Susannah: 166, 224, 225, 267, 383
  Joseph: 129, 268, 269, 381
  Joseph: 129, 269
  Joseph: 269, 270
  Joseph the smuggler: 265, 271, 272
    his wife: 272
  Mary (Cook): 269
  Mary (Flint): 269
  Richard: 129, 240, 270, 271
  Robert: 122, 240, 268
  Robert (Gent): 267, 269-273, 381
  Thomas of Lewes: 166, 268, 269
  Thomas: 166
Merrion House (see also Great Sanders): 147
Midhurst Cottage: 388, 389
Mill-lane: 351
Miller's Stores (see Byner's & Durud): 32
Mine-pit field: 10
Moat Lane: 31, 314, 338
Monk:
  Robert: 360, 441, 442
  Bill: 474
Montagu, Lord (see Anthony Browne)
Montalet: 406
Moon:
  Mr.: 378

Moore:
   Alan (Sir): 14, 157, 158
   Eithne: 157
   Gillachrist: 157, 158, 461
   Mary (Burrows): 158
   Milicent: 157
   Norman (Dr): 157
Morgay: 88
   Woods: 87, 240, 422
Mosley:
   Ann: 379
   Robert
   Spencer: 379
Mosley's: 360, 361
Mot:
   Robert: 99, 100, 101
   Thomas: 42
Motkyns (Motekyn): 223, 224
Mountfield: 153, 233, 260, 293
   Court: 332
Mount Joy: 54, 229
Monkebo (see Balcombe Green Forge)
Mullens of Westfield Place: 292, 328, 431
   Cyril: 462
   Major: 354, 431, 486
Muntz: Hope
   The Golden Warrior: 56
Murray:
   Anne (Witham): 308
   James the General: 307, 308
   James, the younger: 308
Myrtle Cottage: 405

## N

Nairn:
   Charles: 231
   Jane (see Plummer)
   Richard (Dean of Battle): 219
National Maritime Museum: 158
National Trust: 17
Nash, John (tailor): 378
Nature-trail: 313
Neatenden:
   Brickyard: 384, 385
Netherfield (see also Darvel): 75

Newble:
   Bob: 370
   Fred: 370, 376
   Gertie (Ditch): 370, 376
Newcastle (see also Pelham):
   Duke of: 165, 284
New England Lane: 410, 432
New Road (see also Turnpike Road): 17, 67, 71, 337-343, 433
Nightingale: 488
   landlord of Queen's Head: 292, 454
   John: 290
   Alfred: 290
Ninfield: 264, 285
Nixon:
   Adrian: 112
   General: 112, 113, 401, 462
   Lady: 112, 113
Noble:
   Elizabeth: 199, 490
   John: 199, 476, 477, 490
   Rev. W. H.: 199, 296, 476, 477
Normandy: 39, 61, 73, 74
   Robert of: 73
Normans: 41, 48-55, 79, 97
   Conquest: 38, 63, 73
Northiam: 39, 40, 85, 141, 196, 215, 216
Norton's Farm: 81, 311-313, 338
Nurse:
   District: 363, 389
   Laker (see Kenwood)
   Susan (see Martin)

## O

Oakwood, Gill: 54
Oaklands: 225, 239, 294, 350, 356, 380, 452, 475, 476, 482
   Auction: 480
   Drive: 32, 339
   House
   Park: 14, 18, 31, 158, 238, 310, 324-336, 423, 455, 458

Oast-house: 150, 152, 167, 168, 234, 323, 335, 436-438
Old Thatch: 116-119, 153, 349, 356, 365, 391
Oliver: 348
  Annie Laura: 364
  Argent: 172
  Elizabeth: 172
  George: 240, 248
  Goody: 175
  Nicholas: 171
Orchard Cottage: 411
Overseers: 317, 319, 320, 321
  Accounts: 28
Owen, Rev. Edward: 108, 198, 485
Oxen: 38, 81
Ox-ploughs: 81, 312
Oxenbrigge, Richard: 27

**P**

Paine:
  Phineas (blacksmith): 130, 347, 348, 351
Pankhurst:
  James and Esther: 491
Parish:
  Clerk: 34, 211, 220
  Council: 33, 295, 447, 448, 464, 469
  Records: 28, 169
  Registers: 155, 187-189
  Roads: 339
Parker:
  Geoffrey: 111, 409, 464
  John: 409, 493
  William: 409
Park Shaw: 333, 383
Park View: 356, 357, 358, 359, 360, 361
Parliament: 160, 202, 211, 255-259
Parsonage (see Rectory)
Parsons, Anna: 167
  Thomas: 167
Patry, Edward: 167, 168, 415

Paygate: 340, 342, 343, 422, 432
Peacocke, Thomas: 282
Pelham:
  John, Sir: 74, 196
  John Buxton Pelham, 8th Earl of Chichester: 75
  Thomas, Sir: 165
  Baron Pelham, Duke of Newcastle: 283
Pennygrove Wood: 90, 233, 422
Pepper:
  James: 118, 321, 356
Pepys:
  John: 195
Pestalozzi Children's Village: 10, 331, 452, 482-484
Petley: 70
  Woods: 11, 65, 71, 277, 301, 338, 413, 415-417
Pevensey (see also Anderida)
  Castle: 74, 141
Phillips:
  Fred: 362
Pickering:
  Rev. Peter: 196, 282, 284
Pinnock: 33, 422
Piper, William (fellmonger): 359, 360
  Eliza: 359
Plan of 1632, The: 102, 103, 104, 166, 208, 210, 213-254, 241
Plummer: 488
  Elizabeth: 219
  Isabella (Browne-Wright): 188, 197, 219, 231
  Jane (Nairn): 219
  John: 219, 220, 285
  Lucy (Botting): 219
  Martha (Everndon): 218, 229
  Mary: 219, 220
  Samuel (1): 218, 219, 277, 282, 283
  Samuel (2): 219
Plumtree Cottage:
  Mrs. Beeching of: 475, 477
Polhill:
  Edward: 161, 194
  William: 87

Police:
  Constable Graves: 388, 389
  Constable Gearing: 388, 389
  Sergeant Dallaway: 388
  Station: 446
Pooke: 211, 225
Poor: 169-182, 202, 204, 205, 206
  house: 174, 178-182, 410
  law: 174
  Overseers of
  Rates: 169
Poppinghole: 43, 234
  Farm (also Yorkshill): 248, 443, 476, 477
  Lane: 209, 240, 246, 466
Post:
  Boys: 373
  man: 374, 375, 408
  masters: 371, 372, 374, 461
  office: 372-375
Pottery: 12
  castor ware: 25
  1st to 4th centuries: 24, 416
  native: 24, 25, 416
  Norman: 24
  Samian: 24, 25, 416
Powdermill: 300-306, 465
  at Battle: 301-304
  off Brede Lane: 304-306, 335, 471-472
  at Sedlescombe: 17, 67, 231, 266, 301-304, 351, 477
  Farm: 140, 437
Powdermill Farm, Little: 67, 68
  House, Battle: 303
  Reservoir: 17, 18, 38, 138, 151, 334, 471-473
  Runners: 301
  Valley: 334
  waterwheels: 301
Pralle, John: 71
Pralles, Richard: 152
"Pralles": 74
Pratt: 235, 328, 339, 448, 488, 491
  Arthur: 198, 409, 448, 464
  Bessie: 245
  Cecily: 49
  Harriet: 198, 288, 370, 371, 448
  Rev. John: 107, 110, 146, 180, 197, 198, 221, 231-235, 243,

Pratt, Rev. John—cont.
  245, 288, 376, 408, 491
  Rev. Joseph John: 370
  Mary: 110, 197, 198
  Mary Anne (Bucknell): 448
  Richard: 198, 235, 409
  Sophia: 198, 448
  Violet: 409
Precious Field: 45, 151, 422, 487-491
Presbytery: 298, 402, 462
Pump, The: 198, 372, 447-450, 460, 461, 486
  Cottage: 362, 363, 390, 449, 477
  house: 362, 363, 385, 387, 389, 449

Q
Queen:
  Anne: 281
  Elizabeth 1: 114, 141, 169, 170, 192, 317, 430, 439
  Elizabeth 2: 459
  Mary Tudor: 255
Queen's Head: 31, 32, 142, 168, 210, 290, 320, 375, 379, 439-441, 453, 454, 458, 467

R
Railway: 372
Randalls Farm: 431
Rape: 72, 80, 82
  of Hastings: 60, 72-78, 118, 127, 204, 206, 207, 214, 256
  Lords of the (see also Pelham and Chichester): 41, 72, 73, 87, 91, 94, 127, 283, 402, 403
Raper, Mr.: 57, 58
Rat's Castle (see also Battle Barn Farm): 422
Ray, John: 127, 128
Rectors: 190-201, 461
  Edward Barton: 160
  James: 98, 190
  John
  John Ball (Bell)
  Ralph: 44, 98, 190
  Roger: 98, 190
  of Brede: 320

Rectory (Parsonage): 136, 277, 292
Red Barn Cottages: 383-38
Reed:
 John: 176-277
 Thomas: 179, 404
 William: 321, 339
Reid:
 Rev. Ernest: 198, 273, 330
Revolt: 133-137, 317-323
Ribbon dance: 457
Riccards:
 Farm: 17, 67
 Lane: 249, 433
Richardson: 140
 Henry: 45, 378, 444
 John (miller): 443
 Thomas (miller): 152, 443, 444
 William (miller): 444
Ringfold: 402
River (see Brede)
River line: 17, 65
Riverbridge Cottages: 19, 179, 290, 388
Robertsbridge: 421, 461
 Abbey (see also Abbey): 74, 83-90, 98, 99, 189, 425
 Abbot of (see Abbots)
 Estate: 248
 Fair: 84, 134, 451
 Furnace: 28, 86, 87, 185
Robertson Street Congregational Chapel, Hastings: 445
Rofes and Garrantay: 125, 224
RoHAS: 117-119, 125, 128, 227, 241, 245, 246, 366, 368, 371, 374, 393, 406
Roman: 20, 21, 26, 32, 97, 137, 309, 339
 Bath: 25, 311
 British ironworkings: 9, 20, 21, 24, 25, 32, 82, 89, 309
 coins: 32, 310
 Road: 9, 20-34, 210, 314, 344
 Statuette: 310
 tiles: 25, 311
 villa: 25, 36, 90
Rose:
 Cottage: 298, 362, 387, 407, 449, 480, 495
 lands: 349, 363, 367, 407, 480

Rother:
 Estuary: 12, 13
 River: 21, 62, 83
Round-frocks (smocks): 210, 318, 319, 327, 328, 418, 419, 453
Royal Oak:
 Inn: 31, 260, 321, 337, 338
 Order of: 260
 Sign of: 260
Royal Military Canal: 14
Ruskin: 325
Rusty Brook: 25, 245
Rye: 303, 430, 439, 458
 estuary
 harbour: 357
 Grammar school (see also Peacocke): 430
 Mayor and Jurats of: 14
 town: 14, 16, 21, 138, 141, 208, 226, 258, 265

S

Sackville: 139, 141, 149, 152-158, 173, 193, 208, 221, 228, 256, 329, 488
 Anne: 154, 221
 Sir Christopher: 153
 Constance: 153
 Elizabeth: 156
 Joan (Downton): 154
 John (1): 102, 158, 166, 170, 223
 Sir John: 155
 John (2): 154, 155, 223
 Margaret: 106, 155, 156
 Richard: 430
 Col. Thomas: 30, 105, 106, 139, 154, 155, 185, 223, 256
 Sir Thomas: 30, 104, 153, 155, 171, 172, 204-206, 211, 215, 250, 281, 327
 Funeral helm: 156
Sackville Cottages: 147, 238, 390, 394, 395, 396
St. Mary's School, Baldslow (Holmhurst): 326
Salehurst: 306
Sanders (Sandre) (see also Great Sanders), John: 77, 147

Savill:
  Cecil: 401, 455, 469
  Edith: 380, 401, 455
  Sir Eric: 401, 455
  Gardens: 401, 455
Sawmills: 427
Sawyer: 355
Saxon: 72, 190, 263, 391
  pottery (see Pottery)
  Shore, Count of: 26, 35
Saxons: 26, 38, 47-55, 79, 97
  East: 36
  South: 35, 36
  West: 36
Sayer:
  Carlile: 311-316
School: 281-299
  house: 297, 407
  masters: 281-299
  mistresses: 281-299
  Trustees of: 281
  Terrace: 373, 392
School Hill Cottages (see Thimble, Magpie and Cherry Tree Cottages): 462
Scottesland (or Scotch Down): 91, 92, 370, 422
Searle, Eleanor: 63, 65, 66, 75, 92, 242, 357
Sedlescombe: 36, 38, 46, 65, 72, 73, 82, 85, 169, 265
  Bridge: 18, 31, 32, 165, 264, 283, 303
  Green: 17, 33, 39, 63, 76, 138, 141, 166, 211, 212, 344, 372, 391, 439, 441, 447, 481
  harbour: 12, 16, 21
  Place (see Hancox): 156
  Street: 9, 20, 21, 38, 97, 167, 210, 211, 277, 300, 344, 387, 392, 417, 442, 481
  village: 9, 15
Seizin of the Rod: 129, 232
Sellens:
  Mr: 180, 445
  Reg: 316
Sellens & Cramp: 292, 374

Selmes: 339
  David: 175, 188, 243, 244
  Henry: 374
  Sam: 175
Senlac: 48, 58, 72
Sesse (see Cess)
Share Wood: 432
Sharpe (see also Brabazon & Combe):
  Anne: 110, 323
  Hercules: 31, 107, 110, 167, 224, 238, 270, 323, 339, 406, 423
Sheather:
  Dame: 216, 281
  "Bumper": 71
  John: 210, 222, 253
Sherralds (Wisteria Cottage): 354, 365, 379, 380, 398, 446, 474
Sidney:
  Sir Philip: 99, 145
  Sir William: 84, 86, 145
Simmonds:
  George, the elder: 66, 328, 349, 350
  George, the younger: 66, 350, 454, 457
Sinden:
  Mrs.: 306
  William: 306
Sittings Plan 1632: 30, 202-213
Skinner: 209
  Andrew: 247, 250
  William: 246, 247
Skinner's Farm (see Bellatkin)
Slaughters (see Spilsteds)
Sloane, Sir Hans: 278
Sluter:
  James: 150, 227
Smith:
  "Bangy": 372, 431
  Charlie: 472, 473, 485, 486, 492
  Eliza: 233, 234
  George: 375
  Hannah: 485
  Jim: 415
  John and Mary: 495, 496
  Lottie: 431, 445, 486

Smith—cont.
 Richard: 89, 198, 233, 234, 240, 242, 339, 362
 Spencer: 485
 "Strawberry": 477
 Tilden: 64, 89, 126, 232, 233, 240, 339, 367
 Tilden (younger): 234
 Will: 375, 408
 Smith, Hilder, Scrivens & Co.: 234
Smiths of Strawberry Hill: 248
Smithy: 117, 351
Smugglers: 261-266, 303, 313
 Gangs: 262
 Hawkhurst 264, 265
 Jacob Walters: 264
 Kingsmill: 264
 Stephenson of Rochester: 264
Smuggling: 261-266, 333, 335
 brandy: 263
 guns: 141
 tea: 15, 262, 264
 tobacco: 263
 wool: 261, 262
Snow:
 Henry
 Thomas: 283
Snuff-mill: 313
Soan:
 Charlie: 357, 373, 462
 Fred: 357, 373
 Fanny: 373
 Jim: 462
 heirs of: 226
Socknersh Manor: 161
Solar: 116
Soldiers: 263, 264, 303
Spears: 488
 George: 351
 Henry: 321
Spencer-Chapman:
 Col. Freddy, D.S.O.: 484
Spilstead (Slaughters): 172, 192, 209, 221, 226, 227-235, 228, 233 234, 235, 236, 247, 249, 408, 409, 438, 444
 Cottages (also Stream House): 235, 242, 243

Spilstead (Slaughters)—cont.
 Farm: 63, 67, 145, 195, 228, 241, 243, 338
 John: 181, 231
 Sally: 181, 231
 Stephen: 231
Spray (see also Wicks):
 Adrian: 177, 178, 315
 Elizabeth: 315
Spray's Bridge: 31, 313, 315, 337
Spray's Green: 18, 178, 315
Springfield Cottage (see Brede Lane Cottages)
Stace:
 Charles: 403, 405
 Mary: 403
 Thomas: 351
Staple:
 Cross: 21, 30, 34, 45, 278, 364
 Cross Inn: 45
 Cross Windmill: 45, 364, 378
 Hundred of (see Hundred)
 Millers: 443, 444
Stapeley:
 Anthony: 258, 259
 Anthony, Colonel: 259
 George (baker): 364
 John: 258
Star:
 Goodman: 175, 242
 Jo: 242
 his wife: 242
Statute of Westminster: 27
Steam:
 carriages: 341
 rollers: 342
Stoolball: 451, 452
Storms (see Hurricane)
Straker:
 Wealden iron: 86, 139, 143, 310, 339, 416
Strawberry field: 244
Strawberry Hill Farm (see also Bellatkins): 246-248, 364
Stream:
 Cottages (see Spilsteds)
 House: (see Spilsteds)
 Lane: 18, 31, 149, 210, 227, 229, 236, 249, 320

Streatfield: 85, 246
  Wood: 86
The Street (see Sedlescombe)
  Street Farm: 361, 387
Surrey Archaeological Society: 25
Swailes Green: 34, 85, 97, 234, 465, 486
  Farm: 240, 241, 248, 430, 467, 477
  House: 209
Swales, Little: 241
Sussex:
  Archaeological C o l l e c t i o n (SAC): 14, 27, 57, 107, 134, 161, 176, 202, 214, 260, 262, 275, 279, 281, 301, 310, 337
  Archaeological Society (SAS): 25
  Archaeological Society Museum (see Barbican House)
  Record Society (SRS): 42, 76, 85, 88, 145, 152, 357, 413
  County Magazine: 141, 142, 168, 264, 319, 320, 403, 419
  "Weekly Advertiser": 304, 306
  Express: 353
Swing, Captain: 318
Symes:
  John: 157, 367

T
Tailor: 212
Tanhouse:
  Durhamford: 152, 245, 348
  Pump house: 235, 358
Tannery: 62, 93, 95, 114, 120, 121, 252, 357-360
Tanning: 123, 357-360
Tanyard: 123, 348, 357-360, 375
  Cottage: 124, 362
  House (see also Park View): 126, 327, 350, 356, 357, 361
Tanner's Wish: 229
Taylor:
  Charlie: 348-353, 481
Telham:
  Hill: 18, 48, 140
  Mill: 275
Tenterden: 141

Thimble Cottage (School Hill Cottages): 405
Thomas: 488
  and Sons: 168, 362, 364, 365, 374, 383, 410, 445, 469
  Charlie: 240, 362, 492
  Georgina: 492
  Dennis: 349, 362, 383
  Frank: 68, 383
  Mr. Ted: 125, 127, 383
  Robert (carrier): 291, 362, 386
  Will: 383
  Mrs. F.: 374
Thorne, Sir John: 37, 99, 107, 139, 147, 155, 159, 160, 165, 214, 220, 228, 235, 242, 245, 268, 281, 380, 425, 486, 494
Thorpe: 339
  Arthur: 236, 409
  Edmund (minister): 30, 165, 193-196
  John: 183, 195
  John: 236, 405
  Mary: 183, 401
  Nancy: 236
  Nicholas: 42
  Phyllis: 236
  William: 126, 236, 403
Thorpe's Catalogue: 69, 70, 91, 93-95
Till:
  George: 304
Tillingham, River: 40, 143
"The Times": 142, 319
Tithe Barn: 95, 142, 329, 363, 364
Tithe Map: 43, 56, 122, 126, 167, 189, 221, 225, 244, 245, 349, 362, 373, 401, 406, 422, 441
Tithes: 320
Tithing: 42, 77
Tithingman: 41, 42, 66, 77
Toll:
  charges: 340, 341
  gate: 314, 411
  houses: 340, 341, 342
Torr:
  V. J.: 368, 369
Tournament: 308
Tower of London: 14, 257

Tradesmen: 173, 344-391
Treasure: 9, 56
Trevelyan, "Social History of England": 174, 281
Tudor Rose (see Cherry Tree Cottages)
Tuppenny:
 the Blacksmith: 288, 346, 445, 446
Turner, William: 325, 326, 367
Turnpike road (see also Toll): 31, 32, 67, 89, 311, 312, 314, 332, 337-342, 442
Tyltonsbath (see Iltonsbath)
Tyshurst:
 Moses: 251, 253
 John: 253

U

Uckham (see Wickham)
Ulwin, the Saxon: 82, 238

V

Vale Marlowe (see Claytons)
Van (see Avann)
Veness: 375
Vermin: 185
Victoria County History: 91, 148, 166, 228, 368, 439
Vidler:
 James: 152
Village Hall: 452, 463, 468, 469-481
Vinehall: 87, 89, 233, 240, 320, 321, 332, 418, 421, 430

W

Waghorne: 362, 400
 John: 88, 126, 366
 Robert: 119
 William (butcher): 366
Waller's Wish: 252
Walter, son of Lambert: 80, 81, 91
War:
 Napoleonic: 317, 459
 World I: 421, 427, 444, 451, 457, 460-463, 469
 World II: 454, 458, 474-479, 480

Warner:
 Rev. John: 110, 198, 213, 288, 328, 402, 453, 491
 William Mead: 110
Waste ground: 165, 183, 424
Waterlands: 224
Watson:
 family: 239
 Samuel: 373
 Simon (tanner): 245
Watts:
 Farm: 38
 Hill: 37
 Palace Lane: 37, 38
Wattus Rex: 37, 38
Wayside cottages: 425
Wealden:
 Forest: 9
 Iron (see Straker)
Webster:
 Sir Augustus: 328
 Sir Godfrey: 37, 69, 233, 322
 Sir Thomas: 87, 369
 Sir Whistler: 87
Well (see The Pump)
Well field (see also Burnt House field): 43, 229
Wendy Mill (Belle Vue): 388
Wenestan: 82, 87, 430
Werste (see Ewhurst)
Westfield: 197, 204, 229, 284, 287, 288, 305, 322, 327, 337, 430, 431
 Forge: 14, 16, 138, 140
 Place: 18, 332, 430, 431, 462
 village: 9, 21, 163
 lane: 311
Westons: 167, 285
 Albert: 362
 Henry: 111
 James: 225, 381
 John: 375
 Robert: 225, 367, 392, 397
 Thomas: 111, 225
 William (carpenter): 379, 404
 widow: 244, 251
Weston's house: 243, 244, 251
West Wind (see Cherry Tree Cottages)

Whatlington: 17, 39, 46, 62, 65, 82, 85, 97, 150, 156, 229, 232, 233, 260, 327, 337, 414, 443, 476
  Church: 14, 413
Wheelwright: 117, 123, 211, 355, 356, 380, 381
White (see also Everndon):
  Mary: 215, 250
  William: 215, 250
Whydown: 92, 267, 323
  Cottage: 336, 411
  Hill: 31, 32, 107, 332, 338, 410, 432
  House: 411
  Poultry farm: 444
Wickham: 62, 91, 92, 229, 232, 242
  Hill: 28
  lane
  Olivia de: 65
Wicks:
  Samuel: 177, 178, 315
  Thomas: 177, 178, 315
Willard:
  Mrs. Harriet: 343
William:
  the Conqueror: 41, 49-56-61, 62, 72, 73, 75, 78, 79
  Rufus: 61-62
Wilton:
  Percy: 373, 376
Winchelsea: 12, 13, 14, 133, 138, 140, 141, 215, 274, 357
Windmills (see Hancox, Staplecross): 265, 377
  Beacon: 378

Windmill Cottage: 377
Winter:
  Caesar: 158
  Charles (schoolmaster): 287
Wisteria Cottage (see Sherralds)
Wolseley, Viscountess: 168
Women's Institute: 470, 480
Woodman's Cottage: 404, 406, 477
Wool (see Smuggling): 165, 176, 180, 261, 262
Worge:
  George: 220, 231, 300
Workhouse (see also Poor):
  at Battle: 181, 182
  Accounts: 231, 360
  Cash book: 179
  Matron, Mrs. Eldridge: 179-181, 427

X, Y, Z

Ypres:
  Battle of: 158, 330
Yeoman:
  Richard: 241
Yew-tree Cottage: 316, 338
Yorkshill (see Poppinghole)
Young Wives:
  Fair: 454, 455
Yssoldon (Issoltun) (see Eu):
  Ralf: 74
  William: 74

*Map of the area around Battel (Battle), Sussex, showing:*

HUNDRED OF ... (Hurst Green, Bridge, Parsonage, Bodyham, Court lodg, Bodyham Castle)

Buissill, Rotherbridge, Silver hill, Salehurst, Bodyham Lordp, Enchurst Pla, Brasses

SHUR, Tidhurst, Slatting ham, S Walter, Rotherbridg Furnace

Darvel Furnace, Court Lodg, Munfield, Tine hall street, Tine hall, Staple Cross, Beacon Win

HUNDRED OF ALL, Darvel, Gr. Saunders, Handcocks, Castleman Oak, Bread Fu, Sedlescomb

NETHERFIELD, Woodvile, Durha fo Beech, Parsonag, Whartling ton, Peetly

Reach Furnace, Watch Oak, Marlly, HUNDRED OF Bathurst, Old Mill

Stevens Creuch, Battel, BATTEL HU, Battel Abby, Looss, Hedgland, Woods, Bale

Powder Mill, S. Richards hill, Park Gate, Powder Mill, Tellham, Bridgesel green, Relscomb, BALD

Catsfield, Catsfield Plac, Crowhurst, Lavenders, Parsonage, hill, Wenfield Stocks, Ingerham, Pathly, Hollington